BRIEF CONTENTS

C O N T E N T S

CHAPTER 3
Learning to Parent 70

CHAPTER 4
Becoming Parents 108

PART II

Parenting at Developmental Stages 209

CHAPTER 7

Parenting Children from Birth to Two Years 210

CHAPTER **8**

Parenting Children in Early Childhood: The Years from Two to Five 241

CHAPTER **10**
Parenting Early Adolescents 307

CHAPTER 11
Parenting Late Adolescents and Young Adults 338

PART III
Parenting in Varying Life Circumstances 377

CHAPTER **12**
Parenting and Working 378

CHAPTER **13**

Parents by Adoption and Parents by Reproductive
Technology 407

CHAPTER 14
Parenting When Unmarried 429

CHAPTER 17
Parenting in Challenging Times 491

PREFACE

The ninth edition of The Process of Parenting has been an exciting and challenging one. Research of interest to parents continues to grow at a rapid pace with observations of families interacting at home, studies of preschool children's behavior at home in countries around the world, and children followed in schools for extended periods of time. In addition, neurophysiological and neuroendocrine research tell us more about sources of challenge and stress in children's and parents' lives and sources of comfort and help. Studies of children's development provide more details about children's early efforts and capacities to understand the world, the ways in which their thinking is like that of older persons, and the ways in which it is uniquely characteristic of childhood. Studies of couples, unmarried parents, and families reinforce the importance of all family members' positive involvement in children's lives. Finally, innovative parenting programs have increased dramatically. These programs range from in-home programs including all family members, important friends, and community officials to county-wide programs including all members of the community. Insightful research and innovations in programs appear so frequently that in this revision, it has been necessary to return to chapters already revised to include new material. Because new material continues to appear as the book goes into production, the INSTRUCTOR'S MANUAL, will include new studies.

There are several new features in the ninth edition. First, it includes more studies of parent-child relationships and parenting in other countries and cultures as well as more reviews of international policies and programs relevant to parents. This information provides insights regarding parenting in this country and its effects on children and increases our knowledge of policies and programs that have potential benefit for parents and children here.

Second, there is greater attention to the social context in which parent-child interactions occur. The 2008 recession has resulted in decreased employment and income for parents, loss of homes and moves for many families, and increased stress related to all these changes. In addition, decreased government income has resulted in fewer resources for programs that help parents and children, e.g., child care and recreation. The growing inequality between children whose families are in the lowest quintile of income and those in the highest, has increased social scientists concerns about a two-track childhood, some children having many advantages and some few or none.

A third new feature, related to the second, is the inclusion of family stress theory and a focus on interventions designed to reduce negative feelings related to family stress and parental conflict that can arise and be so devastating to all family members. There is also an emphasis on the actions we can all take in our communities and daily lives to support parents because so many organized programs are disappearing and in this economic climate, few are likely to be added.

A fourth feature is the emphasis on new parenting programs and interventions that are evidence-based and shown to be effective with individuals, families, and communities.

A fifth new feature is the addition of First Person Narratives that illustrate research concepts or processes discussed in the chapter in terms of real-life experiences of individuals. For example, we refer to accounts of people trying to get pregnant and adopt in Chapter 4, young adults talking about growing up in gay and lesbian families in Chapter 16, children's experiences in divorced and remarried families in Chapter 15, a memoir of a young woman spending part of her childhood in homeless shelters with her mother in Chapter 17. The aim is to translate the drier research into everyday life experiences even though some of the accounts are by researchers who blend their personal experiences with discussions of research.

The ninth edition continues to emphasize the powerful ways parents contribute to children's positive growth and development and to buffer children from the negative effects of stressful experiences of all kinds: negative genes, early maturation for girls, economic downturns, discrimination and prejudice, divorce, and natural disasters.

This edition continues to emphasize teaching parents to use sensitive, responsive behaviors with children as the major intervention with children. This does not mean accepting and tolerating all behaviors of children but it does mean connecting with children with positive words and actions to change the behaviors that require change because they are unsafe or hurtful to the child and others.

Although much new research documents the importance of parenting, few parents have had training to succeed in this important activity. Our society requires that people demonstrate competence to drive a car, cut hair for pay, or practice any profession. But nowhere does society require systematic parenting education, which may matter most of all.

The aim of the ninth edition of *The Process of Parenting*, like that of earlier editions, is to help parents and caregivers translate their love and concern for their children into effective parenting skills. The book strives to bring to life the child's world and concerns, so parents can better understand what their children may be thinking and feeling. The book also describes the myriad thoughts and feelings—positive and negative—that parents have so that they can better understand themselves. Finally, the book highlights the influence of the social context on both parents and children.

APPROACH OF THE PROCESS OF PARENTING

I have selected topics and written this book from the points of view of a parent, a clinician, a researcher, and a teacher of parenting skills. I have the firm conviction that anyone who wants to invest attention and effort in becoming a competent, caring parent can do so in his or her own way. The basic prerequisites are the desire to succeed, the willingness to invest time and energy in becoming an effective parent, and patience to persist because the results may come slowly. The results are well worth the effort. My experience as a clinician has shown me that children face many difficult situations; with a loving, supportive caregiver, children can live life fully and happily even if temporarily engulfed by trauma.

Children are not the only ones enriched by adults' efforts to be effective parents. Helping children grow is an intense and exciting experience that brings special rewards to us as parents. Our physical stamina, agility, and speed increase as we care for infants and toddlers. Our emotional stamina grows as we deal with our own intense feelings toward our children and help children learn to express and modulate their feelings. Our intellectual skills grow as we answer young children's questions and, later, help them learn school subjects. In helping children grow, we gain for ourselves an inner vitality and richness that affects all our relationships.

ORGANIZATION

As in the past, the book is divided into three parts, but the chapters in the first part have been reordered, and the chapters in the third part have been reorganized into shorter chapters focused on more specific topics.

Part I, General Concepts, Goals, and Strategies of Parenting, includes six chapters. Chapter 1 continues to describe the roles and interactions of the three participants in the process of parenting: child, parent, and the social system. It describes the powerful role parents play in children's lives and the dynamic influence of the social context that shapes both parents' and children's behaviors and interactions. Chapter 2 goes into depth concerning the many social and cultural influences that impact children and parents, and the individual ways in which these influences are interpreted and incorporated in people's lives.

Chapter 3 describes how parents learn to parent from their own experiences with family members in childhood, from professionals, friends, the media, history, science, theories and parenting experts, and research. Chapter 4 outlines how parents become parents, the activities they engage in during the prepregnancy period to prepare for a healthy pregnancy, and the healthy lifestyle they maintain during pregnancy to minimize stress and enhance the baby's development. This chapter also describes what parents can do to have a child when a pregnancy does not occur after trying for more than a year.

Chapter 5 focuses on maintaining close family relationships, relieving stress, and promoting warm, close ties as these bonds are the basis of family life. While establishing close ties, family members have to find ways to cope with negative feelings from lack of time, stressful events, family conflicts, or parents' problems with depression or substance abuse.

Chapter 6 describes all the actions parents take to establish healthy routines, promote positive behaviors, and control negative influences impinging on the family from TV and social media. It describes three kinds of parenting programs that address family, couple, and community needs.

Part II, Parenting in Developmental Stages, includes Chapters 7–11, which describe children's behavior from birth to young adulthood. Each chapter describes children's development in that period, the particular parenting concerns and tasks, and actions parents can take to help children develop to the fullest.

Part III, Parenting in Varying Life Circumstances, focuses on how family contexts shape children's development, parents' concerns and tasks, and effective actions for parents in each situation. Chapter 12, Parenting and Working, concerns ways parents' work impacts parenting and strategies parents have found effective in to accomplish their goals.

Chapter 13, Parents by Adoption and Parents by Reproductive Technology, describes the special challenges in parenting when additional help has been required to have children, ways to incorporate biological parents who may or may not have been part of the family, and ways to meet challenges.

Chapter 14, Parenting When Unmarried, describes the special circumstances of teen parents and cohabiting and single parents living alone for many reasons. Chapter 15, Parenting in Divorced Families and Remarried Families, describes the grief and sadness that often accompany divorce and impact remarried families if the feelings are not dealt with. Common dilemmas and solutions are described. Chapter 16, Parenting in Lesbian and Gay Families, focuses on the many challenges these families meet but, in spite of them, parent in ways that enable children to thrive. Chapter 17, Parenting in Challenging Times, concerns how to help children, and their parents, face adverse and painful situations: illness, death, victimization, maltreatment, foster care, homelessness, national disasters, and service of family members in the military.

CHANGES TO THE NINTH EDITION

Chapter 1: Parenting Is a Process. New sections or information on

- public interest in parenting
- public views of changes in family structure
- growing concerns on increasing disparities in resources available for poor children
- effects of inequality on social life
- twenty-first-century challenges for parents
- twenty-first-century century supports for parents
- parents' role in launching children on extended pathways of development
- intergenerational transmission of parenting

Chapter 2: Cultural Influences on Parenting. New sections or information on

- ways similar major cultural themes are reflected in different countries
- dynamic nature of cultural influences
- ways cultural values are transmitted
- ways everyday activities of young children communicate and also reflect social values

- parents' reports of young children's qualities in different cultures
- parents' reports of children's behavior problems in twenty-four countries
- cultural influences on older children's activities and interests
- social construction of race
- patterns of acculturation
- negative stereotype threat
- influence of social class on patterns of children's consumption
- community programs for helping low-income families and neighborhoods

Chapter 3: Learning to Parent. New sections or information on

- what parents learn about parenting in childhood
- what parents learn about parenting from media and other sources
- neurobiological mechanisms that promote adaptation
- effects of temperament on effects of parenting behaviors
- experiences that increase executive functioning
- family systems theory
- family stress theory
- parenting stress theory

Chapter 4: Becoming Parents. New sections or information on

- prepregnancy planning for children and leading a healthy lifestyle
- decision to parent in married and unmarried parents
- prenatal development of child
- managing parental stress during pregnancy
- new ways of offering obstetrical care to reduce stress for mothers
- new parenting programs to include married and unmarried, low-income mothers and fathers in the transition to parenthood
- recommendations for improving parenting programs

Chapter 5: Nurturing Close Family Relationships in a Technological Society. New sections and information on

- transmission of feelings in the family
- encouraging close relationships between brothers and sisters
- resolving parental conflicts constructively
- effects of sudden economic loss on families—economic stress model
- managing daily stresses and negative feelings
- parents with ongoing negative moods and feelings—effects of depressed and substance-abusing parents' behaviors and ways to help families

Chapter 6: Supporting Children's Growth and Development. New sections and information on

- parents' role in children's growth
- parents' beliefs about parenting and children
- children's individual qualities
- parenting programs to help control children's weight gain

- role of exercise in learning and health
- children's media use
- multitasking
- using social media
- parents' media use
- family life and media use
- coercive discipline in the United States and around the world
- Triple P-Positive Parenting Program
- Parenting Program for couples

Chapter 7: Parenting Children from Birth to Two Years. New sections or information on

- babies' abilities to observe and understand more than we thought
- effects of parents' behavior on babies' sleep patterns
- comparison of attachment parenting, sensitive parenting, and more structured parenting on babies' crying and sleeping patterns
- Pikler method of caregiving in infant and toddler years
- effectiveness of parenting programs for expectant and new parents

Chapter 8: Parenting Children in Early Childhood. New sections or information on

- children's fears and ways they cope with them
- effects of excessive family stress on children's behavior
- children's and parents' responses to children's emotional upsets
- children's views of moral behavior
- children's lying
- ways parents promote empathy, fairness, and inclusiveness

Chapter 9: Parenting Elementary School Children. New section or information on

- importance of positive school atmosphere for children's achievement
- children's optimistic view of others' behavior
- children's awareness of ethnic bias
- bullying
- relationship between lack of sleep and attention and emotional problems in adolescence
- collaborative problem-solving approach to deal with children's behavior in many situations
- effectiveness of school-based programs in promoting positive social and emotional behaviors

Chapter 10: Parenting Early Adolescents. New sections or information on

- effects of neurotransmitters on children's emotional moods
- changes in brain structure and functioning
- society's pressures on girls
- effects of discrimination on early adolescents
- development of behavioral control in this period

Chapter 11: Parenting Late Adolescents and Young Adults. New sections or information on

- information on teens' safety precautions and high-risk behaviors
- adolescent sexual activity
- adolescent high-risk behaviors
- school's influence on teens' sleep patterns
- relationship between number of hours worked and teens' school behavior
- relationship between stress, well-being, and community activities
- formation of ethnic identity
- family interventions for substance abuse and aggressive behaviors
- return of young adults to live with parents
- parenting strategies for living with young adults

Chapter 12: Parenting and Working. New section or information on

- benefits and supports for working parents in other countries
- reasons for benefits given to American parents
- diversity of current workforce
- patterns of daily life
- patterns of daily life in dual-earner families
- work patterns of single mothers
- children's stress levels at day care
- ways to improve working parents' lives
- investing in growth or remediating problems

Chapter 13: Parents by Adoption and Parents by Reproductive Technology. New sections or information on

- experiences prompting adoption or ART
- changes in nature of adoption
- transracial adoption within and outside the United States
- parents' concerns about effects of adopted children's early experiences in institutions
- importance of counseling all parents participating in adoption
- effects of contact with searched-for biological parents
- family communication patterns in adoptive families
- telling children about use of ART and surrogate in conception
- reasons parents do not discuss surrogacy

Chapter 14: Parenting When Unmarried. New sections or information on

- public's attitude about changes in family structures
- teen parents' transition to parenthood
- teen mothers' relationships to own mothers
- teen mothers' relationships with babies' fathers
- parent training for teen fathers

- characteristics of unmarried cohabiting parents and single unmarried parents
- problems of children of unmarried parents
- programs to promote parents' and children's effectiveness
- psychological and economic resources of single mothers by choice
- transition to parenting and parenthood of single mothers by choice

Chapter 15: Parenting in Divorced Families and Remarried Families. New sections and information on

- grief process in divorce
- children's views of divorce and remarriage
- school programs for children of divorce
- advice to parents from children in divorced families
- advice to parents from children in stepfamilies

Chapter 16: Parenting in Lesbian and Gay Families. New sections or information on

- vulnerability in the absence of legal protections
- decision to parent and pathways to parenthood
- transition to parenthood
- parenting in lesbian and gay families
- children's responses to parents' sexual orientations
- young adults' reports of growing up in lesbian and gay families
- dissolution of parents' relationships
- strengths of lesbian and gay families

Chapter 17: Parenting in Challenging Times. New sections or information on

- family stress theory in understanding the effects of trauma in family members
- national survey of children experiences of victimization, maltreatment, disasters
- Multisystemic Therapy for families coping with abuse and neglect
- community interventions and their effectiveness in decreasing abuse and neglect
- impact of disasters on children and children's and family members' responses to terrorist attacks
- homeless families
- challenges for military families

FIRST PERSON NARRATIVES

Most chapters contain First Person Narratives describing a book telling of an individual's personal experience pertaining to issues mentioned in the chapter. For example, Chapter 4, Becoming Parents, describes three books detailing parents' successful or unsuccessful paths to parenthood, and Chapter 15, Parenting in Divorced Families and Remarried Families, presents books on children's advice to divorced and remarried parents on how to proceed to minimize the pain for children.

The purpose of the narratives is to make the dry concepts talked about in the research literature more real to students and to illustrate what these concepts mean in people's everyday life experiences. In some instances, the narratives are by researchers who tell of their own personal experiences and also describe their work and other research. For example, in Chapter 15, Robert Emery describes both his own divorce and the clinical and research work he has done.

PROBLEM SOLVING

A portion of each of the chapters in Part II deals with common problems children experience and parents must handle. Because each child is a unique individual, parents require a variety of strategies and techniques for handling problems, depending on the child and the circumstances; a problem-solving approach is presented in Chapter 6 that consists of defining the problem specifically, getting the child's point of view, making certain the problem is the child's and not the parent's, maintaining positive interactions and good times with children, considering possible actions, taking action, evaluating the results, and starting again, if necessary.

THE JOYS OF PARENTING

In addition to describing what parents do, the book describes how parents feel as they raise children. Stages of parenthood are identified, and interviews with parents provide information about what parents wish they had known about parenting before they started. The book also emphasizes the joys that parents experience. In 1948, Arthur Jersild and his colleagues at Columbia University observed that most research on parenting was focused on the problems parents experience and little attention was given to "the cheerful side of the ledger." Because this is still true today, I try in this text to redress the imbalance.

INTEGRATED COVERAGE OF PARENTING CHILDREN WITH SPECIAL NEEDS AND SUPPORTS FOR PARENTS

The ninth edition continues to present a more complete picture of parenting children at specific ages by having material on children with special needs in chapters throughout the book. For example, the discussion of attention problems is in Chapter 9 concerning the elementary school years and the discussion of depression is in Chapter 11 on late adolescence. Similarly, material on supports for parents is included in appropriate chapters—such as supports for parents of infants in the chapter on infancy.

SPECIAL FEATURES

New features of the book include First Person Narratives. In many chapters, there are practical questions of interest and significance to parents such as, Do the first three years of parenting count the most? What do parents do if they think their child is not developing according to the usual timetables of growth? When in conflict should parents stay together for the sake of the children?

SUPPLEMENTAL MATERIALS

Instructor's Manual and Test Bank: Accompanying the book is an instructor's manual and test bank. The manual includes for each chapter, 3 power point lecture outlines, 2 role playing suggestions, 2 topics for group discussions, suggested outside speakers, and video resources. A Test Bank of matching, true/false, multiple choice, short answer, and essay questions is available. Please contact McGraw-Hill for more information.

PowerWeb: Child Psychology: Accompanying new copies of the book is a pass-code to access *PowerWeb: Child Psychology* at www.dushkin.com/powerweb. *PowerWeb* includes current articles, curriculum-based materials, weekly updates with assessment, informative and timely world news, Web links, research tools, student study tools, interactive exercises, and much more. If you have bought a used copy of the text, you can purchase access to *PowerWeb* at www.dushkin.com/powerweb.

ACKNOWLEDGMENTS

Writing acknowledgments is one of the pleasures of completing a book. As I read manuscript and page proofs, I am constantly reminded of all the people who have helped make this book a reality.

I wish to thank all of the clinicians and researchers who gave generously of their time not only for the interviews themselves but also to review the excerpts and clarify points: Susan Harter, Emily Visher, John Visher.

I thank the following people for a review of the ninth edition of this book, as their comments enabled me to make more insightful revisions:

Fatemeh Zarghami, St. Cloud State University; Kristen Benson, North Dakota State University; Judith Brake, Ozarks Technical Community College; Deborah J. Handy, Washington State University; Elizabeth Rhodes, Florida International University; Amy Spilkin, University of California—San Diego; Jerry Cook, California State University—Sacramento; Amy Reesing, Arizona State University.

Special appreciation goes to Robert Kremers, the former Chief of the Department of Pediatrics of Kaiser Medical Center, for his willingness to place questionnaires about the joys of parenting in the waiting rooms. I thank the many anonymous parents who completed them there and in parenting classes. Most particularly, I express my gratitude to all those parents I interviewed about the joys of parenting and the ways they changed and grew through the experience. I gained valuable insights about the process of parenting, and their comments enliven the book immeasurably. These parents are Michelle Brown, Steve Brown, Kevin Carmack, Laura Carmack, Mark Clinton, Wendy Clinton, Judy Davis, Douglas Dobson, Linda Dobson, Jill Fernald, Otie Gould, Warren Gould, Caryn Gregg, Robert Gregg, Michael Hoyt, Henrietta Krueger, Richard Krueger, the late Patricia Landman, Jennifer Lillard, Kathy Malone, Chris McArtor, Robert McArtor, Charles Nathan, Jean Oakley, Paul Opsvig, Susan Opsvig, Sherry Proctor, Stewart Proctor, Robert Rosenbaum, David Schmidt, Nancy Schmidt, Moshe Talmon, Anthony Toney, Patricia Toney, Steven Tulkin, Raymond Terwilleger, Elizabeth Whitney Julie Whitney, Kenneth Whitney, Leon Whitney, Richard Whitney, Barbara Woolmington-Smith, Craig Woolmington-Smith, and Iris Yotvat-Talmon.

My coworkers at the Kaiser Medical Center at Hayward were supportive and helpful throughout. Evelyn Kobayashi and Maricela Gehrke our medical librarians, have been essential in gathering articles and books: pediatricians and pediatric advice nurses have given helpful information about parents' concerns. I greatly appreciate the support at Kaiser, especially Jerome Rauch, former chief of psychiatry, and current chief, Adam Travis, who promote an atmosphere in which creativity flourishes.

I am extremely grateful to the staff and the freelancers at McGraw-Hill who take the manuscript and turn it into an appealing book for students. I appreciate the help of Sponsoring Editor Debra Hash, Project Manager Robin Reed, and Developmental Editor Craig Leonard, who have worked hard to organize the review process that guided the revision and kindly shepherded the book through the details of permissions and tables. I also appreciate the hard work of the production staff, Kala Ramachandran and her team that delivers the final product.

I am grateful to the late Paul Mussen, who thirty years ago suggested that I use comments from researchers to make material more vivid for students. His concern with the social forces impinging on parenting has continued to influence my thinking.

Finally, I owe debt of gratitude to my daughter Margo who was so essential as a computer consultant and assistant who took care of the technical obstacles along the way and gave helpful feedback. I wish to thank all my family and friends for their thoughtfulness and company. I want to thank my patients for sharing their lives and experiences with me. I hope they have learned as much about life from me as I have learned from them. Most particularly, I want to thank my children, who are now grown and live away from home. They are very much in my mind as I write, and I relive our experiences together as I explore the different developmental periods. I find that I have learned the most important truths of parenting from our interactions. I believe that when I have paid attention, they have been my best teachers.

I

General Concepts, Goals, and Strategies of Parenting

1

Parenting Is a Process

Test Your Knowledge: Fact or Fiction (True/False)

1. As the wealthiest industrialized country in the world, our rate of infant mortality is lower than that of other industrialized countries.
2. The American public disapproves of the changes in family life over the last fifty years and is pessimistic about the future of marriage and the family.
3. Because of the many changes in the forms of family life over the past thirty-five years, parents' spend less time with children and adolescents, and so young adults now do not feel as close to their parents as their parents did to their parents in 1970.
4. In a large survey, parents report many more joys and satisfactions than problems in raising children.
5. In societies with great disparities between those at the top with many resources and those at the lower rungs who have few resources, there is more crime, more physical illness, more substance abuse, and shorter life spans.

Parenthood transforms people. After a baby comes, a whole new role begins, and parents start a new way of life. What is parenting really all about? Why do people undertake this new and demanding role? How does society help or hinder parents? In this chapter we explore parenting as a cooperative venture among parents, their child, and society. We define parenting and describe the roles of parents and society in rearing children. The chapter describes parents' important influence on children's lives and the ways children change their parents.

Over four million babies are born each year in this country, and Americans have strong feelings about how they should be raised.[1] In early 2011, the *Wall Street Journal* published an article, "Why Chinese Mothers Are Superior," an excerpt from a parenting memoir *The Battle Hymn of the Tiger Mother*, in which Yale lawyer Amy Chua described her strict upbringing of two daughters, then fifteen and eighteen, not allowing them to have play dates or, go on overnights, not accepting less than first place in all academic work.[2]

The response was immediate and intense.[3] The newspaper received almost 6,000 comments on its website in the next week, more than any other article had engendered, and continued the discussion the following week with Ms. Chua's responses[4] to some of her critics as well as Ayelet Waldman's article defending the permissive Western mother.[5]

Newspapers reviewed Ms. Chua's book, and columnists commented on her philosophy. Within a month she was a featured speaker at the World Economic Forum in Switzerland, debating former Harvard President Larry Summers,[6] and in May of 2011, *Time* magazine named her one of the 100 Most Influential People of the Year.[7] We describe the nature of the debates in the third chapter, but here we simply note that the intense reaction to a clearly stated parenting philosophy speaks to the importance of parenting in adults' lives and to the strength of beliefs about how to rear children.

WHY DO ADULTS TAKE ON THE JOB OF PARENTING?

Would you apply for this position?

> Wanted: Caregiver to rear one or two children from birth to maturity. The job is a seven-day-a-week, twenty-four-hour-a-day position. No salary or benefits such as sick or holiday pay, no retirement plan. The caregiver must supply all living expenses for self and children, and in the event of any absence, even for a few minutes with younger children, must supply substitute care. There is no opportunity to meet child or children in advance of taking the position to determine compatibility. Motivation for the job and satisfaction in it must come from within the applicant as neither children nor society regularly express gratitude and appreciation.

Although such a newspaper advertisement might get few applicants, in everyday life the parents of more than four million babies accept such a position each year! And many exert extraordinary effort and pay thousands of dollars for help in getting pregnant or in locating children to adopt so they can take on this job.

The advertisement describes the time commitment and selfless nature of the job that takes over parents' lives as, at the same time, they continue their roles as spouses and partners, extended family members, friends, and workers. Most parents would say parenting never ends; they feel that as long as they live, they will be trying to help their child grow and be happy. So why take on this daunting role?

People are drawn to parenting for several reasons. First, we appear to be preprogrammed to respond positively to babies.[8] The young of all species have a quality of babyishness—heads are proportionately larger; foreheads and eyes are more prominent; cheeks are fatter; limbs are shorter in relation to the torso; and

Parents say an important reason for having children is to feel the joy and excitement of helping them learn and grow.

there is a quality of clumsiness to their movements. Everyone is not equally attracted to babies, and the fact that there may be a biological contribution to the attraction does not mean that people are required to have children. It suggests only that there may be a biological contribution in addition to the social prescriptions for parenthood.

Second, society's strong encouragement is a major influence in having children. Society needs children to flourish and continue, and so it emphasizes the positive value of having children. More than work or marriage, society describes parenthood as a sign of maturity and adulthood.[9] Social pressure for parenthood has varied over historical time and across cultural groups. Currently, in some European countries and in Japan, pressure is increasing because the population is diminishing.[10] In our society most couples expect to have children, but as we shall see in Chapter 11, many young adults no longer see parenthood as a defining characteristic of adulthood.

While no one should feel pressured to have children against their will, a little push to have children may be beneficial. And the reason is this. Most parents describe profound joys and satisfactions with their children. One father said, "It is the first time in my life I know what the term 'unconditional love' means. The wonder of this little girl and nature! I have never experienced anything like that. It is 'Yes' without any 'Buts.'"[11] Yet such pleasures are difficult to experience with other people's children and difficult to know in advance of having children. As one father said, he would really have regretted not having children. Society tries to make sure few have that regret.

Reasons Given for Having or Not Having Children

When asked, men and women, parents and nonparents alike, give similar reasons for having children, and the reasons appear in similar order in different ethnic groups.[12] People want children:

- to love and be close to
- to feel excitement at children's growth and developing skills
- to feel a greater sense of self-growth, of being more sensitive, more caring
- to satisfy society's expectations of being adult and responsible
- to feel a sense of creativity and accomplishment in helping childen grow
- to meet moral or religious expectations
- to feel greater security in times of sickness or old age

Rural residents and African Americans are more likely to list children as providing economic help and security in old age. As we shall see throughout the book, extended families are major bulwarks in stressful times. When people lack close family ties, they must create strong units of support.

Reasons given by couples for not having children center on three broad factors:[13]

- Restrictions (loss of freedom, loss of time for other activities, increase in work load)
- Negative feelings in relation to children (worries concerning their health and well-being, difficulties with discipline, fear of disappointments in children or in self as a parent)
- Concerns about the child being poorly cared for

Joys and Problems with Children

The largest study of joys and problems in child-rearing found that, by and large, parents get what they hope for in parenthood. Arthur Jersild and his colleagues interviewed 544 parents.[14] While the study is sixty years old, it is the only extensive study of parenting joys as well as problems. Parents reported more than twice as many joys, 18,121, as problems, 7,654, in rearing children. The most common joys described are

- Children's special qualities as a person
- Companionship and affection
- Pleasure in watching the child grow in intellectual and social skills
- Feelings of satisfaction in helping them grow and in the general role of parent
- Satisfactions in seeing sibling closeness

The list shows that parents' joys are the everyday life experiences and interactions readily available to all parents and not to children's outstanding or spectacular achievements available to only a few parents.

The problems parents described in Jersild's study centered on:

- The child's difficult personality traits
- Difficulties in getting cooperation in routines
- Concerns about sibling conflicts
- Disappointments in self as a parent

Interestingly, the difficulties did not prevent the closeness that is the main reason parents want children, as only a small percentage of parents (15 percent) reported lack of closeness with the child as a problem. Eighteen percent of parents reported health issues as a problem, but few parents (only 2 percent) reported good health as a satisfaction.

As we talk about parents' many activities in helping children grow, and the work and the effort involved, it is important to remember that there are many more satisfactions than problems in parenting; we just do not talk about the joys as much. Special sections in this book draw attention to these joys.

DEFINITION OF PARENTING

We define parents as individuals who nourish, protect, and guide new life to maturity.[15] Parents make "an enduring investment and commitment throughout their children's long period of development"[16] to provide responsible caregiving that includes:

- An ongoing attachment and relationship with the child
- Material resources such as food, clothing, and shelter
- Access to medical and dental care
- Responsible discipline, avoiding injurious and cruel criticism and harmful physical punishment
- Intellectual and moral education
- Preparation for taking on responsibilities of adulthood
- Assuming responsibility for child's actions in the larger society

Parents provide care in **direct** interactions with children (e.g., feeding, teaching, playing with children).[17] They also provide care in **indirect** actions that can take many forms. For example, parents serve as advocates for children in the community by ensuring good schools and education for children as well as libraries and playgrounds for after-school activities.

PARENTING IS A PROCESS

While parents provide care and resources for their children, parenting is not a one-way street in which the parent directs the child to maturity. Parenting is a **process** of action and interaction between parent and child; it is a process in which both parties change each other as children grow to adulthood.[18] Society is a third dynamic force in the process. It provides supports and stresses for parents and children and can change in response to the needs and actions of parents and children.

The child, the parent, and society all influence the process of parenting, and, in turn, are changed by it. Let us look at the contributions of each.

The Role of the Child

Children's physical immaturity at birth and for many years thereafter requires that parents and society care for them and meet their physical and social needs for a long period if children are to survive.

Babies' physical needs for shelter, food, clothing, and warmth are similar around the world, but they can be met in many different ways, depending on the environment and the cultural values of the society in which babies are born. Psychological and social needs are more complex.

Urie Bronfenbrenner and Pamela Morris[19] believe a child has basic psychological needs for:

- An ongoing relationship with at least one adult who has a profound love for the child and a lifetime commitment to provide care
- A secondary adult who joins in the emotional attachment and care and provides emotional support and encouragement for the other caregiving adult
- Stable and consistent interactions with caregivers and objects in the environment that enable the child to develop more complex behaviors and gain greater knowledge of the world

The child need not be biologically related to the caregiver or live in a two-parent family, but the caregivers must have a long-term attachment and love for the child who is seen as special and irreplaceable. And caregivers must have support in their caregiving.

In addition to their basic human needs, children's individual qualities—their gender, temperament, physical health—affect both what parents do and the effects of parents' actions on children. For example, the mother of fraternal twins, a boy and a girl, commented that if she had had either child alone, she would have thought that she was either the best or the worst mother in the world. Her daughter was a quiet, adaptable, easygoing baby, happy with whatever her mother did, and her mother felt she was an excellent mother. Her son was an intense, colicky baby, and nothing his mother did seemed to make him happy in the first few months so she felt very inadequate as his mother. She was the same person with the same skills, but her behavior had a different impact on each child as a result of the child's temperament, and her impact on the babies affected how she felt about herself as a mother.

A child's health influences parenting. Genetic or birth complications can interfere with babies' basic abilities to nurse, to adapt to stimulation, and to sleep. Soothing and caring for babies is more complex, and parents have the added burden of worries about their children's health.

Another factor in the parenting process is the "goodness of fit" between the child's qualities and those of the parent and family.[20] For example, the behavior of a slow-moving, slow-to-adapt child may present a problem in an active, boisterous, on-the-go family, but no problem in a family where most members are quiet and slow-moving.

Children's Importance to Parents and Society   As we noted earlier, children meet parents' basic needs for closeness, sense of accomplishment, and maturity in life. Parents grow as they undertake new activities and become more involved in community activities to meet children's needs.

We do not often think about how children meet critical needs for society, but they do. Children maintain traditions and rituals, and transmit them to the next generation. Very important, they grow into economic producers who support the aging members of society as well as their own children. As Richard Lerner, Elizabeth Sparks, and Laurie McCubbin write, "Children constitute 100 percent of the future human and social capital on which our nation must depend."[21]

The Role of the Parent

Parents' basic role is to provide responsible caregiving, as we described earlier. Society gives parents primary authority in meeting children's needs because parents are assumed to have their dependent children's best interests at heart.[22]

Parents bring a complex set of needs and qualities to the process of parenting. Unlike children who come to the parenting process fresh and inexperienced, parents[23] come with a history of relationships and with many other responsibilities that influence their behavior as parents. They bring:

- Their gender and temperamental qualities just as children do
- Their personal qualities such as sociability and self-esteem
- Their relationships with their parents and siblings
- Their level of physical health and psychological stability
- The relationship they have created with each other
- Their relationships with their broader social network of extended family, friends, and coworkers
- Their problem-solving skills
- Their work skills and satisfaction with their work

Parents' Importance to Children and Society   We explore parents' vital importance to children in an expanded section later in the chapter. Parents meet society's needs as they rear children who will maintain society. They provide around-the-clock care for eighteen years, and they pay all children's expenses. When society is forced to intervene in family life, it is difficult if not impossible, as we shall see, for society to provide the level and continuity of personal care that parents happily give children.

The Role of Society

Children live in families, and families live in neighborhoods and communities in a larger society that provides values and standards of conduct for all three parenting partners—parent, child, and society.[24] Society is a dynamic force that changes in response to economic and social changes that, in turn, affect parents' and children's lives. First we describe society's demands of parents and children and then look at changes that have affected forms of family life.

Legal Definitions of Roles   Although we are a diverse society, the legal system's demands of parents, child, and society apply to all groups and are as follows:[25]

Parent

- A parent is defined as the biological mother of the child and the man to whom she is married, regardless of whether he is the biological father or as a person who, by adoption, has obtained the legal right to take on the responsibility of care for a child in the absence of or with consent of the biological parent.
- A foster parent has been given the funds and the responsibility to care for a child for a specific period of time under supervision of the state.
- An unwed biological father's rights vary depending on the state in which he lives; he had no rights until 1972 when the Supreme Court stated his rights depended on his level of involvement in the child's care; states interpret that requirement differently.
- Prebirth figures assisting in the reproductive process—egg donor, sperm donor, surrogate mother—usually relinquish parenting rights prior to birth but the law is vague here.

In cases of conflict about parenthood, the biological tie is the first consideration provided the parent is fit, but it is not the only consideration.

Society not only defines a parent, but also the basic requirements of parenting. Because parents are expected to make most of the decisions, society imposes few, but important, requirements. Generally, according to law,[26] parents must provide:

- Childhood immunizations before the age of five
- Ongoing medical care
- Education between the ages of five and eighteen
- Accepted forms of discipline for behavior
- Education so children become law-abiding citizens

Society acts if it determines parents are being neglectful, abusive, or putting the child at risk. Child protective agencies can remove children from parents' custody and charge parents with crimes if it feels parents have endangered their children. In addition to holding parents responsible for their behavior, society sometimes holds them legally responsible for their children's actions—paying fines when children do not attend school, making restitution when children have destroyed property.

Child

- Is considered inexperienced and dependent on parents
- Is expected to follow parents' rules and requests
- Is thought incapable of making informed decisions, and so, prior to a child's eighteenth birthday, parents must give consent for routine medical care, driver's license, entry into the military and marriage

Most states have made exceptions to this general rule and permit teens to seek treatment for substance abuse, pregnancy, contraception, reproductive health, and mental-health counseling without parental consent. Furthermore, parents cannot obtain information about their teens' medical care in these areas.[27]

Society acts to ensure that children and teens obey parents' rules.[28] Children and teens can go to juvenile detention for repeatedly violating reasonable parental rules or running away. While teens cannot make many decisions, they are increasingly being considered responsible for violent crimes and are charged, sentenced, and jailed as adults would be.

Most often, society looks at family issues from the point of view of the parents, but at the same time tries to keep in mind the best interests of the child. The child's interests are usually the main concern in custody issues.

Although society demands much of parents and children, society provides only limited services to help them meet the demands.[29] See Box 1-1 for parents' descriptions of contradictory expectations.

Society

- Provides free education to children from the age of five to eighteen
- Gives specific tax exemption for each child in the family
- Gives tax credit for child-care expenses
- Any other assistance is given only if a parent or child has a disability or is living in poverty

Although we think of ourselves as a society that cares for children and honors parents, the United States is the only industrialized country in the world that does not provide health care for children and parents, though it does for people over age sixty-five.[30] It is one of only five or six countries that do not provide paid maternity leave at the birth of a child.[31] Many countries provide a family allowance for each child, regardless of income, schooling beginning at age three, and a high percentage of child-care expenses. Because our country provides so few benefits, our poverty rates are among the highest in the industrialized world.[32]

Our lack of benefits has consequences. Lack of health care for all children and parents is a factor in this country's having the highest rate of infant mortality among the developed countries. Our rate of infant mortality (the number of deaths of a child under one year of age per 1,000 live births) is more than twice as high as that of Japan, which has the lowest (6.1 compared to 2.8).[33] Mortality rate is of concern because the factors that lead to infant death are the same factors that lead to chronic problems among those infants who live.

Box 1-1
UNREALISTIC EXPECTATIONS FOR CONTEMPORARY PARENTS

Society's roles for parents can be demanding. Here a mother and father identify problems they see in society's expectations of them.

Judith Warner, author of *Perfect Madness: Motherhood in the Age of Anxiety,** describes the heavy burden society's role prescriptions place on mothers. The Mommy Mystique, as Warner terms society's demands, makes mothers totally responsible for their children's development and well-being. Mothers are expected to be physically available to children at all times, to meet all their needs for physical care, love, and stimulation, and then, to see that children have access to the best physical, social, and educational programs. Mothers must excel in their role so their children can succeed in our competitive society. Mothers are failures if their children have difficulties or cannot achieve high levels of success. Such total responsibility for a child's well-being is especially hard for contemporary mothers who have been raised to have strong commitments to their work as well.

While society demands much of mothers, it gives little help in meeting its expectations. Quality, affordable day care is often not available, especially for mothers who work part-time; little after-school care is available for older children, so much of mothers' pay goes for substitute care while they work.

The expectations and lack of help in meeting them create tremendous stress for mothers as they run around frantically trying to accomplish all their tasks. The role demands also arouse intense anxiety in mothers about their children's future performance and guilt whenever children fail to keep up with other children or develop problems. The expectations also affect children as they sense that their mothers feel stress and tension around them.

Warner believes this situation will not change until parents band together and insist on programs that reduce maternal stress like affordable quality day care, tax credits and benefits for part-time workers, and a more parent-friendly workplace with flexible hours and work.** Still others believe the stress can be managed when individuals make informed choices as to how to balance work and family commitments. Jennifer Regen Bisbee wrote in response to an article by Warner that she could understand Warner's complaints but wondered why she did not use the word "No" to manage the stress. She limits her children to one after-school activity so the family can have a manageable daily schedule. "No, I tell myself, I will not take on another client right now, which would mean more money but also more nights away from my children."*** She believes parents have to accept the fact that they can't do everything right now.

Joe Ehrmann identifies a misguided role expectation for men.**** A former NFL football player who became an inner-city minister in Baltimore following the cancer death of a much-loved, younger brother, he has observed that society values and teaches a "false masculinity" that gives boys and men approval for excelling at physical games, attracting and impressing women, and building up financial wealth. Boys are taught to compete and win, and to hide their feelings, especially when they feel hurt. But masculinity emphasizing power and dominance prevents men from developing close relationships and becoming loving husbands and fathers. Such masculinity does not bring any lasting sense of worth and happiness in life. Genuine masculinity, he believes, depends on creating close relationships and caring for others and a cause beyond oneself.

(continued)

Box 1-1
CONTINUED

Ehrmann believes that in the context of high school football, he and co-coach businessman Biff Poggi and the eight assistant coaches can encourage adolescents' positive relationships with others by teaching them three basic behaviors: (1) to take responsibility for their actions, (2) to "lead others courageously," and (3) to "enact justice on behalf of others." The boys learn responsibility by being on time, following team and school rules, and meeting academic standards. They also take responsibility for finding and developing their skills to the fullest. The boys learn to care about each other also include others in their group. Ehrmann terms this program that he carries out at a secular, private high school "Building Men for Others."

Ehrmann and the coaches give the boys the experience of being nurtured and cared for and encourage them to care for each other and for others in their lives.

*Judith Warner, *Perfect Madness: Motherhood in the Age of Anxiety* (New York: Penguin, 2005).
**Judith Warner, "Mommy Madness," *Newsweek*, 21 February 2005, 42–49.
***Letters, *Newsweek*, 7 March 2005, 15.
****Jeffrey Marx, *Seasons of a Man's Life* (New York: Simon & Schuster, 2003).

What Do Parents Want Society to Provide?

In a large national survey of European American, African American, and Latino/a parents, only 6 percent thought government and employers were doing enough to help parents.[34] Eighty-four percent thought the government should do more, and 76 percent thought employers should give more help. Their requests fell into four broad categories:

- financial help in terms of increasing the tax exemption for each child, the tax credit for child care, and the removal of sales taxes on items necessary for children like diapers
- changes that would give them more time with families—e.g., tax incentives to employers to encourage part-time and flex-time schedules, requiring employers to give paid maternity and paternity leave, allowing parents to take two extra weeks without pay each year to participate in children's activities
- laws increasing children's safety and providing health care, requiring safety devices on guns, controlling crimes against children like kidnapping
- positive messages that support parents' values[35]

Parents worry that society barrages their children with messages about sexual activity, drugs, and alcohol that undermine parents' goals of rearing responsible, caring children. Forty-seven percent of parents in a 2002 national sample considered protecting children from negative social influences their biggest challenge as parents.[36] Though crimes against children are statistically low, 50 percent of parents worry a lot about them.

Joint Efforts among Partners in the Process of Parenting

The following example illustrates the ways the three partners contribute to children's development; we use as an example children's attention span, an important quality for learning, emotional regulation, and behavioral control.

Children Contribute Their Genetic Make-up and Constitutional Qualities   Children's genetic make-up increases the likelihood of certain behavior. Children, for example, with the gene DRD4 7-repeat allele are more likely to have attention problems.[37]

Parenting Plays a Role   Parents' insensitive parenting is more likely to promote noncompliant and aggressive behaviors in children with DRD4 7-repeat allele gene whereas children without the gene do not show such behavioral responses to parents' insensitivity.[38] When, however, parents of toddlers with the DRD4 7-repeat allele learn more sensitive, responsive parenting, their children, when preschoolers, do not develop noncompliant and aggressive behaviors associated with this gene.

Environmental Factors Play a Role   A nursery school program lasting one or two years, termed Tools of the Mind, increased children's executive attention.[39] Emphasizing dramatic play to encourage symbolic and imaginative thinking, self-talk to guide behavior, and strategies to facilitate memory and attention, the program resulted in children's having significantly higher scores on measures of flexible problem solving and complex memory skills than children in schools with a typical state curriculum. A five-session computer-training program for children of the same age also increased children's executive attention and overall intellectual level.[40]

Finally, an elementary school teacher designed special desks and stools to increase attention and focus on work by permitting students to be more physically active.[41] She thought students were expending too much effort to contain their movements in class, and they needed an outlet for their physical energy. The desks and stools are adjustable so students can sit or stand, and flexible foot rests attached to desks allow them to move their feet at will. Students and teachers believe the desks help students focus attention and get work done, and controlled research is under way to validate their impressions. The school principal believes the results of the controlled study will be positive. "We just know movement is good for kids. We can measure referrals to the office, sick days, whatever it might be. Teachers are seeing positive things."[42]

How Do Partners in the Process of Parenting View Each Other?

Parents are thrilled to be parents, and in a 2002 survey, 96 percent say they would not trade being parents for the world.[43] At the same time they evaluate themselves as doing only a fair or poor job in raising their children, and this is a similar trend from 1996 to a 2010 poll, in which both parents and nonparents blame parents far more than teachers, schools, and government for children's school problems and failures. In 1996, almost two-thirds of parents and nonparents alike thought parents have children before they are ready for the responsibility and half the sample thought parents spoil children and fail to give them appropriate discipline.[44]

The public does not believe parents are failures, but rather that they are overwhelmed with pressures of work and family and need help. Nonparents and parents believe that a parent's job is more difficult than in the past because children face problems with drugs and alcohol, more sex and violence in the media and the world outside the home, and more gangs in school.

The most positive views of parents' effectiveness come from children. About 60 percent of teens between the ages of twelve and seventeen say that parents are doing a good or excellent job in rearing children (only 36 percent of parents say this about themselves).[45] These teens say parents are there for them and are affectionate. In another sample, children and teens reported that both mothers and fathers love, appreciate, and care for them and do a good job of balancing work and family, but these children's main concern is that parents are too stressed and tired.[46]

Summarizing observations from a study of new parents, Jay Belsky, agreeing with children's positive assessments of parents, wrote that he worried about how little the public acknowledged all the financial and emotional sacrifices parents made as they reared children. "Ills that plague the American family are complex and have many sources. But I think one major source is that our society no longer honors what I witnessed every day—the quiet heroism of everyday parenting."[47]

The Social Context of Parenting Today

We all know parents and children, but we are less aware of the third partner—the dynamic social context that changes with historical time and with the family's life circumstances and influences both children and parents. We first look at the changes of family life over time and then look at the social factors affecting parents today.

Changes in Family Life in the Last Two Hundred Years

Vern Bengtson points to four major forms of family life in the last two centuries.[48]

- **The extended farm family** of parents, children, and extended family was the primary form of family life in this country until the late nineteenth century; it was a productive economic and social institution based on law and custom.
- **The nuclear family** of parents and children, based on companionship and love, had as its primary purposes socializing children and meeting family members' emotional needs; it arose as industrialization and urbanization increased and families moved off the farm at the end of the nineteenth century; it was the predominant form of family life until the 1970s.
- **Diverse family forms** such as dual-career families, single-parent families, and stepfamilies arose in the 1970s as social and economic changes requiring more than one parent's income to support families led to women's entrance into the workforce and increasing secularism permitted greater acceptance of divorce and of childbearing outside marriage.
- **Multigenerational families** relying on two or more generations to sustain youth have arisen in the 1990s as young families face greater economic difficulties with unstable employment, increasing housing and child-care

Multigenerational families rely on two or more generations to provide strong emotional ties and resources for children.

costs, and reduced incomes in single-parent families, and emotional resources are stretched with the demands of work and family. "For many Americans," says Bengston, "multigenerational bonds are becoming more important than nuclear ties for well-being and support over the course of their lives."[49]

Demographic changes in the population underlay these shifts. In the last 100 years, the lengthening of the lifespan from 49 years for women and 46.4 years for men in 1900 to an average of 80.4 years for women and 75.4 for men today has provided an additional thirty years for adults to be involved with younger generations.[50]

In this same period, the average number of children per family has dropped from 4.1 in 1900 to 1.93 in 2009.[51] The age structure of the population now resembles a bean pole, according to Bengtson, with equal proportions of people at all ages. Thus, adults of many ages are available to nourish the small number of children. Grandparents and great-grandparents step in and meet children's emotional needs for closeness. Referred to as "latent kin networks" or the "family national guard," they "muster up and march out when an emergency arises regarding younger generation members' well-being."[52]

Despite all the changes in family structure, adolescents and youth feel as much solidarity with mothers and fathers in 1997 as their parents did with their parents in 1971, according to data from the Longitudinal Study of Generations collected on four generations of working and middle-class families from 1971 to 1997.

Figure 1-1 compares the early life experiences of Generation 3 (termed Baby Boomers) with the life experiences of their children, Generation 4 (termed Gen Xers), including feelings of family solidarity with mothers and fathers. Baby Boomers grew up in families with more siblings, with fathers and mothers having less education, with mothers more likely to be full-time homemakers, and with fewer divorces than their Generation X children. Yet the family solidarity scores of Baby Boomers in 1971 were very similar to the scores of their children with them in 1997.

■ **FIGURE 1-1**

HISTORICAL CHANGES IN FAMILY STRUCTURE AND PARENTAL ATTRIBUTES: "GENERATION X" COMPARED WITH THEIR BABY-BOOMER PARENTS AT THE SAME AGE

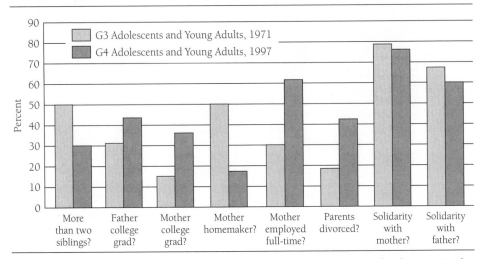

From: Vern L. Bengtson, "Beyond the Nuclear Family: The Increasing Importance of Multigenerational Bonds," *Journal of Marriage and Family 63* (2001): 11. Reprinted with permission.

Children not only feel close to parents, they maintain similar values with regard to achievement as well. Maternal employment has not changed self-esteem or values with the exception that Gen X young women have higher occupational aspirations than did either their mothers or Gen X young men.

Claude Fischer's analysis of survey data from 1970 to 2010 supports Bengtson's conclusion that despite all the social changes, adults are as close to family and friends as they have ever been. The activities may change, for example, less entertaining at home and more phoning and e-mailing, but the close connections remain.[53]

Living Arrangements of Contemporary Families

Parents and children live in the many different family constellations listed in Table 1-1.[54] Children may live with two parents, one parent, or no parents. Parents may be biologically related to children or may be adoptive parents. Parents may be married or cohabiting. Assisted Reproductive Technology, described in Chapter 4, means conception is not limited to heterosexual couples so parents may be heterosexual or gay/lesbian/bisexual or transgendered in sexual orientation, single or partnered. Adoption agencies too have broadened criteria for adoption so parents may be older or disabled. We discuss the impact of these many forms of family life in Part III of the text.

■ **T A B L E 1-1**
LIVING ARRANGEMENTS OF CHILDREN IN THE UNITED STATES: 2010*

Family Form	Percentage of All Children
Two-Parent Family	**69%**
Two biological/adoptive parents married	60%
Two biological/adoptive parents cohabiting	3%
Biological/adoptive mother, stepfather	4.2%
Biological/adoptive father, stepmother	1.8%
One-Parent Family	**26%**
Mother alone	21%
Mother cohabiting	2%
Father alone	2.4%
Father cohabiting	0.6%
Not Living with Biological/Adoptive Parent	**4%**
Grandparent	2.2%
Other relative	0.8%
Foster care	0.3%
Other	0.7%

*Adapted from: www.childstats.gov/americaschildren/famsoc1.asp. Table Family 1.B: Percentage of Children Ages 0–17 Living in Various Family Arrangements, 2010.

In 2010, the general public reported greater acceptance of these family changes than rejection of them.[55] See Table 1-2. Cluster analysis of the responses reveals that:

- 32 percent of the public reject almost all changes in the two-parent married couple family as bad for society
- 31 percent accept the changes as unimportant or good for society
- 37 percent say the changes generally make no difference with the exception that a single mother's raising a child without a man involved is bad for society

One suspects that the public is disapproving of single motherhood because of concerns about the difficulties both single mothers and their children encounter without the financial and psychological resources of two parents. Regardless of attitudes about family changes, most of the respondents—67 percent of the whole sample and even 60 percent of those who disapprove of the changes—are optimistic about the future of marriage and the family as an institution.

■ **TABLE 1-2**
PUBLIC'S ATTITUDES ABOUT CHANGES IN FAMILY STRUCTURES*
PERCENTAGE OF RESPONDENTS WHO THINK EACH OF THE FOLLOWING
TRENDS IS:

Item	Good Thing for Society	Bad Thing for Society	Doesn't Make Much Difference	DK
More women not having children	11	29	55	5
More unmarried couples raising children	10	43	43	3
More single women having children without a male partner to help raise them	4	69	24	3
More gay and lesbian couples raising children	12	43	41	4
More people living together without getting married	9	43	46	2
More mothers of young children working outside the home	21	37	38	4
More people of different races marrying each other	25	14	60	2

*Adapted from: Pew Research Center: Social & Demographic Trends, "The Public Renders a Split
Verdict on Changes in Family Structure," downloaded from www.pewsocialtrends.org/2011/02/16.

Ethnic and Racial Diversity of Families

This was already a multiracial and multicultural country when the English settlers
arrived in Virginia and Massachusetts in the early seventeenth century. Twenty-five
thousand years earlier, immigrants from Asia had trudged over the Bering Straits
and settled in North, Central, and South America.[56] Spanish settlers came to Florida
in the sixteenth century, bringing with them African slaves. Waves of immigrants
have continued to come from around the world, bringing with them many different
cultural traditions. We continue to add about a million immigrants to our population each year so that currently one in about every eight citizens is an immigrant.[57]

Of the thirty-eight million foreign-born people in this country in 2009, approximately 71 percent have authorizations to be here, and 29 percent do not.[58] Social
scientists have concerns about the stress and limited resources of families here
without authorization, about the fears and anxieties of children living in these families, and about the trauma they experience through deportation and separation of
family members.[59]

The country has many opinions as to how to handle the problem of the 29 percent
of unauthorized immigrants, but at present no resolution. A recent poll indicates

about two-thirds of Americans want unauthorized immigrants to have a path to citizenship though a significant number of these people (42 percent) want border security and immigration laws enforced at the same time.[60]

Currently, 66 percent of our population described themselves as nonHispanic/white, 16 percent Hispanic, 13 percent African American, 4 percent Asian, and 1 percent Native American; 1.8 percent of the population identified themselves as being of two or more races.[61] Ethnic minorities will increase in the population as their birth rates are higher than that of European Americans. Between 2000 and 2009, births to African American, Asian American, and Latina women accounted for 79 percent of our population growth.[62] Their higher birth rates are the major reason that the United States does not suffer from the decreasing birth rates of European countries. We look at these cultural influences on parenting in Chapter 2.

Economic Diversity

We are an economically diverse society.[63] The median family income in 2008 was $63,366, but there was a wide range of incomes depending on ethnic group with Asian Americans having a median family income of $80,101; European Americans, $70,835; Latino/a Americans, $43,437, Native Americans, $43,190, and African Americans, $41,874. The median income figure does not reveal the great disparity between households with the most and least income. The top 5 percent of households have income approximately nine times the income of the lowest 20 percent ($180,000 per year compared to less than $20,712 per year in 2008). Children are the poorest in the population, and currently, one of every five children lives below the poverty line of $22,025 per year for a family of four.[64]

The disparity in resources of children in the wealthiest and poorest families raises social scientists' fears of a two-track childhood for American children with one track living with well-educated parents with good jobs and incomes, in stable marriages, and the other track living with parents with less education, less stable marriages, less income, and greater stress levels that decrease children's physical and psychological well-being.[65]

Further, British epidemiologists Richard Wilkinson and Kate Pickett found that countries like Britain and the United States with the greatest income inequality have higher rates of violent crime, mental illness, drug and alcohol abuse, teenage pregnancies, and physical illness, as well as shorter lifespans than those countries with greater equality.[66] Income inequality affects the well-being not only of the poorest within a country as would be anticipated, but it also affects the well-being of the wealthiest individuals. Those individuals with the lowest status in a greater equality country like Sweden have lower death rates than the wealthiest segments of the population in England and Wales, countries of great inequality.

Why does inequality in a country have such devastating effects? Wilkinson and Pickett believe that we are social creatures, sensitive to social hierarchies, and low status arouses feelings of inferiority that, in turn, create stress, especially for those with the fewest resources. Stress, as we shall see in Chapter 3, increases stress hormone levels that, when chronically elevated, decrease physiological and intellectual functioning, reducing immune responses and triggering physical illness. On the other hand, greater equality among groups increases feelings of trust and support from others if needed, thus reducing stress and its negative effects on behavior.

While as a country we cannot quickly change families' income levels, we can work, as we shall see, to provide greater feelings of community and trust in each other regardless of income level. Box 1-2 describes an example of the ways individuals reach out to provide support for children when families cannot.

Twenty-first Century Challenges for Parents

Raising children is a demanding job at any time, but the first decade of the twenty-first century has brought parents stressful new challenges.

Fears over National Safety and Security   Since the terrorist attacks on the United States and deaths of more than 3,000 people on September 11, 2001, we have lived with fears of further killings through bombs, chemical warfare, and shootings. While the first terrorists were from outside the country, most recently citizens within the country have been charged with shootings and plans to blow up buildings and homes. Every time we go to an airport or train station and are urged to report suspicious activities, we are reminded of our vulnerability to unknown people who want to harm us. Parents have to cope with their own fears and help children cope with their fears. We discuss how to do this in Chapter 17.

Economic Insecurity   In 2008, the world experienced the most severe recession since the Depression of the 1930s.[67] In the United States, the unemployment rose to 10 percent in 2009. Forty-four percent of families experienced a job loss, a reduction in hours, or a pay cut in the 2009–2010 period; many families also lost their homes.

Unemployment is expected to stay at a high level for several years because the economy is not generating the millions of jobs needed to return to the more usual unemployment rate of 5 to 6 percent. Extended unemployment and numerous moves bring stress and changes for all family members. Stress increases because the government and community agencies that help families at these times also have less revenue available to provide help. We discuss how to manage the stresses and demands in Chapter 5.

Globalization   While this country is experiencing economic loss and insecurity, some developing countries in Asia and South America are growing at a much higher economic rate and are experiencing prosperity, arousing doubts about our future place in the world. Students from developing countries work hard in school and now surpass American students' achievement. They compete for graduate school and occupational positions that were routinely filled by Americans.

While our country used to have the highest rate of college graduation, we now rank twelfth among thirty-six developed countries.[68] Only four (New Zealand, Spain, Turkey, and Mexico) of thirty countries have a lower rate of high school graduation than the United States, where only seven in ten students graduate.[69] Those students who do remain in school do not perform as well on international tests of reading, math, and science as students in most other industrialized countries.

Box 1-2
HELPING HANDS ENABLED IMPOVERISHED YOUTH TO DREAM AND ATTAIN HIS GOAL*

Ryan Green's journey illustrates how community members can step in and help families nurture children. Born to African American parents who later divorced, leaving his mother to support her two boys with low-paying jobs, and with little musical interest or training until junior high school, Ryan Speedo Green was an unlikely candidate to become a Metropolitan Opera singer. Yet, in 2011, at the age of twenty-five, he was one of five winners of the Metropolitan Opera National Council Auditions, and he auditioned and was accepted into their small Young Singers program where he will be trained and prepared to sing, hopefully with the company.

During Ryan's childhood, his mother was emotionally and financially stressed, and the family moved frequently, living in a trailer park and later in a run-down, drug-infested area. He was an angry, defiant elementary-school boy who bullied others and turned over desks in classrooms when he did not get his way. His unmanageable behavior resulted in a special class placement where his teacher, Mrs. Hughes, introduced him to books that captured his interest and motivated him to read and learn.

Fighting with his brother at age 12, he threatened to knife and kill both his brother and mother. Ryan's threat was so detailed that a psychiatric evaluation resulted in his going to Juvenile Detention for two months. He has "blocked out" much of this experience, but he has clear memories of the phone calls his teacher, Mrs. Hughes, made to him twice a week during his stay; they kept his spirits up.

When he returned to school in junior high, he began to achieve in regular classes. He played football, and the coach suggested choir as an easy credit. In choir, the director encouraged all his students to apply to the prestigious Governor's School for the Arts, a special public high school. Ryan had little interest in music, and his singing was unremarkable but he was accepted because they needed more boys' voices in the classical division.

He initially felt out of place because he lacked the training of the other students, but when he was 14, Mrs. Hughes and her husband, who was the executive director of the Governor's School, paid Ryan's expenses for the school trip to hear *Carmen* sung at the Metropolitan Opera House in New York. The toreador's powerful performance captivated Ryan and changed his life. Ryan determined to be an opera singer who could move audiences in the same way.

He confided his goal to Mr. Brown, the choir director, who offered to give him free singing lessons three times a week and served as a father figure for him during adolescence. With this preparation, he attended and graduated from the music program at the University of Hartford and from a graduate program at the University of Florida.

While earning a small salary as a bass-baritone singer in a traveling Colorado company, Ryan entered the Metropolitan Opera auditions and worked his way up to the semi-finals. During the week of intensive practice for the finals, the conductor was so critical of Ryan's pronunciation of Italian, the Met provided special tutoring for the correct pronunciations, and a donor provided special funds for final performance clothes that Ryan did not own. The audience fell in love with him and his performance, and his proud mother was in the audience to see and hear his success.

Although his mother had few resources to identify or nurture her son's musical talent, teachers and others stepped in to provide the help he needed to reach his goal.

*From: Daniel Bergner, "Sing for Your Life," *New York Times Magazine*, May 22, 2011, 20–28, 48.

Government agencies put pressure on teachers, parents, and students to raise achievement scores, creating stress for everyone. Teachers feel they are teaching only for testing, many students feel overburdened and uninterested in school, and parents feel responsible and forced to pressure children.[70] We discuss these issues in Chapters 5 and 9.

Increasing Use of Technology   Electronic devices like laptops, BlackBerry™ smartphones, and multipurpose cell phones enable parents to take their work with them wherever they go. Parents' work extends beyond the eight-hour day and becomes part of family life and recreational time. For both parents and children, the advances in mobile and online technology increase the use of media. One can talk or text to friends and others at any time or place. As a result, in the last five years children and teens increased their direct use of media from six hours and twenty minutes a day to seven hours and thirty-eight minutes. Since they are multi-tasking with media about a third of the time, children's and teens' daily total media exposure time is currently ten hours and forty-five minutes, seven days a week.[71] Census data and other surveys suggest parents' media exposure is ten to twelve hours a day.[72] How to balance family life and work, healthy, satisfying activities with media use presents a greater challenge for families today and we discuss that further in Chapter 6.

Twenty-first Century Social Supports for Parents

Parents have access to special supports to help them deal with challenges, sometimes from the very source that creates problems.

Technology   Electronic media enable parents and children to be in close touch. The Internet also gives parents and children enormous amounts of information quickly and conveniently. Parents can consult professionals' websites for advice on any parenting problem. If a child has a rare disease, the latest research is available and often contact with the researchers and other patients with the disease is possible.

The Internet not only informs, it also connects people with others for organized action, as has occurred in political battles in other countries. In unprecedented ways it has enabled parents to contact and plan actions with other parents. We use the example of parents' increasing concern that children lack playtime. Parents who want recess returned to their local school can contact the website playworks .org to get research to support their position, to find out what has worked in other school districts, and to find other parents to work with. They can plan events more easily and make changes quickly.

Nonprofit Organizations   Many people have set up organizations to provide underfunded or innovative services for children and families. For example, if parents want greater understanding of the importance of play and fun in children's lives, they can contact ultimateblockparty.org, which spearheaded a play day in

New York's Central Park. It drew fifty thousand families to play and receive a Playbook with many examples of playful activities easily carried out in everyday life.[73] If parents believe there are no safe playgrounds in their area, they can contact kaboom.org that has built more than 1900 playgrounds in low-income areas and ask for help.

Focus on Supporting Children's Positive Growth   State, national, and international agencies have focused more intensively on promoting positive aspects of development—children's physical and emotional health, intellectual and social competence, and participation in community activities. In "Thriving across the Life Span," Matthew Bundick and his colleagues describe programs that promote positive development in people of all ages.[74] Anne Petersen describes how international programs promote capabilities in youths in developing countries where the majority of the world's young people live.[75]

The Search Institute in Minneapolis carries out a broad range of activities with parents, children, and community officials in this country and abroad to create "Asset-Building" communities and experiences to provide all the nutrients for children's and teens' optimal development.[76] The institute identifies children's internal psychological assets that lead to healthy development, assets such as positive self-esteem, motivation for learning, social competence, and conflict resolution skills. Their focus is primarily on children and youth in the elementary school and adolescent years.

The institute also identifies community supports or external assets that can help all children develop their internal assets and help parents rear children. External assets include such supports as safe and caring neighborhoods, caring school climates, safe playgrounds, constructive youth programs, and opportunities for youth service. Such communities may counteract the stress and mistrust Wilkinson and Pickett describe as characteristic of an unequal society like ours. The institute has found that developing children's and adolescents' strengths has added benefits of decreasing high-risk behaviors like substance abuse that are so worrisome to parents and society at large.

Individuals from the Search Institute work both from the bottom up—with children, teens, and parents—and from the top down—with public officials and administrators—by:

- providing tools like surveys to find out community needs and resources for programs, e.g., posters reading "150 Ways to Show Kids You Care"
- facilitating communication between individuals and groups working on a topic
- providing training and consultation in the process of program development
- conducting research on program effectiveness

We will cite examples of their projects throughout the text but here we briefly describe an initiative in Multnomah, Oregon, to illustrate how people and communities proceed. Residents and community leaders were concerned at the results of the Search Survey showing that very few young people believed their community valued them, in part because newspaper coverage of teens often focused on their high-risk behaviors. A newspaper staff member asked two young people to brainstorm new ideas to improve communication. As a result, a reporter was assigned full-time to cover teen issues, a new weekly column reported teen activities, and the paper began to integrate teen workers throughout the company. The Asset-Building organizers sought partners with other media companies like radio and television stations, theaters, and bus advertising companies to join in publicizing asset-building activities, encouraging greater enthusiasm and participation in making teens an important part of the community.

HOW IMPORTANT ARE PARENTS IN CHILDREN'S LIVES?

In 1998, popular writer Judith Rich Harris sparked great debate with her statements that parents had far less influence on children's development than they imagined because genetic influences and peers accounted in large part for the way children turned out.[77] In response, researchers conducted studies to reveal parents' critical role in providing a protective environment for children's growth, stimulation for optimal development, and advocacy for children's interests in society. Here we review recent longitudinal research detailing parents' important role in setting children on developmental pathways, either positive or negative, that extend years into the future, impact several areas of children's behavior, and are passed on to the next generation.

Launching Children on Extended Pathways of Development

Research indicates that when parents provide warm and sensitive care to their infants, forming secure attachments with them, as toddlers, these children more easily develop self-regulation that enables them to form friendships in preschool and adjust to the rules.[78] Children develop self-esteem and enter school confidently where their behavioral and emotional control promote learning and school friendships. So from the security of the parent-child relationship in infancy, children's good feelings in social relationships expand to peers and to teachers. Competence in social and emotional regulation expands to children's competence in academic learning, which as we shall see later, is a protection against high-risk behaviors in adolescence.

Conversely, when children live in poverty with depressed mothers who lack energy to be sensitive, responsive, and stimulating caregivers, their children are more likely to start a pathway of negative experiences and difficulties.[79] As toddlers, they are angry and aggressive with mothers and others. As preschoolers, they are more likely to alienate their mothers, teachers, and peers with their aggressive and poorly controlled behaviors. They enter school, and these same behaviors make it hard for them to learn so they fall behind other students who do not want to play with them. By the time they are in the third grade, they are more likely to be academically delayed, rejected by peers and alienated from teachers. It is not surprising they more often report feelings of loneliness and anger.

When parents' relationships with children change, then children's behavior changes. For example, when mothers who attended a program to prevent the negative effects of divorce and were able to change the qualities of their relationships and their ways of disciplining their children then children's behavior improved.[80] Children whose mothers became warmer and more accepting felt less anxious and less worried in late middle school, and in late adolescence they were less anxious and had increased self-esteem. Children whose mothers became more effective disciplinarians became less angry, less noncompliant, and less impulsive in late childhood and as late adolescents, were more likely to have better academic grades and less substance abuse.

In another study, mothers who attended a fourteen-week parenting program to prevent sons' problems following divorce experienced many changes in their own lives and their children experienced change as well.[81] Following the sample for nine years, researchers were surprised at the many benefits that followed mothers' learning both to set consistent, fair limits and to create a positive relationship with children, encouraging them and providing stimulating activities. Mothers' depression decreased. Boys' depressed feelings and noncompliant, aggressive behaviors decreased, and their friendships at school increased. Over the nine-year period mothers' educational and occupational levels increased, and their incomes steadily improved. So becoming a more effective parent triggered many other positive changes in mothers' lives as well.

Intergenerational Transmission of Parenting

Longitudinal studies including three generations of families reveal that parents' child-rearing strategies, both positive and negative, influence not only their children's behaviors, but appear to be passed on to the next generation and impact their grandchildren.[82] Grandparents who are hostile and harsh in their parenting encourage anger, impulsivity, and noncompliance in their children who are more likely to grow up to be hostile, harsh parents whose children develop the same noncompliance and irritability their parents showed as youth.

Positive parenting techniques of listening to children, responding openly, and having assertive rather than harsh discipline helped children develop academic competence and success in high school.[83] When these adolescents became parents themselves in adulthood, they used their parents' positive methods, and their children developed the same academic success and competence in school they had experienced.

While genetic and constitutional factors certainly play a role in the behaviors children develop, changes in parents' ways of responding to children are related to changes over time in children's behavior. Further, mothers' parenting changes appear to increase mothers' general personal effectiveness as well (see Box 1-3).

Box 1-3
SHOULD A PARENTING LICENSE BE REQUIRED?

Given the important influence parents have in children's lives, should we require parents to get a license in order to have children? Although some behavior geneticists minimize parents' role in children's behavior, David Lykken was not among them. Despite the fact that his work has demonstrated high heritability for certain traits, he nevertheless believed that parents have such a profound influence on children's lives that parents should be licensed to have a child. Having studied criminal behavior and its antecedents, he was convinced that immature, impulsive parents doom a child to a life of difficulties.

> Most of the 1,400,000 men currently locked up in American prisons would have become tax-paying neighbors had they been switched in the hospital nursery and sent home with a mature, self-supporting, married couple. The parent with whom they did go home would in most instances not have been fit to adopt someone else's baby. . . . For evolutionary reasons, human beings are reluctant to interfere with the procreational rights of any person, no matter how immature, incompetent, or unsocialized he or she might be. In consequence human beings tend not to think about the rights of a child to a reasonable opportunity for life, liberty, and the pursuit of happiness."*

Lykken would require prospective parents to get a license, just as adults have to do to drive a car or operate a truck. Similar to the requirements for adoptive parents, a parenting license would require proof of (1) legal age, (2) marriage, (3) employment or economic independence, and (4) no history of violent criminal behavior. If parenting courses were available, a certificate of completion would be required as well. Proof of marriage was required because Lykken believed the biggest risk factor for adult problems is lack of a biological father. If couples object to marriage, they can sign a legal contract indicating they plan to stay together for twelve years to provide stability in the child's life. Gay or lesbian parents can appeal to a family court for a license. If parents had a child without a license, the child would be removed and placed for permanent adoption. If a divorce occurred after the child was born, the child would remain with the parents.

To critics of licensure, Lykken replied that no system will eliminate all problems, but he insisted, "Parenthood is both a privilege and a responsibility. The privilege of parenthood would not be determined by test scores or family trees, but by behavior. . . . If you wish to have a child, all you have to do is to grow up, keep out of trouble, get a job, and get married."**

Few might agree with the specifics of Lykken's plan, but how would *you* go about balancing the needs of the child with the rights of the parent?

*David T. Lykken, "Parental Licensure," *American Psychologist 56* (2001): 885–886.
**David T. Lykken, "The Causes and Costs of Crime and a Controversial Cure," *Journal of Personality 68* (2000): 598.

MUST PARENTS REPEAT THEIR PARENTS' BEHAVIORS?

As adults, parents worry about repeating negative behaviors and ways of relating learned in childhood, but research shows parents can deal with their feelings about their parents' behavior and adopt new ways of relating. A group of parents who experienced early hardships and difficulties in their relationships with their parents were able to find new ways of solving problems and interacting with others.[84] With the emotional support of a therapist, spouse, or friend, these parents, as adults, were able to look at their childhood experiences, identify the negative emotional experiences, and accept that their parents could not give them what they needed or wanted. With insights and acceptance of what had been, they were then able to create the kinds of relationships they wanted to have with their sons and daughters. Their sad and depressed feelings about their childhood experiences, while painful, did not limit them. They acknowledged the pain and went on to develop the flexible, warm style of parenting they desired.

Even if parents experience abuse as children and have a higher risk of being abusive than a parent who did not experience abuse—between 25 to 35 percent grow up to maltreat their own children—still, the majority do not adopt their parents' behavior.[85] And those parents who feel they are on the verge of hurting a child can learn new behaviors.

And this is true in other areas as well. Even though the risk is increased, the majority of children who grow up with an alcoholic parent do not, themselves, become alcoholics. Steven Wolin found that some families with an alcoholic parent acted deliberately to prevent transmission of alcoholic behavior to the next generation by protecting family rituals and routines like Christmas and birthdays from the alcohol abuse of the parent.[86] Parents who grew up with an alcoholic parent but did not transmit alcoholic behavior on to their children had healthy patterns of communication; parents talked together about their goals and planned satisfying holidays and routines, sometimes by doing the opposite of what had been done when they were children. Such planning prevented the development of alcoholic behavior in their children who are the grandchildren of alcoholics.[87]

And when parents are absent, their children need not be psychologically limited. In a continuation of his interview on Box 1-1, Joe Ehrmann describes how adolescents can handle the real losses they have experienced when parents were not present in their lives. He advises that even if fathers leave their families, and mothers and children struggle to manage, teens have to take responsibility for their own responses to painful events. "Even though your dad walked away, you've still eventually got to assume responsibility for yourself. And you've got to assume responsibility not to do that to your kids the next go-round. . . ."[88]

As noted, working with a therapist helps parents change. As we have just seen and will review in Chapter 6, parenting groups focus on ways to change. And, drawing on insights from neurobiology, attachment theory, and parent education classes, child psychiatrist Daniel Siegel and teacher/educator Mary Hartzell's book, *Parenting from the Inside Out: How a Deeper Self-Understanding Can Help You Raise*

Children Who Thrive, shows parents how, through awareness of their present feelings and reflections on the sources of these feelings, they gain self-understanding that allows them to be the parents they want to be. "By freeing ourselves from the constraints of our past, we can offer our children the spontaneous and connecting relationships that enable them to thrive."[89]

They encourage parents

- to live in the present moment with children; focusing on the feelings and perceptions as they occur.
- to look beyond the child's external behaviors to understand the internal ways the child thinks and feels.
- to appreciate what parent and child are experiencing, and then to choose actions that meet children's basic needs.

When parents react to children's behavior with intense feelings they do not understand or in ways they do not approve of, parents can look for the unresolved feelings left over from other situations that interfere with parenting. In such situations, the authors recommend journal writing about the situation because the reflection of writing often gives parents insights and understanding. Sometimes, others' comments, including the child's, provide insight. "Our children are not the only ones who will benefit from this making-sense process; we ourselves will come to live a more vital and enriched life because we have integrated our past experience into a coherent ongoing life story."[90]

HOW RAISING CHILDREN HELPS PARENTS GROW

Parents write about their intense love for their children. They write about stress, but less often about the positive changes parents allude to when they talk about how parenting has changed them (see Box 1-4). These parents use such phrases as "a better person," "more patient," "more kind," "more responsible," "more oriented toward the future."

Katherine Ellison's recent book, *The Mommy Brain: How Motherhood Makes Us Smarter*, describes the many positive changes mothers especially, but fathers and nonrelated caregivers experience in their personalities and behavior as a result of caring for children.[91]

Reviewing studies and interviewing researchers, Ellison identified five areas in which abilities improve:

- Observational skills and sensitivity to others' behaviors
- Efficiency
- Resiliency
- Motivation
- Social skills

Mothers are more sensitive to infants' cries, can identify their own infants' cries from those of other infants in the hospital, can identify their infants' clothes by smell. In one study, they are better able than nonmothers to read the body language

Box 1-4
HOW PARENTING HAS CHANGED ME AS A PERSON

"It has changed my priorities, my perspective. I am much more protective. If I see someone driving like an idiot, I get much more upset. I feel more like a regular person, more grown up."   FATHER OF A TODDLER

"Now I'm officially grown up. It's kind of funny because I am a forty-year-old person who is just feeling grown up. For me, it's being less caught up in myself, more unselfish, I don't do everything I want to do all the time, and that's changing and it's okay. I used to resent that. I'm less self-centered, less concerned with myself and how I'm doing, how I'm feeling, what's up. Now I am thinking more about him. For both my husband and me, I don't know whether this is going to change, but we are more oriented toward the future."   MOTHER OF A TODDLER

"My own personal sense of the meaningfulness of life in all its aspects has really gone through a dramatic change. It's just been so gratifying and meaningful and important to have this other little life, in a sense, in my hands, to be responsible for it."   FATHER OF A TODDLER

"It has changed my sense of the past. I appreciate more of what my parents must have gone through for me. No matter what their problems or shortcomings, gee, they had to do all this for me."   FATHER OF A TODDLER

"It's that overused word *maturity*. It happened for both of us, my husband and me. We look back on our lives before our son and afterwards. Our whole lives were what we wanted, every hour of every day. Along came the baby and, by choice, there was a reverse, almost 100 percent. We don't go out like we used to. It seems like an agony sometimes, but we are growing up as a couple and a family. It's very enriching."   MOTHER OF A TODDLER

"It has changed me for the better. It matured me, really at the core. I am much more responsible because I want to be a good example for them, provide stability for them. It has helped me to see into myself. I recall things I did as a child, and I understand better what was happening then. It has changed the kind of things I think of as fun."   FATHER OF ELEMENTARY SCHOOL–AGE CHILD AND EARLY ADOLESCENT

"Having children makes you more patient, more humble, better able to roll with the punches because life is not so black and white. You can't just base your life on platitudes. You have the experience of having things go not the way you would have them go, having your children do things you would not have them do, and you have to roll with that. You learn it; it either kills you or you go on, and you have a different view of life. You become more patient, and, I think, more kind."   MOTHER OF EARLY AND LATE ADOLESCENTS

"I want to be a good father so it makes me evaluate what I do and say; I look at mistakes as you would in any important and intense relationship, so it certainly makes me more self-examining and more aware of myself and how I am being experienced by the other person. It is also a challenge to be tolerant when I don't feel very tolerant. So in developing certain interpersonal skills, I think being a parent has helped me to become a better person."   FATHER OF ELEMENTARY SCHOOL–AGE CHILD

and identify the emotional reactions of an adult. Mothers appear more responsible and more understanding of themselves and others in the period after having children.

Ellison believes these changes are most dramatic for mothers because of the numerous hormonal changes during pregnancy, the birth process, and later, during nursing, but clearly hormonal changes are not required because fathers respond to infants' cries in ways similar to those of mothers. They too increase in their ability to read body language and identify emotional reactions.

Mothers, fathers, and teachers identify four similar ways in which children have changed them.[92] First, children have heightened their awareness of environmental issues, and motivated adults to change bad habits like smoking or drinking. One mother said, "It wasn't so much that he [her son] would say anything, it was just how he would look at me, like he was really worried when I smoked. It would kill me. He cared so much. He really helped me to care for myself better. I haven't had a cigarette in over a year."[93]

Second, children have helped parents to understand and integrate experiences from their own childhoods. They may hear themselves saying or doing things their parents did and understand their parents better. Or they may use such an experience as a wakeup call for the need to change their behavior with their own children.

Third, adults say they have become more knowledgeable and more creative in helping children learn and master tasks. Fourth, children's awe and wonder at life trigger parents' wonder and awe. When adults interact with children, the familiar categories and concepts adults use to organize the world can be challenged and even cracked open by the child."[94]

So, we grow in many ways as a result of caring for children. As researchers studying the satisfactions and problems of parenting wrote, "Perhaps no other circumstance in life offers so many challenges to an individual's powers, so great an array of opportunities for appreciation, such a varied emotional and intellectual stimulation."[95]

MAIN POINTS

Parenting is
- nourishing, protecting, and guiding new life
- providing resources to meet children's needs for love, attention, and values

Reasons for having children
- love, affection, and stimulation
- creative outlet, proof of maturity, and sense of achievement
- proof of virtue and economic advantage—joys that far outweigh problems of rearing children

The process of parenting involves
- three partners: children, parents, and society
- children who have their own needs and temperaments but meet parents' and society's needs

- parents who rear their children while also maintaining marriages, work, and social relationships
- society defines roles, enforces basic requirements for parents, and serves as a powerful source of support or stress for children and parents

The social context of parenting

- has shifted from extended farm family in the nineteenth century to nuclear families for much of the twentieth century to diverse families in the 1970s and more recently a shift to multigenerational families
- is very diverse in terms of parents' living arrangements, racial and ethnic background, and economic resources
- presents twenty-first century challenges of national and economic insecurity and increase in technology at home, but also provides special supports
- has not weakened bonds of solidarity between the generations

Parents are

- the single most important influence and resource in a child's life
- not the only influences on children's behaviors, as media, communities, and social events outside the family influence children's behavior and development as well
- stimulators and providers of nourishing environments that enable children to achieve their maximal potential even when genetic factors make special efforts necessary
- advocates who can make social changes to help children
- so influential that some suggest people be required to have a license to become parents
- difficult for state institutions to replace

When parents have difficult experiences with their parents in childhood, they

- are not doomed to repeat them with their children
- can gain self-understanding and reparent themselves as well as get guidance from professionals, parenting groups, and friends

Raising children changes parents who

- become more observant, sensitive, efficient, resilient, and socially skilled
- gain greater understanding of self and are motivated to correct bad habits
- feel a new sense of awe and wonder in the world

EXERCISES

1. Interview your parent or parents, separately or together, about the joys they anticipated having with you before your birth. Did they experience them or others in addition to them? Were they surprised at any of the joys? If possible, interview a grandparent or grandparents about the joys they anticipated with your parent and ask them the same questions. Were the joys the same for the two generations of parents? Were there differences, and if so, what were they?

2. From the year of your birth, trace the social influences acting on your parents as they raised you. For example, for the 1980s, such influences might have included the increased rate of women's participation in the workforce, the high rate of divorce and remarriage, the drop in skilled-labor jobs. Look for the effects of social change on your daily life and the ways your parents cared for you. For example, if your mother worked, describe the day care arrangements. If your parents divorced and/or remarried, describe how child care was affected.

3. Suppose that you had to obtain a license in order to have a child, as David Lykken suggests. What would you require for such a license?

4. Go online to nytimes/motherlode.com and read two articles by Lisa Belkin. Summarize the article and reader comments.

5. Read the newspaper for one week and cut out all the articles of interest to parents, including news and feature articles. The articles might cover a broad range of topics—solving children's behavioral problems, laws relating to parents' employment benefits or to the rights of parents in the workplace, laws regarding who is recognized as a parent at times of divorce or death. Describe what these articles tell you about the parenting experience at the beginning of the twenty-first century.

ADDITIONAL READINGS

Benson, Peter L. *All Kids Are Our Kids: What Communities Must Do to Raise Caring and Responsible Children and Adolescents*, 2nd ed. San Francisco: Jossey-Bass, 2006.

Chua, Amy. *Battle Hymn of the Tiger Mother*. New York: Penguin, 2011.

Ellison, Katherine. *The Mommy Brain: How Motherhood Makes Us Smarter*. New York: Basic Books, 2005.

Lewis, Michael. *Home Game: An Accidental Guide to Fatherhood*. New York: Norton, 2009.

Wilkinson, Richard and Pickett, Kate. *The Spirit Level: Why Equality Is Better for Everyone*. London: Penguin, 2010.

CHAPTER

2

Cultural Influences on Parenting

CHAPTER TOPICS

In this chapter, you will learn about:

- Definition of culture and cultural influences around the world

- Two cultural models of parent-child relationships

- Dynamic nature of culture and how culture is transmitted from one generation to another

- Sources of cultural influences in the United States: race, ethnicity, socioeconomic status, religion

- Cultural diversity and experiences of immigrant and ethnic minority groups

- Ways to reduce discrimination and manage its effects

- The influence of socioeconomic status and economic hardship on parenting

- Ways to intervene to mitigate effects

Test Your Knowledge: Fact or Fiction (True/False)

1. To stabilize social functioning, cultural influences are passed from one generation to the next with few changes.
2. Writing short essays on personally important, positive values helped African American middle-school students maintain self-confidence and improve their academic performance.
3. Poverty status influences more aspects of children's development than racial or ethnic background.
4. The self-esteem of people in different ethnic groups reflects the general regard their group receives from society at large.
5. Parents do not realize how important it is to children to have culturally valued possessions.

Culture provides a nest for all the parent-child interactions we look at throughout the book. In this chapter we look at the many ways cultural forces shape the process of parenting. We look at common features and diversity in how parents socialize children around the world and in different social groups within this country. We examine the experiences of immigrants in the process of adaptation to American culture, and the heavy burden that prejudice and discrimination place on those who encounter it and those who witness it.

Culture is a system of values, beliefs, ways of thinking, routines, rituals, and institutions established by a group or population.[1] The group can be as small as a neighborhood, school, or community or as large as racial, ethnic, and social status groups. Culture provides ways of looking at the world ignoring some things and focusing on others. Culture shapes what we talk about, what we remember, how we conceptualize our lives. Along with other influences, culture determines patterns of feelings and behavior in everyday life. As we saw in Chapter 1, culture is a dynamic force responding to social, political, and economic events and shaping the meaning of these events for us.

Culture provides a developmental niche that includes (1) the physical and social settings for parents and children, (2) the psychological characteristics valued in parents and children, and (3) recommended parenting practices and behaviors for family members.[2] So, culture shapes a broad range of parental behaviors, from the more general values parents teach to the concrete aspects of daily life such as where children eat and sleep.

CULTURAL THEMES AROUND THE WORLD

People have looked for ways to organize and understand cultural influences and their effects, and surveys of many ethnic groups have revealed two general models of social relationships. No one country or group perfectly illustrates either model, but groups tend to have more features of one than the other.

Two Cultural Models

The independent/individualistic model and the interdependent/collectivist model provide frameworks for understanding how cultural values influence what parents do with their children.[3] Table 2-1 outlines these two general models of social systems as they apply to parenting behaviors.

The interdependent/collectivist model is the older and more widely followed model and emphasizes the importance of the social group. The self is defined in terms of membership in the social system, particularly the family or community group, being a son or daughter, grandchild, brother or sister, and an independent, autonomous self does not exist apart from the group. Thus, the model is termed group centric or sociocentric. The group seeks harmony among its members. An individual's main form of action in the group is to understand others' needs and adjust or accommodate to them, thus fulfilling one's duties and obligations to others. One feels connected to others when one is adjusting to their needs, showing the

■ **T A B L E 2-1**
CONTRASTING CULTURAL MODELS OF PARENT-CHILD RELATIONS*

Developmental Goals	Independence	Interdependence
Developmental trajectory	From dependent to independent self	From asocial to socially responsible self
Communication	Verbal emphasis	Nonverbal emphasis (empathy, observation, participation)
	Autonomous self-expression	Child comprehension, mother speaks for child
	Frequent parental questions to child	Frequent parental directives to child
	Frequent praise	Infrequent praise
	Child negotiation	Frequent parental directives
Collaborative problem solving	Division of labor	Shared multiparty engagement
Parents helping children	A matter of personal choice except under extreme need	A moral obligation under all circumstances

*From Patricia M. Greenfield, Lalita K. Suzuki, and Carrie Rothstein-Fisch, "Cultural Pathways through Human Development," in *Handbook of Child Psychology*, 6th ed., eds. William Damon and Richard M. Lerner, vol. 4: Child Psychology in Practice, eds. K. Ann Renninger and Irving E. Sigel (Hoboken, NJ: Wiley, 2006), p. 676. Copyright (C) 2006. Reprinted by permission of John Wiley & Sons, Inc.

commitment to the relationship. Being attentive to many people's wishes as well as one's own duties to others encourages a holistic way of thinking and approaching situations, focusing on the entire picture rather than on particular parts.

This model dates back to the hunter-gatherer society that involved close contact with a small group of people for a lifetime.[4] Parent-child relationships emphasized physical contact between mother and child with nursing for three or four years and cosleeping. Children were gradually transitioned to multiage groups, sometimes involving sibling care. Although young children were indulged, as they grew older, they were expected to internalize and follow the rules of parents and other authorities, and parents were active teachers and socializing agents. This model has been widely practiced in Asia, Sub-Saharan Africa, and South America.

The independent/individualistic model of social systems, characteristic of Europe, North America, Australia, and New Zealand, emphasizes the importance of the independent individual who defines the self in terms of personal choices, goals, and achievements.[5] This system is a self- or ego-centric system, and interpersonal relationships are mainly interactions to influence people, to persuade them to one's point of view or to help them in a positive way. One feels connected to others as one influences them. The emphasis on the self, action, and goal achievement encourages analysis of situations into parts and logical strategies to achieve goals as opposed to holistic forms of thought.

This model is thought to have developed from Greek civilization that centers on the importance of the individual, personal agency, careful, logical analysis of situations into separate parts, but was eclipsed until the religious Reformation in Germany and England and the changes of the Industrial Revolution emphasizing the importance of the individual and personal choice and action. The model has been reinforced in pioneer groups who have settled new countries that require individuals to be self-directed and self-sufficient. In the independent model, parents nurture infants but from the earliest days encourage autonomy by having babies play and sleep alone. Parents actively stimulate children to explore, learn, and become self-sustaining, productive, competent adults who enter into relationships with other adults by choice.

Each social system provides stresses and supports. In an interdependent system, stress comes from trying to understand others' points of view and restraining one's own thoughts, feelings, and actions to accommodate others; the advantage of the system is that the support of the group is always available to help in times of need. The stress of the independent system comes from the anxiety of seeking to achieve and the lack of guaranteed help in adverse circumstances. The positive side of the system is that people are free to have their own interests and pursue their goals without the burdens of others' expectations.

Variations in Cultural Themes

These models are put into practice in different ways depending on the particular country.[6] For example, in Asia, Chinese parents emphasize the emotional interdependence and harmony that exists between parent and infant, but they demand that toddlers learn others' expectations of them. Parents actively teach children what to do, pointing out mistakes in behavior, reviewing them in detail so that children will know how to avoid them in the future. As children grow older, parents emphasize learning and mastery of material but also want children to develop a passion for knowledge, using it to help the group.

Chinese people tend to emphasize harmony in two-person relationships while Japanese people are absorbed in the group. Social pressures in China more often come from authority figures whereas in Japan, pressures come from peers.[7] The Japanese are less irritated by social constraints than the Chinese and positively value the sense of order that comes from knowing one's duties and obligations. Japan has become a capitalist country but retains its social values in its management style of company loyalty, team spirit, and cooperation among workers.

In Sub-Saharan Africa, parental theories emphasize mother-child closeness and nursing lasting for three years. As infants become more mobile, there are more caretakers involved in their care.[8] Some social scientists feared that multiple caretakers would dilute the attachment relationship between mother and child, but that does not appear to be the case. Children become securely attached to their mothers, who provide security and a safe basis for exploration even when there are other caregivers.

In African countries, concern for the group is reflected in parents' emphasis on a child's capacity for socially responsible behavior like being able to carry out an errand at a young age without supervision. Social responsibility is a combination of such qualities as social insightfulness, empathy, quick thinking, and the capacity for independent action to help others. Although this trait has great value to parents, we know much less how it is instilled.

While we think of Northern Europe and the United States as having similar child-rearing practices because they follow an independent model, comparisons of parenting infants in the Netherlands and Boston reveal differences in early caregiving.[9] Dutch parents strongly believe that regular daily schedules are important for themselves and for their babies. Regular routines and long hours of sleep, they believe, help children become competent and independent. Parents put their babies down to sleep at the same time every night, expect them to sleep, and babies sleep. American mothers have conflicted feelings, encouraging babies' independence in sleeping alone, but believing sleep patterns are innate and related to infant temperament, consequently gratifying them. At six months of age, Dutch babies get two hours more sleep each day than American infants, and significant sleep difference continues through early childhood. The regular schedules and extended sleep of Dutch babies may play a role in Dutch toddlers' maintaining a state of quiet alertness and calm during daytime observations when American toddlers are observed to be in a state of active alertness and greater arousal during most of the day.

Dutch and American parents also interpret special time with children differently. Dutch parents have special family time at dinner each night when everyone is present, and children are present from the earliest days of life even if colicky or difficult. Parents look forward to the time that children will participate more actively. American parents interpret special time as a time each parent spends separately with each child so it is a partner event rather than family time. These parents share a general model of parent-child relationships that is carried out in slightly different ways that have behavioral consequences.

The Dynamic Nature of Culture

These are broad models of behavior, and people's behavior changes in response to life experiences. For example, in the 1870s, a group of Japanese people seeking greater economic prosperity voluntarily migrated to Hokkaido, a remote island off the northern coast of Japan.[10] Succeeding on the island required initiative, energy, ingenuity, and independent thinking. The descendants of these settlers, when tested on measures of cultural orientation, resembled Americans more than they did Japanese from the mainland.

Patricia Greenfield believes that many parts of the world are currently in the process of shifting from interdependent/collectivist societies to more independent/

individualistic societies because of increased urbanization, increased use of technology, and greater education required to participate in a more complex industrial society.[11]

Greenfield believes many societies will shift completely to the independent/individualistic model with continuing urbanization and industrialization in agrarian societies, but others believe it is possible to merge the two models and have individuals who seek personally chosen goals in an independent fashion, yet stay strongly connected to families. They point to studies showing that with a little priming, we can take on the behaviors of the other culture. When people are primed, for example, to give individualistic responses by circling all the first person singular words in paragraphs, they respond to laboratory tests in a more independent fashion than those who are primed for an interdependent response by circling first-person plural words.

Social psychologist Richard Nisbett, who has carried out extensive research in the area of cultural psychology, believes that interdependent and independent societies can blend their orientations in such a way that both "are represented but transformed—like the individual ingredients in a stew that are recognizable but are altered as they alter the whole. It may not be too much to hope that this stew will contain the best of each culture."[12]

As cultures change and emphasize new values, research suggests it is important that individuals retain meaningful connections with their traditional roots. Social scientists in Canada were able to link the psychological adjustment of adolescent Native Canadians with the level of cultural continuity in their communities. They examined the suicide rates of 196 Native communities. Those Native communities and tribes that were able to preserve their past and maintain control over their land, their government, and community services conveyed a sense of cultural continuity. These communities and tribes had very low, or zero rates of suicide in comparison to Native communities that could not create a sense of continuity between past, present, and future and had much higher rates.[13]

THE TRANSMISSION OF CULTURAL VALUES

Socialization "is the process through which children acquire the beliefs, values, practices, skills, attitudes, behaviors, ways of thinking, and motives of their culture that together help children develop into effective and contributing members of the group."[14] Anthropologist Melvin Konner believes there are four general ways that individuals are socialized to their culture's values and practices:[15]

- cultural habitation—living in the culture, carrying out the daily routines and rituals, copying what others do, experiencing the rewards and consequences of the behaviors—teaches culture much as living in a foreign country for a year
- learning through social interactions with other people who explain the customs, include individuals in group activities, show them how to perform the activities, give explicit instructions

Children first learn about their cultural heritage from interactions with family members.

- emotional enculturation—learning through positive emotional attachments to others, identifying with them, wanting to be like them and please them by taking on their behaviors and having fears of strangers and other anxieties reduced through following rules and receiving protection from caregivers

- cognitive enculturation involves learning through symbols that shape perception and thinking, e.g., use of language, narratives, and stories that shape the way individuals understand the culture and think about the world

Rituals, defined as repeated patterns of behavior that have symbolic meaning for the family, are major ways that cultural and ethnic groups pass their values and traditions on to the next generation.[16] Rituals arouse feelings and a special sense of belonging when they are carried out. Rituals include special family traditions like vacations or birthday celebrations, family celebrations of major secular or religious holidays, and community-wide celebrations of important traditions.

Exposed to all these forms of enculturation, children actively construct a view of the world and their place in it.[17] Based on what parents teach, what children experience, what they see happen to those around them, what they learn from interactions with individuals outside their own group, children construct a cultural *scheme* of the world.[18] This is an active process in which parents present expectations, and children resist, refuse, and most often incorporate them.

The anthropologist Jean Briggs writes,

The notion that meaning inheres in culture and that people receive it passively as dough receives the cookie cutter is rapidly being replaced by the idea that culture consists of ingredients, which people actively select, interpret, and use in various ways as opportunities, capabilities, and experience allow.[19]

Everyday Activities That Teach Young Children Cultural Values

While there is great variety in the living conditions and caregiving practices around the world, as the 2010 movie *Babies* documented, there are still common experiences that enable babies to develop basic skills. All babies begin social smiling at about the same time; they become attached to parents and use them as a secure base for exploration, and they develop language.[20] One- to three-year-old children in very different cultures like rural Canada, rural India, and rural Peru all develop social-cognitive skills of attending to others, understanding their intentions, imitating what they do, and helping them.[21] Differences appear in the third year in skills with external symbols like pictures and using objects for pretend play. Canadian children who had early and extensive experience with books and pretend play showed these behaviors about a year in advance of children in India and Peru with minimal experience, suggesting that culturally specific skills involving objects and abstract symbols vary more depending on particular learning experiences.

Jonathan Tudge sought to identify how cultural and social influences provide resources for three-year-old children and shape what they do, and how children's responses create variations within all groups.[22] He initiated a complex study observing the activities of three-year-old children around the world, selecting, as best he could, comparable cities of about 200,000 people in each country and obtaining volunteers for separate middle-class and working-class samples in collectivist countries such as Russia and Estonia, developing countries such as Kenya, Brazil, and South Korea (though it is also a collectivist country), and individualistic countries like Finland and the United States where Tudge had separate samples of European American and African American middle- and working-class children.

He trained observers in each country to systematically and carefully record each child's activities for twenty hours that, in a week's time, covered the child's day from waking until going to sleep at night. The observations focused on four activities: (1) play, (2) lessons of an informal sort about academic matters and the way objects and the world worked, (3) conversations about things occurring in the past or the future, thus requiring greater cognitive skill than talking about ongoing activities, and (4) work. These four activities took up about 70 percent of children's time; the remaining time was spent in eating, bathing, and sleeping. His samples and systematic observations of activities increased the likelihood differences between countries were due to cultural forces and not to comparing urban middle-class children in one country with poor, rural children in another.

Observations revealed:

- children in all countries and groups spent about 60 percent of their time in play, most frequently with other children, but they differed in what they played with; most children had toys and educational materials like books to play with but in Kenya they did not and played with objects in the natural or adult worlds like bottles, jars, and sticks

- work was being carried out by others in about 23 to 35 percent of the observations, but children engaged in work only 8 to 15 percent of their time

- children engaged in conversations between 5 and 10 percent of their time with one exception—children from Finland talked almost twice the amount of time of other children

- children engaged in lessons between 5 and 11 percent of the time with children in Finland and Brazil having even smaller amounts of time at 3 and 2 percent

- children most often initiated their play activities but others most often initiated their lessons, conversations, and work

- in all countries, television viewing was associated with decreases in time in pretend play, in play with educational kinds of toys or objects, and in conversations

- social class differences in other countries resembled those in this country with middle-class children having more lessons, more pretend play, more work, and in four countries, less television watching than working class children

Children absorbed cultural influences from the intersection of their countries' activity patterns, children's social status, and the child's own personal interests. Although all children engaged in similar activities, the pattern of these activities differed somewhat with Finnish children learning more about their culture from conversations and less from lessons, Russian children learning more from work, conversations, and lessons, and less from play, South Korean children learning more from play and work and less from conversations, Kenyan children learning more from lessons and work and less from conversations, and Brazilian children learning from conversations but less from work and lessons, and American and Estonian children learning from a balanced pattern including all activities.

We do not know how these differing activity patterns affect the development of abilities, but we do know that Western parents' reports of their children's personal characteristics reflect common qualities valued in Western countries, with differences depending on the particular country.[23] Sociable, loving, active, and strong-willed are adjectives used by all groups of parents of toddler-preschoolers in six Western countries, but each country has additional qualities that reflect its values with Dutch parents' describing their children as having long attention, being agreeable, and regular, and American parents' describing their children as being intelligent, cognitively advanced, and adaptable.

Parents' reports of young children's problem behaviors in twenty-four countries around the world reveal that Danish, Dutch, Korean, and Finnish parents report the fewest problem behaviors and parents from Taiwan, Chile, and Lithuania report the greatest number with American parents' being at the mean.[24] Common problem behaviors reported in twenty-two of the twenty-four countries are "Can't stand waiting," "Demands must be met immediately," and "Wants a lot of attention."

Despite variations in culture, observations and parents' reports reveal children around the world engage in many common activities and develop some common behaviors with differences reflecting a particular country's values and resources.

Everyday Activities of Older Children and Adolescents

The biggest factor in how older children around the world spend time is the country's level of industrialization.[25] In non-industrialized countries, children spent more time in chores and paid work, often done in the company of parents and family members. Once countries were industrialized, children's major block of time was spent in schools and in doing homework, so there is a growing percentage of time spent out of the company of parents as children go through adolescence.

Around the industrialized world, television watching consumes about the same amount of time with similar gender and social differences. Boys watched more TV, and children in higher social groups watched less.

Leisure time can be categorized into structured and unstructured activities. Sports, artistic activities, clubs, civic activities are structured activities. Americans exceeded all countries in the amount of time spent in sports; this too related to gender and social status with boys and children in higher social groups engaging in more sports.

Parents in Asian countries encouraged their children, freed from work, to spend long hours at school and in studies that would lead to productive work and economic gain. American youth were permitted to spend time in leisure activities that were structured, like sports or artistic activities, or unstructured activities like free play and getting together to talk with friends. The value of structured activities may be that they help children develop initiative and self-regulation.

There are more cultural similarities than differences in the people children spend time with. In most industrialized countries, time spent with families decreased as children went off to school. While Asian youth spend most of their out-of-school time at home studying, American children spend more time with peers and adults outside the home as they go through adolescence.

MAJOR SOURCES OF CULTURAL INFLUENCES WITHIN THE UNITED STATES

We are a country teeming with cultural influences from many sources.

Race

Up until about 1970, race was considered a category based on external differences like skin color and hair texture, which were thought to be rooted in biological differences.[26] Because there was much variation within racial groups and few differences between racial groups, and because most of us carry genetic markers from more than one race, race is now considered a social construct, a way of categorizing people to identify and justify social position. Because it is a social construct, race is considered a fluid concept subject to redefinition and change.

Analysis of data from the National Longitudinal Survey of Youth illustrates how changeable race is.[27] At the end of yearly interviews with the study members, interviewers categorized the race of the respondent as white, black, or other, and two times during the study, respondents were asked to identify, in 1972 their "origin of descent," and in 2002, their race and races, and whether they were of Hispanic ethnicity.

Comparisons of interviewer classifications from year to year revealed that if persons categorized as white in the previous year reported being unemployed, incarcerated, or impoverished, they were less likely to be categorized as white in that year and more likely classified as black. For example, 96 percent of white people who did not report incarceration were reclassified as white in that year, but only 90 percent of people who reported being incarcerated that year were reclassified as white. The 6 percent difference was significant and not due to recording errors that were estimated at one-quarter of 1 percent as that was the error rate of gender recording.

Of equal interest, individuals' self identifications changed when they reported being poor, impoverished, or incarcerated over the period from 1979 to 2002. For example, 97 percent of individuals who identified themselves as white in 1979 and did not experience poverty between 1979 and 2002 continued to identify themselves as white in 2002. Only 93 percent of those who identified themselves as white in 1979 and experienced poverty in the intervening years identified themselves as white in 2002. So race is a changing concept related to changes in social conditions.

The Census Bureau data reflects this concept of race.[28] In 1990, the Census Bureau recognized four racial groups: American Indian/Alaskan Native, Asian/Pacific Islander, Black, and White. In 2000, a government directive broadened the categories, making a separate category for Pacific Islander, adding a category, Some Other Race, and offering respondents the opportunity to check more than one race. In that year also, the Census Bureau began to ask if the person was of Hispanic origin, and if so from what area. People of Hispanic origin were considered an ethnic group, not a racial group.

The *Statistical Abstract* states in its section on population,

> The concept of race, as used by the Census Bureau, reflects self-identification by people according to the race or races with which they most closely identify. These categories are sociopolitical constructs and should not be interpreted as being scientific or anthropological in nature.[29]

In 2000, about 2.4 percent of the population or seven million people identified themselves as being of two races, and the figure for 2010 is not yet known. Pittsburgh Steeler Superbowl star Hines Ward described how hard it was growing up as a biracial child of a Korean mother and African American father.[30] All groups rejected him—African Americas didn't want him as a friend because of his Asian mother, and European and Asian American children did not include him because they considered him African American. So, finding a sense of identity was hard. And then once I got involved in sports, color didn't matter."[31] Many colleges have established organizations like the University of Maryland's Multiracial and Biracial Student Association that presents talks and provides a place for students to discuss their own experiences and find support from others with similar identity issues as young adulthood is often a time when this is explored.[32]

Ethnicity

The term *ethnicity* refers to "an individual's membership in a group sharing a common ancestral heritage based on nationality, language, and culture. Psychological attachment to the group is also a dimension of ethnicity, referred to as '*ethnic identity*.'"[33] Previously considered racial groups are now considered broad ethnic groups including many subgroups. For example, the European American ethnic group includes people of German, Irish, Eastern European or Italian descent with different cultural emphases. Native Americans include members of more than four hundred tribes. Asian Americans include Hmong, Filipino, Chinese, Japanese, and others. The Latino group includes people from many different countries in Central and South America as well as from the Caribbean Islands. Conversely, an ethnic group may have members in more than one racial group. For example, some Latinos fall in the Caucasian racial group, but others fall in the African racial group. We discuss immigrant groups in a later section.

Social Status

Based on individuals' education, occupation, and income, social status is perhaps the most powerful influence shaping parents' child-rearing behaviors. Belief in the American dream that ability and hard work determine success makes it difficult to accept that social position can be such a force in children's experiences growing up, but several studies suggest this is so. For example, researchers comparing the home environments of four ethnic groups—European Americans, African Americans, Latinos, and Asian Americans—found that while ethnic differences influenced what parents did, social status reflected in families' resources overshadowed ethnic differences in the homes, with parents' providing poor children fewer books, musical instruments, and lessons, but also giving less attention and physical affection. Of the 124 items describing the home and parenting, 88 percent were affected by poverty status, and only fifteen items were unaffected. The effects of having few resources were similar across all ethnic groups.[34]

Religion

Religions are not discussed in detail because they are so numerous in this country, but it is important to note that religious groups form cultures that provide niches for development and prescribe ways of life—no alcohol, no caffeine, prayers several times a day—that parents pass on to children.

Box 2-1
FIRST PERSON NARRATIVE*

Unlikely Brothers: Our Story of Adventure, Loss, and Redemption by John Prendergast (JP) and Michael Mattocks is the story of how two men dealt with a major childhood loss—the loss of a father's love—and how, after many ups and downs, each crafted a meaningful adult life. The culture each man inhabited, in JP'S case, middle-class, Irish Catholic, suburban Philadelphia culture, and in Michael's case, the inner-city, African American culture of Washington, D.C., provides both supports and additional stresses that shape how each man responds to the loss.

The lives of the two men intersect when twenty-year-old JP, a Georgetown University student, becomes six-year-old Michael's Big Brother. Their thirty-year relationship, most often close but at a few crucial times not close, gives each man a unique role in the other's life. The book describes how adolescence affects each man and the role temperament plays in their response to loss and difficulties. The book powerfully details the sustaining force of family members' love for these men, and how little acts of interest and rejection by people in the community have profound effects on directing young people's lives. JP becomes a peace activist focusing on events in Africa, and Michael enters the world of the drug dealer for a decade and then leaves it.

Both men come to terms with their losses. Michael becomes the loving and responsible father he never had in his life, and JP finds stability and peace in a second marriage with desires for becoming a biological father though he has already cared for and mentored nephews, little brothers, and children around the world.

Their stories provide many reasons for believing that desired outcomes lie just beyond enormous challenges when in the company of brothers and other family members who love you.

*John Prendergast and Michael Mattocks, *Unlikely Brothers: Our Story of Adventure, Loss, and Redemption* (New York: Crown Publishing, 2011).

Other Cultural Influences

Other cultural influences include geographical areas with distinct cultures found in areas of the North, South, East, and West, and rural–urban areas of residence also exerting cultural influences.

Personal Identity and Reference Group Orientation

William Cross describes how culture influences self-concept. He distinguishes two aspects of self-concept: *personal identity* (PI), which includes such factors as self-esteem and general personality traits, and *reference group orientation* (RGO), which includes cultural group identities such as gender and ethnic identities, group awareness, and group attitudes (see Figure 2-1).[35] He discusses RGO primarily

■ **FIGURE 2-1**
SCHEMATIC OF THE TWO-FACTOR THEORY OF BLACK IDENTITY*

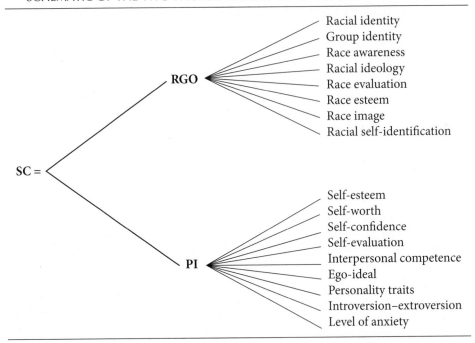

Note: Self-concept (SC) = personal identity (PI) + reference group orientation (RGO)

*From William E. Cross, Jr., "A Two Factor Theory of Black Identity," in Children's Ethnic Socialization, ed. Jean S. Phinney and Mary Jane Rotheram (Beverly Hills, CA: Sage, 1987); Figure 6.1, p. 122. Children's Ethnic Socialization: Pluralism and Development by Phinney, Jean S. Copyright 2012 Reproduced with permission of SAGE PUBLICATIONS INC BOOKS in the format Textbook via Copyright Clearance Center.

in terms of racial identity, to explain why people of the same ethnic group with equal commitments to that group may have very different attitudes about ethnic identity—that is, they have very different RGOs.

He states that RGO may be prominent in some groups and not in others— for example, some European Americans think of themselves only as Americans, whereas others have a strong ethnic identity as Italian Americans or Irish Americans. Some people have a strong religious RGO, and others do not. Cross shows the usefulness of these concepts in understanding gender identity. Two women might be similar with regard to self-esteem and self-worth, but one may have a strong RGO as a feminist and interpret much of her experience in light of that group identity, while another woman might not and thus perceive situations differently. Or the same person may have a shift in RGO over time as life circumstances change. For example, teenage girls experience what is termed gender intensification (see Chapter 11), and adapt their behavior to meet societal prescriptions regarding gender-related behavior to a greater degree than they did at an earlier age so their RGO of gender would be more prominent in adolescence than in elementary school.

CULTURAL THEMES AND VARIATIONS WITHIN THE UNITED STATES

Reviewing cultural influences within the United States, Catherine Tamis-LeMonda and Karen McFadden point to the broad framework of values established early in our country's history and shared nationally as important principles: personal freedom, the right to individual expression and to pursue individual goals provided they do not infringe on others' rights, and the right to equal treatment.[36]

Variations among Ethnic Groups

European American families are the most likely to follow the independent/individualistic model of social relationships, but even within this large group there is variation with some group like Italian Americans highly attached to family and the group.

Most ethnic groups within this country have a more interdependent/collectivist approach to social relationships.[37] The emphasis on family closeness and connectedness is seen in Latino/a focus on familism, the loyalty and solidarity felt with immediate and extended family, in Asian Americans' focus on family obligations and duties, in African Americans' closeness with extended family and "fictive" kin who are not relatives but have family status like "auntie" and "uncle," and in Native Americans' attachment to the family, the tribe, and to the natural environment.

The equality existing in many European American families with all members vigorously asserting personal opinions, desires, and goals is less routinely practiced in many ethnic groups where there is a more hierarchical relationship between parents and children. Parents have a controlling role, insisting on respect and obedience to their rules and regulations. As one African American mother said to her son, "I am not your friend. I am your mother. Maybe someday we'll be friends, but now I am your mother, and I expect you to do what I say."

In many ethnic groups, there is less emphasis on individual achievement and a greater emphasis on actions for the benefit of the family or the group. Young adults would be expected to contribute to the family finances and needs of individual members even if this meant postponing education.

Table 2-2 presents basic demographic characteristics of the six major ethnic groups in this country. One can see that European Americans, Asian Americans, and Middle Eastern Americans have above-average resources in terms of income and education. The recent downturn in the economy has affected most those groups with fewest resources with increases in poverty levels greatest in African American and Latino groups. Differences in resources and education are related to higher rates of infant mortality, greater numbers of health problems, and shorter life spans.[38] We discuss the problems of poverty in a later section.

IMMIGRANT FAMILIES

Today 23 percent of children in the United States (nearly one in four) live in immigrant families.[39] These children, however, are rooted in American life. Most were born in the United States and 64 percent live with at least one parent who is a United

T A B L E 2-2
DEMOGRAPHIC CHARACTERISTICS OF SIX ETHNIC GROUPS AND TOTAL POPULATION*

Characteristic	Total	NA	Whites**	AfA	LA	AsA	MEA***
%Pop. 2009	100	1	66	13	16	4	1
Median Age	37	30	38	31	27	35	33
Education: 2008							
%HS. Grad.	85	76	90	81	61	85	84
%Coll. Grad.	28	13	30	18	13	50	41
Income: 2008							
Median Fam.	63,366	43,190	70,835	41,874	43,437	80,101	52,000+
%Fam. in Pov.	10	20	7	21	19	8	17
%Child in Pov.	18		15	34	30	14	
Number of Children: 2009							
Avg. Per couple	1.93		1.88	2.02	2.13	1.71	
Avg. Single Mo.	1.74		1.58	1.55	1.58	1.61	
Avg. Single Fa.	1.55						
Children under 18: 2009							
Two-par. fams	70		75	40	68	86	85
Single Female	25		21	54	28	11	8
Single Male	4		4	5	4	3	7
%Infants Born to: 2007							
Teen mothers	10	18	10	17	14	3	3
Single mothers	40	65	35	71	51	17	17

*Despite the fact that the years are sometimes different, all statistics unless otherwise noted are from: *Statistical Abstract of the United States: 2011*, 130th ed. (Washington, D.C.: U.S. Government Printing Office, 2010).

**The term white refers to Non-Hispanic whites; not all are European Americans.

***Data for Middle Eastern Americans come from Census, 2000 Special Report, Augusta Brittingham and G. Patricia de la Cruz, "We the People of Arab Ancestry in the United States," U.S. Census Bureau, March 2005. Available on www.aaiusa.com.

†Income data based on 1999 figures so 2007 figure would be much higher.

States citizen. It is estimated that 11 percent of children are unauthorized residents, and 18 percent were born in the United States but have an unauthorized parent. Immigrant children join a resident population of ethnic minority children and together constitute about a third of all children in this country. It is estimated that by 2030, this group will make up the majority of children in the United States.

Immigrants to this country experience *acculturation*, defined as a process "of learning about a new culture and deciding what aspects are to be retained or sacrificed from the culture of origin."[40] Because culture is multidimensional, immigrants must attend to many new aspects of experience—language, food, customs, and social attitudes. Adaptation can be difficult.

Four patterns of acculturation have been identified:[41]

- Integration—features of the culture of origin are maintained and features of the new culture are included
- Assimilation—complete adaptation to new culture and abandonment of culture of origin
- Separation—features of the culture of origin are maintained as closely as possible with isolation from the new culture
- Marginalization—immigrants cannot retain their culture of origin because of pressure to give it up and adaptation to new culture is hindered because of obstacles like discrimination

A study of the attitudes and behaviors of five thousand immigrant youths in thirteen countries revealed that the largest number of youths fell into the integrated category, using both the old and new languages, having a positive identification with both cultures and friends from both cultures. The separated category was the second largest group of youth who retained their identity to the culture of origin, preferred the language of origin and friends from that culture. The third largest group of young people assimilated to the new culture, adopting the new language, new customs, and a negative identity with the culture of origin. A final group of youth did not appear engaged with either the new or the old culture.

In the process of acculturation, parenting behaviors and practices appear to change more quickly than parenting cognitions, that is, immigrant parents adapt the new country's parenting behaviors but not necessarily their beliefs. The behaviors of young immigrant children will more closely resemble the behaviors of children in their new culture.

Overall, immigrants who retain some aspects of their traditional culture appear to have better physical health, better psychological adjustment, and overall more educational success than those who quickly give up the behaviors of their traditional culture.

Unauthorized Immigrants

Approximately 5.5 million children have at least one unauthorized parent, and one million of these children are themselves unauthorized, but the majority of children with an undocumented parent are themselves citizens because they were born here.[42]

The undocumented status of parents affects children's development in many ways. The family lives in a sort of twilight zone, afraid of being discovered, ejected from the country, and separated from family and friends. Parents are able to get only the lowest paid jobs and have no protections at work or in housing. Because family members fear detection, they do not enroll their children into programs like government-subsidized child-care programs that increase cognitive skills of low income children even though they are entitled to enter the program.

Parents' difficulties affect young children's cognitive development and by the age of two years, children already show decreases in skills related to parents' depression and distress and their work schedules.

If children themselves are unauthorized, their lives become difficult and constricted as they grow older. Without a birth certificate, it is hard to get a driver's license, and one must have a Social Security card to apply for a job. Many of these children were brought here at a very young age and may not have known they were unauthorized until they had need of a birth certificate.

An Integrative Model of the Experiences of Immigrant and Ethnic Minority Groups

Cynthia Garcia Coll and Laura Szalacha present a model of child development that describes the experiences of immigrant and ethnic minority children.[43] They consider these two groups together because they believe both groups are treated as outsiders in the culture. Figure 2-2 presents the model combining an ecological and interactionist approach to describe these children's experiences growing up. Social position, based on social class, race/ethnicity, and gender, triggers a community response. In the case of minority and immigrant children, their social position is associated with racism and discrimination, which lead to inadequate resources reflected in poor schools and violent neighborhoods with few community and economic resources. The disadvantaged environment fails to promote an adaptive cultural community and thus inhibits families' functioning and children's development.

A recent, carefully controlled, national longitudinal study documented the unequal resources provided to low-income children in our society.[44] Following a sample of low-income African American children and low-income European American children from birth to age ten with comprehensive assessments of their environments and development, researchers reported that even within a sample made up of low-come children, African American children experienced more social risks from living in poorer households, experiencing less sensitive and more authoritarian parenting, having lower quality child care settings in early childhood, more disadvantaged neighborhoods, and lower quality schools than European American children living in low-income families. Differences in school environments contributed significantly to the achievement gap between poor European American and African American children, and poorer school quality contributed to an increasing gap in mathematical skills in the school years.

Garcia Coll and Szalacha define racism broadly as any restriction or exclusion or bias that deprives individuals of basic human rights and freedoms in any sphere of life. Racism includes both prejudice, defined as negative thoughts, feelings or

■ **F I G U R E   2-2**
AN INTEGRATIVE MODEL OF CHILD DEVELOPMENT*

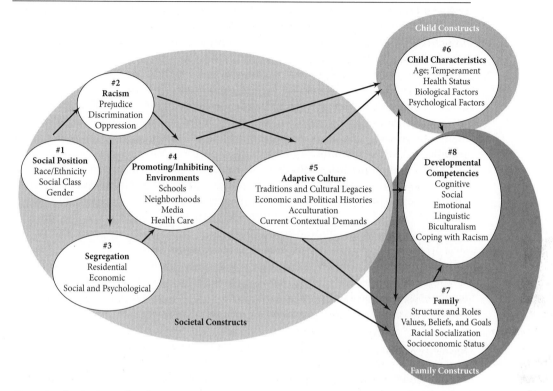

*From: Cynthia Garcia Coll and Laura A. Szalacha, "The Multiple Contexts of Middle Childhood," *The Future of Children 14*(2) (2004): 83.

judgments about someone based on the person's race, religion, or nationality, and discrimination, defined as unfair treatment because of race, religion, or nationality.

Schools, according to Garcia Coll and Szalacha, are the most important socializing influences on children apart from their families, and are made up of three nested environments: (1) the classroom, with teachers, peers, and learning materials; (2) the school; and (3) the school district. Even if schools are poor and lack many resources, they can promote learning when teachers are warm and focused on helping each child learn. When there are large percentages of children like themselves, children are less worried about discrimination or rejection, but negative school experiences can greatly reduce the positive attitudes and motivation present when children start school.

Neighborhoods can promote development, providing libraries and community centers that offer after-school and vacation care when they have resources. Even when poor and segregated from the rest of the community, they can promote social cohesion by protecting the customs of the culture from the negative reactions they might receive in a more diversified community.

Popular media, they believe, can have positive and negative features. It can increase self-esteem and prosocial behaviors as children see their group positively portrayed in the media and when prosocial behaviors such as empathy and understanding are modeled for children. Media have negative effects when they present models of aggression, discrimination, and prejudice. These issues are discussed in greater detail in Chapter 5.

Diversity can be a risk or a protective factor. Garcia Coll and Szalacha believe research has frequently viewed diverse groups through "the lens of deficit." Children of ethnic groups are often studied in terms of aggression, delinquency, attention deficits, and hyperactivity. The difficulties are seen as residing in the children rather than in the system that has not made available resources to provide health care, good schools, and safe communities.

"High family cohesion, strong sense of family obligation, strong ethnic pride, and high value of education are some of the characteristics that have been observed in outsider families that can be positive influences on children's development through middle childhood."[45] While some children from these families are overrepresented in high-risk groups, most children are not, even though their families and communities lack the advantages thought necessary for healthy development.

In addition to systemic changes to make more resources routinely available to these families, interventions should be multilevel ones that involve schools, neighborhoods, and families together. Parents can be engaged to target their goals and find ways to work with community agencies to achieve them.

Negative Stereotype Threat

Being members of a group considered to do poorly on a task increases individuals' stress levels and decreases their performance on the task. African Americans suffer the negative stereotype of being considered poor students, and researchers devised an intervention to counteract the stress that accompanies such a stereotype and may interfere with the academic achievement of African American children.[46]

At the beginning of seventh grade, they asked European American and African American students to write short essays either on a positive personal value that was of importance to them like family or friends (the experimental group) or on a neutral personal value or daily routine (the control group). After doing this twice, the fall grades of African American students' writing about a positive value increased, and those of the control group did not. The effects were greatest for the low-achieving African American students, and were nonsignificant for European American students who generally were not experiencing stress from a negative stereotype.

The groups wrote a total of five short essays during the seventh grade year, and half of each group wrote two to four essays in the eighth grade year to see if booster shots helped. The grade point averages (GPA) of students were obtained at the end of eighth grade in their core classes of science, social studies, English, and math. As is typical in middle school, grades of all the groups decreased, but the grades of African American students who wrote essays about positive values in seventh grade decreased less steeply. At the end of two years, the low-achieving African American students who wrote about positive values scored half a grade point higher and they were significantly less likely to be in a remediation program than those who wrote on neutral topics. Booster essays in eighth grade had no effects on grades. Again, writing essays did not improve the grades of European American students.

The researchers speculated that low-achieving students became discouraged at their initial low performance level, believing they were confirming the negative stereotype. Discouragement resulted in continuing poor performance and triggered a vicious negative cycle of low performance, discouragement, and worsening performance. Writing the essays appeared to interrupt the downward spiral and enabled students to feel more confident about themselves. With increased confidence, their performance improved, leading to greater confidence and sustained effort, and greater academic achievement.

While parents may not ask children to write essays, they can talk with their children about the activities and experiences their children enjoy and value positively, giving them confidence through conversations rather than writing.

Discrimination

Many children fear being excluded and rejected because of their race and/or ethnic background. In a national sample of fifteen- to seventeen-year-olds, 15 percent of white children, 23 percent of African American, and 37 percent of Latinos/as reported that discrimination because of race and ethnic background was a very big concern, and among thirteen- and fourteen-year-olds, the comparable figure was 32 percent of the sample, not broken down by ethnic background.[47] Experience of discrimination was the strongest predictor of poor psychological and social adaptation in a large group of immigrant children.[48]

Feeling discriminated against brings a variety of feelings. A five-year longitudinal study following African American early adolescents from the ages of ten to fifteen enabled researchers to track the feelings that follow perceived discrimination. At each assessment at about ages ten, twelve, and fifteen, early teens reported the frequency of perceived discrimination in the preceding year.[49] Discriminatory events included such experiences as racial slurs and insults, physical threats, and false accusations. Youths also filled out measures of depression and problem behaviors, and both parents and children filled out a measure of the parents' nurturant and involved parenting behaviors.

Latent growth curve modeling revealed that (1) increases in perceived discrimination were positively associated with increases in depressive symptoms and conduct problems, (2) children from higher socioeconomic-status families were more likely to perceive increases in discrimination over time, (3) both boys and girls who perceived discrimination had increases in depressive symptoms but the link between discrimination and conduct problems was stronger for boys than for girls, and (4) effects of perceived discrimination decreased when children had warm relationships with parents, prosocial friends, and school engagement. However, even, with warm parents and good friends, perceiving discrimination was related to increases in depressive feelings and conduct problems.

In African American families followed for two years, mothers reported their experience of discrimination at each yearly assessment as well as their physical problems, depressive symptoms, and their parenting behaviors.[50] Mothers who perceived discrimination reported an increase in stress-related physical problems that, in turn, were related to an increase in depressive symptoms and a decrease in their positive parenting strategies. Parenting interventions with their twelve-year-old children helped to decrease mothers' psychological stress and depressed moods.[51] Mothers focused on paying attention to children's point of view and feelings. They learned communication skills, consistent discipline, and monitoring teens' whereabouts. Early adolescents learned to follow household directions, set goals, complete homework, and avoid risk-taking peers. The program led to improvements in mothers' moods and early adolescents' regulated behaviors.

What can parents do when they worry about their children's experience of discrimination? Having open relationships with children enables them to tell parents what is happening in their lives so they and their parents can problem-solve specific upsetting incidents. Parents' acceptance and support is a main protective factor in insulating children from psychological problems because of others' cruelty and can help in situations of discrimination. In Chapter 10 we discuss a helpful program in greater detail. In general, parents help children feel good about themselves and their ethnic group and find ways to manage barriers and discrimination and to achieve their goals.

Actions Parents Can Take to Promote Fairness and Justice

Around the world, nations are dealing with the effects of migrations and the resulting increases of multicultural influences within their countries.[52] We include interventions from their efforts to promote justice as well as programs within this country. These programs benefit all members of a society not only because they promote the moral imperative of equal treatment for all individuals but also because they decrease the discrimination and unfair treatment stresses to the bystander as well as the victim as we shall see in Chapters 9 and 10.

In understanding prejudice and discrimination, it is important to realize that in the preschool years, children view their own group positively.[53] Just how easily young children form a sense of being in a special group was highlighted in a study in which researchers gave preschoolers either red or blue T-shirts.[54] In the control classes, the children wore the T-shirts for three weeks with no mention made of them. In the experimental classes, the T-shirts were used as general identifiers—"Reds and blues, it is time to go to lunch." Or "Reds and blues, it's time to go to recess." There was no positive status or value attached to the shirts or to the groups of children wearing them. Still, at the end of three weeks, children in both groups developed a positive feeling for their group; it was special, with the experimental group showing a stronger in-group bias.

It is later in the early elementary school years that children come to attach negative views to outgroup members while continuing to prefer their own group. This is the primary reason for intervening in the preschool years before children begin to view outgroup members negatively.

Parents and teachers decrease prejudice and discrimination by increasing cross-group interactions with peers, increasing adult-child conversations at home and at school about group differences and fairness, and by attending to children's cognitive, social, and moral reasoning.[55]

Having increased contact with peers of different ethnic and cultural groups promotes greater understanding among group members and reduces prejudice. Joining in activities of common interest like hiking, swimming, or music increases understanding, and working on cooperative activities to achieve a common goal promotes positive behaviors and friendships with partners that, in turn, reduce prejudice.[56] Even hearing about cross-group friendships between someone in your group and the outgroup can reduce prejudice.

Parents at home and teachers at school can provide information about differences among groups to promote understanding of the history, values, and special difficulties of each group. Specifically teaching children about difficulties groups have experienced, like the racial discrimination of African Americans, increases empathy and decreases prejudice.[57] Classroom programs can also decrease exclusion and discrimination. In the Netherlands, a multicultural curriculum sought to increase children's understanding of group differences and to educate students on the reasons for eliminating discrimination seen in name calling and exclusion from activities, and finally to emphasize the social and moral imperative of equal treatment for all. Students later showed less ethnic bias. In the United States, the Teaching Tolerance project has provided students and teachers with free resources and a magazine that teach respect and social justice for all students. The materials raise awareness of discrimination and increase behaviors to counteract it.

For young children of many countries, Sesame Street has developed a series of programs promoting awareness and appreciation for other cultural groups within the countries. They have focused on countries with high degrees of conflict like Northern Ireland and promoted with a variety of characters, issues of respect, social inclusion, and mutual respect for members of all groups. Parents can carry these themes out at home, reading stories, playing games that convey the same messages.

Third, to increase programs' effectiveness, parents and other adults pay attention and seek to understand, through conversation and observation, children's forms of reasoning about what group membership means to them, to other people, what is fair to others and to oneself, and what equal treatment means to them. As children grow older, friendships and groups focus on common interests and similar activities so interventions at older levels may require more planning and more encouragement. We continue to discuss these issues as they apply to different age groups in Chapters 8, 9, 10, and 11.

The Self-Esteem of Ethnic Groups

Jean Twenge and Jennifer Crocker, concerned that prejudice and discrimination have led to both low levels of self-esteem and negative self-concepts in ethnic groups that society described negatively, carried out a meta-analysis of studies to determine the levels of self-esteem in five ethnic groups in the United States.[58] They looked at 712 comparisons of self-esteem among African Americans, European Americans, Native Americans, Latinos, and Asian Americans and found the rank

Working together with children of diverse cultures promotes positive behaviors and friendships with partners.

ordering of these groups on inventories of self-esteem presented in Table 2-3. This table also presents the factors that influence self-esteem scores.

The rank ordering of the groups on self-esteem does not follow the pattern of society's general regard for the group. Despite higher levels of education and income and community respect for their levels of achievement, Asian Americans report the fewest positive self-perceptions. Although they experience great discrimination, African Americans make many positive statements about themselves. Of interest is the fact that the socioeconomic status of the subjects reduced the differences among the groups. High-status individuals of all groups resembled each other in their levels of self-esteem.

■ **TABLE 2-3**
RANK ORDERING OF ETHNIC GROUPS WITH RESPECT TO SELF-ESTEEM SCORES AND FACTORS INFLUENCING SCORES*

Rank Order of Self-Esteem Scores High Self-Esteem	Self-Esteem Scores Vary Depending on
1. African Americans	1. Age of person
2. European Americans	2. Education
3. Latinos	3. Geographical location
4. Native Americans	4. Year scores obtained
5. Asian Americans	

*From: Jean M. Twenge and Jennifer Crocker, "Race and Self-Esteem: Meta-Analyses Comparing Whites, Blacks, Hispanics, Asians, and American Indians, and Comment on Gray-Little and Hafdahl," *Psychological Bulletin 128* (2002): 371–408.

With respect to age, the differences in self-esteem among the five groups were smallest in elementary school and grew larger through high school and into the adult years. This suggests that initially, all children tend to make positive statements about themselves, but as they grow older, they become more socialized in their culture's views of what is appropriate to say about oneself. Self-esteem scores decreased with age in those groups, namely Asian Americans and Native Americans, that emphasize an interdependent self and minimize the importance of the self.

Examining self-esteem in relation to the subjects' geographic area of residence and the years of data collection yielded interesting findings. The self-esteem of African Americans and Asian Americans was highest in areas where that group had greater concentrations of population. For example, African Americans' self-esteem was highest in southern states that had the greatest numbers of African Americans. This is similar to the finding that African American students at African American colleges have higher self-esteem than do African Americans at European American colleges. Asian Americans living on the West Coast, where there are higher concentrations of Asian Americans, reported higher self-esteem than did Asian Americans in other parts of the country.

The subjects' cohort (year of birth) and the subjects' age at the time the data were collected also related to scores on self-esteem. In 1980, about twenty years after the civil rights movement began in the United States, African American scores on global self-esteem inventories began to rise. Twenge and Crocker speculate that the emphasis on the experiences and contributions of African Americans to this country, and the civil rights movement's emphasis on group pride and self-respect, affected children who absorbed these messages in the 1960s and 1970s. As they got older, they retained the high self-esteem that the data collected after 1980 reflected. Cohort differences are found for other groups as well. The most recently born Asian Americans and Latinos have rising self-esteem scores and differ least from European Americans.

The authors conclude that a variety of cultural factors explain self-esteem in different ethnic groups. First, the cultural influence of the ethnic group itself plays a role. Scores are highest for groups that have an individualistic orientation that emphasizes independence, setting personal goals, taking control to achieve these goals, valuing uniqueness, and seeking to stand out from others, and lowest in groups with an interdependent orientation that does not emphasize positive self-statements.

Social factors also affect the cultural groups' beliefs. First, as ethnic group members reside longer in this country and are exposed to its individualistic orientation, their reports of self-esteem begin to resemble those of European Americans. Second, self-esteem increases when groups receive positive messages from the communities in which they live. When political and social movements emphasize a group's contributions and when groups feel support from large numbers who share their cultural orientation, then self-esteem increases. Since individuals of higher status in all groups make positive comments about themselves, we can speculate that higher education, a major marker of status, brings with it an increasing appreciation of the self.

THE INFLUENCE OF SOCIOECONOMIC STATUS

Socioeconomic status (SES) provides a developmental niche for parent-child relations just as racial and ethnic backgrounds do.[59] Three factors—parents' occupation, education, and level of income—make up SES. Although income at or below the poverty level affects parenting (see the next section), income closer to the average appears less influential in shaping parenting beliefs than do education and occupational status. The influence of social status, like that of culture, is not fixed because education, occupation, and income can all change.

Summarizing the research on the influence of SES on parenting, Erika Hoff, Brett Laursen, and Twila Tardif state that higher SES parents are more likely than lower SES parents to have a child-centered orientation to parenting. They seek to understand children's thoughts and feelings and to make them important partners in the process of parenting. They elicit opinions and encourage children's participation in making rules. Lower SES parents are more parent-centered than are higher status parents. They see themselves as authorities and want children to comply. When children do not obey, such parents may be harsh and punitive.

A second major finding is that differences in SES correlate with more differences in verbal than nonverbal interactions between parents and children. For example, an hour each month Betty Hart and Todd Risley visited the homes of forty-two European American and African American families of professional, working-class, and welfare backgrounds and recorded the words spoken to and by children from the ages of one to three years.[60]

Recorded observations indicated no gender or racial differences in language acquisition, but they did reveal large differences based on social group. Although all children in the study experienced quality interactions with their parents, all heard diverse forms of language spoken to and around them, and all learned to speak by the age of three, the differing amounts and kinds of language heard in the homes surprised the investigators.

- professional parents spoke about three times as much to their children as did welfare parents and about one and a half times as much as did working-class parents; children in professional families heard about 487 utterances per hour; children in working-class families, 301; children in welfare families, 178.

- the emotional tone of the conversations also reflected startling differences; professional parents gave children affirmative feedback (confirming, elaborating, and giving explicit approval for what the child said) about thirty times an hour, or every other minute. In working-class families, children received affirmative feedback fifteen times an hour, or once every four minutes; welfare parents gave children positive feedback six times an hour, or once every ten minutes.

- professional parents gave prohibitions about five times an hour, and welfare parents about eleven; children in welfare families heard twice as many negative comments as positive ones, whereas children in professional families heard primarily positive comments and rarely any negative ones.

These findings have important implications for the development of self-concept and general mood as well as for language development. Language differences in the home at ages one to three strongly predicted vocabulary growth and intellectual development when the child was about nine years of age. The most important predictors of vocabulary and intellectual competence were the emotional tone of the feedback and the amount of linguistic diversity the child heard.

Encouragingly, the study shows that all parents have the capacity to promote language and intellectual development, because they already have the ability to speak and interact with children effectively. In homes where parents are inclined to say little and what they do say is negative, increasing conversations with children and providing more positive feedback to them will help not only language development and intellectual growth but also the development of self-concept and general mood.

Annette Lareau went into the homes of middle-class (those with managerial jobs or jobs requiring college level skills), working-class (those with unskilled, lower-level, white-collar jobs with little or no managerial responsibility), and poor parents (those receiving public assistance) of European- and African-American background.[61] She and her research assistants observed interactions occurring over many hours on about twenty occasions with each family, following the children and families at school events and doctor visits as well. Like Hart and Risley, Lareau found many elements of family life common to all social groups and found too that socioeconomic differences overshadowed the influence of ethnic background.

Table 2-4 presents the features common to families of all social levels. Table 2-5 describes the features of a parental philosophy of "concerted cultivation," which Lareau believes is characteristic of middle-class families, and features of a parental philosophy of "accomplishment of natural growth," characteristic of working-class and poor families.

■ **TABLE 2-4**
CHARACTERISTICS OF ALL FAMILIES REGARDLESS
OF SOCIOECONOMIC STATUS*

1. Enormous time and effort expended by parents
2. Challenges children face in process of growing up
3. Times of fun, laughter, happiness, emotional closeness, and comfort
4. Rituals regarding favorite meals, television shows, toys, games, and outings
5. Large percentage of time spent in routines such as eating, dressing, daily chores, homework
6. Tragedies such as premature deaths, auto accidents
7. Differing temperaments among family members
8. Differing levels of messiness and neatness among families
9. Atmosphere of safety, security, and hominess

*Adapted from: Annette Lareau, *Unequal Childhoods: Class, Race, and Family Life* (Berkeley: University of California Press, 2003), 237–238 and 274.

■ **T A B L E** 2-5
TYPOLOGIES OF DIFFERENCES IN CHILD REARING*

	Child-Rearing Approach	
	Concerted Cultivation	*Accomplishment of Natural Growth*
Key Elements	Parent actively fosters and assesses child's talents, opinions, and skills	Parent cares for child and allows child to grow
Organization of Daily Life	Multiple child leisure activities orchestrated by adults	"Hanging out," particularly with kin, by child
Language Use	Reasoning/directives	Directives
	Child contestation of adult statements	Rare questioning or challenging of adults by child
	Extended negotiations between parents and child	General acceptance by child of directives
Interventions in Institutions	Criticisms and interventions on behalf of child	Dependence on institutions
	Training of child to take on this role	Sense of powerlessness and frustration
		Conflict between child-rearing practices at home and at school
Consequences	Emerging sense of entitlement on the part of the child	Emerging sense of constraint on the part of the child

*Reprinted with permission. Annette Lareau, *Unequal Childhoods: Class, Race, and Family Life* (Berkeley: University of California Press, 2003), 31.

The children of all families had positive experiences and all parents worked hard rearing children, but parents in different classes exerted energy in different ways. Middle-class parents stimulated children with lessons, trips, and group activities, encouraging their verbal and social skills so children knew how to interact with adults outside the home, how to present their own needs and to persist in an assertive but polite way until adults attended to these needs. They conveyed to children a sense of ease and confidence that they would be treated well in the outside world.

Children in working-class and poor families had advantages at home in the sense they were less pressured and scheduled to attend lessons and activities. These children had more time for free play and often had much closer relationships with family members and cousins than children of the middle class. Still, these children longed to have lessons and trips. The real disadvantages of working-class and poor families came in their lack of self-confidence as they moved outside the home. Many parents felt they did not meet the expectations of middle-class teachers and doctors, and some feared more severe criticism that might remove children from the home for failure to meet middle-class standards of discipline and punishment. Their children did not have the view that all would go well.

Lareau believes the middle-class pressure for lessons and stimulating activities to develop each child's potential to the fullest comes from the changing nature of the country's economy in which only outstanding performance will qualify a child for the shrinking number of well-paid jobs in the economy. She also believes that well-funded community recreational programs can provide working-class and poor children with the athletic and musical lessons and the enriching experiences that middle-class parents provide so that these children too can look forward to a bright future.

Sandra Hofferth believes that the family patterns and child-rearing strategies Lareau attributes to social class are really the result of mothers' education, just one of the components of social class.[62] She and her colleagues observed middle-class and working-class children and families and found that within both groups, it was mothers' education that determined what children did. Even when resources were more limited in working-class families, mothers with education enrolled children in community and church activities that provided the benefits that middle-class children gained from private lessons and country club activities. Hofferth believes it is more useful to consider that it is mothers' education that is the pivotal element because it can be increased.

Recent research suggests that when working-class families adopt the daily family routines of the middle class reflected in valuing reading activities, having regular routines of reading to children, dinner-time conversations, special homework times,[63] and getting extended sleep at night,[64] working-class children's cognitive performance and school achievement resemble that of the middle class.

Sociologist Allison Pugh describes the effects of class and race in determining children's patterns of consumption of culturally sanctioned products and activities.[65] Based on observations and conversations with low-income and upper-income children at an after-school program, an upper-income public school, and a private school, and on her interviews with their parents, Pugh noted that most parents understood the role of highly desirable possessions and out-of-school activities like a birthday party or trip to the movies in securing their child a place of dignity in the social world of their peers and helping children feel connected, important, and cared for. To lack all the culturally valued possessions isolated a child.

Low-income parents managed to give by practicing what Pugh termed "windfall childrearing," giving something special or desired, a "symbolic indulgence" like an item of clothing, when the layoff ended or an absent parent sent child support, a way of making up for the hard times and signaling that the child is loved. These special treats, however, were seen as unpredictable and out of one's control so they were part of life's general instability.

Upper-income parents practiced "symbolic deprivation," not buying everything they could afford because they did not want to appear too materialistic. What parents chose to purchase or restrict often related to their childhood experiences.

Upper-income parents were more likely to spend money for children on activities that would be pathways for developing skills or competencies. For example, though it might require giving up extended vacations, parents would send a child to private school in order to insure an education that would lead to success.

Consumption patterns were part of a broader child-rearing philosophy. Low-income parents wanted children to feel comfortable at school, to fit in, as parents thought lack of anxiety produced learning. They did not send children to better schools out of their immediate area because they were afraid children would feel different, would not fit in, and would find learning harder or because they could not get there quickly if needed.

Upper-income parents focused on children's uniqueness and difference, and expected schools and teachers to appreciate their children's distinctive qualities. Upper income African American parents arranged what Pugh termed an "exposed childhood," enrolling their children in integrated schools where they were among only a few African American students and in leisure activities and sports teams with low-income students so children could feel comfortable with a wide range of people. They did not worry that their child might be "the only one" of their race in school or the only one of their class background in leisure activities. Being exposed to all these activities and differences made them strong.

Because commercial products come to signify emotional connection, belonging, being cared for, Pugh believes it is difficult to reduce attachments to commercial products unless parents bind together as a community and discourage elaborate, expensive birthday parties or expensive Halloween costumes that reinforce status positions and social class distinctions and require poor parents to spend money to give their child dignity that low income often erodes.

THE INFLUENCE OF ECONOMIC HARDSHIP

The previous section included some families who received public assistance, but here we focus exclusively on what happens to families when income falls to the lowest levels.

Who Are the Poor?

The official federal index of poverty developed in the 1960s is the most common measure of poverty; it is based on pretax, cash income and the number of people in the family.[66] The index is determined by the estimated cost of food multiplied by three, as food was found in surveys in the 1960s to absorb about one-third of the family income. The index is considered inadequate because food now is less than one-third of the budget, and other costs such as transportation to work and day care are not considered. However, the index does not include some non-cash benefits of programs like Food Stamps so some people feel the poor have more resources than the Poverty Index suggests. Despite criticisms for over a decade, it is still the official figure. Because the official index is too low, some consider poverty 200 percent of the official Poverty Index.

Children are the poorest individuals in the United States. In 2008, the official poverty rate for children under eighteen was 18 percent (compared with a poverty rate of 10 percent for those aged sixty-five and older).[67] Rates of poverty are higher for children in certain ethnic groups. In 2008, 34 percent of African American and 30 percent of Hispanic children were living in poverty, compared with 15 percent of European American and 14 percent of Asian American children.

Many factors influence rates of poverty. Poverty decreases when parental education increases and when the number of children in the family decreases.[68] Poverty increases when children live in single-parent families, although living in a two-parent family is not a complete protection because in one study, almost half the years children spent in poverty occurred when they were living with two parents.

Three factors seem to push families into poverty: (1) decreases in the number of skilled jobs that can support families, (2) increases in the number of single-parent families, and (3) reductions in government benefits to families.[69]

Jeanne Brooks-Gunn and Greg Duncan refute the argument that the problems of the poor result from parents' genetic endowment or their work ethic.[70] They report that siblings reared in the same family with the same parental attitudes can differ in the age and duration of poverty in their lives and thus serve to control for the effects of parental characteristics on poverty. They found that sibling differences in income during childhood were related to siblings' years of completed schooling, suggesting that income does matter even when genes and work ethic are controlled for.

The Effects of Poverty on Children's Development

Poor children are at higher risk for many problems that include:[71]

- Physical health risks like higher infant mortality, low birth weight, greater exposure to lead poisoning, toxic wastes, poor air quality
- Neighborhoods with poorer day care and schools, greater risks for violence, aggressive peers
- Fewer toys, less verbal stimulation; cognitive delays that appear as early as age two and persist; more likely to have learning disabilities and grade retention
- Greater family instability with more moves; more divorce; more exposure to domestic violence, neglect, and physical maltreatment; more likely to be separated from parents
- Higher levels of neuroendocrine arousal that may underlie learning problems

Poverty status presents not one risk but a cascade of problems that complicate children's lives at every level.[72] At the level of physiological functioning, poverty status is related to lack of resources such as food, healthy housing, and safe neighborhoods. Even when a resource is free, easy to provide, and beneficial like school recess, poor children are less likely to get it.[73]

Diminished resources place a physical demand on children's bodies that is reflected in changes in blood pressure, neuroendocrine secretions, and self-regulatory behavior. These changes begin in young people in elementary school, and as stress and body changes continue, the body over time is damaged.[74] It is the accumulation of stresses that is important for physical changes, not any particular one. Given all the stresses, it is not surprising poor children are described as more aggressive and more worried.[75]

Children who were chronically poor from birth to age nine experienced lower quality of parental care than those who were never poor in that period.[76] Their mothers were less sensitive caregivers, less stimulating, and more depressed. Over time, the quality of the homes decreased further. Children had lower scores on cognitive and language skills and their out-of-home caregivers and their teachers rated them as more aggressive, noncompliant, and more anxious and worried.

In this sample, aggressive behaviors decreased when family's income increased, mothers worked, and had a partner.[77] If mothers worked but gained no increase in income, children's behavior worsened. So, financially beneficial employment improved family well-being and children's socioemotional functioning.

Despite all the difficulties poverty creates for poor children and their families in terms of limited resources and parents' high stress levels, children in poor families feel as close to their mothers and fathers as children in affluent families, feel parents pass on moral values, and eat meals with them as often as children in affluent families report about their parents.[78]

In poor and affluent families alike, closeness to parents, particularly to mothers, and parents' positive support predict children's school competence and subjective sense of well-being. In poor and affluent groups of children, there are subgroups of children who are unhappy and detached from parents. In poor families, there are no resources to get help, and in more affluent families, parents are often too reluctant to seek the help that is available to them because of embarrassment about psychological problems.

Interventions can provide the help that poor families need.

Ways to Intervene

Many interventions promote children's health needs and cognitive delays with such programs as Head Start focused on preschool children and multifaceted Early Head Start, targeting low-income parents with infants and toddlers, providing a full array of services such as health care, home visits, parent education, child care, and family support for twenty months in the first three years of life.[79] Programs have increased parents' skills in the areas of (1) forming emotionally supportive relationships with children, (2) stimulating children's verbal and learning abilities, and (3) finding alternatives to physical punishment.

Three-year-old children in this program performed better on measures of verbal and intellectual abilities, on measures of attention span, and on ability to emotionally engage parents than control children not enrolled in the program. They were also less aggressive. So, in the areas that parents increased in skills, children increased in performance.

Follow-up studies of children attending an intensive, two-year preschool program found that the effects of such programs can last well into adulthood. The High/Scope Perry Project, developed and carried out in Ypsilanti, Michigan, in 1962, enrolled three-year-olds from a very poor neighborhood in a five-day-a-week, three-hour-a-day program that focused on helping children learn active problem-solving skills that included planning activities, doing them, and reviewing what they had done.[80] In weekly home visits, parents got information on how to encourage learning in everyday life situations, like counting change at the grocery store.

Children in the program and in the control group have been followed into their forties. Although the initial differences between the groups at the ages of seven and eight were not impressive, significant differences have emerged in the quality of the lives of these two groups. Program children got higher grades in high school and were more likely to graduate from high school (66 percent as compared to 45 percent in the control group). Nearly twice as many have completed college. They are more likely to be employed (76 percent as compared to 62 percent), more likely to own a home and a car, and earn more ($20,800 as compared to $15,300).

Social achievements are significant as well. Only 28 percent of the preschool group have been sentenced to jail or prison as compared to 52 percent of the control group. Men were more likely to marry and almost twice as many were involved in raising their own children (50 percent compared to 30 percent).

Other preschool programs following students into adulthood have found similar improvements in many areas of life.[81] All these programs have been cost effective in that social gains in income contribute to government revenues, and fewer social difficulties reduce the costs of government services, e.g., prisons.

An innovative Canadian prevention program, titled Better Beginnings Better Futures (BBBF), may serve as a model for successful community interventions in the United States.[82] The central government funded three low-income communities with money, support staff, and a period for community planning so that each community could devise programs to benefit children's long-term development, support families' functioning, and positively impact the community. All communities had high proportions of low-income families, but they differed in the number of immigrants, the geographical area covered, and the percentage of French-speaking and English-speaking schools. Everyone in the community was eligible for services regardless of income level.

Children and their families participated in BBBF programs when children were ages four to eight years. Although each community had its own emphasis, all communities offered free breakfasts, home visiting programs to increase parental support, parenting skills, and family recreational activities, and all had community outreach programs, community social activities, and special celebrations. Some communities put more money into school interventions reducing class size to ten students to each adult because of the number of immigrants with language problems, and some put more money into community programs. Residents in the communities devised the programs in consultation with service agencies and other professionals. Measures of child, parent, family, and community functioning were obtained when children were in Grade 3 (ages eight/nine), Grade 6 (ages eleven/twelve), and Grade 9 ages (fourteen/fifteen).

The interventions helped both children and parents. BBBF children's social and school functioning was higher in Grades 6 and 9 than that of comparison children in communities without the programs, their emotional adjustment was increased, and behavior problems decreased in Grades 3, 6, and 9. Parents reported greater feelings of support and well-being, increased marital satisfaction, and improved family functioning. Positive effects were seen in the use of community health and social services, and more involvement and satisfaction in neighborhood activities. Benefits of the program appeared to increase over time with larger effects seen in outcomes at Grades 6 and 9, and even greater benefits for children who participated five years after the first group.

Economic analysis of the programs revealed that by the time the children were age fifteen, the government had already saved more money than it had spent: $1.31 saved for every $1.00 spent for the programs, mainly from reductions in money spent on remedial education for BBBF children. Most early childhood programs find their savings come from reduced social services in adulthood so one can anticipate savings in the future as well. The program has been so successful that the central government has incorporated the interventions into ongoing government services.

PRACTICAL QUESTION: WHAT HAPPENS WHEN PARENT EDUCATORS AND PARENTS HAVE DIFFERENT VALUES?

Knowing that individuals within different ethnic and social groups may have particular values based on both culture and personal experiences makes us aware of the wide variety of beliefs possible about the goals and strategies of parenting. Tammy Mann, a parent educator, questions the effectiveness of parent educators when the mainstream philosophy of parenting they teach differs from the ideas and experiences of the parents whom they seek to influence.[83]

She lived in the South in a two-parent family. When she was two, the family moved to Detroit accompanied by many aunts, uncles, and cousins, so she grew up with a large extended family who had frequent gatherings. The extended family periodically returned to the South for vacations, traveling together in "caravans."

Mann's parents shaped and controlled their children's behavior without discussions of their children's preferences or ideas. Children had to obey. Such control was to help children grow into accountable and responsible adults. Her parents expected their children to help in the family from an early age. They emphasized respect for elders, manners, and polite behavior to others. Her mother had a strong religious faith, and the family participated regularly in church activities. Education was very important, and both parents wanted their children to go further in school than they had.

As a parent, Mann finds herself maintaining her son's strong connections to the extended family. Though she, with her husband and son, live far from other relatives, she makes sure he visits the extended family in the summer, and all three travel to the South for family reunions. This does not substitute for the warm cocoon of the extended family Mann experienced as a child in Detroit, but she duplicates those childhood feelings for her son as best she can. Because religion has been so important to her and her parents, she delights in her son's spontaneous and easy reliance on prayers as a way of coping with the stress of waking up in the night alone.

She sometimes feels uncomfortable wanting to follow the values that have been such strengths for her and her brother and sisters, because they do not conform to what experts recommend. For example, she does not value independence, individual expressiveness, and achievement above all. Instead, she stresses family connectedness, responsibility to others, a strong religious faith, and educational achievement. She suspects that parents she has worked with in the past may have felt as alienated from mainstream parenting beliefs as she has, and she worries that rejecting "aspects of who we are, in an attempt to become something else deemed 'better,' can be more destructive than practitioners sometimes imagine."[84] She believes parent educators and practitioners must first try to understand families and their values before intervening.

Vivien Carlson and Robin Harwood describe a four-session program to help parent educators become aware of their own cultural orientations and values with respect to parenting and then to use their increased awareness to better understand and help parents.[85] Carlson and Harwood state that many educators are surprised to discover that cultural beliefs are more than a set of beliefs endorsed by a group. Groups pass on unspoken ways of viewing the world, but individuals interpret these beliefs uniquely in terms of their own experience. Thus, educators have to pay attention to the unique beliefs, socialization goals, and values of the parents they work with. They also have to be sensitive when parents' values differ from their own.

In this program, educators learn to ask questions to discover the long-term goals parents have for children, such as independence, social relatedness, respect and deference, and individual achievement. They also learn to identify parents' expectations about milestones, such as children's feeding themselves, being toilet trained, and sleeping by themselves.

During the course of the training, participants come to realize that knowledge of group history and characteristics is valuable, but not sufficient, for culturally sensitive practice. In particular, they appreciate the training emphasis on specific questioning strategies for use in exploring cultural beliefs and values with families, with 95 percent of participants agreeing or strongly agreeing with the statement, "I will use the information about socialization goal categories and questioning strategies in my work with families."[86]

Such information enables educators to provide more effective and relevant services to parents.

MAIN POINTS

Culture provides

- ways of viewing the world
- goals and strategies for parenting
- a developmental niche for parent-child relations

Even though national cultures are dynamic and changing and have their own particular emphasis, cultures around the world have been categorized into two main models of social relationships

- the independent model, stressing children's independence, initiative, and the capacity for setting and achieving goals
- the interdependent model, stressing children's becoming part of a strong social network that nourishes and supports them

Children around the world

- learn cultural values and rules in similar kinds of activities like play, work, conversations, and lessons, though each culture may rely more on one activity than another
- have similar television habits
- are strongly influenced by the level of industrialization in the country which dictates amount of schooling and time spent away from family

Members of ethnic and immigrant groups in this country

- have often experienced prejudice and rejection
- differ in values and strategies of parenting, with European Americans preferring the independent model and many other groups preferring the interdependent model
- differ in levels of self-esteem, with members of individualistic cultures reporting higher global self-esteem and members of interdependent cultures reporting lower global self-esteem
- report higher self-esteem when they feel supported and appreciated by their community

Parents of differing socioeconomic status have

- different views of their roles, with higher-status parents being more child-centered in their approach and lower-status parents being more parent-centered in their approach
- different goals and strategies, with higher-status parents valuing verbal interactions with children, eliciting and understanding feelings, and negotiating differences, and lower-status parents valuing obedience and strict discipline for noncompliance
- similar forms of interactions with children but spend different amounts of time doing them

Poor children

- are more likely to suffer health problems, cognitive delays, abuse, and neglect than are nonpoor children
- lack income that affects the quality of their health care, home environment, and neighborhoods
- tend to experience conflict and tension because their parents face stress from financial pressure

Parent educators benefit from

- exploring their own values about parenting
- programs that help them to pay attention to parents' goals and preferred strategies

EXERCISES

1. Everyone receives many cultural messages from the groups to which they belong, whether determined by ethnicity, religion, geographic area of residence, age, or gender. What groups most strongly influence your views of the world and your general values?
2. Look at the ethnic influences that are part of your heritage. What values of these groups have you incorporated into your own life?
3. Recall the independent and interdependent models of parent-child relations. What are the advantages of each? Which of the two is more appealing to you? Why? Do you think it is possible to combine the best of all cultures into one culture as Richard Nisbett suggested?
4. What are your short-term and long-term goals for parenting?
5. If you were a parent educator working with a parent with a set of values that differed greatly from yours, how would you handle it?

ADDITIONAL READINGS

Lareau, Annette. *Unequal Childhoods: Class, Race and Family Life.* Berkeley: University of California Press, 2003.

Nisbett, Richard E. *The Geography of Thought: How Asians and Westerners Think Differently . . . and Why.* New York: Free Press, 2003.

Pugh, Allison J. *Longing and Belonging: Parents, Children, and Consumer Culture.* Berkeley: Univesity of California Press, 2009.

Thorpe, Helen. *Just Like Us: The True Story of Four Mexican American Girls Coming of Age in America.* New York: Simon & Schuster, 2009.

Tudge, Jonathon. *The Everyday Lives of Young Children: Culture, Class, and Child Rearing in Diverse Societies.* New York: Cambridge Press, 2008.

3

Learning to Parent

Test Your Knowledge: Fact or Fiction (True/False)

1. Sensitive parenting can buffer children from the effects of negative genes.
2. Video feedback of positive mother–child actions can improve mothers' sensitivity and increase the security of the child's attachment to the parent in just a few sessions.
3. Most parents do not want to use their own childhood experiences as guides when they parent their own children.
4. There is little stability in children's temperamental qualities over time.
5. Parents with low incomes do not use media sources for obtaining information about parenting because of the expense.

Providing loving care and attention and supporting children's growth are challenging responsibilities. How do parents learn the skills? In this chapter we explore what parents learn from: (1) childhood experiences with their own parents, (2) the media, (3) history of parenting practices, (4) science, (5) current theories about children's growth and development, and (6) research on parent-child relationships.

Parents' knowledge of children's needs and growth patterns enable them to be more effective and satisfied parents.[1] Knowledge about children enables parents to understand children's behavior so their expectations are appropriate and experiences can be introduced at optimal times to further development. Children of parents with greater knowledge are more competent and have fewer behavior problems. Knowledgeable parents are also able to identify problems early and get help early when it is most effective.

But how do parents learn? When families were larger and relatives lived nearby and one generation lived like the next, parents learned from what their own parents did and from their experiences caring for younger brothers and sisters, or younger nieces and nephews.

Today, parents continue to use their own childhood experiences with their parents as primary guides, but they also turn to religious faith, friends, what parents have done historically, what neuroscience, theories, psychological research, and parenting programs tell parents to do to promote children's growth and well-being.[2] They turn to experts and the media. We review how these sources help parents go about their important job of rearing the next generation; the roles of religious faith and parenting programs are discussed in Chapters 9 and 6 respectively.

WHAT PARENTS LEARN IN CHILDHOOD

When parents were asked what influences their parenting, they gave the responses listed in Table 3-1.

Fifty-three percent of parents said the way they were raised is a major influence, and an additional 30 percent said it is a moderate influence. As we saw in Chapter 1, parents learn the use of specific disciplinary techniques and a general emotional tone of positivity or negativity from their parents, and they also learn values as we described in the previous chapter.

Most important in childhood, they become attached to parents and learn how people relate to each other, how trustworthy people are, how much one can control

■ **TABLE 3-1**
INFLUENCES THAT SHAPE PARENTS' APPROACH TO PARENTING*

Influence	Major	Moderate	Minor	None
Way parents raised me	53	33	11	6
Faith/religious background	41	23	19	17
Professionals like pediatricians/ day caregivers	35	44	16	5
Extended family/close friends	35	42	18	5
Parenting books, magazines, TV, websites	9	3	40	14

*Adapted from: Claire Lerner and Lynette Ciervo, "Parenting Young Children Today: What the Research Tells Us," *Zero to Three 30* (2010): 4–9.

others' actions, how enjoyable relationships are, and how lovable one is. These internal models of what to expect from others influence adult relationships with friends, marital partners, and their own children.[3] When parents are trustworthy, warm, loving individuals who provide help and guidance, children come to adulthood feeling secure and comfortable with other people; they trust them and feel good about having others depend on them; they are understanding and supportive with partners and able to resolve conflicts. With their children they are loving, warm, and sensitive, but they are also able to set limits.[4]

Difficulties in childhood relationships with parents are thought to result in one of three kinds of insecure relationships with people in adulthood. Children who form insecure, avoidant attachments to distant and unavailable parents are more likely as adults to be uncomfortable in close relationships, to maintain distance and minimize the importance of intimate ties. They are less sensitive to their children's needs, especially when children have negative feelings, and they tend to be cool and controlling in their interactions with children.[5]

Children who form insecure, anxious attachments to unreliable, anger-provoking parents remain preoccupied with their intense feelings in adulthood. They worry others do not really care for them, and they feel helpless to resolve the intense feelings. With their children, they are responsive but inconsistent, sometimes warm but sometimes easily distressed and ineffective in helping children.

Children whose parents have experienced loss and deprivations and react in unpredictable, unsatisfying ways with children form insecure, disorganized/disoriented attachments and find it difficult to relate in a consistent, supportive way to their children. This is an extreme form of insecure attachment seen in groups of traumatized parents and also abusing parents. As we saw in the first chapter, parents can take many actions to modify the parenting skills learned from parents.

LEARNING FROM OTHER SOURCES

Table 3-1 shows that next to their own childhood experiences, parents look to their religious faith, professionals, and their friends for guidance. Parents are most likely to seek out professionals such as pediatricians and day care givers when they are first-time parents, parents of children under nine months of age, and single and divorced parents.[6] Parents in these circumstances may feel more pressured and more motivated to seek expert opinion than an experienced parent, one with older children, or one whose spouse is available.

Friends may be people known for many years or people parents meet in relation to their children—in prenatal or parenting groups, in nursery school or school-based activities, in sports. These people as well as friends at work all provide helpful information.

LEARNING FROM THE MEDIA

When they consult media, parents are most likely to turn to magazines, websites, books, and television shows for information on child development and parenting. About 40 percent of parents report using these sources at least once a month, and

25 percent use them several times a month.[7] Parents with high incomes are more likely to use websites, and parents with incomes under $20,000 per year are more likely to watch television parenting programs regularly.

The media give parents techniques for establishing healthy eating and sleeping habits, and they present ways of handling problems as they arise, e.g., how to proceed when children have school problems or depression. They also provide up-to-date information on health issues and disease.

But they can also trigger debates and spark dialogues that help parents and society come to a clearer understanding of parenting issues. We present two issues as examples.

Parents worry about how protective to be of their children. After Lenore Skenazy wrote a brief newspaper article in 2008 about allowing her nine-year-old son to take the subway and bus to get home from midtown Manhattan, a journey he had taken many times with his parents, she received extensive public criticism, and responded with a blog, freerangekids.com. From parents and children's responses and a review of research, she wrote a book *Free-Range Kids: How to Raise Safe, Self-Reliant Children (Without Going Nuts with Worry)*.[8]

She cites statistics showing that children are as safe today as they were when parents were growing up, but parents have become so protective that children grow up with few chances for outdoor explorations and few opportunities to develop self-sufficiency and confidence in going about the world. As a result, we have increases in sedentary activities and children's obesity, and children do not know the joys of independence.

Ms. Skenazy attributes parents' increased fearfulness to twenty-four-hour news cycles that repeatedly highlight crime and awful acts committed against children, to parenting experts who rob parents of their confidence to make sound decisions, and to parents' intense desires to provide children with a childhood free of worry and difficulty. To counteract the fears, Ms. Skenazy encourages parents to teach children how to be safe in a world with risks and how to let them go to enjoy their freedom. Her fourteen Free-Range Commandments include such directives as: Know When to Worry; Turn Off the News; Don't Think Like a Lawyer, Some Risks Are Worth It; Listen to Your Kids, They Don't Want to Be Treated as Babies; Relax.

A second area of concern is how academically demanding to be with children. As mentioned in Chapter 1, *Battle Hymn of the Tiger Mother* describes Amy Chua's reluctant journey from Chinese mother who applied her immigrant parents' strict rules in raising her two daughters to a slightly Westernized mother who finally accepted her stubborn, early adolescent daughter's refusal to follow her mother's regime of violin lessons and practices and a mother who gave her husband and girls the right to review her book and approve what she wrote and published.[9]

Ms. Chua's graphic descriptions of the demands, bribes, threats, and insults that worked well with Sophia, her first-born daughter, but not so well with Lulu, her second-born, horrified many readers who worried about the girls' psychological stability under such pressure for achievement.[10] Her insults and threats, some of which Ms. Chua herself regretted, did not hide the many positive strengths of her family: her extraordinary energy and commitment to helping her children; the love both she and her husband had for the girls and the enjoyable hours the family spent apart from the lessons and practices; the strong and caring bonds with their extended family of grandparents, aunts, uncles, and cousins who traveled long distances to support each other at times of stress and to celebrate with each other at times of joy and success.

Even though she became more open-minded, at the end of her book Ms. Chua still championed her philosophy that children have abilities that develop from hard work and effort, and it is her obligation as a parent to work hard to insure her children work hard to be the best they can be in whatever areas they choose to pursue. When asked about pushing children less talented than her daughters, she gave the example of her younger sister who has Down Syndrome, which delays areas of development. Her mother worked as hard helping Chua's sister with her school work and her piano lessons as she did with her daughters who went to Harvard and Yale. Her sister, now an adult, works, has friends, and plays the piano for them.[11]

Reviewers and readers praised Ms. Chua's honesty and marveled at her confidence in actions that astonished some parents and contrasted so markedly with the more understanding, giving approach sometimes recommended. "No More Mrs. Nice Mom" one reviewer wrote of Ms. Chua's approach.[12] Others saw Ms. Chua's philosophy as one especially useful now to reverse our declining position in global educational rankings.[13] Evaluate her parenting in Box 3-2 at the end of the chapter.

Unlike Ms. Chua, many other parents worry that the demands of hard work required in advantaged school districts create unacceptable levels of stress for students.[14] A documentary titled *Race to Nowhere*, written, directed, and produced by parents in a high-achieving school district, presents a case against long hours of academic work and striving for perfection. Many students eventually dislike school and learning, and a small group become so distressed they leave school or harm themselves. Middle schools and high schools as well as other organizations are showing the film and encouraging conversation between parents and school officials, and between parents and their children, about what level of stress is acceptable and manageable so school can meet everyone's needs.

Parents need not wait until someone writes a book or sets up a website to connect with other parents. One can comment on other parents' blogs (see nytimes.com/motherlode for a list of frequently read blogs) and one can join or create a parenting listserv, a large e-mail list, and pose questions or comments on others' comments.

In gathering information on the Internet, it is best to deal with official sites from organizations like the American Academy of Pediatrics or the Center for Disease Control and with reliable individuals.

LEARNING FROM HISTORY

Parents also learn from the ways parents reared children in the past. When historians first looked at the history of parent-child relationships, they focused narrowly on Western Europe and North America and drew the following conclusions from secondary sources such as religious and medical writings, paintings, and literature of the times:[15]

- apart from the eighteenth century, life was difficult for children
- there was no conception of childhood as separate from adulthood

- parents were indifferent to children's needs
- punishment was harsh and designed to break the child's will

One historian stated that the further back one went in history, the lower the level of regard and care for children, so that parenting in antiquity was described as the "Infanticidal Mode" with children being abandoned, killed or brutalized, and the Middle Ages as the "Abandoning Mode."[16]

Later historians looked at many other civilizations and broadened our understanding of early parent-child relationships. A more detailed examination of parenting in early classical civilizations like those in Egypt, Greece, and Rome concluded that classical parenting:[17]

- was much like our own

- recognized stages of childhood—infancy, early childhood, youth, and adolescence

- involved both parents as important figures with specialized tasks—mothers, generally nurturing and protecting children, and fathers, teaching and guiding children as they took on adult roles

- protected children's health as well as possible, recognizing that children faced special dangers and required special treatments though they had few except prayers, charms, and herbal remedies

Linda Pollock looked at parenting practices as revealed in almost five hundred diaries of parents and children, autobiographies, and newspaper accounts of court cases involving children, all taken from the years 1500 to 1900 in Britain and the United States.[18] She found relationships between parents and children were close. "Parents, although they may have found their offspring troublesome at times, did seem to enjoy the company of their children. . . . It is also clear that the majority of children were not subjected to brutality. Physical punishment was used by a number of parents, usually infrequently and when all else had failed."[19] Restrained discipline was a consistent theme in the diaries and in newspaper accounts and so Pollock concluded most parents were not battering their children.

Parents worried about children's health and education and were ready to help them as needed. Children also felt able to come to their parents with their difficulties. Adolescence brought conflicts between the generations, but parents expected children to have independent thoughts and supported them and maintained contact even when there were differences.

Parents in the seventeenth and eighteenth centuries were increasingly concerned with abstract questions about parenting (e.g., the responsibilities of being a parent, the best methods of discipline, worrying whether they were competent enough to be parents).

While variations among parents at a given time and over time existed, Pollock describes a general continuity in parenting practices and concerns over the last five hundred years—given minor changes due to technological advances such as refrigeration as it affected feeding. She believes the limited variation in parenting practices is due to two fundamental features of child rearing: (1) parents' goal to protect and rear children to maturity, and (2) children's state of extended dependency. "Children . . . make demands on their parents and parents are forced to operate within the context of these demands. The parents in every century studied accommodated to the needs of their offspring."[20]

LEARNING FROM SCIENCE

Recent scientific advances have helped us understand:

- parents' critical role as sensitive caregivers who not only promote children's growth but buffer children from the effects of negative genes and negative life experiences
- complexity of the growth process and the need for parental involvement in more areas and for longer times than previously thought

To illustrate these points, we look at advances in genetics, neurobiology, temperament, and cognitive development to illustrate these points.

Genetics

Prior to the mapping of the human genome in 2000, scientists thought that human beings had about 100,000 genes, each gene had a single, specific function and the sequence of nucleotides on the gene—the genetic code—contained all the vital information needed for effective development and functioning. The complete mapping of the genome revolutionized our thinking. Human beings have only around 20,000–25,000 genes,[21] and each gene is more versatile than thought, producing several proteins depending on messages they receive from other cells, other genes, and hormones triggered by the environment. Genes not only produce chemical changes in their environment, the environment triggers changes in the ways genes function and the proteins they produce. The focus now is on the operations of the gene, and the dynamic interplay between DNA and its environment.[22]

Studies carried out by Marian Bakermans-Kranenburg, Marinus van IJzendoorn, and their colleagues illustrate the complex interaction of genes, the environment, and parenting.[23] They found that insensitive parenting was related to increases in preschoolers' aggressive, noncompliant behaviors but only when children had a particular form of the gene, DRD4 7-repeat allele, which is associated with behaviors like attention problems, poor state regulation, aggressiveness, and Attention Deficit Hyperactivity Disorder (ADHD).

Researchers undertook a preventive program to increase the sensitivity of parents of one- to three-year-olds who already had elevated levels of aggressiveness and noncompliance and were at risk for behavior problems in preschool. Behavioral measures were obtained on all study members at pretest and posttest sessions. Cortisol levels, physiological measures of stress, were obtained at the posttest to determine whether the intervention reduced physiological stress as well as negative behaviors.

Half the families were enrolled in a home intervention program and half were in the control group receiving only six phone calls. In the intervention group's six home visits, a home visitor highlighted parents' positive behaviors with children in areas like paying positive attention, responding sensitively to children's signals, and using distraction, persuasion, and explanations to deal with noncompliance. This form of intervention is described in greater detail in the research section.

Parents' increases in sensitive parenting in the toddler years were related to:

- increases in preschool children's ability to regulate stress but only if preschoolers had the DRD4 7-repeat allele
- decreases in children's aggressive and noncompliant behaviors but only if preschoolers had the DRD4 7-repeat allele
- decreases in aggressive behaviors were greatest for those children whose mothers had the greatest increases in sensitive parenting

So parents' sensitive behavior can prevent the development of the negative behaviors associated with the gene DRD4 7 repeat allele. This research demonstrates the important point that children's genetic makeup plays a role in their responsiveness to parents' behaviors, and children are not equally responsive to what parents do.

Caregivers' behavior can also reduce the impact of traumatic experiences on the actions of children's genes. Childhood family adversity reflected in abuse and neglect appears to modify NR3C1 gene expression so that individuals have greater difficulty managing physiological responses to stress, and as a result are more vulnerable to stressful situations later on in life and more likely to engage in self-destructive behavior.[24] Caregivers' actions described in Chapter 17 can reduce the physiological responses and vulnerability as a result of neglect and abuse.

Neurobiology

In the past, we thought that genetic programming completely controlled brain development and many traits like height and intelligence. Recent developments have shown us that brain development is more plastic, that is, subject to influence from internal and external stimulation, than we had thought, and plasticity is greatest at the most complex levels of functioning.[25]

Neurons and Their Connections   A neuron is the basic unit of communication in the brain, transmitting information from one part of the brain to another and to other parts of the body. It consists of a cell body, an axon (an extended branch of the cell that sends messages to other cells) and dendrites (protruding parts of the cell that receive messages from other cells). Cells communicate with each other across a small gap called a synapse. Endings on the axon release a substance termed a neurotransmitter that triggers a change in the dendritic membrane of the receiving cell so the message is received. At the end of the axon are several branching terminals so messages can go to more than one cell. Dendrites too develop branches with numerous endings to receive messages from many cells. In parts of the cortex, one neuron can have as many as 80,000 synapses or connections with other cells, some close by and others more distant. Myelin, a sheath of fatty tissue, covers the axon to increase the speed of conducting messages. Other cells in the brain like glial cells provide support and nutrients to neurons.[26]

In the prenatal period, most all the neurons we will have in life are formed though some new neurons are formed in adulthood in certain parts of the brain like the hippocampus, involved in memory tasks based on new experiences.[27]

Human beings are equipped with special neurons termed "mirror neurons" found in many areas of the brain.[28] When individuals watch others' actions like picking up a pen or throwing a ball, mirror neurons in the brain fire in the same way that the neurons in the brain of the person carrying out the action fire. An unknown mechanism prevents the observer from actually making the same physical movements.

Similarly, when we see disgusted, sad, or angry expressions, the firing of our mirror neurons triggers reactions in the emotional areas of our brain, and we feel the disgust, sadness, or humiliation we witness in another's reaction.

Mirror neurons serve several important functions. They help us understand what others are doing or are about to do, and how they may feel because we are having the same neurophysiological reactions. Some scientists think mirror neurons help us have empathy for others because at a very real level, we feel their pain. Mirror neurons may also help us learn language because the movements for language are laid down in our brains as we watch others speak and gesture. Difficulties in the functioning of mirror neurons may contribute to developmental disorders like autism in which children do not seem to understand other people's thinking and intentions.

The existence of mirror neurons has enormous implications for parenting because what children observe, they are also experiencing at the neurological level. Parents' and siblings' behavior and other external influences, like television, are affecting children's brains. Mirror neurons may account for such phenomena as the negative effects on children of witnessing domestic violence[29] and others' arguing and may account for the negative effects of mothers' depressive behavior as children take on the behaviors they witness. Mirror neurons may help to explain the negative effects of witnessing violent television shows. A study revealed that when children watched violent television programs, mirror neurons in areas related to aggression fired, and children were more likely to behave in aggressive ways following the show.[30]

One can speculate that mirror neurons may also account for the fact that mothers' positive moods and smiles are able to increase the smiles and moods of their infants, and for the fact that toddlers and preschoolers imitate the caring behaviors of their caregivers.

The Developing Brain   The architecture of the brain is laid down in the first two trimesters of pregnancy, primarily under genetic control but influenced by negative environmental events like toxins and drugs.[31] At birth, the neurons are in place, and the connections controlling the most basic processes are formed, again under genetic control. Many of the connections between neurons, however, have not been formed and develop in the first years of life.

At birth, the brain is one quarter of its adult size, but during the first year, there is such an increase in the number of axons, dendrites, and synapses that at the end of the first year, the brain contains twice as many synapses as exist in the adult brain.[32] Both internal and external stimulation of the brain play a role; experience stimulates cells and activates them to fire, and cells that fire together are wired together and form strong connections.

An overabundance of synapses in the brain leads to pruning or eliminating synapses, and close to 50 percent of childhood synaptic contacts are lost by adolescence. Those synapses that are unspecified or inactive are most likely to be pruned. The rapid growth of synapses after birth, the pruning of unused neuronal connections, and continuing development of new brain connections through new experiences point to the contribution of environmental input in shaping the structure and functioning of the brain.

It was thought that pruning was complete and the brain formed by adolescence, but neuroimaging of the brains of children and adolescents from age four to twenty-two reveals that brain development continues on into the twenties, long after it was thought to end.[33] White matter continues to grow throughout the brain during adolescence, especially in the frontal area responsible for thinking and planning. Continuing brain development in adolescence provides further opportunities for teens' activities to contribute to the formation and strengthening of new neuronal connections. It also means that adolescents' developing brains are vulnerable to substances like alcohol and drugs because development is not complete. Throughout the lifespan, activities and experiences stimulate the growth of axonal and dendritic endings and strengthen connections between cells so we continue to develop though at a slower pace.

Peter Huttenlocher, who has carried out extensive research on brain development, describes the implications of his work for parents.[34] First, early childhood training that is not continued later has dubious value because the early connections will disappear unless maintained with practice. Practice can be varied so it is not boring, but it must be consistent to maintain the connections. Second, there are no critical periods or closed windows for stimulation or environmental input. There are optimal periods when learning and practice may have the biggest benefits, but stimulation has value at all ages. He uses the example of learning a second language. If children learn before puberty, they can speak without an accent. They can learn languages throughout life, perhaps at a slower rate, but they will most likely have an accent.

Third, he states that the brains of children and adolescents may need time for rest and integration of what has been learned to nourish creativity. He writes, "A proper balance of early exposure to an enriched academic environment and time-off may be important for optimum cortical development. At this point, we do not know where this balance lies."[35]

Neuroendocrine Research   Here we review briefly the role of the nervous system in regulating the individual's behavioral state and how social relationships depend on such neural regulation in order to develop fully.

There are now efficient and simple ways to get measures of circulating cortisol, a hormone that is secreted by the nervous system and regulates children's daily pattern of arousal, alertness, and attention.[36] In human beings, cortisol is elevated in the morning and gradually declines during the day and early evening as individuals get ready to sleep. Cortisol levels can change over short periods of time when children confront new tasks and new people. For example, a moderate cortisol increase followed by a decrease is associated with flexible problem-solving, self-regulated behavior, and letter knowledge in preschoolers.[37]

Ongoing stress as occurs in the case of chronic poverty or abuse disrupts the usual patterns of cortisol release and children show atypical patterns with some showing low levels in the morning and throughout the day, and some very high. When levels are continuously low, children appear less alert and attentive and perform less well on cognitive tests.[38]

Cortisol is also involved in the stress response system. The stress response has two components, a fast-acting component involving the sympathetic nervous system that readies the body for fight or flight, and the hypothalamic-pituitary-adrenal response system (HPA), a slower acting component that involves a cascade of hormones that triggers the adrenals to release cortisol as well as epinephrine and norepinephrine.[39] Cortisol is high during stress, and when stress decreases, cortisol binds to receptors to inhibit the stress hormones.

Ongoing stress and high levels of cortisol can result in decreases in the immune system, resulting in illness and in cell loss in the hippocampus, resulting in memory difficulties and poorer academic work.

Stephen Porges believes that in addition to the stress response neural circuit that enables humans to avoid or confront danger, human beings have two other neural circuits that promote adaptation to life.[40] First is the response of immobilization—freezing, shut-down in the face of life-threatening events. It is a more primitive response than the stress response as it involves passive coping and is used when a more active response is not possible or effective.

The third neural circuit, the most advanced, seen in mammals and human beings, is triggered in times of safety; under the control of myelinated fibers of the vagal nerve, it has two functions. First, it damps down the stress response when it is not needed, slowing the heart rate and inducing physiological balance so the body functions efficiently and is able to restore itself and grow. When danger appears, the vagal nerve quickly triggers the stress response to protect the individual. The vagal nerve also controls sensory and motor nerves of the head, neck, and face, those areas of the body most activated in vocalizing and perceiving and responding to other people. Second, this circuit, including hormones like oxytocin, vasopressin, dopamine, and endorphins (the body's manufactured opiods), stimulates social bonding and engagement.

This neural circuit is functional at birth though in rudimentary form, undergoing its most rapid period of development in the first three months after birth and continuing to develop into adolescence. Initially, it is mothers' sensitive caregiving that reduces babies' distress and regulates babies' physiological functioning because babies' systems are too immature to permit self-regulation. As the nervous system matures in the first three to six months after birth, babies develop abilities both to better regulate their physiological functioning and to soothe themselves when distressed.

At birth, the hormone oxytocin, present in breast milk, encourages mothers and infants to bond with each other and form a strong attachment. The hormone stimulates feelings of calm and relaxation; mothers are stimulated to approach their crying infants and stay close, to nurture and care for their infants and feel distressed at separation from them. Oxytocin triggers infants' feelings of safety and security that over time are associated with the presence of their nurturing mothers.

The neural circuit also triggers dopamine and endorphins that people associate with feelings of pleasure and desire, safety and security. Beginning in infancy, humans seek social relationships because they are enjoyable and because social interactions are a major way to damp down the stress response system. However, stressful conditions such as neglectful or abusive or inconsistent care can disrupt the circuit, triggering hypervigilance and physiological instability in babies, making them unable to flourish and grow and fully engage in social interactions. Porges believes that the important point of this kind of research is to show that prosocial behaviors and close ties depend on a well-regulated physiological system that has damped down stress so that the baby can engage with others. As we will see in Chapter 7, a basic parental task following birth is to help regulate the baby's system and allow him or her to engage in mutually enjoyable social interactions.

Temperament

The term "temperament" refers to babies' innate ways of reacting and responding to the world. It is their individual contribution to the parenting process. The formal definition of temperament as "Constitutionally based individual differences in reactivity and self-regulation in the domains of affect, activity, and attention"[41] refers to biologically based differences in how children react to experiences and how well they regulate their reactions. A child's temperament is important because it refers to behaviors that

- are biologically based, arise spontaneously, and require effort to change
- influence children's reactions in many situations
- trigger reactions in parents, peers, and others in the environment
- shape the effects of parents' behavior on the child
- can put a child at risk for certain problems.

Three broad dimensions of temperament are identified in infancy and childhood:[42]

- negative emotional reactivity that includes reacting to experiences with fear, sadness, frustration, anger, or discomfort
- extraversion/surgency that includes reactions of smiling, spontaneity, positive approach to stimulation, and high activity
- effortful control/self-regulation that includes inhibiting behavior, focusing attention, and low intensity pleasure

Stability of Temperament   In general, there is modest stability in these broad behavioral categories over time. Where there is change, it is often not from one end of the scale to the other, but from marked characteristics of a dimension to intermediate behaviors.[43]

A careful study of the stability of high negative reactivity and low reactivity has followed children from four months of age to mid-adolescence.[44] General consistency in behavior is seen in those highly reactive four-month-old infants who cried and squirmed and had strong physiological reactions when confronted with new, unfamiliar stimuli and those who were low reactors. In early childhood and school years, high reactives were fearful, shy, and inhibited, and as teens, they were more emotionally subdued, quiet, cautious, religious, and worried about the future. Those four-month-old infants who reacted little to unfamiliar stimuli were sociable, outgoing, eager to approach situations and make friends.

There were different risks for psychological problems in adolescence for these two groups. Five high-reactive girls were being treated for depression in contrast to only one low-reactive girl, and one high reactive boy was being treated for social anxiety.

Another group that has negative emotional reactivity is the irritable, fussy infant who is demanding.[45] Irritability at six and seven months tended to persist and was related to behavior problems at ages two and three. In Chapter 7 on page (224) we describe an early intervention to modify that behavior.

Several longitudinal studies have identified three groups of children—overcontrolled (similar to high reactive, inhibited children), undercontrolled, and resilient/well adjusted—and found consistency in behavior over time. A New Zealand study followed children from age three to young adulthood and looked at their behavior in significant areas of life—work, romantic relationships, friendships, and social network. Children identified as having confident, well-adjusted, or reserved temperaments at age three were doing well in all areas.[46] Those who were inhibited, cautious, and fearful at age three had good relationships at work and were satisfied with their romantic relationships, but they had fewer friends, fewer interests, and less social support.

Those who were poorly controlled at age three had the greatest number of difficulties as young adults.[47] They were highly impulsive, aggressive, risk-taking people who irritated others. Three- to five-year-olds self-control predicted measures of health, depression, substance abuse, employment and earnings, and law-abiding behavior when these study members were age thirty-two.[48]

Temperament and Parenting   Parents' behavior has different impacts depending on the child's temperament. When mothers of highly reactive infants were protective and nurturant, rocking and holding their crying baby, the child remained fearful and inhibited in the toddler years.[49] When, however, mothers were supportive but firm that the child had to soothe himself or herself, children were much less reactive as toddlers. Other studies have obtained similar results. Parents' nurturant protection did not affect low reactive children's low level of inhibition.

As inhibited children develop a conscience and learn prosocial behavior, they are responsive to parents' rules and regulations so that parents have to use only requests and explanations because children are fearful of not following them.[50]

Parenting of undercontrolled children requires adaptation just as parenting of inhibited children does. When children are relatively active and fearless and have little response to their own wrongdoing, they do not benefit from gentle, persuasive techniques nor do they benefit from punishments that arouse their anger.[51] Instead, they learn rules most easily when parents establish a positive, initially cooperative partnership based on a secure attachment. More securely attached, fearless children comply with what the mother wants because of the relationship, not the specific disciplinary techniques used.

Temperament research indicates that no one set of interventions will help all children. Rather, parents must be sensitive, flexible caregivers who target their behavior to be a good fit with their child's temperamental qualities, recognizing that their child's biological inheritance may present special vulnerabilities for them in development. We come back to this topic in chapters on development, especially Chapter 8 (pages 246), and show the influence of culture—the American culture, for example, is more accepting of the extroverted, active, positive person and less accepting of the timid, fearful, inhibited person—on the child's behavior and the ways temperamental qualities modify children's development.[52]

Executive Functioning

We have seen how important the ability to control and regulate one's behavior is in life. Executive functioning (EF) includes three general skills that are strongly related to effortful control: [53]

- the ability to inhibit habitual behaviors
- the ability to hold and use information in working memory
- the ability to adjust to change and solve problems flexibly

These skills are related to measures of intelligence and predict achievement in math and reading throughout the school years though they are primarily meaures of attention and impulse control.[54]

Neuroimaging techniques reveal that executive functioning skills depend on developments in the hippocampus, the prefrontal cortex and the surrounding areas where memory, attention, and rudimentary problem-solving skills begin to develop in the first year of life. The ability to control behavior and inhibit responses grows in the second year of life and improves dramatically in the preschool years.

Children and adults differ in their EF skills, in part because of genetic predispositions, but also because of life experiences. Parental behaviors early in life help children learn skills in self-regulation as we shall see in Chapter 7. Mothers' ways of playing and solving puzzles with their babies play a role.[55] When babies are twelve- to fifteen-months-old, mothers' respect for babies' tempos, giving babies active roles in play, supporting and helping them to achieve their goals all predict greater attention skills when they are eighteen- to twenty-six-months old.

Patterns of sleep play a role in developing attention skills.[56] Twelve- and eighteen-month-old children who got a larger percentage of their sleep at night as opposed to the day were more advanced in EF skills at twenty-six-months though not in general cognitive abilities. Sleep at night may be especially helpful in promoting brain development that, in turn, affects EF. So parenting behaviors that promote healthy sleep at night may also be promoting executive skills.

A carefully developed nursery school program termed Tools of the Mind increased executive skills.[57] This program, based on Vygotsky's views of intellectual growth (described later in the chapter), developed forty different skills including self-talk to guide behavior, dramatic play to encourage symbolic and imaginative behavior, and strategies to facilitate memory and attention. Compared to control children who had a state curriculum, the Tools children who practiced the skills for one or two years in nursery school performed significantly better on executive functioning tasks such as complex tasks requiring memory of several directions, flexible problem-solving, and the inhibition of habitual responses.

Reviewing many other forms of intervention to improve EF including other school-related curricula such as Montessori programs as well as computerized training and other games, and physical programs such as aerobics, martial arts, and yoga,[58] Adele Diamond and Kathleen Lee conclude that successful interventions require (1) increasing levels of difficulty and challenge that provide the greatest benefits for those who have the lowest score on measures of EF, and (2) increasing the positive emotional tone of classes by arousing feelings of joy, interest, and competence, reducing stress, and strengthening social bonds with other children.

Increasing EF skills can have many benefits for children because more focused control and greater capacity for reasoning increase physical health, academic success, and occupational achievement.

The advances in science we have reviewed help us to see parents' important role in their children's growth in all areas. The experiences parents provide can buffer children against the expression of negative genetic characteristics and help the brain realize its full potential. Parents' daily interactions can promote children's executive functioning that influences all learning. Finally, sensitive parenting directed to the child's specific qualities can help children live comfortably with their unique physiology.

We now look at what theories tell us about how children incorporate the biological, emotional, psychological, and social influences in their lives.

LEARNING FROM THEORIES OF GROWTH AND DEVELOPMENT

Theories describe children's growth and development and the factors thought to stimulate healthy growth. Although theories do not provide step-by-step directions for parents, they do help parents understand children's needs and the many ways parents meet them and contribute to children's growth. In most instances, theories are complimentary, each contributing important information on different facets of children's growth. Box 3-1 at the end of the theories section describes how each theory might handle a problem.

Theories are grouped according to the emphasis they give to (1) parents and external influences, (2) children's internal characteristics, and (3) interaction between children's internal qualities and external influences.

Theories Emphasizing Importance of Parents' and External Influences

We include attachment theory, learning theories, and Vygotsky's Theory.

Attachment Theory London psychoanalyst John Bowlby developed attachment theory in the 1950s to focus on the quality of parent-child relationships that promote healthy development. Attachment is defined as "an enduring affectional tie that unites one person to another, over time and across space,"[59] and gives the infant feelings of safety, security, and protection and provides a safe base from which to explore the world.

Adults' behavior determines the quality of attachment between parents and children. When parents are accepting, emotionally available, and sensitive in meeting babies' needs, children (about 62 percent in U.S. middle-class samples) form secure attachments to them. In laboratory situations, they are happy and secure with parents, protest when they leave, and are happy and seek closeness when they return.

There are three forms of insecure attachment:

- *anxious-avoidant* attachments (about 15 percent in U.S., samples)—being unconcerned when parents leave and uninterested in their return as parents are intrusive and overstimulating

- *anxious-resistant* attachments (10 percent in U.S. samples)—strong protests when mothers leave and difficulties establishing closeness when mothers return, alternately seeking the mother and resisting closeness as parents are insensitive to babies' cues and often unavailable

- *disorganized/disoriented* attachments (about 13 percent in low-risk families but higher in high-risk families with problem behaviors like abuse and few resources)—occur in families in which parents appear frightened or traumatized, and as a result may appear frightening—children's behavior seems disorganized because at times, they happily approach the mother as a securely attached infant would, and at other times, they avoid the parent.

They also appear disoriented because they show signs of confusion as to how to respond, sometimes "freezing" or "stilling" when near the parent.

Since attachment classifications depend on the quality of the parent-child relationship at the time, attachments are stable for long periods of time, e.g., from one year to late adolescence, when family life and relationships are stable. When infants or older children experience many changes, especially negative changes that weaken the quality of the parent-child ties like divorce or family illness, stability of attachment is lower.[60] However, attachments can change in a positive direction as well; mothers' increases in confidence and feelings of security led to more secure attachment to children.[61]

In addition to insuring infants and children will stay close to the parent and remain responsive to parents' protective guidance, attachment relationships also provide a framework for babies' understanding of the world, teaching them how people relate to one another.[62] Babies develop expectations of how well others will

Children learn from observing what other people do and imitating them and are most likely to imitate warm, nurturing models.

understand and respond to them, and how much influence they will have on others. They develop a sense of their own lovability when others respond positively to their overtures, and they anticipate similar responses from adults in new situations. When babies are ignored or rejected, they may develop a sense of unworthiness and helplessness. When interactions make up consistent patterns, babies acquire a sense of order and predictability in experience that generalizes to daily activities and to the world at large.

The benefits of early attachments extend to the future. Securely attached infants are more curious later in childhood than are insecurely attached ones. They attack a problem vigorously and persistently but accept help from others and are not aggressive. Children with early insecure attachments tend later to be more anxious and have tantrums when presented with problems.

While attachment initially referred to early parent-child relationships, its use has broadened to apply to parent-child relationships throughout the lifespan and to relationships with significant others like friends, teachers, caregivers, and marital partners.

Attachment theory helps parents understand that (1) attachments are formed with important people throughout the lifespan, (2) the way parents treat babies creates long-lasting expectations about the way the world will treat them, and

(3) attachments depend on the quality of the parent-child relationship at the time and will change as circumstances improve or damage the quality of the relationship.

Learning Theories   These theories emphasize the specific forms of environmental stimulation that promote children's growth and give a very important and active role to parents.[63] Children's role may vary from blank slates who learn all behavior from external rewards and punishments to more active learners who interpret the environment around them and select goals and models to imitate. Still, the major force for development is seen as coming from outside forces that teach and produce behavior change.

American learning theorists focused on how behavior changes as a result of the positive or negative consequences that followed the behavior. They note that behaviors increase when positive consequences followed consistently and decrease with consistent negative consequences. They identify kinds of rewards—material, like food or a toy, extra privileges, like staying up, and social rewards, like attention or physical affection. They find personal attention to be a most important reward for children and adults alike. If children do not get attention for positive behaviors, they will seek attention through irritating behaviors like whining and arguing.

Social learning theorists found that children learn even when there is no reward at all. They observe people around them and imitate them. For example, babies will not play with a toy if the mother has looked at it with disgust. Observation of behavior alone is enough to stimulate imitation. Children are most likely to imitate models who are warm, nurturing, and powerful. In extreme circumstances when there is no model of warmth to copy, children will imitate a hostile, cold model.

Social learning theorists like Albert Bandura focus on the active nature of the learner who chooses goals to pursue and reflects on performance.[64] In understanding the process of learning, the learner's thoughts and interpretations of the environment are as important as environmental rewards and punishments.

Learning theories help parents understand (1) Their important role in modeling appropriate behaviors for children and structuring the consequences that teach children new behaviors; (2) parents' importance as role models because children copy parents whether parents are carrying out approved or disapproved behaviors, (3) children want parental attention and will seek it by negative means if they do not get it for positive behaviors, and (4) the conditions under which children learn best.

Socioculture Theory   Lev Vygotsky gives parents a central role in supporting children's growth, but one that differs from the role given by learning theorists.[65] Every culture, he believes, has a view of the world and the way to solve problems. Language, art, and everyday routines all reflect the cultural worldview that children learn from parents and daily experiences. He believes that knowledge, thought, and mental processes such as memory all rest on social interactions with knowledgeable partners.

Whatever children learn, Vygotsky believes, they first experience in a social interaction with someone, usually a parent, teacher, or peer, and then internalize the social interaction at the individual and psychological level. For example, preschoolers learn about their culture from taking on society's roles in dramatic play with their peers. They learn what mothers, fathers, and policemen do, and their language and knowledge grow as they take on these roles.

Vygotsky describes a unique concept called the *zone of proximal development.* There is a range of actions a child can perform alone, demonstrating a capacity that is clearly internal. This is what we consider the child's level of ability. But Vygotsky points out that when a more experienced person guides or prompts the child with questions, hints, or demonstrations, the child can respond in a more mature level not achieved when the child acts alone.

So, a child has potential that emerges in social interaction guided by an experienced partner. For example, a child learning to talk may use a particular number of words spontaneously. That would be the child's verbal ability. A mother, however, might increase the number of words or the length of the sentence by prompting the child to use more words, saying "The doggie?" and waiting for "runs" or "goes bowwow." Adults' teaching has the greatest impact, Vygotsky believes, when it is directed to the child's learning potential at the high end of the zone of proximal development.

Vygotsky believes language plays an important role in mental development. Language develops in social interaction and serves several functions. It influences others' behavior. Adults and children talk to each other and say what they need or want or what is upsetting them.

Language also serves as a guide to what to do. Parents can use language to help children remember sequences of actions in terms of steps. Children initially guide their own behavior with words they hear from others. They then talk aloud to themselves as others have talked to them and guide their behavior with their speech when they are alone. A toddler will say, "No, no," to herself as a way of stopping forbidden action, and gradually the speech becomes internal or inner speech that becomes thought in the older child. So language is the forerunner of thinking and a means of regulating behavior.

Dramatic symbolic play also helps children to grow because they are interacting with their peers and have to play by rules and adjust to others' actions, so symbolic play develops imagination and self-control in relationships with others. Peers play an important role because in cooperating with each other to achieve a goal, children learn the give and take of social relationships.

Vygotsky's theory helps parents understand (1) Their important role in conveying their culture's view of the world and how to live in it; (2) their role as experienced partners in guiding children to more advanced behaviors; and (3) the very important role of language both in reflecting the culture's values and in advancing children's ability to think and reason.

Theories Emphasizing Importance of Children's Internal Qualities

We now turn to three theories that emphasize the important role of children's inner qualities in shaping development—evolutionary theory, Piaget's constructivist theory, and Freud's theory of psychosexual development.

Evolutionary Developmental Theory   Psychologist emphasize how our evolutionary heritage influences our behavior today.[66] Evolutionary psychologists draw on Darwin's concepts of natural selection, the process whereby adaptive characteristics increase in frequency in a group because those behaviors enable individuals to survive, grow to maturity, reproduce, and pass along their genes to the next generation. Evolutionary psychologists provide insights about contemporary social life by showing how our human genetic history influences our needs and behavior today.

They trace the origins of family life back thousands of years to the time we lived in small hunting-gathering tribes that required physical activity and agility in its members and depended upon organized, cooperative, social behaviors. Complex social behaviors required a large brain that meant the child had to be born earlier in a less mature state so that the body of the mother could accommodate the size of the child's head in the birth process. Being born in a less mature state required an extended period of dependence on caregivers, and that, in turn, encouraged father's ongoing protection and support. Thus, a family system of mother, father, and children was born.

Early conditions of life also fostered the development of heavy parental investment in children. For immature children to survive, mature, and reproduce, caregiving had to extend for the long period of child dependency so the children of parents with heavy investments in rearing their children increased because of their ability to survive.

In contemporary life we see a similar advantage for children whose parents make heavy investments in parenting[67] When children grow up in harmonious families with resources to provide many opportunities for development—lessons, trips, advanced schooling—children postpone sexual activity and mating, produce fewer children, and invest heavily in those they have. Conversely, when children grow up in conflicted families with limited resources and few opportunities for skill development, they reach puberty early, invest heavily in sexual and mating behaviors, and invest less in parenting behaviors. One way to increase parental investment for those growing up in families with limited resources is to provide opportunities for growth and development.

Evolutionary developmental psychology helps parents understand that (1) as human beings we have selected tendencies based on our past history that make certain contemporary adaptations more or less difficult—e.g., see Box 3-1 for the ways that evolutionary developmental theory provides insight on school problems—and we must take that heritage seriously as we make social interventions; and (2) our strong attachment and closeness to nurturing family members has had and continues to have survival value.

Constructivist Theory **Jean Piaget** profoundly changed our views of children's intellectual growth by showing that children think about the world differently from adults. Though different, their thinking is understandable as it proceeds through a series of predictable stages.[68]

Piaget emphasized the child's active construction of knowledge. Learning about the world is not a passive process of taking in what one sees and hears. Intellectual competence is a dynamic process in which the child explores the world, takes in information, and organizes it into internal structures called schemes. This process of taking in and organizing information is termed *assimilation*.

As children obtain new information, they find their internal schemes inadequate and modify them to account for the new information. The process of changing internal schemes to incorporate new information is called *accommodation*.

Box 3-1
THEORIES' VIEWS OF SCHOOL PROBLEM

This box contains what each theory's view might be of a boy or girl who is having difficulty in the first grade staying in his or her seat, settling down, and completing class work. The child has always been an active participant in school programs and had many friends. There are no medical, learning, or family problems.

Attachment, learning, and Vygotsky's theories would focus on what parents and teachers can do to increase children's level of functioning at school. Parents can structure the home—good sleep habits, quiet place to do work—so children can learn at school. Both parents and teachers can use a reward system to increase positive behaviors.

Attachment theorists would believe the child's problem-solving abilities and self-control are related to attachment relationships in the present and in the past and would foster secure attachments at home to support confident, curious, problem-solving school behavior. They would encourage teachers to interact with the child in a warm, sensitive, responsive way to form a secure attachment so the child has an available, reliable source of help, a secure base from which to move forward independently.

Vygotsky's approach would also focus on what teacher and parents might do but would focus on joint interactions with the child, engaging and supporting the child's behavior at the high end of the zone of proximal development. Language would be emphasized to help the child engage in self-talk to guide his or her behavior and get the work done. Efforts would be made to engage the child with peers in cooperative learning and imaginative play to advance thinking and executive skills.

Evolutionary, Piagetian, and Freudian theorists would look at children's qualities as sources of problems but use external influences of parents' and teachers' actions to solve the problem. *Evolutionary* theorists would highlight young children's needs to engage in rough and tumble play and motor activity rather than sedentary, culturally invented activities like reading. They would see the solution as more time in recess and active play during the day, and research confirms that increasing physical exercise and frequent breaks through the day increase learning even if the breaks do not involve active physical exercise.*

Intellectual growth is a constant interplay of taking in new information (assimilation) and modifying internal structures (accommodation) to achieve a balance or equilibrium between the individual's structure of the world and the world itself. *Equilibration* is the active process by which the individual achieves this effective balance.

An example of this process is seen in the child's growing understanding of the concept of persons. Initially all adults are "mama" and "dada." Eventually, the child will have an understanding of a world of adults with many different names—grandma, grandpa, auntie, uncle, teacher, coach, principal. Some are family members who will give you special consideration, and some are not.

Piaget described growth in terms of four major periods in which the child takes in and processes information in distinctive ways:

- *the sensory-motor period*, the first eighteen to twenty-four months of life, known as the *sensori-motor period*, the child's own body, perceptions, and

Piaget's theory emphasizes the teacher's role in organizing a classroom in which children's way of reasoning is respected and children can have an active role in constructing knowledge. Children would be given projects and small experiments to carry out in class to promote a greater understanding of the world through active discovery.

Freud would identify children's anxieties from many sources at school and home as the source of the school difficulties—e.g., teacher's behavior, competition with peers, bullying. The solution would be to help the child identify and cope more effectively with the source of the anxiety.

Erikson, bioecological, and family systems theorists would include the emphases of all previous theorists but would go on to include social/cultural milieu of the classroom, school, neighborhood as a source of problems and means of remedying them. Children's ethnic group or gender may not be valued; e.g., girls' math and science interests and boys' creative writing may be discouraged. Bioecological theorists would look at the mesosystem, the relationship between parent and the teacher. Can they communicate and understand each other? Do they share common values about what is most important for students to learn, so they can work together to help the child adjust?

Family systems theorists add a focus on events in the extended family as a source of children's tensions and anxieties in school—maybe a grandparent has moved or is ill.

Just as one would look in many places for the sources of the difficulties, one would look at several ways to address them. In addition to all the individual interventions parents and teachers could carry out with the child, bioecological theorists would encourage parents to get involved in parent–teacher–community organizations to provide resources that enable children to engage in many physical activities in a safe atmosphere.

*Anthony D. Pellegrini and David F. Bjorkland, "The Role of Recess in Children's Cognitive Performance," *Educational Psychologist* 32 (1997): 35–40.

actions are the focus of interest, and the schemes consist of action patterns such as kicking legs or opening and closing hands; gradually, actions become more complex and months later, the child acts to achieve a purpose—reaches to grasp a toy; at the end of the first year, babies come to understand the permanence of objects, meaning babies understand objects exist even if out of the baby's sight; this concept leads to increased exploration of how objects work and where they might be when they are not visible.

- *the preoperational period* from about age two to age seven, children move from immediate experience of objects, people, and whatever is present at the moment to representations or thoughts of what is not immediately present; they can represent what they see or hear with language that increases in number of words and in the complexity of sentences to express thoughts; although children are curious and ask many questions, they pay attention to only a small number of characteristics of objects, usually to sensory features, so their concepts are limited; for example, they may think a tall, thin glass holds more liquid than a short, fat glass because they pay attention only to the the height of the glass.

- *the period of concrete operations* begins at about age seven, when children can think more logically about concepts and are not so bound by the appearance of objects. They grasp relationships among objects and easily arrange a series of sticks by lengths with little trial and error. Children can think more logically and form classes, because they have a keen interest in understanding how things work.

- *the period of formal operations*, at ages twelve to fourteen, is when children begin to think more abstractly; not only can they think logically about tangible objects, they can think more abstractly about possible or hypothetical situations, about what might happen in the future. They can think about their own thoughts and about the thoughts and reactions of others. They become more concerned about abstract concepts like justice and engage in volunteer activities.

An example of the different ways of thinking in these stages is seen in children's responses to the question, "What do you think with?" Children five or six years old say they think with their mouth or their ears because they speak thoughts with their mouths or hear others' thoughts with their ears. Children age eight or nine will say they think with their heads but they describe thoughts as material things like inner "little voices in their heads." Children age twelve will say they think with their heads and describe thoughts as immaterial—they are just there in their heads.[69]

Piaget's theory helps parents understand (1) They must take children's view of the world into account in their interactions with children; so, for example, parents will not expect a toddler to understand the abstract concept of danger and future consequences—that if I run in the street or if I pull the pot off the stove, I will be hurt), and (2) that children need opportunities to explore objects and activities and to think their own thoughts about the world in order to grow.

Freud's Theory of Psychosexual Development   Freud revolutionized the way we think about children's experiences in early childhood.[70] In treating people with emotional problems, Freud observed he could trace many adult symptoms to anxieties about experiences occurring in early childhood. Concluding that what happened in early childhood had lifelong effects on adults' personalities, he set about describing the significant dimensions of childhood. He focused on children's impulses, particularly sexual impulses and their sources of gratification. Children were viewed as pleasure-seeking creatures who had to tame their impulses to conform to parents' and society's demands.

Freud divided childhood into five psychosexual stages that unfolded over time from birth to adolescence. The ways children attempt to gratify each stage's impulses and others' reactions to their attempts shape adult personality. Each stage is named after the area of the body that is the primary source of stimulation and gratification at that time. The stages are: first, the oral stage, with pleasures of nursing and taking in food; then the anal stage at the time of toilet training, with pleasures associated with tightening and releasing the anal musculature; then the phallic stage in the preschool years when genital stimulation predominated over oral and anal gratifications; then latency in the early elementary school years, when sexual feelings were thought to be dormant; and finally the genital stage in adolescence when sexual development and sexual feelings were thought to mature fully.

Freud believed that the outcome of the Oedipal conflict or family romance occurring in the preschool years is a major determiner of personality development. Just as children begin to feel competent and effective, they experience a failure that can permanently damage their self-regard. In these years, the child wants to be romantically involved with the parent of the opposite sex, to marry the parent and have a new family.

While this love flourishes, preschoolers feel very competitive with the same-sex parent. Freud believes children want to surpass and outperform the adult, and they talk a lot about how grown-up and powerful they are. They are angry at the same-sex parent for standing in the way, and wish that parent would disappear. They feel guilty and anxious about their anger and seek reassurances that the same-sex parent has not been a victim of their aggressiveness. Eventually, the child deals with the anxiety by giving up the opposite-sex parent as a love object and identifying with the same-sex parent as a model. As the child takes on the behaviors of the same-sex adult, the moral conscience and society's commands become internalized in the form of what Freud calls the superego that shapes the behavior of the id, the repository of impulses, and the ego that uses reason to control behavior.

Although Freud did not give direct advice to parents, he emphasized the importance of appropriate gratification of children's natural impulses—demand feeding, permissive attitudes about thumb sucking and toilet training, acceptable outlets for aggressive impulses—without criticism or punishment.

Freud's theory helps parents understand (1) Children have internal needs that drive behavior and neither they nor parents have complete control, and (2) parents have a powerful role in understanding children's inner needs and helping them find acceptable ways to gratify their impulses; parents are authoritative guides and supporters on the path to maturity, not generals commanding the course of growth.

Theories Emphasizing Both Internal and External Influences

In this section we discuss three theories—Erikson's Lifespan Theory, Brofenbrenner's bioecological theory, and family systems theory that stress the interaction of the child's inner qualities and outer social forces—from the genes to governmental institutions to historical time—that shape children's growth and affect parents' behavior and responsiveness to their children. While parents do not control these forces, they do take active roles to manage the effects of these forces in their everyday lives.

Erikson's Lifespan Theory of Development
Erik Erickson emphasizes the importance of cultural and social influences on growth, lifespan development, and attention to the positive and healthy aspects of ego development.[71]

■ **T A B L E 3-2**
ERIK ERIKSON'S EIGHT STAGES OF LIFE*

Ages	Crisis	Virtue
0–1	Trust versus Mistrust	Hope
1–3	Autonomy versus Shame, Doubt	Will
3–5	Initiative versus Guilt	Purpose
5–12	Industry versus Inferiority	Competence
12–19	Identity versus Identity Diffusion	Fidelity
19+	Intimacy versus Isolation	Love
25+	Generativity versus Stagnation	Care
65+	Integrity versus Despair	Wisdom

*Erik H. Erikson, *Childhood and Society,* 2nd ed. (New York: Norton, 1963); Erik H. Erikson, *Insight and Responsibility* (New York: Norton, 1964).

Erikson, a Freudian analyst expands Freud's stages into eight stages (see Table 3-2). In each stage physical and psychological capabilities appear and are the focus of development. A developmental crisis or turning point occurs in each stage, and depending on the balance of positive and negative experiences, leads to the development of the positive or negative basic attitudes of that period (e.g., trust or mistrust, autonomy or doubt/shame). Stages of growth emerge from within the person but require support from the environment for healthy growth to occur.

Individuals have both positive and negative experiences in the process of meeting needs, and both kinds of experience are important for optimal growth. Without some frustrations, we never learn how to cope with difficulties. However, for healthy growth, the balance should favor the positive. When this occurs, a strength or virtue develops.[72] Erikson does not believe that we resolve each crisis once and for all. Later experiences can change earlier resolutions for better or worse. Stress in adulthood, for example, can disrupt mature ways of coping so a person may show immature behaviors. Positive experiences in adulthood can reverse mistrust or doubt developed in childhood.

We focus on the qualities in Table 3-2 that develop when the appropriate experiences and positive environmental support occur; if experiences are primarily negative and support is lacking, negative qualities will develop. In the first years of life when all goes well, children develop trust, autonomy, and initiative. In the elementary school years, children attend school and are industrious and productive.

In adolescence, children incorporate sexuality into their expanding sense of self and develop a sense of identity—a feeling of sameness and continuity of self—that is a central concept in Erikson's scheme. Individuals also incorporate society's views of who they are—as men, women, and members of particular religions and ethnic groups. Individuals need to have their identities validated by their parents and society; otherwise, they remain confused, uncertain of who they are and where they are heading. When positive identities are formed and validated, teens develop fidelity—defined as loyalty to one's choices whether they be persons, goals, or ideals. When life events or family members or society are not supportive, individuals may develop a negative identity, a feeling of worthlessness.

Erikson conceived of three stages in adulthood. In the first, young adults establish intimate personal ties with an agemate. Intimate relationships involve mutuality and surrender of the self to the relationship. The virtue that develops in this period is love and involves transferring the love experienced in the developing years of childhood to adult relationships.

This is followed by a period of creating new life—generativity. In the past women experienced this primarily in the family setting, creating a home and children; men in the past have done so in their work. Now parenting and work are significant creative activities for both sexes. The virtue that develops is care—concern and attention to what has been created even if that requires sacrifice.

In the final life stage, the focus returns to the individual's personal experience. Individuals must come to terms with their lives and be satisfied with who and what they are and what they have done. When this occurs, individuals develop a sense of integrity and wisdom about life. Erikson believes children and grandchildren will be able to face life when parents can face death.

Erikson's theory helps parents understand (1) that psychological growth continues in adulthood and resolutions of old conflicts are possible later in life; (2) that children are active, adaptive individuals who go through stages of growth to become independent, giving individuals concerned with other people and the world around them; and (3) parenting is important to both the child who experiences it and the parent who gives it.

Bioecological Theory of Development   This is the most inclusive system for understanding children's growth and the many factors affecting parents and children. The late Urie Bronfenbrenner, a systems theorist, emphasized the ecology or the environments that human beings encounter in daily life as they grow and develop.

Bronfenbrenner describes a process–person–context–time (PPCT) framework for understanding development.[73] *Processes* are the daily interactions the child has with people, symbols, and objects in the environment. Processes are the engines of development. A father's feeding a baby, a child's exploring a toy, and a child's learning a skill from a coach are examples of such processes.

The *person* has many characteristics such as age, gender, ethnicity, temperamental dispositions, abilities, and resources that influence their behavior and responses to others.

Bronfenbrenner's major contribution has been to describe the nested systems that make up the child's environment:

- the *microsystem*—the pattern of daily activities and interactions the child has with symbols, objects, and people who are primarily parents and siblings in the early period of life and then other caregivers, teachers, coaches, and friends.

- the *mesosystem*—the pattern of relationships and interactions between two or more settings that a child participates in (e.g., the interrelationships between parents at home and teachers at school, or between parents at home and caregivers at day care).

- the *exosystem*—system that influences the child but with which the child does not participate in—parent's work, government agencies; for example, parents' work policies can determine parents' time with children after birth and later their participation in children's school activities.

- the *macrosystem*—the broad, culturally shared beliefs about how things are done; the cultural context in which microsystems, mesosystems, and exosystems exist.

In addition to processes, persons, and context, Bronfenbrenner's system includes the concept of *time*, to refer to the importance of regularity and stability in interactions in the child's life, and to the timing of an event in a child's development. Poverty or divorce may have very different consequences for a toddler and an adolescent. Time also refers to the historical time that exerts an influence on development. While historical time influences individuals and the contexts of their lives, people can modify the effects of historical time. For example, when economic recession reduces government resources, community members can work together to provide services.

For the last decade of his life, Bronfenbrenner, who died in 2005, expressed concern at what he termed the "growing chaos" in children's and families' lives and the resulting decline in competence of those coming of age in the twenty-first century.[74] Bronfenbrenner believes that as a society we need to commit more resources to programs such as the G.I. Bill of Rights that helped all families after World War II to get educations and to own homes. He also points to Head Start as a program that strengthens and empowers children and families.

Bioecological theory helps parents understand (1) that forces outside the family—historical events, economic factors, social institutions like work—impact parents' care of children; (2) importance of regularity and stability in children's lives; and (3) improvements in parenting come not just from changing what goes on in the home but also what goes on in society.

Family Systems Theory   A family, regardless of its structure, is a system made up of interdependent members who interact and affect each other in a mutually responsive way. An event in one family member's life has a ripple effect, touching all members, and their reactions, in turn, affect the person who initially experienced the event. Thus, a parent's job loss affects the couple's relationship and children, as we saw in the last chapter when we looked at the effects of economic hardship. A child's or parent's illness has a similar broad impact on the family. Difficulties in relationships between two or more family members can spill over and affect everyone. Parents' conflicts affect children's feelings of emotional security or intense conflicts between adolescent brothers and sisters affect the quality parents' marital relationships.

Philip Cowan, Douglas Powell, and Carolyn Cowan identify six dimensions of the family system.[75] We have added a seventh to include all those individuals who play a role in bringing the child to life for parents who adopt or use assisted reproductive technology:

1. each parent and already existing child with his or her individual traits
2. present and past quality of each parent's relationship with members of the family of origin, and grandparents-grandchildren relationships as well

3. parents' relationship with each other and their abilities to communicate and solve problems together, whether single or married, together or separated

4. quality of the relationships between brothers and sisters, if they exist

5. relationships between parents and other important people in their lives—coworkers, work supervisors, friends

6. relationship between each parent and each child in the family

7. relationships with individuals like birth parents who give children to adopting parents and those who donate eggs, sperm, or a surrogate womb to help bring the child to life; they can be a part of the family as occurs in open adoptions or ongoing relations with donors

Families try to maintain a balance between supporting close relationships within the family and meeting the demands from the social context, but there is always a certain tension because members are always in the process of growth so the family system is changing to accommodate their needs and fit with new social contexts.

Reuben Hill formulated a family stress theory termed the ABC-X model that describes the process that occurs when families respond to family change or to an external stressful event.[76] A stressor event (A) occurs. The level of stress the family experiences (X) depends on the family's resources (B) for coping with the event, and the family's perception (C) of the event. So, the specific level of stress (X) triggered by the stressor event A varies from family to family depending on B and C factors.

A son's dropping out of college serves as an example of how the model works. This event will be perceived as highly stressful in a family with many personal and financial resources (B) and the expectation that the son will go to law school and join his father in his law practice. The family perceives (C) dropping out of college as the end of their ambitions for their son and his entering the family practice. Another family experiencing the same event with the same resources perceives (C) the event as a sign that their son has developed goals of his own and is ready to take independent action to achieve them. Their level of stress (X) is very low.

Yet another family with few financial resources (B) and an elderly and ill grandparent to care for views (C) their son's leaving school as a sign of his caring and his willingness to sacrifice his own goals to help the family. While they are sad this sacrifice is necessary, their appreciation of his love and feelings of obligation to them reduce the stress they might feel to a low level.

When confronted with stress, families have several coping strategies available:

- direct action to change the situation—e.g., learn skills to cope with the stressor, get additional resources

- change one's interpretation of the event or of one's ability to manage it, e.g., see the stressor as less serious and one's abilities to cope, greater

- manage feelings triggered by stressor event—seeking emotional support

Coping with stress is a process that occurs over time while the family still maintains its usual activities of maintaining closeness and communication, supporting each other in daily life. Effective coping enables the family to adapt to the stressor event and manage it so that the family returns to its previous level of functioning. Family theorists believe it is possible that through coping with a stressor event, the family can learn new skills and develop new strengths so that the family rebounds and achieves a higher level of functioning than before the stressor. The concept of resilience refers to the ability to rebound and become more skillful as a result of dealing with stress.

Gary Peterson, Charles Hennon, and Terrence Knox apply the concepts of family stress theory to increase our understanding of stresses of parenting.[77] They point to three kinds of stressor events (A) in the process of parenting:

- normative stressors that are part of everyday life like the stressors of caring for dependent young children or the stressors from developmental transitions like the transition to parenthood or having children become adolescents
- nonnormative stressors that are unpredictable events that disrupt everyday life like parental divorce or a child's life-threatening illness
- chronic stressors that are atypical events, persisting over time and placing an ongoing burden of stress on parents, e.g., marital conflict or a child's having behavioral problems like ADHD

Parental resources (B) include parents' abilities and strengths and the resources and strengths of the extended family and community. When these resources are positive, parents are better able to cope with stress, but when these resources are negative or lacking, then families are vulnerable and find coping difficult or impossible, and the family's functioning decreases. The two most important resources in families are the parents' marital relationship and support from extended family and the community. When these resources are positive assets, families can cope with any stress as we shall see in subsequent chapters, and when they are absent or negative, families have increased stress. Resources are potential sources of help or hindrance until they are drawn upon. Many families have identical levels of resources, but one family uses them, and another family does not.

Parents' perceptions (C) of stressor events play a large role in determining parents' level of stress, especially when it comes to dealing with children's behaviors. Parents' perceptions, rooted in their past experiences, their cultural traditions, and family and community expectations, play an especially powerful role in determining the meaning or significance of their children's behaviors. For example, Asian parents have a favorable view of their child's shyness, seeing it as a sign of the child's sensitivity and cautiousness, and so they are positive and supportive of their shy children whereas North American parents view their child's shyness negatively as it does not meet the culture's expectation of independence and social outgoingness so they are critical and sometimes rejecting. Children's behavior is the same, but the parents' view of it changes its significance.[78]

In dealing with stressors, parents' coping strategies include taking direct action, changing their interpretation of events, and managing feelings aroused by stressors. Cultural groups differ, however, in their willingness to discuss children's difficulties with outsiders or seek help from schools or other agencies, and so some families rely on families for help. Other parents are quicker to get help from professionals as experts in what to do.

Parents sometimes reframe stressors as challenges and opportunities to increase their parenting skills, and they take action by learning skills in parenting education groups. Other families may define the child's problem behavior as a temporary behavior that the child will grow out of so no action or worry is required.

Whatever the mechanisms of coping, the aim is to stabilize family members' behavior by returning the family to its previous level of adaptation or by achieving a new and higher level of functioning as is reflected in the concept of resilience.

We will use Peterson, Hennon, and Knox's application of stress theory to parenting as we examine parents' behaviors in a variety of situations in coming chapters.

Summary All these theories deepen parents' understanding of their role in children's lives and the many factors that affect how parents carry out this role. Parents are not only models of behavior and providers of appropriate consequences for behavior, they are insightful, authoritative guides who understand the pressures children experience as they grow, and they provide support and direction for them. Parents are influenced by the historical time they live in; the social world they inhabit and bring to the child; the child's experience at the physical, emotional, social, and behavioral levels; the nourishing quality of the environment; and the lessons people outside the family teach children. So parents can rightly consider themselves as the stabilizing and guiding center of a wide array of influences on children's lives.

Looking at the ways the theories would approach a common childhood school problem, we see that each theory has insights on possible causes and remedies and that the insights are complimentary rather than contradictory. While no one child would require the insights of all these theories, still all theories are useful in understanding the many different children who have first grade problems. This illustrates an important point in parenting—there is rarely only one reason and one remedy for children's problem behaviours. All these theories help us understand some children.

CONSULTING EXPERTS

Psychologists Haim Ginott[79] and Thomas Gordon[80] wrote early popular parenting books focusing on effective methods of communicating feelings to meet the child's needs and strengthen the parent-child bond. Ginott establishes and enforces limits in an impersonal way and Gordon encourages parent-child problem-solving sessions when conflicts arise. We discuss their methods of communicating with children in Chapter 5.

Rudolf Dreikurs, a child psychiatrist and one of the first to organize parents' groups, advises both establishing close relationships and setting limits.[81] Dreikurs believes that children have built-in capacities to develop in healthy ways. Their strongest desire is to belong to a group, and from infancy, they seek acceptance and importance within the family. Each child, however, develops a unique path to family acceptance. Parents influence children by gaining their cooperation, using encouragement to stimulate development of children's inner resources, and applying natural and logical consequences to provide limits for children's behavior. We discuss his concepts in greater detail in Chapters 5 and 6.

Toward the end of the twentieth century, child psychiatrist and psychoanalyst Stanley Greenspan emerged as a major expert.[82] He has been a careful observer who has described children's motor, language, intellectual, social, and particularly their emotional development from birth on. He was one of the founders of the organization Zero to Three, which focuses on the development and needs of children in this period. In addition, he has been concerned with children who have special developmental needs (e.g., children with autism), discussed in greater detail in Chapter 8.

He has written a number of books describing patterns of development and parents' important role in helping children master challenges in each area and developing appropriate skills. He has also turned his attention to advocating for social policies that support parents and children. With T. Berry Brazelton, he coauthored the book, *The Irreducible Needs of Children*,[83] so that parents and public policy experts could lobby for reasonable supports. He and Brazelton want society to pay attention to parents' needs by providing additional resources for families' growth. They focus on what society must give parents to help them rear children.

The twenty-first century has brought us parenting experts on television. Dr. Phil,[84] *Nanny 911*,[85] and *Supernanny* offer parents guidance on child-rearing matters, and like their predecessors, they are both parent- and child-centered in their approach. Dr. Phil is a psychologist, but the nannies are unique among the experts in being individuals whose expertise lies in their having a lot of hands-on experience with many families, living in or spending long days with the children and their parents. In contrast to twentieth-century experts, these experts go into the homes and videotape parents and children interacting prior to the advice and after it. They observe how parents put the advice into practice and fine-tune parental behaviors. Perhaps because these experts go into people's homes and follow up, they are direct with their suggestions.

The nannies are among the most realistic of the experts in knowing the amount of effort change requires. They spend one day observing and drawing up a plan for change and the rest of the week modeling and guiding parents' interactions with children. They also show parents how to organize the home and daily routines.

Nannies Deborah Carroll and Stella Reid describe the "No-nonsense School of Parenting" that teaches parents how to "grow up and be parents"[86] as follows: "We believe that children need lots of love, but they also need lots of House Rules, giving structure to their days. This means strict limits tailored to children's personalities, and lots and lots of positive reinforcement rather than constant nagging and negativity. We'll show you how to confront your family problems head-on with firm but loving discipline, clear and effective communication, and the implementation of family rules. We'll teach you how to stop making excuses, avoid tackling problems that may seem insurmountable, and how to stop giving in when your children are whining and crying.

"Paradoxically, imposing *more* order on children allows them the freedom to thrive and stretch their wings and to grow up to be happy, healthy, and loved."[87]

RESEARCH THAT GIVES PARENTS DIRECTION AND SUPPORT

Few parents have heard the names of Diana Baumrind or Gerald Patterson; yet their research work, carried out over decades, has provided a solid base of empirical evidence for experts who believe that love, nurturance, and understanding must be combined with firm, consistent limits if children are to flourish.

Baumrind identified three patterns of parental behaviors associated with varying levels of preschool children's competence: authoritative, authoritarian, and permissive. In all age groups, in all ethnic groups in this country, in all types of family structure, authoritative parenting has had positive benefits for children.[88]

Authoritative parents exercised firm control over the child's behavior but also emphasized independence and individuality in the child. Although the parents had a clear notion of present and future standards of behavior for the child, they were rational, flexible, and attentive to the needs and preferences of the child. Their children were self-reliant and self-confident and explored their worlds with excitement and pleasure.

Authoritarian parents employed similar firm control but in an arbitrary, power-oriented way without regard for the child's individuality. They emphasized control without nurturance or support to achieve it. Children of authoritarian parents, relative to other groups of children, were unhappy, withdrawn, inhibited, and distrustful.

Establishing a warm parent-child relationship helps parent create a consistent positive reinforcement program that prevents negative cycles of behavior.

Permissive parents set few limits on the child. They accepted the child's impulses, granting as much freedom as possible while still maintaining safety. They appeared cool and uninvolved. Permissive parents sometimes allowed behavior that angered them, but they did not feel sufficiently comfortable with their anger to express it. As a result, anger built up to unmanageable proportions. They then lashed out and were likely to harm the child more than they wished. Their children were the least independent and self-controlled and could best be classified as immature.

Both authoritarian and permissive parents had unrealistic perceptions of children. "While Authoritarian parents tended to view children as having responsibilities similar to those of adults and Permissive parents tended to view children as having rights similar to those of adults, Authoritative . . . parents saw the balance between the responsibilities and rights of parents and the responsibilities and rights of children as a changing function of stage of development."[89]

Authoritative parents also interpreted the parental role as including the responsibility to teach children that in their relationship, each had to treat the other as they wished to be treated, and children were expected to behave the same way in their relationships with others outside the family.

The research of Gerald Patterson and his colleagues at the Oregon Social Learning Center also encourages parents to give both love and limits. Their research initially focused on helping families with aggressive children who defied parents at home and teased and bullied children at school.[90] Observers in the homes recorded patterns of family interaction. Parents learned about behavior modification techniques. Parents and child drew up a contract of rewards and negative consequences to increase positive target behaviors and decrease negative behaviors. The program led to positive behavior change in the family and to fathers' taking more active roles in controlling children's behavior.

Combining their observations with insights from attachment research on the importance of sensitive caregiving and maternal warmth, Patterson and his coworkers have sketched a process of development that leads to children's compliance or noncompliance as follows.[91] Sensitive parents, responsive to their children's needs, form secure attachments to their children; they therefore create early in life a climate of mutual responsiveness in which children are willing to comply because parents attend to their needs and wishes. The children act out of the commitment to the relationship with their parents. Throughout the learning process, parents give children the encouragement and support needed to persevere in the often frustrating learning process.

Like mutual responsiveness, the process of coercion begins with the interactions between the mother/caregiver and infant. Either partner can start the process and both keep it going.[92] Typically, the infant is irritable and fussy, and the mother, for whatever reason, is negative and unpredictable in her response. This increases the infant's irritability. The infant comes to see the world as an unrewarding, unsupportive, unpredictable place. Or the mother may be depressed and pay little attention to the infant who becomes irritable and negative and triggers further negativity on the mother's part.

The infant develops into a noncompliant, negative toddler who fails to follow rules. Eventually other family members are drawn in to the negative cycle. The noncompliant toddler becomes the impulsive, defiant preschooler who then becomes the aggressive, bullying elementary school student.

To counter a negative cycle, Patterson and his colleagues have taught parents to use a supportive, consistent, positive reinforcement program to create a sensitive, caring relationship between parent and child. Once a warm relationship is established, then parents can actively teach desirable habits primarily through the use of positive statements and consistent consequences. Though they believe that temperamental qualities of parent and child affect the interactions between the two, they also believe that behavioral interventions can and do modify parents' and children's behavior.

An extensive series of studies carried out by Dutch researchers Femmie Juffer, Marian Bakermans-Kranenburg, Marinus van IJzendoorn, and their colleagues combine the insights of attachment theory and Patterson's coercion theory and apply them directly to helping parents facing special situations—adoptive parents, parents of preterm children, insecure mothers, and low-income parents.[93]

The interventions, Video-Feedback Intervention Positive Parenting (VIPP) with the added module VIPP-Sensitive Discipline (VIPP-SD) and a third with an extensive discussion of attachment (VIPP-R), all have a common format of having a clinically trained intervener go into the home for four to eight sessions to videotape the mother and child interacting in play and family routines, identifying positive forms of interaction and highlighting them for parents each week. Building a positive relationship between the intervener and parent is critical to the success of the program.

Each session has a theme. The first two sessions are focused on the child's behavior and learning to read the child's signals, and the next two sessions are focused on the mother's responses (e.g., paying attention to the sensitivity chain—child sends a signal, mother responds, child sends back a positive response that shows mother how important she is for the child's well-being). Each week's video is searched for examples of positive behaviors that illustrate the next week's topic. Explicitly pointing out mother's skill emphasizes mother's competence as a caregiver and her expert knowledge of her child and encourages mother to stay involved in the program.

Because the program directly targets the parent's behavior to increase sensitive responses, the baby's positive reaction provides ongoing reinforcement for the mother and the program can be a short one. Video fragments of mothers' positive behaviors are used to convey to mothers that they are competent and the experts on their child, and they are used because they have found that parents identify more with themselves than with paid model illustrations of the actions.

And the program is effective.[94] Mother's sensitivity and secure attachments increased as a result of the interventions in numerous samples that include around 1,500 families. Interventions were most effective when the child was over six months. The authors believe their program is successful in helping mothers because it communicates and promotes a world in which attachment figures are available, reliable, and trustworthy and the self is worthy of love and care.

Summary   The history of parent-child relationships over the centuries, much of the theory, and careful research agree that parents' love, nurturance, consistent guidance, and limits are needed to support children's growth that is determined by the maturation of the child's nervous system in a stimulating, supportive environment provided by parents. We explore in greater detail how parents establish close relationships and support growth in Chapters 5 and 6.

Box 3-2
HOW DO YOU EVALUATE TIGER PARENTING?

No one, not even Ms. Chua, agrees with her insults and extreme threats. Putting them aside as they are not a necessary part of the approach, how do you evaluate tiger parenting after your reading of theories and research? What are its strengths and drawbacks? Would you say Ms. Chua is an authoritative or authoritarian parent? While a case can be made that she is authoritarian—my way or the highway—insisting on strict control of children, a case can also be made that she resembles an authoritative parent who gives strong support to attain high parental standards in an atmosphere of love and a begrudging acceptance of her children's individuality.

Many readers of the book worried about the negative effects of Ms. Chua's methods on her children—depression, anxiety about mistakes, lack of creativity, as well as possible self-harm if one failed.* Yet the descriptions of the girls, their challenging arguments with their mother, speeches or notes in the book, as well as a friend's description** of Sophia suggest they are flourishing. Early descriptions of the families of children with high self-esteem may, in part, explain why:

> The treatment associated with the formation of high self-esteem is much more vigorous, active, and contentious than is the case in families that produce children with low self-esteem. Rather than being a paradigm of tranquility, harmony, and open-mindedness, we find that the high self-esteem family is notable for the high level of activity of the individual members, strong-minded parents dealing with independent, self-assertive children, strict enforcement of more stringent demands, and greater possibilities for open dissent and disagreement. This picture brings to mind firm convictions, frequent and possibly strong exchanges, and people who are ready to assume leadership and who will not be treated casually or disrespectfully. The parents apparently start with many of these characteristics as part of their personality structure, and by early adolescence their children are well on the way to being assertive persons in their own right.***

Many readers urged an approach that combined strategies suited to the particular child's needs. Ayelet Waldman expressed that point of view: stating that strong parental demands empower some children to achieve and weaken others; intense nurturance helps some children blossom and saps the energy of others. "Amy Chua and I both understand that our job as mothers is to be the type of tigress each of our different cubs needs."****

*"Our Readers Roar Back," *Wall Street Journal*, January 15–16, 2011, C2.
**Molly Gibson, "Letter to the Editor," *New York Times*, January 20, 2011, A 26.
***Stanley Coopersmith, *The Antecedents of Self-Esteem* (San Francisco: Jossey-Bass, 1967), 252–253.
****Ayelet Waldman, "In Defense of the Guilty, Ambivalent, Preoccupied Western Mom," *Wall Street Journal*, January 15–16, 2011, C1.

MAIN POINTS

Parents' childhood experiences

- provide models of ways people relate to each other
- are not, if negative, unchangeable

Media

- provide current information in areas of interest to parents
- raise issues and spark debates that make parents think

The history of parent–child relationships over the centuries reveals that parenting

- over centuries has shown a general continuity with parenting today
- continuity is shaped by two factors: (1) parents' goal to help children survive and flourish and (2) children's needs

Science has helped us understand the complex relationship between

- genetic, neurophysiological, psychological, and social factors in children's development
- parents' actions and their effects on children's development and the fact that there is no one way to rear children given the individual's unique makeup

Theories emphasizing the role of external influences on development view parents as

- providers of a secure emotional base for exploration and learning
- models of behavior that children copy
- dispensers of positive and negative rewards that encourage learning
- partners in social interactions that stimulate growth and knowledgeable guides who provide experiences that help children achieve their maximum potential
- transmitters of culture

Theories emphasizing the role of internal influences on development view parents as providing

- emotional support and guidance so children learn to satisfy natural impulses in socially acceptable way
- daily regime and environment that is compatible with genetic heritage
- stimulating environment and freedom for child's active learning
- guiding children's growth as a mentor

Theories emphasizing both internal and external influences of development

- focus on all levels of experience from genes to internal drives to societal organization and historical time
- stress the ways the environment, and parents as part of the environment, support internal growth patterns

- identify many important people in children's lives from immediate family to extended family to parents' work colleagues to governmental officials
- identify many different kinds of external influences like agencies, communities, social climate and give parents active roles in helping children integrate all the influences impinging on them

Researchers studying parent-child relationships in the laboratory as well as at home find

- authoritative parenting that includes (1) nurturance and attention to children's individuality and (2) behavioral demands and limit-setting help children achieve social responsibility and competence
- authoritarian parenting that makes many demands of children but gives little support to achieve these demands is associated with unhappiness, inhibition, and distrust in children
- permissive parenting that allows children freedom of impulse expression but does not teach or support self-control and self-regulation is associated with immaturity and dependence in children
- positive and negative cycles of parent-child interactions are established early in life, depend on the qualities of both parents and children, and require the actions of both partners to keep the processes going

Parenting interventions relying on video-feedback of home behaviors have been successful in increasing children's development because they

- focus on parents' skills and existing competencies
- encourage parents' sensitivity and responsiveness to children
- create a positive cycle of interactions between parent and child

EXERCISES

1. Which of the theories of children's development seems most useful to you in understanding children's growth and development and why?

2. Choose a television parenting program (*Nanny 911, Supernanny, Dr. Phil*) and watch three episodes. Summarize what parents learn by watching. How much support do parents get for change? How effective do you think the suggestissons are?

3. Erikson's theory of lifespan development focuses on the importance of positive experiences and strengths. Review your own life in terms of the positive experiences you have had and the current strengths you have developed. For example, you may have developed a love of the outdoors from camping activities with your family, and feel you have developed independence and a love of the environment.

4. Do you feel the concept of attachment helps you to make sense of your experiences in life within and outside the family? Why or why not?

5. How would your parents evaluate Tiger Mother's child-rearing approach? Would their evaluation differ from yours? How?

ADDITIONAL READINGS

Brazelton, T. Berry, and Greenspan, Stanley I. *The Irreducible Needs of Children.* Cambridge, MA: Perseus, 2000.

Carroll, Deborah, and Reid, Stella with Moline, Karen. *Nanny 911.* New York: Regan Books, 2005.

Chua, Amy. *The Battle Hymn of the Tiger Mother.* New York: Penguin, 2011.

McGraw, Dr. Phil. *Family First.* New York: Free Press, 2004.

Skenazy, Lenore. *Free-Range Kids: How to Raise Safe, Self-Reliant Children (Without Going Nuts with Worry).* San Francisco: Jossey-Bass, 2009.

4

Becoming Parents

In this chapter, you will learn about:

- How adults form couple relationships and decide to parent

- How age and gender influence conception

- Main forms of assistance in creating new life

- Child's and parents' experiences during pregnancy.

- Parents' experiences in the transition to parenthood

- Parenting programs that improve parents' partner relationships

Test Your Knowledge: Fact or Fiction (True/False)

1. About 50 percent of pregnancies in the United States are unintended.
2. Skin-to-skin physical contact between mother and newborn following birth helps to settle the newborn's physiological system.
3. Fathers' age and lifestyle influence the rate of birth defects in their children.
4. Prospective parents talk over their ideas about child rearing before they have children so they can work out their differences.
5. Parenting programs for couples with infants have similar positive benefits whether couples are married or unmarried.

Each individual who becomes a parent does so within unique circumstances. This chapter describes the many paths to parenthood in our contemporary society. We look at how parents come into parenthood and the many factors in their lives that influence their experiences as they make the transition and adjust to parenthood.

Parents' paths to parenthood reflect social changes occurring in the last fifty years. In 1970, 89 percent of babies went home from the hospital with married parents who had either conceived their child or adopted a child born in this country.[1] That currently remains the most common form of family life for newborns, but only 60 percent of babies go home to it, and 20 percent go home with unmarried mothers who are cohabiting with the biological fathers, and 13 percent go home with mothers who are romantically involved with the father though not living with him. Only about 7 percent of unmarried mothers have no involvement with the father.

About 1 percent of mothers reported having adopted a child in the course of a year,[2] and 1 percent have used assisted reproductive technology (ART) to have a baby.[3] Currently, many persons unable to adopt in the past—lesbians, gays, single parents, disabled parents—are now able to adopt children who sometimes come from many different countries. In addition, ART has made it possible for couples, single persons, gay/lesbian partners, parents in their fifties to create and bear new life. One of the most basic desires in life—to have a child—meets the most advanced technological changes in ART.

In this chapter, we look at the pathways to parenthood, to factors that affect fertility, conception and a healthy pregnancy and delivery, and at how parents reduce the stress that can accompany parents' transition to parenthood. We also look at parenting programs seeking to prevent problems that arise at this time so that babies and parents get off to a good start.

FAMILY FORMATION

Currently, parenting has few requirements; even those imposed in the past by such physical characteristics as age are changed with technology, so how do we know parents are ready to have children?

Readiness to Parent

Recall David Lykken's requirements for a parenting license described in Chapter 1.[4] He considered adults ready when they were over eighteen, married, employed, and without a history of violence because he believed these qualities enabled parents to provide the stable structure that children need to develop. Many argued with him, but he put the rights of the child before the rights of the parents.

Christoph Heinicke identifies three psychological qualities of parents that provide "an optimal parenting environment": (1) parents' feelings of self-esteem; (2) their capacity for positive, mutually satisfying relationships with others, especially with the partner; and (3) their capacity for flexible problem solving.[5]

Research with teen mothers suggests a fourth important quality: cognitive readiness for parenthood.[6] Measured in the last trimester of pregnancy, teen mothers' knowledge of children's growth and major developmental milestones, their realistic expectations of children, and their attitudes about parenting predicted their children's cognitive and socioemotional skills as they moved through childhood.

A further qualification for parenthood is a healthy lifestyle because by the time parents know the mother is pregnant, three to six weeks of important prenatal development have occurred and mother's and father's exposure to drugs and environmental toxins can affect the growing child before the pregnancy is known. Further, research is showing that what the mother does within the year before conception has an effect on the fetus. Mothers' high fiber, low-fat diet in the year before conception significantly lowered babies' risks of neural tube and brain defects.[7]

Box 4-1
PROGRAM FOR STRESS RESILIENCE*

Step 1. Get regular physical exercise
Step 2. Get adequate sleep
Step 3. Eat healthy food
Step 4. Learn relaxation techniques
Step 5. Prevent stress
Step 6. Develop problem-solving skills
Step 7. Learn conflict resolution skills
Step 8. Develop positive qualities of psychological stability—self-acceptance, satisfaction with life
Step 9. Stay connected with family, friends, people in the community
Step 10. Get help if there are problems with domestic violence, depression, or substance abuse

*Adapted from: Michael Lu, *Get Ready to Get Pregnant: Your Complete Prepregnancy Guide to Making a Smart and Healthy Baby* (New York: Harper, 2009).

Obstetrician Michael Lu is so concerned about the importance of potential mothers' and fathers' living a healthy lifestyle and learning to manage stress in advance of conceiving that he has written a book, *Get Ready to Get Pregnant*, alerting parents to healthy foods, toxins to eliminate in the home,[8] and ways to eliminate stress that negatively affects conception and pregnancy. Lu emphasizes that seven days after fertilization, before a mother can know she is pregnant, the placenta, the main organ that attaches the baby to the mother and filters all substances that go to the baby, begins to develop. Problems in placental development can cause problems later in the pregnancy. Even if parents come for care as soon as they could possibly know of the pregnancy, the placenta, the heart, and the nervous system are already developing, and a doctor's care at that point cannot reverse any damage.

Groups of parents do not differ in why they want children, but they differ in their readiness, the efforts they must make to become parents, and the resources they have to provide for children. The way an individual or family initiates a pregnancy reflects problem-solving and planning skills that set the stage for the child's development both before and after birth.

Pathways to Parenthood

In the past, the traditional pathway to family formation was school completion, self-supporting work, marriage in the early twenties, followed by children one or two years later. Many pathways to family formation have replaced the traditional one because young adults stay in school longer, cohabit more frequently, marry and have children later, and bear more children outside of marriage.[9]

Our information about how young people form families comes in part from large longitudinal studies that follow participants from high school graduation to their early or mid-twenties, chronicling patterns of schooling, work, intimate partner relationships, and parenthood. Using the National Longitudinal Study of Adolescent Health data on study members when they were eighteen and twenty-three, researchers plotted the common pathways young women took as they established stable work patterns and families.[10] Through latent class analysis, they identified seven pathways and the personal and social resources that predicted these pathways.

The most common pathway between eighteen and twenty-three was to continue schooling and then transition to the workforce for an increasing number of hours until full-time participation occurred with no family formation. A second common pathway was to leave school and go directly to full-time work with no family formation, and a third was to enter the workforce on a more part-time basis and cohabit with a partner without children. These three pathways together characterized about 62 percent of the whole sample.

Three other, less frequent pathways characterized mothers who made up about 20 percent of the sample. One pattern was to work part-time, enter marriage by age twenty-one, and then have children. This was the traditional pattern of the past that described only a small percent of this sample. Another was to work part-time and become a single mother, and a third was to cohabit with a partner and have a child. A final pattern described about 6 percent of the sample, who did not go to school or work, or marry, but instead lived at home, possibly because of a special difficulty.

Data reveal that those young women with many personal and social resources—positive relationships with their parents, high self-esteem, friends, school success—postpone families. Their parents are educated and have prepared them to do well in school, and they are establishing satisfying patterns of work, friendships, and leisure activities. When they marry, they are more likely to rate the relationships as satisfying than those who marry early.[11]

Young women who have children alone or in married or cohabiting relationships are more likely to be those with fewer resources or plans.[12] They value a child as a social resource—someone to love, to care for, provide a grandchild for grandparents, someone to care for them in their old age. These women have fewer resources to provide for children because they have less education and less extensive work experience. Many obtain further schooling later, but it is more difficult.

A longitudinal study tracking both young men and women from eighteen to twenty-five yielded very similar findings.[13] By the time most young adults have turned age thirty, they have finished school, are working, have left home, and are married so they get to the place that their parents achieved at younger ages.[14]

Women's and men's paths are similar, and there is greater gender equality in their activities than in the past. European Americans participate in schooling and work in greater numbers than African Americans and members of other ethnic groups and that gives them greater resources for rearing families. Finding ways for parents in groups with few resources to increase their resources and decrease the stress that often accompanies limited income and support is a major social task.

Childlessness

Although 80 percent of women in 2006 had children by the time they were age forty to forty-four, 20 percent were childless.[15] The figure was higher—27 percent—for those women with graduate or professional degrees and lower—18 percent—for those who did not go beyond high school. Women appear more accepting of childlessness then men, especially women with education.[16] In one study, of those who were childless in the age group forty to forty-four, half were voluntarily childless, and half, involuntarily childless.[17] The voluntarily childless are generally of European American backgrounds, employed full-time with higher incomes, not religious, and comfortable with being childless. Latinas are underrepresented in this group.

Childlessness creates long-lasting distress primarily for women who want children but are not able to conceive and have no children in adoptive, foster, or step-families.[18] Women who did not have a strong desire for children or the need for biological children did not have the same level of distress.

DECISIONS TO PARENT

Half of all pregnancies are unintended, defined as not wanting any child or not wanting a child at this time, and result from either contraceptive failure (48 percent of unintended pregnancies) or failure to use contraceptives (52 percent).[19] Half of unintended pregnancies are terminated through miscarriage or abortion so that about two-thirds of babies born are from intended pregnancies, and many of the unintended babies are welcomed by the time of birth.[20]

Unintended births are of concern because mothers are less likely to seek prenatal care in the first three months and more likely to continue habits such as smoking and drinking alcohol that place the fetus at risk.[21] They are more likely than mothers who planned babies to have babies who are premature, low-birth weight, or small-for-gestational age, and they are also less likely to breast-feed their babies. When mothers get appropriate care throughout pregnancy, differences in the two groups of babies disappear.

You might think that married couples have planned or intended births and unmarried couples have unplanned or unintended births. Not so. Seventy-nine percent of births to married couples are intended, 54 percent of births to unmarried women cohabiting with the biological fathers are intended, and 39 percent of births to unmarried women who are not cohabiting are intended.[22] About 15 to 19 percent of unmarried teens intended to get pregnant and have babies.[23] So let us look at how subgroups of prospective parents form families.

Married Parents

Women with college educations, in comparison with women of high school educations and less, are more likely to marry by age thirty and marry men with college educations, have greater incomes, stay married, and plan their children.[24] From the moment of conception, children born into these families enjoy more structured, less stressful family lives. Mothers are more likely to get prenatal care, to have positive moods during pregnancy, and to feel more satisfied with their relationship with the father.[25]

As they are observed over the course of the first two years of their child's life, mothers report less depression than unmarried cohabiting mothers, and they are observed to be more sensitive parents.[26] Married mothers who did not plan the birth reported more depression during pregnancy, and their husbands reported less marital satisfaction in the relationship.[27] An unexpected pregnancy may be especially difficult to manage for married parents because they are accustomed to a predictable, organized lifestyle and an unplanned pregnancy requires flexibility and adaptability.

A longitudinal study of married fathers' feelings about the pregnancy—did not want a baby or waited too long for a baby—shaped fathers' behavior and his interactions after the baby was born.[28] Fathers who did not want the pregnancy were less warm with infants, and those fathers who wanted babies sooner were more nurturing and caring with their babies. Fathers who were more involved in prebirth activities—going to doctor's visits, seeing a sonogram or ultrasound of the baby—were more involved in all aspects of infant care when babies were three months old. Getting fathers involved in prenatal activities increased their involvement in care after the babies came, regardless of their attitudes about the pregnancy.

Cohabitating Parents

Mothers with high school education or less, in comparison with college-educated women, are more likely to cohabit with the father. Couples often begin to cohabit without discussion of what living together means.[29] Many slid into the relationship, spending a few nights together regularly and then living together, seeing it as an alternative to being single, not as an alternative to marriage. Cohabiting with the child's father increases intended and unintended pregnancies for European and African American and Latina mothers groups, but Latinas are more likely to plan births with cohabiting husbands than the other two groups, and European American women are more likely to marry the fathers than African American or Latina mothers.[30]

About a third of these relationships end in marriage within two years and about half the relationships will end within two years.[31] Fifty percent of children born into cohabiting parent families are likely to experience parents' separation by age nine compared to 20 percent of children living with married parents. These relationships are also more likely to include children by more than one partner. In one sample, 59 percent of unmarried parents had a child by a previous relationship in comparison to 36 percent of all parents giving birth to a child, and in 20 percent of unmarried families, both parents had children by a previous relationship.

As noted, pregnancies in these families are less likely to be planned, but the planfulness of the pregnancy does not impact the well-being of cohabiting parents during the pregnancy as it does married parents; whether planned or unplanned, cohabiting couples reported more negative feelings than married couples who planned the pregnancy.[32]

Comparing the moods and parental behaviors of cohabiting parents to the moods and parenting of married biological parents over a two-year period revealed that cohabiting mothers reported more depression and showed less parental sensitivity in interactions with their young children.[33] The mediating variables that seemed to account for the relationship between parental mood and parenting behaviors were the conflict and ambivalence in the cohabiting parents' relationship. So even a cohabiting relationship that continues for two years is associated with parental ambivalence and conflict that depress mothers' moods and affect their parenting.

Unmarried Unpartnered Mothers

This is a very diverse group that includes teen mothers who most often have unplanned pregnancies, and older, highly educated, single mothers who are having a baby by choice using ART. We discuss this group in greater detail in Chapter 14. Births to unmarried mothers are twice as likely for African American women and Latina women as for European American women. African American women are more likely than the other two groups to have births when not cohabiting with fathers.[34]

Single Fathers

There are a new group of single parents less studied, and that is single men who have impregnated a woman who wants to give the child up for adoption. The biological father wishes to have custody and raise the child as his, but laws in many states set a very narrow window of time in which fathers can register to claim paternal rights to adopt the child.[35] Currently, fathers have brought suits to obtain custody in several states.

State registries have increased in the last ten years to protect the rights of the child to permanent placement, to protect adoptive parents from having a child taken from them after several years as happened in the early 1990s, and to give fathers rights too. The registries, however, are little publicized and hard to locate, with varying windows of time for registration, some as little as five days from birth, others until the adoption petition is filed. Further, registries may give fathers rights only within a county or state so that if the mother takes the child out of state, the father has no rights. Fathers are at a disadvantage in knowing about registries and registering within the time limit so Congressional legislation has been considered to establish a national registry for fathers.

Carefully Planned Babies

Parents who adopt or use ART must plan very carefully to have a baby. Parents may be married, gay/lesbian/transgendered partners, single women and men and either heterosexual or gay/lesbian, disabled. These parents form a heterogeneous group, but all must consider carefully many factors: their psychological and financial resources, support systems, strategies for finding a child, weathering the procedures, either adoptive or physical, to have a child. And many adults and couples have experienced all pathways to having a child—conceiving naturally, using ART, and adoption. These parents often, but not always, have more resources, and they demonstrate commitment, persistence, and planning in having a child, and these qualities predict a stable transition to parenting. As we will see in Chapters 14 and 16, the diligence and effort parents expended to become parents may make them especially sensitive and effective parents as children grow.

Separation of Marriage and Parenting

As noted, marriage is in part related to economic factors. People with education and good incomes marry in large numbers and remain married. They link marriage and children together in that order. People with fewer resources highly value marriage, but see it as a distant goal they hope to achieve some day when they have secure jobs and money for a home and established way of life.[36] Relationship problems with the prospective spouse like domestic violence and substance abuse are also reasons given for not marrying.

Although marriage is a distant goal, many low-income mothers believe child bearing can occur in the present, and there is no stigma to having a child outside of marriage. Children bring emotional satisfactions so unmarried mothers go ahead and have the baby, considering marriage a future possibility but not a requirement for having a child. Economic resources, though necessary for marriage, are not viewed as a requirement for having children: being there and caring for them is enough.

The problem with this separation is that, as we noted in Chapter 1, it fosters two tracts for children's development with one group of babies starting out with many advantages that promote development, and one group with many risk factors that impede the child's future growth and development.[37] The separation of marriage and children has occurred because birth rates have remained constant and marriage rates have declined so more babies are born outside of marriages, but we do not know precisely why the marriage rate has declined. It may be economic forces reducing the number of skilled jobs that support a family or it may be social factors that have led women to postpone parenthood but then to choose it outside the context of marriage rather than forego it completely.

Because living in families with many transitions and disruptions presents a risk factor for children's development, parenting programs are now focusing, as we shall see, on giving unmarried men and women relationship as well as parenting skills that permit them to be joint parents whether married, living together, or separated. Since almost all babies are conceived in a romantic relationship, there is a foundation of positive feeling between parents that can lead to effective coparenting.

Unwanted Parenting

When mothers have *unwanted* children, defined as the mother's not wanting to have any children or not wanting to have more than she has, mothers are less happy, more prone to depression, and have greater difficulties rearing not only the unwanted child but also their siblings.[38] Mothers who bear unwanted children are less likely to spend time with them when they are young and more likely to spank them. Difficulties in mother-child relationships continue so that even in adolescence and young adulthood, mothers are less affectionate and less supportive with their children.

In a long-term study carried out in Czechoslovakia, children whose mothers had twice requested but were twice denied abortions to terminate the pregnancy had significantly more problems and less enjoyment in life than did children whose parents wanted them.[39] In elementary school, the unwanted children had fewer friends, more behavior problems, and poorer school performance even though they had equal intelligence. In adolescence, the differences between the two groups widened, and in young adulthood, individuals unwanted before birth were less happy with their jobs and their marriages. They had more conflict with coworkers and supervisors and less satisfaction with friends. They were discouraged about themselves and their lives, but many took the positive step of getting help for their problems.

At age thirty, there were still differences between unwanted and wanted children, but the gap had narrowed. Women who were unwanted, however, were more likely to be single or divorced, unemployed, and having difficulties in parenting than women who had been wanted. There were few differences between the two groups of men. At age thirty-five, unwanted children continued to seek more psychiatric treatment than wanted children. Adults who were unwanted as children did not develop such problems as alcoholism or criminality, but they were underrepresented on indicators of well-being and excellence.

While the average tendency for an unwanted child is to have some difficulties, the following anecdote represents the love many children experience despite their being unwanted initially.

One man described his mother's finding out she was pregnant with twins after World War II but both his parents felt barely able to raise the two children they already had after just surviving the Holocaust and losing so many family members as well as all their resources. The doctor told his mother she might die if she had an abortion.

> "So here I am. Knowing why I was born has never made me feel insecure or unwanted. My life is so filled with blessings and difficulties like everybody else's, and I have two devoted parents who would move mountains for me."[40]

CONCEPTION

Though most women have minimal trouble getting pregnant, some individuals and couples have difficulty and feel deeply disappointed. Although the usual estimate of infertility, defined as an inability to get pregnant after twelve months of unprotected sexual relations, is 10–15 percent.[41] Forty percent of infertility is thought to result from women's problems, 40 percent from men's problems, and 20 percent from difficulties with both individuals. A large telephone survey of women, ages twenty-five to fifty, revealed that in the course of their lives, 35 percent of women experienced infertility, most often before the pregnancy with their first child.[42] Infertility was not related to race, age, income, employment, or marriage. Thirty-seven percent of the women got fertility assistance, and 92 percent of the group eventually conceived. As we noted earlier, those who feel most distressed are those who want a child but never have one.

Age and Conception

Increasing age is related to increasing difficulties in conception. Young mothers and fathers in their teens and twenties have few difficulties conceiving. The age of first-time mothers has been increasing and is now twenty-five.[43] In the past, women

> ### Box 4-2
> ### FIRST PERSON NARRATIVES OF PATHS TO PARENTHOOD
>
> These three books describe paths to parenthood or blocked paths to parenthood and highlight the diversity of contemporary adults' experiences in becoming parents.
>
> Holly Finn's *The Baby Chase: An Adventure in Fertility** describes her struggles to become a single mother by means of sperm donation and in vitro fertilization (IVF). Although Ms. Finn, a forty-one-year-old writer and communications director at the Skoll Foundation, knows and reports the many negative reactions to her endeavors, she also wants young women to understand that pregnancy postponed until the mid- or late-thirties may be pregnancy foregone as chances of conceiving healthy babies decrease with age. Her young adult choices would have been different, she believes, had she better understood age-related fertility problems.
>
> Her story is a poignant and touching one and helps those who have not had direct experience with IVF procedures to better understand the physical, psychological, and financial demands made on the women, married or single, who use them. It also helps people avoid the insensitive, upsetting comments to women who have difficulties in conceiving and bearing the children they want.
>
> Annie Murphy Paul's *Origins: How the Nine Months before Birth Shape the Rest of Our Lives*** is both a memoir of her second pregnancy and a careful compilation of studies and interviews with researchers detailing the many ways that prenatal experiences impact our health and well-being for decades. Ms. Paul, a journalist, wife, and mother of a three-year-old boy, used each month of her pregnancy to discuss different factors like toxins, medications, and stress that affect the developing fetus, emphasizing that substances not affecting mothers can have disastrous effects on children.
>
> Her access to twenty-first-century health care and resources enabled her to deal effectively with stress and low moods that arose during the nine months. Increasingly aware of the vulnerability of mothers and developing children in our fast-paced society, she makes many recommendations, described in the text, for enabling all women and their children to have healthy pregnancies and births.
>
> David Marin's book *This is US: The New All-American Family**** chronicles his struggles to adopt three foster children, brothers, ages two and eight, and their four-year-old sister. Mr. Marin found himself in his forties with one failed marriage, no potential wife and mother, and jobs and activities that had taken him around the world but left him with a strong desire to experience the joys and frustrations of fatherhood and family life.
>
> His own father died suddenly of a heart attack at a young age before Mr. Marin had a chance to have a father-son relationship he could remember. For years he feared he too would die young, but when he reached his early forties, healthy, with a good job, and an intense fear of growing old alone, he decided this was the time to adopt and experience a relationship from the perspective of a father.
>
> His book describes the warm, loving relationship that immediately developed between him and the three children. Though the children had been in a series of foster homes and he had little experience with parenting, the four of them managed very well. Frustrations came from working with the Social Services agencies, even with his outstanding social worker who got him and the children through the years
>
> *(continued)*

Box 4-2
CONTINUED

it took to finalize adoptions, and from people in the community who questioned and commented on the fact that he, a red-headed, pale-skinned, single man was adopting three brown-skinned Mexican American children. What was not immediately apparent to them was that he too was a Latino man with a Puerto Rican father.

The adoption took place six years ago, and Mr. Marin and his children are all thriving. Skills he learned and choices he made as a parent illustrate sensitive parenting at its best.

*Holly Finn, *The Baby Chase: An Adventure in Fertility* (published by Byline.com in 2011, available as an Amazon Kindle Single).
**Annie Murphy Paul, *Origins: How the Nine Months before Birth Shape the Rest of Our Lives* (New York: Free Press, 2010).
***David Marin, *This Is US: The New All-American Family* (United States: Exterminating Angel Press, 2011).

over thirty-five having babies were usually having the last of their children; now, many mothers are having their first. In 2007, approximately 600,000 babies were born to women over thirty-five, and 22 percent of the babies were born to first-time mothers.[44] Factors that account for the growing number of older first-time mothers include feminism, a general postponement of childbearing, the large number of Baby Boomers in childbearing age, advances in contraception, better health among women, advances in reproductive technologies, and better obstetrical care.

Nevertheless, women over thirty-five more often have difficulties with conception of a first pregnancy.[45] Spontaneous abortions increase from 25 percent at age thirty-five to 50 percent at forty-five, and mothers over thirty-five have greater percentage of genetic abnormalities in the fetus, so screening for such abnormalities are routine for them. Like teenage mothers, older mothers have a greater likelihood of pregnancy complications such as diabetes and low birth weight babies, but these can be treated as they can be with younger women.

Like women, men have a biological clock, and conceiving a child when the father is over forty increases the risks of spontaneous miscarriages as well as risks of a child with autism, bipolar disorder, and schizophrenia.[46] Further, older fathers' children may have increased risks of breast and prostate cancer.

Although older parents face difficulties in conception, they have many advantages as parents. Compared with younger parents, they have more education, higher status jobs, and, as a result, greater incomes with more money available to spend on their children.[47] Further, older parents tend to be in more stable marriages and to be more attentive and sensitive parents. Because they are older and have had more experience in life, they find it easier to put children's behavior in perspective and not become frustrated over little things. Yet older parents' work and community responsibilities make incorporating an unpredictable, time-consuming young child into their lives more difficult.

Gender

In the past we have emphasized mothers' role in fertility and ensuring babies' health, but as noted fathers' behaviors are important too. Just as mothers who smoke, drink alcohol, and use drugs put children at risk for birth defects, similar behaviors on fathers' part do the same.[48] Men's lifestyle changes as noted, father's increasing age presents difficulties with conception, higher rates of miscarriage,[49] and children's risk for mental health problems.[50]

Assisted Conception

Prospective parents seek assistance with conception because they very much want to bear a biological child. While the procedures were originally developed to help married couples having difficulties with conception, the procedures have made biological parenthood available to people who could not have had biological children fifty years ago. Single women without partners and gay and lesbian singles and couples very much want that opportunity now.

There are several levels of assisted conception.[51] The interventions can result in a child that is genetically related to both parents (when the parents' eggs and sperm are used), to one parent (when one parent's egg or sperm is used along with a donor's egg or sperm), or to neither parent (when both donor egg and sperm are used). Initially, assistance takes the form of supporting natural processes by artificial insemination, inserting sperm directly into the woman's reproductive tract with an instrument, and by chemically stimulating the ovaries to produce more eggs, increasing the likelihood of pregnancy.

Assisted Reproductive Technology (ART)   The National Center on Birth Defects and Developmental Disabilities uses the term ART to refer to the more advanced methods of assistance in which eggs and sperm are handled outside the body.[52] In vitro fertilization (IVF) involves removing eggs from the woman's body, fertilizing them in a petri dish with sperm, and then implanting them back in the uterus. This procedure is used for many reasons, for example, for women who have blocked fallopian tubes. More advanced techniques include introcytoplasmic sperm injection (ICSI), removing an egg and injecting a sperm directly into the egg and then transferring the fertilized egg into the uterus. This has enabled many infertile men to become fathers.

Advances in ART have enabled scientists to make diagnoses of genetic disorders prior to the implantation of the fertilized egg in the uterus.[53] Known as preimplantation genetic diagnosis (PGD), the procedure of taking one cell from the eight-cell embryo and testing it for genetic diseases such as Tay-Sachs disease and implanting only embryos without the genetic defect permits parents to know that the embryo is healthy at the start of the pregnancy. Parents do not have to wait several months to do amniocentesis to determine if the fetus is healthy. Since there can be some error, couples may choose genetic tests later in the pregnancy to increase their confidence that the baby is healthy.

In 2006, there were more than 138,198 ART procedures performed and about 52,000 infants were born as a result.[54] Currently, there is concern that infants born of ART procedures may have a higher risk of birth defects than children conceived naturally.[55] In ART procedures resulting in a single birth, there was an increased number of children born with heart defects, cleft palates, and gastrointestinal defects. Despite the increase, the risk of any birth defect remains very low. Still, parents considering the procedures should be aware of all possible risks.

Donor Assistance   Donor assistance adds to the possibility of having a baby.[56] There are sperm donations from men and egg donations from women and, more recently, fertilized embryo donations. Further, a surrogate mother (or birth mother) may carry the fertilized embryo to term for the mother. The surrogate may also, but not necessarily, donate an egg for fertilization.

Sperm donations were the first form of donation; stored in sperm banks, the donations provided healthy sperm that could be matched with the characteristics of the prospective parents. Traditionally, the donors were anonymous, but more recently, banks have asked donors whether they would be willing to be contacted when the child reaches age eighteen. Since the early 1980s, egg donations have also been available through clinics. Because medications are used to stimulate and remove the eggs, egg donation is a more complicated procedure than sperm donation. Perhaps for that reason, egg donors are sometimes friends or relatives of the parents rather than anonymous donors, and they may well sustain an ongoing relationship with the parents.

Donor embryos have raised concerns. These are embryos that couples had frozen, in reserve for their use in the event they did not conceive from the embryos that were implanted. The couples had the children they wanted and no longer needed the embryos. There are approximately 400,000 such embryos in the country, but only about 2 percent have been donated to other couples.[57] Although couples originally felt they would be willing to donate, they decline to do so years later, saying they would feel too uncomfortable knowing they had children being raised by others, and that their children had brothers and sisters they might not know.[58]

A religious organization called Snowflakes has encouraged couples to release these embryos to other parents for adoption and keep some form of contact with the families after the birth as happens in open adoption.[59] The organization insists receiving families get counseling about doing this, and the two families can set criteria for an ongoing relationship. Other organizations have concerns that the term embryo adoption means that the embryo has the same status as a child, and thus far that is not true, as some are donated for research.

PGD has been used to identify embryos with genetic makeup that could, at birth, provide a genetic match to save the life of an existing sibling with an incurable genetic disease. For example, a child with Fanconia anemia, a genetic disorder that leads to the child's early death, can be saved with a perfectly matched bone marrow transplant. Parents have successfully sought help to produce siblings with genetic makeup that saves the life of an existing one.

While most would agree to the use of PGD to prevent or cure illness, there are concerns that it can be used to create designer babies with the preferred sex, height, intelligence, or hair color.[60] Lori Andrews, a lawyer specializing in the legal aspects of reproductive technologies, worries about polls that indicate that 43 percent of responders think it is acceptable for parents to select the physical characteristics of their children, and 42 percent believe it is acceptable to select intellectual traits. She worries that down the road people may shop for a baby like a car.

> She writes that babies represent new life; they are unknown quantities when they are born. Sometimes they bring unanticipated delights, and sometimes they bring unexpected challenges. Parents' job is to love their children unconditionally, no matter who they are. "Parents, above all, should not be saddling their babies with admission standards for birth.[61]

Legal and Ethical Issues of ART   ART has created legal and ethical dilemmas that are currently solved on a case by case matter in the courts.[62] For example, should sperm donations be anonymous or should we follow the rules used in Europe? Britain and the Netherlands have recently banned anonymous donations of sperm, and any child at age eighteen now has the right to look up and seek the donor father. In Sweden, individuals conceived by donor eggs or donor sperm have the right to identifying information at age eighteen and can contact the donor if they wish. In the United States, there is currently a move to adopt the policies of Sweden. The Sperm Bank of California, for example, already requests permission from donors to give children identifying information when they are eighteen, and 80 percent of donors have agreed. Other questions arise about donor sperm. Should the use of one man's sperm be limited? Currently it is unlimited, and one man has created 150 children.[63] Who owns eggs, sperm, and fertilized embryos? Can eggs, sperm, or fertilized embryos be used after divorce or death to create children? Should unused fertilized embryos be given to couples seeking to have children? Is it baby selling if models or Harvard students advertise their eggs for $50,000? Should clinics help women in their sixties become pregnant even though they may not live long enough to raise the child? Is it ethical to use PGD to create tall, or smart, or curly-haired children or children of a certain sex to meet parents' requests? At present the United States has few recognized guidelines to resolve these issues. As Debora Spar documents in a recent book, *The Baby Business,* creating babies is a $3 billion industry in the country—without guidelines.[64] We discuss these questions and parenting children of ART in Chapter 13.

PREGNANCY

Nine months of pregnancy give parents time to prepare for the baby's arrival even though a month or two of that time may have elapsed before the pregnancy is confirmed.

Highlights of Prenatal Development

We give a few of the developmental milestones of prenatal development to show how quickly development begins and how responsive babies are to what happens in their first homes. A baby's growth is off to a fast start with both the brain and the heart beginning to develop in the third week following fertilization, before many parents know there is a pregnancy.[65] In the first eight weeks, all the major organs of the body begin to develop. The heart beats from the fourth week on, and the brain and the nervous system send out impulses. Lungs and digestive system and sex organs begin to develop. Facial features—eyes, ears, nose, lips, tongue, and even the beginnings of milk teeth are present. By the twelfth week, the baby has a well-formed body and is active though mothers cannot feel the movements.

Development of the systems laid down in the first trimester continues in the second trimester.[66] Babies are more muscular and movements are stronger and more varied, slow, and squirming, sharp kicks, and slow hiccoughs. Babies establish a sleep-wake cycle similar to that of the newborn. Babies can hear noises, and a loud noise or music can stimulate a spurt of activity.

In the third trimester, babies gain weight and make final preparations for birth. By the seventh month babies are sufficiently developed so that most can live if born prematurely and cared for in specialized neonatal units. In the last three months, babies gain about five pounds or more and receive substances to immunize them against many diseases. Mothers' blood provides immunity against all the diseases they have had and from the placenta comes gamma globulin to fight other diseases.

As there is less room in the uterus, movements are smaller. Much activity focuses on practicing the reflexes that will be used after birth—breathing and sucking especially—even though mothers' blood supplies all the oxygen and nutrients required. Children suck their thumbs and breathe, excreting the fluid taken in with breathing. After birth, they can recognize their mother's voice reading a story read to them twice a day in the last six weeks before birth. In addition to hearing, the child can make eye movements, but we do not know what the child sees.

Highlights of development in the second and third trimesters illustrate the increasing responsiveness and competence of the fetus to emphasize that all these activities need the support of a nurturing environment in the mother's womb and in the home that supports parents.

A Healthy Lifestyle

The first act of parenting is to live a healthy lifestyle that consists of appropriate levels of exercise, healthy eating habits, and avoidance of damaging substances like cigarette smoke, alcohol, and environmental toxins.[67] While in many ways mother and child form a symbiotic unit during the pregnancy, it is also important to realize that even in the early months they are two separate organisms and substances that may not harm the mother in any way, e.g., the medication tetracycline may harm the growing baby.

We describe major groups of hazards to mother and child in Table 4-1, although there may be additional hazards depending on a parent's health status. In addition to infections and nonprescription drugs, we also list environmental toxins. Numerous prescription drugs affect pregnant women, and pregnant women are advised to check all drugs with their physician, including any herbal or nutritional supplements as they too can have damaging effects on the fetus.

Chief among the healthy habits to promote growth is good nutrition that not only promotes a healthy pregnancy for mother and child and growth of the developing fetus, but also affects the child's development after birth. Studies in developing

■ **TABLE 4-1**
RISKS IN PREGNANCY*

Infections	Sexually Transmitted Diseases
Chicken Pox	Chlamydia
Cytomegalovirus	Genital Herpes
German Measles or Rubella	Gonorrhea
Hepatitis B	Human Papillomavirus (HPV)
Human Immunodeficiency Virus	Monilial Vulvovaginitis
Listeriosis	Trichomonal Vaginitis
Toxoplasmosis	
Varicella	

Drugs	Environmental Toxins
Alcohol	Lead
Amphetamines	Mercury
Caffeine	Polychlorinated Biphenyls (PCBs)
Cocaine	Glues and Solvents
Ecstacy	Pesticides
Marijuana	X-rays
Nicotine	

*Adapted from: Glade B. Curtis and Judith Schuler, *Your Pregnancy Week by Week*, 5th ed. (Cambridge, MA: DeCapo, 2004).

countries and in low-income groups in this country have found that nutritional supplements to mothers during pregnancy have increased birth weights of babies and have also improved performance on cognitive measures after birth.[68]

Prenatal healthy nutrition also programs the baby's metabolic system for the future. Too few or too many calories can have negative effects for decades. For example, Dutch babies whose mothers were pregnant with them during the starvation period at the end of 1944 showed immediate effects at birth in terms of increased stillbirths, birth defects, and infant mortality, but as older adults, these Dutch babies showed higher rates of diabetes and heart disease than individuals whose mothers had adequate nutrition during pregnancy.[69]

Conversely, pregnant obese but nondiabetic mothers with high blood sugar levels force the fetus to produce high levels of insulin to process the sugar that passes from mother to child. Babies of these mothers are larger at birth, and produce more insulin, thus predisposing them to childhood obesity and its subsequent problems. Current research in England provides medication to obese mothers to maintain normal blood sugar levels, eliminating the fetus's need to produce large quantities of insulin and the resulting changes in endocrine functioning.[70]

Managing Stress

In the next chapter we discuss dealing with depression and substance abuse that complicate pregnancy and family life, and here we focus on both moderate and severe stress. When pregnant mothers experience high levels of stress like mothers did in Hurricane Katrina, losing homes, struggling through water, being without electricity, they had increased risk of preterm infants and low birth weight babies.[71] Researchers following the children of mothers pregnant during a severe ice storm in Canada in 1998, termed the nation's worst disaster, found similar low birth weights in the babies of mothers who experienced high levels of stress, but also found ongoing effects on children's development through childhood. At age two, children of highly stressed mothers had poorer cognitive and language skills than babies whose mothers experienced low stress levels. Researchers were surprised to find continuing effects in cognitive tasks when children were ages five and ten.[72]

Moderate levels of stress affect the fetus depending on when during the pregnancy they occurs. High levels of pregnancy-specific worries—e.g., worrying about the health of the baby, possibility of miscarriage, one's own health—experienced in the first trimester appear to program the baby's neural system in ways that affect mental growth in the first year of life, as measured by lower performance on cognitive tasks at twelve months.[73] High levels of pregnancy-specific worries in the third trimester, when babies normally have heightened levels of cortisol in preparation for birth, appear to facilitate babies' motor and neurobehavioral development measured in the first two weeks of life and in another study, accelerate cognitive skills measured at the end of the first year.[74]

Obstetricians find stress so prevalent among pregnant mothers that they refer many to a form of obstetric care termed Centering Pregnancy.[75] Ten mothers, all at the same stage of healthy pregnancies, meet at the same intervals as individualized obstetric care for a two-hour session that includes the usual blood, weight, and urine screening procedures, but then includes a group meeting in which a midwife's or obstetrician's brief presentation is followed by discussions that enable mothers to ask questions and talk about their feelings with other mothers who may have been having similar experiences. This program provides support for highly stressed mothers and has resulted in a 33 percent reduction in preterm births to these mothers as compared to mothers receiving standard care.

Support systems are important to all mothers. When pregnant low-income mothers reported supports in dealing with problems, they were less likely to experience stress and depression than those who had few supports to help them meet their needs.[76] Middle-class pregnant mothers who reported more positive experiences of daily life like getting a compliment or a friendly smile were better able to manage a simulated stressful laboratory interaction than women who reported fewer.[77]

Parents' Experiences during Pregnancy

Pregnancy involves many physiological and psychological changes. Physical changes include changes in levels of fatigue, sleep and eating patterns, size, shape, and emotional reactivity, to mention only a few. Parents begin to accommodate to the demands of the life growing within the mother. The changes are easier to adapt to when parents have deliberately taken on the challenges rather than having been forced to adjust to them.

Ellen Galinsky, a consultant and lecturer in child development, found herself changing after her children were born and finding no pertinent research to describe parents' changes, she interviewed 228 parents with different experiences of parenthood—married, divorced, step-, foster, and adoptive parents.[78] These parents did not represent a random sampling but were a broad cross-section of the population. On the basis of the psychological reactions parents reported, Galinsky describes pregnancy as the period of image-making; parents form ideas of what they will be like as parents and what the baby will be like. Even in the early months their images may clash with reality. Parents may not feel as excited as they anticipated even though they had planned the baby or mothers may feel sicker than they expected. Throughout parenthood, parents have to adjust their images of what they expect to fit the reality of what is happening. That process starts in pregnancy and continues.

In the next three months, Galinsky believes that parents prepare for parenthood. They think of the changes in their roles that will occur after the baby comes. They look at their own childhoods, think how they want their child's life to be similar or different from what they experienced. If they already have a child, they wonder about how a brother or sister will adjust or how they will be able to love more than one child. They may form new friendships with other parents-to-be, and older friendships may fade into the background.

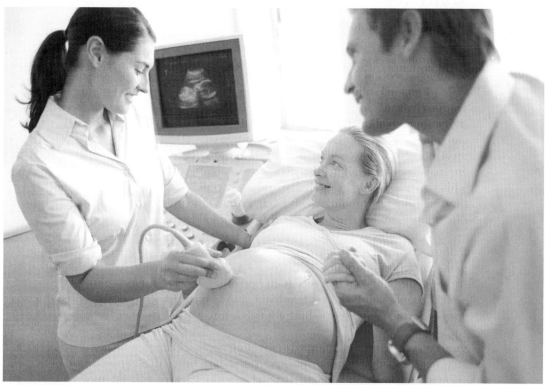

Nine months of pregnancy gives parents time for the baby's arrival.

In the last three months of pregnancy, their thoughts turn to the birth, and they begin to worry about what it might be like. During this time, childbirth classes help parents make realistic preparations for the birth and arrival of the baby and parents in the classes often form an ongoing support group to talk about worries and stresses.

Recommendations for Supporting Families during Pregnancy

Based on fetal research and interviews with researchers, journalist Annie Murphy Paul strongly advocates greater protection and concern for pregnant women and their babies,[79] and others would include fathers as well, so that all babies have optimal starts in life. Investing in expecting families would require making quality prenatal care for all, making healthy foods available in all neighborhoods, controlling and eliminating harmful environmental toxins, more clearly labeling over-the-counter medicines that are harmful to fetuses, effective treatment programs available for substance-using mothers, effective screening and treatment programs for parents with psychological problems such as depression and anxiety, and having special provisions for pregnant women at times of emergencies so they are cared for and provisions they need are provided.

ADJUSTMENT TO PARENTHOOD

The arrival of a baby changes every aspect of adults' lives, from finances to sex life, sleeping habits, and social life. Although many first-time parents report that nothing could have adequately prepared them for the experience, knowing what to expect can still help parents cope.

The Power of Positive Relationships

Throughout this book, we will see that positive relationships sustain parents as they care for their children. Positive relationships with their own parents and with each other enable parents to be more loving and effective parents.[80] Furthermore, positive relationships with children are related to children's healthy growth.

When mothers and fathers feel support from each other, their competence as parents grows, and interaction with the baby becomes more effective. Father-infant interactions and fathers' competence, particularly, are related to feeling support from mothers (see the interview with James Levine). Even basic activities are influenced by the quality of the marriage. Mothers experience fewer feeding difficulties when their husbands are supportive and view them positively, whereas marital distress is related to inept feeding by the mother.[81]

Ingredients of a positive relationship between married parents, and presumably cohabiting and single parents as well:[82]

- parents' agreement on role arrangements regardless of whether traditional or egalitarian

INTERVIEW
with James Levine

James Levine is the director of the Fatherhood Project at the Families and Work Institute. He served as a principal consultant to Vice President Al Gore in drafting the federal initiative on fatherhood, created by executive order in 1995.

What are the best ways to get men involved in parenting?

There are several issues. I think the absolute key is the couple's expectations of what the father's role will be. If the mom doesn't expect the dad to be involved, and the dad doesn't expect to be involved, that's a prescription for noninvolvement. If Mom doesn't expect Dad to be involved and Dad might want to be involved, he won't be involved. The mother is the gatekeeper in the relationship. Many women say they want husbands to be involved, but in effect, they want them to be involved as a sort of mom's subordinate or assistant. Mom's the manager, telling Dad how to be involved as opposed to assuming Dad will be involved and will learn the skills to be a father. It is important for mothers to back off and be in the background, and let fathers be with children.

So, one key to involvement is the couple's dynamics. I don't mean to blame Mom, but there is a system here—men and women as a system—and one starts here in terms of making a supportive system for fathers' involvement.

Then let's look at men in terms of men and the system outside the couple. All the research we've done shows that men today define success on two dimensions: being a good provider and, equally important, having good relationships with children. So if you look at the values men bring to parenthood, there are generally agreed-upon desires to have close relationships with their children. But, aside from the couple relationship, there are two obstacles. Men sometimes feel incompetent as to how to do this; they need skills. And, second, their work sucks them up in spite of their best intentions to give time to relationships with children. They spend a lot of time working, not to avoid forming relationships with children, but as a way of caring for children.

A key to change is changing the cultural clues men get about being fathers. Looking at this from an ecological and systems point of view, we can ask, "What are the cues that men get about parenting across the life cycle?" The expectations others have about them have a lot to do with shaping their behavior. For example, prenatally if men get expectations from the health-care system that they are expected to be at prenatal visits, they will be there. Mostly, however, they get the message they have no role during the pregnancy. Yet, research has shown that one of the best predictors of good prenatal care for the mother is whether the partner is involved with prenatal care.

We have found in our work with low-income men that when men understand how vital their role is even before the child is born, they can change their level of involvement. Knowing how important their role is with their babies increases the motivation of low-income men to be involved.

So at the time of birth and afterward, if the pediatrician sends messages that he or she wants both parents at visits—"I need to know both of the baby's parents. I want to see you both, not just the mother"—that message shapes the father's behavior. Same thing at preschools or day care. They can also send messages that they want both parents, not just mothers, to be involved.

(continued)

INTERVIEW with James Levine

(continued)

So it is the expectations that are embedded in daily interactions that are the real keys to fathers' involvement. If you look at the face-to-face interactions with maternity nurses and pediatricians, embedded in dialogues with doctors, health-care providers, and teachers are messages about expected involvement. If more messages expect fathers to be involved and daily interactions offer support for fathers' involvement, fathers will be involved.

- couple's ability to communicate with each other—to express thoughts, feelings, and needs in ways each partner can hear and respond to, can be a touch, or an action

- focusing on what is good about the situation or the action of the other person and what needs to be done to improve the situation, avoiding negative criticism and angry exchanges

These parents discuss different points of view and express themselves forcefully, but they stay focused on how they can make needed changes and improve the situation, and they avoid assigning blame for problems.

Changes the Baby Brings

A great deal goes on during the early months. Parents are highly involved in the nurturing stage of parenthood, caring for the child, and accepting their new role as parents.[83] They worry, "Am I doing okay?" "Am I the kind of parent I want to be?" Gradually, parents incorporate other parts of their lives—work, extended family, friends—into their caretaking activities. Parents may find it difficult, however, to give each other the support that is so crucial in coping during this period. New mothers and fathers had similar complaints: (1) tiredness and exhaustion; (2) loss of sleep, especially in the first two months; (3) needing to adjust to new responsibilities; (4) feeling inadequate as a parent; (5) difficulty in keeping up with the amount of work for baby and home; (6) feeling tied down, and (7) worries regarding finances.[84] Neither parent anticipated the many changes that would occur in their lives when their babies arrived, in part because they did not realize how much work is involved in caring for an infant.

Forming a Coparenting Alliance

James McHale and his colleagues observed a group of middle-class, educated families as they made the transition from the last trimester of pregnancy through the first two and a half years of the child's life,[85] focusing on the coparenting alliance parents built as they reared their children. Coparenting is parents' ability to work together, to cooperate and coordinate their efforts to provide care for children. The quality of the marriage predicted the coparenting alliance parents would build after the baby came, coparenting is more than a measure of marital adjustment. It is a measure of parents' ability to plan and coordinate efforts to care for their children. The researchers did find that some couples were able to build a coparenting alliance even though they were experiencing difficulties in their marriages. They did this by attending to their partners' perceptions, feelings, and desires and tried to coordinate their child-rearing efforts with those of their partners.

In their interviews and assessment measures in the last trimester of pregnancy, McHale and colleagues focused on parents' views of their family of origin and how their parents coparented and on parents' expectations of what their family would be like when the baby came. The researchers were surprised that many of the parents had negative views of their parents' coparenting and were committed to making changes in their own families. In talking about attachments to their parents, many prospective parents expressed feelings of rejection, distance, and detachment from their parents. These negative feelings did not predict their future hopes or behavior when parents were able to gain a broad understanding of their parents and talk about their relationships with them in a coherent way.

When parents could not move beyond these early experiences and handled them by pushing them out of their thoughts or dismissing their importance, or continuing to brood or dwell on them, then these parents were more likely to be distanced and detached about the future they would build. Men and women who felt rejected by fathers were very negative in their expectations of forming a coparenting alliance. McHale and his colleagues emphasized it was not the family of origin or where parents came from that predicted the future but how prospective parents handled their feelings about the early events that predicted the future.

The researchers were also surprised how little parents had talked to each other about their parenting beliefs and values before the child's birth. Parents did not really know how the other parent felt about letting the child cry or where a child should sleep. Frequently, parents had little understanding of their partners' beliefs so there were marked discrepancies between parents' actual beliefs and what the other parent predicted they were. It was the discrepancy between what parents thought was the right thing to do with babies and toddlers that produced intense feelings and conflicts.

All parents were a little anxious. It was primarily those parents who struggled with additional issues concerning their parents or difficulties in their marriages that had significant problems. In envisioning the kinds of services most beneficial to parents, McHale suggested that interventions to help parents communicate and discuss issues around caring for children would be the most helpful. While traditional home visiting programs improve parent-child interactions and marriage communication programs improve couples' abilities to talk about their relationship, neither kind of program targets the ability of the couple to coordinate their efforts and work together. Thinking back later about what might have helped at the time of the baby's birth, parents said having a greater understanding of the other parent's cultural beliefs about parenting would have helped.

Adjustments of Parents Who Have Premature Children

In addition to the usual stresses of the birth of a baby, parents who have premature children face additional challenges. Unlike most parents, who have nine months of preparation for parenthood, parents who have premature births are often plunged into parenthood in unpredictable ways.

They may have little or much to manage. If children are only a few weeks premature, parents may have few problems. If a child is born at twenty-four or twenty-six weeks after conception, however, the child might stay in the hospital for an extended period of time. His or her parents must consider whether the child will survive and whether long-term problems will develop. They also face the ongoing

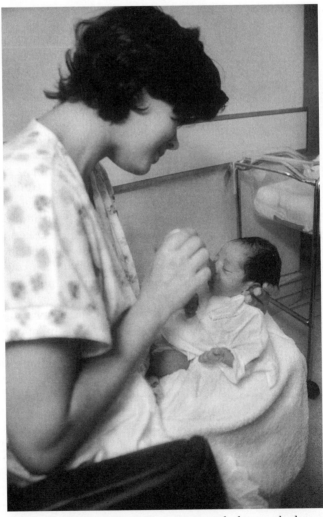

Parents of premature children are advised to interact with them and take over as much of their children's care as possible in the hospital.

stress of dealing with hospital and medical personnel and the changing medical status of their child. Further, when the child comes home, they may need to make changes to address their child's special needs.[86]

Innovations in neonatal nurseries have had success in creating more womb-like experiences for premature babies born two to three months early.[87] To create an individualized hospital care plan for each baby is a complicated process—training staff and parents to carry it out, and monitoring the child's response—but research indicates great benefits for the baby. The program, begun within seventy-two hours of birth, lasted until the child reached the corrected age of two weeks. (Corrected age is the child's age from the date of expected arrival, not from the date of actual birth.)

Parents and staff do everything possible to reduce stress, to physically support the child with much Kangaroo Care (KC) time (skin-to-skin between mother and child); often two nurses carry out procedures—one holds and supports the baby, while the other does the procedure. When babies who received the experimental care were at a corrected age of two weeks, they had better neurobehavioral functioning and increased coherence between frontal and other brain regions than control babies, and when corrected age was nine months, experimental babies' development was significantly advanced. They scored in the 73rd percentile for overall development when control babies scored at the 39th.

Parents of babies in Neonatal Intensive Care Units also benefitted from special psychological help to prevent the traumatization that can occur when parents view the medical interventions, pain, and discomfort babies endure. A one-time intervention with mothers whose babies were in intensive care focused on identifying mothers' sources of stress, explaining the emotional upheavals that parents experience, identifying supports mothers can draw on, and offering ongoing assistance as needed during hospitalization. At discharge, 27 percent of mothers in the intervention groups showed clinically significant signs of psychological trauma compared to 59 percent of control group mothers who had access to chaplains' visits and could request psychological help if they wished it.[88]

KC benefits not only premature infants but also the whole family after they leave the hospital.[89] Skin-to-skin contact between mother and infant for at least an hour a day for a period of two weeks increased families' interaction patterns when infants were three months of age. KC was related to increases in mothers' sensitivity to their infants and in their ability to adjust their stimulation to the babies' needs and to increases in affectionate touching between parents and between parents and child. At three months of age, infants were less irritable than infants in a control group who did not receive KC, and there was greater reciprocity in the relationships between parent and child. It is thought that the physical contact helped the mother understand the baby's needs better and enabled her to give more sensitive care; as a result she felt more confident and positive toward both the baby and her husband. Mother's positive touching of her husband increased his positive touches with her and the baby.

A very brief version of this intervention has proved useful for full-term infants as well. Infants who received one hour of KC with mothers about twenty minutes after birth were found to have more organized motor movements, to sleep better, and have less crying following KC.[90] The benefits were observed for up to four hours. For full-term infants, KC helped to reduce the stress associated with all the physiological changes at birth and appeared to help newborns achieve greater regulation of their physiological state. More study is needed on the effects of KC during the first postnatal weeks and its effects on mother-infant interactions and babies' focusing skills.

Parents of premature babies use the same strategies as parents of full-term babies to ease the transition to parenthood. Support from friends or from those dealing with similar situations, clear communication between parents and between parents and professional workers are especially essential.

Parenting Programs That Ease the Transition to Parenthood

As early as the 1950s, research documented declines in couples' relationships following the birth of a child and the decline continues to be noted in research down to the present time. Childbirth classes that include both mothers and fathers have become a routine part of preparing for the birth, but these classes primarily prepare couples for labor and delivery.

Pioneers in this area of research, Carolyn Pape Cowan and Philip Cowan began their work with couples in the 1970s, organizing parent groups that did not seek so much to develop specific skills as to give parents opportunities to discuss their parenting experiences and reduce stress.[91] The groups consisting of four couples expecting their first child and two professionals began in the last trimester of pregnancy and continued for six months until the child was three months old to provide support for parents as they created their families. Parents talked about sources of stress and well-being and ways to increase closeness between the couple. After the births, the parents brought their babies to the group sessions. Following the couples over five years, the Cowans found that participation in the couples groups significantly reduced marital decline for wives and husbands; couples were still together at the end of three years when those in the control group experienced a divorce rate of 15 percent. At the end of five years, the divorce rate was similar for the two groups. The Cowans have expanded this intervention to include parents whose children are about to enter elementary school, and we review that work in Chapter 8.

Their initial studies were all done with middle-income married parents. In extending their program to include low-income, married and unmarried parents, of many ethnic backgrounds in groups, the Cowans have used two forms of intervention: the couples groups they have used in the past and groups of fathers only.[92] Fathers met with clinically trained leaders for sixteen weeks to discuss fathers' importance to children's development, ways to improve fathers' relationships with children, and ways to deal with fathers' feelings. Couples' groups included the same topics but in addition focused on parents' satisfactions in their relationships with each other.

In an eighteen-month follow-up, parents in the control group who received only a lecture about fathers' importance showed the usual decline in couples' relationships with each other, a decline in fathers' involvement, and an increasing number of parent-reported behavior problems in children. Men in the fathers' groups reported increasing involvement in children's care and fathers and mothers reported no increase in children's behavior problems. However, parents' relationships declined over time. In the couples groups (should be groups), parents reported similar increase in fathers' involvement and, no increase in children's behavior problems, and they reported an additional benefit of stable level of partner satisfaction without the decline the other two groups experienced.

When asked in an interview what parents can do to ease the transition to parenting, the Cowans suggested:[93]

- address unresolved couples' issues before they become overwhelming
- organize a realistic and mutually agreeable division of who does what work in the home
- nurture the couple relationship as well as the relationship with the infant; check in with each other every day, find out how the other person is feeling

When asked what recommendations they had for life education workers, the Cowans answered:

- make a greater effort to involve fathers in parenting programs
- go beyond the usual curriculum of infant development and parenting skills and talk about parents' feelings about their relationship and strategies for maintaining a satisfying couple relationship
- include measures of the child's development so we can see how improving relationships and increasing skills and knowledge impact children's development

Developed by nurses to serve as a vaccine to prevent the difficulties many parents face after the birth of a child, Becoming Parents Program gives parents information on the same three topics and also includes building and drawing on a support system.[94] The program has been used with middle-class and low-income parents, and married and unmarried parents of many different ethnic groups. In post-birth follow-ups with families, couples report fathers are involved with parenting, parents feel satisfied with their relationship, parents get more sleep, and they report less depression.

PRACTICAL QUESTION: WHAT CHANGES CAN PARENTS ANTICIPATE FOR THEMSELVES?

Parents continually develop new behaviors as they rear their children and as they deal with their frustrations as parents. So, it is not surprising that creating these new responses leads to permanent changes in parents themselves.

Galinsky has divided parenthood into six stages in which parents focus their emotional and intellectual energy on the task of that period.[95] These stages differ from most in that a parent can be in more than one stage at a time with children of different ages.

The six stages, with their timing and tasks are:

- Image-making, during pregnancy and sometimes later in anticipation of children's growth, parents anticipate what baby will be like, how they will respond, prepare for changes in themselves and their lives
- Nurturing, birth to about eighteen months, parents focus on caregiving and meeting children's physical and emotional needs, balancing babies' needs with theirs and setting priorities
- Authority, eighteen months to about four, parents set rules and structure for children's lives and help children learn to accommodate to them
- Interpretive, four to adolescence, parents teach children about life, instilling values and morals interpreting experiences outside the home with other adults and children
- Interdependent, adolescence, parents share power with their increasingly independent children
- Departure, children leave home for college or work, parents evaluate their effectiveness as parents, where they have succeeded and where they might have acted differently

We have discussed the image-making stage in this chapter and will discuss the other stages in greater detail in later chapters.

SUPPORT FOR PARENTS

Various kinds of support can help parents adjust to parenting. When parents successfully meet the demands of their new roles, they feel competent and effective. These feelings of self-efficacy can continue, influencing ongoing parenting in beneficial ways. Family and friends provide informal sources of support as well as information, advice, and direct help in the form of shopping, cleaning, and cooking so parents can get some rest. Other, more formal sources of support consist of classes and support groups that we reviewed earlier in this chapter.

Most couples are referred to classes at hospitals or in the community prior to the arrival of the baby. Even programs given in hospitals at the time of the birth can provide information that increases parents' competence in caring for their babies. Such information focuses on babies' states and their repertoire of behaviors, the ways they send signals to parents, and how parents learn to understand and respond to the signals. Especially helpful are tips on when to "engage" with babies (when they are fed and alert), when to "disengage" (when babies turn away, fall into a drowsy state), how to feed infants, and how to deal with crying.[96] A brief behavioral parent training enables parents to help their newborn develop healthy sleep patterns and improves parents' confidence.[97]

When parents conceive a child and bring him or her into the world, they embark on one of the most life-changing experiences of their lives. Whether well or poorly planned, the child elicits new behaviors from parents and at the same time brings a host of new pleasures to them. When parents work together with each other or with supportive friends and relatives, when they communicate expectations, experiences, and feelings as they care for the baby, the baby brings parents and friends and relatives closer together to share life experiences in a more intense, meaningful way than previously known. Babies demand a great deal, but they give much in return.

MAIN POINTS

Becoming a parent involves

- assessing parental readiness in terms of time and psychological resources
- couples' planning children and resolving differences
- single adults' planning children
- accepting a child if unplanned
- resolving ambivalence so the child is wanted, not rejected

Changes in adoption policies and assisted reproductive technologies

- mean that people who would have been childless in the past can now have children
- raise questions about children's rights to know their biological roots

Timing of children

- depends on the psychological qualities of parents rather than their age
- affects a child's later adjustment—if parents are not mature, a child may develop later problems

Babies bring

- new routines and responsibilities
- great pleasures
- a special appreciation in parents who experienced infertility

Dimensions underlying a parent's transition to parenthood include

- balancing individuality and mutuality
- communication skills
- positive attitudes
- agreed-upon division of labor
- parents coming to terms with their own childhood experiences
- forming a coparenting alliance

Parents experience greater ease in the transition when they

- maintain intimate bonds with their partner or a supportive friend or relative
- share expectations, feelings, and workload with partners
- line up support from friends and relatives
- adopt an experimental attitude toward solutions—trying them and seeing if they work

EXERCISES

1. Imagine that you and your partner were discussing your readiness to have a baby. What factors would make you feel that you are ready? How would you handle a disagreement between the two of you as to whether to have a baby or not? Suppose you both felt strongly about your opinion, what would you do?

2. Describe your expectations of parenthood. What changes will it require of you? Do you think your expectations are realistic? Describe the activities that you do now that might prepare you for being a parent—taking a course in parenting, learning to solve conflicts in a positive way, practicing communication skills with friends, learning about children and their needs. Are there other things you could be doing?

3. Plan out the support system you would organize for yourself and your partner if you were having a baby in three months. Whom would you include? How involved would your relatives be? How much extra expense would such a system create?

4. Imagine that you are six months pregnant and investigate the childbirth and parenting groups available in your community. Are there groups like those organized by the Cowans? Do they include married and unmarried couples?

5. Imagine you and your partner required donor insemination or egg donors. Investigate the resources in your area and the requirements for people using them.

ADDITIONAL READINGS

Cowan, Carolyn Pape and Cowan, Philip. *When Partners Become Parents*. New York: Basic Books, 1992.

Ehrensaft, Diane. *Mommies, Daddies, Donors, Surrogates*. New York: Guilford Press, 2005.

Finn, Holly. *The Baby Chase: An Adventure in Fertility*. Byline.com Available as an Amazon Kindle Single, 2011.

Lu, Michael. *Get Ready to Get Pregnant*. New York: Harper, 2009.

Marin, David. *This Is US: The New All-American Family*. United States: Exterminating Angel Press, 2011.

McHale, James. *Charting the Bumpy Road of Coparenthood: Understanding the Challenges of Family Life*. Washington, DC: ZERO TO THREE, 2007.

Paul, Annie Murphy. *Origins: How the Nine Months before Birth Shape the Rest of Our Lives*. New York: Free Press, 2010.

Spar, Debora. *The Baby Business: How Money, Science, and Politics Drive the Commerce of Conceptions*. Cambridge, MA: Harvard University Press, 2006.

5

Nurturing Close Family Relationships in a Technological Society

---

CHAPTER TOPICS

In this chapter, you will learn about:

- Family Closeness and Good Feelings
- Creating Closeness through Understanding and Expressing Feelings
- Transmission of Feelings in the Family
- Encouraging Closeness through storytelling and play
- Mutual Problem Solving
- Resolving Parental Conflicts Constructively
- Effects of Sudden Economic Loss on Families

- Managing Daily Stresses and Negative Feelings
- Parents with Ongoing Negative Moods: depressed and substance-dependent parents
- Substance-Dependent
- Developing a Support System
- How Do Children Define the Good Parent?

Test Your Knowledge: Fact or Fiction (True/False)

1. Families most often transmit negative feelings from one person to another, but less often transmit positive feelings. (T)
2. Sudden economic loss affects families and children in this country but not in other countries where governments provide financial benefits and services. (F)
3. Coaching children in understanding and expressing feelings helps children develop effective social skills and maintain physical health. (T)

4. Children become distressed when parents fight even if parents find a compromise and are happy about it. (F)
5. Parents today put in more hours of work on the job and at home but find more time for child care. (T)

Parents in all ethnic groups give the same primary reason for wanting children—to love them and feel close to them. This chapter describes how parents create close bonds with children and at the same time manage the daily hassles and frustrations of life and the larger social forces that impact families so children feel loved and cherished.

When a representative group of adults was asked in a survey, what, if anything, had emotionally strained them the day before, the most common response was, "Family." When the same group was asked what provided the previous day's pleasure, an even larger number responded, "Family."[1] This chapter focuses on how to maintain family relationships and create family routines that nurture the pleasures of close ties and minimize the stresses. We identify those patterns that foster family well-being, and those factors that create stress, and then we suggest specific ways to reduce the negative feelings.

FAMILY CLOSENESS AND GOOD FEELINGS

In Chapter 3 we saw that close social relationships bring great pleasure, reduce stress, and improve health and well-being.[2] For most people, families are the first and most frequent providers of closeness.

Physical Touch and Closeness

Physical closeness brings feelings of pleasure and relaxation, and we first learned about these physical benefits from studies with animals and newborn infants. Rats whose caretakers handled them gently had great resistance to stress and survived surgeries that killed rats without such handling.[3] Preterm infants who received deep-pressure massages several times a day in the hospital gained weight faster, were awake and more active during the day, more alert and responsive during a developmental assessment, and were discharged from the hospital sooner than infants who did not receive massages.[4]

In the first few weeks of life, infants who receive extra carrying and physical closeness cry less than babies who are not carried so much, and they are more visually and aurally alert.[5] When parents massaged their colicky babies for fifteen minutes before bedtime, when compared to nonmassaged colicky babies, their babies were more alert and less irritable during the day, fell asleep faster, and awoke fewer times during the night.[6]

Although there is less research on the benefits of touch for older children and adults, existing studies indicate that giving infant massages has benefited the adults

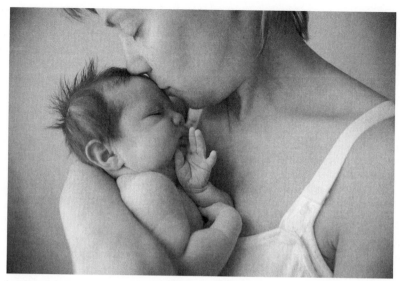

Physical closeness and touch brings feelings of relaxation and emotional closeness for both participants.

who gave them.[7] After giving massages, depressed mothers were more alert and responsive in their interactions with their children, and elderly volunteers who learned to give infant massages reported that they felt less anxious and depressed, slept better, and were more socially active, and benefits increased over a month.

Finally, a recent Magnetic Resonance Imaging study documented that holding their husbands' hands, as opposed to strangers' hands, decreased stress from anticipated mild shocks and produced changes deep in the brains of happily married women.[8] Within this sample, those women in extremely close marriages experienced the greatest relief from stress because additional areas of the brain were stimulated when they held their husbands' hands. So, highly satisfying relationships can be especially beneficial.

Physical touch is important, then, and can be maintained with toddlers and older children with night-time massages, hugs, physical play that fathers often engage in, and a hug or pat on the shoulder for older children.

The Power of Positive Feelings

Happy feelings do not have just fleeting effects but confer long-term benefits as well. Researcher Barbara Fredrickson believes each positive emotion broadens individuals' experiences and leads to new capacities and abilities.[9] Joy stimulates play and creativity; interest encourages exploration and learning; contentment fosters appreciating experiences and understanding their importance to individuals' growth; pride builds connections with others to share what has been achieved, and love, described as an amalgam of all the positive emotions shared in relationship with others, stimulates play, creativity, exploration, and learning together.

Positive emotions also appear to undo the effects of negative feelings by calming cardiovascular arousal triggered by anger, sadness, or fear and by enabling individuals to put negative experiences in a broader perspective, thus minimizing their effects on the person. Feeling positive, the person is able to make plans and take action.

In addition, positive emotions also contribute to the important psychological quality of resilience, defined as functioning effectively and achieving good outcomes when confronted by adversity.[10] As positive emotions broaden attention, creativity, and cognitive skills, they contribute to the effectiveness of people's coping mechanisms, an important aspect of resiliency. Finally, small daily events provide pleasure, which triggers an upward spiral of feeling good, taking action to meet goals, meeting goals, feeling good.

Positive thoughts are important as well. If children simply think of some pleasant event for a short time, they resist temptation more successfully and respond to unfair treatment with fairness and generosity.[11] In addition, happy feelings inoculate children against the effects of negative events.

Since so many benefits flow from positive feelings, we focus attention on how to nurture these feelings in our homes with family members.

Emotional Closeness

Parents create closeness when they love the child as a special person and feel the love their child has for them. Dorothy Briggs describes the psychological climate that enables children to feel their parents' love: "Nurturing love is tender caring—valuing a child just because he exists. It comes when you see your youngster as special and dear—even though you may not approve of all that he does."[12] Children are loved simply because they exist—no strings attached, no standards to meet.

Parents form close relationships with children of all ages in two basic ways—by providing sensitive, responsive care that meets the child's individual needs and by becoming an interactive social partner. Sensitive care and forming a social partnership take many forms, depending on the age and unique qualities of the child, as we discuss in subsequent chapters.

CREATING CLOSENESS THROUGH UNDERSTANDING AND EXPRESSING FEELINGS

Haim Ginott wrote, "Emotions are part of our genetic heritage. Fish swim, birds fly, and people feel."[13] Feelings help to define who we are as distinct individuals so to feel close to people, we need to understand their feelings. Babies come into the world with emotions and feelings that serve as signals to others of what infants are experiencing. Long before they have language, children communicate with others through smiles, laughs, cries, and frowns. And they respond to the feelings of those around them.

Parents differ in their attitudes and thoughts about how important feelings are in life.[14] Some parents have a heightened awareness of their own and their children's feelings and believe feelings signal that change is required. Anger serves to initiate action in frustrating situations, and sadness slows a person down to have time to cope with loss. These parents feel comfortable with their feelings, and they coach children to manage their feelings.

Other parents feel uncomfortable with feelings and handle the discomfort in one of three ways:[15]

- dismissing the importance of feelings and making light of or ignoring them
- disapproving and punishing the expression of feelings
- accepting all feelings, no matter how inappropriate the form of expression

Children of dismissive and disapproving parents have a hard time trusting their own judgements. By learning that their feelings are wrong, they come to believe there is something basically wrong with *them* for having the feelings. Because they have little experience in acknowledging and dealing with their feelings, they often have difficulty controlling them and solving problems.

Finally, children whose parents accept all feelings and often comfort the child when the child experiences a negative emotional reaction receive little teaching or guidance in how to express feelings appropriately because their parents seem to believe that expressing feelings in any form—whether appropriate or inappropriate—will take care of the problem. Their children do not learn to cope with feelings constructively and have difficulty making friends and concentrating and learning in school.

So, the three types of response—ignoring or criticizing feelings so they occur as little as possible and accepting all expressions of feeling without providing guidance for expression—lead to similar kinds of problems for children, such as the inability to regulate feelings and to feel comfortable with themselves and others.

John Gottman and his coworkers found that when parents coach their five-year-old children in how to deal with feelings, the children function better physically and psychologically when they are eight years old. They perform better academically and are socially more competent with peers. They are physically healthier as well, perhaps because coaching helps children modulate their emotional reactions, which in turn helps their physiological system function better. Coaching consists of five key steps:[16]

Step 1: Parents recognize when they are having a feeling, what that feeling is, and when others are having feelings.

Step 2: Parents consider feelings as opportunities for intimacy or teaching. When the child is upset, happy, or excited, parents see this as an opportunity to be close to the child and to teach the child how to express feelings appropriately.

Step 3: Parents listen empathically and validate the child's feelings without trying to argue the child out of the feeling.

Step 4: Parents help the child verbally label the feeling. The child may be confused about what he or she is feeling and labeling gives the child a word for the strong emotion; it is not telling the child how to feel. Labeling a feeling while the child is experiencing it appears to have a soothing effect on the child's nervous system. Labeling feelings also helps a child see that he or she can have two feelings at the same time.

Step 5: Parents set limits while helping the child solve the problem. Parents limit the way feelings are expressed; by means of I-messages explained in a section that follows. Parents do not, however, limit the child's having the feeling itself but they limit its expression. Anger is acceptable, but hitting a sibling is not. Parents help the child think of possible actions to express feelings and ways to achieve his or her goals in the situation.

Gottman speculates that talking about emotional reactions has positive benefits for children because the verbal expression of feelings helps children plan appropriate actions and eliminates the consequences of inhibiting negative emotional reactions.[17]

Active Listening

Active listening, a specific tool parents use in coaching, is Thomas Gordon's term for what parents do when they reflect their children's feelings.[18] Parents listen to children's statements, pay careful attention to the feelings expressed, and then frame a response similar to the child's statement. If a child says she feels too dumb to learn a school subject, the parent might feed back that she feels she is not smart enough. Here is one of Gordon's examples of active listening:

CHILD: I don't want to go to Bobby's birthday party tomorrow.
PARENT: Sounds like you and Bobby have had a problem maybe.
CHILD: I hate him, that's what. He's not fair.
PARENT: You really hate him because you feel he's been unfair somehow.
CHILD: Yeah. He never plays what I want to play.[19]

The child confirms the parent's response if it is accurate, and, if it is inaccurate, the child corrects the misinterpretation. The parent can continue active listening to understand what is happening to the child.

Gordon also gives the example of a teenage girl who refused to eat dinner. When her father used active listening to understand her feelings, she revealed she did not want to eat because her stomach was in knots. She was worried that her boyfriend was going to choose another girlfriend who was more popular and comfortable with boys than she was. She wanted to be more outgoing but was afraid of making a fool of herself. After talking about her feelings, she decided she would take a few chances and be more outgoing. So her father's active listening moved the conversation from a dinner refusal to talking about a serious problem and then considering a way to deal with it.

Sometimes, active listening helps the parent to better understand the situation. One mother reported that her son at college called home and complained about two different courses, the teachers, and the workload. The mother said, "Sounds like this semester is not much fun." Her son immediately said, "No, it's good." and went on to describe an enjoyable course and a good campus job, so the mother's view changed as a result of listening and reflecting feelings. Active listening has many advantages. It helps children express feelings in a direct, effective way. As feelings are expressed and parents accept them, children feel understood and accepted.[20] Listening to children's feelings is sometimes all that is needed to resolve the problem. Often when we are upset, sad, or angry, we simply want to express the feeling and have someone respond, "It is really painful when a friend walks off with someone else and leaves you behind." The response validates the feeling as being justified and important, and frequently that is all we want.

Active listening requires persistence, patience, and a strong commitment to attend to both the child's words and accompanying behavioral clues. Furthermore, there are times when active listening is not appropriate:

- when a child asks for specific information, give the information
- when a child does not want to talk about feelings, respect the child's privacy and do not probe
- when the child has no more to say

One of the mothers in Haim Ginott's parenting group raised the question of reflecting back feelings of great sadness over a loss.[21] Is this wise? Does it help children? Ginott responded that parents must learn that suffering can strengthen a child's character. When a child is sad in response to a real loss, a parent need only empathize, "You are sad. I understand." The child learns that the parent is a person who understands and sympathizes.

I-Messages

When a parent is angry, frustrated, or irritated with a child's behavior, the parent can communicate his or her feelings constructively with an I-message rather than nagging, yelling, or criticizing. Using I-messages also provides a model for children in how to express feelings so problems are worked out. The I-message contains three parts: (1) a clear statement of how the parent feels, (2) a statement of the behavior that has caused the parent to feel that way, and (3) a statement describing why the behavior is upsetting to the parent. For example, a parent frustrated with a teenager's being late for family dinner might say, "I feel upset and frustrated when your lateness delays dinner for all of us, because we want to eat together and have fun hearing what everyone did today, and you are not here."

To use I-messages well, parents have to spend time analyzing their feelings and becoming more aware of exactly how they feel and why. Gordon points out that anger at a child, often hides other feelings like disappointment, fear, frustration, or hurt. When a child comes home an hour late, the parent may launch into a tirade. The anger covers the worry that grew into fear during the hour of waiting; Gordon believes expressing worry is more helpful than yelling angrily.

What should a parent do if a family member pays no attention to I-messages? First, be sure the person can pay attention to the I-message. Do not try to communicate feelings when a child or partner is rushing out of the house or is already deeply immersed in some other activity. If an I-message is then ignored, send another, more forceful message, in a firm tone of voice.

Sometimes, the person responds to an I-message with an I-message. For example, when a parent expresses distress because the lawn is not mowed, the daughter may reply that she feels annoyed because mowing interferes with her after-school activities. At that point, the parent must "shift gears," as Gordon puts it, and reflect back the child's frustration by using active listening.

I-messages have several benefits. First, when people use I-messages, they begin to take their own needs seriously. This process benefits all family relationships because parents feel freer—more themselves—in all areas of life. Second, children learn about the parents' reaction, which they may not have understood until the I-message. Third, everyone has an opportunity to solve problems in response to I-messages. Even toddlers and preschoolers have ideas, not only for themselves but also for others.

I-messages can convey appreciation—"I feel pleased when you help me with the dishes because then we have time to go to the store for your school supplies." I-messages are also useful in heading off problems and in helping children see that their parents have needs, too. These messages, termed *preventive I-messages*, express parents' future wants or needs and give children an opportunity to respond positively. For example, if a parent says, "I need quiet so I can drive the car," the child learns what to do to be helpful.

Although closeness is enjoyable for and helpful to children, some parents do not feel good about themselves or some of their own qualities, causing them to wonder if their children might not be better off remaining distant from them. They fear that their children will pick up their bad qualities. Research on close and non-close relationships among adolescents and their parents reveals that children who feel close to their parents are less likely to take on the parents' negative qualities than are children who feel distant. Parents' negative behaviors are a more potent influence on children when parents and children are not close.[22] Thus, even when parents have many self-doubts and self-criticism, closeness with them and all their failings is still a positive experience for their children.

Transmission of Feelings in the Family

Living closely together, family members are affected by each others' emotional reactions. Detailed observations of all family members' emotional responses and activities over an extended period of time enable researchers to describe the patterns of emotional transmissions in the family.

Daily diaries and experience sampling methods (family members report their activities, interactions, and feelings) yielded a picture of how family members influence each others' moods for hours and sometimes for a day. Reed Larson and David Almeida summarize a series of studies to understand how feelings spread through the family and conclude:[23]

- family feelings are often transmitted by one person in one direction without a reciprocal response from the other person
- parents' negative feelings are more likely to be passed on to children than positive feelings
- a powerful person's anger may lead to feelings of anxiety and vulnerability in a less powerful person
- fathers' feelings have the most impact on family members; fathers express feelings to mothers who accept them, and to children who also accept them
- fathers bring stress home from work and negative feelings spill over on to all family members

- married and single mothers appear better able to contain stress from work and are less likely to bring stress home from work
- depressed feelings are more likely to be expressed to marital partner than anxiety, and depression in one partner is likely to depress other partner's positive feelings
- marital conflict spills over onto relationships with children; fathers' marital dissatisfaction is more likely to color parent-child relationships than mothers' marital distress; single mothers do transmit negative feelings to their adolescent children who experience anxiety and anger
- when families have resources and members are not stressed, they are less likely to transmit negative feelings
- when justified reasons exist for negative feelings, like irritability caused by physical illness, family members stop the transmission of negative feelings
- when stressed mothers have time alone to relax and restore their energies, they do not pass on negative feelings to children

The patterns of emotional transmission in families suggest ways to help families minimize the transmission of negative feelings. For example, developing resources that provide emotional support and reduce stress reduces the transmission of negative feelings, and later in the chapter we describe supports that help all families. Because negative feelings are so readily passed around in families, and positive feelings are not, even though they are highly beneficial for everyone, we emphasize the activities that bring good feelings to family members. We also see that when family members understand the sources of feelings—like an exam or poor health—they do not transmit negative reactions; there is an emphasis on understanding others' emotional reactions.

Encouraging Closeness and Good Feelings between Sisters and Brothers

Sisters and brothers do not always enjoy good times together, and are often ambivalent about each other. Having observed sibling relationships over time, researchers designed a program for four- to eight-year-old brothers and sisters to increase their good times together, focusing on seven skills to enhance the quality of their interactions.[24]

The first three skills involve starting play—initiating, accepting, or declining overtures to play. The fourth skill is taking the point of view of the other person, and the last three skills focus on managing feelings—identifying and regulating feelings, and problem-solving conflicts. Brothers and sisters ages four to eight years came to four group play sessions at a laboratory, meeting with three other sibling pairs four times.

In group sessions, children learned to identify their own feelings and those of their brother or sister, and learned how to manage them. Group leaders used modeling, role-playing, coaching, and skills training to encourage new behaviors. Children practiced and rehearsed the behaviors—how to understand the other child's desires, how to say "Yes" to the other's invitation to play or how to say "No" in a nonantagonistic way. Children got coaching and immediate feedback on their responses. They learned to use self-talk to control their own immediate emotional reactions at times of conflict and to express their own points of view, finding solutions that satisfied both siblings.

Parents watched the group sessions through a one-way mirror and received coaching on how to reinforce the skills at home and how to reduce conflicts between children. Parents learned to help children identify feelings, calm themselves when they were upset, and then find appropriate expression of feelings and their behavior. A final coaching session took place at home to put the skills into practice in daily routines.

Following the five sessions, parents reported brothers and sisters interacted more warmly and less aggressively. Parents who do not have access to such a program can encourage talk about feelings at home, especially when emotions are highly aroused, encouraging ways to regulate feelings, using creative activities like drawing, storytelling, and imaginative play to reduce stress so children can problem-solve more effectively.

STORYTELLING

Telling stories draws family members close to each other. As Susan Engel writes, "We all want to know who we are and how we came into our world. We all want to know that we were recognized, that we are singular and special. And we each learn this, in part, through the stories we are told about our beginnings."[25]

Storytelling begins at birth. Babies hear the stories others tell, and as soon as they can talk, they tell their own stories that initially consist of only a few words about an event—"Played house. I baby."

Observations reveal that mothers and toddlers tell about nine stories each hour. In addition to telling stories to others, young children, as they play, often construct ongoing stories of what they are doing. By the time children grow up and are in college, they tell as many as five to thirty-eight stories each day.

Engel says parents can encourage children's participation in storytelling by listening attentively, expressing interest with smiles, gasps, facial expressions, and repetitions. Parents collaborate in the stories by asking open-ended questions that encourage elaboration, and they expose children to a variety of stories and poems that stimulate children's stories.

Stories serve several purposes.[26] They shape our views of ourselves, other people, and events in our lives. Stories tell us about the world and our culture and the values that hold our families together.

Mothers and fathers who tell dinnertime stories about happy times with their families of origin report satisfactions in their marriages, and show more positive feelings to children.[27] In attempting to tell stories about their personal experiences, family members sometimes struggle to make sense of their experiences, and the effort is worth it because, "Families that are able to make sense of their experiences, pleasant or challenging, however, provide their children with a meaning-making system that can better prepare them for an unpredictable world."[28]

Play

Every day should include some family time to relax and play in ways that depend on the ages of the children. A longitudinal study of children's activities and behavior in the first six years of life found that those children who in infancy and early childhood had opportunities to engage in productive play developed greater self-control and were less likely to have behavior problems in first grade.[29] The exact reasons for the positive effects of play are not known. Play may create feelings of pleasure and joy that enable children to relax and adjust to others' demands more easily or it may drain off tension so there is less negative emotion to control.

Play with parents may only be twenty minutes, but it should be a time in which parents do not make demands on children or insist on certain behavior, a time during which parents follow children's leads and play under their direction. Within safety limits, children can do what they want, and parents engage without giving corrections or criticism. Children spend so much time in the day doing what parents or other caregivers request that it is important to have a time simply to play and interact for fun. With older children, the play time may be just conversation, but it is nevertheless time set aside for pleasurable activity. The family may select card games or other games appropriate for all family members.

Richard Louv believes parents and children should spend some time outdoors as we, as a society, have become disconnected from the joys and physical and psychological benefits of time outdoors[30] so that even when families have large yards, people go outside only 10 percent of the time they spend at home.[31] His grass-roots campaign to "Leave No Child Inside" is described in *The Last Child in the Woods*[32] and gives families many suggestions for ways to improve communities so that parents and children have more access to the joys and calming effects of the natural world (see www.childrenandnature.org).

MUTUAL PROBLEM SOLVING

Mutual problem solving is a strategy that helps families resolve family members' conflicting feelings and find solutions that meet everyone's needs. Thomas Gordon describes this method as a useful one for parents and for children.[33]

The method begins with the person most concerned about the problem using an I-statement to describe the problematic feelings or actions or behaviors from his or her point of view. A mother may say to the whole family, "I get frustrated and upset when I have to be in charge of the housework each week and follow up to see if everyone has done their job because it takes a lot of my time to check and be told, 'I am going to do it now,' and find out later, it wasn't done. What can we do to solve this problem?" Everyone can give suggestions; the family can choose a solution and carry it out.

The aim of problem solving is to find a win-win solution agreeable to all concerned. There are six steps to the problem-solving process:

1. defining the problem, both parties make I-statements,
2. generating possible solutions,

3. evaluating possible solutions,

4. deciding on the best solution,

5. implementing the decision, and

6. doing a follow-up evaluation.

When an agreed-on solution is not followed, a strong I-message of disappointment or frustration is expressed by one of the parties. Perhaps a different solution is needed or perhaps some changes need to be made to the one selected. Gordon advises against the use of penalties to enforce agreements between parents and children. Parents should assume children will cooperate instead of starting with a negative expectation expressed in the threat of punishment. Children frequently respond well to trust.

RESOLVING PARENTAL CONFLICTS CONSTRUCTIVELY

The family system begins with the relationship between the parents, and that relationship is the basic support for each parent as he or she deals with the challenges of life—working, rearing children, and caring for elder parents all at the same time. Even if parents are not together and had only a fleeting relationship at the time of conception, a positive coparenting relationship is a beneficial force in children's lives and an important support to the other parent rearing the child born of the relationship. Resolving conflicts with the other parent is as important for children as if parents lived together because the negative feelings between parents hurt and worry children.

Parenting behaviors and children's well-being are closely related to the quality of parents' relationship to each other. Studying family interactions in representative samples of families, researchers found that parents in happy marriages generally had effective parenting skills and their children functioned well.[34] When conflicts arose and parents resolved them with compromises and positive feelings, children felt secure because the parental relationship appeared stable and satisfying to both partners.[35]

But the most disruptive, stressful aspect of family life for parents and children alike is unresolved, destructive marital conflicts that undermine parents' and children's sense of emotional security. When parents cannot resolve their disagreements and they remain unhappy, angry, or sad, children's stress, as measured by cortisol and changes in heart rate, increases, and aggressive behaviors and poor emotional control increase as well.[36] Researchers speculated that living with parental hostility, tensions, and difficulties increased children's feelings of vulnerability and their symptoms of nervousness. Following children who had insecure representations of parents' relationships, as seen in the stories they told in response to a standard set of story stems, researchers found children developed attention problems that over time were reflected in school problems with peers and difficulties in complying with classroom rules.[37]

No matter how old or young the children, destructive parental arguing has an impact on them. Even babies six to fourteen months old, who cannot understand the words, can grasp the emotional tone in arguments, and they react emotionally.[38]

When parents resolve their differences in a cooperative, positive way, babies have little interest in parents' discussions and show no distress or frustration.

When, however, infants are in rooms with disagreeing parents who argue in destructive ways, babies become focused on parents' interactions. When parents are angry, babies express distress, and when parents are depressed and withdrawn, babies feel frustration. Babies' react more strongly when they are being held by the arguing parents than when they are on the floor nearby, and researchers speculate that babies are absorbing parents' tensions through the quality of their touch as well as from the emotions expressed verbally. Babies who have been exposed repeatedly to parents' arguing are less able to regulate their feelings when parents argue than babies without that exposure.

Over time, parents' unresolved conflicts with each other affect their parenting skills so they become overcontrolling and less warm with their children so their older teens are more withdrawn and depressed[39] or suffer from low-self-esteem.[40]

Researchers who have carried out many of these studies have become so concerned about the widespread effects of marital conflicts on parents and children that they have developed a four-session preventive program to teach parents how to solve marital disagreements constructively so parents are respectful of each others' emotional needs and seek to find win-win solutions. These changes, they believe, lead to greater marital satisfaction for parents and greater emotional security for children, thereby reducing children's depressed moods, their difficulties in schools, and in relations with peers.[41]

After the initial assessment, couples attend four sessions, lasting about two to two and a half hours each. Each session includes a didactic session of thirty to forty-five minutes, a one-on-one coaching session with a facilitator to train the couple and practice constructive problem solving, and reviews of diaries of conflict resolutions that occurred in the previous week. The four main objectives of the program are to help couples:

- identify constructive and destructive ways to solve problems and effects of both methods on couples' feelings and behavior
- understand the effects of marital conflict on children's feelings of emotional security and the benefit to children of constructive problem solving
- identify constructive and destructive marital behaviors and their effects on children
- understand the effects of marital conflict on parenting and secure parent-child attachment relationships

A self-study control group of parents received two written publications that covered all the material provided to the couples in the four-session group. All parents filled out assessment forms at the completion of the program and at six and twelve months later. At the follow-up assessments, parents in the extended groups also got a booster review of the treatment material. The prevention program improved parents' ways of handling marital conflict, and improvements were sustained for at least a year. Parents' marital satisfaction increased, and their parenting improved, as did children's level of adjustment.

The positive benefits this program provides for parents and children demonstrate the importance of parents' expressing emotional support to their partners and seeking solutions that meet both parents' needs.

EFFECTS OF SUDDEN ECONOMIC LOSS ON FAMILIES

In Chapter 2, we talked about the stresses of poverty. Here we discuss the stress of sudden economic loss occurring in families affected by social forces like the widespread loss of farm revenues in the 1980s or the economic toll of the Great Recession of 2008. Parents who have worked and enjoyed sustaining incomes suddenly lose the jobs they were trained for, the economy is not generating new jobs, and the economic future looks uncertain. While family experiences under these conditions of economic hardship share some similarities with the experiences of families in poverty in terms of worry about paying basic expenses, they differ in that families had a comfortable way of life, and many friends in their communities may continue lifestyles these families used to enjoy so there is an ongoing comparison of what was, what was lost, and what may never come again. Children continue to go to school with their friends who have not experienced the sudden loss though many friends may have suffered also.

In the 1980s, economic forces led to severe loss of farm revenues in Iowa; many farmers lost their farms, and related businesses went bankrupt. Researchers recruited a sample of two-parent families with two children, one of whom was a seventh grader and the other, a sibling within four years of age.[42] Researchers observed the psychological and social experiences of the families over a five-year period, with follow-ups for an additional ten years, and developed what they termed the Economic Stress Model (ESM) to describe parents' and children's psychological reactions at home and at school.

Drawing on family stress theory, researchers described the major stressor event as economic loss of farm income that triggered parents' individual psychological reactions to the stress, e.g., depression, anxiety, anger. Parents' distress in response to the event increased marital conflict that in turn affected parents' parenting strategies and children's psychological adjustment. When pressures from the economic losses triggered depressed, angry, and irritable feelings in parents, then marriages became more unstable, and spouses were less supportive of each other. Marital tensions spilled over into parenting relationships, and parents sometimes withdrew from children, not monitoring their behavior as well, and not being as emotionally supportive as they had been in the past. As a result, children had more problem behaviors.

Some of the farm families were described as resilient, overcoming the negative effects of the stressor, and parents used two ways of adapting that helped the whole family.[43] The first was maintaining a positive marital relationship; parents cooperated with each other and provided positive emotional support to each other. Marital support increased parents' feelings of self-esteem and self-confidence, and they experienced little distress from the economic pressures. The second positive way to adapt was to use problem-solving strategies to deal with the specific problems. Couples who used these strategies experienced a sense of mastery that suppressed the stress of the economic losses. So a supportive marital relationship and the use of problem-solving strategies buffered families from the emotional distress and tension that occur when income disappears.

Since economic pressures affected them less, resilient parents could maintain warm, nurturant parent-child relationships that supported children's functioning. Their children reported little emotional distress, and were able to perform well in school, had close friendships, and avoided aggressive and delinquent behaviors. Even if parents were tense with each other and harsh in their parenting, children who had warm relationships with siblings or with adults outside the family still avoided problem behaviors like drinking. So positive emotional relationships with parents and with others like siblings or adults in the community buffered adolescents' functioning at times of economic stress and marital tensions.

The ESM has been found useful in understanding family reactions to economic downturns in rural and urban areas of the United States[44] and in other countries like Finland,[45] South Korea,[46] and Turkey[47] that differ from American society. Finnish researchers were surprised at the usefulness of the ESM in understanding the marked psychological reactions to job loss because the government provides basic financial security so job loss has much less economic impact on families in Finland than it does in the United States.

Finnish social scientists speculate that one reason the model works so well in predicting stress levels and children's psychological adjustment is that people in both Finland and the United States place great value on consumption as a sign of status so they feel great psychological distress when they lose discretionary income and cannot participate in this activity. A second possible reason for the similarity of reactions to job loss is that Finland, like the United States, is a country of small nuclear families, and when one or both parents lose a job, children do not have the reassurance of many extended family members to provide psychological support while parents cope with the problems.

Economic crises in the late 1990s in South Korea and in 2001 in Turkey provided an opportunity to test the usefulness of the ESM model in understanding marital responses to economic loss in traditional societies where husbands are the primary breadwinners and where men have social outlets outside the family in drinking establishments (South Korea) and coffee houses (Turkey). In these cultures, job loss and economic strain, so damaging to feelings of self-esteem, directly predicted marital problems for men without the mediating feelings of emotional distress that may have been drained off in social activities with men outside the home. For women, however, economic strain produced emotional distress that predicted marital conflict. So cross-national studies indicate that economic loss is a profound family stressor in many different forms of society.

The 2008 recession in the United States, termed the Great Recession, continues to produce enormous stress for parents and children.[48] In a national poll of 708 unemployed adults in the summer of 2009, 71 percent of the jobless reported their financial situation was "fairly" or "very" bad, almost 70 percent reported they were more stressed than usual, 56 percent said their children's lives changed as a result of parent's job loss, 55 percent reported problems sleeping, 48 percent reported more arguments with family and friends, and 46 percent reported feelings of shame

■ **TABLE 5-1**
PERCENTAGE OF PARENTS AND CHILDREN REPORTING STRESS SYMPTOMS*

Symptoms	%Children 8–12	%Teens 13–17	%Parents Est.**	%Parents
Difficulty sleeping	39	49	13	47
Headaches	30	42	13	34
Eating problems	27	39	8	27
Increased worry	26	45	23	42

*"APA Stress Survey: Children Are More Stressed Than Parents Realize," downloaded from: apapracticecentral.org/update/2009/11-23/stress-survey.aspx downloaded July 19, 2011.
**Percentage of children estimated by parents to have symptoms.

or embarrassment at being unemployed.[49] We see here the emotional distress and tension that spill over into arguments that can impact children's psychological adaptation to parents' unemployment.

In an American Psychological Association poll including adults and a subsample of parents and their children, both parents and children report increased worries from 2008 to 2009 and an increase in physical symptoms as well.[50] Table 5-1 reveals that almost half the sample of teens reported increased worry, headaches, and difficulties sleeping; these figures were slightly higher for teens than for their parents. Fewer children between eight and twelve years reported increased worry and physical symptoms, but still, between a quarter and a third of elementary school children reported problems.

Note in Table 5-1 that parents greatly underestimate their children's levels of worry and difficulties, believing only a small number of teens have headaches and problems sleeping, when in fact almost half the teens and a third of younger children report such symptoms. Although parents generally understand the specific stressors for children, namely, completing schoolwork and getting good grades, family's having enough money, and concerns about physical appearance and weight, they again underestimate how many children worry about these areas—44 percent, 30 percent, and 22 percent of children respectively report stress in these three areas, but only 34 percent, 18 percent, and 17 percent of parents report children worry about these problems.[51]

Parents are not aware for several reasons. Sometimes children do not tell their parents for fear of increasing their stress levels. One child told her teacher she was worried about having to move and leave her friends, but it was many months before she could tell her mother her worries, the major one being that the family would be homeless.[52] That was mother's worry too. Sometimes, parents dismiss a child's tentative statement about a worry, not having time to listen or not wanting to know that children are in pain because parents feel they cannot do anything about it. Often, parents think children are too young to worry about these things, but they do.

If parents do not know children are worried, they cannot take action to help children cope, and it is parents' support that is helpful. Listening to children's feelings, reassuring them that parents can handle the family problems, pointing out the specific supports the family has available to them, monitoring what is happening in their lives, being warm and supportive in helping children solve their daily problems, finding fun times that do not cost money but bring pleasure and laughs for all are parental actions that enable children to cope with economic stress. Just as parents' mutual support reduces much of the stress of economic worry for them, parents' positive support and caring helps children manage stress, as was seen in the resilient Iowa families.

MANAGING DAILY STRESSES AND NEGATIVE FEELINGS

We are aware that strong emotional reactions like anger or depression affect children's behavior, but we may not be so aware that even negative moods in the course of daily life—such as those caused by the overall challenges of parenting—can also adversely affect parents' interactions with children and children's behavior. Here we look at these daily stresses that are more frequent in the lives of most parents than the large stressors.

Lack of Time

Box 5-1 summarizes changes in patterns of family life as gleaned from analyses of survey data and parents' time diaries from 1965 and 2000.[53] In brief, parents give increasing hours to work and to children and accomplish this by decreasing the amount of time parents spend together as a couple and in leisure activities of their own.

A study using videotaping to understand the daily lives of American families followed thirty-two Southern California, two-parent families with two children during all their waking hours at home for a one-week period. When they analyzed the tapes, researchers found, "Well, life in these trenches is exactly what it looks like: a fire shower of stress, multitasking and mutual nit-picking."[54] In addition to being loving caregivers, parents served as teachers, coaches, and social directors for children. Confirming the information in Box 5-1 that parents focused attention on children, the time each parent spent alone with a child (mothers, 34 percent of time at home and fathers, 25 percent) was parents' most frequent home activity. Mothers spent 23 percent of their time doing housework; fathers, 18 percent; children spent only 3 percent. Stress was least in those families in which mothers and fathers had definite tasks to carry out, but greatest in families who negotiated who would do what on an ongoing basis.

Family members spent only a small amount of time—14 percent—in a room together and rarely ventured into their backyards, which were more peaceful than the homes. Stress, as measured by cortisol sample, decreased rapidly for mothers when they had opportunities in the evening to talk with their husbands about the day's events; fathers' stress levels decreased more slowly in conversations with their wives. Yet parents had only 10 percent of their time alone together.

Observations from this study suggest, as do parents' time diaries, that families feel less stress if parents have more time with each other. Perhaps if children do more household chores, parents will have more time for each other. Families might also feel less stressed if they spent more of their time outdoors as Richard Louv recommends.

Box 5-1
SUMMARY OF CHANGES IN WORK AND FAMILY ACTIVITIES, 1965–2000*

- Both men and women spend increased number of hours in paid work
- Both men and women spend more time with children in direct care and leisure activities
- Both men and women decreased the time they spent with spouses and with friends and community organizations
- Parents enjoy their time with children but 50 percent worry they do not spend enough time with children
- Fifty percent of parents want more time with spouses and 50 percent of fathers and 75 percent of mothers want more time for themselves
- Leisure time (that time available after eating, sleeping, work/school, home care activities) available is 41 hours weekly for children; 35 hours weekly for fathers; and 32 hours weekly for mothers; for parents, leisure time is available in small amounts of time
- Children spend more time weekly (19 hours) in unstructured activities like watching television than in structured activities (8 hours) like sports, artistic activities, clubs

*Suzanne M. Bianchi, John P. Robinson, and Melissa A. Milke, *Changing Rhythms of American Family Life* (New York: Russell Sage, 2006).

Table 5-2 shows that cross-nationally mothers consistently perform more household work and child care than fathers do.[55] The differences are least in countries like Denmark and France where government benefits strongly support families so neither parent works long hours. The differences are most marked in Italy with a

■ **T A B L E 5-2**
AVERAGE NUMBER OF HOURS PER WEEKDAY MOTHERS AND FATHERS SPEND IN BASIC ACTIVITIES*

Country	Paid Work Mothers	Paid Work Fathers	Domestic Work Mothers	Domestic Work Fathers	Child Care Mothers	Child Care Fathers	Total Hours Mos.	Total Hours Fas.
Australia	2.1	7.7	4.6	1.8	4.1	1.3	10.8	10.3
United States	3.5	7.8	3.8	1.6	3.6	1.3	10.9	10.7
Italy	2.1	7.9	4.6	0.6	3.1	1.0	10.8	9.5
Denmark	3.6	6.2	3.1	2.0	3.1	2.0	9.8	9.7
France	2.2	6.0	3.5	2.0	2.6	0.8	8.8	8.3

*Adapted from: Lynn Craig and Killian Mullan, "Parenthood, Gender, and Work-Family Time in the United States, Australia, Italy, France, and Denmark," *Journal of Marriage and Family 72* (2010): 1344–1361.

very traditional culture in which mothers do almost all the housework and child care, and fathers give most of their time to paid work, and in Australia and the United States where government does little to support families.

American mothers and fathers do indeed work hard. When compared to mothers in other countries, American mothers put in almost the maximum number of hours in every sphere of activity, and fathers, while giving many hours to paid work, also do significant amounts of domestic work and child care. So, it is not surprising American families feel stressed. While American parents do have leisure time available to them, it is usually in small chunks so parents have to plan to use it wisely. Unfortunately, many parents use 40 percent of their leisure to watch television that fails to bring a high degree of satisfaction.[56]

Everyday Negative Moods

Minor daily hassles at work or with children contribute to parents' negative moods that in turn affect parenting and children's behavior. Negative moods bias what parents recall about children's past behaviors, shape parents' interpretations of current behavior, and cause parents to discipline children more harshly.[57]

Hassles do not have to be intense or prolonged. In one study, even a briefly induced negative mood reduced mothers' positive comments and verbal interactions with their children during play and laboratory tasks.[58] In another study, being distracted by a simple task involving anagrams resulted in parents' being less positive, more irritable, and more critical of and interfering with their preschoolers.[59]

The hassles that generally trigger a negative mood stem from the daily challenges of parenting rather than major difficulties with children.[60] Hassles fall into two broad categories: (1) the effort required to rear children—continually cleaning up messes, changing family plans, running errands to meet children's needs—and (2) the challenge of dealing with irritating behaviors such as whining, sibling fights, and constant demands.

Parents' personality characteristics, their coping styles, and the amount of support available to them can intensify or decrease stress.[61] Outgoing, sociable, optimistic parents are less likely to respond to hassles with negative moods. Parents who use avoidant coping styles, who wish stress would go away so they wouldn't have to deal with it, experience increased stress. Parents who use positive reappraisal of the situation, who feel they are learning from the situation and becoming more skilled, experience decreased stress and retain their self-confidence.

PARENTS WITH ONGOING NEGATIVE MOODS

All parents have trouble with negative moods in response to stress or family problems. However, some parents suffer with ongoing negative moods like depression, anxiety, and anger that impact children and families on a daily basis. Here we talk about two groups—parents who suffer from depression and parents who are substance-dependent; sometimes parents suffer from both problems. Approximately one in six children lives with either a depressed or substance-dependent parent or both as estimated from statistics described below.

Depressed Parents

Depression is a mood disorder that has as its central feature depressed mood or loss of pleasure and interest in usual activities. To have a diagnosis of Major Depressive Disorder, depressed mood must be accompanied by at least four other symptoms like disturbances in eating and sleeping, loss of weight, energy, and concentration, feelings of guilt and worthlessness, preoccupation with death and thoughts of suicide, lasting for at least two weeks and resulting in an inability to function.[62] Milder symptoms of this kind lasting over a longer period of time justify a diagnosis of dysthymia.

Approximately 10 to 17 percent of mothers have major depressive symptoms during pregnancy, about 7 to 10 percent of mothers have a major depressive episode following the birth of a child, and up to 80 percent of mothers may suffer from postpartum blues.[63] Four percent of fathers in a large sample[64] had a major depressive episode in the first two months following the birth as well, and 7 percent of fathers of one-year-olds endorsed symptoms of depression.[65] For adults in general, at any given time, about 6 percent of women and 3 percent of men suffer from depression.[66]

While past research has focused on mothers' depression, particularly in the early years of children's lives, research interest has expanded to include fathers and to look at the effects of both parents' moods throughout childhood and adolescence. While in the past, there was much interest in the genetic predisposition to depression that parents passed on to children, more recent research has focused on the family environment depressed parents provide for their children.

Risk Factors   Parents' depression affects children in three ways:[67]

- direct biological effects of mothers' depression in pregnancy on infants' neuroendocrine system and patterns of brain wave activity—stress hormones are higher in infants of mothers depressed in last trimester of pregnancy and in the months following birth, children have atypical patterns of frontal brain activity
- genetic predisposition to depression
- social context of children's development—parents' withdrawn, unresponsive behavior with children, harsh and intrusive parenting behaviors, marital conflict, use of avoidance as a means of coping with problems

When compared to children of nondepressed mothers, children of depressed mothers are more likely to[68]

- be fussier, more irritable and tense, less happy as babies
- have higher rates of insecure attachments at twelve months
- have problems with anxiety, withdrawal, social difficulties as preschoolers
- continue to have similar problems in school and also have problems with attention to academic work

Studies looking at how depression is transmitted from one generation to another identify parenting behaviors, marital conflicts, and patterns of family interaction as major factors.[69] Parenting strategies of depressed parents appear to be a main way to transmit problems early in life. Even if children inherit a genetic risk for depression from birth mothers diagnosed with major depression, toddlers do not show the fussy, irritable, unregulated behaviors thought to be the forerunners of depressed symptoms in children when adoptive mothers are highly responsive to their infants. Toddlers at genetic risk did develop the fussy behavior at eighteen months when adoptive mothers were low in responsiveness to their infants. However, adoptive mothers' depressive symptoms during infancy in the absence of genetic risk predicted toddlers' fussy irritability.

When depressed mothers of toddlers were able to maintain positive, responsive interactions with their children, guiding them firmly without harshness, their children's behavior problems decreased over the next three years.[70] Depressed mothers who had nondepressed friends were most likely to maintain positive parenting, perhaps because their friends served as models for parenting. These depressed mothers also found play dates and friends for their children with children of nondepressed mothers.

Studying families with depressed parents over a two-year period suggests that parents' depression initiates a process similar to that of an external stressor like economic loss.[71] Parents' depression triggers parents' feelings of insecurity in close relationships that, in turn, increase marital tension and conflict that is associated with parents' withdrawal from children. Children view the withdrawal as rejection of them and experience negative feelings and adjustment problems. Parents' depression does not trigger children's adjustment problems directly, but it is children's feelings of rejection that trigger adjustment problems.

Depressed mothers of early adolescent children appear more negative, more critical of their children and less positive with them whereas nondepressed mothers of early adolescents appear more positive and less negative.[72] Children in the family appear to model the behavior of their mothers so children of depressed mothers are also more negative and critical.

Protective Factors   Research indicates that the following features of the social context serve as protective factors for children of depressed mothers so they are less likely to experience difficulties:

- effective medication treatment so mothers' depression goes into remission[73]
- parents' use of responsive, positive parenting[74]
- positive marital bond[75]
- patterns of open family communication[76]
- parents' use of active problem-solving strategies to deal with problems instead of avoidance coping strategies[77]
- children's not blaming themselves for parents' problems[78]

Interventions   The first step is to get the depressed parent effective treatment because children's behavior problems improve when parents get treatment. At the same time that the depressed parent gets help, interventions need to be provided to families and children to minimize children's difficulties.

A very effective home intervention in the first year of babies' lives, using the kind of Video-Feedback Positive Parenting program described in Chapter 3 but including eight to ten sessions and massage therapy for infants, focused on helping mothers become more sensitive and responsive to their babies.[79] Home visitors modeled positive behaviors, interpreted babies' behaviors more accurately for mothers, reviewed tapes with mothers, and helped them become more sensitive to their infants. The babies developed secure attachments to their mothers and became more socially competent than babies of depressed mothers who did not have this intervention but did have treatment for their own depression. Treatment for depression by itself does not appear to change the quality of parent-child interactions.

Clinicians designed a prevention program to help depressed parents talk with their children about depression and organize family routines to prevent children's developing depression and the problems associated with it.[80] The thrust of the program designed for children eight and older was to help the family talk about parents' depression, what it was, how it affected all family members and changed their lives, and to emphasize it was nobody's fault. While no one caused the depression, there were things the family could do to make the situation better. A primary purpose was to help children avoid self-blame for parents' problems and thereby reduce children's tendencies to worry and brood.

Parents were guided in helping children form friendships and engage in activities outside the home. Parents were also helped to have more open family communication with their children, paying attention to indications of children's distress and worry and helping them deal with their feelings. Children reported greater understanding of parents' problems. In viewing parents' depression more objectively, children appeared better able to separate themselves from their parents' problems and not feel so responsible. As a result, they felt less self-blame and had fewer worries. Parents' reported changing their behavior in the family, and children benefitted with improvements being greater at the end of the second year than at the end of the first and were maintained over a four and a half year period.[81]

Other researchers following the children of depressed parents into adulthood urge clinicians to see depression as a family affair and to encourage depressed parents to adopt a more active approach to dealing with problems and to teach their children a more active style of coping also.[82] Parents were encouraged to respond to problems not by avoiding them but by clearly identifying the problem, generating solutions, and evaluating the effects of each.

One can see here that the interventions to help depressed parents and their families are the actions all families take to function at their best.

Substance-Dependent Parents

Substance dependence is defined as the compulsive use of substances like nicotine, alcohol, opiates (heroin), and stimulants (amphetamines and cocaine) despite significant negative effects on daily activities, psychological functioning, and health and safety. Physiological dependence on the substance is often present but not essential to the diagnosis of substance dependence.[83]

Approximately 10 percent of pregnancies are affected by alcohol or drug exposure, and a significant number of children live with substance-dependent parents.[84] It is estimated that approximately 9 percent of adults have a substance-dependence problem; 7 percent suffer from alcohol dependence, about 1 percent suffer from drug dependence, and another 1 percent suffer from both alcohol and drug dependence.[85] In addition, many substance-dependent adults also suffer from psychological problems like depression or anxiety.

Risk Factors   Like depression, substance dependence of parents affects children in three main ways:[86]

- the biological effects of drugs directly affect the baby's development in utero, and mothers' physical health, if she is the user, may impact the course of the pregnancy and the prenatal care that she gets

- genetic effects that may predispose child to impulsivity and later substance use; also genetic mutations that may occur as a result of substance abuse

- effects of the social environment substance-dependent parents provide for children and parents' ability to care for child when using; substance dependence is associated with economic instability and poverty, marital conflict, domestic violence, physical abuse, increased likelihood of having a parent with additional psychological problem like depression

It is not surprising that children of substance-dependent parents are at greater risk for biological, intellectual, psychological, and social problems as they grow up. From birth, they may be more irritable and difficult to soothe, and their caregivers may have reduced abilities to give sensitive, responsive care as they are less regulated themselves.[87] Research on a large cohort of children, tracking the effects of risk factors at age one (e.g., maternal mental health, maternal substance abuse, poverty) on children's early development by age three found that it was not any one factor that impacted children's development negatively, but the accumulating number of risks that had the greatest impact.[88] For example, the percentage of children at age three who had scores above the cutoff in anxious/depressed behaviors increased with the number of risk factors: 0 risks (9 percent of children), 1 risk (14 percent), 2 risks (16 percent), and 3 risks (27 percent). Children living with a substance-abusing parent frequently have many risk factors in their lives.

From infancy, children of substance-dependent parents have greater problems managing anxiety and depressed feelings and controlling aggressive behaviors.[89] These problems are likely to continue into early childhood and the school years, when many of these children develop academic problems because of problems with attention and impulsivity.

Michigan researchers combined data from three longitudinal studies that included a sizeable sample of children of alcoholic parents and compared the number and kind of stressors they experienced from the preschool years into young adulthood with a control group of children whose parents were not alcoholics.[90] They found that, compared to controls, children of alcoholic parents experienced:

- a greater number of stressful life events; stress was more severe and began early in life
- stressor events recurred
- many stressor events fell in the area of family interactions and financial problems
- some stressful events resulted from parents' impairments—parent's being arrested or going to jail, neighbors' saying bad things about parent
- stress continued in young adulthood for the children of alcoholics as they were more likely to have family problems, difficulties getting work, and financial problems

Adult children of alcoholics also experience parenting difficulties. Philip Cowan and Carolyn Cowan report that, to their surprise, 20 percent of the parents in their study of couples becoming parents grew up with an alcoholic parent. Although none reported current problems with alcohol, "on every index of adjustment to parenthood—symptoms of depression, self-esteem, parenting stress, role dissatisfaction, and decline in satisfaction with marriage—men and women whose parents had abused alcohol had significantly greater difficulty."[91]

The parents also passed on effects of their growing up to their children (the grandchildren of the alcoholics). Parents saw their preschoolers as less successful, even though objective measures suggested these children functioned as well as others. Growing up in the homes of alcoholic parents who were critical and negative in their views gave these parents unrealistic expectations of their children, so they viewed their typical children as lacking in competence. Over time, one suspects their view will impact the child's behavior and he or she will be less successful.

Protective Factors   In recent years, researchers have begun to look for protective factors that predict resilience in the face of the many stressors these families face.

When living with alcoholic fathers, toddlers who had early secure attachments to mothers at twelve months were less likely to show aggressive and noncompliant behaviors at twenty-four and thirty-six months of age than those toddlers who lived with alcoholic fathers and had insecure attachments to mothers.[92]

When children ages six to twelve lived in families with an alcoholic parent, but the family was able to maintain family cohesiveness and stability and children had secure attachments to parents, parents and observers in school noted these children had fewer social and intellectual problems than those children living with an alcoholic parent in a disorganized family atmosphere, with little support and little emotional security.[93]

Researchers speculate that it is the lack of these positive experiences of family cohesion and stability and close attachments to parents along with parents' depression that account for many of the negative effects associated with living in a family with an alcoholic parent. If parents can protect positive interactions and enjoyable times with children, maintaining family activities and rituals that promote healthy behaviors, children do better.

Interventions　The many risk factors and negative effects for children of substance abusers' behaviors suggest that treatment of substance-dependent adults needs to involve family members and be directed to helping spouses and children even when children are very young.

Many parents who abuse substances feel shame and self-contempt, especially young mothers who are pregnant so they sometimes deny substance problems and do not seek treatment. Women who entered residential treatment and stayed for more than six months when they were pregnant remained abstinent six to twelve months after leaving the program.[94] In addition to treatment for substance dependence, these adults often need psychiatric treatment for the other psychological problems that accompany the substance dependence like depression.

Treatment of substance-dependent mothers often includes attention to parenting skills and to increasing mothers' knowledge of children's development. A review of the effectiveness of parenting programs for substance-dependent mothers of children from birth to age five reveals that while the majority of these programs were effective in helping mothers maintain abstinence, they had little impact on mothers' behaviors with their children or on children's development even though programs were giving information on child development and training parents' skills in behavior management.[95] The one exception in the review was a program that focused on the emotional and mutually responsive relationship between mothers and children.

Researchers then designed an attachment-based parenting program emphasizing the importance of the mother's accurately understanding and responding to children's needs and behaviors.[96] The parenting program was part of an extended, multifaceted outpatient treatment program for heroin-addicted mothers and their toddlers, lasting twenty-eight to forty weeks and providing treatment for substance abuse, psychological problems, and parent-child relationship problems.

The first goal of the program was to form a positive, supportive relationship with the mother, providing her with a therapist who made referrals for services and helped to solve problems.

With a positive bond established, the focus was to help mothers become more reflective about their own reactions to their children and events and help them to be more sensitive and responsive to their toddlers' behavior. Through questioning, and active listening, therapists drew out mothers' underlying beliefs about themselves, their children, and the events that occurred in their lives. Mothers were encouraged to examine and question these beliefs and to develop a fuller picture of their child's behavior. As mothers became more reflective about their behavior and their children's reactions, they became more sensitive and responsive to their children's distress, and children did not have to work so hard to communicate their needs to get parents' help. There were indications mothers' psychological adjustment and substance abuse improved as well. In many ways this program was a longer version of the attachment-based, positive parenting program developed in The Netherlands (see pages 103 in Chapter 3).

Since many adults with substance abuse problems do not have insurance coverage for treatment programs, county, state, and community programs are especially important sources for treatment. One of the most effective treatment programs, available free of charge, is Alcoholics Anonymous that for decades has provided a variety of services for families and children as well as for substance-dependent adults. Their emphasis on helping the family understand the problems aims as the depression program did, to remove the responsibility from spouses and children so they do not blame themselves for a problem they cannot control. Their website, www.aa.org, gives information on services for the individual and family available around the world.

In the electronic age, the Internet provides information on the nature of substance abuse, its causes and treatments, and guidelines for helping friends and family members. An excellent website that children and teens can consult is www.kidshealth.org; its well-written presentation in question-and-answer format covers all the questions a worried child or teen or parent might ask as well as guidelines of what to do to help both the substance abuser and the concerned family member.

DEVELOPING A SUPPORT SYSTEM

When parents receive support from friends, relatives, and each other, they experience less stress and fewer negative moods. The support may come from organized parenting groups, discussed in the next chapter. Or support may come from family members like a spouse, grandparents, extended family, neighbors, and the community, including the broad Internet community.

Grandparents as Supports

Outside the child's nuclear family, grandparents are the most important figures in most families. Grandparents influence grandchildren directly when they serve as caregivers, playmates, and family historians who pass on information that solidifies a sense of generational continuity. They are a direct influence when they act as mentors to their grandchildren and when they negotiate between parent and child. They influence grandchildren indirectly when they provide both psychological and material support to parents, who then have more resources for parenting. Grandmothers who do not live with grandchildren but have high levels of contact with them can provide the indirect support grandchildren facing certain risks need.[97] For example, preschool grandchildren who were easily frustrated and emotionally reactive children at risk for social problems were able to develop abilities to compromise and cooperate with others when they had contact with grandmothers. Also relationships with grandmothers appeared to protect children from the effects of mothers' harsh parenting. When preschoolers whose mothers used harsh discipline had contact with grandmothers, they did not develop the noncompliant, aggressive, defiant behaviors that children of these mothers often show. Grandmothers' love, affection, and support buffer these children with special risks so they are able to develop competence.

Because minority families interact more with extended family members, more information on the role of grandparents in such families is available than for other families. The extended family often includes one or both grandparents. Grandmothers

Grandparents provide positive emotional support for both parents and grandchildren.

help families nurture and care for children in a less structured, more spontaneous way than is possible when only two generations are present. The grandparents' role depends on whether one or both parents live in the home.[98]

In general, contacts between grandparents and grandchildren vary, depending on the age, health, and proximity of the grandparents.[99] Grandparents typically see their grandchildren once or a few times a month. Although a few studies suggest that only a small percentage of grandparents enjoy close, satisfying relationships with their grandchildren, many other studies indicate that young adults generally feel close to grandparents (averaging 4 on a 5-point scale of emotional closeness) and that "the grandchild–grandparent bond continues with surprising strength into adulthood."[100]

Geographic proximity is the most important predictor of the nature of the relationship.[101] When grandparents live close by, contact naturally increases. When grandparents are young and healthy enough to share activities, grandchildren feel close because of the shared fun. At the same time, when grandparents are older and in poorer health, grandchildren feel close because they can help them.

Gender plays a role in such relationships. Grandmothers are more likely to be involved with grandchildren than are grandfathers, and they appear to play a powerful role in children's well-being.[102] Anthropological research presented at an international conference on grandmothers indicates that the involvement of grandmothers and older female kin enhance the lives of their grandchildren. In one study, the presence of the maternal grandmother increased childhood survival at age six to 96 percent; the survival figure for homes without grandmothers was 83 percent.[103] The presence of the paternal grandmother did not change the childhood survival rates.

When grandchildren are very young, they see grandparents as sources of treats and gifts. When grandchildren are in elementary school, they look to grandparents to share fun activities with them, and in early adolescence, they also take pleasure in sharing a variety of activities with them. Grandchildren often see grandparents as more patient and understanding than their parents, and contemporary grandparents try to live up to this expectation.[104] They seek to be supportive to grandchildren rather than intrusive and critical. A grandparent can become particularly close at times of family change and serve as confidant and advocate for the child who could become lost in the chaos of events (see Chapter 14).

Community Supports for Parents

Most people in the community realize that raising children in today's world is a hard job. Over 70 percent of a national sample of 1,400 adults reported that adults in the community can play an important role by forming relationships with children, conversing with them, encouraging them to do well in school, and commenting on their positive behaviors. Only 5 percent, however, take any actions like this in their community.[105]

So parents have to organize their own community support network for their children. Suggestions for how to do this are presented in Box 5-2. In Chapter 3, we discussed the Internet community that parents can consult for help as was just done with substance-dependent parents; websites were given that can be extremely useful to families with a variety of problems. We discuss community support for parents in Chapters 9, 10, and 13 as well.

How Do Children Define a Good Parent?

Thus far we have looked at close relationships from the point of view of how a parent promotes them. Let us look at the qualities children of different ages say they want in the "good parent" or "good mother."

Preschoolers interviewed about the qualities of a good and a bad mommy and daddy suggest that good parents are physically affectionate and nurturant, especially in providing food for children. In addition, good parents like to play games with their children and read to them, and they discipline them—that is, they keep children from doing things they should not, but they do not spank them or slap them in the face. Bad parents have the opposite qualities. They do not hug or kiss, do not fix food, do not play games. They hit and do not let children go outside. Bad parents are also described as irresponsible—they go through red lights, throw chairs at people, and do not read the newspaper.[106]

As children grow older, they continue to value physical nurturing and affection, but they also appreciate qualities reflecting psychological nurturing. Mothers' good qualities include "understanding feelings and moods," "being there when I need

Box 5-2
BUILDING COMMUNITY SUPPORT FOR CHILDREN*

Parents and children profit when adults in the community take an interest in children and take actions to engage in relationships with them and support them in their activities. When such support is not immediately available, parents can take the following actions to create it for children.

- Encourage extended family members to take an interest in your children. Invite them to your children's special events—birthdays, school, and athletic events. Invite them to join you and your family for events of mutual interest.
- Take an active role in supporting the friends of your children. Tell their parents about their special qualities or positive actions that you have observed. Ask the children about their interests and views about things.
- In your neighborhood, set an example of how you want adults to relate to your children by relating in that way to other children and their parents. Get to know children's names, their special interests—hire teenagers to do extra chores, organize and participate in block parties that include all generations. Organize families to accomplish a needed neighborhood chore such as cleaning up debris after a storm or shoveling snow on sidewalks.
- As appropriate, encourage older children to ask parents of friends about career satisfactions, advice about specific colleges or graduate schools, or part-time jobs.
- Get to know your neighbors. Help them get to know your children and have your children get to know them (e.g., speaking politely to them, offering to do favors for them). As appropriate, involve neighbors in your children's lives. Invite them to events in your home such as a dinner or watching a sporting event of interest. Invite them to school events of interest.

*Adapted from: Peter C. Scales, Peter L. Benson, and Eugene C. Roehlkepartain, *Grading Grown-Ups: American Adults Report on Their Real Relationships with Kids* (Minneapolis, MN: Lutheran Brotherhood and Search Institute, 2001), 57.

her," and "sticking up for me." Children continue to emphasize the limit-setting behaviors in a good mother—"She makes us eat fruit and vegetables," "She yells at me when I need it"—but they want their mother to consider their needs and wishes in setting the rules. Older children still enjoy mutual recreational time—playing, joking, building things together. Finally, as children get older, they appreciate the teaching activities of the good mother.[107]

When early adolescents and their parents talked in a group about their definitions of a good parent, they agreed on several qualities. Early adolescents' definitions touched on three main themes: attention to the child's feelings and individuality, spending time together, and parents' self-control. For early teens, the good parent is one who "listens," "respects you for who you are," "gives you a hug when you are sad." These teens emphasized spending time together, going places together, and having a parent who "knows when to be silly, not always serious." They saw the good parent as one who "manages their temper," "doesn't bark at you," "knows when to stop talking," and "tells you what they want you to do before you have to do it."

In sum, children's descriptions of the good parent point to three main areas: being a sensitive caregiver, a social partner, and a person with self-control.

MAIN POINTS

Physical touch and closeness
- help infants stabilize their functioning after birth
- help colicky babies with sleep problems develop longer sleep periods at night and greater alertness during the day
- help adults reduce anxiety and depression and reduce stress

Positive feelings
- help people be more understanding and sympathetic
- contribute to later psychological health and physical health
- contribute to problem-solving skills and social skills

Close emotional ties rest on the parent's love for the child
- as a unique person
- as expressed in sensitive daily care and in becoming a social partner
- in the sharing of feelings and thoughts and stories about what is happening

Understanding and expressing feelings
- involves listening to children's feelings and expressing one's own
- is avoided by parents who are dismissive, disapproving, or laissez-faire
- involves five steps of identifying, labeling, and validating feelings and helping the child find appropriate ways to express them
- helping brothers and sisters to use these skills to have better relationships

Mutual problem solving
- involves respecting and understanding others' feelings and points of view
- finding solutions that satisfy both individuals' needs
- evaluating results and changing if necessary

Resolving marital conflicts constructively includes
- awareness of widespread effects of conflicts on partner and children
- talking with respect and empathy for others' feelings
- using humor and kindness to find solutions that meet everyone's needs

Sudden economic loss affects families through a chain of events that follow from the stressor:
- stressor triggers depression in parent that disrupts marital bond
- marital tension spills over onto parenting, and parents becomes harsher and less involved with children

- children develop behavior problems
- that need not be negative if parents maintain a strong, supportive marital bond
- and are similar in different countries with different social organizations

Managing daily stresses includes dealing with

- stress from lack of time with family members
- daily hassles

Strategies for dealing with negative feelings include

- using family time for satisfying activities
- using communication skills to express feelings appropriately
- developing a support system
- learning to deal with negative feelings

Depressed and substance-dependent parents

- affect children's development through the biological, genetic, and environmental influences parents' behavior has on children
- reduce the risks to children when parents have a positive marital bond and form a stable, cohesive pattern of family interactions
- reduce risks to children when they get treatment that controls their symptoms
- reduce risks when they use positive, sensitive parenting strategies and stay engaged with children
- without treatment increase the risk of their children's having similar kinds of problems from an early age and extending into adulthood

Children see the good parent as

- a sensitive caregiver and effective limit setter
- a social partner
- a person with self-control

EXERCISES

1. Imagine a time when you were a child and felt very close to one of your parents (if you like, you can do the exercise for each of your parents), and describe your parent's behavior with you. What qualities of your parent created the closeness? Share these qualities with class members. Is there a common core? If you do this exercise with each of your parents, note gender differences. Have your mother and father at times shown different qualities of closeness with you? Have your classmates experienced differences in their mothers' and fathers' behavior toward sons and daughters?

2. Imagine a time when you were a child and felt distant from one of your parents (again, you can do this for each of your parents), and describe

your parent's behavior with you. What qualities of your parent created the distance? Again, share these qualities with class members and find the common core. Are these qualities the opposite of qualities that lead to closeness, or do they represent a variety of dimensions? Do the qualities you discovered in Exercises 1 and 2 support what clinicians and researchers say is important?

3. Take turns practicing active listening with a classmate. Have a partner active-listen as you describe one or several of the following situations, and then you active-listen as your partner does the same: (a) Describe a time when you were upset as a child, (b) describe negative feelings in a recent exchange, (c) describe scenes you have witnessed between parents and children in stores or restaurants, (d) follow the directions your instructor hands out for what one child in a problem situation might say.

4. With a classmate, practice sending I-messages. Again, choose from a variety of situations: (a) Recall a situation when a parent was angry at you when you were growing up and describe I-messages your parent might have sent, (b) recount a recent disagreement with a friend or instructor and give appropriate I-messages. (c) describe public parent-child confrontations you have witnessed and devise appropriate I-messages for the parents, (d) devise I-messages for problem situations presented by your instructor.

5. Plan three fun activities for a family of four, including two children, aged five and eight. One activity should be in the home, one in the outdoors, and one in the community.

ADDITIONAL READINGS

Bianchi, Suzanne M., Robinson, John P., and Milkie, Melissa A. *Changing Rhythms of American Family Life.* New York: Russell Sage Foundation, 2006.

Doherty, William J. *The Intentional Family.* New York: Avon, 1997.

Engel, Susan. *The Stories Children Tell.* New York: Freeman, 1999.

Gottman, John M., and DeClaire, Joan. *The Heart of Parenting: Raising an Emotionally Intelligent Child.* New York: Simon & Schuster, 1997.

Honore, Carl. *Under Pressure: Rescuing Our Children from the Culture of Hyper-Parenting.* New York: HarperCollins, 2008.

Louv, Richard. *Last Child in the Woods: Saving Our Children from Nature-Deficit Disorder,* rev. ed. Chapel Hill, NC: Algonquin Books of Chapel Hill, 2008.

6

Supporting Children's Growth and Development

CHAPTER TOPICS

- Parents' Roles in Supporting Children's Growth
- Creating a Collaborative Family Atmosphere
- Influences on Parents' Behavior
- Healthy Lifestyles
- Getting the Benefits Media Can Provide
- Tool Chest for Dealing with Parent-Child Conflicts
- Parenting Programs
- Keeping Children Safe

Test Your Knowledge: Fact or Fiction (True/False)

1. Parents believe they are doing as good a job raising their children as their parents did with them.
2. When people see signs that others do not follow rules, they are less likely to follow rules.
3. Parents who spank their children have not learned to use positive methods like reasoning when children fail to follow family rules.
4. Children's media use climbed rapidly and reached its present height in 2004 where it has remained with only a slight increase in the last several years.
5. Effective, evidence-based parenting programs are available no matter where parents live.

Parents want children to be healthy, responsible individuals, caring of others and themselves, and believe it is their responsibility to help children develop these qualities. With the hectic pressures of life today, however, parents report they are not doing as good a job as their parents did.[1] They would like more skills to do the job and to control outside influences, like television, that interfere with what they are trying to teach children. This chapter focuses on how parents can accomplish their goals.

In this chapter we look at the many roles parents take on to rear their children to become responsible, caring adults according to the values of their cultural group.

PARENTS' ROLES IN SUPPORTING CHILDREN'S GROWTH

In the last chapter we saw that parents' positive emotional relationships with each other and with their children, and the emotional tone of the family, are the heart of the social context in which children develop. Here we look at the many other actions parents take to help children grow.

Models for Children

Folk wisdom has long advised parents to do and be what they want their children to become. As we saw in Chapter 3, mirror neurons make it likely that children will copy parents' behavior, and as we shall see in this chapter and others, children copy parents eating behaviors, their exercise habits, and their values.

New research suggests that not only do people copy what they see others do, they also copy what they think others have done based on seeing the results of their actions.[2] In studies in the community, Dutch researchers demonstrated that people are more likely to litter or steal when they see signs other people have broken community rules. For example, 33 percent of people threw flyers they received on the ground when no graffiti appeared on a building wall, but 69 percent of people littered when graffiti appeared on a wall next to a sign saying "No Graffiti." People were twice as likely to steal an envelope sticking out of a mailbox showing a 5 Euro note when graffiti covered the mailbox or when papers littered the ground as when there was no graffiti or littering (27 percent compared to 13 percent). While these studies were done with adults, children are as likely to be influenced by signs of disorder as adults.

So children copy what they see others do and what they think others have done based on signs of order or disorder, so parents have to be sure their behavior and the environment they provide for children reflect the qualities they want children to develop.

Socializers of Children's Behavior

Parents help children learn the cognitive and social-emotional skills needed to become valued members of the social community, a process termed socialization. Joan Grusec and Maayan Davidov describe five kinds of parenting behaviors that socialize children:[3]

- relieving children's distress so they feel protected
- establishing reciprocal interactions and agreeing to children's reasonable demands so they learn to reciprocate when others make requests

- using appropriate disciplinary techniques so children develop self-control
- matching teaching style to children's developmental level so they internalize what is taught
- including children in social and cultural activities so they learn family and culture's values and a sense of social identity

Parents carry out these behaviors so children not only learn to manage their feelings and behavior to comply with society's rules but also have the capacity to enjoy good feelings and behave in giving ways to others.

Initiators of Children's Developmental Pathways

George Holden describes parents' roles in child rearing as initiators and supporters of children's developmental pathways or trajectories.[4] Recall in Chapter 1 we saw that parents' interactions with children can set children on a developmental trajectory, defined as a path of behavior extending through time. For example, harsh, critical parents tended to stimulate anger, impulsivity, and noncompliance in their children who grew up to be harsh, critical parents.

Pathways may encompass a broad range of behaviors like the pathway to academic success or the pathway to social competence, or they may include a narrow range of behaviors like the pathway to soccer success. Many pathways begin in infancy or early childhood like the pathway to emotional competence, but some may begin later like the pathway to community service.

Parents initiate pathways by the activities and experiences they organize and provide for children. This sounds like a very planned undertaking, and for some parents it is. They think about children's needs and their own cultural values, e.g., wanting children to follow in the family tradition of being health-care providers or athletes, and they consciously decide what to do, giving a little child a doctor's kit or a baseball bat. For other parents initiating a pathway is less planned, and in some cases is triggered by outside events that set both parents and children off on a pathway as happened when sudden economic loss triggered a host of negative changes that were shaped by parents' abilities to remain supportive marital partners and active problem-solvers.

Children's temperamental qualities and their behaviors also influence trajectories; for example, some children may be more irritable and have a harder time learning self-control so require more support and guidance from parents in order to progress on the path. Children's own interests may initiate a pathway that parents then support.

The advantage of Holden's model of parents as initiators of developmental trajectories is that it includes a great variety of activities and roles for parents such as teacher, coach, adviser, social director, model, mediator, and consultant. The model also emphasizes how certain behaviors may put a child on a path that sustains the behavior. For example, as we will see, parents put children on a path to emotional, social, and academic competence when they ensure babies and young children eat healthy foods, get sound and adequate amounts of sleep, and engage in physical activity. For these reasons we focus on these seemingly unimportant daily activities.

INFLUENCES ON PARENTS' BEHAVIOR

Experts' views of parents' roles are not the only influences on parents' activities.

Parents' Beliefs about Children and Parenting

As we saw in Chapters 1 to 3, many influences—values and goals of cultural and social groups, personal experiences in families growing up, media, friends, experts, and children themselves shape parents' beliefs about how they should carry out their many roles.

When parents believe that children can control their behavior and actions and that misbehavior is due to children's deliberate decision to get their own way, then parents are harsher and angrier in disciplining their children than those parents who believe misbehavior is due to immaturity.[5] When mothers have great concern about spoiling and being too responsive to their six-month-old infants, they are less likely to provide the amount of nurturance infants require to regulate their feelings, and these babies are less likely to regulate their feelings and behavior as toddlers.[6]

Sometimes parents change their views based on their experience with their children. Two-thirds of mothers of three-year-olds report they changed their views about spanking since having children.[7] Half the group became more positive about spanking because they felt their strong-minded and independent child needed a strong parental action to get their attention and change their behavior. The half who became more negative about spanking changed because they felt their child did not respond well to the spanking.

Parents' beliefs themselves may become risk factors for children. If parents believe very strongly in not spoiling a child, or see an infant determined to thwart parent's control, then harsh physical punishment may be more likely.[8] As we shall see later in the chapter, many parenting programs seek to influence parents' beliefs about children.

Children's Qualities

As we emphasized in Chapter 3, and it is important to recall, children's genetic/temperamental constitution influences both parents' behaviors and parents' effectiveness. For example, fussy, irritable infants may place more demand on parents for action, and children's responsiveness may shape the effectiveness of parents' actions.[9] Children with the DRD4–7 repeat allele react more strongly to the quality of the parenting they receive: when parents are insensitive, children react negatively and become more noncompliant and disruptive; conversely, when parents are sensitive, children respond with greater regulation. Children who have heightened sensitivity to the autonomic or adrenocortical nervous systems are also more sensitive to their environments.

So parents must anticipate that their actions may not have the same results with their children as other parents experience with their children, and that is why parents have to reflect and evaluate the effects as we describe in a problem-solving process at the end of the chapter.

CREATING A COLLABORATIVE FAMILY ATMOSPHERE

Psychologists have identified a family atmosphere of collaboration that enhances children's growth and enables them to learn the lessons parents most want to teach.

An Emotional Climate of Mutual Responsiveness

Parents create a family culture of cooperation and mutual responsiveness from the earliest days of the child's life. Sensitive parents provide responsive care that meets children's individual needs. Such care creates harmonious parent-child relationships and helps to establish a secure attachment between parent and child.[10] That attachment, in turn, encourages cooperation and a willingness to attend to parents' requests since parents attend to children's.

Although it is easier to establish an atmosphere of receptive compliance when children are infants, it is possible to create such an atmosphere when children are elementary-school students and teenagers. Recall the discussion of Gerald Patterson's work in Chapter 3, which indicated that parents can create a positive atmosphere of collaboration with school-aged children by paying positive attention to their behavior, spending time in enjoyable activities, encouraging them in their activities (discussed on page 102),[11] and engaging in problem solving when problems arise. All these actions increase children's willingness to listen and comply with rules.

Routines

Thomas Weisner, a cultural anthropologist, believes that regardless of what culture one lives in, parents promote family well-being and children's growth when they establish everyday routines and activities that:

- meet everyone's needs with the least amount of conflict
- are within the family's resources of time and money to perform regularly
- meet cultural goals and values
- are sustainable on an ongoing basis[12]

No matter how useful a routine might be to a family, if the family does not have the time or the money to carry it out regularly—e.g., daily exercise at a community health club—it is useless to plan it. It is better to schedule activities like family walks at a local park two evenings during the week and a hike one afternoon on a weekend, activities that fit the family time and money budget. Similarly, it might be fun to stay up late at night and sleep in in the morning, but children have to be on time for school.

Routines are defined as regularly occurring patterned interactions that accomplish a practical goal—eating, getting sleep, carrying out chores.[13] Routines may not have symbolic or emotional investment for families in the beginning, but often they become important family rituals, special ways of carrying out tasks that everyone enjoys—special family dinners and breakfasts, special bedtime routines.

Making children partners in routines as soon as they can participate contributes to a collaborative atmosphere.[14] Parents can show infants how to cooperate in dressing by guiding them through the actions in a playful way and letting them push their arm through a sleeve or stick their head out of the top of a shirt. Toddlers like to help, and many parents discourage their participation because everything takes longer, but finding small tasks to include young children in routines helps them develop a clearer idea or a script of the behaviors that make up the family routines around eating, picking up, and cleaning.

Parents can talk about the rules and the reasons for them so children can understand why they are important. Even when children are young and cannot understand the exact words, the tone of voice indicates there is a routine to follow.[15] As children gain greater verbal understanding, clarity about the purpose of the rules and the effects on others when rules are not followed help children remember the rules and follow them. Talking when everyone's emotions are calm increases the likelihood children will hear and take in what parents are saying. Conversation in the midst of conflict is not as useful.

At times of actual misbehavior and rule breaking, verbal strategies of discipline have many benefits. Children's social and emotional competence grows and they are able to internalize the rules when mothers remain calm, use reasoning, and avoid threats and physical force. Forcing children with yelling and angry gestures increases children's frustration and defiance.

Routines structure family life, and are especially important at times of transition, e.g., to parenthood or to single parenthood. Single parents who maintained routines around eating, bedtime, and doing things together felt more successful as single parents, and their children functioned better.[16]

Organized routines also increase children's academic competence.[17] For example, routines of dinnertime meals, reading aloud and for pleasure, and homework routines made up what was termed the "intimate family culture" and when carried out from the beginning of school significantly predicted children's reading skills in Grade 3; most of the variability in scores was attributed to family income and ethnicity. When children from families with fewer resources had the intimate culture of families with middle-class resources, children with limited resources improved in reading at the same rate as middle-class children. Box 6-1 describes the many psychological benefits to family members of having regular family meals together and how parents and communities can protect these routines.

Encouragement

Drawing on the insights of Alfred Adler, the first of Freud's followers to modify psychoanalytic theory and focus on individuals' healthy, purposive, and social behavior, Rudolf Dreikurs proposed positive child-rearing strategies that rely on

Box 6-1
FAMILY MEALS NOURISH MORE THAN OUR BODIES*

Family mealtimes, lasting on average twenty minutes and occurring in the majority of homes three to five times a week, serve as an example of how simple activities that are part of everyday life can be powerful forces in promoting children's development and well-being when they are consistent, well-planned, and enjoyable occasions without the distractions of television and other electronic devices.

Having family meals together predicts many positive aspects of children's development. For all children, family mealtimes are associated with healthier eating habits and better health. For young children, organized mealtimes predict language development; for school-aged children, academic achievement; and for teens, reduced risk of smoking, marijuana use, and alcohol abuse. It is thought that the benefits come from the family's being together, sharing events of the day, and growing closer through better understanding of each others' lives. When the television is left on, as some parents do to decrease conflict between children, some of the health benefits are lost.

The topics of conversation change as children grow older. With young children, parents can talk about what happened at home and in the neighborhood; when children are school-aged, school activities and time with friends can be major topics as well as planning family activities on the weekend. As children move into adolescence, parents can talk with them about current events and, possible work activities as well as teens' social activities. Parents talk about their lives as well. They can share work anecdotes that help children understand what it is parents enjoy about their jobs; children often hear much about the stresses of work, but they do not hear about the satisfactions. Families can also talk about community volunteering and selecting an activity that the family can do as a whole.

Home and community obstacles interfering with regular mealtimes include parents' work schedules that prevent getting home for dinner, children's school schedules with sports and other activities at the dinner hour, and family's busy schedules that allow little preparation time for meals. Parents can surmount the obstacles by coordinating work schedules so that one parent is at home for meals. Parents and children can use food shopping, selection, and preparation as times spent together bonding and learning more about nutrition and healthy foods.

Researchers make six recommendations for community actions to support families' efforts in establishing regular mealtimes together:

- support local zoning laws and food labeling programs that allow for healthy food choices in all neighborhoods
- communities and schools work together to reserve one night a week for family meals either with no school or community events scheduled at mealtimes or scheduled events include the whole family and dinner, sending a strong message that family meals are important
- primary care providers like pediatricians talk with parents and educate them about the importance of such actions as turning off television and cell phones, expecting appropriate dinner table behavior of children, encouraging conversations with children of all ages

(continued)

> **Box 6-1**
> # CONTINUED
>
> - advertising and marketing industries encourage healthy eating, partnering with communities to publicize benefits of family mealtimes and healthy foods
> - state and local governments can work to promote food sufficiency for all families and promote healthy mealtimes in under-served communities
> - encourage the Federal government to include healthy family mealtimes as part of its reauthorization of the Child Nutrition Act.
>
> *Adapted from: Barbara H. Fiese and Marlene Schwartz, "Reclaiming the Family Table: Mealtimes and Child Health and Well Being," *Social Policy Report 22* (2008): 3–9, 13–18.

encouragement to stimulate children's built-in capacities to develop healthy, effective behaviors.[18] Because children naturally seek to develop their abilities and become competent and important members in the family, parents' main tasks are to provide an environment for growth and to avoid the use of parental power to force or punish children.

A central feature in the growth-promoting environment is encouragement, which Dreikurs defined as "a continuous process aimed at giving the child a sense of self-respect and a sense of accomplishment."[19] Parents' tone of voice in speaking to children, their gestures, their affection, their willingness to play with children all communicate to children that they are valued and well-loved family members.

Parents provide encouragement when they (1) give children independence to act on their own—even babies can have opportunities to amuse themselves, feed themselves, and as toddlers, share in family chores so they learn their own capabilities, (2) identify the child's positive contributions and help—"It's a real help when you empty the waste baskets," or "Thank you for taking the napkins to the table," and (3) teach children to ask for what they need so parents can better meet the needs. "Tell me what is upsetting you so we can see what can be done."

Parents encourage children by teaching them how to do basic self-care routines and chores—like dressing themselves or making a bed. Parents anticipate that children will need time to develop skills, and they do not criticize or tear down children's confidence with statements like, "I can do it for you faster," or "You are too little to set the table." When children are frustrated with the process of learning, parents call attention to the challenge of the task and to the gains the child is making. "Practicing the piano is hard in the beginning, but you are learning all the scales, and you are able to play more pieces."

In all families, children make mistakes. Dreikurs describes parents' tendencies to overemphasize these errors by pointing out every minor mistake and continually telling children what they must do to improve.[20] Under such a regime, children may feel they have to be perfect in order to gain acceptance and such a fear can keep children from trying activities because mistakes are so painful. Dreikurs believes children need to learn the courage to be imperfect, to accept mistakes.

INTERVIEW
with Susan Harter

Susan Harter, a professor of psychology at the University of Denver, has spent twenty years studying the development of the self and self-esteem and has written numerous articles and chapters on the subject.

You have done a great deal of research on self-esteem. More than any other quality, I would say, parents hope to help children develop self-esteem. What can they do to promote it in their children?

We have identified two broad themes that impact children's self-esteem. First, the unconditional support and positive regard of parents and others in the child's world are particularly critical during the early years. What do we mean by support? It is communicating to children that you like them as people for who or what they are.

That sounds relatively easy but is in fact extremely difficult. Most of us as parents are far more skilled at providing conditional regard or support for children even though we are unaware we are doing it. We approve of our child if he cleans up his room or shares or doesn't hit his brother. So our support is conditional on his conduct. However, it isn't perceived by children as supportive at all. Basically it specifies how the child can please the parents. That does not feel good to children.

Unconditional regard validates children as worthy people and lets them know they are appreciated for who they are, for their strengths and weaknesses. It also involves listening to them, which is very validating to children as well as adults. So many well-meaning parents, and I make the same mistake, preach at their kids because we think we have a lot to say. We think we're teaching when we are really preaching. We don't refrain from talking; we don't shut up, listen well, and take the child's point of view seriously.

With unconditional support early on, children internalize positive regard so that when they are older, they can approve of themselves, pat themselves on the back, give themselves psychological hugs—all of which contribute to high self-esteem.

Another major part of self-esteem, beginning at about age eight, is feeling competent and adequate across the various domains of life. One does not have to feel competent in every domain in order to experience high self-esteem. Rather, one needs to feel competent in those domains that he or she judges to be *important*. Profiles of competence for two children in the different areas of athletic, social, and intellectual competence can look very similar, but one child can have high self-esteem while the other can have low self-esteem. They both can feel competent in the same areas and feel inadequate in the same other areas. What distinguishes the low self-esteem child is the fact that areas of incompetence are very important to his or her feeling of being worthwhile; thus the child doesn't feel good about himself or herself. The high self-esteem child feels the low areas are very unimportant and so still feels good about himself or herself.

According to Dreikurs, mistakes are incompletions, not failures. They are signs that the child is trying to do something, exerting effort, but is not quite ready to do the task completely. The child may need more time to learn or practice a skill. Though unfortunate in that they take up time and sometimes cost money, mistakes are valuable because a child learns what is not effective. In addition, many warm family memories center on mistakes that were overcome. So parents help children figure out what the next step is.

Sensitive Discipline

Femmie Juffer, Marian Bakermans-Kranenburg, and Marinus Van IJzendoorn have combined concepts of attachment theory with the learning concepts of Gerald Patterson described in Chapter 2 to help parents and children gain control of impulsive, aggressive, inhibited behaviors. While designed for parents of toddlers, the program's positive emphasis in discipline can be adapted for parents of older children. The program emphasizes the following basic guidelines for parents:[21]

1. Use reasoning to help children understand the need for rules and routines and the benefits for all that come from following the rules, saying, for example, "We all need to go to bed at our bedtime, even Mom and Dad, so we will get enough sleep and have energy to play and work tomorrow."

2. Help children refocus attention on positive alternatives when they are frustrated—e.g., when children are hungry and insist on eating cookies just before dinner, parents can say, "Why not help me set the table so we can eat sooner," or "You can clean a carrot and eat that."

3. Pay attention to the many times that children follow rules and engage in positive actions, and express appreciation for their behavior.

4. Empathize with children's feelings, desires, and stage of life and verbalize what you think they might be feeling. "I know it's hard to have your little brother grab your cars and play with them, then forget where he left them, so you can't find them." Or, "I know it's hard to have to do chores before you leave the house on Saturday morning. Maybe we can find a different time."

5. Help children withdraw from a tantrum or angry confrontation by taking a time-out in the living room or hallway. Parents must stay calm and say they will be available for talk or play when the time-out is finished. When they are young, children spend one minute for each year of children's age in time-out. With older children, parents and children can take a time out to cool down and discuss the problem in half an hour or later.

6. Talk to children during routines, explaining them, answering questions, especially if the routine is not a happy one like going to the dentist.

7. Give children advance warnings when it is time to shift activities and give choices when possible.

8. Be available for play and fun.

HEALTHY LIFESTYLES

In the United States, life expectancy increased from forty-five years in 1900 to seventy-eight years in 2007,[22] resulting primarily from the prevention of illnesses through immunizations, improved nutrition, increased exercise, and better housing and drinking water and not from improved medical treatment of illnesses.[23]

Establishing physically healthy environments and health-promoting behaviors are major parental tasks though only 68 percent think it is essential to teach healthy eating habits, and 51 percent think it essential to teach good exercise habits.[24] Genetic factors and cultural values regarding physical appearance and activity play a role in how easily or how diligently habits are practiced. Still, establishing healthy eating, sleeping, and exercise habits in children promotes competent functioning in all areas and prepares children for a lifetime of health.

Parents initiate a pathway to health for their children by providing a healthy environment with nutritious foods, modeling healthy behaviors, establishing routines that enable children to develop healthy habits, and helping children overcome roadblocks on the pathway to health like watching too much television. Young parents themselves, however, often do not practice healthy eating and exercise habits. Pressed for time, they get less exercise than young adults without children, and mothers report eating more sugar-sweetened drinks and high-fat foods so they have higher mean Body Mass Indexes (BMI) than women without children.[25] Health-care providers are advised to encourage young parents to follow healthy exercise and eating habits both to improve their health and to enable their behaviors to serve as models for their children.

In talking with parents about the importance of these activities, health-care and parent educators are encouraged to go beyond talking about fitness and fatness, and emphasize the other benefits that come from physical activity and sleep such as intellectual skills, social skills, and emotional well-being.[26]

Safety

Safety measures are the first concern because injuries are the leading cause of death in children and teens and kill more children than all other diseases combined, and many injuries are preventable.[27] Not only do children die from injuries, they also suffer physical trauma requiring hospitalizations, ongoing medical care, lengthy recuperations, and lifelong impairments. Initially people thought injuries were the result of random accidents. About forty years ago, however, safety experts realized that like illnesses, injuries could be prevented.

Figure 6-1 describes the major health hazards to children and teens, and actions parents take to reduce injuries. Injury prevention is stressed in parenting books for parents of young children, but receives less attention in books for parents of teens.[28]

In addition to providing a safe home and teaching safety habits, parents monitor their own behavior so that their cigarette, alcohol, and drug use do not present a risk to children as well as to their abilities to care for their children.[29]

Eating

Eating nutritious foods in moderate amounts promotes motor and cognitive development in childhood and adolescence. Poorly nourished children are less physically active and they perform more poorly on measures of attention span and short-term memory.[30] Adults poorly nourished in childhood continue to show lower performance on cognitive tests than well-nourished adults.

Healthy eating habits are especially important now because currently between 20 and 30 percent of children in developed countries are overweight.[31] California's

■ **FIGURE 6-1**
WAYS TO PREVENT ACCIDENTS AND INJURIES*

Bedroom

1. Install devices that prevent windows from opening and child from getting out or falling out.
2. Cover electrical outlets.
3. Inspect toys for broken and jagged edges.

Bathroom

1. Keep safety caps on all bottles.
2. Keep medicines, aspirin, rubbing alcohol in locked cabinets.
3. Adjust water heater so water is not scalding hot.
4. Use rubber mats in bath and shower.
5. Keep bathmat next to tub and shower.
6. Do not allow young child alone in bath.

Living Room

1. Cover electrical outlets.
2. Check safety of plants.
3. Put rubber-backed pad under small scatter rugs.
4. Pad sharp edges of tables.
5. Have screen for fireplace.

Have lock for door.

Stairs

1. With young child, block off tops and bottoms of stairs.
2. If necessary, mark top and bottom steps.

Kitchen

1. Keep vomit-inducing syrup on hand.
2. Store soaps, cleaners, all poisonous chemicals in locked cabinet.
3. Have guard around burners or use back burners on stove so child cannot pull contents onto self.
4. Unplug all appliances when not in use.
5. Store sharp knives in safe place.
6. Store matches out of child's reach.

Dining Room

1. Cover electrical outlets.

Garage-Workroom

1. Keep tools out of child's reach.
2. Keep poisons locked up.
3. Store paints and other toxic materials out of child's reach.
4. Store nails and screws in safe place.

General

1. Install smoke alarms in house.
2. Have fire extinguishers in kitchen, most rooms in house, and garage.
3. Keep firearms out of home; if in the home, keep ammunition and unloaded guns in separate locked cabinets; become aware of firearms in homes the child visits and be sure they have same precautions.
4. Keep poison control, fire, and police department telephone numbers by the telephone.
5. Learn infant, child, and adult cardiopulmonary resuscitation and how to access 911.
6. Never allow buckets of water to remain after use when infants and young children are in home, as children can drown in them.
7. Discourage use of infant walkers.
8. Use currently approved automobile safety restraints for children of all ages and parents.
9. For all children and adolescents, use helmets for bicycling, skate boarding, and in-line skating; use appropriate padding and safety equipment for all sports.
10. Teach children pedestrian safety in parking lots, street corners; do not let children under six or seven cross the streets by themselves.
11. Have fire escape routes planned from home in event of fire, and make sure children know them well.
12. Never believe that children under five can be water safe, even if they have had lessons; be sure that children over five have swim lessons; but no child should swim alone, and even adults should always be encouraged to swim with another person present.
13. Discuss the role of alcohol in car and water accidents with early and late adolescents.

*From: The American Academy of Pediatrics Committee on Injury and Poison Prevention, "Office-Based Counseling for Injury Prevention," *Pediatrics 94* (1994): 566–567.

Children learn positive eating habits at home.

state-mandated data collected on BMI of all California students reveals that in 2008, 38 percent of children between the ages of eight and seventeen were overweight (above the 85th percentile), and 20 percent were obese (above the 95th percentile).[32] Ethnic differences in being overweight exist with 28 percent of European and Asian Americans' being overweight and 12 percent obese as compared to 39 percent of African Americans, 42 percent of Latino students, and 46 percent of Native American students being overweight and 21 percent, 26 percent, and 24 percent of these groups, respectively, being obese.

Overweight and the intake of fatty foods are related to the development of many physical problems like heart disease and diabetes that compromise the quality of children's lives in adulthood. Pediatricians are becoming more active in taking BMI measures of all children yearly and discussing with all parents the actions they may take so their children maintain healthy weights—an hour of exercise a day, family mealtimes, reducing television time, eliminating TV at meal times, and getting adequate amounts of sleep. Box 6-1 describes the many benefits of family mealtimes, and the ways communities can support families in having these times together.[33]

When children are overweight, a program titled Parenting Eating and Activity for Child Health (PEACH) for parents of children five to nine years of age puts parents in charge of changing the family habits around food consumption and activity.[34] Eight sessions provide parents information on food selection, eating habits, activity levels, increasing children's self-esteem, and decreasing teasing. After the sessions, four phone calls to the family support parents' efforts. Overweight children whose parents attended this program lost 10 percent of their weight and were able to maintain the loss for the next eighteen months. Giving parents four sessions on parenting skills at the beginning did not improve the results. Children were never seen in the program, but parents' actions helped them reduce their weight.

Exercise

Physical activity increases children's physical fitness and health, as well as their self-esteem and it decreases anxiety and stress.[35] Physical play with other children also contributes to social skills. Physical well-being in childhood predicts overall long-term physical health, reducing the risk of heart disease, osteoporosis, and in women, breast cancer.

Exercise also increases children's attention span and their ability to inhibit responses. A recent study with preadolescents found that twenty minutes walking on treadmills improved performance on tests requiring cognitive control and on reading achievement.[36] A Chicago high school instituted a program of twenty minutes of treadmill walking before students went to difficult classes and found that it improved academic achievement significantly.[37] If a treadmill is not available, jumping rope gets the heart rate up and serves the same purpose.

Many influences, both physical and social, contribute to physical activity. Genetic factors such as gender—boys are more active than girls—play a role.[38] Social factors, such as the safety and the social cohesiveness and social bonds of the neighborhood,[39] school policies regarding recess, and resources for physical activity, play a role. Having friends who are physically active can encourage sports and outdoor activities.

Again, however, parents play a major role as models, and their influence is critically important. Physically active mothers tend to have children who are physically active. Parental inactivity is a strong predictor of child inactivity as young as the preschool years.[40] Families are strongly advised to begin exercising together to get the benefits of exercise and reduce the problems brought on by being sedentary.

Sleep

Sleep is necessary for life. Rats deprived of sleep die faster than rats deprived of food.[41] Sleep is so important that newborns spend sixteen to twenty hours a day sleeping, and by the time children are two years of age, more than half their life—fourteen months—has been spent in sleep. Similarly, throughout childhood and adolescence, adequate, good-quality sleep is related to physical, cognitive, and emotional well-being.

Though sleep is essential, a survey by the National Sleep Foundation found that toddlers get on average two hours less than the minimum amount of sleep recommended and preschoolers get four hours less on average.[42] Further, 18–21 percent of schoolchildren report feeling tired during the day, and 63–87 percent of adolescents report they do not get as much sleep as they need. So, parents must be diligent in helping children get sleep.

Though sleep is very important, its function is not well understood. Several theories exist.[43] First, it is thought that, during sleep, the brain repairs itself, restoring depleted energy levels, repairing damaged cells, and growing new brain connections. Sleep is also thought to consolidate recent learning in long-term memory. Sleep is related to the regulation of metabolic processes related to obesity. Finally, healthy sleep is related to daily alertness and reduced accidents (e.g., while driving).

Sleep promotes healthy cognitive growth. Twelve- to eighteen-month-old toddlers who got most of their sleep at night performed better on measures of executive skills at eighteen and twenty-six-months than toddlers who got more of their sleep during the day.[44] When school children add one hour of sleep to their nightly pattern, whatever that pattern is, their improvement on cognitive measures is the equivalent of two years of growth.[45] Other work demonstrates that adequate amounts of sleep reduce racial and social differences on cognitive tests.[46] When schoolchildren from different ethnic and social groups get adequate amounts of sleep, their performance on Woodcock-Johnson tasks is similar. When sleep is disrupted, traditional performance differences between racial and social status groups appear on these cognitive tasks. The performance of European Americans and high social status groups is less affected by decreased sleep than that of African American and lower social status children.

Helping children develop healthy sleep habits is a critical task for parents not only because poor sleep patterns are associated with lack of alertness, poor attention span, and poor memory as well as learning problems,[47] but because sleep problems are also associated with emotional problems such as aggressiveness and depression as well.[48]

Sleep is a family affair. Parents' warmth, stability,[49] and marital harmony influence amount and quality of children's, teens', and young adults' sleep.[50] In order to sleep well, children seem to need to feel emotionally secure and relaxed and not vigilant. Because parents' actions differ depending on the age of the child and parents' values, we take up the topic of sleep in the appropriate age-related chapter. Here we simply emphasize parents' critical role in ensuring that their children develop healthy sleep habits to prevent the behavioral, learning, and emotional problems associated with sleep deprivation, which is becoming increasingly common in our society.

A Healthy Lifestyle Is a Simple Lifestyle That Requires Effort to Achieve

In Chapter 3 we discussed that we live with a genetic inheritance that developed tens of thousands of years ago when we lived a physically active life in small bands of closely attached people who ate simple foods and slept long hours (see page 89). Our fast-paced, multitasking society that stimulates us as many of the twenty-four hours a day as we choose makes it hard to meet our inborn needs for physical activity, simple foods, long hours of sleep, and close, emotionally secure contact with our families.

Though the healthy lifestyle is a simple one, effort and attention are required to achieve it. And lack of time and increased stress often interfere with the effort despite our best intentions. But for food, physical activity, and sleep, we have to plan carefully so our needs are met. This means managing the technological devices that crowd into our homes so we get the best of what they can offer us, and barring the negative influences from entering.

GETTING THE BENEFITS MEDIA CAN PROVIDE

Families live in a media rich world that includes books, magazines, television, handheld video game players, iPOD/MP3 players as well as computers, laptops, cell phones, and car video screens. Innovations in these devices make it possible for family members to have immediate communication with people around the world and to have access to entertainment at any time of the day regardless of where they are.

Media can be a positive force, increasing skills and knowledge, drawing family members and friends closer together, or it can be a negative force, crowding out activities like exercise and reading we know are beneficial for children and families and increasing the risk of negative behaviors like aggressiveness.[51] The impact of media on children's lives depends very much on the ways parents incorporate media in family life for it is parents who make decisions about media availability and use.

In this section, we look first at the availability and use of media technology, focusing primarily on children and adolescents, and their multitasking and use of social media. Parents' media use is also described briefly. Then we review what we know about the effects of media use. Most of the studies focus on the use of television, and there are fewer systematic, well-controlled studies on newer media. We look at rules around media use and how families develop agreed-upon strategies to include media use in family life. Finally, we describe how parents interact in the community to promote healthy media use.

Media Availability

In 2009, the average home with children from ages eight to eighteen years included three to four CD/tape players, four televisions, three radios, two to three VCRs/DVD players, two video game consoles, two computers, and one TIVO. Seventy-one percent of children this age had televisions in their bedroom, and 30 percent, computers as well.[52] Thirty-three percent of children under six have televisions in their bedrooms, 23 percent, a VCR/DVD player, and 5 percent, a computer.[53]

Mobile media are available as well with 76 percent of children ages eight to eighteen years having iPOD/MP3 players, 66 percent, a cell phone; 59 percent, hand-held video game players; and 29 percent, a laptop.[54] Children are rarely separated from media devices and spend more time in media use than in any other activity except sleeping.

Media Environment

Two-thirds of children report that the television is on during meal times, and almost half report that in their home, the television is on most of the time, even if no one is watching.[55] Children's television viewing greatly increased in homes where the television is left on most of the time (3.17 hours per day) as compared to 1.42 hours for children living in homes where the television is left on little or none of the time when no one is watching.

Parents of children under six also report encouraging children's media use for several reasons.[56] It gives parents free time to do chores, relax, and watch television themselves. Media use also provides a way to interrupt children's bickering and rule breaking. And some parents use media to calm children down and help them sleep. Some believe video games are ways for fathers and sons to bond and have fun together.

Families today live in a media-rich environment.

Media Use

Children under Age Six   Media use starts early and grows through the toddler years, according to a national survey of one thousand parents of children under age six.[57] Although the American Academy of Pediatrics discourages screen time for children under age two, the average child that age has about an hour of screen time per day, rising to two hours per day at age two and remaining there.[58] Screen activities are the most frequent activity of young children and twice as much time is spent in them as in reading activities.

Children between Eight and Eighteen   In 2009, a representative national sample of 2,002 children from grades three to twelve answered detailed questionnaires about the availability and their daily **recreational, non-school-related** use of media, and a subsample of 700 children kept a weekly diary of media use as well.[59] This was the third wave of survey data collected by the Kaiser Family Foundation to get a clear understanding of media use among children ages eight to eighteen years. Table 6-1 summarizes the amount of time spent in each media activity, for the years 1999, 2004, and 2009. The total figures of media use and exposure of 2009 excluded daily cell phone activity so total time could be comparable from one survey to the next, but cell phone use figures for 2009 are listed separately in Table 6-1 and can be added to those above to get a complete picture of media use. Total time does include the time spent watching videos and playing games on computers and consoles.

Since children use more than one media at a time, they condense the equivalent of ten hours and forty-five minutes of media exposure into seven and a half hours a day. Even excluding cell phone use, these figures are an increase of two and a quarter hours of media exposure in the last five years, an increase made possible because new technology enables users to take media every place they go and view programs whenever they wish.

■ **T A B L E 6-1**
AVERAGE AMOUNT OF TIME CHILDREN AGES EIGHT TO EIGHTEEN SPEND IN
MEDIA ACTIVITY IN A TYPICAL DAY*

Medium	2009	2004	1999
Television	4.29	3.51	3.47
Music/Audio	2.31	1.44	1.48
Computer	1.29	1.02	0.27
Video games	1.13	0.49	0.26
Print	0.38	0.43	0.43
Movies	0.25	0.25	0.18
TOTAL MEDIA EXPOSURE	10.45	8.33	7.29
Multitasking proportion	29%	26%	16%
TOTAL MEDIA USE	7.38	6.21	6.19
Talking on cell phones	0.33		
Listening to music on mobile media	0.17		
Playing video games on phones	0.17		
Watching television on phones	0.15		
Texting on cell phones	1.30		

*From: Victoria J. Rideout, Ulla G. Foehr, and Donald F. Roberts, "Generation M2: Media in the Lives of 8- to 18-Year-Olds," (2010) Henry J. Kaiser Family Foundation, January, 2010. www.kff.org., 3.

There are age, gender, and ethnic differences in media use.[60] As children move into early adolescence (eleven to fourteen years), media exposure dramatically rises to almost twelve hours a day packed into about nine hours of time. The major increases are in video games and television. This high level decreases slightly to 11.23 hours in later adolescence, but it remains much higher than the levels of eight- to ten-year-olds—7.51 hours of media exposure packed into five and half hours.

Each day, boys have fifty-five minutes more of media time than girls, primarily spent playing video games on consoles or computers. Girls listen to more music than boys do and spend six minutes more in social networking. The differences in video games and listening to music are similar to those found in 2004.

Marked ethnic differences appear in all areas of media consumption except print matter. The thirteen hours of media exposure that both African American and Latino/a youth average per day is four and a half hours more of media exposure than the 8.36 hours averaged by European American youth. African American and Latino/a youth watch more television and movies, play more video games, and listen to more music than European Americans. These ethnic differences were present in surveys in 1999 and 2004, but have become more pronounced in 2009. There are few significant ethnic differences in the likelihood of parental rules about amount of time spent with media, but European American parents are more likely to impose rules about content of media than parents of African American and Latino/a children.

Multitasking

Seventh to twelfth graders spend about 29 percent of their media time using two or more media at the same time—watching television and looking at a magazine, or using the computer and listening to music.[61] Instant messaging is not included in the 2009 total tabulations to match previous survey data collected in 1999 and 2004; if it were included, it would figure prominently in multitasking. Multitaskers are most likely to be living in a media-rich environment with televisions and computers in their bedrooms and access to cell phones and wireless Internet services.

While 31 percent of youth report they are using another medium most of the time that they are doing their homework, more than half report never multitasking or only a little while doing homework.[62] Listening to music and watching television are common media used during homework.

Research suggests there is a limit to the amount of information that the brain can take in at one time, and when we do two things, we devote decreased resources to each. Fewer facts were recalled about news stories, for example, when they were presented in the CNN format with other information crawling along the bottom of the screen than when stories were presented one at a time in a simple visual format.[63] Similarly, more facts were recalled from a lecture when students had their laptops closed than when laptops were open and students were encouraged to get more information from the Internet during the lecture.

Studies of problem-solving skills in adults who multitask show that multitaskers, when compared to non-multitaskers, have greater difficulty ignoring or shutting out irrelevant information, and they take longer on a task of discriminating stimuli like odd from even numbers because they are not as efficient in juggling problems[64] They appear very sensitive to incoming information, highly alert and responsive to what is new so that focus and attention are difficult.

Using Social Media

Social media include social networking sites like Facebook and Twitter, gaming sites and virtual worlds like Club Penguin, chat rooms, blogs, video sites like YouTube, as well as cell phone texting. Table 6-1 lists the amount of time youth reported in some of these activities in the 2009 Kaiser media survey.

Like other media, social media have many educational and social benefits. Adolescents can organize study groups to do homework or other school projects, organize extracurricular and social activities, post pictures, share photos, and blog about what they are doing.[65] Youth use social networking to deepen friendships with their offline friends and maintain close friendships with children they may know but do not see daily, e.g., friends from a previous school or from nonschool activities like community sports teams or photography or other classes. Through sharing their activities and reactions, teens' sense of identity grows and intimacy increases with those who keep in close touch and reciprocate with their own information.

Gwenn O'Keeffe and Kathleen Clark Pearson describe four risks for adolescents in using social media: (1) peer-to-peer risks (e.g., cyberbullying), (2) inappropriate content such as sexting, defined as sending or receiving sexually explicit pictures or messages, (3) lack of understanding of privacy issues, and (4) outside influence of marketing and other groups.[66]

Many parents may not be technologically savvy, and many do not know what their children are doing on social sites so they cannot help their children deal with the risks. James Steyer says, for example, only 4 percent of parents thought their children checked their social sites more than ten times a day, when in fact 22 percent of teens reported they did, and only 2 percent of parents thought their children had posted a naked picture when 13 percent of teens reported they had done that.[67]

What occurred with Margarite, a fourteen-year-old, eighth-grade girl in Lacy, Washington, illustrates the risks for teens.[68] After receiving a picture of her new boyfriend without his shirt, she posed nude in front of her bathroom mirror and took a full, frontal picture of herself with her cell phone, and sent it back to him. Shortly thereafter, they broke up, but he mentioned the picture to a girl he thought was Margarite's friend, but their friendship had ended over a dispute about another boy. Margarite's supposed friend pressured the boy to send her the picture. He initially resisted but finally did send it, and within minutes, she attached a text message to the photo, "Ho Alert! If you think this girl is a whore then text this to all your friends," and she and another girl sent it out to all their friends. Within twenty-four hours, hundreds of students had received the photo. Parents called the school, fearful that their children would be charged with a felony for receiving a sexually explicit photo of a girl under eighteen. The parents of the children involved in sending the photo were dumbfounded; they had no idea their children were doing this.

School and police officials investigated, and while the teens could all have been charged with a felony for sending a sexually explicit picture of a fourteen-year-old girl, the district attorney decided to consider Margarite a victim who made a poor decision to send a boy a picture but had no idea that it could spread as it did, and the other three as guilty of a misdemeanor, requiring community service. The three would have to create public service messages about the risks of sexting, and then attend one session with Margarite to talk about the incident. Margarite, the teens, and their families all agreed to that resolution.

While Margarite initially left that school, she later returned and was in a class with the girl who sent the photo, but Margarite had called her to say she was returning, and the girl apologized again. At the family meeting with all the children and parents at the time of resolution, Margarite's father with whom she lived said, "I could say it was everyone else's fault, but I had a piece of it, too."[69] He recognized that his lack of involvement in her use of the phone and texting played a role in what happened.

One of the teens who wrote public service messages advised parents to talk to their children, find out what they are doing with cell phones and texting, and have a dialogue so parents can express their feelings about the legal and social risks of media use and ways to minimize risks to teens' reputations, and teens can express their feelings. The message writers advised teens to listen more to parents' views because parents know more about life.

When children and youth begin to use social sites, parents and children need to discuss ground rules for such use, with parents explaining the risks, what is legal/illegal, the permanence of digital material even when there is a delete button and it appears gone, the regrets that youth have about what they have posted or written—39 percent of teens say they have posted something they regret.[70] Parents and children can find agreement and continue discussion about how well the rules work or do not work.

Parents have to create an atmosphere of trust so that children will come to them when something bad happens in the course of social networking. In Chapter 10, we take up cyberbullying in detail, but the biggest protection for children in media use is their confidence and trust that they can talk with their parents if they break the rules or something bad happens to them while using media. Even if parents have indicated an openness to talk, children may fail to disclose what happens, and be at a disadvantage in dealing with it. Parents can reassure children that even if they do not approve of what teens have done, they will help them deal with it.

Parents' Media Use

In 2005 and 2006, parents of children under six years of age reported an average of two and a quarter hours of screen use per day.[71] Thirty percent reported none or less than an hour per day, and 42 percent reported more than two hours per day. Children whose parents had more than two hours a day of screen time also had increased screen use (30 minutes more) compared to children whose parents had less than an hour of screen time.

In contrast to these figures that describe limited media use, census figures from 2003 to the present indicate that Americans ages eighteen and older (for movies, television, and video games, children twelve and older are included) consistently used in-home and mobile media about ten hours a day with multitasking counted as separate times of use.[72] A recent survey reported adults had about twelve hours a day of media exposure at home, adding in the time they were using several media at separate times.[73] So, parents' media exposure at home appears to be just slightly more than the 10.45 hours of their children. Census data indicate television, radio, and the Internet occupy the most time.

Some marital therapists have grown concerned that technology is a major reason for marital conflict and also emotional distance as parents get in the habit of communicating through e-mail and texting.[74] An Italian study found that those couples with televisions in the bedroom had sex half as often as those who did not. For these reasons, some therapists suggest having periods when no electronic media is used except for work or school assignments. We discuss this suggestion later.

Media's Impact on Children' Activities and Development

Parents want to know what the effects of media use are on children's behavior and ongoing development. The impact of media uses depends, in large part, on how children and teens use it, what they do with it, and its impact depends somewhat less on the amount of time spent with the media or the specific device used.[75]

■ **T A B L E 6-2**
MEDIA USE AND BEHAVIORS ASSOCIATED WITH SUCH USE*

Media	Associated Behaviors
Background TV, on but nobody watches	Children watch more TV, read less, and are less read to**
Television/video with children age 0–3	Children do not learn easily from media, need direct action with person
Heavy media use	Increased attentional difficulties but not clinical deficit disorder, poor school grades
Viewing educational media, children ages 3–18	Increases in academic achievement, literary skills
Specialized computer video games, children ages 5–18	Enhance attention, enhance visual spatial reasoning, problem solving
Media demonstrating prosocial themes	Increase in altruism and tolerance
Increased viewing media showing aggression and violence	Increase in child aggressive behavior and increase in adult physical aggression for men and women***
Increased viewing media with sexual content	Additional research needed to establish clear link with earlier sexual activity
Viewing media with smoking/ alcohol advertisements or characters smoking/drinking	Increase in underage cigarette/ alcohol use

*Unless otherwise noted, findings from: Jeanne Brooks-Gunn and Elizabeth Hirschhorn Donahue, "Introducing the Issue," *The Future of Children 18* (2008): 3–10.

**Victoria Rideout and Elizabeth Hamel, "The Media Family: Electronic Media in the Lives of Infants, Toddlers, Preschoolers, and Their Parents," Kaiser Family Foundation Report No. 7500, May 2006. www.kff.org.

***L. Rowell Huesmann et al., "Longitudinal Relations between Children's Exposure to TV Violence and Their Aggressive and Violent Behavior in Young Adulthood, 1977–1992," *Developmental Psychology 39* (2003): 201–221.

Table 6-2 summarizes behaviors associated with media use and the ages of children using them and reveals that positive behaviors are generally associated with positive stimulating media that teach and develop new skills, and negative behaviors are associated with negative content that parents do not want children to emulate.

Media use is significantly associated with behaviors listed in Table 6-2, but it is important to recall that association does not mean the direct cause of the behavior.[76] Both media use and the behavior may be the result of a third variable not presently known, or media use may be just one step in the process of developing the listed behavior.

For example, parents may be under stress from parents' ongoing unemployment and be less stimulating and less diligent in monitoring media use so that a child spends extended time watching television programs with aggressive themes that reflect his irritability. When playing with peers he adopts the aggressive behavior he has seen on television. So family stress plus the exposure to television violence increased aggressive peer play.

However, even if not the only cause, changing children's television exposure can sometimes trigger behavior changes. School programs that increase children's awareness of media uses and encourage reductions in their use have reduced elementary school children's television use, in turn reducing playground aggressiveness and weight gain.[77]

Parents' Rules about Media Use

Parents can limit the number of media in the home and locate them in places to reduce their use. For example, televisions and computers can be removed from bedrooms and located in family living areas.[78] Parents can use V-chips, video game ratings, and computer filters to control programming, and they can turn media off during all meal times and when no one is watching.

Parents can follow the recommendations of the American Academy of Pediatrics that discourages any media for children until they are two years of age, and for children and teens recommends no more than one or two hours of quality programming per day.[79] Rules have an impact. Those children reporting rules of any kind have about three hours (2.52) less media use per day.[80]

Still, parents have fewer rules about media use than might be expected. Parents of children under six years of age are more likely to have rules about media use than parents of older children. Sixty percent of parents with children under six have rules about how much their children can watch and 85 percent have rules about the content of programming.[81] These rules seem to have an effect as children in households with rules watch thirty minutes less of television a day than children in homes with no rules.[82]

The majority of children ages eight to eighteen report they do not have rules about media use with the exception of rules about what one can do with a computer with 52 percent of children reporting their parents have rules about that. Parents are most likely to have rules for younger children eight to ten years of age—only 3 percent of children that age report they have no rules at all, whereas 30 percent of children between fifteen and eighteen report they have no rules.

Parents can institute rules about cell phone use in light of recent research. A panel of researchers from the World Health Organization has said that cell phones are "possibly carcinogenic" because recent work found cell phone use is associated with an increased risk for glioma, a form of malignant brain cancer.[83] The link is not firmly established, but there is sufficient evidence to indicate that it is wise to minimize the contact between head and cell phone by using a hands-free headset or by texting instead of making voice calls.

Reasons for following laws against cell phone use and texting while driving should be discussed in detail with teens as they may not be aware that distracted driving ranks with drunken driving and speeding as major causes of fatalities and injuries in car accidents.[84] In 2009, cell phone use was involved in 18 percent of fatal car crashes. Teenagers account for the largest percentage of distracted drivers involved in fatal crashes.

Parents' interactions with children around media use can be effective.[85] Reading with children and talking about what is being read increase children's reading and comprehension. Parents' discussions with children about TV and movies influence children's interpretations of what they see.

Family Life and Media Use

Children become active participants in the family media culture, using a variety of devices for learning and entertainment from very early ages. Many young children begin to demand the products they see advertised, and this continues throughout childhood and adolescence so parents have to have ongoing conversations about what they will and will not buy. Parents, especially parents of young children, control the purse strings and can refuse to purchase the objects despite children's protests.

Sometimes parents become alarmed at family media use because every family member is present in the room, but no one is paying any attention to anyone else; each is glued to his or her individual screen. Yet media offers the possibility of connecting families closer together. For example, grandparents often participate more fully in their grandchildren's lives through Facebook and other social media, talking, playing online games, seeing pictures, aware of all the family activities. As one mother wrote, "Grandparents and grandchildren have plenty in common. They have free time, disposable income for gadgets and gizmos, and a keen interest in staying in touch with people."[86]

Robin Dunbar, an evolutionary anthropologist, writes that social media can connect the family as it was 150 years ago, when people were born in a community, surrounded by family, living there until death with a close group of people known since childhood.[87] He says that by keeping friends from different locations and experiences—previous neighborhoods, camps, community activities—children and adults build networks that follow them through life, and people in the network all come to know each other through postings and comments they share. He says social media "allow us to reintegrate our networks so that, rather than having several disconnected subsets of friends, we can rebuild, albeit virtually, the kind of old rural communities where everyone knew everyone else."[88]

In order to get these benefits and not be overwhelmed by the pressures of online activities, some families have imposed digital holidays of one kind or another. After Mrs. Broadnax noticed that her family sometimes went several days without speaking in the evenings, she imposed a weeklong period in which neither parent nor the girls, ages four and twelve, used any electronic media except that required for school or work demands.[89] The family was very awkward the first evening at the dinner table, not knowing what to talk about. Conversation and interactions became easier the next night, and at the end of the week, the family decided to extend the holiday for another five days. Mrs. Broadnax was delighted when she came home one evening and found her husband and the girls playing a trivia game. They were using the computer screen for the questions, but they were talking and having a good time together.

Another mother made a rule that every night after dinner, the family went outside with no digital equipment and took a walk with the dog. She thought family members found it easier to talk when they were not face to face, and that everyone felt better in the outdoors. Her son commented, "I notice when my mom goes outside, her feelings get really calm."[90]

To include media in social interactions with family members, parents and children can watch television programs together, talk about shows or video games, and surf the Internet together. Parents can use these interactions as opportunities to learn about children's thinking and interests and have children learn about parents' interests. Using media together enables family members to discuss laws about appropriate use, matters of privacy, and ways to minimize risks from media while still enjoying the benefits.

When parents model appropriate media use and use media for learning and family interaction, children can understand parents' concerns about the media and may be more willing to follow rules and share upsetting experiences they have had with other people on the Internet.

Community Action

Parents can also take community action with other parents and community organizations to get the kinds of programs they want for their children on television and on other media. Restricting negative content in the media is difficult as was seen in June 2011, when a Supreme Court decision invalidated a California law restricting the sales and rentals of violent video games to minor children under eighteen.[91] The justices decided 7–2 that the law limited the free speech of game makers.

Parents have had success, however, in promoting positive behaviors through media campaigns describing the benefits of the behaviors and delivering the messages in many forms throughout the community—radio, television, buses, billboards.[92] For example, the Consortium to Lower Obesity in Chicago Children (CLOCC) developed a city-wide program promoting the "5–4–3–2–1 Go!" campaign to increase healthy eating, healthy television consumption, and healthy exercise. The message is: 5 servings of fruits and vegetables, 4 servings of water, 3 servings of low-fat dairy, 2 hours of television, and 1 hour of exercise per day. The program has appealed to other communities as well.

Patricia Greenfield makes an important point that no one medium—be it books, television, video games, or computers—can provide all the cognitive skills a person needs. Special video games may play a role in developing visual processing and visual motor skills and in increasing attention span. Reading excels in developing thoughtfulness, reflection, and critical analysis of material, qualities society requires in accumulating and evaluating information and knowledge. Reading also helps to develop imagination and creativity. She concludes that, "The developing mind still needs a balanced media diet."[93]

TOOL CHEST FOR DEALING WITH PROBLEM BEHAVIORS

No matter how skilled the parent or how good the parent-child relationship, children sometimes do not want to do what is asked, and parents must deal with the conflicts that arise. The problem-solving method described in Chapter 5 is helpful in resolving differences. Verbal strategies of dealing with problems are preferred because they enable children to learn the reasons behind rules and requests and to understand principles that can be used in other situations. For example, if parents talk about why it is important for children to be ready to go to school in the morning, children can then generalize the importance of promptness to other situations in school or with friends.

We give a number of strategies for parents' use depending on the situation and their values. These tools should all be used in a family atmosphere in which good behavior receives attention and appreciation. Attention alone is enough reward for some children to increase the positive behaviors you want, thus preventing conflicts. Sometimes in the busyness of everyday life, parents rush from one problem to another and pay attention only when the child is not doing what is requested. Thus, the child hears only what requires changing. So first, parents must be sure they are giving attention to the many ways their child follows their requests.

When actions are required, the following choices exist in addition to the problem-solving strategy. We begin with natural and logical consequences because it requires primarily that parents let children learn from the consequences of their actions.

Natural and Logical Consequences

Rudolf Dreikurs described the method of natural and logical consequences as an alternative to parents' use of power and punishment. The terms *natural consequences* and *logical consequences* are used jointly and interchangeably but have slightly different meanings.[94] Natural consequences are the direct result of a physical act. For example, if you do not eat dinner, you experience hunger. If you do not put your dirty clothes in the laundry, they are not washed. Parents mainly have to stand aside and let the natural consequences occur—let the child remain hungry until the next meal or wear dirty clothes.

Logical consequences are events that follow a social act. For example, if you lie, other people will not believe you. If you misuse the family car, your parents will not trust you with it. Natural and logical consequences are directly related to the act itself and are not usually imposed by others. Exceptions exist, however. If a natural consequence presents a risk to a child—for example, running out into a busy street could result in being hit by a car—parents generally use a logical consequence. If a child starts toward the street, the child is restricted to playing in the house.

Natural and logical consequences differ from punishment in several ways. They are directly related to what the child has done—no clothes in the laundry basket results in having no clean clothes. A punishment may have no logical relationship to what the child has done—a spanking is not the direct result of refusing to eat a food but is the result of the parent's authority. Logical consequences do not place moral blame or pass moral judgment on the child. The child has made a mistake and pays the price. The parent stands by as an adviser rather than a judge.

When a parent establishes a logical consequence, it has to be one that he or she can accept when the child experiences it. For example, if a teen is told that the logical consequence of not getting homework turned in on time is that she will have to stay in on the weekend and complete it all even though there is a desirable party on Friday night, then the parent has to stand by the consequence even though the child is sad and angry, and the parent would like to see the child go to the party.

Contracting

Parents can also use a behavioral contracting system. Just as parents want children to perform certain behaviors, so children want to attain certain objects, activities, and privileges. Parents offer desired rewards in exchange for the performance of certain activities. For example, if a child does his chores (making his bed, clearing the table) without reminders, he earns an extra 15 minutes of time for playing. Likewise, an older child may be given use of the family car on the weekends if she maintains acceptable school grades and arrives home at the prescribed times. Contracting is similar to mutual problem solving but differs in that parents are more authorities who agree to dispense privileges and rewards in exchange for actions rather than joint problem solvers.

Negative Consequences

Recall our discussion of learning theories in Chapter 3. Negative consequences are used to decrease behaviors that are not desired. If attention to positive behaviors and the preceding methods have not worked, parents can institute a negative consequence to decrease the likelihood of the behavior's recurrence. There are six general principles for using negative consequences:

1. Intervene early. Do not let the situation get out of control.
2. Stay as calm and objective as possible. Sometimes parents' anger and frustration are rewarding to the child. Parents' emotions can also distract the child from thinking about the rule violation.
3. State the rule that was violated. State it simply and do not argue about it.
4. Use a *mild* negative consequence. A mild consequence has the advantage that the child often devalues the activity itself and seems more likely to resist temptation and follow the rule in the future.
5. Use negative consequences consistently.
6. Reinforce positive social behaviors as they occur afterward; parents do not want children to receive more negative than positive consequences.

The following negative consequences range from mild to severe. First, ignoring might seem the easiest in that the parent simply pays no attention to what the child says or does. It requires effort, however, because the parent must keep a neutral facial expression, look away, move away from the child, and give no verbal response or attention to what the child says or does. Ignoring is best for behaviors that are not harmful to anyone. For example, children's whining, sulking, or pouting can be ignored.

A second is *social disapproval*. Parents express in a few words, spoken in a firm voice with a disapproving facial expression, that they do not like the behavior. When children continue disapproved behavior, parents can institute a consequence—removing a privilege, using the time-out strategy, or imposing extra work. When families have contracts, children agree to carry out specified chores or behaviors in exchange for privileges. When certain behaviors do not occur, children lose privileges.

Finally, *time out* is the method best reserved for aggressive, destructive, or dangerous behaviors. It serves to stop the disapproved behavior and to give the child a chance to cool off and think about the rule violation. The time-out method has many variations. The child can be requested to sit in a chair in the corner, but many children get up. If the child is required to face the corner, parents can keep a young child in the corner for the stated time. With older children, parents may want to add the rule that if the child does not comply with time out for one parent during the day, making the presence of both parents necessary, then the child will spend twice the amount of time in time out. The time need not be long. For young children, the number of minutes in time out should equal the number of years in age. It is best to have only two or three behaviors requiring time out at any one time. Otherwise, a child may spend a great deal of time in the corner for too many different things. Further, both parents and all caregivers need to agree on the two or three things that will lead to time out so the child receives punishment consistently.

When children get older and have many toys and recreational pleasures in their rooms, such as stereos and computers, restriction to their room is not an effective punishment. For these children, it is better to substitute extra work or chores that have a constructive outcome such as cleaning the garage or devoting time to a community activity.

Ineffective Forms of Discipline

A review of over three hundred studies identifies four kinds of problems in disciplining children: (1) inconsistent discipline, referring to inconsistency both on the part of one parent and between two parents; (2) irritable, harsh, explosive discipline (frequent hitting and threatening); (3) low supervision and low involvement on the part of the parent with the child; and (4) inflexible, rigid discipline (use of a single form of discipline for all transgressions regardless of seriousness). All four forms of ineffective discipline are related to increases in children's aggressive, rule-breaking behavior that then frequently leads to social difficulties with peers.[95]

Coercive Discipline

Coercing, forcing disciplinary strategies for dealing with children's misbehavior, include both verbal and physical punishment. These methods share many features and are often used together. In a sample in which 59 percent of mothers of four-year-olds spanked children with their hand, and an additional 8 percent with an object, 93 percent of mothers yelled at children two or more times a week.[96] Verbal and physical punishment are found in countries around the world like China, India, Philippines, Kenya, Italy, as well as the United States,[97] and they are less frequently used than the positive strategies of teaching good behavior, reasoning, negotiating, and loss of privileges. Parents begin to use verbal and physical punishment in the first year of children's lives[98] and gradually increase their use through the preschool years, but reduce their use as children enter school and later move into adolescence.[99]

Parents use these methods for several reasons. Parents know, and more often use, positive strategies, but they become frustrated and angry when children cannot comply with their requests. A major part of the problem is that many parents have unrealistic expectations of children's abilities to control their feelings and behavior.[100] For example, 20 percent of parents think children can control their emotions and not have tantrums by two years of age, and 43 percent expect this by age three, but research shows it is not until the ages of three to five that children have such skills. Forty-seven percent believe children can share and take turns by age two, when again, this does not occur routinely until the ages of three to five.[101]

Parents may also have unrealistic expectations of the power of verbal explanations and reasoning with children in the first two years of life.[102] Children's level of verbal understanding and the ability of words to control children's actions may not be as advanced as parents assume, and children may need more active physical guidance as well as the words to achieve what parents want.

A second major reason for the use of coercive punishment is parents' difficulties in self-control either because of major psychological problems like depression and substance abuse or because they are coping with financial stresses and difficult problems like children's health and developmental issues without sufficient support from their partner, family, friends, and community.[103] Parents are least likely to use coercive methods when they have positive emotional moods and children are developing well.[104]

Cultural values and approval moderate the effects of verbal and physical punishment. African American parents use more verbal and physical punishment than parents of other cultures, but their children do not seem to develop negative behaviors from it.[105] It is thought that the warm, supportive emotional relationships of many African American families help children to see the punishment as a sign of concern about children's developing acceptable behavior rather than a sign of rejection and lack of love. When families of other ethnic groups are warm and supportive or when countries value punishments, then the negative effects associated with their use in older children is absent or reduced.

Verbal Punishments   Verbal punishments include yelling, shouting, shaming, scolding, and making derogatory remarks to children. Babies' fussiness at one year predicted parents' verbal punishments at ages one, two, and three years.[106] African American parents were more likely to scold and verbally punish their children than European American and Latino parents. In contrast to physical punishment, however, verbal punishments of children under three are not related to problems with aggressive behaviors, and when used by emotionally warm and responsive mothers, they appear to stimulate cognitive growth, perhaps because of the interaction.

When mothers of older children, ages eight to twelve, use such methods as shaming, yelling, and expressing disappointment, both they and their children report increased aggressiveness and anxiety in the children.[107] When such measures were approved by the culture, the negative relationships were less marked.

Physical Punishment   Physical punishment is defined as "the use of physical force with the intention of causing a child to experience pain, but not injury, for the purpose of correcting or controlling the child's behavior," and includes spanking, grabbing, hitting, or shoving a child.[108] Parents' attitude toward spanking when children are six months old predicts their use of spanking when children are in preschool.[109]

Our understanding of physical punishment as a disciplinary technique is less detailed than we would like because the measures of physical punishment in studies often refer only to presence or absence in the past week or month and do not describe the severity or circumstances of its use. We rarely have information on how both parents use this method, and when we do, we get a greater picture of family aggression in representative samples.

Box 6-2 reveals that the effects of physical punishment differ somewhat from those of verbal punishments. Spanking in the first year is related to aggressiveness at age two and slightly lower performance on a cognitive test at age three though spanking at age two does not appear to have these effects.[110] In another study of spanking in the first two years of life, the children of European American mothers who spanked had problem behaviors after entering school at age five, but the children of African American parents who actually spanked more did not show these effects nor did Latino children who received the least amount of early spanking.[111]

The general findings in the preschool years are that use of mild physical punishment of a slap or two on the buttocks with the flat of the hand does not cause problems in children's behavior, but if punishment continues on when children enter school, then they are likely to become more aggressive and noncompliant.[112]

In summary, both verbal and physical punishments occur more frequently in families under stress without mutual support from the other parent or from other family, friends, or community. Parents know and use more positive methods of discipline, but their own unrealistic expectations or their own emotional problems or stresses prevent their relying on these methods all of the time.

The vast majority of health professionals and parent educators discourage the use of coercive discipline although there are a small minority who recommend the methods when positive means fail.[113] Coercive strategies have few documented positive behaviors associated with them, and they do not help children to internalize the values parents want children to learn.

Box 6-2
STUDIES ON PHYSICAL PUNISHMENT (PP) REVEAL THAT:

- looking at PP in 6 countries (China, Thailand, India, Philippines, Italy, and Kenya) reveals that its negative outcomes for 8–12-year-old children were similar in terms of predicting increases in aggressive behavior and anxious feelings though the effects were not as strong when the culture approved harsh punishment[114]
- in the United States, rates of PP vary between 45 percent of parents using it to 94 percent[115]
- in the United States, rates of PP vary with

  age of child, with younger children 2 to 5 experiencing more PP than children over 5[116]

  gender of child with boys experiencing more PP than girls[117]

  gender and age of parent with mothers using more physical punishment than fathers, and younger parents using more than older parents[118]

  ethnicity of parent with African American parents more likely to approve and use PP[119]

  income of family with low income families using more PP[120]

  emotional characteristics of child with fussy infants and disruptive preschoolers more likely to receive PP[121]

  emotional characteristics of parents with depressed, psychologically distressed, substance-using parents more likely to use PP[122]

  region of country with parents in Southern part of the United States, more likely to use PP than parents in Northeast[123]

  religious views with people belonging to conservative Protestant groups more likely to use PP than Catholics[124]
- effects of PP on children's behavioral adjustment vary with age of child and with family and cultural context of PP

  infants and children under 3 show mixed results with children spanked at one year of age showing more aggression at age 2 and less cognitive skill at age 3,[125] but children spanked at 2 not showing these effects; in another study European American children who were spanked in the first two years showed more behavior problems after entering school four years later but African American and Latino children who received more spanking did not[126]

  preschool children who receive mild PP (slap or two on buttocks with flat of hand) do not have increased risk of behavioral problems[127]

  school-aged children and teens who receive PP are more likely to be described as aggressive and anxious and girls were more likely to report depressed feelings[128]

  warm, emotionally supportive family atmosphere reduced the negative effects of PP in all ethnic groups in this country[129]

(continued)

Box 6-2
CONTINUED

- when both parents asked about use of PP as well as physical shoving and
  pushing with marital partner, PP occurred in an atmosphere of family
  aggression in which:[130]

  65 percent of children were spanked; 13 percent by father only, 23 percent by
  mother only, 29 percent by both parents

  *71 percent of families reported at least one parent physically aggressive with
  other*; 28 percent of families had two aggressive parents, and 43 percent had
  one aggressive parent

  85 percent *of families in sample* reported some form of physical aggression,
  and only 15 percent reported none; in 13 percent of families both parents
  were aggressive with each other and both spanked their child

---

The most important step is to help parents decrease the use of these punishments because even parents who use them would rather not because they do not find them effective.[131] To start the process of decreasing coercive discipline, parents can use positive disciplinary techniques to create a collaborative family atmosphere as described earlier in this chapter. Parents pay attention to children's positive behaviors and devote time to enjoyable family activities. When parents discipline children, they use nonphysical means of problem solving, contracting, earning privileges, and time outs for behaviors that must be stopped. They use these techniques consistently, without anger or criticism or belittling the child, and they supervise children to make sure children follow through with behaviors. Even if children protest loudly, parents persist with nonphysical discipline. Gradually, parents and children emerge from the vicious cycle of escalating conflict and physical discipline.

Parenting programs that we discuss in the next section are a major way to help parents learn to avoid damaging verbal and physical interventions, but stopping such interventions does not automatically put in place the strategies for a happy, well-functioning family life that promotes growth. Parents must see the importance of positive family routines and actions as they seek to eliminate negative coercion, and they need more support for themselves.

PARENTING PROGRAMS

Just as people take courses in driving to get a license or in cooking to master basic skills, parents seek to learn skills in parenting programs. Parenting programs can be divided into those targeted for the general population of parents and those directed to parents with special difficulties or to parents of children with special needs like parents of twins or multiples, parents of premature children or parents of children with attention deficit hyperactivity problems. We discuss parenting programs throughout the book, and here we focus on three researched-based programs that target different groups of parents.

The Triple P-Positive Program

The Triple P-Positive Program is a well-established, evidence-based, multidimensional parenting program developed over a twenty-five year period by Matthew R. Sanders and his colleagues at the University of Queensland in Australia.[132] Often presented on a community-wide basis and founded on social learning theories, the program seeks to increase parents' knowledge about children and to give parents skills that enable them to rear children more effectively and with less parental stress.

A primary aim of the program is to help parents develop the capacity for self-regulation defined as a process in which, "Individuals are taught skills to change their own behavior and become more independent problem solvers in a broader social environment that supports parenting and family relationships."[133] Self-regulation means parents are active agents in choosing the goals of behavior change, monitoring their progress toward the goals, and holding themselves accountable for meeting their goals. Becoming active problem solvers increases parents' confidence as they see they can succeed in making the changes they want. Parents learn to attribute success to efforts and not to some uncontrollable event like luck or genes. Parents teach their children the self-regulation skills they have learned.

Triple P-Positive Parenting Programs emphasize many of the positive behaviors we have discussed in this chapter and Chapter 5. The five core principles of the program are that parents:

- provide a safe, protected, stimulating environment for children
- provide a positive learning environment in which parents respond to requests for help, information, and support so children can learn to solve problems themselves
- use authoritative discipline with clear rules, reasoning, willingness to discuss disagreements in a calm way, using logical consequences and time out and not using spanking or physical punishment
- discuss their underlying beliefs about children and how realistic they are so parents can develop realistic expectations of children and select appropriate goals
- practice self-care as they make changes and learn new skills in cooperation with the other parent

The program seeks to increase the protective factors in family life—close positive relationships between parents, fun family times, active teaching so children learn skills and become problem solvers. At the same time, the program aims to reduce the risk factors in family life—marital conflicts, arguing and shouting at children, and physical punishments.

Because parents set their own goals and the methods they want to use to achieve them, the program has been successful with different cultural groups and in many different countries like Japan, Germany, Switzerland, and the United States, where it is effective and highly rated by both European American and African American parents.

The program is available in a variety of formats: a community-wide level, groups, individual sessions, in day care, school, medical and mental health settings, with parents who want to prevent problems as well as with parents who have had instances of child maltreatment or parents who have children with special problems like developmental delays.[134] The program is also used as a self-directed program with telephone contact for parents who do not have courses available in their geographic area. Wherever the program has been used and in whatever form it has been presented, it has predicted parents' and children's behavior changes that are sustained at follow-up assessments from three to twelve months later.

The program provides a remarkable range of services that are documented to have large effects that are maintained over time. It is currently being offered in this country as a community-wide program in South Carolina.[135] In nine counties, several hundred service providers in day care settings, schools, medical, and mental health facilities have been trained and are offering the program. Three measures of its effectiveness will be tracked in the nine counties and contrasted with the comparable figures in nine control counties not having the program. Prior to the introduction of the five-year, community-wide Triple P-Positive Program, the eighteen counties did not differ on these three measures: (1) child out of home placements, (2) child injuries documented as the result of maltreatment, and (3) number of child maltreatment cases. Preliminary analysis at the end of the first two years indicates that the nine counties using the Triple P-Positive have had significant and large reductions in these three measures of maltreatment, and both African American and European American parents are highly satisfied with the program.

The program has a website where any parents can seek tips for parenting or involvement in their program. It is: www10.triplep.net/?pid=20.

Parenting Programs for Couples

Impressed with the effects of their six-month groups described in Chapter 4, the Cowans began another intervention study at the time of the child's entrance into elementary school.[136] Groups began when the child was four years old and about to enter school within a year.[137] The groups met for two hours, and the study lasted for sixteen weeks. Although the parents were well-functioning volunteers who had not sought mental health services, their scores on measures of depression and marital satisfaction still suggested they were experiencing stress in their daily lives.

Parent groups consisted of four couples and two mental health professionals and focused on five topics central to parents' and children's adjustment: (1) parents' sense of self and their relationships, (2) with each another, (3) with their parents, (4) with their children, and (5) the life stresses and supports they experienced. In each session, parents had time to raise questions or problems. Researchers devised two forms of the parenting groups. In one group, leaders were told to focus on marital issues and parents' relationship as a couple in the open-ended discussion periods; in the other group, leaders emphasized parents' relationships with their children.

The control group consisted of parents who were offered a yearly consultation with the staff couple who did their initial interview before their children entered kindergarten, during kindergarten, and then during first grade. Compared to children of control parents, children whose parents were in the intervention groups were more competent in kindergarten and first grade. They had higher academic achievement, fewer behavior problems, and more positive self-concepts. Both forms of the intervention groups were related to positive behaviors in children in kindergarten and first grade. Benefits were still evident ten years later. Group parents were happier and communicated with each other more effectively. Teachers rated children as less aggressive and less hyperactive.[138]

Strong African American Family Program

Gene Brody and his coworkers at the University of Georgia surveyed rural African American families' concerns.[139] The families identified early sexual activity and adolescent substance use as areas of great concern to them. Researchers set up a training program to help parents and their eleven-year-old, early adolescent children develop skills to avoid these behaviors. Titled the Strong African American Family Program, the program consisted of two-hour sessions for seven weeks. Parents and children met separately for an hour and then jointly for an hour to practice the skills learned.

Parents learned nurturing parenting skills, ways of monitoring and controlling children's behavior, adaptive strategies of racial socialization, and strategies for communicating information about sex and substances as well as parents' expectations in these areas. Children learned the value of following household rules and doing chores, adaptive ways to counter racism, the importance of having a future orientation of setting and achieving goals, ways to counter and resist the temptations of substance abuse and early sexual activity, and ways that those who did not engage in these activities differed from those who did. Families in the control group received three pamphlets in the mail regarding early adolescent development, ways to manage stress, and ways to encourage exercise.

Seven months after the parenting program, parents and children who received training demonstrated more behaviors associated with protective factors against substance use and early sexual activity than did those in the control group. Parents gave children more general information on the topics of early sexual activity and substance abuse and talked more about their own expectations of children in these areas, and were more positive and supportive with children in this age period. Compared to youths in the control group, youths in the program had greater acceptance of parents' rules, a greater orientation to the future and to setting goals, and a more negative view of those who use substances and engaged in early sexual activity. The future behavior of these early adolescents will be tracked to see whether parents' and children's attendance at the programs and development of protective factors against substance use and early sexual activity reduced the rates of these behaviors in children as they progress through adolescence. In Chapter 10, we describe the adaptive ways researchers taught early adolescents to combat racism.

The evidence from parenting programs is that they help to develop useful parenting and personal skills, and they change the quality of family life. Though directed to parents, the programs have been highly successful in impacting children's behaviors even when children are not included in the program.

Camille Smith, Ruth Perou, and Catherine Lesesne reviewed the history and present state of parent education and concluded that,

> Parenting is open to change, but it is not easy to change. . . . What has become clear from the research over many years is that the fundamental principle that parenting education programs (both universal and targeted) must stress is the importance of relationships. Relationships are among the most significant influences on healthy growth and psychological well being. The quality of the parent-child relationship has long been acknowledged to be one of the most powerful predictors of optimal child development. Warm, responsive parenting is associated with later child language development, cognitive development, school success, and behavioral adjustment. Conversely, parents who are less involved and affectionate with their children are more likely to experience many more academic and behavioral problems with those children as they grow in years. . . . It is imperative that we stress the key component that should be a part of every parent education program: the importance and significance of the parent-child relationship.[140]

Problems arise, and parents often wish they had a single solution to each kind of problem they encounter in child rearing—one way to handle temper tantrums, one way to deal with teens' rebelliousness. Unfortunately, there is no one formula that all parents can use to raise all children. Each child, as well as each parent, is a unique individual.

When parents have difficulties, a seven-step problem-solving approach seems most useful. This approach allows parents to choose interventions that take into account the child's age and temperament as well as the family's social values and living circumstances. It also enables parents to encourage the qualities that they and their ethnic group value. Here are the seven steps:

1. Spend pleasurable time daily with the child
2. Specifically identify any problem; observe when and how often it occurs
3. Question yourself on the reality of the problem; is it the child or your own expectation that creates a problem
4. Get your child's point of view
5. Agree on an intervention and carry it out
6. Evaluate the results of the intervention
7. Start over again if necessary

As we conclude this chapter on supporting children's growth, it is good to keep in mind the words of Arnold Gesell and Frances Ilg:

> When asked to give the shortest definition of life, Claude Bernard, a great physiologist, answered, "Life is creation." A newborn baby is the consummate product of such creation. And he in turn is endowed with capacities for continuing creation. These capacities are expressed not only in the growth of his physique, but in the simultaneous growth of a psychological self. From the sheer standpoint of creation this psychological self must be regarded as his masterpiece. It will take a lifetime to finish, and in the first ten years he will need a great deal of help, but it will be his own product.[141]

Parents have the privilege of serving as guide and resource as their child creates a unique "psychological self."

PRACTICAL QUESTION: HOW CAN WE KEEP CHILDREN SAFE?

Parents become concerned about their safety as children spend more time away from parents and home, going to and from school or to friends' homes. They want to help children be independent and safe in the world, yet they do not want to frighten them and make them afraid of strangers and new experiences.

Fostering children's awareness of danger, sense of caution, and preparedness for unsafe situations does not mean making children live in fear. Children can learn that even though most people in the world are good and helpful and many situations are safe, some people and experiences are not, and everyone must learn to protect him- or herself from dangers that arise. Parents can help by putting this knowledge in perspective for children. Life has always involved danger of some sort, and many objects or experiences that are positive also have dangerous aspects. Cars are useful—they get us to work, to stores, to hospitals—but they can be dangerous if they hit us while we are crossing the street. The answer lies not in eliminating cars, because before we had cars, there were dangers from horses and horse-drawn vehicles. The solution is to take precautions to minimize the dangers and enjoy the benefits.

Families need to develop a set of instructions, to be discussed and revised as necessary, regarding certain dangerous situations. A one-time discussion is not enough; parents must periodically review instructions with children. Children can learn these safety rules gradually—for example, when and where they may go alone or what they should do if bothered by someone on the street or in a store, even when parents are nearby. Learning safety rules can become as natural to children as learning to brush their teeth. Parents emphasize teaching children the skills to deal with the environment, to make them competent and independent.

Although parents worry that talk of possible fearful events will damage the child, the risks that come with ignorance are much greater. Parents can begin with simple discussions of traffic safety—where, when, and how to cross the street. They can move from that topic to others of importance for the child. Television may prompt some discussion. Grace Hechinger recommends playing the game "What If?"[142] Parents ask a variety of questions and give children chances to develop solutions to difficult situations. "What if someone takes your backpack?" "What if a stranger approaches you on the street and starts talking to you?" Parents should not be upset if their children's initial answers are impractical, because they can guide their children in learning more reasonable responses.

Parents should have clear safety rules on (1) behavior if there is a fire at home; (2) traffic behavior, whether on foot or on a bicycle; (3) boundaries within which the child can come and go freely and outside of which an adult or parent must be present; (4) behavior in public with strangers; (5) behavior at home if strangers telephone or come to the house; (6) behavior when the child is a victim or witness of muggings by peers or adults; and (7) behavior when sexual misconduct occurs. Home behaviors at the time of fires, for example, should be practiced just as they are in schools or workplaces. Lenore Skenazy's book on rearing independent children has more suggestions for parents.[143]

If children are victimized—their bike is stolen, their money is taken, a stranger approaches them—parents' reactions can help speed the healing process. When parents listen to children's reactions and help children take constructive action, such as notifying the police, they help children cope. When parents' responses are exaggerated ("This is horrible!") or detached ("I cannot deal with this"), children get no help in coping with their feelings. If they cannot talk about how they feel, they will find it difficult to work out their feelings. Active listening and simple I-messages ("If that happened to me, I'd be really upset") give children a chance to say what the experience meant to them. Sometimes children need to describe the event several times and each time they do, more details emerge, as do more feelings. Gradually, after the incident, children regain their self-confidence. If a child's eating, sleeping, or play habits change or if marked changes in schoolwork or personality continue for some time, professional help should be sought.

An important step in promoting children's safety is working with people in the community. Developing community awareness and programs gives everyone a positive feeling of working together, which does much to banish fear. Promoting public safety programs with school and police officials and organizing block-parent programs to help children in the neighborhood are useful steps. In block-parent programs, one house in the neighborhood is designated as a house where children can come if they need help or reassurance when no one is home.

Family members grow stronger when they face problems and work together to deal with them. Sense of community grows when families and agencies cooperate to make the environment safe for children.

MAIN POINTS

Parents' roles in helping children are:
- Modeling approved behaviors
- Socializing children's behaviors so they meet culturally approved goals
- Initiating children's developmental pathways
- Influenced by parents' beliefs and children's qualities

A collaborative family atmosphere
- rests on responsive, sensitive parental care of children
- rests on secure relationships between parents and children and is never too late to establish
- includes children as partners in routines that benefit whole family
- rests on conversations about rules and future events
- draws on the process of encouragement

Healthy lifestyles
- prevent injuries and illnesses by providing a safe home and healthy routines
- require parents' efforts to model and structure daily routines for eating, exercise, and sleeping

- help develop intellectual and social skills and emotional regulation

Children's media use

- occupies seven and a half hours a day for children between the ages of eight and eighteen, and up to four hours for children under age six
- includes social media that can create greater intimacy with relative and offline friends
- includes social media with four main risks: peer-to-peer like cyberbullying, sexting, privacy issues with few total deletions of material, and marketing influences
- has positive benefits of teaching children, giving them literacy and number skills, modeling examples of positive actions
- can be related to negative consequences such as increased aggression in childhood and adulthood and early initiation of sexual behaviors; irregular sleep and reduced attention span when children use too much media or media of poor quality
- can interfere with close family relationships unless parents regulate use
- has great potential for learning and bringing people and families closer together

Tool chest for dealing with problem behaviors includes

- natural and logical consequences
- mutual problem solving and contracting
- using negative consequences such as ignoring, loss of privileges, social disapproval, and time out

Nonabusive spanking

- is often the result of parents' unrealistic expectation of children
- is used by large majority of parents at one time or another but most often by young parents under stress and without support
- detrimental effects depend on the context of the parent-child relationship whether it is culturally approved and age of child
- often occurs in the context of family aggression

Ineffective forms of discipline

- inconsistent discipline and harsh, explosive discipline
- low supervision of the child and rigid, inflexible discipline

Parenting programs

- can provide support groups for parents and reduce the stress of parenting
- teach specific skills to parents
- enable parents to reduce children's behavioral difficulties
- help parents create a more positive collaborative family atmosphere
- increase parents' self-confidence and feelings of competence
- can prevent problems from developing because parents become more skilled
- whatever else they include must focus on the importance of the quality of the parent-child relationship and ways to improve and nourish it

Keeping children safe requires that parents

- teach children about potential dangers, ways to minimize them, and ways to respond if they occur
- work with other agencies and people in the community to provide a safer community for everyone

EXERCISES

1. As you go about your daily life, observe parents interacting with their children in a grocery store or at a restaurant or other public place. Are parents on a cell phone? Are parents talking or listening to children? What are parents saying? Is it mostly dos and don'ts? Is it about something the family will be doing in the future? What messages might children get from parents' words? If you saw only these interactions in public places, what would you conclude about the relationships between parents and children?

2. Write a parents' guide for talking to early adolescents about using social media. Describe the risks and benefits of such use and how you would advise parents to minimize the risks.

3. Watch the television show *American Idol* or any other popular show of your choosing. What messages does that show convey about the meaning of life, values of daily living, moral behaviors? Does that show teach or model positive or negative behaviors, or both? If you have teenagers, would you want them to watch it?

4. Follow the 5–4–3–2–1 Go! plan being used in Chicago to encourage healthy living. How hard did you find it? Did you see any benefits from getting regular exercise and reducing television time?

5. Investigate the parenting programs available in your area. What is the range of programs in terms of cost, length, content? If possible, attend one meeting and give your evaluation of the class.

ADDITIONAL READINGS

Fischer, Claude S. *Still Connected: Family and Friends in America since 1970.* New York: Russell Sage Foundation, 2011.

Goleman, Daniel. *Emotional Intelligence.* New York: Bantam, 1995.

Johnson, Simon. *Keep Your Kids Safe on the Internet.* New York: McGraw-Hill/Osborn, 2004.

Nelson, Jane. *Positive Discipline.* New York: Ballantine, 1987.

Skenazy, Lenore. *Free-Range Kids: How to Raise Safe, Self-Reliant Children (Without Going Nuts with Worry).* San Francisco: Jossey-Bass, 2009.

II

Parenting at Developmental Stages

7

Parenting Children from Birth to Two Years

CHAPTER TOPICS

In this chapter, you will learn about:

- Parenting the newborn
- Development in the first two years
- Parent-child relationships

- Promoting children's growth in all areas
- Support for parents

Test Your Knowledge: Fact or Fiction (True/False)

1. Duplicating conditions in the womb helps calm newborns so they can settle into their new world more easily.
2. Because fathers relate differently to infants, infants are not as likely to become attached to them as they are to mothers.
3. Colic (frequent bouts of unsoothable crying in the first twelve weeks) is related to the ways parents interact with babies.
4. Mothers' harsh, negative caregiving in the first six months of life predicts young adults' negative self-descriptions as being impulsive and aggressive.
5. Parenting programs for new and expectant parents reduce parents' stress but do not increase their skills or promote the development of their babies.

What are babies like? How do they relate to parents and shape what parents do? How do parents support children's rapid growth in these first two years of life? Who and what support parents in their important roles as caregivers of the next generation?

After living nine months in warm fluid with necessities automatically provided, babies are thrust into a cold, dry world, required to breathe and eat on their own, and arouse others to provide the necessities of life. In two short years, they develop from newborns struggling to adapt to their new world to assertive toddlers who walk, run, and talk and love their parents but have definite ideas of their own. They know what they want and go get it. This chapter charts how parents become gentle soothers, loving caregivers, active social partners, and persuasive guides who set firm limits.

THE NEWBORN

During the first three months, babies' physiological rhythms and states are not organized and only gradually settle into more organized patterns. Parents feed and help newborns maintain calm states for sleeping and seeing the world.

The average newborn:

- sleeps about sixteen to eighteen hours a day, with a range from ten to twenty-two.[1]

- spends about 50 percent of their sleep time in active, REM sleep (rapid eye movement sleep, sometimes termed dreaming sleep, thought to stimulate the brain), and 50 percent in non-REM quiet sleep (when the body is relaxed and still).

- sleeps increasingly longer blocks of time, permitting longer periods of waking time to investigate their new world, even if they initially only use their eyes to do so.

Babies also cry and appear distressed. Again, great individual differences exist. In newborn nurseries, babies cried from one to eleven minutes per hour, with a daily average of about two hours. Hunger and wet diapers were significant causes, but the largest single category of causes was "unknown."[2]

In the first six weeks, infants' crying increases to about three hours per day, mostly concentrated in the late afternoon or evening hours,[3] then decreases to an average of one hour a day at three months. Although hunger seems to be the predominant cause, "unknown" remains the second-highest category for this age.

Ways to soothe babies and help them settle in are described in Box 7-1 and in the section "Parenting Tasks and Concerns."

Early Social Reactions

Babies come into the world preprogrammed to respond to human beings.[4] They see most clearly at a distance of 8–10 inches, the average distance of a parent's face from the baby when being held, hear best in the range of the human voice, and move in rhythm to human speech. They recognize their mother's voice, and quickly show a preference for her face.

Newborns respond to others as well. Babies a few hours old respond to the cries of other newborns and often cry themselves in response.[5] When less than a week old, they can imitate an adult's facial expression of sticking out a tongue, fluttering the eyelids, or opening and closing the mouth, suggesting a rudimentary sense of self as a human being capable of imitating a person and having the motor control to do it.

VOICES OF EXPERIENCE

What I Wish I Had Known about the First Two Years

"I remember when we brought him home from the hospital, and we had him on the changing table for a minute, and I realized, 'I don't know how to keep the engine running.' I wondered how could they let him go home with us, this little package weighing seven or eight pounds. I had no idea what to do. I kind of knew you fed him and you cleaned him and kept him warm; but I didn't have any hands-on experience, anything practical. In a way, I would have liked them to watch me for a day or two in the hospital while I change him, to make sure I knew how to do it. It's kind of like giving me a car without seeing whether I could drive it around the block." FATHER

"I wish we had known a little more about establishing her first habits about sleeping. The way you set it up in the beginning is the way it is going to be. Having enough sleep is so important. We went too long before we decided to let her cry for five minutes. Then she got into good sleep habits." FATHER

"I wish I had known how it would change things between me and my husband. The baby comes first, and by the time the day is over and he is in bed, we have two hours together, but I just want to curl up and take care of myself." MOTHER

"I wish I had known about how much time babies take. It is like he needs twenty-four-hour attention. For an older parent who is used to having his own life and is very set in his ways, it is hard to make the changes and still have some time for your own life." FATHER

"She had this periodic crying at night in the beginning, and you are caught in the raging hormones and somehow I thought if I just read Dr. Spock again or if I read more, I'd understand it better. And we joked about reading the same paragraph in the book over and over. We needed reassurance it would end, and at three months it ended. That was the hardest part." MOTHER

"Someone said, when you have a child, it's like two appointment books—his appointment book and yours. And first you do everything in the kid's appointment book; and then when you're done, you do everything in the kid's appointment book again. I wish I had known they weren't joking. I knew that it would be a challenge, and in some ways I wish I had known more. But in other ways I think if I had really known exactly how hard it would be sometimes, I might have been more reluctant or waited longer, and that I would really have regretted—not doing it." FATHER

"I wasn't prepared for all the decisions. Is it okay if he does this or not? He's trying to do something; shall I step in so he doesn't hurt himself, or shall I let him go? It's making all those choices, making sure what I feel." MOTHER

"I wish I had known what to do about climbing. He climbs all over everything. I have the living room stripped bare, but I wonder if this is the right thing." MOTHER

"I wish I had known how much time they needed between one and two. They are mobile, but they are clueless about judgment. I think it was one of the most difficult times. Even though she did not get into a lot of trouble, sticking her finger in the light sockets, still she takes a lot of time and watching, so the transition to two was great." MOTHER

Box 7-1
WOMB SERVICE*

Pediatrician Dr. Harvey Karp's book, *The Happiest Baby on the Block*, can improve many parents' lives by giving them tools to calm and soothe their newborns. Dr. Karp describes a five-step method that helps newborns settle into their new world more easily, especially those newborns with intense temperaments who find it difficult to soothe themselves.

Dr. Karp believes that newborns would benefit from another trimester in the womb because at birth their neurological systems are still immature and easily overwhelmed with the forms of stimulation they experience. They need the "womb service" they are used to. In the womb, babies are folded up in the tight uterine support surrounding them; they hear the noise of blood coursing through arteries and veins, the sounds of stomachs gurgling, and sometimes background voices. They move in many different ways as mothers go about their daily activities.

When they are born, their little bodies are out in space with arms and legs moving wildly; they miss the enfolding support of the uterine walls, especially when lying on their backs. Often, it is deadly quiet and dark, like a cave. And they can only lie there; they can't move around on their own. So, until the nervous system develops and gives babies greater ability to regulate themselves, as it gradually does in the first three months, babies find it hard to settle in, and many cry.

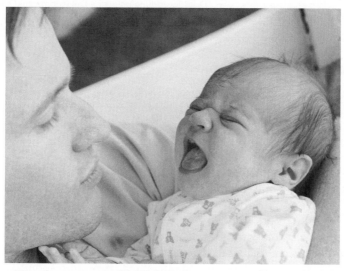

Dr. Harvey Karp suggests several steps for calming a crying baby.

Dr. Karp's method is to duplicate as closely as possible the characteristics of life in the womb because reminders of that time trigger a child's powerful calming reflex. This reflex, Dr. Karp believes, is essential to a healthy pregnancy and delivery. If fetuses had tantrums and frenzies of activity and flailed around forcefully, they would increase their risk of having the umbilical cord wrapped around their necks or wedging themselves in odd positions that would be difficult to change in the uterus or birth canal.

(continued)

Box 7-1
CONTINUED

His five-step program is to be done in a specific way:

1. Swaddling—securely wrapping the baby in a receiving blanket (have pediatrician rule out congenital hip problems that swaddling could affect**)
2. Side/stomach position for holding the child—in the stomach position, the child is held against the body so he or she feels pressure on the stomach; the child is always placed on his or her back for sleeping
3. Providing a *shhhh* sound that duplicates noises in the womb helps babies—some parents use a vacuum cleaner or dust buster, but parents can make shushing noises
4. Swinging or some form of rhythmic motion such as jiggling, dancing, rocking, or carrying the child in a sling
5. Sucking on a pacifier or breast or finger

These five steps together makeup what Dr. Karp calls the Cuddle Cure to soothe babies. He believes these steps copy what many other societies do naturally to calm babies.

*Adapted from: Harvey Karp, *The Happiest Baby on the Block* (New York: Bantam, 2002).
**Susan T. Mahan and James R. Kasser, "Does Swaddling Influence Developmental Dysplasia of the Hip?" *Pediatrics 121* (2008): 177–180.

Early Parent-Child Relationships

In addition to feeding babies, keeping them warm, and getting them to sleep, parents also soothe babies and help them regulate their physical system. As noted in Chapters 3 and 4, physical contact with mothers regulates infants' hormonal levels, sleeping and eating patterns, and heart rate.[6] Music and singing to infants also reduce stress and regulate arousal level.[7]

In their early interactions, parents shape infants' emotional reactions, encouraging positive moods and smiling and discouraging negative moods with such phrases as, "Don't cry."[8] Babies copy their parents' emotional reactions, responding with joy and interest to mothers' happy faces, with anger and a form of fear to mothers' angry faces, and with sadness to mothers' sad faces. Over time, mothers' positive expressions are related to increases in babies' smiling and laughter.

As infants' behavior becomes more integrated, parents respond sensitively to babies' rhythms and moods. Parents engage babies in face-to-face interactions, and become social partners, looking for periods of alertness and babies' readiness to respond before playing games. These social interactions stimulate babies' emotional, cognitive, and social growth.

Turn taking involves waiting and adjusting to other people's behavior, and is an early form of self-control predictive of the child's self-control at age two.[9] Babies learn social routines and develop expectations of what others will do.[10] Babies as young as three months become distressed if these expectations are not met. When, for instance, a parent of a three-month-old adopts a still, impassive facial expression, the baby responds negatively and often tries to elicit the anticipated reaction by smiling or vocalizing. If this does not work, the baby turns away.

These interactions as social partners create mutual understanding and a shared state of meaning termed intersubjectivity. In the state of shared meaning, the baby uses the parent as a social reference for responding to experience.[11] For example, babies will not play with a toy if the mother has looked at the toy with disgust.[12]

Coparenting

James McHale's observations of mothers and fathers with their three-month-old babies revealed parents were sensitive and responsive, but cautious in their interactions.[13] Even at this early age, parents already reported differing views about what to do—where the baby should sleep, how long the baby should cry before being picked up, how they should divide the work. Couples who incorporated both parents' points of view in solutions formed a cooperative, warm alliance that supported both parents. Those parents who were in the process of forming an alliance were not in conflict, but were out of synch with each other, sometimes jumping in at the same time to get the jobs done and sometimes withdrawing at the same time. These parents did not feel they got positive support from the other parent.

In this middle-class sample, 24 percent of mothers and 13 percent of fathers reported clinical levels of depressive symptoms. Some reported decreases in marital satisfaction. Depression and marital distress decreased the warmth and cooperation between the parents and reduced their ability to work together.

When parents anticipated lack of cooperation and support from the other parent before birth, they were less likely to form cooperative relationships after the birth, but only if the baby were irritable and fussy. Negative predictions did not come true when babies were easy and adaptable, possibly because it was easier to provide care and parents received positive feedback from babies and the other parent about their caregiving skills.

McHale believes that if parents are having a hard time working together, they should make every effort to talk to each other about their attitudes and feelings. If they cannot settle their differences, they should seek guidance as the difficulties are likely to continue and eventually will affect the child's behavior.

Managing When Babies Are Born Prematurely

Premature babies and their parents have been through a lot in the hospital as we described in Chapter 4.[14] Now at home, parents have a demanding job. Because preterm babies left the protective womb early, their systems are not ready for the level of stimulation they experience in the world.[15] They may be unresponsive much of the time, or they may react intensely to stimuli full-term babies can absorb. So, parents have a very narrow range of behaviors that will be intense enough to stimulate but not overwhelm the baby.

Both mothers and fathers naturally adapt their behaviors to meet preterm babies' needs. Compared with other parents, they are more active in holding and touching babies, directing their attention. They may appear overstimulating as they try to compensate for their child's special needs. Over time, preterm babies come to resemble full-term babies in their development, but mothers of preterm babies use different strategies to promote growth. For example, they may hold babies more to encourage mutual gaze and responsiveness, because preterm babies respond with more gazing when being held.

Parenting behaviors are associated with babies' development.[16] When mothers remain sensitive to babies and engage in cooperative interactions, babies' social skills and behavior like eating well are similar to those of full-term babies. When mothers become overcontrolling and intrusive with infants, then babies have more troubles like eating difficulties. A study following a sample of preterm babies born before thirty weeks found that parents' positive parenting behaviors—their warmth, their sensitivity, and their ability to coordinate their efforts with children, and support children in their activities—were related not only to children's emotional regulation and positive mood at age two, but also to their toddlers' cognitive skills.[17] When parents laugh and smile and share positive emotions with their children, when they match their behavior to what the child is doing, then children's neurobehavioral development is advanced and reflected in greater competence, perhaps because sensitive parenting appears to scaffold children's actions and create connections so children learn more effectively. The one area in which negative affect and frequent directives had a positive association was with motor development. The greater directives and less positive tone, however, may have been the result of having a very active infant.

Preterm infants' cognitive development illustrates the powerful effect a mother's attitude has on the baby's growth. When mothers felt that their role was important and that they were doing a good job, and when they felt positively about the baby, their husband, and life in general, their babies developed well.[18] The attitudes of mothers of full-term babies were only moderately related to the baby's progress. Parents' responsiveness and social stimulation of preterm babies are related to children's academic and social success through young adulthood.[19]

Parents of premature babies need to understand their strong and important role and the child's capacity for healthy growth, for our culture seems to hold subtle negative beliefs about preterms. When mothers were told an unfamiliar six-month-old baby was premature, they were more likely to rate the child as smaller, less cute, and less likable, even when the child was actually full term.[20] In brief interactions, they touched the child less and offered a more immature toy for play. What is startling is that the babies' behavior changed with these women, and they became less active. College students watching videos of the interactions could tell immediately whether the child was described as full term or preterm.

Such stereotypes may influence friends and relatives who in turn affect the parents.[21] Mothers who do well tend to adopt and nurture an optimistic attitude about the long-term outcome for the child. Professional support that discusses possible difficulties and coping strategies is at times disruptive for these mothers, although such help is useful to women who feel under stress with their infants.[22]

Because preemie babies start life with special problems, parental overprotectiveness is not unusual in the first several months, as the child grows and becomes stronger. If overprotectiveness persists after the first year or exceeds what the pediatrician considers reasonable, however, parents have developed a problem and need help in standing back and giving children freedom to grow.

DEVELOPMENT IN THE FIRST TWO YEARS OF LIFE

In this section, we discuss babies' physical, intellectual, language, and emotional development, as well as development of self, in the first two years. All these areas of development are closely intertwined in the early months and years as advances in one area make possible advances in other areas. Growth in physical and motor coordination enables babies to get around and explore more objects in greater detail, thus enhancing intellectual growth.[23] Crawling to people enables babies to initiate more social contacts and to become a more active partner. More social contacts and vocal interactions promote language development.

Observers have identified three periods of major reorganization in babies' development over the first two years of life.[24] They occur at about three months, seven to nine months, and eighteen to twenty months and are related to neural changes that enable babies to become more effective social partners and more efficient learners. As we shall see, babies begin learning early in life and have incredible capacities for observations and reasoning.

Physical and Neurophysiological Development

On average, the baby grows from 21 inches at birth to about 33 inches at the end of two years, and birth weight increases to about 29 pounds. Growth includes increasing organization of behavior as well.

Three months: The increased myelination of nerves in cortical and subcortical neural pathways and the increase in the number of neuronal connections at three months of age improve the child's sensory abilities and coordination, bringing greater control of behavior. The nervous system appears more integrated. Voluntary behaviors replace reflexes. Babies are more awake during the day and are more skilled in manipulating and playing with toys and objects.

Eight months: Increased myelination of neurons in the motor area and in areas of the brain controlling coordination of movement underlie babies' abilities to sit alone, to crawl, and finally to walk between ten and eighteen months. Development of the prefrontal cortex and in areas responsible for organization of behavior enable babies greater attention span and skill in inhibiting behaviors.

Eighteen months: Increased brain myelination is related to rapid advances in language and the development of representational thought.

Intellectual Development

As noted in Chapter 3, Jean Piaget and Lev Vygotsky focus on early development. Piaget emphasizes the child's changing capacities for incorporating stimulation and active exploration of the world.[25] Infants learn from the actions of their own bodies (e.g., learning about spatial relations by working to get fingers to their mouths for sucking). Babies reach for objects in the environment, manipulating them, seeing how they work, and gradually becoming problem-solvers who observe what happens when they drop objects on the floor or throw them in water.

Even before babies are able to crawl and move around, they are careful observers of what goes on around them, and they understand more than we thought. Babies at six months, for example, already have a rudimentary sense of quantities and numbers.[26] How do we know? Babies pay attention to and look longer at what is new and unfamiliar to them so by measuring the length of time they look at stimuli, we can tell whether a stimulus is new or familiar. After becoming familiar with a picture of 16 dots, babies lose interest but become alert and interested when they view only eight dots, which they view as different. They become increasingly alert and interested when the number of car horn beeps change. After viewing visual patterns, eight-month-old, babies developed expectations about the ways visual patterns changed and were able to use social cues to rule out distracting stimuli.[27]

By eight or nine months, babies have learned that people and objects are separate from them and exist even when they are not seen. Object permanence, the term for this new understanding, is essential to the concept of a coherent world. As babies move and explore objects, they form intentions and goals (e.g., get a toy, grab the cat).

In social play with parents babies learn that others too have goals and intentions.[28] They learn that when a parent looks off at an object or points, they can share the adult's gaze and focus on the object too. They also learn that parents can understand their goals and provide feedback as necessary. So, at about nine to ten months, they seek information and help by referencing parents' facial and emotional expressions. If confronted with what looks like a dangerous cliff, for example, they will not crawl toward it until the mother encourages it. By eighteen months, toddlers can understand others' have different desires and respond in terms of what others would like.[29] For example, when adults indicate they prefer broccoli to the Goldfish crackers that toddlers prefer, children give adults the broccoli when they hold out their hands. At fourteen months, they would hand them the crackers that they themselves enjoyed.

In the middle of the second year, babies begin to use symbols such as mental images and words to represent their experience so they are not limited to the present and what they see. Toddlers engage in pretend, fantasy play, copying the actions of parents and brothers and sisters in play. This is the beginning of representational thought.

Vygotsky emphasizes the importance of social interactions.[30] Parents establish routines that draw children into the culture and teach them basic values, as we saw in Chapter 3 with regard to American and Italian families. Parents simplify play so babies can participate, giving toys they can manipulate so skills increase. Vygotsky also emphasizes the importance of language. Words give children tools to communicate with others and enable them to represent their experience in words that are internalized into thoughts.

Both Piaget's focus on active exploration of the world and Vygotsky's focus on social relationships provide parents with guidelines to help children learn and reach their full potential.

Language Development

Infants' emotional reactions—their smiles and cries—are early forms of communication. Gradually, babies develop cooing, babbling, and repetition of syllables, such as *ma-ma* or *da-da-da*.[31] By five months, babies use their vocalization to capture adults' attention and expect adults to respond socially.[32] When adults adopt a still face, babies increase their vocalizations, and if there is no response, they cease vocalizing. By eight months, babies attend to sequences of syllables in languages even if the language is made up or foreign to the babies.[33] Identifying syllable sequences is most likely how babies begin to segment flowing speech into words. The rhythm of natural speech helps segment words, and infants learn even more when the words are sung to them rather than spoken.

At about ten months, children attach words to objects that interest them and visually stand out.[34] Parents advance children's language when they label objects children are already focused on. In the second year, children attend to the speaker and what the speaker is looking at or pointing to. Parents can increase children's verbal skills if they have the child's attention and are very clear in communicating the object they are labeling.

The amount, content, and form of parents' language influence what children understand and talk about.[35] Researchers found that the typical parenting routines in all families provide only a very limited vocabulary. Thus, children with the most advanced vocabularies live in families where parents talk a great deal and use a rich variety of words. When mothers are trained to elaborate on what children say and encourage children to talk in more detail about events, then children demonstrate richer memories of events.[36]

Most important is the emotional tone of the language.[37] Thirteen-to eighteen-month-old children whose families directed primarily positive, affirming words to them were observed to use primarily positive words with family members two years later. Conversely, children whose families directed primarily negative, critical words to them used similar words with their family members.

On average, by their first birthday, babies have two or three words and by eighteen months, fifty words.[38] At age two, they have a vocabulary of about three hundred words, but at all these ages, they understand many more words than they themselves use. By age two, toddlers have also made the leap to putting two words together to form a sentence.

Emotional Development

At birth, infants' emotional repertoire consists of three general states: contentment, alert interest, and distress/irritability.[39] In the next three to four months, emotional states develop into more differentiated and specific emotions: contentment into joy, distress into sadness at the loss of pleasure, and anger in response to frustration. Fear develops at seven or eight months, and parents see it most clearly in stranger anxiety, which develops about that time. Babies are able to identify people as newcomers in their environment, and they are fearful of them. This subsides by the end of the first year. By the end of the first year, babies express a range of emotions—interest, surprise, joy, sadness, anger, fear, and disgust.

Anger   Parents most want to know how to handle children's negative feelings. In the second year, toddlers become more self-assertive, and at times defiant. Even when mothers are supportive and offer choices, children refuse to comply with requests and insist on their point of view. Researchers conclude that defiance at this age appears part of healthy development.[40]

Aggressive behavior increases in the years between one and three, and then gradually decreases after the third birthday. Before age two, boys and girls are equally aggressive, but from two years of age, boys are significantly more aggressive than girls.[41] Florence Goodenough asked mothers to keep diaries of young children's anger outbursts and found that many factors influence the occurrence of anger.[42] Outbursts peak in the second year and are most likely to occur when children are hungry or tired or when they are ill—when reserves are down for physical reasons, tempers flare and are usually short-lived—most last less than five minutes—and, with young children under two, the aftereffects are minimal; with increasing age, children sulk and hold on to angry feelings.

Parents whose children had the fewest outbursts:

- had a tolerant, positive home atmosphere with realistic expectations that children would be independent, curious, stubborn, and have individual needs.
- anticipated problems and found ways to prevent them.
- helped children conform by preparing them for changes in activities, announcing mealtimes in advance so children had ten minutes or so to get ready.
- had a consistent daily routine and consistent and fair rules.
- were firm when a real conflict arose.

Parents whose children had many outbursts

- were critical and disapproving with children.
- were inconsistent and unpredictable, basing decisions on their own wants rather than the child's needs.
- ignored children's needs until a problem forced them to respond.
- imposed a routine regardless of the child's activity of the moment and forced the child to act quickly in terms of their own desire.

Handling Negative Feelings   Toddlers use many coping strategies they:

- look away and soothe themselves.
- call or pull parents to whatever they want fixed.
- use words to express feelings and get feedback from parents.
- use transitional objects like stuffed animals or pieces of cloth to provide comfort in times of distress—the use of such objects peaks in the middle of the second year, when as many as 30 to 60 percent of children have them.[43]

Empathy   Newborns cry at the distress of other newborns, and by six months express a preference for those who help others.[44] After watching a puppet show in which a circle humanized with eyes tries to climb a hill, is helped by a square which pushes the circle up, but hindered by a triangle which pushes the circle down the hill, a six-month-old preferred to play with the helpful square and ignored the triangle.

Toddlers go beyond crying at others' distress—they take action.[45] They touch, cuddle, or bring the child something he or she would like. Toddlers' concern is most frequently directed to family members, particularly to mothers. Toddlers do not express much concern when they cause distress. They intervene to help or remedy the situation, but they do not feel guilty for causing the problem.

Happiness and Affection   From the start, babies enjoy people and making things happen—getting a parent's attention, kicking a mobile.[46] Exercising their developing skills gives babies' great pleasure in life. They are often unconcerned with failures—recall how hard a child works to master crawling or walking, not getting discouraged or giving up. Unconcerned with others' reactions, they do not appear to make value judgments about their own actions in the first year.[47] Although children begin to develop standards for behavior in the second year, still, their main response is one of delight in what they do.

Although they most enjoy pursuing their own goals, they also enjoy meeting adults' expectations. In one laboratory study, toddlers responded quickly and enthusiastically to adults' requests to arrange toys in a certain way.[48] Later, when allowed to play freely, toddlers happily repeated the tasks. The researchers concluded that the pleasure of accomplishing a goal is a powerful motive for their obeying commands.

Affection also increases in this period. Toddlers pat, stroke, and kiss their parents, particularly mothers. They are also affectionate to animals and younger children.

Development of the Self

The self goes through developmental stages, as described by Susan Harter.[49]

- Birth to four months: the self emerges as infants coordinate visual, sensory, and motor responses and begin to act on the world, for example, by making a mobile move or making a parent laugh.

- Four to ten months: infants have an increasing sense of self as doers and social partners attached to parents. When caregivers react positively to babies' bids for attention, babies have a greater sense of control over events.

- Ten to fifteen months: babies become increasingly differentiated from caregivers and find a greater sense of themselves as agents who make things happen. Although attached to parents, they move off, using parents as secure bases for exploration in the world.

- Fifteen to eighteen months: "me-self" develops. Toddlers begin to internalize how others respond to them—that is, they start to react to themselves as others do. Children at this age recognize themselves in a mirror, identify photographs of themselves, and respond strongly to others' reactions to them.

- Eighteen to thirty months: toddlers develop a greater understanding of what influences others to act; as a result, they gain a greater sense of the separation between the self and others. Their language reflects their feelings of being separate persons. By age two, they use pronouns such as *I*, *me*, and *mine*, and they describe their physical appearance and actions—"I run," "I play," "I have brown hair." These verbalizations increase self-awareness.

Development of Self-Regulation

As we have seen, self-control too begins to develop in the earliest days of life.[50]

- In the first three months of life, infants regulate arousal states of wake and sleep and the amount of stimulation they get; they also soothe themselves.
- From three to nine months, infants modulate sensory and motor activities and continue to soothe themselves, looking away from what upsets them or sucking on fingers or hands. As they reach out, form intentions, and develop a rudimentary sense of self, their capacity for control begins to emerge.
- From nine to eighteen months, infants show awareness of social or task demands and begin to comply with their parents' requests. As infants act, investigate, and explore, their sense of conscious awareness begins to appear. These trends continue in the second year.

Researchers found that babies in the first year obey their mothers' commands when they accept and are sensitive to babies' needs.[51] Mothers who respect babies as separate individuals and tailor daily routines to harmonize with the children's needs, have babies who are affectionate and independent, able to play alone, and (even at one year) able to follow their mothers' requests. Thus, even at this early age, a system of mutual cooperation between mother and child is established.

Toddlers are most successful in avoiding forbidden activities when they direct their attention away from these objects or activities—looking elsewhere, playing with their hands, finding an acceptable substitute toy.[52] A substantial number of two-year-olds can wait alone as long as four minutes before receiving permission to touch.[53]

Peer Relations

Children pay attention to peers, smiling and glancing at them in the first year.[54] In the second year, children's social skills advance significantly. Toddlers imitate each others' actions, take turns, engage in imaginative play. They also have conflicts. Toddlers argue over toys and activities. Many of the conflicts involve outgoing toddlers who are learning cooperative ways to initiate activities.

Social behaviors of this period may persist into the preschool and early school years. Inhibited children tend to remain shy and fearful; poorly controlled toddlers often continue to have difficulties with peers, and socially skilled children maintain their social competence.

THE PROCESS OF ATTACHMENT

In Chapter 3, we described attachment as an enduring tie that binds the child to the parent, who is a source of security for the child. We also saw that secure attachments promote positive behaviors. How do parents establish such bonds?

An analysis of sixty-six studies on infants' attachments to mothers (as mothers were the focus of most studies) found four important contributors to secure attachment in the first year:[55]

- *Sensitivity* (ability to perceive the infant's signals accurately and respond appropriately and promptly to the child's needs)
- *Mutuality* (positive harmony and mutuality in relationship)
- *Synchronicity* (coordinated social interactions)
- *Positive attitude* (emotional expressiveness, acceptance, and delight in the child)

Mothers' sensitive, responsive caregiving in infancy not only promotes secure attachment but also reduces resting levels of stress hormones that, in turn, promote greater attention, self-regulation, and cognitive competence at age two.[56] In contrast, fathers' negative parenting of their six-month-old infants triggers higher levels of stress hormones when babies are aroused and higher resting levels of stress hormones at age two.[57] Mothers' negative, harsh parenting in infancy is related to these children's self-descriptions of inattentive and aggressive when they are young adults.[58] The negative interactions in infancy appear to set the stage for toddler noncompliance and angry battles with mothers, and later aggressive behavior problems as reported by kindergarten teachers.[59] Box 7-2 contains interventions.

In the toddler years, parents:

- maintain a state of mutual understanding through continuing sensitivity and availability as a secure base for exploration.
- become teachers and guides for children, balancing support and guidance with increasing independence for the child.
- stay one step ahead of the child's level of interaction and when the child confronts a new barrier, the parent steps in to give just the right amount of help so the child solves the problem and moves on. This form of guidance is termed *scaffolding,* or balancing the child's weakness (see Chapter 6).[60]

Gender Differences in Parents   Research shows that mothers and fathers relate differently to infants in terms of both quantity of time spent and the kinds of activities engaged in with infants.[61] Data collected in the 1980s and 1990s showed that, even though many mothers had jobs, they spent more time with children. In these studies, fathers spent, on average, only 40 percent as much time with children as mothers did.[62]

Data collected from a national representative sample in 1997 reveal that fathers in intact families now spend more time with children.[63] On weekdays, fathers of infants spent 60 percent as much time as mothers in activities and in being available for activities with infants, but on weekends, they spent 80 percent as much time. Fathers do proportionately less caregiving than mothers, but they spend exactly the same amount of time in social activities. In addition to caregiving and play and social activities, fathers also do household chores and teach children.

Box 7-2

INTERVENTIONS TO INCREASE SECURE ATTACHMENTS FOR IRRITABLE BABIES AND THEIR MOTHERS

Concerned that irritable temperament puts babies at risk for insecure attachments with their mothers, Dymphna van den Boom recruited a sample of one hundred irritable babies and their mothers in The Netherlands to intervene to decrease that risk. Babies were identified as irritable infants at the tenth and fifteenth days after birth with Brazelton's Neonatal Behavioral Assessment Scale and randomly assigned to a control or experimental group.*

When infants were between six and nine months, the experimental group received three home visits in which Dr. van den Boom observed mother–infants' interactions and made suggestions to increase mothers' sensitivity and responsiveness. She increased mothers' attentiveness to infants' signals and appropriate responses to them. She also suggested effective ways for mothers to soothe babies when they cried, and explained why it was important to do so. She encouraged mothers to play with their babies to increase pleasurable interactions and reduce the negative quality of interactions. Each visit lasted two hours, and was focused on the individual behaviors of each mother–infant pair.

After the intervention, experimental group mothers were significantly more sensitive, stimulating, and attentive to their nine-month-old children, and their babies were more sociable and more able to soothe themselves. They cried less and explored more. When infants were twelve months of age, 62 percent of babies in the experimental group had secure attachments, while only 22 percent of infants in the control group had secure attachments.

Children and mothers were seen again when children were eighteen, twenty-four, and forty-two months.** Mothers in the experimental group continued to be more attentive, responsive, and supportive, and fathers showed similar behaviors. Their children were more cooperative and involved with peers than children in the control group.

In speculating about the reasons for the long-lasting benefits of the brief intervention, van den Boom attributed the effects to mothers' learning how to attend, interpret, and respond to children's behaviors in sensitive ways. Increases in mothers' sensitivity increased the security of the attachments, and that security also contributed to positive behaviors as children moved outside the immediate family. One suspects that success came partly from the very specific suggestions tailored to each mother–infant pair.

*Dymphna C. van den Boom, "The Influence of Temperament and Mothering on Attachment and Exploration: An Experimental Manipulation of Sensitive Responsiveness among Lower-Class Mothers," *Child Development* 65 (1994): 1457–1477.
**Dymphna C. van den Boom, "Do First-Year Intervention Effects Endure: Follow-up during Toddlerhood of a Sample of Dutch Irritable Infants," *Child Development* 66 (1995): 1798–1816.

Though they show different amounts of involvement, mothers and fathers are equally competent as caregivers.[64] Fathers can be as sensitive as mothers in their interactions with infants, reading and responding accurately to babies' cues. Babies drink as much milk in fathers' care as in mothers'. Mothers are more likely to hold babies in caregiving activities and to verbalize than are fathers. Mothers are thought to provide a "holding environment" for infants as they regulate their system and develop increasing skills in interactions with people and objects.[65]

Fathers are more attentive visually and more playful in physically active ways than are mothers.[66] Fathers are most likely to be highly involved in caregiving and playing when the marital relationship is satisfying and their wives are relaxed and outgoing. Both fathers and mothers give mostly care and physical affection in the first three months, when babies are settling in. As babies become less fussy and more alert at three months, both parents become more stimulating and reactive.[67]

TASKS AND CONCERNS FOR PARENTS OF INFANTS

Marc Bornstein describes four main tasks for the parents of infants:[68]

- Nurturant caregiving: providing food, protection, warmth, and affection
- Material caregiving: providing and organizing the babies' world with inanimate objects, stimulation, and opportunities for exploration
- Social caregiving: engaging and interacting with infants—hugging, soothing, comforting, vocalizing, playing
- Didactic caregiving: stimulating infants' interest in and understanding of the world outside the parent-child relationship by introducing objects, interpreting the surrounding world, and giving information

T. Berry Brazelton and Stanley Greenspan add that both parents and children require a community that supports parents' efforts and children's growth.[69]

We look here at two main tasks of parenting: (1) establishing an optimal level of arousal for infants, and (2) promoting infants' self-regulation.

ESTABLISHING AN OPTIMAL LEVEL OF AROUSAL

Reducing time spent in crying and establishing healthy sleep patterns promote a state of arousal that enables babies to respond to people and to the world around them. Although parents in the United States most often rely on the independent model of caregiving, behaviors characteristic of the interdependent model, such as nursing for a year and carrying babies, have increased.[70] So, let us look at which strategies work best to reduce crying and promote healthy sleep patterns.

Crying

As noted, crying increases from about two hours at birth to three at six weeks and decreases to about one at three months of age. Those mothers who responded immediately to the cries of the baby had babies who cried less at six to twelve months. Conversely, ignoring a baby's cries seemed to increase the amount of crying.[71] Mothers' immediate response to babies' distress when babies are six months of age not only decreases crying but also promotes babies' social competence and their ability to regulate their behavior at age two.[72]

VOICES OF EXPERIENCE

The Joys of Parenting Children
in the First Two Years

"I love babies. There is something about that bond between mother and baby. I love the way they look and smell and the way they hunker up to your neck. To me it's a magic time. I didn't like to babysit particularly growing up, and I wasn't wild about other people's babies, but there was something about having my own; I just love it. And every one, we used to wonder, how are we going to love another as much as the one before; and that is ridiculous, because you love every one." MOTHER

"There is joy in just watching her change, seeing her individualize. From the beginning it seemed she had her own personality—we see that this is not just a little blob of protoplasm here; this is a little individual already from the beginning. She has always had a real specialness about her. It was exciting to see her change." FATHER

"I think it's wonderful to have a baby in the house, to hear the baby laugh, sitting in the high chair, banging spoons, all the fun things babies do. They seem to me to light up a household. When there's a baby here, a lot of the aggravations in the household somehow disappear. Everyone looks at the baby, plays with the baby, and even if people are in a bad mood, they just light up when the baby comes in the room. I think there is something magical about having a baby in the house." MOTHER

"There is the excitement of baby talk becoming real words." MOTHER

"I enjoy that she directs me more than I could sense. Before, there was a 'yes' or 'no' response, but now there is more back and forth. If I dress her, she shows me she wants to sit or stand—'Do it this way' is what she seems to say. Before, she was tired or not tired, hungry or not hungry, okay or not okay. Now there is much more variation." FATHER

"I've heard of this, and it's true; it's rediscovering the child in yourself. Sometimes, it's the joy that he and I hop around the couch like two frogs on our hands and knees. Or we're in the bathtub pretending we are submarines and alligators. Sometimes he likes to ride around on my shoulders, and I run and make noises like an airplane or a bird. And I am not just doing it for him, but we are doing it together, playing together." FATHER

"I was just blown away by the way he tries to help other children. From a very young age, he has done this. Now, when a little girl he sees everyday cries, he takes her one toy after another and says, 'This is? This is?' meaning, 'Is this what you want?' until he gets her to stop crying by giving her something she wants. He's very people oriented, very affectionate, and seems so secure." MOTHER

"Watching her grow, seeing her grow, seeing the different stages, I just take pleasure in everything she does now, because I know she will be on to a new stage soon." MOTHER

"As he gets older, I relate more, play more. He is more of a joy. Some of the joys are so unexpected. I would stop myself and open up and think, 'Oh, this is my son, he's so joyful. He's smiling for no particular reason.' I am not that joyful, but he's joyful for no reason. He reminds me of joy." FATHER

What strategy is most effective in terminating crying? Caregivers around the world follow similar methods—soothing babies by "rocking, patting, cuddling, swaddling, giving suck on breast or pacifier."[73]

Supplemental carrying in a sling for three extra hours per day from three to twelve weeks decreased crying, but not in all studies of crying.[74] In one study, carrying not only reduces crying, but increases secure attachments at one year.[75] Low-income, inner-city mothers who from birth carried their babies in slings rather than infant seats were more vocally responsive with infants at three months and at thirteen months and had higher rates of secure attachments (83 percent) than mothers using infant seats (38 percent with secure attachments). Myron Hofer, who has studied the effects of maternal behavior on the infant rat's neurological and regulatory systems, believes that the movements experienced in slings help develop the child's vestibular sense of balance and motion in space, contributing to a child's sense of emotional security.[76]

When healthy babies cry more than three hours a day for more than three days a week for more than three weeks, they are said to have colic.[77] No one knows what causes it, and it may be the highest end of normal crying behavior, as it has the same pattern of increasing after birth, peaking at six weeks, and decreasing at three months.

Babies' crying upsets parents as they feel helpless to comfort their babies. Primarily parents are advised to search for patterns of soothing activities, some of which work some of the time. Parents use Dr. Karp's Cuddle Cure (Box 7-1), rock, carry, and soothe babies.

Pediatrician William Sammons has observed that babies gradually have the ability to calm themselves, sucking on fingers and wrists or focusing on objects or walls[78] and encourages parents to engage in a mutual partnership with babies so that infants can find their own ways to calm themselves. Jodi Mindell believes that if parents have tried everything, they should give themselves a rest. It is possible that in the rest, babies may find their own ways to self-calm. We discuss strategies for reducing crying and the effects of crying on parents in a later section.

Sleep

In most parts of the world, infants sleep with a parent (co-sleeping), and most toddlers and older children sleep with or near a parent. Surveys reveal that, in the United States, infants in middle-class families sleep alone in bassinets, and by six months of age, most sleep in their own rooms.[79] While co-sleeping has occurred more frequently in American families with less income and less space, a growing number of more advantaged parents sleep with their babies, perhaps to reduce babies' crying or to stay connected with the child at night.

A longitudinal study of sleeping patterns in England revealed four patterns of sleeping from birth to age four: never co-sleeping (66 percent), co-sleeping only in the first year (13 percent), cosleeping after the first year (15 percent), and co-sleeping for the entire four years (6 percent).[80] Thus about one-third of the sample co-slept at one point, and co-sleeping was associated with increased breastfeeding.

A New Zealand longitudinal study of sleep patterns in the first twelve months of life was designed to give clinicians empirical data for discussing sleep issues with parents and revealed that infants typically consolidate their sleep times in the first five months of life. Criteria for sleeping through the night are:[81]

- sleeping five hours or more at night,
- sleeping eight hours from midnight to 8:00 A.M., and
- sleeping the social pattern that conforms to the family from 10:00 P.M until 6:00 A.M.

Fifty percent of babies met criteria 1 and 2 by three months of age, and criteria 3 by five months. By twelve months, 87 percent, 86 percent, and 73 percent met criteria 1, 2, and 3 respectively.

When babies are expected to sleep in their own cribs—whether in parents' room or their own—the general approach is to help babies develop healthy sleep habits so they get the amount and quality of sleep they need. Drs. Richard Ferber[82] and Jodi Mindell,[83] directors of children's sleep disorder clinics, believe parents have a major role in establishing children's healthy sleep habits.

Since most babies (and adults) awake briefly several times during the night, babies must fall asleep in ways they can duplicate to return to sleep on their own in the middle of the night. If they develop the habit of falling asleep while nursing or being rocked, they will be unable to duplicate those conditions in the middle of the night and will cry.

About six weeks after birth, parents begin a regular bedtime routine that precedes the evening sleep time even if they do not establish a regular bedtime until the child is about three to five months, when sleep patterns have stabilized.[84] The aim is to have a consistent sequence of calming activities that prepare the child for sleep. Since our inner clock is based on a twenty-five-hour cycle, we need a regular schedule to keep to a twenty-four-hour day, and babies must depend on parents to set the schedule.

Infants and children often cry and object to being left in bed. Both Ferber and Mindell agree that parents should enter the bedroom to reassure the child that everything is okay; parents do n ot return and engage in previous activities. Mindell says parents can go in as often as they want to reassure the child, and Ferber has a more structured program for entries.

Although co-sleeping is associated with increased breastfeeding, the American Academy of Pediatrics does not recommend it because Western beds are not designed for that and infant deaths are attributed to parents' rolling over on the child or the child's being wedged between the mattress and wall or trapped between the headboard and the mattress.[85] Currently infant beds that can be attached to adult beds lack safety standards.

There are common safety rules regardless of where babies sleep, with some additional ones for co-sleeping.[86] All babies should:

- sleep on a firm mattress and not on soft chairs or sofas, waterbeds, or pillows
- have only light coverings; comforters, quilts, or heavy blankets can suffocate or overheat the baby
- sleep in a crib meeting national standards to prevent wedging or entrapment; when put to sleep, their feet should be at the foot of the bed
- be put to sleep on their backs to prevent suffocation; the Back to Sleep rule

- in the first year be put to sleep for naps and at night with a pacifier as research suggests that for unknown reasons a pacifier decreases sudden infant deaths; a pacifier should not be forced or reinserted if it falls out

Co-sleeping parents are advised not to sleep with babies when they have physical conditions that decrease their arousal at night (e.g., sleep apnea; extreme fatigue; alcohol, drug, or medication use). Parents are also advised not to put co-sleeping babies next to toddlers and older children.

Attachment Parenting

In contemporary society, co-sleeping is one facet of a larger system of *attachment parenting,* which incorporates many aspects of the interdependent model of caregiving. Pediatrician William Sears encourages parents to accept their babies' dependency needs and meet them appropriately. He describes the five Bs of attachment parenting in infancy: (1) bonding with the infant at birth, (2) breast-feeding, (3) bed sharing (cosleeping), (4) baby wearing (carrying the baby in a sling), and (5) belief in the baby's cry as an important signal. The five Bs keep baby and parents physically connected so parents can learn who their child is and be able to respond in a sensitive, caring way.[87]

> With attachment parenting, parents and children find their needs in cooperation with one another, thus creating a family-centered lifestyle. A key benefit of this responsive style of caregiving is that both parents and children feel that they are getting their "cup filled," as some parents say. Children feel whole and secure, while parents feel more relaxed and confident.[88]

Attachment parenting does not require that a caregiver be at home full-time, and there is much advice on how to combine attachment parenting and working. Parents are advised to create a community of caregivers who share the parents' values and will behave in the same way toward the baby when the parents are not there. Such caregivers would give breast milk the mothers have pumped, carry the children during the day, and respond quickly and attentively to children's cries.

Advocates believe that "experienced attachment parents who have seen their children through early childhood and beyond describe this gentle nurturing style as a completely fulfilling way of life."[89] Research certainly supports elements of attachment parenting—the importance of sensitive, responsive care and the decrease in crying that comes from increased early carrying—but it is not clear that co-sleeping and prolonged carrying of the child are beneficial, nor is it clear that immediate gratification of desires is essential or wise for all babies. Recall that soothed fearful and inhibited children maintained those behaviors when firm support to learn self-soothing appeared more useful in helping them overcome the behaviors (see Chapter 3).

Parenting, Infant Crying, and Sleeping

Researchers in England and Denmark followed parents and babies for twelve weeks after babies' births, collecting diaries of their own behaviors and babies' feeding, daily activities, crying, and sleep for four consecutive days when babies were ten days, five weeks, and twelve weeks of age.[90] The sample consisted of three groups of parents who, prior to the births of their children, had selected one of three forms of infant care.

The London community sample selected a form of Western or European care in which parents were more likely to put babies in strollers or seats to play alone when alert, let babies wait before responding to their cries, and put them to sleep in their own beds at night (82 percent at ten days and 89 percent at twelve weeks), and less likely to breastfeed (70 percent at ten days and 37 percent at twelve weeks).

The attachment parents breastfed (95 percent at ten days and 85 percent at twelve weeks) and breastfed babies more frequently, held babies more than 80 percent of the time (16 hours and 29 minutes in 24 hours), responded more quickly to babies' crying, and co-slept with babies most of the night (73 percent at ten days and 70 percent at twelve weeks). The parents in the Copenhagen community sample were like attachment parents in responding quickly to distress, and more likely to cosleep at least part of the night with children than London parents, but held children less often (9 hours and 44 minutes at ten days as compared to 16 hours). These differences in behavior patterns of parents and babies continued to be seen when babies were five weeks of age.

The study revealed that:

- the amount of time parents spent playing and interacting was similar in all three groups at ten days
- the percentage of babies with unsoothable crying and colic was similar in all three groups at ten days and five weeks and decreased in all three groups by twelve weeks, confirming the view that unsoothable crying and colic are not related to parenting
- babies in all three groups reduced their crying by about one-third between ten days and twelve weeks
- infants of London parents at ten days and five weeks spent 50 percent more time fussing and crying than babies of Copenhagen and attachment parents, but reduced their crying by twelve weeks of age
- infants of London and Copenhagen parents were more likely at twelve weeks to sleep five or more hours at night without waking and crying than babies of attachment parents who continued to cry and wake their parents at ten months

Each form of care had some benefits. Infant crying was reduced in babies of both Copenhagen and attachment parents, suggesting it was the greater holding time and greater responsiveness to distress that decreased crying as these two groups differed in frequency of feeding and co-sleeping. The Western parenting of London parents was effective in establishing longer hours of sleep. The infant care of Copenhagen parents was as successful as attachment parenting in reducing crying and as effective as that of London parents in establishing longer hours of sleep. Recall that parents selected infant care practices before they knew their children's crying and sleep behaviors. Parents can choose infant care practices based on these empirical findings. Box 7-3 presents an additional method.

Box 7-3
FIRST PERSON NARRATIVE

Ruth Anne Hammond's book, *Respecting Babies,** is her story of learning about, applying, and becoming a teacher in the method of rearing infants and toddlers developed by Hungarian pediatrician Emmi Pikler, and brought to the United States by early childhood educator Magda Gerber. Ms. Hammond learned of the method in a childbirth preparation class when she was pregnant with her first child, and was so impressed with it that she and her husband immediately adopted it and joined a parent-infant class led by Magda Gerber. Ms. Hammond then went on to become a certified teacher in the method known as the Resources for Infant Educarers (RIE, pronounced "rye") that is based on the belief that, "What adults do with infants and toddlers either supports or undermines their inner drive to learn and to develop their unique capacities as human beings."** In classes and groups, parents and caregivers learn how to "provide the necessary scaffolding for infants and toddlers to maximize their capacity for self-regulation and purposeful activity."

Ms. Hammond describes how she and other parents focus on the quality of the interactions with babies, observing how babies are reacting and feeling, engaging them as active partners in all activities, talking to them, telling them what is happening and what will happen in soft, calm tones of voice. Parents provide regular, consistent routines so babies can anticipate what will happen. In one chapter, Ms. Hammond describes how parents touch babies and young children with care and sensitivity, supporting their bodies so they are comfortable and able to explore in the safe environments parents provide.

While interacting requires time and sensitivity, without multitasking, she describes how parents do depend on babies' abilities to amuse themselves and explore and learn so parents are not responsible for teaching babies every moment. Once babies have a safe environment and oversight to be sure their activities are safe, they are allowed to play and learn about their world.

Ms. Hammond talks about how sensitive interactions and consistent routines avoid the overstimulation and overactivity that make it hard for babies and toddlers to settle down at night and soothe themselves so they can fall sleep. She also describes how the approach enables toddlers to learn to regulate their behavior. Although this approach has not been subjected to a controlled study comparing it to other child-rearing programs as was done with attachment parenting in the study just discussed, there is much research evidence to support the different elements of the program: sensitive, responsive caregiving, talking to babies, opportunities for play and exploration, healthy sleep routines. Her experiences and those of other parents provide many thoughtful insights about care for infants and toddlers. One of the interesting observations, for example, is that babies may be very uncomfortable on their tummies until they have arm strength and can lift their heads and support their trunks. Before that, it is hard to see and play. One box is entitled, "Try Tummy Time Yourself." It is true, it is not comfortable for seeing and playing until one has very strong arms, trunk, and head control. They advise letting babies put themselves in tummy time when they can roll in and out of it themselves. Until then time on their backs is more supportive of play.

*Ruth Anne Hammond, *Respecting Babies: A New Look at Magda Gerber's RIE Approach* (Washington, DC: ZERO TO THREE, 2009).
**Ibid., page 1.

PROMOTING SELF-REGULATION

Now we turn to a task that parents find challenging and demanding: helping children develop the ability to control their own behavior.

Encouraging Compliance

Parents first create an atmosphere of mutual responsiveness and receptive compliance. Secure attachments to children and sensitive caretaking create a climate in which children are more likely to comply.[91] When noncompliance occurs, parents use reasoning and explanations—low-power techniques—that result in a sharing of power. Sharing power with children has a strong impact because it communicates essential respect for the child as a person.

Parents take many other actions to encourage self-control and self-regulation, including:[92]

> *Modeling*—showing the behaviors you want your child to learn
>
> *Consistent daily routines that help children learn rules*—it is much easier for babies to calm down for sleep if every night a child has a bath, nursing, a song, rocking, and bed in that order rather than an unpredictable rotation of these activities
>
> *Preventive actions to head off potential problems*—parents divert children's attention from tempting but forbidden activities by suggesting interesting substitutes (e.g., in grocery stores, suggesting children pick out the family items on the shelf when they are bored)
>
> *Conversations about rules and reasons for them*—when everyone is relaxed and there are no conflicts, conversations about rules and how people feel when rules are broken help children to understand what is expected and why

Establishing Rules

Parents generally introduce rules that dovetail with the toddler's increasing abilities. Research reveals that

- at thirteen months, rules center on safety for the child, for other people (no hitting, kicking, or biting), and for possessions.
- at about eighteen months, the rules expand to include behavior during meals, requests to inhibit behavior and delay activity, and early self-care.
- at about twenty-four months, rules center on polite behavior and helping with family chores (putting toys away) are included.
- at thirty-six months, children are expected to do more self-care, such as dressing themselves.[93]

Children's compliance with safety rules is high and increases with age. The time and involvement required for promoting all areas of self-regulation are enormous, and parents of two-year-olds intervene eight to ten times per hour to gain compliance.

Such parents need a great deal of energy and support.[94] When parents have difficulties in encouraging rule compliance, guidelines in Chapter 6 provide strategies for them.

Temperament and Early Parenting

In the early months of life, babies' reactivity and emotionality strongly influence what parents do and the effects of parents' actions. We discussed this relationship generally in Chapter 3, and here we discuss how temperament affects what parents do in the first two years. We have already described the effects of babies' fussy, irritable behavior on parents' caregiving. When parents lack success in soothing babies, they may withdraw or become harsh and restrictive in discipline, increasing babies' irritability and negative mood. This is especially true when parents have limited economic resources. When parents are older and have more economic resources, parents are more likely to be patient and supportive with babies, the very qualities that are likely to decrease fussiness and irritability.[95]

When young infants are fearful and inhibited in response to new and unfamiliar people and events, sensitive parents are nurturant and protective with their infants, so infants tend to remain fearful and inhibited. The children who decrease in fearfulness and inhibition over time have parents who are both supportive and sensitive, yet expose children to new events, encouraging them to develop coping strategies.[96]

When inhibited, fearful children become toddlers, they are very responsive to parents' instructions and rules.[97] They need only gentle support to internalize the rules. When parents are assertive and directive, using power harshly at times to dictate to children, toddlers become so emotionally stressed they do not learn the rules.

Fearless children who are energetic, curious, self-directed, and independent also fail to respond to power-assertive, restrictive discipline.[98] They learn rules most easily when parents form close, warm, harmonious relationships. Children then follow the rules to maintain the caring and responsive relationship they have with parents.

Harsh, power-assertive discipline is not effective in helping children learn to regulate their reactions and behavior, especially children with temperamental problems. Parents are most effective in helping children develop self-control and self-regulation when they are warm and sensitive, have harmonious relationships with children, and are gently supportive yet firm in encouraging children to develop coping strategies.

Play, Reading, and Fun

Family fun turns out to be very beneficial for children's growth as well. We know children need toys and objects and opportunities to explore in order to learn about the world. But children benefit also from pretend play, especially with parents. For example, when mothers and fathers engage in imaginary play with their toddlers, toddlers play in a more sophisticated way than they do when playing alone.[99] And they learn from such play. Parents and toddlers talk about what they are doing, and language skills and social understanding increase.

A comparison of mother-toddler play in European American, South American immigrant, and Japanese immigrant families reveals universal patterns of play with

Fun activities are very beneficial for children's growth and development.

exploratory and pretend play found in all three groups and children's play being more sophisticated when playing with mothers. In all three groups, boys engaged in more exploratory play when they played alone but not when they played with mothers.[100] Interestingly, research shows that engaging in interactive, productive play in the early years promotes self-control[101] and reduces the risk of behavior problems later in school.[102] As we noted in Chapter 6, it is not exactly clear how play produces positive benefits.

Parents' daily reading to children promotes vocabulary growth and increases intellectual skills.[103] So fun activities, like playing make-believe games, has long-lasting intellectual benefits and important emotional benefits in the form of greater self-control.

PARENTS' EXPERIENCES IN FACING TRANSITIONS

Parents adjust their prebirth images of themselves as parents with the reality of their daily nurturing of their baby.[104] When expectations have been unrealistic, adjustments are painful. Parents of young toddlers face another transition—to Galinsky's authority stage (see Chapter 4). This lasts from the child's second to fourth or fifth year. In dealing with their own feelings about having power, setting rules, and enforcing them, parents have to decide what is reasonable when children mobilize all their energy to oppose them and gain their way and when it is best to compromise.

McHale returned to observe parents' ways of interacting with their one-year-olds and each other.[105] While parents were more confident in interacting with children and all couples had developed some form of coparenting alliance, all parents reported they wanted to improve. All parents wanted more time with the family and for the family to be a major priority. Additionally, fathers wanted mothers to be more relaxed and patient, and mothers wanted fathers to spend more time in child-care and family activities, and to volunteer to help without being asked.

This sample was an advantaged one in which 35 percent of mothers did not work outside the home, an additional 42 percent of mothers had part-time employment, and only 23 percent of mothers were employed full-time. Parents had settled into a pattern in which mothers were the primary organizers and managers of family life, and fathers helped out when asked. Rarely were fathers partners in planning and carrying out child care, and as a result about one-third of mothers felt overwhelmed.

When parents disagreed about parenting behaviors, they were more likely to be critical and outspoken than they were when babies were three months old. Beliefs about parenting expressed during pregnancy predicted these behaviors. When parents anticipated disagreements in their interactions, disagreements occurred after the births. Parents who were very unlike in parenting beliefs were most likely to have disagreements when babies were twelve months old.

Warm, cooperative coparenting alliances established at three months tended to continue. Marital distress seemed the main factor in decreasing the collaboration. There were, however, a small group of parents who were unhappy in the marriage but made a strong commitment to work with the other parent for the child's well-being.

PROGRAMS TO HELP PARENTS WITH SPECIAL STRESSORS

Even advantaged parents like those in McHale's study felt stress and depression in meeting babies' needs, especially when babies are irritable and hard to soothe. So let us see how parenting programs help parents deal with all the changes and new responsibilities.

Effectiveness of Parenting Programs for Expectant and New Parents

A meta-analysis of 142 studies of the effectiveness of parenting programs found that, "Early parenting education programs for expectant and new parents produce a significant positive effect on all assessed outcomes."[106] Outcomes included: reducing parents' stress, increasing parents' skills as caregivers, promoting babies' cognitive, social, and motor development, improving parents' mental health, and the couple's adjustment. The meta-analysis also reviewed follow-up studies and found that positive effects of the programs were maintained over an interval of twenty-nine months.

Another kind of parenting group including both mothers and fathers for weekly meetings over a six-month period from the last trimester of pregnancy to the end of the third month after the birth focused on how couples were managing the changes involved in becoming a family.[107] The programs sought to prevent the drop in marital satisfaction that is typically seen after a couple have a baby. Couples who participated in the couples' groups showed significantly less decline in marital satisfaction than control couples who did not have the intervention. One of the reasons for the success of the program may have been that it gave couples a chance to anticipate the changes and think about how to manage them.

Programs to Help Parents with Babies' Crying and Sleep Difficulties

Meeting babies' needs successfully makes parents feel confident about themselves as parents. They feel good about their partners, and they love their babies.[108] Fortunately, most parents experience this positive cycle of feelings.

But as many as 20 percent of parents have irritable, distressed babies who cry more than three hours per day and don't sleep. These parents feel stressed and exhausted, doubt their own skills, and feel others are critical of them. In focus groups, they say more than anything, they want people to listen to their concerns with empathy.[109]

An interdisciplinary program in Chicago, The Fussy Baby Network, has formed to help these parents so they and their babies can get off to a good start.[110] The network provides many services—preventive education classes to give information and parenting skills, professional assessment of babies' development to identify existing problems, interventions needed to help babies, assessments of parents' mental health, and training and consultation for parents, often in the home.

Three principles guide network activity. Professionals provide (1) an emotionally safe place for parents to express their concerns and obtain referrals, (2) a collaborative relationship in which parents' insights are sought, and parents develop their own strategies, and (3) support in moving forward in small steps. The long-term objectives are to increase parents' confidence, their knowledge and understanding of their baby, and to promote positive relationships among all family members. Their core message to parents is, "You are not alone. You are a good parent." "You are handling a hard situation well."

Parents report stress drops from an average score of 4.59 (on a scale of five) to 0.93 when the program ends.

Parents at Risk for Abuse of Infants

Parents at risk for maltreating children benefit from special programs. In one study parents were identified at the child's birth on the basis of two factors:[111] (1) a child's risk for health problems (because of prematurity or low Apgar scores at birth) and (2) parents' risk for poor care (e.g., history of partner violence, substance abuse or mental illness, victim of physical abuse, past involvement with Children's Protective Services). Parents were assigned to one of three groups: a control group that was given information about community services, a home visit (HV) group, or an enhanced home visit (EHV) group. The HV program provided parent education, anger management skills, and establishment of a social support network. The HVs occurred approximately every two weeks for a year and covered such topics as setting and reaching family goals, obtaining health-care and medical services, parenting skills, and managing finances. Parents were trained to support children's healthy development in the areas of physical, language, and socioemotional growth.

In the EHV program, parents received all the services of the HV program, and at the beginning of each HV, they also received additional psychological training for dealing with children's behavior. Researchers have found that when parents at risk for child abuse confront problems with children's behavior, they see themselves as helpless in confronting powerful children who are determined to defy them and get their own way. They blame themselves or the child for the problem.

The additional training was designed to empower parents and help them develop confidence in their abilities to care for their children in a competent way. The program had two specific aims: to help parents (1) change their perceptions of their children's behavior and (2) develop problem-solving strategies for coping with children's problem behaviors. At the beginning of every HV, parents described a recent problem with children, and then the home visitor asked why they thought the behavior occurred. For example, a parent might say that a baby was crying for a long time because she was mad at the parent or because the parent was a bad parent. Home visitors continued to elicit parents' reasons for the child's behavior until parents gave a benign or non-blame interpretation of children's actions—for example, the child is crying because the formula needs adjusting or he needs to eat more often. Home visitors never pointed out parents' misinterpretations.

Home visitors then asked parents to think about actions to reduce the problem. Was there something they could do immediately or did they need more information? Conversation continued until parents came up with a specific action to carry out. At the next visit, parents reviewed the results of the action and fine-tuned the solution as necessary.

At the end of the year the rates of child abuse and harsh parenting (defined as frequency of physically abusive tactics or spanking/slapping) and child health differed in the three groups: Parents in the EHV program were less likely to physically abuse their children (4 percent) than parents in HV (23 percent) and control groups (26 percent). Infant spanking and slapping (legally not abusive) also decreased—only 18 percent of mothers in the EHV program spanked infants, as compared to 42 percent of mothers in the HV and control groups. The rate of spanking in EHV mothers is similar to that of college-educated mothers. The differences between the groups were most striking in the caregiving of medically at-risk infants.

Children's physical health (defined as freedom from physical health problems in the first year) improved with the addition of services to families. Physical health was highest for children in families receiving EHV, then for those with HV, then for those children in the control group. Added services made a difference. Further work is needed to replicate the results of the study and to follow children's well-being for a longer period of time to note the length of the intervention effects.

The intervention programs cited illustrate that it is possible to shift parents' child-rearing attitudes and behaviors, and that changes in the direction of positive, supportive parenting improve children's health and behavior.

WISDOM OF AND FOR PARENTS

The programs reviewed indicate parents have the capacity for positive caregiving, as even brief interventions had profound effects in triggering a positive or benign cycle of interactions between parent and child. For example, when mothers carried babies in slings from birth, the rate of secure attachments at one year was similar to that in advantaged, college-educated samples. When low-income mothers of irritable six-month-old babies received three two-hour visits focusing on positive forms of interaction, mothers and infants had high rates of secure attachment at one year and positive forms of family interactions and social play with peers at age three. These interventions unlock parents' inner capacities for giving loving care.

We have seen that most parents experience stress, and so all families benefit from supportive services. A wise network of family and friends is sometimes sufficient. Parents with financial assets are increasingly hiring baby coaches who come into the home and advise on routines for healthy sleeping, eating, and discipline. Parents of more modest means often rely on community organizations such as Zero to Three.

Zero to Three is a national organization that supports "the healthy development and well-being of infants, toddlers, and their families."[112] The nonprofit organization seeks to inform and educate parents, professionals who work with parents of infants and young children, and public policymakers regarding young children's needs. The organization holds annual training institutes to bring the latest research to professionals who work with young children and families. It also has developed educational materials for parents that reflect "the belief that parents are the true experts on their children." Thus, each parent must develop his or her own way of promoting a child's growth. Their parent pamphlet, titled "What's Best for My Baby and Me?" presents information on babies' temperament and its effect on behavior, possible interpretations of babies' behavior, and a three-step approach to parenting infants and young toddlers.[113]

All these programs enable parents to learn effective responses for their particular child and contribute to parents' feelings of competency and parental self-efficacy, defined as the belief that one can perform appropriate parental behaviors and influence the child's development.[114] Parental self-efficacy is positively related to parents' satisfaction in the parenting role and to the quality of care parents give children. It also serves as a buffer against stressful factors in the social environment and in the child's development. When difficulties arise, parents believe their behaviors make a difference, and they act.

MAIN POINTS

In the first two years, infants

- gain control over their bodies and learn to sit alone, stand, walk, and run
- take a lively interest in the world around them, reaching out to grasp and explore objects and the world

- develop language gradually from cooing and babbling in the early months, to words at one year and two-word sentences by age two
- develop a wide range of emotional reactions; at the end of the first year, they express anger, fear, joy, pleasure, curiosity, and surprise, and by the end of the second year, they show more affection, more eagerness to please, greater resistance to parents' directives, and great delight in their accomplishments

Effective parents

- are nurturant, material, social, and didactic caregivers
- are available, attentive, sensitive partners who synchronize their behavior with the child's individual needs
- soothe babies and help them regulate their physiological states
- form enduring attachments with their children
- stimulate development when they play and converse with children
- interact with infants in different ways, with mothers holding babies more and doing more caregiving and fathers being more playful and physically stimulating

Parents regulate children's behavior effectively when they

- establish an atmosphere of mutual understanding
- act to prevent problems
- introduce safety rules before other rules
- use low-power techniques such as reasoning and explanation when noncompliance occurs

Parents likely to have trouble establishing secure attachments with infants

- have a negative, critical approach to children that arouses stress hormones and sets in motion a negative cycle of interactions
- have difficulty effectively timing responses to children, either withdrawing or overstimulating them
- can be helped with interventions that provide education, opportunities for the parent to get to know the child, and talk with other parents and gain support

Preterm babies

- make special physical and psychological demands on parents
- have a narrow range of optimal stimulation that is neither over- nor understimulating
- receive long-term benefits from parents' attention and stimulation

As they incorporate infants into family life, parents

- often do not anticipate the stress produced by the number of changes needed
- seek support from each other and their social network
- experience many joys

EXERCISES

1. Recalling the father's comment on page 212 that he knew so little about babies that he should not have been permitted to take one home from the hospital, work in small groups to devise an outline for what new parents should know before they leave the hospital. Compare suggestions among the different groups.

2. Go to a toy store and spend an imaginary $150 on toys for an infant or toddler. Justify your choices. If possible, go again and spend money after reading Ruth Anne Hammond's book, *Respecting Babies*. Would your choices be different?

3. Go to a supermarket or a park on a weekend and observe parents and infants or parents and toddlers. Note how the children respond to the environment around them, to parents, and to passersby. Try to find children about the same age to see how individual differences among children determine responses to the same environment. Observe parenting behaviors, and describe their effects on the children.

4. Go to local hospitals and agencies to determine what kinds of instruction or hands-on training is given to parents to provide safe environments for infants and toddlers.

5. Interview mothers or fathers about how much time they spend with their infants and toddlers each day. What is the family schedule? Who does what? What do they most enjoy doing with their young child? What do they see as the greatest joys and stresses of having children?

ADDITIONAL READINGS

Brazelton, T. Berry and Greenspan, Stanley I. *The Irreducible Needs of Children.* Cambridge, MA: Perseus, 2000.

Galinsky, Ellen. *Mind in the Making: The Seven Essential Life Skills Every Child Needs.* New York: HarperCollins, 2010.

Gopnik, Allison. *The Philosophical Baby: What Children's Minds Tell Us about Truth, Love, and the Meaning of Life.* New York: Farrar, Straus and Giroux, 2009.

Hammond, Ruth Anne. *Respecing Babies: A New Look at Magda Gerber's RIE Approach.* Washington, DC: Zero to Three, 2009.

Karp, Harvey. *The Happiest Baby on the Block.* New York: Bantam, 2002.

8

Parenting Children in Early Childhood: The Years from Two to Five

---

CHAPTER TOPICS

In this chapter, you will learn about:

- Children's development
- Relationships with parents, siblings, and peers
- Managing sleep, aggression, withdrawal, and developmental delays
- Parents' experiences and supports

Test Your Knowledge: Fact or Fiction (True/False)

1. Poverty not only reduces physical resources such as books and toys in the home, but also affects the amount of positive attention children receive.
2. Like adolescents, preschoolers believe it is acceptable to break parents' rules about wearing items of clothing because clothing is a matter of personal choice.
3. Almost all children are physically aggressive in the years from two to three.
4. The moment with the most potential for causing emotional trauma for a child with special needs is when the child realizes that society views his or her differences as signs of inferiority.
5. Parent-child interactions account for only about 10 percent of the emotional distress preschoolers experience at home.

In this chapter, we look at how parents help children make sense of the world around them and support children's growing sense of self. Parental behaviors to help children learn to regulate their behavior and promote positive relations with peers and others outside the home are examined. We also discuss how and where parents get support as they raise their children.

By age two, children have learned the basic skills of walking and talking. They want to understand all that is going on. Their sense of personal identity grows, and they are forming a sense of gender and ethnic identity as they play with other children, share activities, and engage in pretend play. They learn to control their emotional reactions and their behavior. Parents help children advance in all these areas and prepare them for the transition to school and learning outside the home.

PHYSICAL AND NEUROPHYSIOLOGICAL DEVELOPMENT

Between ages two and five, children grow more slowly than before, but still, they grow from about 34 inches and 29 pounds at age two to 42 inches and 42–45 pounds at age five. Children's brains are active and primed for learning. Compared with an adult brain, a three-year-old's brain has twice as many synapses (connections among brain cells), is two and a half times more active, requires more glucose, and has more neurotransmitters (chemicals that facilitate the transmission of information from one cell to another).[1] At puberty, children's brains begin to eliminate little-used connections in a process called pruning so the number of synaptic connections is reduced to that found in adult brains. Brain development increases children's motor control, attention, and memory, which underlie advances in motor, cognitive, and personal–social functioning.

INTELLECTUAL DEVELOPMENT

Children are active and verbal. Increased attention span and increased memory enable children to focus on activities for a longer time and recall more detailed sequences, so thinking becomes more complex. Children can distinguish real events from imagined ones and from dreams and nightmares.[2]

Children continue to explore the world through action, but now use questions to get information. Children ask as many as seventy to ninety questions an hour.[3] Many are "why" questions: "Why does the sun come up in the morning?" "Why can't I fly like a bird?" And children expect answers. If answers are not satisfactory, they ask again.[4] As they seek guidance, preschoolers assess the accuracy of what the person has said in the past; they rely on those who have demonstrated knowledge.[5] When children's actions do not achieve their goals, they recall the successful actions of others and use them.[6]

Verbal skills, the ability to control attention and effort, and persistence when frustrated all contribute to learning and parents play a strong role in helping children develop these skills as we describe in a later section.[7] Neuroendocrine levels also play a role. Moderate cortisol arousal followed by down-regulation was associated with measures of flexible problem solving, self-regulation, and letter knowledge.[8]

By the preschool years, some children have developed what is termed mastery motivation, a strong desire to investigate objects and problems and achieve mastery of them.[9] Children high in this quality persist with challenging tasks and take pride

VOICES OF EXPERIENCE

What I Wish I Had Known about the Years from Two to Five

"I wish I'd known how to react when they lied. You know kids lie, but it hurts me terribly. It was a very painful experience even though I know I did it." MOTHER

"I wish I had known how much frustration comes just because kids are kids and you have to be tolerant. They don't have the attention span for some things. They might want to do something with you, but they can only do it for about fifteen minutes. You have to go places prepared with all his things or with things to keep him entertained. In the car on a trip, we have a lot of things for him to do. When you plan ahead, you can still be spontaneous at times. You learn that if you are prepared, things really don't have to be a hassle." FATHER

"Everything. I wish I'd known more about communication, how to talk to your children, and the most effective way to help them grow with a strong ego, a good sense of self. We were raised with a lot of 'Do this and don't do that' demands and commands. Trying to get in touch with your child's feelings so you really do understand how they feel about things is really hard to learn. I don't know how you can learn it without the experience of actually having a child. But I'm continually learning how to understand her feelings about things." MOTHER

"I think it is incredible that we don't teach anything about being a parent. I have to learn it as I go along, because I want things to be different for them than they were for me growing up. I can't use my own experiences as a guide." FATHER

"I wish I had known how to handle things like believing in Santa Claus. I didn't know whether to encourage it or not or when to tell her there was none. She learned gradually, I think, but she doesn't want to tell her little brother yet." MOTHER

"[I] wasn't prepared for all the decisions. Is it okay if he does this or not? He's trying to do something; shall I step in so he doesn't hurt himself or shall I let him go? It's making all those choices, making sure what I feel." MOTHER

"There is anxiety, a feeling of vulnerability I have never felt before. If he gets sick, what are we going to do? If he has a little sickness, we just hope the doctor is doing the right thing. We went through a great deal in the past few weeks choosing a nursery school for him, and we hope we have done the right thing, but is this the one for him?" FATHER

"I wish we had—because he is our first child—more of a sense of the norms. What is okay versus what is a problem and what is really bad? Is this normal, is this just kids being kids? He pushed someone at school three times; is this par for the course or is this a problem? We don't know when we are reacting and when we are overreacting." FATHER

in solving problems, and they learn more in the course of a year in preschool. Children are most likely to develop this motivation when parents are warm, encouraging, and open in conversation with their children.

LANGUAGE DEVELOPMENT

Children progress from having about fifty words at nineteen months to having ten thousand words at age six, in the first grade, learning an average of 5.5 words per day.[10] The length of sentences grows from two words at age two to complex sentences of several words, with clauses.

Parents promote children's vocabulary and intellectual performance when they:[11]

- talk a lot with their children
- refer to many topics
- use a variety of words and ask questions
- give children positive feedback about their behavior

Children's verbal skills in the preschool years are important because they predict children's verbal IQ and reading skills in the third grade[12] better than vocabulary growth.[13]

Adults' conversations with children not only develop skills, but also convey information about how others think and feel, values about gender and racial matters, and the child's behavior in the past so the child has a sense of autobiographical memory.

EMOTIONAL DEVELOPMENT

Children's understanding of people increases.[14] Toddlers' understand that people's feelings often lead to actions, and conversely, actions lead to feelings—"I give a big hug, Baby be happy." "Grandma mad. I wrote on wall."[15] Preschoolers go beyond toddlers' understanding and see that others' thoughts often determine both feelings and actions.[16]

Preschoolers' greater awareness of others' reactions to their behavior enables them to see how well their behavior meets others' standards. The "self-evaluative" emotions of pride, shame, and guilt develop.[17] Children feel pride and happiness when they accomplish what they set out to, shame when they fail to meet external standards and their weaknesses or inadequacies are exposed, and guilt when they violate the rules of right and wrong. Guilt depends on an internalization of the rules and develops toward the end of the preschool years.

Children are self-conscious and concerned about others' reactions to their judgments.[18] They do not want to stand out from others, and like adults, when placed in a laboratory situation in which their judgments of the size of an object differ from the group, they abandon their own correct judgment to agree with the group, but only if their judgment is given publicly so others know what it is. If their judgment remains private, they maintain their independence. In judging their actions, children, even in these early years, develop one of two approaches—the global performance orientation or the specific learning orientation.[19] When children have a global performance orientation, they believe failure and success reflect their value as a person; they feel great when they succeed or bad when they fail. When children fail, they avoid the activity with reasons like, "I can't draw" or "I'm a terrible runner."

Other children have a specific learning orientation. They look at success or failure as a single action that did or did not succeed. It is not a reflection of their value as a person; a failure means they need more information or practice. These children are confident and willing to work hard to learn because they believe they can learn with greater effort or new strategies.

Aggressiveness

A very careful study of physical aggression (hitting, kicking, destroying property) based on mothers' ratings of their children from ages two to nine as well as information from many sources revealed:[20]

- the majority of children (70 percent) were low or very low on physical aggression for the whole period,
- only 3 percent were consistently high for the whole period, and
- half of the moderately aggressive two-year-olds learned self-regulatory skills and were at a low level of aggression by age five, and the other half maintained a moderate level of aggression.

The lives of highly aggressive children were very stressful from birth to age two as compared to the lives of children low in aggression. The mothers of highly aggressive children were more likely to be: single, depressed, with low income and limited education, less sensitive, less stimulating, and less responsive in their parenting. In contrast, nonaggressive children came from homes where there were emotional support and few stressors. Mothers were educated, psychologically stable women described as responsive and warm in their caregiving. These family characteristics continued to differentiate the aggressive and nonagressive children from ages two to nine.

The most aggressive children between ages two and five continued to be aggressive at age nine and had many additional problems as well—academic, social, and emotional. Fifty-eight percent of these children were rated below grade level in school performance and a sizeable number had trouble paying attention and complying with mothers' or teachers' requests. Children high on aggression did not get along well with peers, teachers, or mothers. In addition, children described themselves as lonely and angry. So these children experienced many early and ongoing deprivations and continued to struggle in several arenas as they grew older. Those children low in aggression at age nine got along well with others, performed well academically, and reported few worries.

Later in the section on Parents' Tasks and Concerns we discuss positive parenting strategies to reduce aggressiveness in both boys and girls, but it is clear that significant childhood aggression comes not just from parents' behaviors but is associated with parents' psychological stability and living conditions that require other additional support.

Fear

Fears are a natural part of life as children grow up. In the early years of infancy, fears of noise and strangers are most evident, but these anxieties gradually fade. In the preschool years, children experience fears of animals, the dark, harm from imaginary creatures, and natural disasters such as fires and storms. Those young children who are the most fearful in the least-threatening situations are those most at risk for later anxiety disorders.[21] In stories preschoolers themselves attribute different levels of fear to people according to age. In a scary situation babies have the highest level of fear and adults are seen as having little fear. Among adults, dads are seen as having less fear than moms.[22]

Biological, psychological, and social factors underlie preschoolers' inhibition. Unique patterns of brain activity and physiological reactivity seen in infancy appear to predispose these children to anxiety and fear and the resulting behavioral wariness and withdrawal.[23]

Parents' behavior plays a role as well. Studies have shown that when mothers of inhibited two-year-old toddlers responded in a "suffocatingly warm" and overprotective way that prevented their children from becoming independent, their children's inhibited, fearful behavior continued through the preschool years.[24] Some overprotective mothers shift their behavior in the preschool years and become more power-assertive, directive, and harsh in trying to force children to overcome their fearfulness. Mothers who were warm and nurturant with their physiologically reactive and inhibited toddlers, teaching them strategies and calmly encouraging them to become more independent had children who, in the preschool years, gained greater autonomy and had fewer worries.[25]

Culture too plays a role.[26] North American culture views inhibition and social withdrawal negatively as children are not conforming to the cultural ideals of independence, self-assertive achievement, and social outgoingness. In Chinese culture, children's wariness and inhibition are viewed positively as signs of sensitivity and cautiousness. Parents are positive and supportive. They are not overprotective or harsh with their children even though Chinese children are far more inhibited than North American children in laboratory situations and so children do not view themselves negatively or feel unloved. Shyness and sensitivity in ten-year-old Chinese children are, in fact, related to social and school success and to psychological adjustment.[27]

Talking with preschoolers about what reduced fears, researchers learned that when fears are of real things like animals (snakes, sharks), children prefer to take action. Boys want to fight the scary animals, but girls want to avoid them.[28] When fears are of imaginary creatures like ghosts, children prefer to use psychological ways of coping by reminding themselves such creatures are not real.

Once a bad event happens, even three-year-olds can predict that a person would worry that a bad event could happen again in the future, but they cannot explain verbally that the future worry is related to a negative event in the past.[29] Four-to six-year-olds can verbalize that connection. They are also able to understand that a person who does not have that history of a past event would not worry about its happening in the future. Thus, even at this young age, they have insights into the ways individuals' past experiences influence their future expectations.

With both aggressive and fearful, inhibited children, parents are most helpful to their children when they are positive, supportive, and provide encouragement to their children as they learn to manage their feelings and develop new behaviors.

Chronic Stress

We now know that experiencing chronically high levels of stress with high levels of cortisol affects children's brain development and decreases self-regulation, memory skills, and learning.[30] Because many young children are exposed to excessive stress in economically deprived living conditions and traumatic conditions following disasters, more focused efforts are made in these years to enroll these children in preschool programs that increase children's executive functioning (EF), emotional regulation, and effortful control. Recently implemented programs like Tools of the Mind and other preschool programs have demonstrated success in improving these skills over a short period of time though they have not been in existence long enough to demonstrate the adult benefits of older, more broad-based programs that increase education and stabilized adult lives and decrease rule-breaking behavior.[31] Parents are well-advised to be sure their children who qualify enter the programs that strengthen EF skills.

Children's and Parents' Responses to Upsets

Parent-child interactions account for 70 percent of children's upsets at home, with sibling and peer conflicts accounting for only 20 percent of the distress.[32] When upset, children's most common form of response is crying. Parents' usual response to the distress is not to comfort but to give the child a practical, problem-solving response so that the child can deal with the situation. When children are angry or sad, mothers who help children refocus their attention and also join with the child to find a way to reframe the situation decrease the intensity of the upset.[33] While 43 percent of parents expect children to control their feelings by age three, such control is still developing from ages three to five and sometimes when frustrated, children need support and comfort.[34]

Empathy

Children's ability to respond sensitively to others' needs increases as they grow. Toddlers and preschoolers are better able to understand sources of emotional reactions, and use strategies to go more directly to the source of the problem.[35] Children learn empathy from parents' modeling it and from books and stories that have moral themes.[36] Fairy tales, universal favorites of children, present models of kind, caring behavior that triumphs over evil and cruelty.

THE DEVELOPMENT OF THE SELF

In early childhood, children continue to define themselves in terms of their physical characteristics and their actions, but they are beginning to organize their self-perceptions and see themselves in more general though dichotomous terms such as good or bad, smart or dumb.[37] Most children continue to focus on their positive qualities and see themselves as "all good," but preschoolers who have experienced abuse are more likely than other children to consider themselves bad.

Preschoolers need not have experienced extreme stress such as abuse in order to have doubts about their skills. In one study, preschoolers who said other children did not like them or accept them were more likely to live in families where mothers were cold and angry in their interactions with children and children observed conflict between parents.[38] Children seemed to take mothers' view of them very much to heart and believe that since mothers were irritated with them, others would be too. Sadly, preschoolers' self-perceptions predicted their kindergarten teachers' ratings of them as being angry, sad, withdrawn, and unable to get along with others.

Children high on self-esteem show confidence in exploring new situations and adaptability when they meet with frustration and stress.[39] Children low on self-esteem are inhibited in exploring and initiating new activities and are unable to manage stress and frustration appropriately. Parents' warmth and sensitive responsiveness promote high self-esteem, as does their modeling adaptable, confident behavior.

Gender Identity

Gender identity is defined as an individual's personal experience of what it means to be a boy or girl, man or woman. Physical, social, and psychological factors contribute to gender differentiation. Physical factors include genes, which, in turn, trigger hormones that lead to the development of internal and external sexual characteristics and also influence behavior.[40] Societies and their subcultures transmit beliefs about what is appropriate for boys and girls through prescriptions of child rearing, and parents contribute their influence as well. Gender identity, however, "is not simply something imposed on children; at all points of development, children are actively constructing for themselves what it means to be female or male."[41]

Even infants of three or four months can distinguish men from women and by one year, they can link men's voices with men's faces and women's voices with women's faces. Between two and two and a half, toddlers announce proudly, "I am a boy" or "I am a girl." They gradually learn, usually between ages three and five, that gender is stable across time—they will always be a boy or a girl. Somewhere between ages five and seven, they also learn gender is consistent—they are girls whether they have short or long hair, wear skirts or pants.[42]

When they identify their gender and see it as an important part of themselves, children begin to develop a gender schema, defined as an organized body of knowledge of what it means to be a boy or a girl. By age two, toddlers have learned to label men, women, boys, and girls and have begun to associate gender labels with objects, activities, tasks, and roles. Conversations with two-year-olds, however, reveal they have little interest in the general qualities of men and women but focus on the activities of specific individuals.[43] Preschoolers, however, make many gender-stereotypic comments.

Up to about eighteen months of age, boys and girls show no differences in such behaviors as aggressiveness, toy play, large motor activity, and communication attempts, all of which exhibit gender differences in the next year.[44] Beginning at age two, boys prefer active pursuits and building activities, and girls prefer arts and crafts and reading. In the third year, boys and girls begin to play in same-gender groups, and this continues into the school years.

On average, boys tend to be more active and aggressive than girls. Girls are found to be more helpful and sometimes more fearful. Caroline Zahn-Waxler refers to the gender issues in problem behaviors as the problems of the warriors and the worriers.[45] We discuss parents' behavior in encouraging gender differences in children's behavior in a later section.

Ethnic Identity

Similar to the stages of gender identity formation, children also go through stages of forming a sense of ethnic identity, defined as a psychological attachment to "a group sharing a common ancestral heritage based on nationality, language, and culture."[46] When the group has an easily noted characteristic such as skin color, children can correctly identify membership in their group by age three. When an ethnic group lacks perceptually distinct characteristics, as for example with ethnic groups from similar geographical areas such as Northern Europe, ethnic group awareness occurs later at age five and reliable self-identification by age seven.

In the process of forming a sense of ethnic identity, children first identify their ethnic group, then see themselves as a member of the ethnic group, gradually learn what is distinctive about their own ethnic group, and finally, by around age seven, realize their ethnic identity is a stable part of them and will not change.[47] Children may develop ethnic identity at an earlier age if ethnic issues are frequently talked about at home.

Children benefit when parents help them form a positive sense of ethnic identity. For example, when children received messages of racial pride, and their homes were rich in Afrocentric items like books and magazines, then children's problem-solving skills were more advanced, and they had more knowledge on a measure of achievement.[48] Those parents who reported giving strong measures of racial pride also reported fewer behavior problems with their children.

THE DEVELOPMENT OF SELF-REGULATION

Children learn the rules of life from interactions with their parents, their brothers and sisters, and their playmates. They learn about conventions and accepted routines from parents, and they learn about moral actions—such as sharing, teasing, helping, not fighting or stealing. Very early in the preschool years, they are aware of the difference between rules that concern kindness and basic consideration of others and rules having to do with social convention, like what clothes to wear.[49]

Significantly, they are more impressed with the importance of kindness to others than with social conventions. While preschoolers feel it is important to follow parents' moral rules like the rule against stealing, and say they would feel bad if they broke it, they are already like adolescents and believe that choices of free-time activities and clothing are personal choices, and children can disobey parents' rules in those areas and still feel good about themselves.[50]

Even though children have a clear idea of right and wrong and want to follow parents' requests, preschoolers evaluate actions by their outcomes. If wrongdoers successfully achieve their ends, preschoolers assume they feel good about that. Preschoolers may know an act is wrong but not necessarily feel wrong or bad for doing it.[51] Children at this age are particularly happy to evade punishment while still getting what they want.

Most parents have a moral rule about telling the truth, and so parents want to know about children's lying, which is most often studied in laboratory settings in which children are asked not to look at a toy or under a cup while the experimenter leaves the room for a moment. Either video recording or objects spilling from under the cup if it is turned up enable the examiner to know what has happened. About 80 percent of preschoolers peek or lift the cup. About two-thirds of those who violate the rule lie about doing so when asked.[52] The younger children cannot cover their lies well, and will say correctly what the toy is and not have a reason for knowing that. When children are six or seven, they can sustain the original lie with further lies, giving plausible reasons for how they know. Those children who have the most advanced understanding of how others think and the most advanced EF skills so they can remember what they have said and inhibit their responses are most skilled in sustaining their lies. Similar results are found with Chinese children as well.[53]

When these studies were carried out in West Africa with preschoolers from a permissive school and preschoolers from a punitive school that relied on much corporal punishment, again about 80 percent of children peeked, but 94 percent of children in the punitive school lied about peeking compared to 56 percent of those in the permissive school. So a punitive atmosphere encourages lying.[54]

Behavioral control is an important quality to develop as an extensive study of children's behavior in the years from three to six with follow-up at age twelve documents.[55] Undercontrolled children, identified on the basis of mothers' ratings and about 20 percent of the sample, failed to cooperate with others, did not comply with adults' requests, did not collaborate with peers and instead, were aggressive. Lack of control was associated with lower performance on cognitive tests in preschool, and academic performance declined over the elementary school years. Further, these children were unhappy much of the time. Age was a factor here, as the majority of younger children described as undercontrolled did not show that behavior two years later.

Those children most likely to improve in control were those living in families with fewer stresses. Children whose behavior was initially adaptable and resilient and became undercontrolled over a two-year period lived in families with external stresses such as loss of family income or family instability. The source of stress was not so important as the number of stresses. As in the case of aggressive children, it is hard to learn self-regulation and self-control when the family is coping with many external stressors.

PARENT-CHILD RELATIONSHIPS

Parents' behavior is central to children's growth and competence. Parents' behavior in the first two years of life influences children's competence in the preschool period, and parents' interactions with children in the preschool years influences how children will fare when they are in elementary school.

Ross Parke and Raymond Buriel believe that parents meet role expectations and socialize children in three ways: (1) as an interactive partner with the child, (2) as a direct instructor, and (3) as a provider of activities and opportunities that stimulate children's growth.[56] Let us look at parents' activities in terms of these three roles.

Attachment

Parents are interactive partners, continuing to provide sensitive parenting to maintain the attachment that gives children a sense of security and trust in relationships with others. Although attachment quality in the first two years influences preschool attachment, preschoolers' present circumstances and the quality of their current relationships with parents are what most influence preschoolers' sense of security and social adaptation.[57]

Positive Parenting

In addition to fostering secure attachments with children, sensitive, responsive parenting (described in Chapter 6) also increases children's willingness and ability to internalize family rules and values and regulate their behavior.[58]

When both parents use positive parenting, they create a family atmosphere of mutual reciprocity and cooperation that benefit not only the parent-child relationship but the relationship between the parents as well. Yet, two-thirds of parents in one sample report that they have concerns about their own and their spouse's anger and irritability with their preschoolers.[59]

Vygotsky's emphasis on scaffolding and working with children at the high end of the zone of proximal development (see Chapter 3) contributes to the positive approach because parents:[60]

1. Adjust the task to challenge but not overwhelm the child (e.g., in the beginning just getting the covers pulled up is considered making the bed; it does not have to be perfect)

2. Problem-solve with the child—raising questions, wondering about possible options

3. Give the amount of help needed until the child gains the skill and then withdraw help

4. Give encouragement to counterbalance the frustration sometimes involved in learning

Parenting programs that emphasize establishing warm secure parent-child attachments in infancy and in the toddler-preschool years emphasize maintaining the close emotional, cooperative bond while at the same time encouraging verbal and cognitive growth through Vygotsky's suggestions for scafffolding and support are effective in promoting verbal, cognitive, and emotional growth in low-income children both those who were full term as well as those who were Very-Low-Birth-Weight babies.[61] Mothers who use this combination of warm, secure positive parenting strategies and autonomy support provided by Vygotsky's strategies in the toddler-preschool years promote children's attention and EF skills as measured at age four.[62] This combination of parenting strategies also contribute to the authoritative parenting Diana Baumrind (see Chapter 3) found so effective in rearing competent preschoolers.[63]

Parents' use of authoritative parenting depends in part on their relationship with their own parents.[64] Parents who reported anger and little love in their relationships with their parents appeared to have negative views of relationships in general, to be less supportive of their marital partner, and be more critical and authoritarian with their children. When mothers were unhappy with their parents, daughters and sons were more likely to be described in kindergarten as withdrawn, sad, and depressed. When fathers were unhappy with their relationships with their parents, sons and daughters were more likely to be described in kindergarten as angry and noncompliant.

Socializing Gender Roles

Parents teach children about gender roles in many different ways. First, parents model gender behaviors in their direct interactions with children.[65] Mothers carry out more caregiving activities and are more nurturant in everyday activities; fathers are often more direct and assertive. These differences were seen in European American and Latina/o parents and in parents of multiethnic backgrounds.[66]

Second, as interactive partners, parents may stimulate gender-stereotyped behavior indirectly when they respond to boys and girls differently. Although mothers and fathers treat boys and girls alike in many ways—they are equally attached to sons and daughters and use authoritative strategies with both[67]—they also reveal subtle differences in how they respond to boys and girls.[68] For example, mothers are more responsive to irritable infant sons than daughters; they talk more to daughters than to sons and use more supportive speech. Such differences in behavior may indirectly reinforce the gender-related behaviors of assertiveness in boys and verbal skills in girls.

Third, parents may sensitize children to gender issues in conversations. One study found that mothers drew their two-year-old toddler's attention to gender categories, labeling the gender of people, talking about the characteristics of boys and girls and men and women even when children were not particularly interested.[69]

As we saw in Chapter 2, simply identifying a group has a powerful impact on preschoolers' thinking about membership in the group. When nursery school teachers made many gender references to boys' and girls' organized classroom activities, e.g., lining up by gender, having separate boys' and girls' bulletin boards for just a two-week period, children developed more stereotypes of the opposite gender, had more negative views of them, and played less with them than preschoolers in classrooms that minimized references to gender.[70]

Play with fathers is more active.

Even though mothers of preschoolers express many egalitarian beliefs and rarely make gender-stereotypic comments,[71] by age four preschoolers make many gender-stereotypic comments, as writer Peggy Orenstein discovered when her Thomas the Tank Engine–loving daughter abruptly gave up her overalls and trains and turned to princess dresses and dolls.[72]

Fourth, as educators, parents teach children directly about gender-appropriate behaviors. They have books that show activities for boys and girls, and a variety of toys are available. Such teaching does not always succeed.

Fifth, and most important, parents influence children's gender-appropriate behavior through their encouragement of different activities and interests.[73] Until recently, boys were encouraged to be more active in sports than were girls, and such activities were thought to build boys' skills in teamwork and cooperation. When girls were highly active like boys, they received more negative responses from adults. Today, both boys and girls receive more encouragement for physical activity.

Finally, mothers and fathers seem to elicit different behaviors from boys and girls.[74] Observing preschool boys and girls in playroom interactions with mothers and fathers separately revealed that parents did not reinforce or encourage sex-stereotyped behavior, and boys and girls did not consistently behave in sex-stereotyped ways with both parents, but in play with fathers, both daughters and sons showed more male-stereotyped behavior; they were more boisterous, assertive, aggressive, and noncompliant.

Since children receive gender socialization from peers and teachers in school, parents need to be sure they convey their values to children at home.

Socializing Ethnic Identities

Parents, as we noted, help children form a sense of ethnic identity. In conversations, parents identify the group to which the family belongs, talking about its distinctive qualities and expressing pride in the group's history and accomplishments.[75] Parents provide books, toys, and pictures that describe the group's values and history. They also introduce children to culturally appropriate ways of doing things such as dressing, cooking food, dancing, and relating to adults. If the group has a distinctive religion, children begin to participate in it.

Even though children are young, parents start to send messages about pride in the group's culture and values, and hearing these messages promotes children's social and academic competence.

Promoting Empathy, Fairness, and Inclusiveness

As we saw in Chapter 2, preschool children prefer their own ingroup, but do not yet view outgroup members as negatively as they will in the elementary school years. Parents' teachings and actions in this age period can play a critical role in preventing the exclusion and negative stereotyping seen in the elementary school years.[76]

We have seen that preschoolers follow parents' moral rules against hurting others, and stealing from them, and parents can justify fairness and inclusion of all children as following the dictates of a moral rule. Through questions and comments, parents can engage children's empathy in understanding how excluding or labeling playmates and calling them names are hurtful actions that are not fair. When asked, preschoolers can tell a time when they were a victim of a mean act, and also give an instance when they themselves carried out a mean act, sometimes against a friend.[77] When victims, they are well aware of the hurt and sad feelings, but when perpetrators, they frequently justify their actions in terms of achieving their own goal. Parents have to help children see that they are breaking a moral rule when they cause hurt or painful feelings for others, just as they violate it when they hit or kick someone.

See Box 8-1 for ways to explore children's feelings about a possible rule, "You Can't Say You Can't Play." What would it be like if parents established that rule with brothers and sisters. It might not always be followed but can lead to conversation about children's view of moral interpersonal behavior and heighten awareness of the importance of fair treatment.

Box 8-1
FIRST PERSON NARRATIVE

Award-winning kindergarten teacher Vivian Gussin Paley decided to institute a rule that she thought would prevent the hurt feelings she saw in her kindergarten children who were told, "You can't play. We don't want you in our game," and would also prevent the formation of a social structure in which certain children were always excluded. Ms. Paley discussed the rule with students in each grade before instituting the rule in kindergarten, and the book *You Can't Say You Can't Play** is a distillation of her conversations with children from ages five to ten about the fairness, benefits, and workability of such a rule.

When first announced, only four of the twenty-five kindergartners approved the rule, and these were the children most often left out. The children who objected to the rule argued free-play companions should be their personal choices, not children forced on them by the teacher's rule. Ms. Paley explained she thought being excluded from play was hurting children's feelings and making it hard for them to learn in school, and so it was fair to protect children from such hurt. In talking about the possible rule, most children described being hurt by friends as well as children who did not like them, and also hurting friends because they wanted to make new friends.

Before putting the rule into practice, she talked with children in all grades in the school about it and brought their thoughts back to the kindergartners. Older children thought nursery school children and kindergartners could follow such a rule, but they were already too mean and set in their ways to change.

Despite her hesitations and uncertainties about the rule, she put it into practice because of her deep concern about the ways social exclusion had hurt her as a child and hurt her students each year. The children adapted to the rule with minor protests, and violations of the rule led to more discussion, and a classroom in which all children were included in games, but were still excluded at story time when a child could refuse to have another child play a role in the story he or she made up. Ms. Paley decided to change that too and say every child had to have some role in a story or the next one acted out. While there were initial protests Ms. Paley noticed that including everyone in acting out stories led to children's being much freer in taking roles in the stories because they no longer had to focus on being chosen. Parents can read the book that includes a series of magical fairy stories illustrating the benefits of inclusion and implement such a rule with siblings at home or encourage their preschools and kindergartens to adopt such a rule.

*Vivian Gussin Paley, *You Can't Say You Can't Play* (Cambridge, MA: Harvard University Press, 1993).

Parents can also emphasize inclusiveness in family activities like reading together the histories of different ethnic and cultural groups in the area, attending their cultural celebrations, parades, and food festivals so children early in life begin to enjoy exploring the cultural traditions of all people. As the world comes closer together and as we become an increasingly diverse country, we can all enjoy the pleasures and surprises of coming to know other groups and appreciating the ways we are alike and the ways we are different.

Conversations

Conversations convey information directly about values, as we saw in talking about gender or race, and in subtle ways, as seen in a comparison of family conversations with two-year-olds in Taiwanese middle-class families and Irish American middle-class families living in Illinois.[78] Careful analysis revealed common themes and differences in the conversations of the two groups observed at home. All families engaged in personal storytelling with their two-and-a-half-year-olds, talking about pleasurable family events such as trips to the zoo or the market. In both groups, children received attention, affectionate comments, and physical hugs. All families talked about illnesses and physical mishaps such as nosebleeds.

In Taiwanese families, conversations were seen as teaching opportunities. Parents corrected grammar and pronunciation. Moral and social misbehavior were the focus of attention in 35 percent of the narrations. The present misdeed triggered discussion of past misdeeds of a similar sort, with an important moral lesson or guideline drawn at the end of the narration.

In Irish American families conversations were sources of entertainment and affirmations of children's positive qualities. Misdeeds were the focus of only 7 percent of narrations. They were described only briefly, presented in the most positive light as signs of curiosity or self-assertion and quickly passed over. Irish American parents were concerned about rules and talked about them, but serious discussions of a child's misbehavior were done in private when outsiders were not present and the child would not lose self-esteem.

These conversations illustrate how parents subtly convey attitudes about misdeeds and their consequences, about success and the meaning of failure or mistakes. Parents' conversations create an atmosphere, in the case of the Taiwanese families, one centered on striving to avoid mistakes and improve, and in Irish American families, one centered on self-assertion and success.

PARENTS' STIMULATION OF CHILDREN'S COMPETENCE

In Chapter 6, we talked about the intimate family culture that prepares preschool children to learn in the school setting—involvement in reading activities and having dinnertime conversations.[79] Board games with children can teach factual knowledge (e.g., numbers and basic math concepts) that helps prepare children for school.[80]

Parents also stimulate growth when they play with children.[81] Physical play peaks when children are one to four and, for boys, is related to social competence and popularity with peers in the preschool years. Such play, however, is related to abrasive peer relationships for girls. Interactional and object play involve more verbal interactions and more symbolic pretend play as children grow older. In pretend play, children learn the routines of everyday life; as in earlier years, parents emphasize turn-taking and other kinds of reciprocity. In this play, parents also help children take on roles more knowledgeably.

Both interactional and object play help children develop emotional, social, verbal, and intellectual skills. For example, for children between twenty-one months and four years of age, symbolic play with mothers predicted social skills at five and a half years.

RELATIONSHIPS WITH SIBLINGS

In the preschool years, children often experience the birth of a little brother or sister. The birth brings changes not only to the preschooler, but also to the parents, who often feel overwhelmed incorporating a second child in the family.

Before the second child arrives, parents are often intensely and positively involved with their first child, forming a tight-knit triangular family unit with the child.[82] The birth of the second child reduces the time and energy parents have for the older child. Furthermore, with increased demands, parents become more directive and controlling with their older child, more parent-centered and sometimes harsh in discipline. Thus, the older child suffers two losses: the loss of exclusive parental attention and the loss of child-centered parenting behaviors.

It is not surprising then that firstborn children often experience anxiety, behavior problems, and conflict with parents and peers following the birth of a sibling. When financial resources are limited, the birth of an additional child further reduces resources for older children, and declines on measures of cognitive achievement and social competence are detectable for these children more than two years after birth.[83] When resources are not limited, children's negative reactions to the birth are usually temporary, and by the end of the first year, 63 percent of preschoolers report wanting another sibling.[84]

The relationships among siblings are emotional, intense, affectionate, and sometimes aggressive. Children are more likely to get along well when parents are sensitive, responsive, and securely attached to each child.

Parents use various strategies to integrate a new child into the family.[85] In some families, fathers attend to the needs of the firstborn, and mothers care for the newborn; in others, the father takes on more household tasks, leaving the mother time to care for both children; and in still others, both parents do all tasks. Some families rely on grandparents, aunts, and uncles to give extra time and attention to the older child.

Although many older siblings feel that mothers favor younger siblings, longitudinal studies of mothers' behavior with their two children when each is age one or two reveal that mothers are quite consistent in the amount of affection and verbal responsiveness they direct to each child at that age, but less consistent in their ways of controlling different children at a given age, probably because they have learned from experience.[86]

Parents promote positive sibling relationships in two basic ways:[87] by creating a warm emotional family climate and by avoiding comparisons between children. Hostility and aggression flourish when one child has reason to feel rejected or unfairly treated or valued.

PEER RELATIONSHIPS

Two-year-olds play with peers, taking turns and sharing. They form stable relationships that can last beyond a year, and such friendships are important emotional attachments that enable them to adapt more easily to changes at preschool or day care.[88]

Preschoolers still spend time watching other children play, engaging in solitary play, drawing, building, and in parallel play.[89] These activities, enjoyable in themselves, help children develop skills for entering play groups of other children. Socially successful children enter groups by first watching what others are doing, playing alongside them, talking to children at play, and then entering play with them. In these years, boys and girls play in gender-segregated groups.

Preschoolers engage in more sociodramatic play that helps their development in many ways. Children talk about the roles they'll play, the actions that will occur; they make up rules they will follow; and they negotiate differences of opinion. From this play children gain a better understanding of others, the usefulness of rules, and negotiating skills. In acting out a variety of roles, they gain a more mature understanding of social behavior.

In the preschool years children form close, stable friendships with children who are like them in age and gender and behave in similar ways. Friends share and cooperate and support each other. They also quarrel and get angry with each other. Although friends have more fights than casual acquaintances because they spend more time with each other, friends handle conflicts differently, disengaging and finding a solution that gives each partner something equal, whereas casual acquaintances fight until someone wins.[90]

Even in early childhood, some children are more socially skilled than others, as they are outgoing and able to regulate their emotional reactions in peer interactions.[91] Secure attachments to parents help children feel trusting and confident in social relationships, whereas insecure attachments increase children's feelings that others are rejecting and neglectful.[92] Parents' monitoring of young children's social interactions and guiding children in how to join in and play with others increase children's social skills.

TASKS AND CONCERNS OF PARENTS

Parents of children aged two to five face new tasks as well as old. Parenting in this age period includes the following:

- Being sensitive, responsive caregivers who foster secure attachments with children
- Helping children learn rules and regulate their behavior
- Helping children manage frustration and challenges so they feel successful
- Stimulating children's growth and competence with books, play, and activities
- Coaching children when they have difficulties in activities and with others
- Providing companionship and guidance in conversation and play
- Accessing and, if not available, advocating for neighborhood services for children and families

The years from two to five can bring frustration for parents and children in the daily routines of sleeping, eating, and tantrums. Problems at home can lead to trouble for children at school or at day care and continue when children enter school. This section emphasizes ways to help children maintain self-regulation through getting optimal amounts of sleep, managing temper outbursts and reducing sibling rivalries, aggressiveness, and social inhibition.

Parents' care is nestled in the social context that surrounds families. As we detailed in Chapter 1, resources in neighborhoods can support parents with young children—libraries to go to, parks for children's play and family activities, places for families to meet and talk and get help from each other as needed. When these are not available, parents can perhaps join together, or be involved in groups to advocate for services.

Sleeping

Healthy sleep at night prepares children for active, happy days, as we described in Chapter 6. A consistent, pleasant bedtime routine continues to be important in these years when children between two and five usually need between eleven and twelve hours per night, and children from four to twelve, about ten hours per night.[93] Many do not get enough sleep and between 10 and 30 percent of children are described as sleep deprived.[94]

Night Fears   In the preschool years many children are afraid to go to bed because of monsters or robbers. Richard Ferber believes such fears reflect anxieties about loss of behavior control around issues such as toilet training, anger regarding siblings, and peer aggression.[95] These anxieties are then expressed as fears of monsters. He states she needs reassurance that nothing bad will occur if she wets her pants or breaks a rule.

> She can best be reassured by knowing that you are in control of yourself and—to the extent that she needs it—of her, and that you can and will protect her. . . . The monsters are in your child's mind, and it is there you should focus your efforts.[96]

VOICES OF EXPERIENCE

The Joys of Parenting Children Ages Two to Five

"When she was four, she was the only girl on an all-boy soccer team. Her mother thought she was signing her up for a coed team, but she was the only girl, and she enjoyed it and liked it even though she is not a natural athlete. She watched and learned and got good at it, and we got a lot of joy out of watching her."   FATHER

"Well, every night we have a bedtime ritual of telling a story and singing to her. This is probably beyond the time she needs it, but we need it."   MOTHER

"He's very inventive, and it's fun for both of us when he tells stories or figures out ways to communicate something he's learned or heard. When his mother had morning sickness, he heard the baby was in her tummy so he figured out the baby is making the morning sickness, pushing the food out."   FATHER

"One of the delights that comes up is reading him stories, telling him the adventure of John Muir, at the four-year-old level. We were talking about places to go, and I said, 'Maybe we could go visit the home of John Muir.' He said, 'Oh, great, then I could go up there and have a cup of tea.' And I remembered I had told him a story about Muir's having tea in a blizzard, and he remembered that. He put that together, and it came out of nowhere. It knocked me over that he remembered that image."   FATHER

"I enjoy her because I can talk to her; we have these wonderful conversations, and she can tell me about something that happened to her today at school that was really neat for her, and I just love to hear about it."   MOTHER

"It's fun to hear him looking forward to doing things with us. He'll ask how many days until Saturday or Sunday because on those days I wait for him to get up before I have breakfast. Usually I'm up and gone before he gets up. He likes to come out and

If the child seems very frightened at night, parents are advised to do whatever is necessary to help the child feel safe and able to sleep, because each night of good sleep makes the next night easier. Parents can spend enjoyable time with the child in his or her bedroom, and move the child's bedtime later so the child will be sleepier. Parents may check in on the child until the child falls asleep to show that they are available. Parents may lie down with the child briefly and may even sleep in the child's room if anxiety is severe. If nighttime fears are the result of a family problem or part of the generalized anxiety seen in many situations, counseling is advised.

Nightmares   Nightmares are scary dreams that occur during light REM (rapid eye movement) sleep, and they result in full awakening, often with the child's having some memory of the dream. The child will call and want comfort. Nightmares are a part of growing up. They peak at about the time children enter school and again at ages nine through eleven. A parent can remain with the child until he or she falls

get up in my lap and share my breakfast, and it's a ritual. He looks forward to that and counts the days." FATHER

"She's really affectionate, always has been, but now out of nowhere, she'll tell you she loves you. She likes to do things with you, and when you give her special attention, one on one, she really likes it. We play games—Candy Land or Cinderella—or just one of us goes with her to the supermarket or to the park. We read stories every night and do some talking. Sometimes I put music on and we dance." FATHER

"The joy comes from the things we do as a family, the three of us—going to see Santa Claus together or to see miniature trains and take a ride. Early in the morning we have a ritual. When he gets up early, he has a bottle of milk and gets in bed with us; the lights are out, and we are lying in bed, and he tells us his dreams and we watch the light outside and see the trees and see the sun come up. We do that in the morning, and it is a quiet joy." FATHER

"One night at dinner, he was watching his little sister, who's one, and he said, 'Do you think when she gets to be a big girl she'll remember what she did as a baby?' I was amazed at the question." MOTHER

"I like going for a walk with her, and we went skipping rocks at the reservoir. I was going to show her how to skip rocks because she had never seen that before. Of course, she wanted to try it, and I didn't think she was old enough to do it. I had found the best skipping rock; it was just perfect. I was going to hold her hand and do it with her. She said, 'No, I want to do it myself.' I thought, it is more important to just let it go. So I said, 'Here, let me show you how.' So I showed her, and she said, 'No, I can do it.' She threw it and it skipped three times! The first time she ever threw one! She wanted to stay till she did it again, and we did a little; but it will be a while before she does that again, I think." FATHER

back to sleep, or perhaps can lie down with the child, but it is best not to make the latter practice a habit.

If nightmares occur frequently, parents can begin to examine what in the child's daylight hours is causing the trouble. Adjustment to a new brother or sister or a change to a new day care may cause stress. Helping the child cope with stress during the day is the surest way to prevent nightmares.

Partial Wakings   As people fall asleep, they move into a deep state of sleep that lasts about ninety minutes, then they transition to a light stage, then return to a deep state of sleep, and gradually during the night, return to longer periods of light-stage sleep in which most dreaming occurs.[97] Children often have difficulty making the transition from deep to light sleep, and sometimes have confusional events in which they are asleep but carry out activities normally associated with the waking state—talking in their sleep, walking in their sleep, screaming and calling for help in a night terror.

It is important not to confuse night terrors with nightmares. In both cases the child awakes in the night, appearing very frightened. The patterns for these two behaviors, however, differ. Night terrors take place during the first few hours of sleep at night—about one and a half to three or four hours after children go to sleep—just as the child enters a light state of sleep; nightmares usually occur much later in the night. In night terrors, the child is not fully awake when he or she calls or cries. The cry may sound like a scream, and so the parents assume the child has had a nightmare. In this case, however, if a parent tries to hold the child, he pushes the parent away; comforting does not help. The child may drop back to sleep automatically and have no memory of the night terror the next day. For night terrors, parents should not attempt to wake the child or offer comfort. They should avoid interacting with the child unless he or she requests it and let the child fall back to sleep. If they believe it was a night terror, parents should not make too much of it with the child, who may be frightened to hear how terrified and out of control he or she appeared. Night terrors disappear as children get older.

Physiological factors are largely at work in confusional events. The best predictor of one is whether the child is sleep deprived. If they are frequent, severe, and present a safety risk, professional help is advised. In her book, *Sleeping through the Night,* Jodi Mindell gives parents guidelines for ensuring safety for children who walk in their sleep, such as locking windows, putting up gates, and bells that can alert parents the child is up.[98]

Since restful sleep is related to children's ability to pay attention and learn, to their maintaining good moods and getting along with their friends, parents' efforts at helping children sleep provide many benefits.

Temper Tantrums

Temper tantrums are common responses to parents' requests. Parents take many actions to increase compliance. They make activities manageable for the child (not doing six errands on a morning the child has a cold); demands are predictable and routines are sensitive to children's temperament and needs.[99] Parents observe what children are doing and step in as frustration begins to increase so they can help the child problem-solve.

Thomas Gordon recommends mutual problem solving to find a solution agreeable to both parent and child at times of conflict.[100] Even when a compromise is not possible and a child is still upset, active listening may be useful. He cites the example of a child who could not go swimming because he had a cold. When the child's mother commented that it was hard for him to wait until the next day, he calmed down.

Behaviorists use a method of ignoring. John Krumboltz and Helen Krumboltz tell of a little boy who learned that, if he cried and whined, his parents would pick him up instead of paying attention to the new baby.[101] When they realized that their actions were creating the problems, they agreed to ignore the outbursts. When the boy learned that he gained nothing by banging his head and demanding what he wanted, the tantrums stopped. Behaviorists insist that parents must be firm and consistent. Otherwise, outbursts will continue, and each time, children will hold out longer because they have learned that they can win by outlasting the parents.

Stanley Turecki and Leslie Tonner distinguish between the manipulative tantrum and the temperamental tantrum.[102] Some children use tantrums to manipulate the parents into getting them what they want, as in the case above. In the case of a manipulative outburst, Turecki recommends firm refusal to give in. Distracting the child, ignoring the outburst, and sending the child to his or her room are all techniques for handling that kind of tantrum.

In the more intense temperamental tantrum, children seem out of control. Some aspect of their temperament has been violated, and they are reacting to that. For example, a child sensitive to material may have a tantrum when he or she has to wear a wool sweater. In these instances, Turecki advises a calm and sympathetic approach; parents can reflect the child's feelings of irritation or upset ("I know you don't like this, but it will be okay"). Parents can then put their arms around the child, if permitted. There is no long discussion of what is upsetting the child unless the child wants to talk. If the situation can be corrected, it should be. For example, if the wool sweater feels scratchy, let the child remove it and wear a soft sweatshirt. This is not giving in, but just correcting a mistake. All parents can do then is wait out the tantrum.

Throughout the temperamental tantrum, parents convey the attitude that they will help the child deal with this situation. Though parents change their minds when good reasons are presented, they are generally consistent in waiting out the tantrum and insisting on behavior change.

Sibling Rivalry

We noted earlier the many reactions children have when a younger sibling is born. Parents use many strategies to help children deal with brothers and sisters, depending on the ages of the children.

When a second baby arrives, parents include the child as a helper so that a more adult-like role can compensate a bit for the loss of all the attention. Getting diapers, entertaining the baby, and giving the baby hugs can be done under adult supervision to ensure safety, as a young child may not understand the infant's need for support. Once beyond the newborn stage, infants take an interest in children and their activities so an older child can have a special role with the baby.

Parents can use sociodramatic play with young children. They can get a small doll for preschoolers and encourage their child to feed it. In the course of feeding babies, parents can verbalize the difficulties of being a baby and not being able to get food for yourself or to older children about what their respective babies like to do or what kinds of days they are having. Such play can be fun and informative and also strengthen relationships between parents and older children.

As children get older, the most basic principle is that parents model the warm responses they want children to show to each other.[103] They also model the use of verbal strategies to understand problems, express feelings, and find alternative solutions.

Gordon's strategies of mutual problem solving create a climate in which children can work out their own problems.[104] One mother whose children were four, six, and eight found that the children, including the four-year-old, devised rules that decreased fighting and name calling. The children were upset by verbal insults and decided they would try to send I-messages. If the situation became too heated, they would go to their rooms to cool off.

Rudolf Dreikurs considers sibling rivalry in detail.[105] He believes that parents can reduce the jealousy among children by making it clear to all that each child in the family is loved for his or her individual qualities and that it is not important whether one child does something better than another. Parents love each child, but a child's trust of that love can be diminished when parents use one sibling's behavior to humiliate another child: "Why can't you be more like Jimmy—he ate everything on his plate."

Dreikurs recommends treating all children the same to reduce sibling fighting. All children should be sent to their rooms if play becomes noisy. If one child complains about another, parents can react so that children feel a responsibility to live in peace. Parents can point out that a child who acts up today may only be trying to retaliate for an incident that happened yesterday. Misbehavior involves all children in the family, and they can learn to take care of each other. When they see that life is more fun when they cooperate and get along with each other, children learn to settle their differences.

All these techniques are important. Parents must decide which ones will work best in a particular situation.

Aggression

Temper outbursts reflect anger, lack of control, and noncompliance, but aggression is out-of-control behavior that is destructive and hurts others or their possessions, as we described earlier.[106]

To reduce aggressive, noncompliant behaviors, parents first foster a positive attachment with the child and second, use Positive Parenting principles to teach children new behaviors. When mothers and preschool teachers participated in a program emphasizing positive responses to replace the negative, critical responses such behavior ordinarily arouses, the aggressive behavior of highly aggressive children declined at home.[107] Mothers participated in twelve weekly sessions, and teachers in a six-day training course. Including teachers was more effective in reducing aggression than training mothers and children alone. Changes were greatest for the most aggressive children and were still notable a year later for children whose mothers attended at least six sessions. At the end of the year, the behavior of 80 percent of the aggressive children fell into a category of low risk for conduct problems. Third, parents teach children specific social skills and skills of emotional control, as described in Chapters 5 and 6. Research indicates that aggressive and disruptive preschoolers want to get along, but they need the proper skills.[108]

Social Withdrawal and Inhibition

We described inhibited preschoolers earlier. Even though withdrawal causes significant problems for children, parents are generally more concerned about aggressiveness. Parents of withdrawn children are often surprised and puzzled at their children's behavior, feeling embarrassed and guilty about it. Believing that shyness is an inborn quality, they tend to use high-power, directive strategies with children to change the behavior. These usually do not work. Such parents can, however, take many positive actions that resemble the effective strategies parents of aggressive children use.[109]

First, they can express a positive attitude toward their child as a person. Parents of withdrawn children tend to be negative in their comments about them, expressing the view that parents have to step in and help children function, but this is not a helpful attitude.

Second, they can be supportive in teaching social skills and encouraging play with others. At the same time, they have to stand back and permit the child to act independently. In their zeal to help their physiologically reactive child, they may have become overprotective, too worried about an upsetting interaction, and therefore too controlling. The child does not have a chance to learn that he or she can succeed independently.

Third, parents have to look at their own behaviors. Do they model a fearful, inhibited approach to new situations and people? Do their own problems interfere with their ability to be positive and to support their child? If so, they need to try to change themselves as part of their attempt to help their children.

A PRACTICAL QUESTION: HOW CAN PARENTS HELP WHEN CHILDREN HAVE DISABILITIES OR DEVELOPMENTAL DELAYS?

These early years involve rapid development in children's skills and abilities. Some children show clear signs of developmental delays at birth. Perhaps a genetic disorder or birth difficulties have resulted in significant problems for the child, and services are provided at birth. Sometimes, however, the delay is identified later, when the child fails to develop certain abilities such as hearing or language.

In the last fifteen years, an increasing number of children have been diagnosed with pervasive developmental disorders, a broad category of disorders, the most common among them being autism and Asperger's disorder.[110] Children with autism have qualitative impairments in three areas: (1) language/communication, (2) socioemotional responsiveness and understanding of others, and (3) stereotyped and restricted patterns of behavior, activities, and interests. These impairments appear in the first three years of life and vary in levels of severity. Children with Asperger's disorder have impairments in socioemotional responsiveness and restricted interests, but their language and cognitive skills are average, and sometimes very advanced. Surveys by the National Center for Birth Defects and Developmental Disabilities find that 1 in every 150 eight-year-old children are diagnosed with one of the pervasive developmental disorders. They are found in all ethnic, racial, and social groups but more frequently affect boys, with a ratio of 4 to 1.

In this brief space, we can only present general guidelines for parents to help children with many forms of disabilities and delays. As soon as disabilities or delays are detected, parents must seek professional consultation for diagnosis. If they feel the diagnosis is in error, they should seek additional opinions until they believe all factors have been taken into consideration. Research indicates that, for most disabilities and delays, the earlier the diagnosis and intervention, the greater the child's progress. Accurate diagnosis is sometimes complicated because it is difficult to tell a significant delay from slow growth within the average range.

Once a diagnosis is made, parents must obtain all available services and monitor that the services are effective in meeting the child's needs. This will be an ongoing task during their child's development because children's needs change with age. Each year in school, parents must monitor services and programs, and all the while, keep accurate records of care, treatment, and progress.

Once services are in place, parents focus on the psychological needs of all family members. Box 8-2 presents brothers' and sisters' reactions and needs when a child has a disability. Parents have many profound emotional reactions to their children's difficulties: sadness that their children must work hard to master skills that come so easily to other children, worry about their children's long-term future, stress from finding time and money to provide resources for children, and sadness that their children may not experience some of the typical joys of childhood and adolescence. Sometimes, they struggle with feelings of guilt that in some unknown way they are responsible for the child's difficulties.

Psychological counseling, often provided when services are begun before age three, can help parents and families deal with the stresses that come from a child's having special needs. This includes helping members of the extended family understand a child's special disability and needs so they can participate in bringing about progress.

At all times, parents provide the love, sensitive caregiving, and security that are the most valuable aids in helping children achieve their maximum potential. Linda Gilkerson and Frances Stott write,

> The moment with the most potential for emotional trauma comes not when the child realizes that he or she is different but when the child discovers that the differences are perceived by society as inferior.[111]

As the child grows and develops, the disability takes on different meanings. At all ages, parents must convey that the child's worth lies in being who he or she is, not in becoming "normal" or like others. Gilkerson and Stott review the "fix-it model of disability" in which the child's value lies in working hard and making progress to become "normal." According to one therapist, children with disabilities must come to see themselves as both intact and disabled at the same time, and to do this they require their families' love and acceptance. Supportive relationships within the family help children develop a sense of themselves as willing, purposive individuals who can act.

A ten-year longitudinal study of children with motor and other disabilities and delays supports the importance of the family emotional atmosphere and parents' sensitive and responsive caretaking.[112] The child's disability predicted growth in intellectual, social, and adaptive skills over this period.

Box 8-2
PARENTING BROTHERS AND SISTERS OF CHILDREN WITH SPECIAL NEEDS

When a child has an ongoing health or developmental problem, everyone in the family is touched and reacts. Parents direct their efforts to getting and providing the best possible care for the child, and they organize family and work life to include the additional activities. They get psychological support for the child with special needs and sometimes for themselves from organizations and professionals. In the stress and pressure of all these activities, it is not surprising that the needs of brothers and sisters are often overlooked.

Yet brothers and sisters of children with special needs have their own stresses and needs, and parents can help in many ways. The exact nature of siblings' responses depends on the specific nature and the effects of the special problem confronting the family. In many ways, siblings' reactions are similar to those of parents. Like parents, they too love and often admire the child with a special problem and feel sad at the difficulties or limitations the child experiences; they wish there were something they could do to make things better. Like parents, they share the restrictions or burdens that a physical or developmental problem places on family activities, and they too experience the general public's reactions to unusual behaviors. Sometimes, they feel guilty they are healthy and were spared special problems. And sometimes, they feel angry at the lack of attention and the burdens of intense feelings that appear to have no outlet.

Adult brothers and sisters of children with special needs have several suggestions for parents to ease the stress for siblings.* Easing siblings' stress is important, according to Don Meyer, founder of the Sibling Support Project, because "these brothers and sisters will likely have the longest relationships of anyone, relationships in excess of 65 years. They should be remembered at every turn."**

Parents are advised to:

- sit down and talk to siblings in age-appropriate terms about the child's special problems—what the problem is, what causes it, what interventions do to help—giving as much information as is appropriate for siblings' ages.
- encourage brothers and sisters to express their feelings about what happens in the family and accept of all feelings, giving children permission to express them, especially negative ones, as many children fear burdening their already-stressed parents.
- include siblings in discussions and plans for treatments insofar as is possible, much as one includes even very young children in the plans for a family event such as a new baby or a grandparent's visit, brothers and sisters should be included in what is happening.
- give brothers and sisters their special time with parents and give siblings time, too, when their needs come before those of the child with special problems, using a babysitter or relatives to care for that child while brothers and sisters have some special activity with parents.
- help brothers and sisters develop their own activities and interests that give them pleasure, increase their skills and make new friends, giving brothers and sisters confidence and a sense that parents care about their development too.

(continued)

Box 8-2
CONTINUED

- model the ways you want brothers and sisters to relate to the child with special needs and accept their help and insights.
- involve brothers and sisters in sibling support groups that enable them to talk to other brothers and sisters who live with a child with special needs. Their age-mates can bring special understanding that parents may not have. In Seattle, Washington, Don Meyer has started a support group that gives information and has discussion groups for children around the country that can be accessed electronically.

*Kate Strohm, *Being the Other One* (Boston: Shambala, 2005).
**Gretchen Cook, "Siblings of Disabled Have Troubles of Their Own," New *York Times*, April 4, 2006, p. D5.

Beyond the disability, however, personal characteristics of the child and the family predicted progress in development. Children's ability to regulate feelings and behavior and express them appropriately, as rated by teachers, and children's ability to remain motivated to learn predicted progress. Sensitive and responsive mother–child interactions predicted growth in social and communication skills.

Parents' stress was related to the extent of the disability and to their child's level of stress as reflected in behavior problems. When children did not develop behavior problems, mothers' stress remained stable and low over the period. Social support and good problem-solving skills reduced parents' stress.

Describing Vygotsky's approach to children's disabilities, Laura Berk writes that it

> is a highly optimistic vision; it accentuates the child's strengths. He underscored the importance of viewing the child not as abnormal or as underdeveloped but rather as having developed differently. . . . With the assurance of others, children with disabilities can realize a wealth of possibilities and unique competencies.[113]

PARENTS' EXPERIENCES IN FACING TRANSITIONS

In these years, parents continue in what Ellen Galinsky terms the authority stage.[114] Many parents, bogged down in battle with their young children, find themselves doing and saying things they vowed they never would—the very words they hated to hear from their own parents when they were children. Parents are shaken and upset as their ideal images of themselves as parents collide with the reality of rearing children.

Parents revise their images of themselves in light of their actual behavior. Because it involves change, this can be a painful process. Parents must change either their ideal image or their behavior to come closer to living up to their own standards. Their images of children change as well. Parents discover that children are not always loving, cooperative, and affectionate. Children can be extremely aggressive—breaking things, hitting, pulling hair.

Parents must also deal with each other as authorities. When James McHale followed up with his parents whose children were now two and a half, he found, "Negative emotion had become a feature of family life during the toddler years in a manner seldom seen in infancy."[115] Several factors accounted for the increase in negative tone. First, fathers were more actively engaged in child care so there were more opportunities for conflicts with mothers over caregiving.

Second, parents were in the process of teaching children basic rules and values for functioning in life. When parents disagreed, each parent was likely to feel strongly about basic values and want to have their view the accepted one. Third, at the same time that parents had strong feelings about children's behavior, children experienced strong emotions and wanted their way. They did not give up easily, and they were skilled at going from one parent to the other to get the answer they wanted. So this was a difficult time for all family members.

Researchers were not surprised at parents' concern about discipline issues, but they were surprised that two-thirds of parents reported that they, their spouse, or both needed to learn greater control of their temper and develop more patience and calm in interacting with family members. Parents also worried when they believed the other parent was hampering their child's development by being too indulgent, too overprotective, too lenient, or not encouraging independence.

Despite their difficulties, parents also report wanting to spend more time with each other and with the family as a unit. Those parents who had a warm, cooperative, cohesive alliance when children were twelve months old continued to work together in the toddler years. There was, however, little relationship between parenting at this time and pregnancy attitudes and coparenting at three months, with the exception that fathers' negativity and the discrepancy between mothers' and fathers' ideas about parenting during pregnancy decreased coparenting solidity in the toddler years. Researchers found that parents did not have to agree in order to work together, but they did need to talk to each other and understand the other parent's view.

Parents' ability to work together affected toddlers' functioning. When parents worked together in a warm, cooperative way, supporting each other and not undermining the other parent's efforts with verbal sniping, then toddlers scored well on a test of preacademic skills and were described at home and at day care as emotionally mature and socially competent.

Parents' hostile and competitive interactions affect preschoolers' views of themselves. They view themselves as unlikeable and unable to make friends with others, and their teachers describe them in similar ways when they are in kindergarten. If parents remain warm and caring with each other when they disagree, their conflicts do not affect children's self-perceptions.[116]

SUPPORT FOR PARENTS

Recall from Chapters 6 and 7 the parents' support groups that Philip and Carolyn Cowan organized to help parents cope with the transition to parenting and then with the transition to the child's being in school.[117] Such groups help parents develop realistic expectations for their children and themselves. As one parent stated, in these early years, one is not exactly sure of what the limits or expectations should be, and these groups can provide information and discuss what the range of individual differences are and which strategies work with various children. Parents can then more easily manage problems and enjoy the time with their children. These groups also give parents an opportunity to talk about relationship issues with marital partners and families of origin. Parents get insights and strategies that release tensions so they are more effective partners and parents. When children have special disabilities or needs, parents can often find national groups devoted to helping parents and children with the problem, and many have local groups that provide support and updated and practical information for parents.

MAIN POINTS

As their motor, cognitive, language, and social skills increase, toddlers and preschoolers
- take a great interest in learning about the world
- develop a greater sense of self and independence
- take pleasure and delight in their new accomplishments
- express emotions such as pride, shame, and guilt
- gradually learn control of their behavior through internalization of rules and standards

As they mature in the preschool years, children's behavior
- decreases in aggressiveness, and undercontrol
- can reveal difficulties in aggressiveness and poor control that persist in the school years
- reflect stressors in family life such as low income and mother's depression
- is competent and resilient when parents form secure attachments and use positive parenting strategies

In these years children's gender and ethnic identities begin to form in stages that
- begin with children's identifying their own group and seeing themselves as a part of the group
- learning about the group and the behavior expected of members
- realizing they will always be part of that group

Parents whose children function well and have secure attachments
- are available and sensitive to children's needs
- grant the child independence within safe limits

- provide models of kind, caring, controlled behavior
- talk with children, answering questions, giving information, getting their views
- play with children to increase closeness and stimulate learning and development

Parents help children learn to regulate their behavior when they

- establish a process of mutual responsiveness
- act to prevent problems
- avoid harsh, critical, directive, and controlling behaviors with children
- introduce rules that dovetail with children's abilities
- use low-power techniques of reasoning and explanations when children do not comply
- use moral reasoning and fairness to encourage inclusive relationships with other children and other groups
- use scaffolding to increase children's attention and executive skills
- work together so children get a consistent set of rules

Problems discussed center on

- sleep
- sibling rivalry
- handling temper tantrums
- dealing with aggression and withdrawal
- helping children with disabilities reach their potential

Joys include the child's

- delight in increasing skills and personal achievements
- helping behaviors
- greater communicativeness

EXERCISES

1. Interview two couples who have preschoolers. Ask them about their children's daily routines and their worries and pleasures regarding their children. What are the sources of stress and support for the parents? Are stresses and supports similar in the two families?

2. In small groups, recall early experiences of gender learning. (a) Did the teachings deal with activities, appearances, behavior, feelings? (b) Who was teaching you about gender-appropriate behaviors—parents, relatives, siblings, peers, teachers? (c) Were you more likely to accept the teachings of adults or of peers? Make a list of the kinds of experiences members had. (d) What similar experiences affect children today?

3. In groups, recall early experiences with siblings. Was there much fighting? Did parents teach children how to get along? Did parents punish children for not getting along? What seems to make for the best relationships with siblings? What roles do siblings play in the life of adults?

4. Watch Saturday morning television programs for preschoolers and decide how much time and what specific programs you, if you were parents, would permit your toddlers and preschoolers to watch. Justify your choices.

5. Interview three preschoolers about their joys in life. What do they like to do best? Do they get to do these things as much as they would like to? How can parents make their lives happier? Are their requests reasonable? Do you think parents are aware of what makes their children happy?

ADDITIONAL READINGS

Bodrova, Elena and Leong, Deborah J. *Tools of the Mind: The Vygotskyian Approach to Early Childhood Education.* Upper Saddle River, NJ: Pearson-Prentice-Hall, 2007.

Greenspan, Stanley I. and Wiedner, Serena. *The Child with Special Needs.* Reading, MA: Addison-Wesley, 1998.

Honig, Alice Sterling. *Little Kids Big Worries: Stress-Busting Tips for Early Childhood Classrooms.* Baltimore: Brookes Publishing, 2010.

Orenstein, Peggy. *Cinderella Ate My Daughter.* New York: HarperCollins, 2011.

Paley, Vivian Gussin. *You Can't Say You Can't Play.* Cambridge, MA: Harvard University Press, 1993.

9

Parenting Elementary School Children

CHAPTER TOPICS

In this chapter, you will learn about:

- Children's development
- Social relationships with parents, siblings, and peers

- Promoting healthy lifestyles, emotional control, school success, and social skills
- Helping children with common school difficulties

Test Your Knowledge: Fact or Fiction (True/False)

1. Adding an hour of sleep to a child's nightly schedule increases memory and reaction time on cognitive tests equivalent to two years of chronological age.
2. Elementary school success serves as a protective factor against the development of high-risk behaviors like delinquency and substance abuse in adolescence.
3. Children around the world, regardless of sex or socioeconomic status, agree with each other on what is upsetting even more than do adults and children within the same culture.
4. Children believe it is okay to violate a moral rule if an adult tells them to do so.
5. Children are best advised to ignore bullies and walk away from them, not giving them the attention they want.

Children's entrance into school marks a new stage in parenthood. Children spend an increasing number of hours in school and with peers. They are absorbing new information and are exposed to new challenges and new values. How do parents foster children's success in this new stage of development?

Children have learned the routines of living—eating, dressing, toileting, verbalizing easily, and taking care of many of their own needs. They now adjust to the demanding world of formal education, and they must create a social place for themselves with new peers as well. They often undertake new interests in sports and music or art. Teachings in the world outside the home may conflict with parents' values. This chapter discusses how parents support children's growth and their participation in learning and new activities and how they help children manage new experiences, especially when they are discouraging or painful.

PHYSICAL DEVELOPMENT

From ages five to ten, girls and boys have approximately the same height, weight, and general physical measurements. At five, they are about 42 inches tall and weigh about 40–45 pounds. By age ten, they stand at about 52 inches and weigh about 75–80 pounds. In the elementary school years, children's coordination is well developed. They ride bikes, skate, swim, play team sports, draw, and play musical instruments. Nearly all the basic skills in the area of gross (running, skipping) and fine (cutting with scissors, drawing) motor coordination are laid down by age seven, and further development consists of refining these skills.

Levels of neurobiological arousal and reactivity influence children's abilities to pay attention and focus on learning in school.[1] Recent studies of neurophysiological functioning and brain development indicate that high levels of emotion may play a role in organizing neuronal groups in the neocortex and in building connections between the cortex and emotional centers in the brain. High levels of emotion also affect learning, and parents' role is to help children regulate their feelings. If children go to school with heightened fear and anxiety, they may not be able to focus and learn. If they go to school with heightened impulsivity and emotional arousal, they may have difficulty attending to and learning new material.

INTELLECTUAL DEVELOPMENT

Three major cognitive changes occur in the elementary school years.[2] First, children learn to reason generally. At about age seven, children become less focused on their own perceptions and more involved in the objective properties of what they observe. They organize their perceptions and reason about a broader range of objects and situations. Because they also more easily adopt the other person's point of view, they understand other people and their reactions better. At the end of this age period, around ten to twelve, thinking becomes more abstract and more closely resembles adults' ways of reasoning.

Second, children at this age organize tasks and function more independently than before. In addition to pursuing goals, children observe and think about their own behavior and reflect on their thinking processes as well. Third, they acquire knowledge in an organized learning environment—school—that sets standards by which they and others evaluate their performance.

In the process of learning children constantly take in, information, and manipulate it developing new strategies for handling it.[3] Part of learning is finding effective strategies for dealing with new materials so children sometimes have to go through

VOICES OF EXPERIENCE

What I Wish I Had Known
about the Elementary School Years

"I wish I'd known how much you need to be an advocate for your child with the school. When we grew up, our parents put us in public school and that was it. Now, you have a lot more options, and the public schools aren't always great; so you realize how active you need to be in order to ensure a good education for your children." MOTHER

"The main thing, I think, is how important temperament is. My daughter was in one school that was very noncompetitive; that's a wonderful philosophy, but it wasn't right for her. She is very competitive, and in that atmosphere she did not do as well. So with the second child, we are going to be more careful to see that there is a good fit between her temperament and what she is doing." FATHER

"I was surprised that, even though the children are older, they take as much time as when they were younger; but you spend the time in different ways. I thought when they started school, I would have a little more time. Instead of giving them baths at night and rocking them, I supervise homework and argue about taking baths. Knowing that things were going to take as much time would have made me less impatient in the beginning, and I would have planned better." MOTHER

"I learned that, especially from five to eight, say, children are not as competent as they look. They really can't do a lot of things that on the surface you think they can. They have language, and they look like they're reasoning, and they look like their motor skills are okay. So you say, 'When you get up in the morning, I want you to make your cereal,' and they can't do it consistently. And so because we didn't know that with the first child, I think we made excessive demands on her, which led to her being a little harsher on herself. Now with the second one, if she can't tie her shoes by herself today, even though she could two weeks ago, we're more likely to say, 'Okay,' instead of 'Well, you can tie your shoes; go ahead and do it.' If you give them a little help, it doesn't mean you are making babies of them; it means they have room to take it from there." FATHER

"I wish I'd known more about their abilities and work readiness. My daughter had some special needs in school. In preschool, I could see there were immaturities in her drawings and writing, but she got lots of happy faces. I thought she was doing better than she was. When she got to school, it came as quite a shock that she was having problems. With my son, I have been more on top, and I ask more questions about how he is really doing, because I want to get any special needs he has addressed. My advice to any parent is that, if at all possible, volunteer in your child's school. I gave up half a day's pay, and in my financial situation that was a real hardship. It is very, very important to keep a handle on not just what is happening educationally, but also who the peers are and what is going on." MOTHER

a process of trying unsuccessful strategies before they find the ones that work. Parents can help children in their problem solving by giving support as children go through the process of finding effective strategies.

SCHOOL

School organizes children's daytime hours and much of children's and parents' evening activities as well. Parents want children to succeed because school achievement has lifelong effects. It determines access to further education, more advanced jobs, and higher incomes. School success has emotional consequences as well.[4] Making friends and developing intellectual skills increase feelings of competence and satisfaction that serve as protective factors against adolescent delinquency and substance abuse. Conversely, school difficulties and peer rejection can be sources of low self-esteem and depression extending into adulthood. Box 9-1 describes how one mother handles such problems.

The Process of Learning at School

Many think children's learning and school achievement depend solely on children's ability and the quality of the teaching. But much like parenting, learning in the school setting is a dynamic process. The participants in the process—the child, parents, teachers/school personnel, peers, and sometimes the neighborhood—hinder or facilitate the process, and all interact and change each other in the process.[5]

Children bring their gender, temperament, and skills, and all the experiences they have had in life. Parents contribute resources, intellectual stimulation, and psychological support. They also bring their personal qualities and all the stressors that impact them and their children. Schools and neighborhoods provide educational resources, teachers, social supports, and stressors that vary in quality. Peers encourage and participate in learning, provide pleasurable social time, or conversely, can arouse feelings of rejection and long-lasting depression.

Parents' Role

First, parents' resources enable children to live in safe neighborhoods, attend quality schools, and have stimulating books, toys, lessons, trips, and tutoring as needed. Their home routines enable children to have healthy food, sufficient sleep, and exercise so children are ready to learn.[6]

Parents' general attitudes about ability and learning influence their children's views of difficulties and their persistence and effort in remedying them.[7] When parents view ability as an internal and unchangeable quality that children have or lack, termed an "entity view of ability," children adopt the same view and lack confidence that they can improve and remedy their problems. They believe failure means they lack ability. When, however, parents believe ability develops in small steps as one learns skills and practices, the "incremental view of ability," children see that developing new skills and exerting more effort remedy learning problems. Emphasizing the process of learning—learning new strategies, making gains—also increases children's confidence.

Parents' beliefs in children's abilities encourage boys and girls to engage in academics, sports, and social activities at school.

Parents' beliefs in their children's abilities (e.g., to do mathematical work or participate in sports), encourage children's feelings of competence in these areas from first through twelfth grade.[8] Parents' beliefs in children's abilities also encourage boys and girls to participate in activities such as sports and music usually associated with the opposite gender.

Parents' involvement in children's learning predicts children's achievement.[9] Involvement includes reading to children, helping them problem-solve how to do schoolwork, and participating in classroom activities and school-wide activities.[10] Parents' involvement promotes children's confidence in their own abilities and thus leads to achievement. Parents balance structuring learning activities that can create dependence with encouraging children's autonomy that promotes initiative.[11]

Parents' ability to remain calm and positive in helping children with activities like their homework enables children to maintain confidence about their learning abilities.[12] Most parents feel frustrated when homework requires their aid, but when parents are critical and negative, children feel helpless and discouraged. Remaining positive and loving toward the child even though feeling frustrated at the homework tasks helps children persist and learn.

Finally, parents are advocates for their children at times of academic or social difficulties. As we will see, parents need to be alert to difficulties so they can work with teachers at the beginning because unaddressed problems continue and exert ongoing effects on learning.

School's Role

Schools are children's homes for up to thirty hours a week, forty weeks a year, and their rules and emotional atmosphere make a difference in children's lives. Children develop strong attachments to teachers and their schools when they are actively involved in the learning process and have opportunities and rewards for developing competencies. Effective teachers, like effective parents, have clear, fair, and realistic expectations of students and emphasize mastery-based learning in a cooperative atmosphere.[13] Effective teachers are especially important for children entering school with limited academic skills, but are fewer in number in poor schools.[14]

Research increasingly documents that the emotional atmosphere of the school, its responsiveness in meeting all children's needs, its fairness and reliance on praise and encouragement, promoting students positive emotional and social skills play a powerful role in increasing students' academic achievement.[15] A positive school atmosphere also decreases children's aggression, bullying, and discrimination against out-groups.[16]

Not only do teachers promote positive learning, they can reduce problems that have already developed. Even when children are identified as being at risk for academic and social problems at the end of kindergarten, having first-grade teachers who offer strong instructional and emotional support enables high-risk students to learn and perform as well as low-risk students.[17] Similarly, first-grade classrooms with a calm, positive, emotional tone reduce the rejection highly anxious boys experience and the depression that highly anxious girls experience in disorganized classrooms with conflict and negative emotional tone.[18]

A recent study documented that an excellent teacher, measured by increasing children's test scores yearly, had a lifelong impact on students' earnings throughout adulthood, their likelihood of going to college, and of having a teen pregnancy.[19] Knowing that classrooms and teachers can have these impacts empowers parents to work with schools to provide learning environments that help children grow and learn in all areas.

Children's Role

Most children start school with positive beliefs about their abilities and capacities to learn. Children in first grade believe that all children can learn and that all they need is effort—those who do best have worked the hardest.[20] When parents encourage an incremental view of learning, children persist when frustrated and improve their work.

School programs too can encourage these children to enjoy the process of learning rather than focusing on the achievements of learning. Such programs reduce feelings of helplessness.[21]

Children's academic and social skills at school entry—in kindergarten and first grade—influence teachers' reactions and set in motion a cascade of events that predict reading achievement in later years.[22] When, for example, children learn to read easily and form positive relationships with teachers, their reading achievement is higher in the third and fifth grades. Conversely, when children experience difficulty and frustration in learning to read, they become aggressive and experience conflict with teachers, and these experiences predict lower reading achievement at the fifth-grade level. Teachers are most likely, in one study, to have conflict with boys and African Americans.

Children's emotional responses decrease learning. Children high in aggression and impulsivity at age five had lower grades in elementary school than those who were low in aggression or impulsivity.[23] Children's feelings of insecurity in their attachments to their mothers and in their parents' marital relationship affected their physiological arousal level, their ability to sleep, and, in turn, their performance on ability and achievement tests.[24] Following children from first through third grade, researchers found that children who entered first grade feeling anxious and depressed and continued to have these feelings, were more likely to be bullied, intensifying their anxiety and depressed moods by the third grade.[25] Aggressive children were more likely to be bullied as well and by the third grade, were also anxious. Researchers urged schools to identify children with highly aroused feelings early and help them develop coping strategies to avoid the continuation of problems.

Peers' Role

Children learn from peers in many ways—through cooperating on classroom projects, observing how others think and reason, and learning negotiating skills in play at recess.[26] Children gain intellectual information, but they also gain social and cultural information on topics such as gender roles. They gain emotional support, and they learn and practice social skills. But peers can also provide social difficulties and negative feelings, as we shall see.

When Home and School Cultures Differ

Schools generally reflect middle-class European American values and patterns of behavior, emphasizing independent work habits, verbal interactions and questioning, and competition. Since we are a society of diverse ethnic cultures, many children come to school with interdependent cultural values and ways of interacting with others, and they may feel uncomfortable in what seems a strange environment.[27]

Not only do children struggle with different values at school, but parents may do so as well. Many parents have the following kind of experience. A principal sees a parent bringing a forgotten library book due that day to his child. The principal points out, not for the first time, that the parent is not teaching his son to be responsible for his books. The father points out, not for the first time, that he is teaching his child the family value of looking out for each other, and that value is of lifelong importance.[28]

Studies of three groups of immigrant families in a Northeastern city find that the immigrant families differ with respect to educational level, family constellation, and reasons for coming to the United States. Their children, however, are remarkably similar in (1) having positive attitudes toward school and teachers, and (2) having positive patterns of academic achievement over three-year periods of time.[29]

Though family values may differ from school values, children of many ethnic groups are able to blend them. For example, some immigrant children who put family obligations first nevertheless see excelling at school as a way to please parents.[30] Parents come to the United States so children can have a better life and school achievement satisfies parents' goals.

Children do not have to come from immigrant or culturally different families to feel alienated from school values. As we described in Chapter 2, many children and parents from working-class families feel a similar distance from some values espoused at school.

Parents must be aware that schools may not understand their values and when conflicts occur, talking to teachers and school personnel can help. Teachers and school personnel in some districts are participating in programs such as Bridging Cultures to reduce such problems.[31]

EMOTIONAL DEVELOPMENT

Children's emotional life is more complex. Children realize that feelings depend, in part, on what led up to the event and how the event is interpreted.[32] They now can experience two or more feelings about an event or a person. They can be happy with Mom for baking a birthday cake, but angry at her for not giving permission to open gifts early. Over time, they learn to integrate their feelings.

Children hide their feelings and give four general reasons for doing so: to avoid negative consequences, to protect feelings of self-esteem, to maintain good relations with others and not give offense, and finally, to observe social conventions.[33] By the age of nine or ten, children have rules, such as smile when you get a gift (even one you do not like) and apologize even when you do not want to.

Children express their true feelings to parents, adult caregivers, and best friends. Children are most likely to express their inner feelings when they are alone with a person whom they trust to respond in a positive, understanding way.[34] Unfortunately, as children—particularly boys—grow older, they anticipate a less positive response from others, even from parents. Thus, older boys are much less likely to express their feelings than are girls or younger boys.

Stressful Life Events

The way children ages nine to eleven around the world rank twenty stressful situations demonstrates that children share perspectives on life that are quite different from those of their parents and often not immediately apparent to parents.

Box 9-1
ONE MOTHER'S EXPERIENCES WITH HOMESCHOOLING

Currently in this country, approximately 2 percent of children from kindergarten through twelfth grade are homeschooled. Parents report their main reasons: concerns about safety, drugs, and negative peer influences (31 percent), desire to provide religious and moral education (30 percent), and dissatisfaction with school/academic programs (16 percent).*

Annie is the mother of Ryan, age nineteen, a second-year student at a city college; David, sixteen, a sophomore at a public high school; Adrienne, sixteen, a junior at a public high school; Jimmy, nine, about to enter fourth grade in public school; and Monique, six, entering first grade in public school. Adrienne and Monique have been adopted in the past three years from an orphanage in Haiti. Annie's husband, George, is a public school administrator.

Annie homeschooled Ryan for nine years from the fifth grade through high school, and David for six years, from the fourth grade through the ninth. David wanted very much to return to high school with his friends from public school, and although this has not been easy for him, he has worked hard to succeed and will continue there. Annie would like to homeschool Jimmy as she believes it would help him, but his father is reluctant at this time.

Why did you decide to do homeschooling?
In the fifth grade Ryan was not reading in school, and we could see that there were issues despite our having an Individualized Educational Plan (IEP) in place for him and doing everything we could to help. He wasn't a behavior problem. He was having trouble with reading and so he tuned out in school. The way he explained it was that it was too stressful at school. He is a quiet person, there was noise, and he could not do the work even though he tested at the gifted level.

He began learning at home where it was quiet. In two months, he was reading easily, and it became his favorite activity. He is gifted in math, and I got him a math tutor to teach him as I could not do it. At city college he is a very serious student, wants to get all As. He is not certain what he wants to do, but he has time to decide.

The year after I began homeschooling Ryan, I began to homeschool David. He was social and liked all the interaction with friends at school, but he had ADHD and was dyslexic and learned in different ways. People said you are crazy to try to homeschool a child who is so active, but in my opinion that was just the kind of child to homeschool. He did not want to leave his friends, but he made new ones through homeschooling organizations so he came to like it. He did want to go to high school because he was "tired of hanging out with mom," but he decided to return a year behind his age group. I would have been happy to continue homeschooling but he did not want to do it.

I feel public school ends up taking children away from the family, and every year they take more time from the family and dictate what the family will do in the evenings and with all their time. Parents feel they have to perform like a teacher and see the work is done.

And the school creates stress. If the child has any problem, the school looks around for who is to blame. Is he having trouble reading? Did you get his eyes tested? Are you

(continued)

Box 9-1
CONTINUED

making him wear glasses? Parents feel like they really have to perform for the school because if there is any problem, it is your fault. What are you doing or not doing?

And when there are difficulties learning, the school sees the child as lacking, imperfect, not right. The school says to the child and the parent, "Try harder!" and the child feels he is trying as hard as he can, and he still can't do it so he feels like a failure. So the child is defined by his ability to do schoolwork, and when kids feel they can't do it and don't fit in, those feelings spill over to the rest of their lives and can create behavioral issues or depression.

My youngest son has all the academic skills, but he doesn't have focus, and he gets distracted. Also he has trouble writing—dysgraphia—so that slows him down. Everyone in the class is told, "Don't distract Jimmy." When the teacher read a story about a boy who had trouble writing, he came home and was very upset because he thought everyone was thinking about him. We started medication to help him focus for only a couple of weeks because he did not notice any difference, and we did not want to use medication even if lack of attention causes issues at school.

What kind of routine did you have when you were homeschooling?
I got information on curriculum and materials from the Home Schooling Group. Ryan liked workbooks, spelling tests, and we went through those. I tried to find what interested the boys, and then focus all the learning skills around that topic, and we would go from the beginning level to the most advanced. Reading, math, and spelling would be focused on that topic.

David is very active so we were on the go a lot. We went to all the museums, we went to parks and to cultural events. And they remembered what they learned through these activities better than they would have from reading about them. I was careful to find out the educational standards and skill levels for children their age and made sure they met them.

As a result of all the things we did and the places we went, my children feel at ease with others. People who don't know they are homeschooled say, "Oh they talk so easily to adults." They are used to relating to people of all ages.

Is there anything the public school can do to make it less stressful for students?
Accept students as they are. We all have differences in how we learn. Give them the activities they like to do and the activities they need to do to learn. Focus the schools on the students. Schools have become businesses with budgets, doing what the government wants, directing what teachers must do to get test scores up. What individual children need is not as important as it should be, I believe. In Jimmy's school there is no time for holiday celebrations; every minute is counted as an instructional minute, all geared to passing the tests so schools can be rated by student performance.

Homeschooling made it possible for my kids to feel good about themselves despite learning differences or maybe because of them.

*National Center for Education Statistics, "Homeschooling in the United States: 2003," Retrieved, April, 2008, www.nces.gov/pubs2006/homeschool/index.asp.

Regardless of sex or socioeconomic status, children from Egypt, Japan, the Philippines, Canada, Australia, and the United States agree with each other on what is upsetting even more than do adults and children within the same culture.[35] Loss of a parent is the most stressful event, and parental fights are highly stressful as well. Embarrassing situations—wetting their pants, being caught in a theft, being ridiculed in class—distress children. Although many students like school, it also causes them anxiety, frustration, and unhappiness, with many children worrying about grades, being retained, and making mistakes. Adults may be surprised at children's sensitivity to embarrassing situations and their concern about school.

Daily journals of elementary school students in the United States reveal that boys are more likely to cite external situations and demands, such as school, chores, interruptions, and environmental factors, as sources of stress and girls, disappointments with self and others and failure to live up to responsibilities.[36]

Loneliness

For a long time, social scientists thought that children could not experience loneliness prior to adolescence, when they became more separate from the family. Recent research, however, finds that five- and six-year-old children have conceptions of loneliness as clear as those of adults.[37] They describe feelings of being sad and alone, having no one to play with. Older elementary schoolchildren give even more poignant descriptions of loneliness ("Like you're the only one on the moon," "Always in the dark," "Like you have no one that really likes you and you're all alone"). Extreme loneliness is related to lack of friends, shy and submissive behavior, and a tendency to attribute social failure to one's own internal inadequacies. Such loneliness, in turn, prevents the child from interacting with others and intensifies the problem.

Cascading Events

Emotional experiences become part of what may be positive or negative cycles of behavior that affect development for many years. When parents express positive feelings in their interactions with their children, their children show more positive feelings in school, and both peers and teachers rate them as helpful and socially competent over a two-year period of observation.[38]

Children who enter kindergarten with aggressive, confrontational ways of reacting to others experience peer rejection in the early grades.[39] Socially adjusted peers leave them out of activities, and they turn to aggressive peers who encourage greater aggressiveness. By the time they are age twelve, the rejected children have developed externalizing behavioral problems. Similarly, withdrawn children may retreat and be rejected and victimized by peers. By age twelve, they are anxious and depressed. Children's aggressive, noncompliant reactions in elementary school are related to poor academic achievement in adolescence and to worry and internalizing problems in young adulthood.[40]

Coping with Problems

In facing problems children are most likely to strike at the roots of the difficulty when the problem stems from peers or school, where they feel they have more control. Children tend to use distraction strategies to adjust to situations they cannot control, such as doctors' visits.[41] Children also tend to use enjoyable activities to buffer themselves from stress. Athletics, being at home with families, and special treats of food all help children to deal with stressors.[42]

Children often seek help in dealing with stressful situations. They "perceive mothers as being the best multipurpose social provider available, in contrast to friends and teachers, who are relatively specialized in their social value."[43] Friends provide companionship and emotional support second only to parents. Teachers provide information but little companionship. Fathers are excellent providers of information, but are generally less available for direct help. Until early adolescence, parents and extended family provide the primary sources of support for African American, European American, and Latino groups.[44] Extended family members are more important for African American and Latina/o children than for European Americans.

THE DEVELOPMENT OF THE SELF

In elementary school, children think of themselves in more general terms rather than concrete physical traits and specific activities, such as "I am popular" rather than "I play with lots of friends." They become capable of integrating behaviors and forming a more balanced view of themselves that takes into account both positive and negative qualities.[45] Instead of smart or dumb, they think of themselves as smart in some things and not so smart in others. Still, they generally have a positive view of their personal qualities and an optimistic view that any negative behaviors can be changed, and they have the same positive views of others.[46] They need only one positive piece of information about a person to view them positively, but five pieces of negative information before they view the person negatively. This general trust in others' goodness may make children vulnerable to strangers' deceptive overtures.

Children also begin to evaluate their behavior in comparison to their peers. In the early grades, comparisons may be overt and direct—"I can finish the work faster than you"—but as children grow older, comparisons become subtler and less direct—"I have more friends than the other girls in my class." And they evaluate their own behavior, as we take up under Self-regulation.

Gender Identity

Psychologists used to think that gender development was largely completed in the preschool years. Studies of older children, however, reveal that gender identity continues to develop over a long time; in fact, it never truly ends.[47]

Children in elementary school reason about the constancy of gender identity in more advanced ways than before, and[48] an increasing number of children explain gender constancy in unchangeable, operational terms such as physical characteristics. In these years, children, particularly girls, are more flexible in their preferences for activities and future occupations than they were as preschoolers, and this flexibility increases with age. However, those boys and girls who are most sex-stereotyped in their behavior at age five remained so at age eight.[49]

While children develop attitudes about what is gender appropriate for their own and the opposite gender, they use their own interests and preferences in determining what is appropriate for them as individuals.[50] For example, six of eight girls who said only men should be doctors expressed an interest in becoming doctors.

The most flexible and tolerant children come from families where parents and same-sex siblings are flexible in their activities. Same-sex peers also play an important role in promoting flexibility and tolerance.

Ethnic Identity

By about age seven, children identify their ethnic group. They learn ethnic consistency and constancy and realize they cannot change their ethnic identity. They construct a sense of ethnic identity much as they construct a sense of gender identity, from experiences at home with parents, at school with peers and teachers, and interactions and observations in the community.[51]

Family routines and activities teach children the distinctive values of their group. Mothers' daily diaries of children's activities in 1997 reveal distinctive activities of four ethnic groups.[52] European American children spend more time playing, more time in sports, and less time studying than the other groups, reflecting the importance of active, social pursuits. They spend more time reading than all but Asian Americans, reflecting the value of general cognitive ability.

African American children differ from other ethic groups in spending more time in church and church activities, reflecting the importance of religion; Latina/o children enjoy more household and family activities, reflecting their group's family orientation; and Asian American children spend more time in educational activities, reflecting a strong drive for academic achievement.

Parents' behavior, verbal messages, and toys and books also shape children's ethnic identity. We discuss African American socialization as more research is available. Homes rich in Afrocentric toys and books stimulate first-graders' cognitive competence and receptive language skills.[53]

Children also learn about ethnic identity from peer interactions. Peer acceptance and, thus, self-perceptions are more positive when children attend schools with higher percentages of African American children, perhaps because children are more likely to be socially accepted and viewed as leaders and less likely to be viewed as fighters.[54] When children have African American teachers, they are similarly viewed in a more positive light. Conversely, when there are smaller percentages of African American children in a class with European American children they are more disliked by the majority group; they prefer their own group and have negative views of European American children in the class. However, prosocial children of both ethnic groups are liked by all classmates.[55]

Children view their occupational possibilities based on what they see around them.[56] As young as age six, African American children can identify occupations with high percentages of European Americans and high percentages of African Americans, and they believe occupations with many African Americans have lower status. In evaluating novel or made-up occupations, African American children give higher status to jobs when pictures show European Americans performing them and lower status to them when pictures show African Americans doing them.

Although they perceive racial segregation in jobs, they do not endorse it and believe that both European and African Americans can do all jobs. Regardless of social class, young children have high aspirations and prefer to work in high-status jobs. By age twelve, children from higher status families prefer high-status occupations, but children from lower status families no longer aspire to high-status occupations, perhaps because they feel they lack the finances to pursue higher education.

As part of forming a sense of ethnic identity children not only learn what it means to be part of their group, but they also come to prefer their own group, seeing it quite positively and viewing other groups less favorably.[57] Studies indicate that in-group favoritism develops first in children by about age five. Children initially prefer their own group without looking at the out-group negatively. Attitudes toward out-groups develop gradually in the early elementary school years. Out-group prejudice appears less likely to develop when children attend a multiethnic school where they have interactions with children of different groups and when they can describe negative qualities about the in-group. Children's ability to recognize negative qualities about their own group seems to enable them to see the positive qualities in other groups. Nevertheless, even when out-group attitudes are not negative, in-group favoritism is so great that out-group children suffer in comparison. Children of ethnic minority groups are much more aware of ethnic bias than European American children who are more focused on gender bias.[58] When children become aware that their group is seen as less intellectually competent, they develop anxiety about their academic performance, but they maintain interest in school.[59]

Self-Esteem

Global feelings of self-worth are related to two independent factors: (1) one's feelings of competence in domains of importance, and (2) the amount of social support one receives from others.[60] Those highest in self-worth feel good about the abilities they value and also feel that others support and accept them. Those lowest in global self-worth feel they lack competence in domains deemed important and report that they receive little social support.

The areas of competence that contribute most to feelings of self-worth are physical appearance and social acceptance by others—namely, parents and peers. Surprisingly, physical appearance and social support continue to be salient across the lifespan for individuals from eight to fifty-five years of age. Elementary schoolchildren also evaluate themselves in terms of their scholastic and athletic competence and their conduct.

Although self-esteem depends on the early positive regard given by parents and caregivers, this regard does not fix it for life. Levels of self-esteem can increase over time as competence in areas of importance to them increase or as support from others increases and decreases under the reverse conditions. Times of change and transition, such as entrance into kindergarten or middle school, can trigger changes in self-esteem. Children maintain self-esteem most successfully when they join or create positive social support or when they increase in other areas of competence.

Recall from Chapter 2 that elementary school children of different ethnic groups resemble each other in self-esteem.[61] As they begin to take on culturally valued behaviors, self-esteem scores diverge, depending on the culture's values. When cultural values stress individualism, expressiveness, and self-assertion, then self-esteem scores stay high, as they do in African American and European American groups. When cultural values emphasize respect for tradition, interdependence with others, and critical self-evaluation, then self-esteem scores drop, as they do in Latina/o and Asian American groups.

THE DEVELOPMENT OF SELF-REGULATION

Elementary school children become more self-critical, and their self-esteem is related to their ability to control their feelings and behavior. They feel guilty when they have broken a moral rule, and ashamed when they have committed both moral and social blunders.[62] Since children do not feel good about themselves when they engage in disapproved behaviors,[63] it is important for parents to help children meet approved standards.

Parents' warm and positive expressiveness help children develop effortful control, defined as the ability to observe and plan behavior, inhibiting inappropriate dominant responses and carrying out less dominant, but appropriate responses.[64] Effortful control enables children to regulate their feelings and their behavior. Following children over a four-year period from ages nine to thirteen, researchers found that parents' positive parenting predicted children's effortful control two years later, and that effortful control predicted low levels of externalizing problems at age thirteen. Table 9-1 lists additional parental behaviors associated with children's self-regulation and prosocial behavior.

■ **TABLE 9-1**
PARENTAL QUALITIES ASSOCIATED WITH CHILDREN'S SELF-REGULATION AND PROSOCIAL BEHAVIOR

1. Being warm and supportive with children

2. Developing mutually responsive relationships with children

3. Helping children understand others' feelings and the effects of their behaviors on others

4. Using reasoning and persuasion to gain children's compliance with rules

5. Including children in family decision making

6. Helping children develop an internal code of rules for behavior

7. Modeling caring and concern for others

Adapted from: Nancy Eisenberg and Carlos Valiente, "Parenting and Children's Prosocial and Moral Development," in *Handbook of Parenting,* 2nd ed., ed. Marc H. Bornstein, vol. 5: *Practical Issues in Parenting* (Mahwah, NJ: Erlbaum, 2002), 111–142.

In the early elementary school years, reasoning about moral and conventional behavior becomes more complex, and children take into account the context of an event. They look at social situations and distinguish certain behaviors as matters of personal choice, other behaviors as matters of social convention, and still others as moral issues.[65] For example, it is morally wrong to deprive a person of a basic right such as access to schooling because of race or gender, but a person has the right of personal choice to choose friends even if someone of another race or gender is not included. Children consider it wrong to violate a moral rule even if an authoritative adult tells them to do it. For example, it is wrong to keep on fighting even if an adult tells you to do so.[66]

PARENT-CHILD RELATIONSHIPS

Children spend more time away from home. While parents and the home remain the center of life activities, friends and extracurricular activities claim more of children's time. Parents spend half as much time with elementary school children and give them less physical affection, compared with preschoolers. Even so, parents enjoy parenting as much as in earlier years, and they report as much caring and regard for children as earlier.[67]

Attachment

Children with secure attachments to parents adapt to school demands and perform well academically, and are socially accepted.[68] Secure attachments provide relationships with:

1. open, sensitive, and reciprocal communication
2. collaborative problem solving
3. support for the child's exploration and autonomy

Securely attached children have lower levels of emotional arousal so they can regulate their feelings and their behavior and focus on learning and relating to others. Patterns of open communication, collaborative problem solving, and autonomous behavior promote learning and positive relationships.

Attachment relationships are generally stable from the preschool to elementary school years, with an overall stability rate of 68 percent.[69] In one study children who moved from secure to insecure attachment experienced a decrease in the amount of time and quality of the mother-child communication process while those children who moved from secure to disorganized attachment experienced more severe stress and loss (intense conflict between the parents, parent's death). Children who changed from insecure to secure attachments developed more emotionally supportive and open communication patterns with mothers than those who remained insecure.[70] So, improving communication and availability increase security, and stresses that interfere with sensitivity and availability decrease secure attachment.

Authoritative parenting that combines parental warmth, firm control of children's behavior, and respect for children's individuality and independence helps children manage the transition from home to school.[71] Mothers' and fathers' authoritative parenting of their kindergartners predicted their children's math and reading scores two years later. Mothers' encouragement of autonomy at the end of kindergarten predicted children's achievement and social acceptance at the end of first grade. Children whose mothers consistently encouraged autonomy from the preschool through the early years of school had high scores on academic and social competence and low teacher ratings of externalizing problems.

Parents' Changing Roles

Because parents no longer have exclusive control of children, they permit children to make decisions that parents monitor, supervise, and approve. Sharing control with children, termed coregulation, serves as a bridge to the preadolescent and adolescent years, when children will assume more control.[72]

Parents gradually allow children greater input on decisions about clothing, schoolwork, activities, and social activities, but less input on chores, health issues, and curfews. This input will increase in early adolescence and surge in late adolescence. Parents are more likely to give girls and easy to supervise children more input than boys and difficult to manage children.[73]

Mothers' and Fathers' Roles

In the elementary school period, mothers and fathers continue to relate to children in different ways.[74] Mothers take major responsibility for managing family tasks—scheduling homework and baths, for example. Mothers are both more directive with children and more positive in their reactions to them. Both parents are similar in being more demanding of boys than of girls and more disapproving of boys' misbehavior.

Fathers, though more generally neutral in affect, continue to engage in more physical play and give more affection to both boys and girls. When fathers have high-status jobs, they have less time to spend with their children, and so low job salience is related to men's playfulness and caregiving.[75] Men are most likely to be involved as fathers when mothers do not take on all the caregiving and managing. Nevertheless, the more skillful mothers are with children, the more skillful fathers become.

Though mothers' and fathers' roles differ, children see them as having many qualities in common. Both parents are described as loving, happy, honest, responsible, self-confident individuals.[76] Fathers are more interested in learning and creativity than mothers, and mothers are more concerned about others' feelings than fathers. Children describe themselves less positively than they describe their parents, but still see many similarities with them. Children are loving, happy, and interested in learning and creativity, but they are far below parents in self-confidence, cooperativeness. responsibility, and honesty. Children described "having good family relationships" as the most important family goal of mothers and themselves, but feel fathers value "educational/vocational" goals most.

When parents make demands on the child, social responsibility increases in boys, self-assertiveness in girls. Diana Baumrind suggests that parents actively encourage characteristics outside the usual gender stereotypes.[77] The natural tendencies for both mothers and fathers are to encourage assertiveness in boys and cooperation and a more dependent role in girls, so parents must make special efforts to encourage a broader range of characteristics. Couples attending parenting groups did become less gender-stereotyped in their behaviors, with fathers becoming warmer and mothers becoming more goal- and limit-setting with children.[78]

Socializing Ethnic Identity

Socializing children regarding racial and ethnic issues includes (1) teaching about the group's cultural values, especially taking pride in the group and its achievements (sometimes termed "cultural socialization"); (2) preparation for bias, helping children deal with bias and discrimination; and (3) promoting skepticism and mistrust of what the majority might do. These aspects of socialization are highly correlated, but they still differ from each other and their effects differ depending on the ages of children.[79]

Parents' messages regarding racial pride and preparation for bias do not have positive outcomes in the early elementary school years.[80] First-grade girls who heard these messages showed an increase in behavior problems. While preparation for bias and encouraging mistrust of the majority group are considered important parenting tasks, there are suggestions that such strategies may have negative impact on early elementary school children with boys' becoming more aggressive and girls', more anxious. However, when fathers of ten-year-old boys engage in preparation for bias, boys appear less depressed.[81] Parents' messages about bias and mistrust were amplified when children live in neighborhoods with few social supports for families.[82]

In these years, children are more likely to get inaccurate and negative messages from other children, the media, and people outside the home, so it is important for parents to encourage a positive self-image and racial pride. When parents acknowledge social restrictions and barriers but at the same time encourage self-development and ethnic pride and help children develop strategies for dealing with barriers, children, particularly older ones, are happy, high in self-esteem, and successful in school.[83] European American parents provide little ethnic socialization for their children because they do not want children to be "race" conscious,[84] and as we saw, children are less aware of ethnic bias. But, again, as emphasized in Chapter 2, parents need to send positive messages about appreciating the special qualities of all people and including them fully in society's activities.

RELATIONSHIPS WITH SIBLINGS

Siblings frequently spend more time with each other than they do with parents.[85] Their relationships improve in the elementary school years and become more enjoyable. The degree of satisfaction depends on the emotional climate in the family, because sibling relationships tend to mirror the ways parents treat each other and the ways they relate to children.[86]

Box 9-2
FIRST PERSON NARRATIVES

When teen-age sisters Sara and Emily Buder read a newspaper article about the cruel bullying Olivia Gardner endured at two schools before she dropped out to do homeschooling, they decided to take action. They checked with Olivia's mother who agreed, and then organized a letter-writing project called "Olivia's Letters," asking their classmates to write letters of encouragement and support so Olivia could know others cared about her, and she could feel good about herself again. They hoped to get fifty letters, but word of the project spread, and eventually, Olivia received four thousand letters, from young and old, boys and girls, men and women.

The book, *Letters to a Bullied Girl: Messages of Healing and Hope,** contains a small number of the letters Olivia received and provides a look at why bullies do it, how bullied people cope with the experience and build happy, successful lives, and how both the bullied and the bullies fare as the years go by. All of the bullies wrote, as adults, to say how guilty and terrible they felt about what they had done. Some explained it as feeling bad themselves and wanting others to suffer; others said it was power gone out of control, others said they really did not realize at the time how wrong it was, and now they make it clear to their children how wrong it is. One wrote he simply had no excuse: he had good parents, a happy life, good friends, a good set of values. He certainly did talk with his children about the pain bullying caused and the strong moral rule against it.

Victims of bullying wrote to encourage Olivia not to take the bullying personally because it was not about her, and the bullies agreed with that. Victims also repeated several times that life was short, not to give any unnecessary thought, worry, or time to the tormenters as they were not worth it. Many wrote to tell Olivia of the happy, fulfilling lives they had with family and children, friends and work as they grew older. Their ways of coping included getting very involved in schoolwork or new interests, and finding one or two friends.

It is a very poignant book useful to anyone who has experienced bullying and to all who want to understand bullying and change their school culture. The example of the many actions one mother took when she learned her ten-year-old son and his friends bullied a boy at lunch serves as an excellent model for all that one family can do within the family, with the victim, and with the school to eventually end the bullying that occurred there.

*Olivia Gardner with Emily and Sara Buder, *Letters to a Bullied Girl: Messages of Healing and Hope* (New York: HarperCollins, 2008).

When parents are positive and treat children fairly, then siblings have good relationships. Conversely, when mothers and fathers are angry with each other, they are more hostile with their children, who, in turn, show anger at their siblings and their peers.[87] Because conflict in sibling relationships during these years predicts a child's level of anxiety, depression, and acting out in early adolescence, improving these relationships when tension arises is important.[88]

Although most research on sibling relationships has been carried out on European American families, research with rural African American families has yielded similar results.[89] When parents have good relationships with each other and positive relationships with their children, the older siblings develop good emotional control and are supportive and caring with younger siblings. Even though these parents work long hours and have financial pressures, when parents are caring with them, the older children also show care with younger siblings.

PEER RELATIONSHIPS

In the elementary school years, children spend about 30 percent or more of their time with peers in a wide variety of settings—school, sports, and interest groups—with less adult supervision than before. They spend more time in rough-and-tumble play than in the preschool years and in group games.[90]

Children are attracted to peers whose interests are similar to theirs, but they also look for friends they can trust to be loyal and supportive.[91] Children continue to prefer positive interactions and to work problems out so that everyone's needs are met. Relationships grow when children can express thoughts and feelings clearly. Friendships are likely to endure when partners are kind and sociable and have low levels of conflict.

While some children are identified as popular, what matters in peer relationships is having a quality friendship with sharing, positive interactions, and willingness to work out conflicts. When shy, withdrawn children have such a friendship, they appear to avoid the negative experiences of rejection and victimization.

Aggressive Children

Some children are physically aggressive, hitting and hurting others. Some children are verbally assaultive—taunting, teasing, and humiliating others. These types of aggression are overt, noticeable, and more characteristic of boys than of girls.[92] Another form of aggression, termed "relational aggression," is more subtle, not easily detectable, and more characteristic of girls. It consists of acts designed to deprive children of friends—spreading untrue rumors about a target child, organizing other children to reject the target child, refusing to be a friend unless the target child does favors. These behaviors are considered aggressive because they are meant to hurt or damage another child.

In one study, about 27 percent of boys were described as aggressive, and of those boys 93 percent were overtly aggressive. About 22 percent of girls were described as aggressive, and of those girls 95 percent were engaged in relational aggression.[93] Only about one-quarter of aggressive children used both forms to hurt children; most relied on one or the other. Note that when relational aggression is assessed, girls are almost equal to boys in aggressive behavior.

Bullying

Bullying occurs when an aggressive child targets a single child or a small group and, though unprovoked, pursues the child(ren) and uses force in an unemotional way, divorced from conflict or disagreement. About two-thirds of aggressive children are overt bullies, and 10–15 percent of all children are victims of overt bullying.[94] As noted earlier, almost all aggressive girls engage in relational aggression, and about 8 percent of all girls are victims of relational aggression.[95] Victims of both forms of bullying share certain characteristics. They tend to be quiet, inhibited children with low self-esteem. Some are physically weaker. Some impulsive, disruptive victims evoke negative reactions from peers.

Some children are both bullies and victims and share the characteristics of both groups.[96] An extensive study of elementary, middle, and high school students' bullying in Colorado surveyed students' personal qualities like self-esteem, their attitudes and beliefs about bullying, and their views of their school cultures. In addition, researchers interviewed students in small groups.[97] Their overall findings were:

- many students become bullies after being victims
- both bullies and victims have low self-esteem and negative views of their schools, believing authorities are unfair, and have few sanctions against bullying
- across all ages bullying is related to getting and keeping power and being victimized is related to being seen as weak or vulnerable
- positive school climate is related to decreases in bullying
- programs for building healthy self-esteem and school success prevent bullying

Children who want to get along with others and use strategies to improve their social skills when bullied are able to assert themselves and form satisfying relationships with other children.[98] Children who seek to demonstrate their value with social success in social relationships feel wounded at bullying and lash back in anger or withdraw in tears.

While individual efforts are important, in a later section we describe a community effort that is effective in combating bullying. See Box 9-2 for personal experiences with bullying.

TASKS AND CONCERNS OF PARENTS

Parenting tasks include new activities as well as previous caregiving behaviors as follows:

- Being attentive, available, and responsive, using authoritative parenting and modeling desired behavior
- Monitoring and guiding children's behavior from a distance
- Structuring the home and daily routines so children have healthy lifestyles
- Encouraging autonomy, new skills and activities, and growing interest in friends
- Maintaining family rituals
- Serving as interpreter of children's experience in the larger world

- Participating in children's activities outside the home in supportive ways (room parent, soccer coach)
- Serving as children's advocate with authorities outside the home
- Sharing leisure activities and fun at home and outside the home

DAILY LIVING THAT PROMOTES GROWTH

Healthy eating, sleeping, and exercise habits affect not only children's physical well-being, but also their intellectual, social, and emotional well-being. These habits are the foundations for positive development, and parents have to establish and monitor them as children lack the self-control to do that.

Parents have no control over what children eat when they are away from home, but they do control the food available at home. Parents can buy healthy foods and model healthy eating habits. If potato chips and soda are available only for parties, children are less likely to beg for them every day.

Sleep is particularly important. Poor sleep is related to school inattentiveness and restlessness that interfere with learning. A recent study indicates that adding an hour's sleep each night to children's existing schedule increases memory and reaction times on cognitive tests the equivalent of two years of chronological age.[99] Children's ongoing sleepiness over a three-year-period decreased children's growth on measures of verbal comprehension and reasoning whereas decreasing sleepiness over the same period was related to growth in verbal skills.[100] Sleep problems at age four predict problems with short attention span, depression, and anxiety in adolescence.[101]

In addition to regular bedtimes and consistent routines, the amount of sleep appears related to emotional warmth and security in the home. Nighttime sleep increases when parents are warm, parents and children eat meals together, and the television is turned off.[102] Disrupted and poor sleep increase when children report insecurity about parents' marital relationship.[103]

Parents' and children's busy schedules make it difficult to set aside time for exercise, but it can be a family activity that brings members closer together. Choosing activities and arranging for everyone's participation can be arranged in family meetings, described in Chapter 5.

Two other areas are important for families. It may seem impossible to fit in, but family game times and reading books together bring families closer together and establish greater feelings of emotional security in children.

In these years, parents talk with children about their moral values and their responses to events that occur in their community. Parents and children can engage together in church or community activities designed to improve, for example, the environment or the school area or solve some other problem. It is a chance to work together and understand each other better and make a positive contribution to solving a problem.

HELPING CHILDREN REGULATE FEELINGS AND BEHAVIOR

In these years, parents undertake many actions to help children manage their feelings, decrease disapproved behaviors and increase approved behaviors.

VOICES OF EXPERIENCE

The Joys of Parenting Elementary School Children

"He's nine, and for the last several months, maybe because I'm the dad, he's come and said, 'Now there's this girl who's written me a note, what do I do?' Or, 'I have an interest here, how do I act?' I never heard any of this from my daughters. Then he says, 'What were you doing in the third grade? How did you deal with this when you were in the third grade?'" FATHER

"Being able to see life through their eyes is fun, sharing the way they see things, the questions they ask." MOTHER

"They are very loving kids. They'll give me a kiss good night and say, 'I'll love you forever.' That's a tradition." FATHER

"It was fun to see him learn to read. First, he knew the letters and then he read a little, and by the end of the year, he could read a lot." MOTHER

"I like watching them when they don't know I'm watching. They're playing or taking something apart. That's when you see how well you've transferred your values to them." FATHER

"It's fun to see the children join in with other kids. They went with their cousins to a July 4th celebration. They got right into a game with children they didn't know." MOTHER

"She wrote poems in school this year. It's amazing. She's quiet, and yet when you see the poems, you realize how much goes on in her head, how observant she is." FATHER

"I like seeing how important family is to them. They enjoy seeing their cousins, they like family to visit." MOTHER

"I'm a kid again. I get to do everything I liked to do all over again." FATHER

"It's fun when she says, 'Mommy, smile at me, make me laugh.'" MOTHER

"I enjoy watching their relationship grow. They are nineteen months apart. They play together a lot. She said to me, 'Sometimes, he's fun to play with and I love him, but sometimes he's a rascal.' They do a lot of imaginary play." MOTHER

"Every night we have a talking time just before he goes to bed, either he and his Dad or he and I. He's a real deep thinker, and he likes to get advice or get a response, and he just needs that verbal connection. So a few years ago when he was five, he was talking about being afraid of death and that he might not be married and he might not have children and that would be the worst. I can hear parts of what he might hear at church or other places like school, and he takes it all very seriously; when it collides, he wants to know what the answer is. They are always things we don't know the answer to either." MOTHER

"I can say, as a father of two girls between five and ten, that to be a father to girls is delightful. It's nice being looked on as a combination of God and Robert Redford. They have a little glow in their eyes when they look at Dad, and it's great. The younger one said, 'When I'm ticklish, you know why? Because I love you so much.'" FATHER

Anger

Dr. Ross Greene has developed a collaborative problem-solving approach to helping children with a wide variety of problems that produce what Greene terms "explosions" at home, school, or with friends.[104] Explosions may be angry, verbal outbursts that upset and alienate others or may involve physical aggression or retreating from challenges in anger or tears.

Greene emphasizes that most children want to do well because life is easier; the outbursts are signs that the child lacks the necessary skills to cope with the situation he or she faces either because skills are delayed or the situation is too demanding; for example, school can make great demands on an active child or a child who is sensitive to criticism and lead to explosions at home or at school. The main tasks for parents are:

- to empathize with the child's problem,
- calmly gather information so parent and child can define the problem and understand its source of the difficulty,
- carry out collaborative problem solving with the child to prevent the problem in the future. The best time to do collaborative problem solving is during a calm time, before the next explosion. Greene believes such problem solving takes practice and has a website, www.livesinthebalance.org, that provides a wealth of material to understand and use his approach with links to many resources.

A ten-year intervention sought to prevent moderate to high-risk kindergartners from developing aggressive psychiatric disorders such as conduct disorder and oppositional defiant disorder, using a variety of interventions to help children and their families.[105] Parents received parent training; children received social skills training, academic tutoring, mentoring, and home visits; teachers received a classroom curriculum and consultation to change the classroom ecology to one promoting social competence to minimize aggressive behaviors. Two years after the program ended, only 18 percent of high-risk children who did not receive the intervention were free of psychiatric diagnosis whereas 32 percent of those who received the services remained free of diagnosis. The intervention was effective for those at high risk for aggressive problems but not for children with moderate risk, in part because those of moderate risk were similar in risk to the general population.

Discouragement

In these years of rapidly developing skills, meeting new friends, and learning in formal settings in comparison with others, discouragement is a common feeling, especially for the more cautious, less confident child. Martin Seligman offers a program quite useful for parents in his book *The Optimistic Child*.[106]

Seligman has documented the nature of pessimistic attitudes that lead to discouragement and withdrawal from challenging tasks. Pessimistic individuals consider difficulty a sign of a pervasive, permanent problem that is one's own fault and is unchangeable. Pessimistic children see a poor math grade as the result of their own stupidity and inability to do math. They sometimes avoid studying because they are discouraged and feel they are no good at the subject.

Parents supply new interpretations of the problem. Perhaps the child did not study enough or needs extra tutoring. Parents can encourage their children to look for solutions to problems and to exert effort to achieve them, as most problems will improve with effort. Parents also must avoid critical personal comments, such as "You never learn at school—you just fool around," that decrease children's confidence.

Lying and Stealing

When parents create a supportive atmosphere in which children can talk about mistakes and misdeeds, and when they offer encouragement rather than criticism, lying and stealing are reduced. Still, almost every child has told a lie at one time, and all parents have concerns about lying and stealing because trust in others is such an important part of close relationships.

Parents express their feelings of concern about dishonesty, accept matter-of-factly that the child has lied or stolen, and problem-solve with the child ways to be more truthful and honest. If a child lies about schoolwork, parents should find out if there are special problems at school. If a child brags about false exploits, parents do well to focus on why he or she needs to do this to feel good. Parents express their belief that their child wants to be honest, and as partners, they need to figure out how to bring this about. Mutual problem solving, as discussed in Chapter 5, is very useful. In this process, the parent becomes an ally and a resource, not an accuser and a judge. The child learns that one can get help when in trouble and that one need not be perfect to be loved.

Promoting Positive Social Relationships

We have seen that parents' secure attachments with children and their use of authoritative parenting predict children's social competence. In contrast, parents of children who are not well liked and/or rejected are reported to use harsh, directive, authoritarian, controlling behaviors with their children. So, positive parenting is a first step in improving children's social behaviors.

When parents believe good social skills are important, model them, and find programs to teach children, social skills improve.[107] Developing new interests and skills such as photography or drawing or getting involved in extracurricular activities are other ways to meet and make friends. Box 9-3 has suggestions many parents can use.

Parents can also seek out behavioral programs for shy and aggressive children. As we have stated, aggressive children benefit from programs meeting the needs of shy children, as aggressive children need to learn how to join groups, how to communicate with peers, and how to validate peers by paying attention to them and helping them. These programs encourage cooperation, develop verbal skills to make requests and suggestions, teach techniques for anger management, and provide opportunities for children to rehearse the skills that increase social competence and peer acceptance. In follow-up studies, children who attended such programs achieved greater peer acceptance and reduced their aggressive responses.[108]

A Problem-Solving Skills Training program has been carefully researched, and attendance predicts significant reductions in problematic behavior at home and at

Meeting and making friends is an important activity at school.

school.[109] Children attend twenty to twenty-five individual sessions that focus on problem-solving skills and ways to settle differences with parents, children, and school authorities. Role-playing, practicing skills, and homework activities help children learn the skills. A parent component, Parent Management Training, consists of sixteen individual sessions for parents and a therapist to plan and practice how to change children's behavior at home and at school. Recently a five-session parental stress component has been added and found to further reduce children's problematic behaviors.

School-based programs seek to promote children's social and emotional competence, and a review of 213 such programs serving more than 270,000 school-aged children found that programs were successful in increasing: (1) children's prosocial attitudes, (2) their skills in identifying and managing feelings, (3) their problem-solving and conflict resolution skills, and (4) their academic achievement.[110]

Controlling Bullying

In the United States we generally deal with bullying at the individual level—a child complains to a parent, the parent goes to the school, and the school often considers what the individual child can do to handle the bully. In Norway, Dan Olweus designed a highly successful school- and community-based program to decrease bullying.[111] School administrators, teachers, parents, and students have roles in the program. Adults create, at school and at home, an environment in which children experience warm, positive attention and firm limits against negative behaviors. Negative behaviors receive consistent, nonhostile, nonphysical consequences, and monitoring occurs in and out of school.

Box 9-3
RICHARD LAVOIE'S STRATEGIES TO DEVELOP SOCIAL COMPETENCE*

Richard Lavoie has long worked with children who have learning disabilities of many kinds. He observed that social difficulties can be closely linked to difficulties in learning. If a person cannot process auditory material, he may not follow conversations well; if he has expressive language problems, he may be slow and awkward in conversations with a friend.

Lavoie points out that if you have trouble with academics, you can always enjoy athletic activities and all the social activities away from school. But a child with poor social skills cannot avoid situations that require these skills. "Any and all activities that involve two or more people require the use of social skills." Furthermore, there is no technology to help a child compensate for social difficulties as there are for learning disabilities (e.g., computers and calculators).

Lavoie has developed a system that parents, teachers, and counselors can use to help a child with social difficulties for any reason.

Lavoie believes that children's social missteps are unintentional—children want to have friends, but don't know how to "tune in" to social situations, join groups, make and keep friends, and resolve conflicts. They need help in all these areas, and each area requires many different skills.

To assist the child, parents take several steps. Most important, they remain calm, nonjudgmental helpers who serve as coaches and mutual problem solvers. As coaches, they help children prepare for difficult situations. If children are going to new classes or new programs, parents and children can go there in advance and become familiar with them. Parents help children rehearse for new social situations such as sleepovers or birthdays. They go over appropriate conversations for upcoming situations, such as meeting new people or giving a gift.

When problems arise, the adult and child together, in a calm, nonblaming way, review what happened and carry out what Lavoie calls a "social skills autopsy"—so termed because it is an attempt to determine the cause and effect of a "social error" in order to prevent its happening again. The social skills autopsy consists of five steps:

1. Ask the child to describe what happened.

2. Ask the child to identify what he or she thinks was the social mistake responsible for the difficulty; often, the child does not know what went wrong in the situation.

3. Help the child identify the particular social error accurately. Put forward alternative options in the situation, and let the child choose an appropriate one.

4. Create a social scenario with the same basic error or moral and see if the child recognizes the problem. For example, if the child got delayed at home and was late for a birthday party, making everyone wait to go to a movie, a similar scene is created in which the parent is late and delays everyone, and the child is expected to identify the error. If he or she fails, another scenario is made up.

5. The child practices the remedy at least once in the coming week—for example, not being late for social activities or sports.

The adult and child are collaborators; the adult asks questions and leads. The process is ongoing because children advance to new social situations and have to learn new skills. But parents are always there as consultants and coaches.

*Richard Lavoie, *It's So Much Work to Be Your Friend* (New York: Touchstone Books, 2005).

Interventions occur at the school, class, and individual level and include the formation of a coordinating group, meetings with staff and parents, better supervision during recess, class rules against bullying, and class meetings. At the individual level, parents, teachers, and students meet to discuss specific incidents and to develop strategies to handle them. Emphasis is on developing effective forms of communication and positive behaviors in all students, not just in bullies or victims.

Evaluated by 2,500 students and their teachers, the intervention program reduced bullying by 50 percent and decreased other antisocial acts as well. Moreover, bullying away from the school did not increase. Students expressed greater satisfaction with their schoolwork, and their social relationships with children increased. The benefits were in some instances more marked after two years than after one year. A similar program in Finland has had similar success.[112]

A program used in American schools where bullying was more common than expected—seen thirty times in an hour of playground observation with twenty episodes encouraged by bystanders—is titled Steps to Success.[113] It decreased bullying and bystanders' encouragement of it significantly and increased children's positive social behaviors. Children in the program reported that adults were more responsive, and there was much less tolerance for bullying and aggressive behaviors.

The Partnership of Families and Schools

In the past, people looked on the school as having primary responsibility for educating children. Parents played a secondary role—raising funds, volunteering in the school, and enriching the curriculum with their input and values. Recently, a partnership model for families and schools has been advanced.[114] Acknowledging the powerful impact of parents' involvement and encouragement on children's educational progress, the partnership model seeks to forge a strong link between parents and the schools. This model rests on six kinds of involvement:

1. Parents establish a home that allows children to (a) be healthy and attend school, (b) be calm and confident enough to pay attention in class and do their work, (c) receive encouragement to perform well, and (d) have home settings that support doing homework and educational projects. Schools provide families with information on effective parenting on school-related issues; they sometimes also provide supportive programs or workshops.

2. Schools keep parents informed of school matters and students' progress and behavior, including notices on students' performance, any difficulties, and any noteworthy behaviors. Schools also provide information on school programs, school needs, and opportunities for parental involvement in projects.

3. Parents, children, and other community members contribute their own special skills to promote children's education, as in cleaning, painting, and giving cultural information of interest.

4. Teachers help parents monitor and help children learn at home. Schools make educational goals and curricula available, show parents how to assist their children, and even give joint assignments that parents and students can carry out together. Teachers are also sensitive to immigrant parents' needs.

5. Parents participate in school organizations and in formal or informal groups that advise educators on school priorities, school improvement programs, and parents' and students' perceptions of problems in the school environment.

6. Finally, parents and schools work with business organizations, local government agencies, and volunteer groups to form partnerships that support school programs.

A PRACTICAL QUESTION: WHAT CAN PARENTS DO WHEN SCHOOL AND PSYCHOLOGICAL DIFFICULTIES INTERFERE WITH ACADEMIC ACHIEVEMENT?

What do parents do when a child's behavior interferes with learning? Space does not permit detailed discussions of the many different problems and conditions—attention problems, learning disabilities, emotional and family problems—that interfere with achievement, but a general plan for dealing with these kinds of problems is described.

School difficulties require accurate diagnosis as the first step in remedying problems. School study teams and school psychologists observe and test the children and provide information to identify the extent and source of the problem. If difficulties do not meet certain criteria or fall in certain categories, schools may refuse to do an assessment. Parents then have to pay privately or seek services in clinics with a sliding scale such as a college clinic.

When specific difficulties are identified, then parents, teachers, and children meet to remedy them. It is important to involve children in the process, as they need to understand specifically what requires changing, and they may have good ideas about how to change. In encouraging new behaviors and skills, parents and teachers identify the specific positive behaviors desired.

The level of work expected must be tailored to children's existing skills and advance as children's skills grow. If assignments are too difficult at the age-appropriate level but are expected nonetheless, then children will grow discouraged and resist doing them.

At the same time that parents help children deal with difficulties, parents also identify children's strengths, inside and outside of school, and help children gain pleasure and satisfaction from them to balance the effort and frustration required by problem areas. For example, sports can channel the energy and frustration of athletic children, and artistic activities such as music or drawing provide outlets for creative children.

Siblings may use school difficulties as a means of teasing or for comparisons that enable them to feel better about themselves and their skills. Parents must stop such behavior and teach family members that all children have their own special strengths, and everyone has one or more areas in which they must strive for improvement. Parents can express empathy for children who must spend long hours, year after year, in an atmosphere and activity that brings frustration.

Having fun daily with family members, perhaps after dinner, relaxes everyone and increases good feelings that sustain effort and motivation for work. See Box 9-4 to see all the actions taken to help a boy with ADHD.

Box 9-4
LIVING WITH ADHD*

In his last two years of high school, Blake Taylor, now a college student, wrote a book about growing up with ADHD, *ADHD & Me*. Diagnosed at age five, he describes not only his distractible, impulsive, and hyperactive actions, and his use of medications but the inner thoughts and emotional reactions that accompanied them. He provides invaluable insights into the experience of having ADHD that help parents, teachers, and professionals better understand the condition.

In the Acknowledgments and throughout the book, he thanks the many people who have helped and supported him—most particularly his mother and family, and also daily caregivers, some teachers and principals, doctors and counselors, coaches, and friends. Despite considerable support, however, he also describes poignant feelings of exclusion and rejection.

Blake emphasizes an active, problem-solving approach to ADHD difficulties. Over his desk, he keeps a fortune cookie saying what sums up his approach, "You constantly struggle for self-improvement." While he recognizes that every person with ADHD is different, he still believes people can learn useful strategies from each other. His suggestions go from the general to the specific. In addition to structure, organization, and routines, he advocates getting nine hours of sleep at night and having a regular exercise program. He found swimming on a team gave him exercise and a whole new group of friends who did not care about ADHD, only about how fast he swam.

In addition to taking control of ADHD symptoms, Blake emphasizes developing new skills and reaching out to others. He urges other children with ADHD to develop social skills—talk to others, make conversation (homework and sibling problems are always good topics). Explain to other children that you have ADHD and the behaviors that go with it—he also had tics to explain. He advises involvement in community activities—he joined a greyhound dog rescue group and made presentations and raised money. He suggests embracing new ways of doing things to overcome rigid thinking.

Blake ends the book with a list of the many gifts that he believes ADHD has added to his life—among them, high energy, humor, creativity, an ability to do a lot of things at once, compassion and empathy, an adventurous spirit. To get the benefits, he has to manage the difficulties. This book gives suggestions that may help other children and families as well.

*Blake E. S. Taylor, *ADHD & Me* (Oakland, CA: New Harbinger, 2007).

PARENTS' EXPERIENCES IN FACING TRANSITIONS

Ellen Galinsky describes this parental stage as the interpretive stage.[115] Parents share facts and information and interpret the world to their children. They teach values and guide children's behavior in certain directions. They decide how they will handle the child's greater independence and involvement with people who may not share similar values.

Parents' behavior at home predicts half the variation in children's adaptation to school.[116] When parents argue with each other, children as young as five years report parents' conflicts, and, sadly, blame themselves.[117] Teachers rate boys and girls as having more behavior problems when marital conflict is covert and expressed as silence or distancing.

Reducing parents' stress from work, marital relationships, and low income improves parenting and children's behavior.[118] Five sessions added to Parent Management Training, described earlier, helped parents identify stresses and find alternative solutions and additional resources that could help (friends, work, community agencies). Possible solutions were tried out as homework. The most common stresses addressed were arranging more time with partner, finding time for oneself, job-related stress, and lack of money. Dealing with parents' stress further reduced parents' and children's problems. Even parents in low-risk, economically stable, two-parent families benefited from talking about their day-to-day relationships with family members in a sixteen-week group, and the quality of children's functioning over a three-year period improved.[119]

Parents also refine their beliefs and values, discarding some and adding others. Children often prompt changes when they discover inconsistencies in what parents say and do. If lying is bad, why do parents tell relatives they are busy when they are not? If parents care about the world and want to make it a safer place, why are they not doing something to make it safe? In the process of answering these questions, parents grow.

SUPPORT FOR PARENTS

Many forms of support exist for parents of elementary school children. Parents work together with teachers and school personnel in parent-teacher associations or local organizations to provide the most effective schools possible. Specialized parent support groups also offer valuable information and resources. For example, Children and Adults with Attention Deficit Disorders (CHADD) provides support for families dealing with ADHD; the Orton Dyslexia Society helps with problems of reading; the Learning Disabilities Association of America, with learning disabilities. In addition, local and state organizations can be helpful.

Parent training programs also provide support, as described earlier. At the Oregon Social Learning Center, Gerald Patterson and his colleagues have worked with married parents, divorced single parents, foster parents, and parent-teacher partnerships to establish structure as well as positive and consistent rewards to help children learn to control aggressive behavior and develop prosocial behaviors at home and at school. These programs are successful and are being refined and expanded.[120]

At all age levels, parents and children find moral support and strength from religious activities. This source of support becomes important at this stage, because children begin to explore moral and ethical issues and are exposed to more ideas about these issues than before. Religious participation provides opportunities for discussing moral principles and applying them to everyday life.

Parents involved in religion can easily include their children. When parents have no affiliation, Joan Beck recommends that parents develop an individual belief system that they share with children as they grow.[121] The process of developing an agreed-upon source of spiritual or secular meaning in life can enrich the entire family.

Religious faith also contributes to feelings of confidence and security. In their study of resilient children who overcame the difficulties of growing up in troubled families, Emmy Werner and Ruth Smith point to the importance of faith:

> A potent protective factor among high-risk individuals who grew into successful adulthood was a faith that life made sense, that the odds could be overcome. This faith was tied to active involvement in church activities, whether Buddhist, Catholic, mainstream Protestant, or fundamentalist.[122]

Children's conception of God adds security to life by providing fallible parents with a backup expert who helps them. "God is my parents' parent and mine, too," said one girl.[123]

MAIN POINTS

As children's competence increases, by the end of this period they have

- acquired all the basic skills in gross and fine motor coordination
- developed more logical thinking abilities so that they can grasp the relations between objects
- learned greater understanding of their own and others' emotional reactions
- gained greater control of their aggressiveness and become less fearful
- learned to remedy situations they control and adjust to situations others control
- come to value themselves for their physical, intellectual, and social competence, developing an overall sense of self-worth and competence
- developed a sense of gender and ethnic identity based on parental teachings, interactions with others, and personal observations

Schools

- are the main socializing force outside the family and can increase growth and competence in all areas: cognitive, emotional, and social
- create stress in children's lives because children worry about making mistakes, being ridiculed, and failing
- promote a strong bond with children by encouraging active participation in learning and activities
- promote learning when they provide a calm, controlled environment and when teachers are gentle disciplinarians with high expectations for students
- often do not reward the values of ethnic groups that emphasize cooperation and sharing among their members even though ethnic minority groups members have high motivation to succeed at school
- can provide positive classroom atmospheres that minimize discrimination

- provide opportunities for social experiences that can be highly rewarding but also can involve bullying, aggressive, and exclusionary behaviors that are painful

With peers, children

- interact in an egalitarian, give-and-take fashion
- prefer those who are outgoing and supportive of other children
- interact more effectively when parents have been affectionate, warm, and accepting with them and less effectively when there is stress in the family
- can improve relationships when they learn emotional regulatory and social skills

Parenting tasks in this period include

- monitoring and guiding children from a distance as children move into new activities on their own
- interacting in a warm, accepting, yet firm manner when children are present
- strengthening children's abilities to monitor their own behavior and develop new skills
- structuring the home environment so the child can meet school responsibilities
- serving as an advocate for the child in activities outside the home (e.g., with schools, with sports teams, in organized activities)
- providing opportunities for children to develop new skills and positive identities
- becoming active in school and community organizations to provide positive environments for children

In Galinsky's interpretive stage, parents

- have achieved greater understanding of themselves as parents and of their children
- develop strategies for helping children cope with new authorities such as teachers and coaches

Problems discussed center on

- helping children meet school responsibilities
- helping children regulate anger and discouragement
- dealing with social problems such as social isolation, aggression, and bullying
- changing rule-breaking behavior such as lying

Parents' joys include

- observing increasing motor, cognitive, and social skills in children
- reexperiencing their own childhood pleasure through their child's experience

EXERCISES

1. Break into small groups of four or five. Discuss (a) how your parents prepared children for school, (b) how parents and schools worked together to deal with problems like bullying, (c) do parents and teachers understand how stressful school can be for children? Identify ways parents and teachers can help children more to adjust to the social and academic demands at school. Share your group's experiences with the class and come up with recommendations for parents and teachers to reduce children's school-related stresses.

2. Investigate the bullying prevention programs available in elementary, middle, and high schools in the community. How effective have they been in decreasing bullying? How often do they involve parents as the Olweus program has to promote positive discipline at home?

3. Investigate the school programs in elementary, middle, and high schools to build children's self-esteem, emotional regulation, and social problem-solving skills. How many include some training for parents, particularly in the middle school years?

4. In small groups, discuss the fears and stresses common to children from ages five to ten. How can parents or teachers help children cope with these fears? What kind of classroom atmosphere minimizes the stresses?

5. In small groups, discuss major activities that built sources of self-esteem in this period for you. Were these athletic activities? Group activities such as Scouts or Brownies? School activities? Come up with recommendations for parents as to the kinds of activities children find the most confidence building.

ADDITIONAL READINGS

Ellison, Katherine. *Buzz: A Year of Paying Attention.* New York: Hyperion, 2010.

Greene, Ross W. *The Explosive Child: A New Approach for Understanding and Helping Easily Frustrated, Chronically Inflexible Children.* 4th ed. New York: HarperCollins, 2010.

Lavoie, Richard. *It's So Much Work to Be Your Friend.* New York: Touchstone Books, 2005.

Seligman, Martin E. P. *The Optimistic Child.* New York: Houghton Mifflin, 1995.

Taylor, Blake E. S. *ADHD & Me.* Oakland, CA: New Harbinger, 2007.

10

Parenting Early Adolescents

Test Your Knowledge: Fact or Fiction (True/False)

1. Students face a mismatch between their developmental needs and the demands of the school environment.
2. Brain development is completed in adolescence.
3. Early adolescents are so busy with friends that siblings' behavior has little effect on them.
4. The ways to help aggressive early teens are similar to the ways to help inhibited shy teens.
5. To help children develop, parents are advised to stay less closely connected to boys and more closely connected to girls.

Adolescence is a time of dynamic changes in physical form, in ways of thinking, in time spent away from parents, in school settings, and in the importance of peers. How do parents support children as they adapt to changes? How do parents maintain close relationships while teenagers are becoming more independent? How do parents of different ethnic groups help their teenagers deal with the specific problems youth confront while establishing their identity in a complex world?

Early adolescence is a period of vulnerabilities and opportunities. Children experience the stresses of many changes. Yet, their thinking is maturing, and they engage in exciting activities on their own and with peers. The challenge for parents is to provide the emotional supports and limits necessary for children's growth toward maturity and greater autonomy.

PHYSICAL AND NEUROPHYSIOLOGICAL DEVELOPMENT

Adolescence begins with biological change. The physical changes of puberty, defined as the age at which sexual reproduction is possible, begin at about eight for girls and nine for boys and extend to the end of the second decade.[1]

Changes in Body and Physical Appearance

The brain triggers endocrine organs to release hormones that affect children's physical growth and secondary sexual characteristics (breasts, body and facial hair), resulting in reproductive maturity. Hormonal changes occur before any outward signs of puberty, so parents do not know at first that puberty has begun. For girls, these changes take place from about age eight to seventeen; for boys, on average, from nine to twenty. Although children vary in the age at which changes take place and their rapidity, the sequence remains consistent.

For girls, a spurt in height accompanies the growth of secondary sexual characteristics and the growth of the uterus and vagina. By the time menstruation occurs, on average at twelve and a half, the breasts and body are well developed. Boys' sexual hormonal secretions begin at about nine to ten; the first visible sign of puberty is growth of the testes and the scrotum that holds the testes. The growth spurt begins about a year later along with the growth of the penis and facial and body hair. Boys' voices change later in puberty.

The onset of pubertal changes, studied primarily in girls because of the clear pubertal marker of menstruation, depends on many factors:

- genetic influences—age of mother's menarche is strongest predictor of daughter's[2]
- physical influences—childhood growth in height and weight, nutrition, and percentage of body fat are predictors
- social influences—economic stresses are related to early and late onset
- psychological influences—family constellation, parenting behaviors, life stress are related to timing[3]

Psychological factors playing a role in the early or later onset of sexual development include:

- mothers' and fathers' positive and supportive parenting in the preschool years is related to delays in both boys' and girls' sexual development[4]
- harsh parenting and stress from low family income are related to girls' earlier menarche[5]
- girls' living in homes without a biological father or with stepfathers or mothers' boyfriends are more likely to have earlier menarche[6]

The timing of sexual development—being early, late, or on time—has psychological repercussions for boys and girls.[7] For girls, being on time is related to greater satisfaction with their bodies and their physical appearance than being early or late. For boys being early is related to feeling satisfied with their size and their physical appearance. Both African American boys and girls reported feeling less satisfied with late maturation, and Asian American and European American early adolescents showed little effect of timing on their body image.

Early-maturing girls have greater difficulties than later-maturing girls.[8] They experience more conflicts with parents and with peers—both boys and girls—because their bodies and interests are more advanced, and they are more prone to social anxiety,[9] depression, and substance abuse than later-menstruating girls. Early-maturing boys may have an advantage because of increased height and muscular strength but research results are inconsistent.

Changes in Sleep Patterns

Pubertal physical changes include changes in sleep patterns.[10] The timing of melatonin secretion changes, and there is later onset of sleep, so adolescents frequently delay going to bed for physical as well as school and social reasons. Parents have to help teens maintain regular sleep schedules to avoid excessive daytime sleepiness that impacts schoolwork, emotional regulation, and social relationships.

Changes in Emotions

Puberty also brings changes in emotional life.[11] Teens are not a cauldron of raging hormones, but following puberty, both boys' and girls' emotional reactions are more intense. The intensity of their negative affect is related to pubertal status, and their "sensation seeking" and attraction to high-intensity emotional experiences is related not to their age but to their pubertal status.[12] Between the ages of ten and fifteen, dopamine, a neurotransmitter that plays a role in feelings of pleasure, increases rapidly in the brain's reward systems, reaching a peak at about fifteen and then declining slowly.[13] Pleasurable events are more intense and exciting than before and early adolescents increase their reward-seeking and sensation-seeking behaviors before executive areas of brain function are fully developed to control behavior. When pursuing pleasure, teens are aware of risks, but focus more on the rewards of the pleasures and sensations they will gain.

Seeking pleasure and sensation may have an adaptive function for teens provided they can stay safe in the process as it enables them to explore new activities and undertake challenges with excitement and confidence.[14] Having followed novelty seekers, social scientists now speculate that when novelty seeking is combined with being adventurous, curious, and persistent, then people can carry out creative activities that benefit the whole group. Intense enjoyment of novelty and change appears related to a form of gene termed the migration gene, but upbringing also plays a role in preference for novelty.

Not only do pleasurable feelings increase in intensity after puberty, but negative ones do as well; girls have a significantly higher rate of depression than boys, a

VOICES OF EXPERIENCE

What I Wish I Had Known about Early Adolescence

"They seem to get caught up in fads in junior high. They do certain things to the max to be part of the crowd. I wish I'd known how to handle that. At what point are these fads okay, because it's important to identify with your peer group, and at what point do you say no? If they are really dangerous, then it's easy; but with a lot of them, it's a gray area, and I wish I'd known what to do better." FATHER

"I wish I had realized that she needed more structure and control. Because she had always been a good student and done her work, I thought I could trust her to manage school tasks without my checking. But she lost interest in school, and I learned only very gradually that I had to be more of a monitor with her work than I had been in the past." MOTHER

"I wish I had known more about mood swings. When the girls became thirteen, they each got moody for a while, and I stopped taking it personally. I just relaxed. The youngest one said, 'Do I have to go through that? Can't I just skip that?' Sure enough, when she became thirteen, she was moody too." MOTHER

"I wish I'd known how to help the boys get along a little better. They have real fights at times, and while they have a lot of fun together and help each other out, I wish I knew how to cut down on the fighting." FATHER

"I wish I knew what to expect. They are all so different, and they don't necessarily do what the books say. Sometimes, I'm waiting for a stage; now I'm waiting for adolescent rebellion, and there is none." MOTHER

"I wish I had known about their indecisiveness. He wants to do this; no, he doesn't. He gets pressure from peers and from what we think is right, and sometimes he goes back and forth. I am more patient about that now." MOTHER

"I wish I had known that if we had dealt with some behaviors when they were younger, we would not have had a problem from eleven to fourteen. He was always a little stubborn and hardheaded, wanting to do what he wanted. But right now, I wish we had done something about the stubbornness because it is a problem. He does not take responsibility, and it gets him into trouble at school. Looking back it has always been a problem, but we did not deal with it." MOTHER

difference continuing through the adult years, and boys have a higher rate of aggressive and violent behavior, possibly related to increased testosterone.[15] We discuss these changes in Chapter 11.

Changes in Brain Structure and Functioning

Scientists have long thought brain development was completed by adolescence,[16] but recent studies with new imaging techniques reveal that brain development continues throughout the second decade of life, especially in the frontal area of the brain, responsible for reasoning, problem solving, planning, and judgment, and is not complete until the midtwenties.

In the beginning of early adolescence, there is a spurt in the number of synapses in the frontal and parietal areas of the brain, perhaps triggered by hormones as girls have a spurt about a year before boys do. As in the early years of development, an overproduction of synapses "may herald a critical stage of development when the environment or activities of the teenager may guide selective synapse elimination in adolescence,"[17] thus allowing adolescent activities and experience to shape brain functions. Being especially responsive to current environmental stimulation and being capable of forming many new connections in the brain at the time of entering adulthood make human beings highly adaptable to their living circumstances.

In the adolescent period, increasing myelination of nerves (covering the nerves with a sheath of myelin), especially in the prefrontal area, speeds conductivity and communication between nerve cells, coordinates attention, emotion, and behavior, and contributes to greater brain efficiency and greater behavior control. "Pruning" or eliminating the least used connections later in adolescence reduces the number of connections and increases the brain's efficiency.

Since the changes in brain structure relating to behavior control occur over a long time from ages ten to twenty-five and are slower to reach maturity than the emotional changes,[18] there is a mismatch, in the early adolescent years, between the highly charged, sensation-seeking emotional system and the slowly developing but not yet mature prefrontal cortex that plans and regulates feelings and behavior. So early adolescents sometimes make impulsive decisions with negative consequences for themselves or others. A study following a large representative sample of 7,600 youths from ages twelve to twenty-four and assessing their sensation-seeking and impulsive behavior by means of self-report measures revealed individual differences in the magnitude of the changes in sensation seeking and impulsivity in these years so not every teen faces the mismatch problem, but many do.[19]

Because early adolescents do not have strong internal "brakes," they need practice in decision-making skills, and at times, parents must step in and be the brakes for their teens, as we shall discuss in a later section.

INTELLECTUAL DEVELOPMENT

Early adolescents' problem solving improves because their working memory and information-processing skills increase, and because they have a broader range of knowledge to use in solving problems. In addition, they gradually become better able to integrate their cognitive functioning with their emotional and social reactions in situations.[20]

Early adolescents between twelve and fourteen enter Piaget's *formal operations period,* when they come to think more abstractly than previously.[21] They reason logically about verbal propositions or hypothetical situations. In this period, adolescents can freely speculate and arrive at solutions by analyzing a problem in their heads. Furthermore, they can enumerate all possible combinations of events and take action to see what possibilities actually exist.

With increased capacity for abstract thought, adolescents turn inward, analyzing their thoughts, feelings, and reactions as well as other people's reactions. They think of the future, what might be happening in the world. They can think of ideal situations or solutions and become impatient with the present because it does not meet the ideal they have pictured. Their introspection, idealism, and impatience with the present all affect parent-child relationships, as we will see.

SCHOOL

At a time of physical and psychological change, many early adolescents go to middle or junior high schools that are typically larger, more demanding, and less supportive in meeting students' needs.[22] Teachers do not know students as well. Assignments demand responsibility and self-direction that many early adolescents do not have, and grading is often based on social comparisons. In addition, friendships may change as children are no longer in the same classes and have little time together. Finally, participation in school activities is more competitive as there are more students to fill leadership roles or team positions.

Often students lose interest in academic subjects, and grades decline. Even when boys and girls achieve good grades, some are reluctant to talk about their interests or their achievements for fear of being thought too smart.[23] Students who have an incremental theory of ability, namely that performance improves with effort, practice, and successful strategies (described in Chapter 9 on page 276), have more positive motivation for schoolwork and their grades are less likely to decline.

Researchers demonstrated the power of an incremental theory of ability with an eight-week workshop given to two groups of seventh-graders who had similar math grades in the spring of their seventh-grade year.[24] Their grades were tracked during the eighth-grade year. One group learned that the brain is like a muscle that changes with experience, and that everything in school is hard at first, but gets easier with practice. These students learned they can choose to practice and, in a sense, get smarter. Students in the other group received general instructions about the brain and processing of memory in the brain.

Prior to the workshops, both groups had decreasing grades, but the students who learned the brain can grow and develop with practice quickly began to improve their grades, whereas the grades of the other group continued to decline. Teachers could see differences in the behaviors of the two groups. Students who thought abilities can grow were more often described as having an interest in learning, asking for extra help, and consistently working hard.

Parents' emphasis on an incremental theory of ability helps children see that no matter what their level of ability in an area, practice and hard work lead to improvement.

EMOTIONAL DEVELOPMENT

Early adolescents' daily reports of their activities and accompanying moods when paged provide a window into the emotional ups and downs of this period. Most studies monitoring moods report that from age ten onward, there is a decline in good feelings and an increase in negative feelings. These changes are relative, however, as early adolescents still have many more good times in a day than negative ones.[25] In one study, negative events rose from 13 percent of all reported events to 20 percent, with 70 percent still being positive.

Early teens generally reported more anxiety and nervousness at school and more positive feelings at home with family members.[26] Those early teens who reported loneliness, low self-esteem, and depression were those who were experiencing unpredictable and upsetting conflicts with friends and family, the people with whom most teens were reporting pleasure. Still, the lonely teens had more positive than negative moods.

Stressful events reported at home and at school create spillover effects.[27] Ninth-graders who experienced family conflicts showed the effects the next day and for the two following days in their schoolwork—failing to turn in homework, doing poorly on a quiz or exam. Conversely, school problems like not doing well on a test and failing to do homework created stress and increased conflict at home the next day and for the two following days. Daily stresses had long-term consequences as well because home and school stress in the ninth grade predicted stress levels and lower grade point average in the twelfth grade.

There are no sex differences between the daily moods boys and girls report. This contrasts with the lower self-esteem girls report, as we will see in the next section. Ethnic differences have appeared in daily moods. Chinese American early teens reported fewer family stressors than children of European American and Latino backgrounds, but when such stressors did occur they were more disruptive of Chinese American children's schoolwork.[28] In another study of daily moods, high ethnic regard was found to buffer Chinese American and Mexican American early adolescents. When they experienced stressors, they felt anxious, but they were able to maintain high levels of happiness.[29]

Positive experiences can serve as a buffer against the effects of worry and low moods. Such experiences provide an "arena of comfort" in which early teens can escape stress, relax, and feel good. When early adolescents from various ethnic backgrounds were asked about their sources of support, all pointed to the importance of close family relationships and friends.[30]

Reed Larson, who has conducted several daily mood surveys, reports concern that many, in one study 27 percent of early teens, reported boredom when beeped, much of the time at school and in study activities.[31] Honor students report boredom as often as do acting-out early teens. Early adolescents, Larson writes, "Communicate an ennui of being trapped in the present, waiting for someone to prove to them that life is worth living."[32] He believes that positive development requires that teens develop initiative, defined as a feeling of internal motivation to engage in challenging, effortful activities that are pursued over an extended period of time. Later in this chapter, we discuss how parents promote this quality in children.

THE DEVELOPMENT OF THE SELF

Early adolescents now think more abstractly than before, and they describe themselves in terms of more general traits ("I'm an extrovert with a lot of friends").[33] Though they may think of themselves as stupid because of poor grades and low creativity, they do not yet integrate this negative quality into their overall picture of themselves. The negative and positive qualities remain isolated as separate traits. This separation may serve as a psychological buffer so the negative traits from one sphere do not influence the overall view of the self.

In this period of change, adolescents begin to explore who they are, what they believe, and what they want. They are in the process of forming what Erik Erikson calls a *sense of identity,* a sense of a differentiated and distinct self that is the real inner "me."[34]

James Marcia describes four ways of establishing identity.[35] There are those adolescents, the majority, who explore new experiences and ideas, form new friendships, and make a commitment to values, goals, and behavior. They gain achieved identity through a process of exploration and commitment. On the other hand, some adolescents choose traditional values without even considering for themselves what they want to do with their lives. They face no crisis or conflict, because they do not want to deal with issues. This commitment without exploration is termed *identity foreclosure* to indicate that possibilities have been closed off prematurely.

A different path is taken by adolescents who experience a *moratorium,* or an exploration without commitment. This is essentially a crisis about what they want to do. They have ideas they explore, but they have not yet made a commitment to act. Finally, some adolescents experience *identity diffusion,* in which they can make no choices at all. They drift without direction.

One study found that adolescent boys who rank high in identity exploration come from families in which they can express their own opinions yet receive support from parents even when they disagree with them.[36] Boys are encouraged to be both independent and connected to family members. Adolescent girls who rate high in identity exploration come from families in which they are challenged and receive little support from parents who are contentious with each other. Girls may need this slightly abrasive atmosphere in order to pursue a heightened sense of individuality rather than follow the path of intensifying social relationships. However, these girls do feel connected to at least one parent.

In early to mid-adolescence, gender differences appear in self-esteem—boys have higher levels than girls do. Susan Harter speculates that in these years the ideal good looks that early teens strive for—tall, thin, willowy, large-breasted bodies—are almost impossible to attain so teenage girls devalue themselves for being unattractive.[37] Since girls, on average, do not get satisfaction from physical activity in sports, they are cut off from a major source of esteem when they devalue their bodies. As we will see in the next section, declines in self-esteem may also be related to feelings of dissatisfaction about their gender identity as well as their physical appearance.

Level of self-esteem has implications for future adjustment as 57 percent of early adolescents with low self-esteem had multiple psychological and behavioral problems when assessed again in their twenties, and only 17 percent were problem-free.[38] Conversely, 56 percent of early adolescents with high self-esteem were viewed as problem-free, and only 17 percent had multiple problems.

Gender Identity

As teens begin to think more abstractly about their own qualities and wonder what others think of them, they wonder how well they meet society's standards for gender behavior. They may feel satisfied with their behavior or they may feel pressure to conform to others' standards of gender behavior. European American teens who feel satisfied their behavior meets cultural standards report self-esteem and social acceptance, whereas those who feel pressure for gender conformity report worries and lower self-esteem.[39] In African American and Latino early adolescents, the relationship with feelings about gender conformity are not so closely related to positive adjustment.[40] It is possible that these youth may be involved in exploring and forming their ethnic identity, and so are less psychologically involved in gender identity.

Although early adolescents are assessing gender conformity, their attitudes about gender roles, on average, grow more egalitarian and flexible from ages seven to thirteen.[41] At thirteen, they reach a plateau that lasts for two or three years, and at about age sixteen, adolescents become more traditional in their views of gender roles. This picture of average changes obscures different patterns of change, depending on children's own activities. Girls and boys who spend time in cross-gendered activities—sports and math for girls and reading and time alone for boys—have less traditional gender role attitudes and interests.[42]

Changes also depend on gender and parents' attitudes.[43] Boys in families with traditional values never adopt more egalitarian views. Boys whose parents have less traditional views of gender roles become more egalitarian, but at age sixteen, they take a sharp turn in the direction of more traditional values and come close to those boys reared in families with traditional values. At that age, the influence of peers' attitudes and the experience of romantic dating seem to affect their gender role attitudes more than parents' views.

Girls, in general, have more egalitarian and less traditional views of gender roles, perhaps because such attitudes permit them to participate in a wider array of enjoyable activities. Girls resembled their parents with less traditional values and never moved in the direction of adopting more traditional values in later adolescence. Girls with traditional parents become more egalitarian from seven to thirteen and at age seventeen make only a slight shift in the direction of more traditional values.

Ethnic Identity

Just as early adolescents are exploring their personal qualities to form a sense of identity and evaluating their behavior in terms of gender typicality, many children include their ethnic group in defining who they are. Drawing on Marcia's dimensions of identity, Jean Phinney describes a three-stage model of ethnic identity formation.[44] In the first stage, children do not think about ethnic matters; they have

Box 10-1
FIRST PERSON NARRATIVE

In his book with Rachel Kranz, *The Triple Bind: Saving Our Teenage Girls from Today's Pressures,** Stephen Hinshaw, professor of psychology, clinician, and researcher, reports his conclusions about the social and cultural pressures girls experience after extensively interviewing them in many parts of the country and analyzing the cultural media affecting girls.

He believes our culture makes impossible demands of girls, demands that discourage the average teenager who feels she will never be able to build a happy life that fulfills the cultural ideals, demands that place vulnerable teens at risk for depression, eating disorders, and self-mutilating behaviors. Because of the rising rates of teenage depression that appear at earlier ages, and the rise in eating and cutting disorders, Hinshaw believes parents and society must provide greater support for all girls and change our cultural messages.

He describes the triple bind as current society's insistence that girls be: (1) typically feminine, nurturant, and well liked by both girls and boys; (2) competitive and successful in school and sports, like boys; and (3) perfect and able to meet everyone's expectations. He analyzes movies and television shows that present these impossible ideals and includes girls' interview responses to the pressures in their lives. The range of experiences among the interviewed girls is varied as Hinshaw was the first to organize and run summer treatment for girls with ATTENTION DEFICIT/HYPERACTIVITY DISORDER. Many of the interviews follow girls over time so we see successive stressors and coping strategies.

Hinshaw also presents remedies for the unrelenting cultural demands that are impossible to fulfill. First, he points to parental and community support that can help girls make adaptive choices about activities to relieve pressure. He believes that involvement in community activities that connect girls to larger causes in the world can help give them a sense of purpose and satisfaction that counteract the cultural demands. He uses his own experiences in coming to terms with hidden secrets in his family as an example of how openness and connection to others in larger purposes has helped give his life rich vitality and can do the same for girls.

*Stephen Hinshaw with Rachel Kranz, *The Triple Bind: Saving Our Teenage Girls from Today's Pressures* (New York: Ballantine, 2009).

no interest in examining their group's history and traditions. If children remain in this state, they show what is termed "identity diffusion," no exploration and no commitment. If children automatically accept others' views of their ethnic group without questioning, they are thought to show "identity foreclosure," commitment to an identity without exploration.

Most early adolescents enter a second stage, termed "moratorium," in which they explore their ethnic group's history and values. This can be a painful stage for some adolescents as they confront the group's difficulties of the past and the burdens of the present. As a result of active exploration, early adolescents integrate their personal experiences and their ethnic heritage and form a sense of achieved ethnic identity. With achieved identity is thought to come a sense of confidence and self-esteem. Recall the Chinese American and Mexican American early adolescents with positive ethnic identities who were able to maintain happy moods at times of stress.[45]

Longitudinal research has confirmed the four forms of ethnic identity and the general sequence of development from a diffuse state through exploration to achieved identity.[46] The research has indicated there is sometimes movement backward as well as forward. A small number of early adolescents abandon exploration and return to a diffuse state, perhaps because ethnic group status may not be uppermost in their minds. A significant number of those who have achieved identity recycle back for further exploration, perhaps because of new information or an upsetting experience.

The psychological effects of perceived discrimination and prejudice have been tracked in these years.[47] When African American early teens perceive discrimination, over time they show feelings of anger, aggression, and depression. When teens have nurturing, warm parents, good friends, and are successful in school, they show fewer effects of discrimination.

The experience of discrimination in early adolescence predicts Chinese American students' reports of depressive symptoms, disengagement from school, and poor school grades in later adolescence; discrimination in later adolescence predicts decreases in socio-emotional development.[48] The effects of discrimination are more marked when students feel acculturated to American society.

THE DEVELOPMENT OF SELF-REGULATION

Following early adolescents assessed as undercontrolled, overcontrolled, or resilients (those who responded flexibly to environmental demands), for four years from ages twelve through fifteen revealed that resilients increased from 39 percent of the sample at age twelve to 51 percent at age fifteen, and there were decreases in both overcontrollers (from 49 percent to 44 percent) and undercontrollers (from 12 to 5 percent of the sample).[49] Resilients and those who became resilient were lower in anxiety than either stable overcontrollers or stable undercontrollers.

Just as they become more controlled, early adolescents' moral reasoning advances to higher levels in these years, and they are less likely to justify actions in terms of meeting their own needs as they did in elementary school. They are more likely to justify their behavior in terms of living up to authority's expectations or others' needs.[50] Their prosocial behaviors increase as they are better able to understand other people and have greater empathy with their experiences. Parents are usually not the recipients of early adolescents' increasing helpfulness. Parents report no change in teens' helping or sharing work at home, and some parents report a decline in these years, perhaps because children spend more time away from home. In these years, helpful, sharing behaviors are often carried out on a regular basis in volunteer activities with youth or church groups.

PARENT-CHILD RELATIONSHIPS

Young adolescents spend about half as much time with parents as they did in the elementary school years.[51] Although there is less time together, parents remain major figures in children's lives.

Parents' Support

Numerous studies document the positive relationship between parents' support and caring and adolescents' cognitive, emotional, and social competence. A recent study included not only younger and older teens in the United States but samples in ten countries in Africa, Asia, the Middle East, Europe, and South America.[52]

In all these countries, teens' reports of parents' support—reflected in comments that parents cared for them, enjoyed spending time with them and talking to them, believed in them and thought they were important—were related to teens' social competence and initiative and to their lack of depression. In many countries it was also related to teens' avoidance of antisocial behavior. In the United States, fathers' support was more predictive of teens' social competence and initiative and mothers' support, more predictive of lack of depression. In most other countries, however, mothers' support was more predictive of both aspects of teens' behavior. Adolescents in other countries listed tangible gifts and financial provisions such as school fees as signs that parents love them, whereas American teens did not.

Studies of parent-teen closeness in ethnic groups within the United States reveal that early teens of European American, Mexican American, and Chinese American backgrounds are equally close to parents, with the exception that European American teens feel closer to fathers than teens in other groups.[53] Closeness, however, is expressed in different ways in each group. In European American families, early adolescents spend more one-on-one time with family members and in leisure time activities with them. Mexican American early teens spend time with parents, working with them and helping them. Chinese American teens spend more time studying each day than helping the family. European American adolescents' time with parents does not interfere with the substantial amount of time spent with peers, which is significantly more than teens from other cultures spend.

Parents' Respect for Early Adolescents' Self-Assertion and Autonomy

While parents' regulation of children's behavior has positive effects, as we discuss in the next section, parents' attempts to control children's private thoughts and feelings are related to early adolescents' feeling dejected and depressed. And not just in the United States. Early adolescents in countries around the world report common reactions of depression and sadness to parents' attempts to control their thoughts and opinions.[54]

With a growing sense of independence, early adolescents assert their desire for choice and self-determination. They argue to get their way about clothes, friends, and when they do chores and homework. They do not challenge parents' moral and social values or their rules about safety issues, but they redefine what parents think are moral and conventional rules for family behavior as matters that should be under their personal control, and they justify their beliefs on the basis of what other teens are doing. While teens disagree openly with parents, the disagreements result in angry relationships with parents in only 5–20 percent of families.[55]

Such behavior is not unique to middle-class, European American teens. Adolescents of Mexican American, Chinese American, and Filipino backgrounds with different beliefs about the authority given to parents and ages for increasing autonomy all report the same level of conflicts at home with parents.[56] The American cultural milieu seems to override families' belief systems so that youth from these ethnic groups behave like European American teens. Furthermore, the European American culture changes the beliefs and expectations with each generation of immigrant families so the beliefs become more like those of European Americans as well.

Parents and children agree that most of the time conflicts end because children follow parents' wishes. In only 18 percent of conflicts do parents follow children's requests, and joint discussion and decisions settle just 13 percent of the disagreements.[57] So in conflicts, children give in, and the relationship between parents and children remains solid.

Judith Smetana, who has investigated parent–teen conflicts for decades in many ethnic groups here and in countries around the world, has this advice for parents:[58]

1. Recognize that children accept parents' basic moral and social values and the need for safety and health rules; having their own beliefs is not a rejection of parents' values

2. Recognize that children's increasing desire for personal choice is part of the process of establishing their own identity and a coherent sense of self

3. Pick your battles and choose to disagree about the most important issues, letting the little things go

4. Give teens opportunities to talk about issues and their reasoning about them with calm and caring parents because such discussions promote decision-making skills; other research suggests that in early adolescence, warm support is most important in stimulating positive behaviors and in later adolescence, engaging in more dialogues about the reasoning process helps.[59]

Regulating and Monitoring Behavior

Research has shown that when parents monitor teens and know where they are, what they are doing, and who they are with, teens are less likely to engage in risk behaviors such as drinking, smoking, and delinquent activity.[60] It was long thought that parental knowledge came from observing and tracking children, but recent studies suggest parents' knowledge comes from adolescents' willingness to tell them what they are doing. This willingness is a part of a reciprocal relationship with parents. When parents behave in a warm, responsive way, children feel accepted and comfortable in sharing information so they are open with parents. When parents have knowledge, they can take effective actions to regulate behavior.

Parents and children agree that teens should share information in areas where parents have authority—namely on moral behavior and other health and safety issues.[61] Both parents and teens agree teens' telling parents how they spend their free time or their money is voluntary because these are personal matters. Early adolescents and their parents believe younger teens have a greater responsibility to disclose what they are doing than older adolescents.

Teens are more likely to disclose when parents are both warm and have clear standards for behavior, and when teens engage in few disapproved activities. Teens feel lying is wrong so they omit details and avoid topics rather than lie outright. Lying more often occurs when parents and teens have poor relationships, when families lack cohesiveness, when teens struggle with impulse control, and families set few rules.

Around the world parental knowledge and monitoring were related to low levels of substance abuse and antisocial activity.[62] It was mothers' knowledge that was particularly predictive of children's behavior. The authors speculate that at times of so many changes in early adolescents' lives, mothers' awareness of what is happening in children's lives is especially important.

Creating Mutually Responsive Dialogues with Early Adolescents

Teens consider parents their first source for information on sexual changes and sexual health. When mothers of fifteen-year-old girls were coached for two ninety-minute sessions to listen more, ask open-ended questions, encourage children to talk, and avoid lecturing, their communication skills increased.[63] Mothers practiced role-playing and applied the skills to discussing issues of sexuality and AIDS with their daughters. Mothers who were coached spoke less, asked more open-ended questions, and were less judgmental than were uncoached mothers. Teens of mothers who were coached did not talk more than teens of mothers who were not coached, but the former teens did feel more comfortable in talking to mothers about sexuality, and they did report more discussion about birth control than did the other teens. Observing mothers and their thirteen-year-old children discuss areas of conflict reveals that children's temperamental qualities like negative emotionality and level of control in late childhood and the present were more predictive of the quality of the discussions than mothers' qualities although mothers' warmth and positivity played a role in having productive discussions.[64]

Observing parents and their twelve-year-olds in problem-solving sessions over a two-year period, researchers found that when parents remained supportive and nurturant and persisted in positive parenting, even when dealing with resistant and negative teens, their children became more flexible, effective problem solvers.[65] When parents avoided engaging in teens' negative overtures, teens' behavior eventually changed.

Promoting Gender Identity

Two clinicians urge parents to encourage less traditional attitudes and behavior for both boys and girls.

Mary Pipher, author of *Reviving Ophelia*, believes that, in the teenage years, girls lose their sense of themselves as individuals and become overfocused on the needs, feelings, and approval of other people.[66] She urges parents to provide homes that offer both protection and challenges to help girls find and sustain a sense of identity. Parents need to listen to daughters and encourage independent thought and rational decision-making skills and to encourage friendships with boys and girls and a wide variety of activities so they develop a sense of identity based on their interests and abilities.

She also encourages altruism to counter the self-absorption that is characteristic of adolescence. Helping others leads to good feelings and to greater maturity.

Clinical psychologist William Pollack believes that boys are socialized from childhood to be strong and tough, aggressive and daring, to achieve status and power and to avoid the expression of feelings like warmth and empathy. He believes that boys are forced to separate from parents too early and that, if they protest, they are ridiculed and shamed. He writes, "I believe that boys, feeling ashamed of their vulnerability, mask their emotions and ultimately their true selves. This unnecessary disconnection—from family and then from self—causes many boys to feel alone, helpless, and fearful."[67]

Pollack advises parents to get behind the masks that boys develop by (1) becoming aware of signs that sons are hiding their feelings, (2) talking to sons about feelings and listening to what they say, (3) accepting sons' emotional schedules for revealing feelings (boys may be slower than girls), (4) connecting with sons through joint activities that can bring parents and sons closer together, and (5) sharing their own growing-up experiences with their sons. Boys need reassurance they are loved for both their strengths and vulnerabilities.

Promoting Ethnic Identity

Parents of different ethnic backgrounds have all the parenting tasks that we have just discussed, and also have a powerful role in helping children develop a positive, affirming sense of ethnic identity.[68]

Parents serve as models for children and as sources of information about ethnic cultures and ethnic identity and ways to cope with discrimination and prejudice. Recall that many children in this age group worry about discrimination for their looks or behavior so even if children do not say anything, the possibility of discrimination is on their minds.

A program with single mothers of eleven-year-old African American children taught general parenting strategies and also included adaptive ways to develop racial pride by:[69]

- Weaving messages giving children feelings of importance and self-worth into daily interactions
- Teaching children about the difficulties and obstacles that exist for their racial group
- Focusing on ways to manage whatever barriers and discrimination children experience
- Focusing on ways to achieve success in activities

When mothers incorporated these messages in the context of warm, nurturing parent-child relationships and firm limit-setting and monitoring, youth expressed

Single mothers of African American children use positive parenting and consistent limit-setting, and their children expressed self-esteem, positive sexual identity, and racial pride.

self-esteem, positive sexual identity, and racial pride. When early teens perceived mothers as being both nurturing and vigilant in monitoring behavior, then they were low in substance abuse and early sexual activity.[70]

When parents maintain ethnic traditions at home and encourage early teens to participate in cultural activities, then Latino youth are more likely to explore their ethnic identity.[71] When this socialization occurs in the context of parental involvement, low levels of harsh parenting and low levels of perceived neighborhood risk, then youth affirm that ethnic identity.

Neighborhoods help or hinder racial socialization efforts. Living in communities with strong ethnic identifications can protect children from the negative effects of discrimination.[72] When neighborhoods are stable and contain a high percentage of people from the same ethnic group, then youth are more likely to affirm their ethnic identity. When neighborhoods are poor and subject to chaotic events, then youth are less likely to affirm their identity.[73]

Family Stressors That Interfere with Effective Parenting and Impact Children's Behavior

When parents cannot get along and disagree, early adolescents experience emotional insecurity that, in turn, impacts children's psychological adjustment.[74] They become fearful, sad, angry, and noncompliant in behavior. When parents argue in the context of an otherwise satisfying marriage and stable family life, children's insecurity is reduced.

For some ethnic group parents, the experience of discrimination sets into motion a train of events that impact parenting.[75] In a longitudinal study in Georgia, mothers who experienced discrimination developed health problems and feelings

VOICES OF EXPERIENCE

The Joys of Parenting Early Adolescents

"Seeing him care for younger children and babies is a great pleasure. He's a great nurturer with small children. He has endless patience." MOTHER

"He is a talented athlete, and his soccer team got to a championship game. He scored the winning goal, and when he took off with the ball down the field, I was very proud of him. It was a unique feeling of being proud that someone I had helped to create was doing that. He had felt a lot of pressure in the game, so to see how incredibly pleased he was gave me great joy." FATHER

"I enjoy the fact that she is very independent and makes up her own mind about things. She is not caught up in fads or with cliques, and I can trust her not to follow other people's ideas. The down side of that is that she resists some of my ideas as well." MOTHER

"I enjoy her sense of humor. She jokes about everyday events, and I laugh a lot around her." MOTHER

"I like that he does things I did, like play the trumpet. He started at the same age I did, and since he took it up, it has rekindled my interest and I started practicing again. This last weekend, we played together. He also brings new interests too. Because he likes sailing, I have started that and really like it." FATHER

"She is in that dreamy preteen state where she writes things. She wrote a poem about the difference between being alone and loneliness. She has a real appreciation of time on her own and how nice being alone can be. I like that because I had that at her age." MOTHER

"It's nice just being able to help them, feeling good because they are being helped out and benefited." FATHER

"It's nice to see her being able to *analyze* situations with friends or with her teachers and come to conclusions. She said about one of her teachers, 'Well, she gets excited and she never follows through with what she says, so you know you don't have to take her seriously.'" MOTHER

"I really enjoy being in the Scouts with the boys. Once a month we go on a camping weekend, and I really look forward to that." FATHER

"I was so impressed and pleased that after the earthquake, he and a friend decided to go door to door and offer to sell drawings they made of Teenage Mutant Ninja Turtles. He raised $150 that he gave for earthquake relief. I was very proud that he thought this up all by himself." FATHER

"I was very happy one day when I found this note she left on my desk. It said, 'Hello!!! Have a happy day! Don't worry about home, everyone's fine! Do your work the very best you can. But most important, have a fruitful life!!!' I saved that note because it made me feel so good." MOTHER

(continued)

VOICES OF EXPERIENCE

The Joys of Parenting Early Adolescents

(continued)

"He enjoys life. He has a sense of humor. He's like a butterfly enjoying everything; eventually he'll settle in." MOTHER

"He's very sensitive, and his cousins two years older than he is ask his advice about boys. They may not take it, but they ask him even though he's younger." FATHER

"It's very rewarding to see them in their school activities. My daughter sings in the school chorus, and I enjoy that, and my son is in school plays." FATHER

"I am very pleased that she is less moody now than she used to be. We used to refer to her lows as 'Puddles of Frustration,' but she has got past that now." MOTHER

"Well, they have their friends over, and we have ping-pong, pool, cards, and we stressed having these things available. I enjoy playing all these games with them." FATHER

of depression that impacted parenting. They were less warm, less able to avoid repetitive arguing, and were less vigilant in monitoring children. Thus, discrimination, experienced by 67 percent of the mothers, decreased their parenting skills.

Happy family times are important because they provide a reservoir of good feelings that sustains all family members through times of conflict and crisis. Family life focuses so heavily on routine chores that outings often provide the best means for members to share fun. Family games, mealtime rituals, and watching certain TV programs together can also provide a sense of sharing and solidarity that adolescents report as highly meaningful to them. Making time for fun and games in a busy schedule may save time in the long run as conflicts and arguing decrease.

RELATIONSHIPS WITH SIBLINGS

As in early years, parents' relationships with their early teens influence siblings' relationships. When parents have warm relationships with children, brothers and sisters have warm relationships with each other.[76] Siblings can be especially important as they are on an equal plane, and they can understand each other better than parents sometimes understand children. Thus, siblings can give positive support, offer advice in dealing with problems, and serve as daily companions. When parents are divorced, siblings may be the most constant features in each others' lives.

As in earlier years, when parents play favorites, siblings are more likely to have conflicts. Aggression is more likely when unsupervised siblings in stressed families act out their angry feelings with each other. Siblings can also encourage deviant behavior in younger early teens.[77] When younger adolescent boys have warm relationships with their older brothers who engage in delinquent activity, they are likely to join them in these activities. With girls, the quality of the relationship has a different impact. Younger sisters who have warm relationships with their older sisters are less likely to copy their older sisters' delinquent behavior. Brothers and sisters are also likely to emulate older siblings' substance use and sexual behaviors.

Though they may copy negative behaviors, children learn positive skills in sharing and negotiating differences, and these carry over into relationships with peers. Children with positive sibling relationships have positive peer relationships and also do better academically in school.

PEER RELATIONSHIPS

Children continue to choose friends whose interests are similar to their own, and they benefit from the greater intimacy that comes from sharing experiences and feeling understood.[78] Friends have as many conflicts as non-friends but they work out differences in mutually satisfying ways. Best friends are even closer and disclose more to each other. They are supportive and loyal. With all the benefits of friendship, it is not surprising that early adolescents with friends are more socially skilled, more confident, and more academically successful than those who lack friends.[79]

Many teens want to be popular, accepted, and well liked.[80] Popular children have many positive qualities; often they are: kind, friendly, helpful to others, easy going, and bright.[81] Research suggests, however, that social success and satisfying friendships do not depend on being broadly popular and sought after. Thirteen-year-olds who considered themselves accepted and liked, even though not rated by schoolmates as popular, had as many friends and were as sought after and socially

Early teens use media to communicate with peers and post personal information.

successful a year later as children designated as popular. The personal feelings of social acceptance may have come from friendships or activities outside school or at church. Whatever the source, children who felt accepted reached out to others and were involved in satisfying relationships. Those early adolescents who had the most difficulties were those who felt unaccepted and in fact appeared to lack connections with others at age thirteen. They tended to feel angry and retreat from social contact so their problems continued over the next year and intensified.

The Internet now provides ways for teens to relate to peers.[82] Approximately 80 percent of early adolescents have access to computers and use them for e-mail, instant messaging (IM), to enter chat rooms, and to post personal information. Patterns of use vary among teens. When teens communicate with already existing friends via IM, they become closer to their friends. Closeness does not increase for those who are primarily communicating with strangers. While self-disclosure over the Internet was easier for socially anxious teens than face-to-face disclosure, socially anxious teens were less likely to use the Internet than socially confident peers. Those who did use it communicated more online than nonsocially anxious teens.

Parents' want to know about their children's friends with some justification.[83] Like siblings, friends can draw a child into deviant behaviors. In addition, with close friends children sometimes engage in what is termed "co-rumination" (dwelling on one's own depressive symptoms over and over); such discussions increase the closeness between friends. While both boys and girls engage in such co-rumination and become closer with friends, girls' co-rumination predicts depressive and anxious feelings whereas it does not predict negative feelings in boys.[84]

In these years, children form cliques, small groups of five to nine members who choose each other as friends.[85] In the beginning of early adolescence, teens spend most of their time in same-sex groups. Girls spend more time than boys talking, and boys more time than girls playing contact sports. Group activities provide sociability and a sense of belonging, promote exploration of the self and achievements, and provide opportunities for learning and instruction. Both self-exploration and learning activities give children the kinds of experiences they need to form a stable sense of identity.

Unfortunately, bullying and harassment continue in these years, and many children fear going to school because of hostile teasing and physical aggression. A longitudinal study analyzed students' reports of being bullied—called names, laughed at, pushed, and robbed—and found that in sixth grade, equal numbers of boys and girls were bullied.[86] More than half the students (57 percent) were sometimes or frequently bullied and only 43 percent, rarely bullied. By the end of eighth grade, boys were the more frequent victims, and bullying had declined to 31 percent being frequently or sometimes bullied.

What did not change over the three years were the emotional reactions to being a victim.[87] Victims and sometimes victims felt unsafe at school, and over time victims developed depression. Witnessing bullying of others impacted students, as those who saw it reported feeling angry and humiliated. Those students who felt only they were being bullied reported the greatest increases in anger and humiliation. They felt like lone targets. We see here that bullying has negative consequences for even those who just witness it.

Box 10-2
WISE AMERICANS' ADVICE TO PARENTS*

After an engaging conversation with a ninety-year-old woman about what she had learned from her long life, sociologist Karl Pillemer, who had studied aging for thirty years, decided to interview a sample of people over sixty-five on the topic of what they had learned from long lives and what lessons they wanted to pass on to younger people. He had interview responses from a thousand people on the important topics of what makes for a happy marriage and a satisfying work life, what are the important lessons for raising children. Pillemer distilled the interviews into five lessons on each topic. The five lessons for parents are:

Lesson 1.   Spend time with children; if necessary and at all possible, give up extra jobs or make other sacrifices to find the time because what children really want from parents is their time; spend the time doing what children would like to do as the point is to share the time in ways that are meaningful to them.

Lesson 2.   While it may be natural for parents to prefer one child, avoid showing favoritism in actions or words; Pillemer observed that older people expressed the deepest pain and hurts in the interviews when talking about a parent's preferring another child in the family; it damaged the relationship not only with the parent but also with the preferred child.

Lesson 3.   Don't hit or spank children; it doesn't work.

Lesson 4.   Avoid rifts or ruptures in relationships with children; try to work out differences and negative feelings before they result in break-ups; if children are teens or older, always take the first steps to heal the rupture.

Lesson 5.   Take a long-term view of relationships with children; the child-rearing years fly by quickly, and when parents are caught up in all the activities of the first eighteen years, they overlook the fact that their relationships with children will continue for forty, fifty, or sixty years so parents should talk and interact with children in ways that promote long-term bonds when both children and parents are adults.

*Karl Pillemer, *30 Lessons for Living: Tried and True Advice from the Wisest Americans* (New York: Hudson Street Press, 2011).

Unfortunately in our technological society, bullying can reach a wider audience via the Internet. Bullies can use websites and personal pages to spread harmful, hurtful messages and hound early adolescents even when they are not in school. In a survey in 2007, one in three teenagers reported they had experienced some form of harassment via the Internet, and the Centers for Disease Control and Prevention is funding studies on electronic aggression among youth.[88] When children tell parents, parents can help to find solutions to the problem. Unfortunately, some children are so upset they tell no one, and take self-destructive action instead. We discuss later how parents can help teens deal with the problem.

TASKS AND CONCERNS OF PARENTS

Parents' tasks expand as they become not only caregivers and interpreters of the social world but also models for an increasing number of behaviors in the world outside the home. Parenting tasks include the following:

- Continuing to be the single most important influence in the child's life
- Modeling self-controlled, responsible behavior
- Being sensitive to the child's needs and feelings
- Monitoring children's activities and behavior
- Communicating information and values on important but difficult-to-discuss topics such as sexuality, substance use, and discrimination
- Making time, being available for conversation when the child is ready to talk
- Giving children more decision-making power
- Providing support as children undergo many physical changes and social challenges, so home is an understanding place
- Sharing pleasurable time

This section describes how parents use active listening skills and behavioral methods to work effectively with young adolescents. It also emphasizes parenting strategies that help children develop initiative and problem-solving skills so they can resolve intense feelings and engage in activities and peer relations that bring good feelings.

Communicating with the Noncommunicative Early Adolescent

We have talked about how important it is to talk with children, but sometimes children come home, go to their rooms, and shut the door. When they emerge for meals or snacks, they say little, answering any question with only a word or two. They do not talk about what they are doing, thinking, or feeling. Children do not seem unhappy, but parents feel they do not know them anymore. Parents may feel hurt when children say little to them but talk for hours on the phone to their friends.

Parents can do many things to promote conversation. First, they can be good models of communication by talking about their own day, friends, and plans. Second, they can ask for comments: "How's school going?" or "What are you and Jenny doing tonight?" If the child answers with one word or two, parents should drop the conversation and wait for another time. Third, they can comment on nonverbal behavior or body language: "Looks like you had a good day today," or "You look happy." Teens may not follow up with any comments, but parents have made an effort.

Once teens begin to talk, parents can listen and reflect teens' feelings, avoiding criticism, judgments of the child or others, blame, or sarcasm. Reflecting the teenagers' feelings helps teens to continue to talk. If teens talk about problems they are trying to work out and want to discuss them, parents can ask open-ended questions and listen.

There are many "don'ts" to the process of encouraging conversation.[89] Don't force the child to reveal her feelings. Don't give advice once the teen has begun to talk. Don't rush to find the solution. Don't hurry to answer questions; delaying an answer can stimulate thinking.

Adele Faber and Elaine Mazlish describe useful techniques when teens begin to talk about discouragement or frustration.[90] They suggest showing respect for the child's struggle with comments such as "That can be hard," "It's not easy," or "Sometimes it helps when . . ." then giving a piece of information: "It helps, when you're rushed, to concentrate on the most important item." Teens are free to use the information or not. Parents have to watch their tone of voice so the information does not sound like advice.

Faber and Mazlish also present interesting alternatives to saying "no." Because teens are sensitive to control and may not like to ask if they often hear "no" in response, having other ways to respond is useful and will encourage greater talkativeness. Suppose a teen wants his mother to take him to the store at 5:30 while she is cooking dinner. Instead of giving a flat "no," she can say, "I'll take you after dinner." If she cannot do it, she can say, "I'd like to be able to help you out, but I have to get dinner on the table and get to that meeting at 7:00." A parent can leave out the "no" and just give information. For example, if a teen asks for an extra, expensive piece of clothing, the parent can say, "The budget just won't take it this month." If there are ways the teen can get the item, the parent can pass that information on: "If you want that as a birthday present at the end of the month, that would be fine."

Using Mutual Problem Solving to Handle Disputes

In the early adolescent years, conflicts with children over a variety of everyday issues require resolution. When parents use mutual problem solving, listening to children's feelings and sending I-messages, parents respect children's views and their individual needs, and at the same time work with the problem situation so both parents and children feel their needs are met.

Knowing that early teens are most likely to argue about issues they believe should be under their control and most likely to accept parents' requests for safe, healthy, and considerate behavior, parents can explain their rules in terms of these reasons. When parents, firm limits on computer and Internet use, requiring that computers be kept in family rooms and monitoring teens' use of them, early adolescents internalize parents' messages and follow their rules.[91]

Health and safety issues should be of paramount importance. In observing how parents both protect children and at the same time find alternative ways to achieve what children want, children learn how to protect their safety and get what they want.

Parents may want to issue orders with the only reason, "Because I said so," but teens need to learn how to reason about these issues, and parents' explanations of their reasoning gives children a model to copy in making decisions. Parents should expect they may have to return to problem behaviors several times, but solutions are more likely to be effective when children have more input.

Encouraging Children's Problem-Solving Skills

We have noted that children's brains are maturing in these years, and planning skills are developing. These skills are important because early teens are often at a great distance from parents and must solve problems on their own.

Problem solving requires the child to define the problem, become aware of his or her feelings and others' feelings and reactions, generate solutions to the problem, choose a solution and carry it out, then evaluate the results, starting over if necessary. Problem solving requires that parents remain calm so that children have opportunities to think and develop their skills. Parents can ask open-ended questions and encourage the child to continue to think of solutions.

Myrna Shure has developed "I Can Problem Solve" programs to teach children from ages four to thirteen to learn to find their own solutions to the problems that bother them.[92] Combining many of the communication skills discussed in this chapter and in Chapter 5 with an emphasis on having children think of alternative actions, these programs help parents avoid highly emotional battles that interfere with good communication and effective solutions.

To solve problems, Shure believes, children must (1) understand others' feelings and underlying motivations, (2) generate new solutions to the problem, (3) anticipate the consequences of each potential solution, and (4) plan behaviors in advance to avoid potential problems. Shure recommends working on only one or two of these skills at a time. Because they are often locked into their own thoughts and feelings of the moment and have trouble seeing different options for action, early adolescents need special help with all of the steps.

If the problem involves them, parents send an I-message that expresses their needs and feelings; otherwise, parents are supportive, refusing to dictate or force solutions. Shure recommends doing this with questions such as "How will the other person feel or react?", "What will happen if you do that?", "What is your plan?", "How will that work?" If children have no answers, parents do not push but instead let children figure the problem out, provided no danger is involved. Where parents have concerns about safety or the necessity of solving the problem now, they engage in mutual problem solving, as described in Chapter 5.

Shure's method helps early adolescents develop the independence and ability to plan that are so necessary for children of this age. Developing initiative has similar aims.

Promoting Initiative

Based on his research with early adolescents and their families, Larson believes that, for positive development in these years, early adolescents must develop initiative, "the ability to be motivated from within to direct attention and effort toward a challenging goal."[93] An important quality in itself, initiative also serves as the foundation for important qualities such as creativity and leadership. Teens, however, experience effort and challenge in activities in which they lack interest, such as schoolwork, and they lack effort and challenge in activities that interest them, such as activities with friends. The task is to find activities that both interest and challenge teens.

Ronald Dahl, who has studied brain and emotional development in adolescence, believes channeling the passions of adolescents into positive activities that engage teens and enable them to use their passions for the benefit of all is an important societal task.[94] Larson believes that structured voluntary activities, pursued over time, are the engaging, stimulating activities adolescents need to develop. The experience of setting goals, organizing activities (often in collaboration with peers), and accomplishing goals leads to the development of independence, decision-making skills, and self-control. These, then, carry over to other activities. For example, participation in voluntary activities in tenth grade predicted an increase in grade point average in later grades. Participants in outdoor adventure programs gained in assertiveness, locus of control, and independence. Furthermore, positive changes continued for as long as two years after the program ended.

Larson speculates that voluntary activities, broadly structured by adults but with direct responsibility given to children for organizing and carrying out the activities, "provided an environment of possibilities for planful action, for initiative."[95] Children develop a language and way of thinking that gives them a sense of agency, of being able to accomplish what they set out to. "Children and adolescents come alive in these activities, they become active agents in ways that rarely happen in other parts of their lives."[96]

Voluntary school activities draw on the problem-solving skills that Shure encourages. Adult leaders in the activities raise open-ended questions that prompt teens to *analyze* and think through the consequences of actions. They are supportive and nonjudgmental. Research shows that when Little League coaches adopt an encouraging attitude, give information on how to improve, provide positive reinforcement for effort as well as for accomplishments, and stress fun and self-improvement rather than winning, players report more enjoyment in playing and greater self-esteem, and they are more likely to sign up for the team the next year than are players whose coaches are not so supportive.[97] Interestingly, positive coaches learned these skills in one three-hour session, and the techniques had the biggest effects on boys with low self-esteem.

Promoting Positive Peer Relationships

Peer acceptance involves both a cognitive understanding of others and oneself and appropriate peer behavior.[98] When children have difficulties—either being too inhibited or too aggressive—problems may exist in how they view people as well as how they behave. Aggressive children, for example, are quick to see others' negative behavior as intentional and therefore worthy of retaliation.[99] Part of the way to help such children is to encourage them to examine their interpretations of others' behavior and adopt more benign views of others' intentions. When they view negative behavior as accidental, children reduce their aggression.

Similarly, shy, inhibited children should be encouraged to review their positive traits and identify the positive contributions they can make to social activities. Peer acceptance requires outgoing behavior that shows respect for others and oneself by listening to others, being open and friendly, having a positive attitude, initiating interactions, and avoiding aggressive, negative behaviors.[100] When children are shy at school and lack friends, parents can encourage friendships away from school—on athletic teams, in artistic activities, or in community or church groups. Parents' highlighting of children's positive behaviors such as kindness and caring with others also increases children's confidence.

On the basis of interviews with adolescents about violence in their schools, James Garbarino and Ellen deLara make many suggestions for parents in combating school bullying and harassment.[101] They advise parents to talk to children about the kinds of negative experiences they have in their school (even if they have not happened to their own children) because many children have witnessed them. Talk to other parents about their views about bullying and form a group to talk to school officials, as described in Chapter 9.

The Internet enables bullies to track rather than trail victims into their homes and to spread rumors far and wide. When children report bullying to parents, and many do not want to talk about it, parents encourage them to save whatever record they have that indicates the source of the bullying. Reports can be made to Internet and phone providers who can follow up and take action because such activity usually violates contracts with them. If bullies come from schools, parents can contact the school to determine what they can do. Consider working with other parents to form a Youth Charter, as described at the end of the chapter.

Handling School Problems

Because all the changes of this period sometimes overwhelm early adolescents, parents' support can help teens identify the source of school problems and a constructive plan to remedy it. Active listening and mutual problem-solving sessions are appropriate tactics. Helping teens organize their study area and study schedules, getting tutoring as needed, or arranging for children to attend Homework Clubs can be potentially useful, depending on the particular circumstances. Computer use has helped some children improve reading skills and grade point averages over time so there may be computer programs or games that can help.[102]

Some schools have organized computerized ways parents can get daily information on students' assignments, work turned in, and grades on tests. They can also be useful in helping parents help children keep up.[103] If, however, parents use the information to criticize and berate students or demand immediate changes, the actions are not likely to help children succeed.

Helping children develop an incremental theory of learning can help. Reminding children of previous successes, reminding them that with any area, the more they learn about it, the smarter they get. Encouraging effort and commenting on gains increase confidence. So parents clearly have many ways to help young adolescents deal with various issues. Table 10-1 reflects many of the strategies this section has discussed.

■ **T A B L E 10-1**
TEN STEPS TO HELP CHILDREN DEVELOP THEIR ABILITIES

1. Understand children's special skills and areas of difficulties.
2. Provide appropriate levels of stimulation that neither bore nor overwhelm children.
3. Teach children that their biggest limitations are the ones they place on themselves and what they can do.
4. Help children learn to ask questions and seek answers.
5. Help children identify what really interests and motivates them.
6. Encourage children to take sensible risks even though there is no guarantee of success.
7. Help children take responsibility for their behaviors—both positive and negative.
8. Teach children to tolerate and deal with frustration, delay, and uncertainty.
9. Help children understand other people's feelings and points of view.
10. Remember that, in helping children realize their abilities, what counts is not financial resources, but the way you interact with children and the kinds of experiences children have in everyday life.

Adapted from: Wendy M. Williams and Robert J. Sternberg, "How Parents Can Maximize Children's Cognitive Abilities," in *Handbook of Parenting*, 2nd ed., ed. Marc H. Bornstein, vol. 5: *Practical Issues in Parenting* (Mahwah, NJ: Erlbaum, 2002), 169–194.

PARENTS' EXPERIENCES IN FACING TRANSITIONS

Many parents report that they do not feel ready to have teenage children. The childhood years have gone so fast, it seems too soon to have a daughter with a mature figure and sons with bulging muscles and low voices. Parents find their children's sexual maturity disconcerting. They are surprised to see sons with *Playboy* magazines and hear girls talking about the sexual attractiveness of boys.

Their adolescents' mood swings and desires for greater freedom throw parents back to some of the same conflicts of the toddler and preschool years. The elementary school years were stable because parents could talk and reason with children, but now they are back to dealing with screaming, crying, moody creatures who sometimes act young but at the same time want more freedom. Parents may feel that they themselves have grown and matured as parents, able to handle crises, only to find themselves back at square one, yelling and feeling out of control with their children.

Though it is difficult to give up certain images of themselves and their children, parents must do so. Children are no longer children; they are approaching physical and sexual maturity. They are not psychologically mature, however, so they still need the guidance parents can give. Parents often have to give up images of themselves as the perfect parent of an adolescent. They recall their own adolescence, the ways their parents handled them, and in many cases they want to improve on that.

Sometimes they find they are not doing as well as they want and have to step back and see where they went off track.

As they mature, early adolescents gain the physical glow and psychological vitality that comes from feeling the world is a magical place. At the same time, parents are marching to or through middle age. It is hard to live with offspring who present a physical contrast to how parents themselves feel. Furthermore, the world is opening up to adolescents just as some parents feel it is weighing them down. Parents have heavy responsibilities, often taking care of aging parents as well as growing children. Parents feel they have little time and money at their own disposal, yet they live with young people who seem to have a great deal of both.

Thus, parents have to be careful not to let resentment of the freedom and excitement of their teenagers get in the way of being effective parents. As parents develop reasonable expectations of the amount of freedom and responsibilities their children are to have, they must be careful not to restrict or criticize out of envy.

To highlight the greater freedom and control children have, Ellen Galinsky calls this the *interdependent stage* of parenting.[104] Parents have several years to work through these issues before their children are launched. When parents can become more separate from their children—can be available to help them grow yet not stifle them in the process—then parents' and children's relationships take on a new richness.

SUPPORT FOR PARENTS

Parents often feel overwhelmed by cultural forces that do not support their efforts to rear children well. For example, the media bombard teens with messages about sexuality that conform to few families' values. William Damon has developed the Youth Charter program to combat cultural forces that make rearing children more difficult.[105] Parents can initiate this program to organize teachers, clergy, police, and others who care about children to develop community practices and standards that promote children's healthy development. Parents' child-rearing efforts serve as a bridge to connect children to community activities at school, with peers, and in the neighborhood. Communities have to be organized to support parents' goals.

Damon outlines a way of organizing concerned adults to identify children's specific needs and work together to find ways to meet them. Standards and expectations are drawn up for children and for the community so that parents and concerned citizens and youth can control teen drinking, vandalism, and early pregnancy and build a community more supportive of children and families. Damon writes,

> Beneath the sense of isolation that has divided our communities, we all share a deep well of concern for the younger generation. If we can find a way to tap into that well, child rearing can become the secure and fulfilling joy that it should be.[106]

MAIN POINTS

In early adolescence, sexual development
- begins and takes years to complete
- is triggered by biological, social, and psychological factors, and, in turn, triggers psychological reactions in young people
- is related to increases in emotional intensity and changing sleep patterns

In early adolescence, brain development
- involves an overproduction of synapses that allow activities to shape brain functioning
- proceeds slowly and is not complete until the midtwenties
- increases the capacities for attention, planning, and problem solving; as it is slower, there is a mismatch between teens' emotional intensity and decision-making skills

Early adolescents
- begin to think more abstractly and analyze themselves and other people
- have daily mood changes related to family interactions and school events that spill over from home to school, and from school to home
- are more involved than previously in peer relationships and cliques

A sense of identity
- depends on exploring a variety of alternatives and making a commitment to values, goals, and behavior
- can be foreclosed if teens make a commitment without exploring their options
- is not achieved when early adolescents experience a moratorium, or explore without making a commitment
- is achieved in youth of racial/ethnic groups when parents are warm and supportive, teach and model racial pride, and discuss ways to deal with mistreatment when that occurs

Peers
- are sought as primary attachment figures when parents are uninterested and give little guidance
- are sought for different kinds of relationships by boys and girls—with girls wanting to talk and express their feelings and boys wanting to engage in group activities with little self-revelation

In this period, parents
- continue to be sensitive caregivers who connect with children and respect their views
- provide role models of ethical, principled behavior and provide accurate information on topics such as sexual behavior and substance abuse

- monitor children's activities and behavior
- give more decision-making power to adolescents
- use mutual problem solving to resolve conflicts

Problems discussed center on

- developing problem-solving skills and initiative
- controlling emotional reactions and dealing with social difficulties
- failures in communication

Joys include

- observing accomplishments in physical, artistic, and intellectual endeavors
- feeling good because the parent has helped the child in a specific way
- observing the child's capacity to take responsibility for self
- emotional closeness

EXERCISES

1. See the video or DVD of the movie *Akila and the Bee* and compare socializing experiences in the three ethnic groups depicted in the movie. What are the roles of parents and community in the different groups? How do adults and the community socialize children for success in the different groups?

2. In small groups, take a survey of students' school experience in the years when they were eleven to fifteen. What size was the school and what grades were included? Have each student rate that school experience from 1, very dissatisfied, to 7, very satisfied. Tabulate the average ratings for each kind of school setting and note whether students were happier when older students were included.

3. Break into small groups and discuss the kinds of experiences that increase the self-esteem of early adolescent years in these changing times. With input from the whole class, write suggestions for parents who want to increase the self-esteem of their early teenagers. What role do electronic media play in increasing self-esteem?

4. Divide into pairs. In the first exercise, have one partner take the role of a parent who wants to talk to his or her early adolescent about safe and appropriate sexual behavior for the teenager, while the other partner takes the role of the teen who wants more freedom to be with peers without parental monitoring. Then reverse roles, and have the second "parent" try to convey values and rules about appropriate uses of substances in adolescent years to the second "teen." In doing this, practice active listening and sending I-messages.

5. Discuss with other students the importance of peers in their early adolescent years. What kind of pressure do peers exert on each other today? What do you think are reasonable rules parents should propose with regard to time spent with peers? At what age do you think dating should begin? Why that age?

ADDITIONAL READINGS

Damon, William. *The Youth Charter: How Communities Can Work Together to Raise Standards for All Our Children.* New York: Free Press, 1997.

Elkind, David. *The Hurried Child.* Cambridge, MA: Perseus Books, 2001.

Hinshaw, Stephen, with Kranz, Rachel. *The Triple Bind: Saving Our Teenage Girls from Today's Pressures.* New York: Ballantine, 2009.

Pollack, William. *Real Boys.* New York: Holt, 1998.

Shure, Myrna B., with Israeloff, Roberta. *Raising a Thinking Preteen.* New York: Holt, 2000.

Strauch, Barbara. *The Primal Teen.* New York: Random House, 2003.

11

Parenting Late Adolescents and Young Adults

Test Your Knowledge: Fact or Fiction (True/False)

1. The United States is alone in the number of young adults who return to live with their parents when they are in their twenties; children around the world are on their own at that age.
2. Teens' decision making improves when they are in the presence of their peers because they pool their ideas and come up with the best solution.
3. More than half of teens of European American, African American, and Latino/a backgrounds have fears of being discriminated against for some personal quality.
4. Having school success in the early grades reduces the likelihood of substance use in adolescence.
5. Our society has an agreed path to adulthood that the majority of teens follow.

Late adolescents continue to mature physically, intellectually, emotionally, and socially. They use parents as consultants and coaches as they move farther away from home in activities, schooling, and jobs. How do parents provide support and at the same time help teens develop the skills that enable them to avoid the possible risk behaviors. How do parents and young adult children create a new balance of power in their relationship? What happens when young adults return home to live?

Late adolescents are becoming comfortable with all the physical changes they have experienced and they look to the future as young adults. They begin many new activities: dating, pursuing romantic relationships, getting jobs, and participating in community activities. In our contemporary society, teens attain adult status at later ages so we follow teens into young adulthood and describe their activities. Parents are adjusting to their new roles in response to children's many changes. They sense their child's impending departure from home with mixed feelings. Still many children return for varying lengths of time as young adults.

PHYSICAL DEVELOPMENT

Throughout the adolescent years and into the twenties, brain development continues in the prefrontal cortical area, with increasing maturation of the reward-seeking circuitry and increasing connections between cells in the prefrontal cortex and between the prefrontal area and other parts of the brain.[1] Executive thinking and planning grow as well but they are not fully mature until the twenties and as we shall see in the section on Intellectual Development, teens still make risky decisions.

We describe teens' sexual and substance use behavior, aggressive behaviors and moods as well as health habits here and discuss regulating them in later sections on self-regulation and parents' concerns.

From 1991 to 2009, teenagers' self-care behaviors improved with more teens' wearing bike helmets, using seat belts, refusing to ride in a car with someone who has been drinking alcohol, engaging in less binge drinking and fewer teens' drinking at all, fewer teens' having sexual intercourse, and more using condoms when they do.[2]

Still, there are great concerns about teens' habits and high-risk behaviors because 74 percent of all deaths between the ages of ten and twenty-four come from four, potentially preventable causes: motor vehicle crashes (30 percent), other unintentional injuries (16 percent), homicide (16 percent), and suicide (10 percent), and because their daily health habits are setting teens on the path to either health or illness later in life.[3] In addition, there are 700,000 teenage pregnancies each year, an estimated 9.1 million sexually transmitted diseases (STDs), and an estimated 6,610 cases of HIV/AIDS in persons fifteen to twenty-four each year. Here we look at adolescent sexual activity, substance use, aggressive behaviors, and negative moods, and health habits.

Adolescent Sexual Activity

Adolescents engage in self-stimulating sexual activities such as fantasizing and masturbation but we know little about these activities, as children are reluctant to talk about them and many feel guilty.[4] Masturbation, which sometimes begins before puberty, is a frequent source of orgasm for boys but not so frequent a source for girls.

Estimating precisely the percentage of adolescents who have same-sex sexual encounters is difficult.[5] Encounters occur prior to adolescence in playful activities or mutual exploration with friends. Of sexually active youth, about 9 percent of boys and 5 percent of girls report same-sex contact, and about half of these contacts are with heterosexual youth. Only about 2 percent of adolescents identify themselves as gay or lesbian in these years.

Sexual activity with a partner of the opposite sex usually proceeds from holding hands to kissing, to touching breasts and genitals with clothes on, then with clothes off, and finally intercourse. A 2009 national survey of public and private school students from ninth to twelfth grades revealed the following sexual behaviors:[6]

	% Girls	% Boys	% Total
Ever had intercourse	45.7	46.1	46.0
Had intercourse by twelfth grade	65.0	59.6	62.3
Sexually active in last three months	35.6	32.6	34.2
Did not use condom at last intercourse	46.1	31.4	38.9
Drank or had drugs before last intercourse	17.1	25.9	21.6
Have had more than four partners in life	11.2	16.2	13.8

Many fifteen- to seventeen-year-olds report big concerns about sexual health issues—51 percent about getting pregnant, 46 percent about getting HIV/AIDS, and 45 percent about getting a STD.[7] Almost all girls and boys believe they can discuss birth control with their partners, but they feel less able to discuss STDs with partners. While teens worry about pregnancy, HIV/AIDS, and STDs, they do not always use condoms.

Both teens and parents are so focused on pregnancy as a problem that they ignore other dangers.[8] Forty-seven percent of boys and 30 percent of girls in one survey believe that oral sex is safe sex. They underestimate the number of teens who contract STDs and the dangers STDs present in terms of other illnesses and later pregnancy complications.

Eighty percent of teens want more information on sexual health issues, particularly about birth control and about the topic of STDs—how to protect themselves and tell if they have them. And very importantly, they want to know how to talk to doctors about sexual health matters. Almost half said they wanted help to know how to resist pressures they feel to have sex.

Sex education classes are a big source of information, but teens also turn to parents, friends, and the media. Knowing that adolescents want more information, parents can provide accurate written materials for reading at home, raise questions in these areas on the basis of news items, and be alert to any hesitant questions teens may ask. They can also inform doctors that teens may want to talk about these issues. Listening and responding in sensitive ways helps teens ask questions.

Substance Use

Table 11-1 gives the rate of substance use reported by a national sample of public and private school ninth to twelfth grade students in 2009.[9] In a national sample of high school students studied longitudinally at the University of Michigan, there

■ **T A B L E 11-1**
SUBSTANCE USE REPORTED IN A NATIONAL SAMPLE
OF ADOLESCENTS IN 2009*

	Tenth Graders	**Twelfth Graders**
Cigarettes		
% used in last 30 days	18.3	25.2
% smoked 10 daily	6.2	8.5
Alcohol		
% used last 30 days	40.6	51.7
% binge drinking last 30 days	22.3	33.5
Marijuana		
% ever used	35.5	45.6
% used in last 30 days	21.1	24.6
Cocaine		
% ever used	5.6	7.9
Percentage Used prescription drug (e.g., Ritalin, Vicodin) without M.D. prescription	18.2	25.8

*Centers for Disease Control and Prevention, "Youth Risk Behavior Surveillance—United States, 2009."
Surveillance Summaries, June 4, 2010. Morbidity and Mortality Weekly Report (MMWR) 2010; *59*
(No. SS-5).

were few gender differences in early adolescence in substance use, but by the
twelfth grade, boys were much more likely to use substances.[10] With regard to ethnic differences, Native American teens were found to have the highest rates of substance use and Asian Americans, the lowest. Of the other ethnic groups, European
Americans report the highest use, followed by Latinos/as and African Americans.[11]

Eighty percent of parents report concerns about children's drug use, and 74 percent
have concerns about alcohol use, the substance teens use most frequently.[12] Alcohol
use gradually rises in adolescence, especially among students having academic difficulties, and family, peers, schools, and neighborhoods play a role in its use.[13] It
continues to increase in the college years especially for those in college.[14] It gradually decreases during the twenties. Binge drinking between the ages of eighteen and
twenty-two is related to desires to get high and escape boredom, and between the
ages of twenty-two and thirty is related to a desire to escape problems.[15]

Alcohol is of concern not only for its role in causing car accidents which are
the leading cause of death and injuries in these years, but also because it increases
the occurrence of high-risk sexual behaviors.[16] Fifty percent of the boys and girls
in the national sample already cited feared they would do more sexually than they
planned because of drinking and drugs, and 25 percent of sexually active teens
said they had done more than they planned and were afraid they might have gotten
pregnant or contracted an STD.[17]

Substance use also decreases learning, with long-term consequences for students.[18] A longitudinal study following African American students from ages six to thirty-three found that, compared to an infrequent/non-user group carefully matched on early demographic and behavioral characteristics, those who used marijuana more than twenty times by the age of seventeen were more likely to drop out of high school, and in their thirties, more likely to continue marijuana use, be unemployed, and parenting a child outside of marriage. While girls were less likely to fall into the category of frequent marijuana use, when they did, the negative outcomes were the same as for boys.

Longitudinal research on substance users reveals that difficulties in elementary school precede substance use in high school.[19] Doing poorly academically in elementary school, being retained, and having deviant behaviors that result in suspension are characteristic of those who will use alcohol and drugs in high school. The inability to meet school demands may increase frustrations already present, whereas meeting school demands may give a sense of competence and confidence that act as protective factors against substance use.

The researchers conclude, "Early academic interventions, additional support for low achieving students, and a focus on personal growth rather than social comparison could be some of the most effective ways to decrease substance use and delinquency when students reach adolescence."[20] This prescription could well apply to decreasing the rate of teen pregnancy, as many girls who go on to have babies as teens perform poorly academically and have few friends in the early elementary grades. (See Chapter 14.)

Qualities of parents and homes contribute significantly to substance avoidance. Teens are less likely to use substances when they come from families in which parents are well educated, compatible with each other, monitor their children's activities, and promote the importance of schoolwork.

Aggressive Behavior and Negative Moods

Table 11-2 describes the large number of both girls and boys who are dealing with aggressive behaviors, and the large number of teens, predominantly girls but with a significant number of boys, dealing with sad, depressed feelings and thoughts about or attempts at suicide. As teens move into young adulthood, these strong feelings accompany them, and we discuss dealing with them later.

Healthy Behaviors

Only 30.9 percent of teens get eight or more hours of sleep a night; only 36 percent are physically active for sixty minutes five days a week, only 22 percent get five more fruits and vegetables a day, and 27.7 percent describe themselves as overweight.[21] So parents have the major role of providing a home that has healthy foods and rules about exercise and sleep.

Schools play a role as well. Early start times contribute to teens' sleep deprivation that, in turn, leads to poorer school performance.[22] Schools that have delayed start times even by thirty minutes find decreases in teens' sleepiness and increases in amount of sleep obtained each night so that those reporting eight or more hours of

■ **T A B L E 11-2**
AGGRESSIVE BEHAVIOR AND NEGATIVE MOODS*

17.5% carried a weapon, knife, gun, or club in the last 30 days

31.5% have been in a physical fight in the last 12 months

19.9% have been bullied at school in preceding 12 months

9.8% have reported being hit, slapped, or physically hurt on purpose by boyfriend or girlfriend (9.1% percent of girls and 11.5% of boys)

26.1% felt sad, hopeless almost every day for a 2-week period, stopped doing at least one activity (33.9% of girls and 19.1% of boys)

13.8% seriously considered suicide (17.4% of girls and 10.4% of girls)

6.3% attempted suicide (8.1% of girls and 4.6% of boys)

*Centers for Disease Control and Prevention, "Youth Risk Behavior Surveillance—United States, 2009." Surveillance Summaries, June 4, 2010. Morbidity and Mortality Weekly Report (MMWR) 2010; *59* (No. SS-5).

sleep increased from 16.4 to 54.7 percent with accompanying decreases in fatigue and depressed mood and increases in motivation and school attendance.

Parents have an important role in all areas of preventing risky behavior and promoting health and we discuss this in a later section.

INTELLECTUAL DEVELOPMENT

Although teens' abstract reasoning and problem solving have improved, teens may have individual theories or misinformation about the issue at hand,[23] and the theories often affect their learning and thinking. Increasing knowledge is not accomplished by just feeding new facts into a receptive learner. First, one must dispel inaccurate theories and then present new facts when the person is receptive and ready to absorb the information. For example, some teens have the false belief that they cannot get pregnant unless they want a child or if they make love standing up, so they find contraceptive knowledge irrelevant.

By their own self-descriptions and by performance on a delay test, children and early adolescents up to the age of fourteen are less oriented to the future, planning less and thinking about it less, but by the age of sixteen, they will resemble adults in their concern for the future.[24] Though sixteen-year-olds will have the same capacity to think about the future as adults, they will not have the same skills and abilities to plan effectively as these skills do not mature until they are in their midtwenties.

Adolescents' growth in attention, memory, abstract reasoning, and organizational skills enables them to plan activities and make decisions more effectively.[25] Teens' decision making is effective when teens are calm and not emotionally aroused, and when they are not subject to peer pressure.[26] Laboratory research shows, however, that when adolescents and college students are in the presence of peers and friends, they take significantly more risks in video game playing and make more

VOICES OF EXPERIENCE

What I Wish I Had Known about Late Adolescence

"I wish that I had got my children involved in more family activities. When they were mostly through adolescence, I heard a talk by a child psychiatrist who said that often when teenagers say they don't want to do something with the family, at times you have to insist because they do go along and enjoy the event. I wish I had known that sooner, because I accepted their first 'No,' when I perhaps should have pushed more." MOTHER

"I had always heard they look for their own independence, their own things to participate in, but until you really experience it with your own, it's hard to deal with it. When you read about independence, it sounds like it's carefully planned out. When it actually happens, all of a sudden they want to do something that they have never done before and which you firmly believe they have no idea how to do. It can be driving for the first time or suddenly announcing they want to go somewhere with friends. I knew it was going to happen, but exactly how to handle it myself and handle it with them so they got a chance to do something new without it being dangerous has been a challenge to me." FATHER

"I wish that I had known that I had to listen more to them in order to understand what they were experiencing. I sort of assumed that I knew what adolescence was about from my own experience, but things had a different meaning to them. What was important to me was not that important to them, and I wish I had realized that in the beginning." MOTHER

"I wish I knew how to raise children in adolescence when you have traditional values and many of the people around you do not. It's very hard to do here in California compared to the South, where we came from. There, everyone reinforces the same values, and it is a lot easier for parents." MOTHER

"I wish I had known to be more attentive, to really listen, because kids have a lot of worthwhile things to say and you come to find out they hold a lot of your viewpoints." FATHER

"I wish I had known it was important to spend time with the children individually. We did things as a family, but the children are so different, and I think I would have understood them better if I had spent time with them alone." MOTHER

risky decisions in solving hypothetical dilemmas involving cheating or shoplifting than when alone.[27] Risk-taking and risky decision making decrease as adolescents mature and become young adults whose risk-taking is the same whether they are or are not in the presence of peers. That the laboratory research accurately reflects teens' greater risk-taking is seen in the greater number of auto accidents teens have despite driver education and training.

Researchers believe it is essential for teens to learn to resist peer pressures in decision making, and to recall that the judgments they make on their own may often be better guides to action than group recommendations when the two conflict. Parents can help teens gain confidence in their own assessments and to rely on them first in group activities.

SCHOOL

The qualities of schools and teachers are especially important as schools become larger and increasingly impersonal.[28] When schools have a mastery attitude toward learning, helping children find ways to improve their performance, emphasizing diverse goals for students, providing support as well as making demands, students perceive teachers as respectful and friendly, feel attached to schools, and engage in fewer delinquent behaviors than those students in schools emphasizing academic competition and an ability orientation to learning. In the latter schools, more delinquent behaviors are carried out, often by students who are not performing well.

Because teens want respect, teachers who respect them are better able to engage them in learning and inspire them to persist when frustrated.[29] Such teachers are especially important for those underachieving students and for those who lack resources, as we see in Box 11-1.

Students of ethnic minority groups often become increasingly frustrated with school because they anticipate a future of limited occupational opportunities due to lack of funds for further schooling.[30] Some students are motivated to increase their grades so they will be able to compete, but others are further discouraged and alienated from school because of discrimination from teachers and peers. We discuss this topic further in the section on ethnic identity.

Involvement in extracurricular activities and sports can increase students' academic motivation. Because students derive feelings of self-esteem and confidence from these pursuits, they persist at frustrating academic tasks.[31]

When parents understand that children's school difficulties can be due to many factors outside their control, parents can problem-solve with children and listen to their concerns and feelings. Parents can work with schools and advocate to get the most effective educational plan for their child.

WORKING

Most adolescents work during the school year, even if only occasionally at babysitting. The effects of working depend on the context of the work.[32] Some adolescents make valuable contributions to their families by working and giving money to their parents. They may feel increased self-esteem at being able to help their families.

Some adolescents work to escape the frustrations of school. They work increasingly long hours, and their motivation for school decreases further. These adolescents may earn steady income but they are at risk for developing behaviors such as smoking, drug use, and minor delinquency behavior. Their failure to get further education limits their occupational future. Two longitudinal studies find that working up to fifteen hours per week seems to have no negative effects, but working

Box 11-1
FIRST PERSON NARRATIVE*

In *Street Life: Poverty, Gangs, and a Ph.D.*, Victor Rios describes his journey from poor immigrant child to life as a gang member, selling drugs, robbing, stealing cars, and most of all, fighting, to life as a college student, a gang counselor, happy husband and father, a graduate student, and finally, a professor of sociology at the University of California, Santa Barbara, doing research and working with gang members to help them build new lives.

He describes the important factors in changing his life: his determined mother who despite a traumatic childhood in Mexico, little education and no English, disappointing relationships with husband and boyfriends, and problems with alcohol, still monitored him as best she could and insisted he return to school when she learned of his truancy because she did not work so hard for him to drop out. "To make my mother proud, to thank her for keeping me alive and sheltered, I decided to go back to school." But not for long as he joined a gang and spent a lot of time with them, gaining a sense of power and meaning in life.

He credits a high school teacher with saving his life when he made the crucial decision to return to school after his best friend's murder. "She taught me to take my struggles and turn them into my strengths," and she got him the resources he needed to remedy his academic difficulties and go to college.

He also describes the critical role that Aztec dancing played in his development when he took it up after witnessing his uncle's murder. It helped heal the pain from the traumas he experienced growing up because it connected him to his cultural past in Mexico and provided a spiritual tradition that gave his life meaning and purpose. It is a short personal book that can be read in connection with his more academic book, *Punished: Policing the Lives of Black and Latino Boys.***

*Victor M. Rios, *Street Life: Poverty, Gangs, and a Ph.D.* (California: Five Rivers Press, 2011).
**Victor M. Rios, *Punished: Policing the Lives of Black and Latino Boys* (New York: New York University Press, 2011).

more than twenty hours a week intensifies the school problems of those who seek work and decreases the likelihood of later schooling, at the same time increasing the likelihood of later substance abuse.[33]

Work seems most beneficial for those teens who work a few hours a week and still participate fully in school and extracurricular activities. Those who balance school, extracurricular activities, and work were more likely to complete a four-year college than nonworking peers and peers who spent long hours at work.

Parents can serve an important role for teens by monitoring the balance of work and school so teens get the benefit of both activities.

EMOTIONAL DEVELOPMENT

Ronald Dahl has described the strong emotional reactions teens have, and the slower development of the emotional and cognitive skills to manage the feelings.[34] Thus, teens need a strong system of social support while they develop these skills.

Teachers, parents, and coaches provide monitoring and are resources as teens integrate feelings and actions.

Extracurricular and community activities bring feelings of competence and confidence.[35] When teens engage in a variety of activities, they develop many different skills that predict success in academic courses and in relationships with peers. Engagement in these activities is also related to lower levels of substance use. To get the benefits of such activities, teens have to be engaged.[36] In interviews, teens said they were most likely to be engaged when they identified with the goals of the program, when they felt they were learning skills, and when they felt a sense of purpose that transcended their own personal needs. These activities advance teens' development when they are structured, give teens ownership of the activities, and hold teens accountable.[37]

While some have feared that children are overscheduled, a recent review of youth activities finds that extracurricular and community activities do not absorb all children's free time.[38] Those European American and African American teens who engage in these activities are more likely to eat meals with parents and discuss issues with them. Teens report higher self-esteem, academic achievement, and lower substance use.

Self-esteem does increase in these years,[39] and depressed feelings decrease.[40] This greater happiness appears to derive from late adolescents' broader perspectives. They interpret experiences in a new light and as a result become more accepting both of family and of themselves. Stress decreases also because teens increase their use of active coping skills (getting information, seeking advice, and getting support) and internal coping skills (thinking about the problem, finding other solutions, accepting their limitations in a situation).[41] From grades eight to twelve, girls who express their true thoughts and feelings with friends and feel comfortable being themselves have greater increases in self-esteem than those who are less expressive with peers.[42] Expressing feelings and being authentic in relationships may show similar positive outcomes for boys as well.

THE DEVELOPMENT OF THE SELF

Midadolescents speak of the many different "me's"—the self with my mother, the self with my father, the self with my best friend, the self with my boyfriend.[43] Seeing their behavior change with circumstances intensifies midadolescents' concerns about "the real me." They feel they express their true selves when they discuss their inner thoughts, feelings, and reactions to events; they express false selves when they put on an act and say what they do not mean. Teens report acting falsely (1) to make a good impression, (2) to experiment with different selves, and (3) to avoid others' low opinions of them. When they believe they have parents' support, adolescents can voice their opinions and express their true selves. Responsive, attentive friends who listen to teens' interpretations of everyday life events with interest enable teens and young adults to understand themselves and their unique qualities and to incorporate their insights into their developing sense of identity.[44]

In late adolescence, teens come to terms with contradictory qualities by finding a more general abstraction that explains the contradiction.[45] For example, they explain changes in mood—cheerfulness with friends and discouragement with parents—by describing themselves as moody. They also come to accept the contradictions as normal—"It's normal to be different ways with different people." As they observe their changing behaviors, late adolescents note the situations in which they show the traits they value and in which they feel support, and they come to seek out these situations.

Gender Identity

When teens achieve physical maturity, they often experience increased pressure to meet gender-role expectations, termed "gender intensification."[46] As we saw in the last chapter, boys become more traditional in gender-role interests at age sixteen, and girls do also, although they remain more egalitarian than boys. Both boys and girls pay attention to the masculine and feminine values assigned to occupations and girls in late adolescence prefer those occupations that have typically feminine values of helping others and allowing much time with family even though girls know they have lower pay and prestige, and boys avoid these occupations.[47]

However, looking at boys' and girls' interests and academic performance provides mixed evidence about change.[48] Boys have greater self-rated competence in sports from first grade through high school. In school subjects, boys rate themselves as having greater math competence but by twelfth grade, boys and girls rate themselves as equally competent. In addition, recent research shows that math performance is similar for boys and girls from grades two to eleven; with a concluding statement in *Science,* "For grades two to eleven, the general population no longer shows a gender difference in math skills."[49]

Behavioral differences in aggression and in depression are found, with boys being higher on aggression and girls higher on depression (discussed later in the chapter). Even within the range of everyday personal qualities, boys' and girls describe themselves differently. Boys' self descriptions emphasize action, and getting ahead in an organized way; they see themselves as more daring, rebellious, and playful in life than girls and, at the same time, more logical, curious, and calm. Girls see themselves as more attuned to people than are boys (more sympathetic, social, considerate, and affectionate) and more emotionally reactive (more worrisome, more easily upset, more needing of approval).[50]

Most girls in junior high and high school, when surveyed, reported at least one experience of sexual harassment (a demeaning joke, touching, comment on one's appearance), academic sexism (negative comments about math, science, or computer abilities), and athletic sexism (negative comments about physical and sports skills).[51] Such experiences occurred usually once or twice.

Boys were the most frequent perpetrators of sexist remarks, but girls also made sexist comments about other girls. Teachers were the most common source of academic sexist comments. Parents too made demeaning comments, with fathers more likely to do so than mothers.

Girls who are unhappy with traditional gender roles are more likely to perceive discrimination than other girls.[52] Latina and Asian American girls reported less sexual harassment than European American or African American girls. The researchers speculate that if boys were surveyed, they, too, would report gender discrimination, particularly if they have less traditional interests.

Gay/Lesbian Identity

Researcher Ritch Savin-Williams describes changes in attitudes about gay, lesbian, and bisexual youth. In the 1970s, they were identified as a distinct group.[53] In the 1980s and 1990s, researchers and the public viewed them as psychologically vulnerable, prone to depression and suicidal thoughts. In the 1990s the public became more understanding and accepting of individuals with same-gender orientations and provided more supports for teens with gay, lesbian, and bisexual orientations, establishing Gay–Straight Alliance support groups, offering counseling in two thousand schools. As a result of greater approval, gay/lesbian teens have increasingly come to think of themselves as like other teens, as adolescents with personal identities who also happen to engage in sexual activities with same-sex partners rather than as having a "gay" or "lesbian" identity.

Failure to arrive at a sexually based identity may also derive from adolescents' having a longer and more fluid process of labeling themselves. In one study following women for ten years, 73 percent of bisexual women, 83 percent of women who gave themselves no sexual label, and 48 percent of lesbians switched their sexual identification during that period, with many bisexual and unlabeled women going back and forth between these two labels.[54]

Around 42 percent of adult men who reported same-sex contact during adolescence did not continue that activity in adulthood, and about half of the gay/bisexual youth report cross-sex sexual experiences in adolescence.[55] Thus, it is not easy to tell who will continue with same-sex activity and incorporate sexual preference into their sense of identity. In general, teens who restrict themselves to same-sex contacts in adolescence are most likely to continue with a preponderance of same-sex activities as adults.

Many adolescents with same-sex attractions get support, but many do not get support and are harassed as we know from the media. Members of teen groups in high school report homophobic attitudes and occasional name calling of same-sex attracted peers.[56] Boys are more negative toward same-sex attracted boys than girls are. There is a tendency for attitudes toward lesbians to be less negative. Although some groups have homophobic attitudes, others are supportive of same-sex attracted peers.

Teens also receive criticism from parents and siblings. Teens who have an early awareness of same-sex preferences and whose behavior is gender atypical receive more early criticism from parents, but once they tell parents of their preferences, they gain more support from them than those who do not disclose their preference to parents.[57] Disclosing teens have less internalized self-hatred and less fear of parents' finding out than the one-third of teens who do not tell parents of their sexual preferences because they fear their reactions.

Several factors influence how families respond to the disclosure of same-sex preferences.[58] When parents have had warm relationships with children in the past, have been sensitive to children's needs yet encouraged their autonomy, teens feel high self-esteem and parental support after disclosing. Parents' acceptance of teens' orientation appears a powerful factor in protecting teens from psychological problems. Family members' abilities to discuss emotional feelings, respect each other, and remain a cohesive group influence the whole family's adaptation. Teens with same-sex preferences are most likely to have psychological difficulties and engage in alcohol and drug use when they experience many areas of stress—with peers, parents, and academic problems at school.[59]

Savin-Williams believes we need to understand better the strengths that enable teens to experience psychological tensions and difficulties in adolescence and yet become loving partners and parents as adults.[60]

Cross-Gender Identity

We know less about this group than we would like. A very small group of children and adolescents have a very strong identification with the opposite gender.[61] As children, they dress and play as members of the opposite gender, want to have friends of that gender, and sometimes insist that they are that gender. As adolescents and young adults, they may insist on living as the opposite gender as well and often express a persistent discomfort with the physical characteristics of their assigned gender and a wish to change them.

Those who persistently act and dress like the opposite gender and feel uncomfortable with their assigned gender are diagnosed with gender identity disorder, sometimes termed identity gender dysphoria.[62] Boys more frequently receive the diagnosis than girls. Adult follow-up of twenty-five girls who received this diagnosis at about age eight found that sixteen of the twenty-five were classified as heterosexual, two as bisexual, four as lesbians, and three continued to receive the diagnosis of gender identity disorder. So a child can have marked cross-sex interests and activities, and still have a heterosexual orientation in adulthood.

Ethnic Identity

Adolescents continue to explore their ethnic identities, achieving a sense of identity toward the end of the decade. The process of identity achievement is a fluid one that depends on many factors. As teens move into late adolescence, those teens with bicultural identity have a clearer understanding of who they are and a more focused sense of ethnic identity than they had in early adolescence.[63]

Many teens who have immigrated from another country switch the ethnic labels they apply to themselves from one year to the next in high school, sometimes using a pan-ethnic label such as Chinese or Asian, and sometimes using an American label such as Asian American.[64] Teens were more likely to use pan-ethnic labels such as Chinese or Vietnamese when they were first-generation immigrants who knew their heritage language.

When teens form a small minority of students in a school, those with strong connections to other ethnic group members find these friends an important influence on the process of their identity formation. When students have friends mostly from the majority culture, their ethnic identity remains very stable with little change in these years.[65] Experiencing discrimination prolongs the exploratory stage for some teens.[66] Teens continue to reflect on the meaning of being a member of their ethnic group. Teens who report high levels of perceived peer and adult discrimination report lower levels of self-esteem and depressed feelings.[67] Feeling support from large numbers of their ethnic group in the neighborhood and at school encourages identity achievement.[68] Longitudinal studies following Navajo youth through high school found that the group was functioning well psychologically, but those teens who experienced discrimination in the ninth and tenth grades decreased in self-esteem, and discrimination in that period predicted increased substance abuse in eleventh- and twelfth-grade boys. Strong connections to the Navajo culture seemed to be a protective factor against substance abuse.[69]

Another longitudinal research following Native American adolescents for a three-year period reveals that teens maintain a high level of self-esteem that increases over the adolescent years.[70] When they feel social support from the community around them, Native American teens not only have a high level of personal self-esteem, but also have a strong bicultural identity that reflects both Native American and European American values.

Studies of African American and Mexican American adolescents in schools where they were the major groups and had positive status found that all students formed a positive ethnic identity, but they differed in the degree to which they valued and identified with the broader American culture.[71] *Blended bicultural* students positively identified with both the majority and their own ethnic group. For example, they saw themselves as African and American and saw no conflict between the identities. *Alternating bicultural* students identified with the majority culture when at school or at other places, but primarily identified with their own ethnic group. A third, smaller group were termed *separated* students, as they did not identify at all with the majority culture, which they felt rejected and devalued them. Among African American students, slightly over half were classified as blended biculturals, about a quarter as alternating biculturals, and 17 percent as separated. Among Mexican American students, about one-third were classified as blended biculturals, almost two-thirds as alternating biculturals, and only 2 percent as separated.

Although a positive identification with both cultures is thought to be important for personal adjustment, the three groups of students did not differ on measures of self-concept, academic grades, and level of anxiety. Thus, there appear to be three pathways to integrating the experience of having two cultures, and the pathways all seem equally related to measures of effectiveness in adolescents.

THE DEVELOPMENT OF SELF-REGULATION

Children's ability to regulate their feelings and behavior continues to foster academic and social competence, but in these years it has health consequences as well. Accidents, assaults, and self-injury are the leading causes of death and injuries, and substance abuse contributes to all three outcomes.

Adolescent self-regulation, however, is based on experiences in past years, and on many factors in the present age period. Teens are most likely to behave impulsively and use substances when they have:

- Been slow to develop behavioral regulation in the years from three to fourteen[72]
- Had academic difficulties in school from the early years[73]
- Low self-esteem[74]
- Lack positive relationships with parents[75]

Factors in the adolescent years that increase high-risk behaviors include:

- Move to a new community with loss of friends and familiar school[76]
- Friends who encourage high-risk behaviors[77]
- Spending long hours at work[78]
- Siblings who engage in high-risk behaviors[79]
- Living in neighborhoods in which there is much deviant behavior[80]

Teens are better able to regulate their behavior when they feel self-esteem from positive activities,[81] spend time with parents,[82] and attend church.[83]

Religious activities are positive factors in teens' lives because they provide a network of relationships with parents, friends, and adults outside the family that are supportive to teens, and they provide a shared vision or goals that increase teens' empathy and altruism.[84]

When all family members participate in religious activities and have warm relationships with each other, teens feel free to think about religion, ask questions, and bring up puzzling issues. Parents listen and give their thoughts on the issues so family members influence each other.[85]

Latinos/as and Asian Americans have a stronger connection to their religious beliefs than European Americans. Latinos/as are more likely to maintain their participation in religious activities during adolescence than Asian Americans and European Americans though all maintain stable religious beliefs.[86]

PARENT-CHILD RELATIONSHIPS

Although parents see less of their adolescents, the dimensions of parenting that predict competence in the preschool years continue to predict adolescent competence, reflected in self-reliant, independent behavior and in the capacity for meaningful relationships with others.

Attachment

As teens mature and explore more and more of the world, parents remain a secure base to which to return, especially at stressful times. In these years, there is a gradual shift in the balance of power as parents cede teens greater autonomy in actions and decision making. Two qualities are thought to foster a successful parent-teen partnership: (1) the ability to communicate with teens, and (2) the ability to allow teens to seek independence while still having a strong relationship with parents.[87]

Parents who are willing to listen to teens have a greater understanding of their children and a greater sensitivity to their needs; teens feel greater support and security. In turn, secure teens are more willing to open up and communicate with parents about their worries and feelings so a very positive process of interaction is established. Teens who have insecure–preoccupied attachments report many symptoms that others close to them do not know. Teens with insecure–dismissive attachments fail to communicate with anyone.

Securely attached teens and their parents are more easily able to engage in problem solving to deal with issues of autonomy, sometimes compromising, sometimes getting one's own way. Anger in these families occurs less often, and when it does, it stimulates discussion to overcome differences and restore harmony.

When teens have insecure–preoccupied attachments with parents, both teens and parents become trapped in angry conflicts, and teens are less successful in establishing autonomy. A negative form of interaction begins in which teens' anger triggers parents' anger, which, in turn, increases teens' anger. While there is some decrease in this pattern at the end of adolescence, these teens often take this angry form of interaction into young adult relationships with partners.[88]

Styles of Parenting

Diana Baumrind's typology of parenting styles continues to predict effective functioning in these years. *Authoritative* parents have strong commitments to children and balance demands with responsiveness to children's needs: "Unlike any other pattern, authoritative upbringing *consistently* generated competence and deterred problem behavior in both boys and girls, at *all* stages."[89] Children from authoritarian homes are less skilled, less self-assured and curious, and more dependent. Children from indulgent homes are less mature, less responsible, and more responsive to peer pressure. Those raised in indifferent homes where parents are not understanding, committed, or demanding are most likely to be impulsive and involved in substance abuse.

While research with large groups of adolescents shows that authoritative parenting has positive benefits across all ethnic groups in the United States and in countries around the world, authoritarian parenting has negative outcomes in European American families but is associated with positive features in African American and Asian American families.[90]

After being partners for many years, most parents can work together to parent teenage children. Still, almost 50 percent say that arguments over teens' behavior is the biggest source of their disagreements.[91] When parents disagree with each other and become negative with children, teens are more likely to engage in impulsive and noncompliant behaviors such as cutting school and using substances.[92]

Ethnic Differences in Emotional and Behavioral Autonomy

Cultures and ethnic groups in this country vary in their timetable for granting teens autonomy. European American families have a timetable for independent actions such as "spending own money as he/she wishes," which is earlier than that of Asian Amerian adolescents and their parents.[93]

Furthermore, cultures vary in their expectations of how responsive teens are to families' needs. Teens in Mexican American families are expected to make sacrifices for their families. Asian American and Latin American families express strong values and expectations that they will respect, assist, and support their families, but in everyday life, "Adolescents from all ethnic backgrounds reported fairly similar relationships with their families and friends."[94]

Dealing with Discrimination

About 64 percent of European Americans, 57 percent of African Americans, and 70 percent of Latinos/as have "somewhat" or "very big concerns" about being discriminated against because of their race, ethnicity, or sexual orientation, and these percentages are similar for boys (62 percent) and girls (69 percent).[95] As we saw in identity development, girls, teens in ethnic-racial groups, and teens with sexual minority preferences all experienced discrimination in these years.

What can parents do? Having open relationships with children enables teens to tell parents what is happening in their lives so teens and parents can problem-solve specific upsetting incidents. As we saw with sexual minority youth, parents' acceptance and support was a main protective factor in insulating children from psychological problems because of others' cruelty and can be useful in all situations of discrimination.[96] The program in Chapter 10 is useful in suggesting that parents focus on helping children feel good about themselves and their ethnic group and find ways to manage barriers and discrimination and achieve their goals.[97]

Serving as Consultants

A parent serves as a reliable resource and consultant for children in areas of importance not only by providing factual information and values, as described in Chapter 10, but also by helping teens develop the confidence to carry out effective behaviors. In addition to giving information, parents are available for conversations about sexual behaviors, jobs, career goals, relationships, and anything else teens want to talk about. Even though it is hard to find time in our fast-paced world, spending fun time together doing what teens want to do gives teens opportunities to ask questions and get the information they need.

RELATIONSHIPS WITH SIBLINGS

Family values and emotional atmosphere influence the quality of sibling relationships. When family values emphasize family closeness, caring, and support, as in Mexican American families, then adolescent siblings spend a lot of time with each other and are daily supports to each other. Relationships are especially close in same-gender pairs, and when children are close in age.[98]

When family relationships are characterized by hostile angry feelings—either parent–parent, parent–child, or sibling–sibling pairs—the hostility seeps through the whole family system, and all members come to resemble each other in negativity.[99] Furthermore, siblings have a tendency for noncompliant, deviant behavior. Older siblings' substance use serves as an example for younger siblings even when economic, social, and family variables are controlled.[100] So there is something very powerful about the sibling example. It can be a protective or risk factor, depending on the older child's example.

PEER RELATIONSHIPS

Teens spend more time with friends, and their relationships with peers differ from those with parents because friends relate to each other on an equal basis; friendships are voluntarily chosen and are often transitory. Teens' peer relationships occur at several levels—there are close and best friends, relationships in small groups or cliques as described in the last chapter, relationships in crowds, and opposite-sex peers in dating and romantic relationships.[101]

Friendships

Adolescents report that their relationships with friends provide intimacy, companionship, and understanding, whereas relationships with parents provide affection, instrumental help, and a sense of reliability.[102] Intimacy increases because friendships involve more self-disclosure, expression of feelings, and support for friends as needed.[103] Friends are expected to tell each other their honest opinions and to express satisfactions and dissatisfactions with the other person. Friends also have to learn to resolve conflicts as they arise. Friendships promote the development of social skills that, in turn, enrich friendships. Intimacy in friendships is related to adolescents' sociability, self-esteem, and overall interpersonal competence.

As teens move into high school, they are likely to join crowds. While crowds can be rigidly structured, inviting only certain people in, then limiting their contact with outsiders, surveys find that two-thirds of teens shift from one group to another between the tenth and twelfth grades. Often the shift is to a similar group—from brains to nerds or druggies to burnouts. Toward the end of high school, teens become less interested in crowds as they form more firm personal identities and pursue their own interests.[104] In addition to fun and pleasure, peer relationships can include pressure and conflict as well. Cliques and crowds and even best friends can pressure each other to do things that teens feel reluctant to do (e.g., drinking).

Conflicts are a daily occurrence in close relationships—an average of eight a day in one survey. In that survey, conflicts were most frequent, in descending order, with mothers, friends, romantic partners, siblings, and fathers.[105] Teens were more likely to negotiate and compromise with friends and romantic partners than with parents and siblings. Conflicts do not sever the relationships with friends.

Dating

Friendships set the stage for dating and romantic relationships.[106] Adolescents learn how to be close to same-sex peers and solve conflicts, then they get to know opposite-sex peers in friendship groups, moving to group and single dating, and finally to romantic relationships. Romantic relationships are usually intense and brief. Because there are almost no studies of same-sex dating, we discuss only heterosexual dating here.

While parent-child attachments have been considered major determiners of the quality of dating and romantic relationships, recent work indicates that the quality of dating relationships is more closely related to the quality of peer friendships. When asked to describe attachment, care received, and affiliation in relationships with parents, friends, and romantic partners, adolescents' perceptions of their relationships with romantic partners were related to their perceptions of their relationships with friends but unrelated to their perceptions of relationships with parents. Parents influence the quality of peer friendships, and the nature of the friendships in turn affects dating and romantic relationships.

The quality of teens' friendships predict the quality of their relationships with romantic partners.

By the time teens graduate from high school, most, though not all, have dated. Dating gives practice in developing feelings of trust and enjoyment with the opposite sex and provides the basis for later romantic attachments.[107] Intimacy, support, and companionship are major satisfactions in dating. As with friendships, romantic relationships often involve intense conflicts, which sometimes trigger feelings of sadness and loneliness. Many teens feel that resolving conflicts brings couples closer together, and so conflicts have positive value.

Teens are most likely to postpone sexual activity when they have close relationships with parents and have positive activities they enjoy.[108] About 40–50 percent of teens have their first sexual experiences in these years, often in romantic relationships but sometimes not. When girls have their first sexual experiences earlier than their peers, then they are more likely to suffer from depression, especially if the relationship is dissolved and involved little emotional commitment.[109] Having first sexual experiences at the normative time or later presents no increased risk of depression for girls. Boys do not appear subject to depression following first sexual experiences.

First sexual experiences change family relationships. Teens' relationships with parents become more distant, and parents and children share less time together in joint activities.[110] Teens also have increased problem-focused interactions with parents. The greater distance between parents and children is related to ongoing sexual activity. When parents remain close to teens and give them room to grow, sexual activity is less likely to continue.

TASKS AND CONCERNS OF PARENTS

In this age period, parents remain supportive caregivers who also grant their teens greater autonomy. Parenting tasks include:

- Being available, responsive caregivers who listen to children
- Serving as models of responsible behavior
- Continuing to monitor and enforce safety rules while supporting and accepting their children's individuality
- Communicating information and values in an atmosphere of open discussion
- Serving as consultant to children as they make important decisions
- Allowing children to separate in an atmosphere of acceptance

The problems encountered during adolescence relate to physical and emotional functioning, social behavior, and family interactions. We now discuss how parents help their children deal with these problems.

Promoting Healthy Behaviors

Parents worry about health and safety issues because they lack direct control to ensure children's well-being. They must rely on modeling healthy behaviors, having healthy family routines, and monitoring teens so they avoid high-risk behaviors.

In the next few sections, we focus on sleeping and eating problems, early sexual activity, drinking, and anger and depression.

Promoting Healthy Sleep Habits

As we detailed at the beginning of this chapter, many factors contribute to adolescents' getting less sleep in these years, including electronic devices like TVs, cell phones, and computers in the bedroom.

Establishing healthy sleep habits is important not only to promote healthy functioning at school and at home, but also to lay down healthy habits because sleep patterns in adolescent years tend to persist into adulthood.[111] For example, when fourteen-year-olds watch TV extensively, they are more likely to have sleep problems at ages sixteen and twenty-two. When they reduce TV watching at age fourteen, they have fewer sleep problems at sixteen and twenty-two.

The emotional atmosphere of the family is an important predictor of teens' sleep. Just as in early years, eating family meals together predicts more sleep each night—each additional hour spent eating together weekly is associated with an additional hour of sleep weekly.[112] Reducing family conflict reduces sleep problems.[113] Those children who live in families with conflict in late childhood and early adolescence are more likely to suffer sleep problems at age eighteen.

Research indicates that parents' supervision and insistence that teens get a reasonable amount of sleep each night predict amount of sleep teens get.[114] Teens may object that it should be their personal choice when to go to bed, but parents' insistence on health issues is persuasive.

Healthy sleep habits are important not only for physical energy and health but also for academic achievement, emotional health and for safe driving.

Promoting Healthy Eating Habits

Teens' social life and food preferences combine to reduce the amount of healthy food teens eat. Skipping breakfast to rush to school, eating at fast-food restaurants or buying high-calorie fatty foods at lunch cafeterias, and getting home late for dinner and eating a frozen meal are cause for concern. When the standard teen diet is combined with lack of exercise, it is not surprising that about 30 percent of teens are overweight.[115]

Parents Actions   Parents focus on establishing positive habits that ensure good nutrition. They encourage healthy eating by serving nutritious food at family meals, having only healthy food in the house for snacks, and arranging family routines and outings that involve walking, biking, or sports activity. Parents can encourage teens to become cooks or active participants in family meal preparations.[116]

With teens' busy schedules, problem-solving situations may be needed to figure out how families can have four or five dinners together each week, how teens can make healthy choices at fast-food restaurants, and how they can include exercise in their schedules.

Eating Disorders   Three kinds of eating disorders are identified and require immediate medical and psychological help. They are anorexia nervosa (extreme thinness because of calorie restriction or purging; less than 1 percent of the population), bulimia nervosa (engaging in binge eating and then purging; (1–2 percent of a community sample), and eating disorders not otherwise specified that includes binge eating and all other eating behaviors that do not meet the strict requirement of anorexia nervosa and bulimia nervosa (about 3 percent of people).[117]

People with eating disorders are at risk for developing other medical problems such as cardiac and neurological problems as well as depression and substance abuse, so parents should always get professional help. If they have doubts about the needs for treatment, parents can go and explain their concerns and get guidance.[118] Many forms of treatment are available with cognitive-behavioral therapy, family therapy, and medications available to arrive at treatments that will address teens' needs.[119]

Promoting Later and Protected Sexual Activity

The very parenting behaviors that encourage social and psychological competence in teens also predict postponing sexual activity—namely, a warm, close relationship with parents and parents' willingness to talk about their values of postponing sexual activity.[120] As we noted, close relationships and shared activities with parents delay the onset of sexual relations and decrease sexual activity after first encounters. Teens' risky sexual behavior also can trigger increases in family activities and heightened parental responses.[121]

Most successful sexual education programs have common elements that parents can use as guides for their behavior.[122] Programs include information about pubertal physiological changes, maturation, and sexuality, interpersonal skills so teens can assert their own beliefs, and giving information on contraceptive devices and their availability.

VOICES OF EXPERIENCE

The Joys of Parenting Late Adolescents

"It's fun to see them discover things about themselves and their lives. The older ones have boyfriends, and I'm seeing them interact with them." MOTHER

"Sometimes the kids have friends over, and they all talk about things. It's nice to see them get along with their siblings as well as their friends. It gives you a good feeling to see them enjoying themselves." FATHER

"I felt very pleased when my son at sixteen could get a summer job in the city and commute and be responsible for getting there and doing a good job." MOTHER

"I like it when they sit around and reminisce about the things they or the family have done in the past. They all sit around the table, saying 'Remember this?' It's always interesting what they remember. This last summer we took a long sightseeing trip, and what stands out in their minds about it is funny. They remember Filene's Basement in Boston, a chicken ranch where we stopped to see friends. One father took the Scouts on a ski trip. They got stuck in the snow on the highway for hours, and the car almost slid off the road. He said, 'Never again.' I said, 'Don't you *realize* that because of those things, the boys will probably remember that trip forever? You have given them wonderful memories.'" MOTHER

"I really enjoy her happiness. She always sees the positive side to a situation. Things might bother her from time to time, but she has a good perspective on things." FATHER

"I really like to see them taking responsibility. Yesterday they had a school holiday, and I was donating some time at an open house fundraiser. They got all dressed up and came along and helped too. The older one coaches a soccer team of

As noted earlier, warm relationships with parents, having available information on safe, responsible sexual activity, and opportunities to talk about it help teens delay sexual activity, and have safe sexual relations when they do engage in it.

Discouraging Substance Use

Earlier in the chapter, we noted that elementary school success and warm relationships with parents serve as protective factors against high school substance use. In addition, parental monitoring discourages use. A large study of Dutch teens and their families finds that teens drink less when parents do not drink, do not make alcohol available in their home, have specific rules about not drinking and enforce these rules.[123] Conversely, when parents drink, make alcohol available in the home, and are permissive about teens' drinking, then teens drink more. Because peer, school, and neighborhood influences impact substance use, new family treatment programs include not only family members but also peer group members

four-year-olds, and the younger is a patrol leader in the Scouts, so they both have responsibility for children." MOTHER

"I enjoy that she is following in the family tradition of rowing. I rowed in college, and my brothers did, my father and grandfather did, and she saw a city team and signed up. She does it all on her own and has made a nice group of friends through it." FATHER

"I can't believe that she has had her first boyfriend and it worked out so well. They met at a competition, and he lives some distance away, so they talk on the phone. He has a friend who lives here, and he comes for a visit sometimes and does lots of things with the family. We all like him, and it is nice for her to have a boyfriend like that." MOTHER

"The joys are seeing them go from a totally disorganized state to a partially motivated, organized state. You can see their adult characteristics emerging." FATHER

"I enjoy seeing my daughter develop musical ability, seeing her progression from beginning flute to an accomplished player who performs, and seeing how much pleasure she takes in her accomplishment." MOTHER

"I enjoy his maturity. He's so responsible. He tests us, but when we're firm, he accepts that. I'm real proud of him because he looks at the consequences of what he does." FATHER

"I enjoy his honesty and the relationship he has with his friends. He is real open with his feelings, and his friends look up to him. He's a leader." MOTHER

"He's not prejudiced. His best friends are of different ethnic groups. People trust him and like him because he's real concerned about people." FATHER

and members from the family's community.[124] Such a program has had significant benefits for Latino/a substance abusers and engaged more African American families in treatment than more traditional treatments.

If parents suspect teens have a drinking problem, they should seek professional help quickly and be included in the treatment, as research does show that parents' behavior affects teens' drinking.

Helping Children Control Aggressive Feelings

Aggressive, rule-breaking boys do continue to have problems through adolescence and into adulthood.[125] They are more apt to abuse substances, to drop out of school, to find getting and keeping a job difficult, and to have driving infractions. Furthermore, they tend to date girls who are also aggressive and to start families early. "It is hard to overemphasize the importance of childhood conduct problems for adjustment failures in young adulthood for males. These failures are pervasive and severe, and the consequences for the young man, his intimate partners, and the children whom he fathers are profound."[126]

What do researchers recommend? As noted in earlier chapters, attentive, fair, supportive, consistent parenting helps boys learn new behaviors to replace the forceful, irritating, negative behaviors learned at home. Social skills programs with age-mates also decrease the aggressive, disruptive behaviors that drive others away.

A third kind of intervention emphasizes learning emotional regulation skills. In one study, aggressive boys who were emotionally volatile—irritating, disruptive, and inattentive to others—had far more problems with peers than did boys who were only aggressive.[127] Thus, these boys must learn to control overreactivity and attend to others' needs. Anger management and communication skills programs can help here.

Treatment for symptoms of depression is important also as rule-breaking boys often suffer depression—45 percent of boys in one longitudinal study—that may well persist into adulthood.[128] The boys who were both angry and depressed were at risk for more severe problems in adulthood than were boys who were either angry or depressed. Thus, help must deal with both sets of problems for a large number of aggressive, rule-breaking boys. Finally, as with substance abuse, new forms of treatment include multisystemic interventions that include the peer group, school personnel, and juvenile justice personnel. Such interventions decrease rule-breaking behaviors and the seriousness of offenses, increase school attendance, and promote positive peer and family relationships.[129]

Helping Children Cope with Feelings of Depression

Depression varies along a spectrum. At the one end are depressed moods—feeling down, being unhappy over an upsetting event such as failing a test or fighting with a friend.[130] The feelings may last a brief or an extended time.

In some cases, depression is a normal response to a loss—a parent's death, parents' divorce, moving to a new location. Children may show signs of depression off and on for months following the event, depending on the severity of the loss, but gradually depression lifts. Depression is sometimes expressed in angry, rebellious, acting-out behavior that masks the underlying condition. Children who are serious discipline problems in school and become involved in drugs, alcohol, and risk-taking behavior are often depressed. They lack self-esteem and feel helpless about themselves and helpless to change.[131]

The most serious end of the spectrum, clinical depression or major depressive disorder, involves depressed mood and loss of interest or pleasure in usual pursuits. Disturbances in sleep, eating, and activity patterns may or may not accompany the depressed mood. Energy level drops, and teens move more slowly and accomplish less than they did formerly. Sometimes clinical depression is accompanied by loss of concentration and poor memory, so school performance may drop. Because they feel less interested and withdraw, depressed children may have fewer friends. These are the main markers of clinical depression.[132] Children may also have thoughts or plans to hurt themselves or, less often, someone else.

Studies suggest that between 10 and 15 percent of children and adolescents show some signs of depression.[133] Because this occurs less before puberty, the majority of young people showing depression are teenagers. In any given year, 8.3 percent of adolescents show signs of depression, about 50 percent higher than the adult rate of 5.3 in a given year. Twenty percent of teenagers report having experienced a major depression that was not treated. As noted in the previous chapter, before puberty, boys and girls are equally likely to be depressed, but after puberty, the rate for girls doubles.

Prior to puberty, suicide attempts are rare, but the rate of suicide increases after puberty. As we saw at the beginning of the chapter, many teens report sad, hopeless feelings with some having thoughts of suicide. Parental warmth and support were negatively related to suicidality.[134]

Many factors are related to depressive states:[135]

- Genetic factors reflected in having family members with depression
- Biological factors such as hormonal changes related to puberty
- Stressful life events such as divorce, discrimination, child maltreatment
- Psychological factors such as inability to manage emotions
- Pattern of family interactions such as lack of parental support
- Peer relationships such as rejection and bullying
- Romantic relationships involving rejection and break-ups

When parents notice signs of depression, they should seek qualified professional help. At the present time, there are several forms of help for depression.[136] Family therapy, individual therapy, and group therapy aimed at helping the child change negative self-evaluations are useful. Medications are often used as well. If parents are uncertain whether their concerns are justified, they can consult a therapist by themselves to determine the severity of the depression and the need to bring the child in.

Following the course of depressive feelings in a large sample of twenty thousand teens from seventh to twelfth grade revealed significant ethnic and racial differences.[137] European American boys and girls had the lowest levels of depressed feelings. Latina girls had the highest level of depressed feelings and Asian American girls had almost equally high rates. Among boys, Asian American boys had the highest rates of depressed feelings, followed by Latino boys. African American boys and girls scored higher in depressed feelings than European American boys and girls, but lower than the other two groups.

All groups decreased in depressed feelings over the six years, but European American boys and girls remained significantly lower than the other three groups, which clustered closely together. Immigrant status did not have a significant effect on the rate of decreasing scores. Despite their coping skills, Asian American, Latino/s, and African American boys and girls enter the young adult years with significantly more feelings of depression that may make it harder for them to achieve their goals.

Mothers' support (there was not a measure of fathers' support) was important in reducing depressed feelings in all ethnic groups.

> For both males and females, and among all race-ethnic groups, higher levels of maternal support were found to be related to lower levels of depressive symptoms. In a sense, mothers' support may be a "race-ethnicity equalizer" because its effect is consistent across all groups.[138]

A school-based program designed to prevent the rise of depressed feelings in the junior high years included coping skills training for students and several interventions for parents to improve parenting skills and parent-teen relationships.[139] The program not only inhibited a rise in depressed feelings in at-risk youth; it also decreased delinquency and substance use.

Promoting Positive Peer Relationships

In the teen years, the quality of parent–child relationships influences teens' orientation to peers.[140] When teens feel they have good relationships with parents and feel that parents allow them a growing role in decision making, teens are better adjusted, less likely to report extreme orientations toward peers, and less likely to seek peers' advice than are teens who feel that parents retain power and control. This latter group of teens seek the egalitarian relationship and mutuality they do not feel with parents. Relationships between fathers and teens are especially predictive of peer relationships, perhaps because fathers and children engage in many recreational activities, and skills learned there transfer to relationships with peers.[141]

Promoting School Success

When adolescents are achieving below their ability levels, studies have found two general approaches helpful.[142] The behavioral technique of regularly monitoring schoolwork by means of a progress report and giving positive consequences such as privileges and rewards helps students raise their performance level. A second strategy is a comprehensive approach to increase teens' study skills, their academic skills (by means of tutoring), and their social skills so they feel more at ease at school. Parents' involvement and use of consequences is also key to such a program. Addressing academic problems alone through tutoring or private therapy has not been as helpful as multifaceted approaches.

Helping Teens Develop a Sense of Purpose

Sense of purpose defined as a commitment to a longer-term goal, an ultimate concern that gives life meaning and guides behavior, is associated with teens' levels of happiness and hopefulness, and with young adults' sense of well being.[143] Impressed with the sense of vitality and direction that some young people show, William Damon interviewed 1,200 adolescents and young adults between the ages of twelve and twenty-two to determine how they developed a sense of purpose in life.

Damon synthesized the parenting actions that encourage a sense of purpose.

> What a parent should do is lead a child toward promising options. A parent can help a child sort through choices and reflect upon how the child's interests match up with the world's opportunities and needs. A parent can support a child's own efforts to explore purposeful directions and open up more potential sources of discovery about possible purposes. These are supporting roles. . . because center stage in the drama belongs to the child. But while the most effective assistance parents can provide is indirect, it is also invaluable.[144]

Specifically, he recommends

- Have conversations about the child's interests and activities and support them
- Listen and pay attention to what arouses your child's interests and support them
- Talk about your own goals and purpose at work
- Talk about the practicalities of accomplishing goals and projects
- Connect your child with mentors in the community
- Support your child's resourceful problem-solving skills and reasonable risk-taking to achieve goals
- Model and support a positive outlook
- Help children develop "a feeling of agency linked to responsibility"

Parents often accomplish these parenting goals in simple conversations while doing an errand or a chore. Being around and available to notice a child's enthusiasm or answer a casual question that triggers more conversation is very important. It is in these little moments that much gets done.

A PRACTICAL QUESTION: HOW CAN PARENTS TELL WHETHER THEIR TEEN HAS A SIGNIFICANT PROBLEM?

Parents want to know the signs of a serious problem. Generally, changes or decreases in a teen's mood and level of functioning at school, at home, and at work can indicate one or more of several possible problems. When parents have concerns, they need to get professional help because these are all serious problems that rarely disappear with time.

Marcia Herrin outlines the early warning signs of an eating disorder: obvious increases and decreases in weight; a sudden and intense interest in diets, nutrition, and nonfat foods; skipping meals; drinking only noncaloric drinks; a frantic pace of exercise or athletic activity; discomfort around eating and meals; preoccupation with physical appearance; low self-esteem; and depression.[145] These behaviors have more meaning collectively than individually. A professional can help evaluate parents' concerns.

Harold Koplewicz helps parents identify depressed teens.[146] He describes the "moody" teen who has lost a boyfriend and is down for days or weeks but recovers and continues her activities and her relationships with friends and family.

> But if the sadness persists—if [she] has become a different person, if she's lost her sense of humor, if her sleeping and eating habits are disturbed, and if she's becoming socially isolated and is suddenly having trouble keeping up with school-work—it may be that the breakup was the triggering event of an underlying depression that needs to be treated.[147]

In addition to such classical signs of depression, Jane Brody points to tiredness, boredom, irritability, temper outbursts, sudden threats to leave home, physical symptoms such as headaches or stomachaches, and anxiety.[148]

Substance abuse may be harder to detect until it becomes a serious problem, because teens often engage in such behavior away from home with peers, and parents can only detect the consequences of it—coming home drunk, a ticket for driving under the influence, loss of interest in school, cutting classes, a drop in grades, a new group of friends, anger and irritability at parents, a decrease in responsible behaviors such as doing chores, and increasing difficulties with others at school or at work.[149] Changes in eating and sleeping and an increased number of physical complaints may accompany drug use as well.

All these problems share many of the same warning signs. With the help of school and professionals, parents can get the best assessment of what is happening to their child and the form of treatment needed.

As parents identify and seek treatment for their children's problems, they often learn that they themselves have the problem but have not recognized or accepted it. Parents of depressed teens may discover, for example, that they themselves have suffered from depression. Parents of a substance-abusing teen may realize that they are problem drinkers. Parents of children with eating disorders may see they have a problem in this area as well. As parents seek treatment for teens, the whole family benefits.

PARENTS' EXPERIENCES IN FACING TRANSITIONS

To understand how parents react and adapt to the changes and turmoil of their children's adolescence, Laurence Steinberg observed 204 families for three years.[150] He found six aspects of a child's adolescent behavior that trigger parents' emotional reactions: puberty and its associated physical changes, maturing sexuality, dating, increasing independence, emotional detachment, and increasing deidealization of the parent.

Parents with the following risk factors were most likely to experience difficulty: (1) being the same sex as the child making the transition, (2) being divorced or remarried (especially true for women), (3) having fewer sources of satisfaction outside the parental role, and (4) having a negative view of adolescence. Protective factors that eased parents' adjustments to their teens' adolescence were having satisfying jobs, outside interests, and happy marriages. The positive supports buffered parents so that, in times of difficulty with children, they had other sources of satisfaction and self-esteem.

Steinberg found that about 40 percent of parents experienced difficulties, 40 percent responded to children's changes but were not personally affected, and 20 percent enjoyed greater freedom as their children became more independent. Based on his research, Steinberg makes the following suggestions to parents for handling this stage of family development: (1) have genuine and satisfying interests outside of being a parent, (2) do not disengage from the child emotionally, (3) try to adopt a positive outlook about what adolescence is and how the child is changing, and (4) do not be afraid to discuss feelings with partners, friends, or a professional counselor.

CRITERIA FOR ADULTHOOD

No single event marks the arrival at adulthood the way puberty marks the beginning of sexual maturity. The legal system typically defines anyone under eighteen as a child and everyone over eighteen as an adult.[151] Adolescents can achieve adult status prior to age of eighteen if they marry, have a child, enter the military, or petition the court to become emancipated minors who can support themselves.

Adolescents (average age sixteen), twenty-year-olds (average age twenty-four), and adults in their thirties and forties (average age forty-two) agree in their descriptions of behaviors a person must achieve to be considered an adult.[152]

The items frequently used to define adulthood focus on three areas:

- independence and responsibility for self
- self-control and self-regulation—using contraceptives, not driving while drunk, not shoplifting
- capacity to protect a family and manage a household.

Items used less frequently to describe adulthood are what might be termed "external markers" of the adult role—marriage, having a child, buying a home, avoiding bad language.

Researchers looking at large samples of people in their twenties identify five markers as signs of adulthood: (1) living independently of parents, (2) completing education, (3) having a stable job, (4) marriage, and (5) childbearing.[153]

THE TRANSITION TO ADULTHOOD

Youths' living arrangements vary. Almost 40 percent of youth live at home and go to college, work, or both work and go to college, and 40 percent go away to school and work elsewhere. About 10 percent are married or are single parents and living away from home, and 10 percent are unclassified.[154]

Trends Common to Those Entering Adulthood

Despite the numerous paths to adulthood, common trends are seen for this group as a whole.

In a diverse sample followed from ages eighteen to twenty-five,[155] psychological well-being improved over the seven years with increasing levels of self-esteem and decreasing levels of expressed anger and depression. In this period, the gap between men and women's scores on depression and anger gradually narrowed. Youth in families with high parental conflict were more likely to be angry and depressed at the beginning of the period, but their scores decreased sharply over the period. Parents' social support and marriage were related to increases in self-esteem whereas periods of unemployment were related to higher depression and lower self-esteem scores.[156]

Alcohol and marijuana use increased into the early twenties, and then began to decrease.[157] While overall well-being improved, this is the period in which serious psychological disorders such as schizophrenia become more prevalent.[158]

Young adults' moods are related to past family experiences. A survey of life satisfaction and positive moods in college students in thirty-nine countries found that young adults enter adulthood in good spirits when they come from families where parents have marriages with good or average agreement between partners.[159] When parents are married and argue or when they divorce and remarry and argue, young adults have lower life satisfaction and more negative moods. When parents argue and divorce, and children grow up in homes with no arguing, their levels of life satisfaction and positive moods resemble those of youth from average marriages.

Parents' Role in Supporting Growth and Development

Parental support takes many forms. Financial or economic support takes the form of paying children's living expenses while they get further training or pay for further education.[160] As children are older, parents offer loans or gifts for cars, deposits for apartments, and down payments on homes. In one large representative sample of children between the ages of eighteen to thirty-four, parents gave an average of $38,000 including the support for living at home.[161] They gave more when children were younger, and less as children moved into their thirties. Families with greater resources gave far more in this period, but even those in the lowest quartile of income gave an average of $9,000 over the sixteen-year period.

Social support is divided into emotional, instrumental, and informational benefits.[162] Emotional benefits include feeling cared for, valued, encouraged, understood, and validated as a person. Instrumental benefits include help with certain tasks such as child care or repairing cars. In the study assessing financial giving, parents also gave an average of 380 hours per year in time to help children—that is an average of 9 weeks of full-time work.[163] Informational benefits include advice about school, referral to resources, or guidance about tasks.

Paths to Adulthood

Researchers following a sample of midwestern European American middle-class boys (42 percent of the sample) and girls (58 percent of the sample) from ages twelve to twenty-four used five markers to describe adult status at age twenty-four: education status, job status, place of residence, romantic relationships, and parenthood.[164] Using Latent Class Analysis of the data, they identified six pathways to adulthood:

Pathway	% of Sample	%M	%F
Fast Starters	12	45	55
Parents without Careers	10	29	71
Educated Partners	19	34	66
Educated Singles	37	47	53
Working Singles	7	53	47
Slow Starters	14	44	56

People in the first three groups live with or are married to partners, and those in the second three groups are single. Three groups—Fast and Slow Starters and Parents without Careers—have children, and the remaining three groups—Educated Partners and Singles and Working Singles—do not. As we can see, more than half of the youth are focused on getting an education, but many are highly focused on work.

Fast Starters are closest to the traditional role of the young adult—having a long-term job, being married, owning a home, caring for children. People in this cluster work longer hours than those in the other groups, and they earn more money though only a small percentage seeks more education to expand their future opportunities. They have been with their partners and spouses for about two years, and they had known them for three years before that. While they report less dissatisfaction with their spouses than other groups, they also report more instances of physically abusive interactions with partners.

Adults in this group spend most of their time at work or with their family and in household activities. They spend less time in leisure activities like sports and reading than the sample as a whole. They also have a lower rate of illegal activities like using drugs or vandalism.

Parents without Careers is a group largely made up of women who either do not work at all or work at short-term jobs, resulting in this group's having the fewest hours worked and the lowest income. The men in the group do have full-time jobs and earn more money, but they do not seek more education so advancement may be limited.

The relationships between cohabiting or married partners began earlier than those in the other groups and have lasted longer. Three-quarters of the group, however, feel the relationships have problems and like Fast Starters, there is a history of physical abuse in the relationships.

Both men and women in the group spend most of their time on family activities and spend the least amount of time on leisure activities. Like Fast Starters they have a low rate of illegal activities.

Educated Partners, like Fast Starters and Parents without Careers, were married or live with romantic partners, but they do not have children. While highly educated, one-quarter continue to seek more education, and as a result, their jobs are less stable and lower paying than those in other groups.

The romantic relationships of this group are shorter-lived than those in the first two groups, but couples dated longer before cohabiting or marrying, and they report the most satisfying partner relationships of all the groups and fewer problems. Because there are no children, their daily activities are more like Educated Singles. Partners report more time in leisure activities and less time in household activities.

Educated Singles are like Educated Partners in many ways except that they do not live with partners and are more likely to live at home with their parents. Thirty percent are currently reenrolled in college courses, and while their earnings are at the mean, their future prospects are expanding because of education and access to higher status jobs.

Like the other two groups of singles, the happiest individuals are those who are in a steady dating relationship with someone. Like all singles they spend little time in household activities and much more time in leisure activities than those living with partners. They are likely to have engaged in some illegal activities like drug use. Though they have a sociable, less settled lifestyle, they are still as responsible as those in other groups for meeting their own needs.

Working Singles, like Educated Singles, are more likely to live at home and feel more comfortable with a steady, caring relationship. Like Fast Starters, they work long hours, and they earn good money in skilled and technical jobs that are secure. About 16 percent are getting more education.

They spend about the average amount of time in household and family activities and more time in leisure activities like sports. Still, they meet all their own needs with the exception of managing a household. So Working Singles are like Fast Starters in making a significant commitment to work, but like other single groups, they are delayed in making commitments to relationships.

Slow Starters are not settled in a stable job. They hold service and office jobs, working fewer hours and earning less money than those in all other groups except Parents without Careers. However, 21 percent of the group is getting more education so future jobs may be more advanced. Slow starters are most likely to be living with parents and not involved in romantic relationships. When they do have relationships, they report difficulties. They spend a lot of time in leisure activities and are the group most likely to violate laws.

Though the group is the most delayed in getting established in jobs, relationships, and independent residence, they are advanced in having children. Almost two-thirds of the group have children. Unlike Fast Starters and Parents without Careers who center much of their time around family and children, Slow Starters devote little time to children.

At age eighteen, several factors predicted the pathways teenagers would take to adulthood. Students' interest and performance in academic courses, their involvement in sports, skill-oriented activities, and community activities all were linked to later membership in Educated Partners and Educated Singles groups. Those who looked forward to marriage and wanted to be married at younger ages were those most likely to be married at age twenty-four. Predicting those who would have children was more difficult. It can be seen, however, that many of those having children early (Parents without Careers and Slow Starters) have fewer financial resources and report more difficulties in partner relationships.

Those eighteen-year-olds whose parents were well-educated and had financial resources were those most likely to be in the Educated groups, but lack of money was not a barrier to education. Good students who were poor still got to college and were in the educated groups.

The research did reveal that while educated groups and Slow Starters are still exploring and making few commitments, still about a third of young people are making significant commitments to work and family at traditional ages.

Those Who Need Special Support in the Transition to Adulthood

Because of physical and psychological problems, learning deficits, and life circumstances, many children received services during childhood and adolescence.[165] As they reach maturity, many of these services decrease or end, and children and their families are left to manage as best they can. Families often do not have resources, and in the cases of children in foster care or the juvenile justice system, family members are often not available.

Though these children have fewer resources than many, they have many needs. Jobs available for high school graduates with no advanced training or skills are few, unstable, and provide few benefits like health insurance. Further, some of these children have additional problems in learning and in skills for independent living.

Recognizing the needs of these groups, federal and state agencies take the supportive role of providing transitional services into the early twenties to give vocational training, life skills for independent living, and self-management skills. These programs tend, however, to be inflexible, providing services according to age rather than needs, and failing to provide families with training and support so they can help children effectively.

Even with such programs, significant numbers of these maturing adults suffer from psychological problems and substance use, instability in living arrangements, and early fertility. Those who have been in special education, about 85 percent of this group, fare better with, for example, only 20 percent experiencing unemployment compared with 50 percent in those exiting foster care or the juvenile justice system. Some people in this group resemble Slow Starters who are living at home and have unstable work histories.

Children who have only health problems have fewer difficulties in attaining adult status than those with learning or psychosocial problems. Researchers find that adolescents with chronic health problems such as asthma, diabetes, arthritis, and cerebral palsy "attain levels of education, income, marriage, and self-esteem that are average for their age group."[166] They show differences in rate of employment, with 73 percent of the healthy group and 67 percent of the group with chronic conditions working, as well as a difference of $1,700 in annual income. On years of education, marital status, and self-esteem, no significant differences between the groups appear.

This does not mean that youth with severe physical health conditions, such as youth who are technology dependent on wheelchairs or other equipment, face no obstacles to achieving adult status. Nonetheless, while they or others with severe conditions have added problems, the majority of teens with chronic physical health problems achieve adult status comparable to others in their age group.

Pathways to Adulthood for Youths from Immigrant Groups

Through telephone and face-to-face interviews with children of immigrants living in New York City, researchers identified paths these youths took to adulthood and compared them with those of native-born European and African American youth.[167] With a median age of twenty-three, these youths came from immigrant families from South American countries (Columbia, Ecuador, and Peru), Caribbean Islands (West Indies, Puerto Rico and Dominican Republic), Russia, and China. Families, on average, had far fewer resources with which to help their children, but their help was critical.

The same paths to adulthood were found in immigrant groups as those we described in midwestern youth—working, going to school, working and going to school, doing neither, while having children, doing both while having children.

However, there were differences among the groups that we illustrate with the marked differences between the Chinese and Puerto Rican youths.

Families from mainland China planned and struggled to get to this country and often came with extended family members. Thus, families often consisted of two parents, and perhaps grandparents, with a ratio of one adult to each child. Families were very cohesive, and marriages were stable. Families worked in relatives' businesses and got help from the extended family. Both parents often worked, and relatives babysat.

Education was highly valued, and families sought out neighborhoods with the best schools possible, sometimes using false addresses to get into another district. In high school years, children were encouraged to apply to good schools outside the neighborhood. Education was stressed as the main path to better lives, and youth saw academic success as a way of repaying parents for all the sacrifices they made to give their children improved lives. As a favorably viewed ethnic group, youth reported their rule-breaking was sometimes overlooked, and they were given many opportunities because the group was assumed to be bright.

Even though parents were not highly educated, their children had high levels of academic achievement.[168] Only three, or 1.6 percent of those aged twenty-two to thirty-two, were high school dropouts, and 75 percent were enrolled in a four-year college or had a B.A. degree. Pursuing education was the primary focus, and the group was less likely to form families and have children than any other group so that at age thirty-two, they had the fewest children.

As American citizens, it was easy for Puerto Rican families to come to this country, return home, and come again so there was less focus on organizing support for a difficult change. About half of the Puerto Rican youth grew up in families with two parents but about 40 percent of the marriages resulted in separation or divorce; almost half grew up in families with a single parent. Because married women often did not work and many parents were single parents, few Puerto Rican youth had the financial resources of two working parents. Parents experienced severe economic stress and racial and class discrimination that forced them to live in the poorest neighborhoods with the greatest dangers and risks of violence and drugs.

There was not a tight and cohesive family to support single mothers who had only themselves and friends for support. Mothers kept children close to them, wanting them to go to neighborhood schools even if the schools were not adequate. Going to poor schools where they were often stereotyped as poor students, many youth lost interest. Local parochial schools were the usual alternative.

Puerto Rican parents had limited education, and they did not see education as the main path to success. Though Puerto Rican parents had the same educational levels as mainland Chinese parents did, their children had lower aspirations than those of Chinese youth. About 25 percent of Puerto Rican youth dropped out of high school, and even 25 percent of children of college-educated mothers dropped out; only 25 percent were enrolled in four-year colleges.

Children were valued, and Puerto Rican youth tended to start families early. One- sixth of the sample were single parents. While it is possible to pursue an education while raising children, it is more difficult, and fewer youth get education beyond high school, limiting them to less stable jobs. Early child bearing started a process of unstable, poorly paid jobs that was similar to that of their parents.

In immigrant youths' paths to adulthood, three family factors played a role in children's successful outcomes: (1) more adults to support fewer children, (2) family's having high educational aspirations for children and encouraging education, and (3) parents' helping children gain access to the best educational opportunities available, seeking out extra services and supportive individuals.

Even if youth have fully formed identities, experiences in educational and job settings can trigger further identity exploration. Experiencing stereotyping or discrimination can stimulate further thoughts about who one is and what being part of your group means. This process can occur throughout the lifespan.

General Parenting Strategies for the Transition Period

While theory and research have traditionally emphasized the importance of separation from the family, current work indicates that whatever the path to adulthood, positive attachments to parents, parents' warmth, understanding, resources, and all forms of support ease the way.[169]

In addition to providing positive support, the main task of this period is to form a new balance in the parent-child relationship to meet children's growing autonomy.[170] Though they rely on parents' assistance, children want to be treated as independent adults.

Negotiating the Issues of Growing Autonomy

Issues range from small ones like whether a college child has a curfew on vacations to large ones like whether children can live at home when they are not going to school or working or whether parents can have access to information about college behavior and problems.

Each issue has to be negotiated on its own merits and on the needs and maturity level of the child as well as parents' needs. As we have seen, some children need additional emotional and family support as they leave high school. Other children eagerly enter independent activities at college, and then become distressed and need additional help. Several universities document increases in the number of students reporting depression, anxiety, learning disabilities, and attention problems.[171] Columbia University reported a 40 percent increase in the number of students coming to the Counseling Center between 1994 and 2002. In addition, alcohol and drug use have increased, with 1,400 college students dying each year from alcohol-related accidents, including alcohol poisoning and car accidents.[172] As in late adolescence, parents provide role models of a healthy lifestyle and help college students get professional assistance as needed.

Whatever the issue, parents, as in all previous stages, listen calmly and use mutual problem-solving strategies to give information and work together with children to arrive at mutually agreeable solutions. Children may be surprised that in this stage, parents' needs are consistently given equal weight to children's when in the past children's needs may have been given greater weight at times because they were still in the process of developing.

THE ACCORDION FAMILY

Around the world, young people who would have left home and started families three decades ago are continuing to live at home or return there after schooling.[173] In some countries like Italy, this results from an economy that does not provide stable full-time work to support independent living. In the United States, extended periods of education or saving for return to education trigger the return home. For some, low-wage jobs make living at home more affordable for the young person and for the parent who needs the income.

Many parents like having their adult children at home because they enjoy their company and they do not have to supervise or monitor them. To get the best from this living arrangement, parents and children need to use the problem-solving methods just detailed so that young people use adult behaviors and share responsibilities with their parents in ways that make sense for each family.

MAIN POINTS

In this period, late adolescents

- reach sexual maturity
- learn about healthy sexual activities, engage in sexual activity, and many have their first sexual intercourse
- think more abstractly but in situations of emotional excitement or under the influence of peers, they can make risky decisions
- get excited at school when permitted active participation and respect
- grow in competence and confidence when they engage in a broad variety of activities
- are likely to become depressed or develop problems such as alcohol abuse if stress is high
- are fearful of experiencing discrimination because of personal or ethnic qualities
- work in large numbers and can gain skills if the work environment is favorable

When late adolescents consider themselves, they

- describe themselves in psychological terms and, through introspection, begin to see patterns in their behavior
- need support from family and community
- reveal gender differences in their self-descriptions, with boys seeing themselves as more daring, logical, and calm than girls, and girls seeing themselves as more attuned to people and more emotionally reactive than boys

Peers

- are major sources of support and companionship and are sought out in times of trouble

- have dating relationships that are often intense but short-lived
- learn to negotiate and resolve problems without ending relationships

Parents

- continue their commitment to children by monitoring, supervising, and enforcing rules, yet at the same time supporting and accepting children's individuality
- serve as consultants and provide factual information on topics of importance to teens
- share more power in decision making with teens so that teens can be more self-governing in the context of warm family relationships and so they can separate with a sense of well-being

Parents' reactions to their children's growth

- stimulate their own growth as parents often rediscover and rework feelings and conflicts from their childhoods
- often stimulate parents to find new possibilities in their own lives
- may bring parents closer to each other

Problems discussed center on

- eating problems
- substance use/abuse
- aggression
- school problems
- depression
- peer relationships
- all point to the importance of warm, supportive relationships with parents to stimulate competent behaviors and protect against high-risk behaviors

Joys include

- observing increasing social maturity and closeness with friends
- enjoying greater personal freedom
- seeing altruistic behavior develop
- watching adult traits emerge

Criteria for adulthood include being

- over eighteen
- financially and psychologically self-sustaining
- taking on adult roles of parent and worker

Paths to adulthood

- include some combination of schooling, work, independent living, romantic relationship, and rearing children
- are termed: Fast Starters, Parents without Careers, Educated Partners, Educated Singles, Working Singles, and Slow Starters

- are similar in youths from immigrant families
- require more support for youths who have received special services
- achieve similar levels of adult status for youth who have had chronic physical illness
- go more smoothly when parents provide emotional, social, informational, and financial support

Positive relationships are promoted

- when parents and children recognize children are adults
- when parents emphasize positive communications, win-win solutions, and doing enjoyable activities together to increase family solidarity

EXERCISES

1. Break into small groups; discuss how parents can help their teenagers get the information that so many teens want about pregnancy, STDs, and contraception availability. List suggestions for parents in short pamphlet.

2. Interview parents about their experience during adolescence and the transition to adulthood. Did they grow up in a city or small town? How much freedom were they allowed? What were the rules for them? What stresses did adolescents at that time face? Whom did they go to for support? How did their parents discipline them? How long did they live at home? Return to class and break into small groups; discuss the ways that parents' experiences differ from those of adolescents of today and report to the class on four major differences.

3. In small groups, describe the most effective discipline techniques parents can use with teens and write ten suggestions for parents of adolescents.

4. Describe three ways you or your friends used to reduce stress as an adolescent. Work in small groups to compile a list of the ten most popular ways to reduce stress, and write a booklet outlining them for teens.

5. If you were a parent of two teenage children, what actions would you take so that your children would have a smooth transition to adulthood?

ADDITIONAL READINGS

Benson, Peter L. *Sparks: How Parents Can Help Ignite the Hidden Strengths of Teenagers.* San Francisco: Jossey-Bass, 2008.

Damon, William. *The Path to Purpose: Helping Our Children Find Their Calling in Life.* New York: Free Press, 2008.

Lerner, Richard M., with Israeloff, Roberta. *The Good Teen: Rescuing Adolescence from the Myths of the Storm and Stress Years.* New York: Stonesong Press, 2007.

Newman, Katherine. *The Accordion Family: Boomerang Kids, Anxious Parents, and the Private Toll of Global Competition.* Boston: Beacon Press, 2012.

Rios, Victor. *Street Life: Poverty, Gangs, and a Ph.D.* California: Five Rivers Press, 2011.

CHAPTER

12

Parenting and Working

CHAPTER TOPICS

In this chapter, you will learn about:

- International perspective on parenting and working.

- Diversity in work-parenting patterns and struggles parents experience.

- The spillover of work to family life and family life to work and how families deal with it.

- Parenting strategies to promote children's growth and parents' well being.

- Types of day care and its effects on children.

- Ways to help working families.

Test Your Knowledge: Fact or Fiction (True/False)

1. Children in dual-earner families report lack of time with parents as the source of greatest stress for them.
2. In a survey, children report employed mothers and fathers as very good at controlling their tempers when children do something wrong.
3. Research shows that, in predicting children's competence, parenting matters much more than day care.
4. Early adolescents are old enough to engage in self-care without negative consequences.
5. The fees for good-quality day care are not very different from fees for mediocre care.

Combining working and parenting is a major challenge for today's men and women. The majority of mothers work from the time their children are infants, and more fathers than ever before are involved in child care. How do parents solve the problems that arise in integrating work and family lives? How do they find child care that promotes children's development? How do they adjust routines to enhance the quality of time they spend with children? How do they adapt to their many responsibilities yet maintain a sense of well-being?

Today, most parents in our society work. In 2009, 77 percent of married mothers with children ages six to eighteen were employed, and 62 percent of married mothers with children under six. The comparable employment figure for single mothers with children six to eighteen was 79 percent and with children under six, 68 percent.[1] About 74 percent of all working mothers work full-time, defined as thirty-five hours or more per week, and 71 percent of mothers with children under six work full-time.[2] In 2009, 94 percent of fathers living with their children were employed, 94 percent, full-time.[3]

In this chapter, we look at how men and women integrate working and parenting, parenting strategies that promote children's development, the day care options available when parents work, the impact of day care on children, and ways parents care for themselves as they raise the next generation.

INTERNATIONAL PERSPECTIVE ON PARENTING AND WORKING

We saw in Chapter 5 that American mothers and fathers have longer hours of work outside and inside the home than parents in other countries.[4] To better understand the challenges facing American working parents, let us review workplace policies that enable parents both to work and to take care of their children. Three major policies can help parents: parental leave at the birth or adoption of a child, leave when children and family members are sick or have educational needs, and childcare.

Benefits Available for Parents

We look here at paid leaves available to parents and to subsidies for childcare and education.

Parental leave at the birth or adoption of a child enables parents to help babies settle into regular sleeping, waking, and eating schedules and benefits both parents and babies.[5] Maternal leaves are associated with increases in breastfeeding that, in turn, decreases infant mortality, sudden death syndrome, and infections, protecting infants and promoting their long-term health. Extended time with babies also decreases mothers' symptoms of postpartum depression.

A 2006 survey of 173 countries revealed all offer paid maternal leave except the United States, Papua New Guinea, Liberia, and Swaziland, and many offer paid paternal leave as well.[6] The 1993 Family and Medical Leave Act (FMLA), under certain conditions, provides American parents with up to twelve weeks of job-protected, unpaid leave in a twelve-month period; leave can be used intermittently, with medical insurance protection, for care of a child at birth or adoption or for medical care for oneself or a family member. The restrictions are that the employee has to have worked at least 1,250 hours in the previous year in a company with fifty or more employees. Several states have passed laws providing additional benefits, e.g., California's Paid Family Leave Insurance Act (PFLI), financed by employee-paid payroll tax, authorizes 55 percent of salary for six weeks with a cap of $987.00 per week and extends benefits to part-time employees and those working in small companies. It does not protect jobs or medical insurance.

Many states have passed laws enabling parents to use their own sick leave to attend to children's preventive, acute, and chronic medical care or to take care of children when they are ill, but only about 47 percent of parents have access to such help.[7] The FMLA provides unpaid leave with job protection, but most parents cannot go without pay to take a child for a medical appointment. Most industrialized countries with the exception of Finland, Switzerland, and the United Kingdom provide paid leave for such health care.

Parents need time off to consult with children's schools and teachers, especially if there is a problem, but provisions depend on the policies of individual companies that sometimes permit the use of vacation time for such activities.

Childhood care by someone other than the mother is required by about 90 percent of the children of employed mothers; for 16 percent, the other caregiver is the father, and 25 percent of children have multiple caregiving arrangements that we discuss later.[8] Juggling these arrangements to provide such care and paying for it are major challenges for working parents of young children, especially single parents who pay twice as high a proportion of income on child care as married parents. The costs of care are such a high percentage of family income that 63 percent of families in one survey rely on free relative care.

The government offers limited help to families. Low-income families may get subsidized care through the federal Child Care Development Fund (CCDF) that provides help to 20 percent of income-eligible children and from block grants to states that can use the money for care and for preschool programs.[9] In addition, low-income children have access to Head Start preschool programs, which are not fully funded so many who qualify are not enrolled in preschool programs. The government provides some aid to higher income families who can set money aside in pre-tax dollars or can ask for a Child and Dependent Care tax credit.

Simple description of what other countries offer is difficult because early childhood care and education are linked sometimes to long maternal leaves so child-care is not necessary before entering the school system at age three. Anglo-Saxon countries like the United Kingdom, Ireland, and Canada, along with Switzerland, resemble the United States and rely predominantly on private care. But still during the first three years of life, the United States, as a country, invests the lowest percentage of Gross Domestic Product (GDP) in care and has the lowest percentage of children in formal care by age five so that many children do not receive any preschool education deemed so important for later learning.

When child-care and educational services are available, single mothers return to work more quickly, and low-income children in high-quality preschools enter school better prepared.

Reasons for Current Benefits

When Congress debated the FMLA act in 1993, arguments against subsidizing parental leave at birth and for children's medical care centered on the costs of such benefits for businesses and the economy in general. If companies had to provide such benefits, they would be less competitive with other countries, and the costs would decrease the number of employees that could be hired, thus increasing unemployment.[10]

Yet an analysis of data from the World Economic Forum revealed that all of the fifteen most highly competitive countries like Japan, Germany, and Canada as well as China and India provide paid maternal leave except the United States, and most provide paternal leave as well.[11] All but four of the most competitive countries also paid for sick leave to care for family members' illnesses. An analysis of the thirteen countries with the lowest unemployment rates in the world revealed all offer paid maternal leave at birth except the United States, and eight of the thirteen pay leave to manage children's health-care needs. So, data analyses do not support fears about the burdens of such programs on businesses and the economy.

DIVERSITY IN WORK-FAMILY PATTERNS

Economic and social changes since the 1970s have created diversity in family work patterns that require many solutions to help parents as no one solution can help all parents.[12]

First, the increasing number of mothers' entering the workforce, especially mothers of children under six, has increased fathers' participation in child care and household activities so now, both parents typically have two jobs with mothers' spending slightly more time at home in child care and fathers' spending slightly more time in paid employment, but both working more than ten hours per weekday.

Second, at the same time, there has been a marked increase in the percentage of children living in single parent homes because of divorce and the sizeable number of children, now 40 percent, born to unmarried mothers. Thus, one parent has responsibility for what two parents often feel pressured to accomplish.

Third, at the same time, the nature of work has changed in this country. The number of semi-skilled and skilled jobs that can support a family has declined, and part-time, temporary jobs without benefits have increased along with jobs at nonstandard evening and night shifts. An increasing number of jobs require education and technological skills. But single mothers, who must work to support their children, on average have less education; 16 percent do not have a high school degree and 30 percent have only a high school degree.[13] So they are eligible for less skilled jobs that lack stability, provide fewer benefits like maternal and sick leave, and require nonstandard hours of work. These single mothers need more stable, steady jobs that provide enough income and benefits to rear children.

Another group of parents obtained more education, started good-paying jobs with benefits but longer hours, and married later. When they have children, they experience a time famine and want fewer working hours. So their challenge is to manage satisfying, demanding jobs while meeting their families' needs.

A fourth social change that affects families is our lengthening lifespans, increasing the number of older parents and relatives who require care at the same time parents are rearing children. Parents with these responsibilities have an additional layer of stress.

So, while some families need more hours of stable work in standard hours, other families want more restricted work hours.

A CONCEPTUAL FRAMEWORK FOR UNDERSTANDING THE IMPACTS OF WORK, FAMILY, AND COMMUNITY ON PARENTS AND CHILDREN

Drawing on Urie Bronfenbrenner's bioecological systems theory (see Chapter 3), Patricia Voydanoff has developed a broad framework for understanding the ways that experiences in the domains of work, family life, and the community influence parents' and children's functioning and well-being.[14]

She describes the microsystem level as the daily, direct interactions parents have in each of these areas—work, family, and community. She also describes the meso-system level as the interrelationships between the areas—the mesosystems of work–family, work–community, family–community, and work–family–community. We see the interrelationships of the areas in this example: the shift from a manufacturing economy to a technology-information-based economy requires workers to have more education, so workers spend more time in school, start stable work later, marry later, and have children later.[15] So work changes impact family life.

Conversely, family life influences work participation. When people live longer and require more care at the end of life, workers reduce their work hours and community participation to care for aging family members.

Within each domain, demands/strains and resources/supports affect parents' performance in that area and their general feelings of satisfaction and well-being. Table 12-1 presents Voydanoff's general framework.

The term "fit" describes the relationship between the demands and the resources to carry out the tasks in a domain. The fit is positive when parents have the abilities and resources to manage the demands and perform at work or at home, and feel good about their performance. Stress occurs when the demands overwhelm the person's abilities and resources to function in that area. The fit between two domains (e.g., work–family fit) results from the combination of the demands and resources within both domains. Two forms of action are possible to attain a positive fit: decrease the demands or increase the resources to meet the demands. For example, when work demands increase for a period of time, extended relatives can step in and do household chores.

Positive Spillover from Work and Community to Family

In addition to providing the resources of income, health insurance, and dependent care credits for rearing families, work binds men more closely to families, making marriages more likely and ongoing contact with children more likely if parents separate.[16] In a cyclical process, being married strengthens men's ties to work and increases the hours they work. Increasing work hours for new, low-income mothers improves their moods and decreases depressive symptoms provided the work is not stressful.[17]

Community programs also contribute to parents' well-being, providing child-care subsidies that enable low-income urban mothers to enter the workforce and

■ **TABLE 12-1**

CONCEPTUAL FRAMEWORK FOR UNDERSTANDING RELATIONSHIPS
BETWEEN WORK, FAMILY, AND COMMUNITY*

	Work	**Family**	**Community**
Time Demands	Scheduled Hours	Child-care Time	Volunteer Time
	Overtime Hours	Spouse Time	Friends
	Nonstandard Work Times	Extended Family Time	
		Household Work	
Demands/Stresses	Job Demands	Marital Conflict	Neighborhood Problems
	Work Conflicts	Children's Problems	
	Job Insecurity	Caregiver Strain	Friend Problems
	Overnight Travel	Unfair Housework	
	Long commute		
Resources/ Supports	Salary	Spouse Salary	Recreational Programs
	Benefit/Health Care	Positive Spouse Relationship	Safe Neighborhoods
	Increasing Skills	Extended Family Help	Friend Help
	Psychological/ Social Support	Positive Feelings Re Self	Positive Feelings Re Self
	Positive Feelings Re Self		
Boundary-Spanning Supports	Flexible Work	Benefits from Spouse Work	Child-care After-School Programs
	Dependent Care		

*Adapted from: Patricia Voydanoff, *Work, Family, Community: Exploring Interconnections*
(New York: Psychology Press, 2007).

enable them to comply with employer needs for additional work hours.[18] Mothers
have fewer scheduling problems, are able to put in overtime, and earn more money.
Community aid also provides programs and services for elder care.

   Work policies that allow parents to work flexible hours and also permit employees to work from home reduce stress that many employees experience. A survey
of International Business Machine (IBM) technological employees in seventy-five
countries around the world revealed that flexible hours and working at home were
beneficial in all countries, regardless of the cultural orientation of the country—
collectivist or individualistic—developing or developed.[19] Establishing work policies that enable parents to have time off during the day to meet family doctor and
school appointments increases parents' performance and well-being at home and

also at work. Even if parents do not use workplace flexible benefits, the perception of having them increases job and family satisfaction.

About 77 percent of parents report that they often or very often feel successful at work. Success is related to having time to get work done but more importantly to being able to focus on work without interruptions, being able to complete a task before getting another job to do.[20] Feeling successful at work is related to autonomy in jobs, positive relationships with coworkers, and feeling the job is meaningful.

Parents' work behavior affects children's behavior and moods. When fathers are psychologically engaged in work but are available at home, and when mothers have control of their work and feel confident, their children are more likely to be described as socially and academically competent in kindergarten.[21] Adolescents whose single mothers entered the labor force and got and kept a good job that paid a living wage for two years reported feelings of mastery and self-esteem while adolescents whose mothers had unstable unemployment for that period had an increased risk of school dropout and declines in well-being.[22]

Parents who felt positive spillover from work to home (about a third of the parents in one study)[23] were those who (1) were married, (2) had jobs that demanded more days per week, (3) experienced less stress and more autonomy at work, (4) had more supportive supervisors and coworkers, (5) had more parental support from family and friends, and (6) felt they were raising their children as they wanted.

Positive Spillover from Home to Work

About 70 percent of parents with children under age eighteen say that their positive feelings about their children often or very often carry over to work, and about one-third say they often or very often have more energy on the job because of their children.[24] The parents who are more likely to have positive spillover from home to work are those who (1) are fathers, (2) put a higher priority on family life, (3) feel they have support for doing their work—they have day care they trust and parental support at times of difficulty, (4) work more days per week but feel fewer stresses and strains at work, (5) have better-quality jobs with more autonomy and learning opportunities, and (6) have more workplace support from coworkers.

Negative Spillover from Work to Home

Negative spillover comes from job demands and working conditions and affects parent-child relationships.

Sources of Work Stress for Parents Sixty-nine percent of parents in one survey reported that they feel a moderate or large amount of work stress, and 55 percent say they feel a moderate or large amount of frustration at work.[25] Stress appears to be related to job demands—working more hours per day and more days per week, having to take work home, having to travel more, feeling pressured to complete work in short periods of time with little control of how it is done, and feeling that the job is meaningless.

Frustration has similar origins but is more related to the daily work schedule than to the total amount of time worked. Inability to focus, feeling unable to make decisions, and feeling that the job entails no learning also increase frustration.

Parents who were most likely to experience negative spillover from work to home were those who (1) put a higher priority on work than family, (2) were more likely to be managers or professionals with relatively large responsibilities at work, (3) had demanding jobs that were difficult to complete on time, (4) had jobs that were too stimulating or not stimulating enough, (5) had less parenting support than did those who did not feel stress, and (6) did not feel support from coworkers or supervisors.[26]

Effects on Family Life and Parenting   Negative working conditions and negative interactions can have fleeting and long-term effects on family life. When mothers of preschoolers had stressful workdays, they were more withdrawn and less attentive when they picked up their children, less caring and loving with them.[27] Children tried to please mothers and engage them in activity but sometimes seemed less happy. Job stress was most upsetting to women who already had feelings of anxiety and depression.

When husbands and wives have negative social interactions at work, they both report greater anger in marital interactions and greater withdrawal.[28] Increased workload also predicted wives' increased marital anger and their withdrawal.

Several studies have focused on longer-term effects of parents' work hours on parenting and children's behavior. An economy in which businesses operate around the clock creates many jobs outside the standard 9 to 5 hours. When parents work outside the standard hours (evenings, nights, and/or weekends), they report greater emotional distress and less effective parenting than parents who work standard hours.[29] Children, age two to eleven, whose parents work nonstandard hours show greater behavioral difficulties as measured by the Children's Behavior Check List. The differences were greatest between families in which both parents worked standard and both parents worked nonstandard hours, but even having one parent working nonstandard hours predicted greater parental distress, less effective parenting, and children's behavioral difficulties.

When mothers work evenings and nights, children's reading scores are lower, and when fathers work night shifts, math scores are lower. The fact that children of mothers with rotating shifts do well academically suggests that ongoing nonstandard hours makes it very difficult to know and monitor children's progress.[30] Nonstandard hours of work of low income single mothers predicted a decrease in children's school performance and an increase in their aggressive and noncompliant behaviors.[31] In another study of single mothers, the length of their commute time predicted children's anxiety and nervousness.[32]

Negative Spillover from Family to Work

Despite the demands family activities make on parents, parents feel much less stress in caring for children than they do at work.[33] Only 6 percent of parents say they feel a great deal of stress in caring for children, and an additional 36 percent say they feel a moderate amount of stress. By comparison, 24 percent experience a large amount of stress at work, and 45 percent experience a moderate amount.

Both parents felt stress at work when daughters lacked after-school supervision.[34] Parents from the ages of twenty-five to fifty-four reported the same levels of negative spillover from home to work, but the sources of stress changed with age.[35] Younger parents with children under age eighteen, those who were unmarried or divorced and lacked partner support, and older parents who were caring for aging parents all reported negative spillover from home to work.

Families with marked stress are the sandwich generation, those caring for dependent children and elder parents. A national survey revealed that between 10 and 13 percent of families fell into that category, with wives' spending 9.5 hours weekly and husbands' 7.5 on care with elder parents in addition to their child-care responsibilities.[36] The study revealed that it was not the objective factors such as the hours worked or the number of children or elders being cared for that predicted parents' stress at home and at work, but subjective feelings of negative reactivity, the quality of the job role, and for women their satisfaction with their care of children that predicted their feelings of depression and dissatisfaction with their overall role performance.

While women reported more depressive symptoms and greater negative spillover to work than their husbands, they also reported greater positive spillover from family to work and feelings of higher job quality. Wives, as in other studies, were more likely than husbands to adjust work to meet family demands—reduce hours, take paid leave for appointments—and report poorer work performance.[37] Both men and women still reported great satisfaction in being able to care for their elder parents at that stage of life.

Resilience in the Sandwich Generation

Couples in the sandwich generation used many ways of coping to prevent stress: they decreased the demands in their lives and increased the resources to support them.[38] At work, they drew on benefits such as dependent care, family medical leave that gave them time off, and flexible work schedules to decrease demands on their time. They drew on the support of friends and community programs like child and elder care or home services to increase resources for handling increased demands on their time.

The key finding of the study was the centrality of spousal support in coping with all the demands and the stress. When wives and husbands were positive and supportive of each other, parents not only felt more life satisfaction and self-satisfaction in their overall role performance, but they adopted the positive parent's coping strategies, felt more comfortable, and were more effective in functioning. A single parent has to build a positive support system with a friend or relative.

Parents' most frequent emotional and cognitive coping strategies are listed in Table 12-2. Structuring priorities and limiting activities reduce demands. Maintaining positive moods by focusing on the positive aspects of life and seeking outside support increase parental resources. While some couples coped by limiting their social activities, their withdrawal predicted lower work performance and decreased well-being.

BOX 12-1
FIRST PERSON NARRATIVE

Michael Chabon,* Michael Lewis,** and Ayelet Waldman*** are writers who have written memoirs about their personal experiences in combining working at home and parenting and their insights about the role of parenthood in one's life. Waldman and Chabon are married to each other, rearing four children together. Lewis is an at-home father rearing three children with his wife. Both Chabon and Lewis comment on the excessive praise they get because they are doing the things like going to the grocery store or attending an exercise group with their child, things women do routinely, for which they never receive praise.

In his description of caring for his infant son in a hospital, Lewis makes an important point: It is through providing physical care for an infant that one becomes deeply attached.

Waldman, a lawyer before she became a full-time writer, describes the conflicts she has experienced combining work and parenting. Waldman's and Chabon's books are interesting to read together because they both describe a common family life from the perspectives of their different roles and personal points of view.

All three authors describe how parenting has changed them as individuals and the interaction between work and family lives. Each book explains how the roles of parent and worker inform each other.

*Michael Chabon, *Manhood for Amateurs: The Pleasures and Regrets of a Husband, Father, and Son* (New York: Harper, 2009).
**Michael Lewis, *Home Game: An Accidental Guide to Fatherhood* (New York: Norton, 2009).
***Ayelet Waldman, *Bad Mother: A Chronicle of Maternal Crimes, Minor Calamities and Occasional Moments of Grace* (New York: Anchor, 2010).

■ T A B L E 12-2
COPING STRATEGIES WHEN CARING FOR CHILDREN AND OLDER PARENTS*

Emotional Strategies Frequently Used by Husbands and Wives

1. I focus on the many good things I have.
2. I try and find humor in the situation.
3. I get moral support and comfort from others.
4. I try to realize that I can't do it all, and it's okay.

Cognitive-Behavioral Strategies Frequently Used by Husbands and Wives

1. I prioritize and do the things that are most necessary.
2. I plan how I'm going to use my time and energy.
3. I take on tasks if no one else is capable or available.
4. I limit my volunteer work.

*Adapted from: Margaret B. Neal and Leslie B. Hammer, *Working Couples Caring for Children and Aging Parents: Effects on Work and Well-Being* (Mahwah, NJ: Erlbaum, 2007), 330–332.

WORKING AND PATTERNS OF FAMILY INTERACTIONS

This section focuses on relationships between parents and children when parents work.

Patterns of Daily Interactions

Parents' levels of satisfaction and stress with work and family rest heavily on how well parents feel they are meeting children's needs.[39] Parents feel good about their parenting when they spend time eating meals, doing homework, and playing with their children. Parents' time diaries over a period from 1965 to 2001 reveal both mothers and fathers are spending more time with children than they did in 1965 despite their increasing participation in work.[40]

Employed parents not only spend time with children, but they interact more intensely with them when they are at home even though they are multitasking about 50 percent of the time at home.[41] Parents watch TV with children while folding laundry, listen to reports about school while preparing dinner, and plan

Employed parents are multitasking about 50 percent of their time at home.

weekend activities on the way to school. Children are included in parents' leisure activities that have become family activities. Parents have decreased time with each other, with friends, and in civic activities. So children of employed parents have more social interactions with peers at day care and more interactive relationships with parents when at home.

Videotaped observations in the homes of dual-earner families with two or more children reveal patterns of reunioning and maintaining physical proximity on weekday afternoons from 3:00 P.M. until the family goes to bed.[42] Only about one-third of parent-child reunions occur at home; many take place at day cares or schools, but one suspects the qualities of reunions there may be similar to those at home. Analyses of the first two minutes after the reunion indicated that most of the interaction between parents and children took place within the first thirty seconds of the encounter so parents have to take advantage of the brief opportunity for connection. Reunions were typically warm and positive with hugs and smiles, and all parents received a warm greeting from at least one child when he or she returned home.

Other response categories included: information reports, logistic requests and behaviors, distraction, and negative behavior like anger. In addition to positive responses to both parents, children were more likely to give mothers information and make requests to do or get something, and to respond to fathers' homecoming with distraction. Children rarely displayed negative behaviors to either parent at times of reunion. Mothers and fathers usually greeted each other positively, exchanging information, but in one-third of couple reunions, distraction was observed. As with children, negative behaviors were rare in the reunion.

Table 12-3 describes the physical proximity of family members during weekday afternoons and evenings. Most striking are the facts that time alone is the most frequent activity for all family members, though mothers spent an almost equal amount of time with one child, and that the family were rarely together as a group. Limited family interactions reinforce the concerns parents expressed in Chapter 6 that although family members were at home together, they were not relating to each other. Couples rarely interacted with each other without children, even though couples report discussing events of the day with each other as very relaxing.

The authors of the study note that although parents want very much to spend quality time with children, they ignore opportunities like those presented at times

■ **T A B L E 12-3**
MEDIAN PERCENTAGE OF TIME FAMILY MEMBERS OBSERVED
WITH EACH OTHER*

Father alone	34	Parents + 1 child	24
Child alone	34	Father + 1 child	22
Mother alone	29	Whole family	14
Mother + 1 child	27	Parents alone	8

*Adapted from: Belinda Campos, Anthony P. Graesch, Rena Repetti, Thomas Bradbury, and Elinor Ochs, "Opportunity for Interaction? A Naturalistic Observation Study of Dual-Earner Families after Work and School," *Journal of Family Psychology* 23 (2009): 798–807.

of reunions or everyday routines to deepen their relationships with children by talking to children about their activities to better understand their lives. Parents also fail to take time to be with each other and talk about their activities.

Special Demands on Single Parents

Most studies of single parents' work patterns and parenting focus on single mothers. Mothers' time diaries show that more single mothers work than married mothers, and they have less time in all activities with children than married parents, but they rated these activities as more enjoyable and satisfying than married parents.[43]

Time diaries of low-income mothers in Chicago, about two-thirds of whom were employed, describe the many responsibilities these working women have and how they meet them with very limited resources.[44] Their activities are concentrated in three areas: child care, work, and transportation. Unlike most middle-class parents who have cars, many low-income mothers depend on public transportation and spend several hours a day getting children to school and day care and themselves to work. One woman spent almost seven hours getting her two sons to a Catholic school, then her daughter to day care, and then herself to work. Another mother who worked an evening shift in a suburban package-loading company waited two to three hours for the first morning bus back to her home in the city three days a week.

These women also cobble together day care arrangements for children as almost two-thirds used two or more caregivers besides themselves, frequently their own mothers. As noted earlier, employed mothers often rely on free relative care because they cannot afford the fees. Older children often provide caregiving for their younger siblings, getting them to school and caring for them after school. They cannot participate in school activities and often have less time for schoolwork so their grades suffer.

Mothers use several strategies to manage the many demands on their time. First, they stagger their obligations. They decide what is most important and carry out additional responsibilities after their main obligation. For example, they focus on the family's health and well-being and organize employment around that, working an evening or a night shift so they can care for children during the day and leave children with a grandparent for the night. Or they postpone getting additional education for work so they can focus on helping children with schoolwork in the evenings.

Second, they use the same strategies all parents use: they expand their resources to meet the demands. They look for a family member or a friend to take care of a sick child or one suspended from school for a week. Mothers also look beyond their immediate neighborhoods for resources to help their families, looking for better schools outside their districts or stores with better products at better prices. Third, they eliminate obligations that are not essential at that time; for example, they put their own needs for rest and sleep at the bottom of the list of things to do.

The lives of low-income working mothers would be less burdened if public agencies where they sometimes go to obtain school vouchers and child-care subsidies were open beyond the 9 to 5 working hours.[45] Community services could help these women by providing reliable transportation, vouchers for all who are eligible for preschool programs, day care subsidies, housing assistance, and health care for adults that also includes dental and eye care, and costs of books and classes for work advancement. Considering mothers' return to school as work activity and paying them accordingly would help these mothers get skills for better paying, more stable work in standard working hours. Having such employment would help children of these mothers as they would benefit from more stable lives.

Agreements and Divergences in Children's and Parents' Perceptions of Parents' Work

Ellen Galinsky, president of the Families and Work Institute, concerned that children's opinions have not been included in the discussions of the effects of parents' work on children and family life, interviewed a representative sample of 605 employed parents with children under age eighteen and surveyed a representative sample of 1,023 third- to twelfth-grade children.[46]

Both children and parents have positive views of working parents. Children rate nonemployed fathers lower than employed fathers in the areas of (1) making their children feel important and loved, and (2) participating in important events in their children's lives. Children tended to give parents higher grades when the family was seen as financially secure.

Seventy-four percent of children felt mothers were very successful in managing work and family life, and 67 percent of children felt fathers were very successful. As shown in Table 12-4, parents received high marks for making children feel important and loved, being understanding, appreciating children, and being there for conversation. Although mothers were overwhelmingly seen as the parent who was there for children at times of sickness, more frequently involved than fathers in school matters, and someone children could go to when upset, the ratings for fathers on other qualities were similar to those given to mothers. Fathers were seen as being appreciative of who the child really was, spending time in conversation, and controlling their temper with the child as well as the mother did.

Parents gave themselves equally high marks in these areas. Children's ratings of parents were higher when they spent more time with parents and when the time with parents was not rushed. About 40 percent of mothers and children and 32 percent of fathers, however, felt that their time together was somewhat or very rushed.

Children were more satisfied with the amount of time parents spent with them than were parents. About 44 percent of mothers and 56 percent of fathers felt they spent too little time with their children, whereas only 28 percent of children felt mothers spent too little time, and 35 percent of children felt fathers spent too little time. The survey asked children to name one wish that would change how parents' working affected the family. Parents expected children to say they wanted more time with parents. Children, however, had three more-important wishes. They wished that parents earned more money, returned from work less stressed, and felt less tired.

Also, when asked if they worried about their parents, approximately one-third of children aged eight to eighteen said that they often or very often worried about their parents, and another third said they sometimes worried. So, about two-thirds

■ **T A B L E 12-4**
STUDENTS'* LETTER GRADES FOR PARENTS' BEHAVIORS

| Letter Grade | A | | B | | C | | D | | E | |
Parents' Behavior	M**	F***	M	F	M	F	M	F	M	F
Being there for me when I'm sick	85	58	8	20	4	12	2	7	1	3
Appreciating me for who I am	72	69	15	16	6	8	4	5	3	2
Making me feel loved for who I am	72	66	16	18	8	9	4	4	1	2
Attending important events in my life	69	60	18	20	7	12	3	4	3	5
Being someone I can go to when I'm upset	57	48	18	19	11	14	6	8	8	10
Being involved in what's happening to me at school	55	45	22	24	11	15	7	10	5	6
Spending time talking to me	48	47	31	25	12	16	5	8	4	4
Controlling their temper when I do something wrong	28	31	31	28	19	18	11	11	11	12

*Students in third through twelfth grades.
**M indicates percentage of students giving mother that grade.
***F indicates percentage of students giving father that grade.
From: Ellen Galinsky, *Ask the Children: What America's Children Really Think about Working Parents* (New York: Morrow, 1999).

of children worry about parents at least some of the time. Children said they worried because they were part of a caring family, but they also worried because they felt their parents had a lot of stress from work. Thirty percent of children aged twelve to eighteen said the worst thing about having working parents was that they were stressed out from work. One suspects that children wanted parents to earn more money so they would feel less stressed.

Furthermore, children saw their parents as less emotionally available to them than parents believed they were, and children were more concerned about parents' anger than parents were. Ninety-six percent of mothers and 90 percent of fathers gave themselves As and Bs for being emotionally available when their children were upset, but only 75 percent of children gave mothers As and Bs and 67 percent gave fathers As and Bs. Only 4 percent of mothers and 5.5 percent of fathers gave themselves Ds and Fs for controlling their tempers, whereas 22 percent of children gave mothers Ds and Fs, and 23 percent gave fathers Ds and Fs.

So parents are sometimes not aware of children's wishes and priorities. Children want parents to be happier and less stressed and available for them emotionally without being angry.

PARENTING STRATEGIES

Monitoring and supervising children's activities is a major parenting task. Although working parents are often not present after school, they can monitor by phone what school-age children do and make certain children engage in approved activities. Studies have found that parents in dual-earner families monitor as carefully as parents in single-earner families.[47] This is important because less-well-monitored boys have lower school grades and less skill in school-related activities, regardless of whether mothers are employed. Girls' behavior is not so clearly related to monitoring.[48]

As we noted in Chapter 10, parents' careful monitoring of their early adolescent boys and girls was related to a lack of externalizing problems such as disobeying and fighting. Careful monitoring counterbalanced the effects of living in an unsafe neighborhood and having a lot of unsupervised activities with peers, two other predictors of externalizing problems.[49]

Galinsky believes parents must consider the quality of their interactions with children.[50] Children want stress-free, focused time with parents. They want parents to be calm, free of anger, and emotionally available to them. Galinsky recommends parents spend time with children by hanging around, being available for conversation and casual play that supports children's interests. Parents improve relationships by listening to children and communicating their own feelings without irritation. Galinsky quotes a twelve-year-old:

> Listen. Listen to what your kids say, because you know, sometimes it's very important. And sometimes a kid can have a great idea and it could even affect you. Because, you know, kids are people. Kids have great ideas, as great as you, as great as ideas that adults have.[51]

Children want working parents to be emotionally available for conversation and casual activities.

Finally, Galinsky recommends that parents talk about their work: what they do and why they like it. Children often do not understand the positive aspects of their parents' work, so they have a limited view of the meaning of work in people's lives. In part, children may be so concerned about parents' stress because they hear mostly negative things about work. Children learn many indirect lessons about work from the way parents discuss their own strategies for accomplishing tasks and getting along with others.

Having more time, not feeling rushed, and focusing on children not only increased parents' feelings of satisfaction and success at home, but, according to parents' reports, their children had fewer problems with anxiety, depression, and inattention.

DAY CARE

As we will see, the context of day care—the child, the family, the setting for care—determines its influence on family life. Adults outside the family have always participated in child care because children require attentive care for an extended time. Thus, Michael Lamb and Lieselotte Ahnert remind us, "Nonparental care is a universal practice with a long history, not a dangerous innovation representing a major deviation from species-typical and species-appropriate patterns of child care."[52]

Patterns of Nonmaternal Care

In the United States where parents receive very limited, if any, paid parental leave at the time of a child's birth, most mothers return to work in the first year, and children enter some form of nonmaternal care. Several forms of care are available:

Relative care—fathers or grandparents living in the home care for the child, or relatives, such as grandparents, care for the child nearby.

Nonrelative family day care—care for infants and children in the home of a nonrelative.

Nonrelative center day care—provides appropriate care and stimulating activities for infants and children and may provide after-school care for children in the elementary grades.

After-school programs—provide supervised care for children in the elementary school years during after-school hours and vacations.

Self-care—care by the child.

Recent data for children under age five with employed mothers reveal that 50 percent are cared for by parents or other relatives, 34 percent in family day care homes, 22 percent in center-based programs, and 3 percent by a sitter at home. Patterns of care vary by the age of the child, with most parents of infants and toddlers preferring care with a relative or in a family day care.[53] As children get older, center-based care becomes the most frequent alternative to relative care.

While most children are in some form of supervised care after they enter school, 15 percent of six- to twelve-year-olds are in self-care on a regular basis, with self-care increasing as children get older—7 percent of children ages six to nine, 26 percent of children ages nine to twelve, and 47 percent of children age fourteen.[54]

Each form of care has advantages and possible drawbacks.[55] Relative care has the advantage that children have special ties to their caregivers and are in a familiar setting. The quality of parental care may be high but can vary if a parent has special stresses or needs, like sleep after working a night shift.

Substitute care at home is expensive but requires that the child adjust to only the new person who is available when the child is sick. As children get older, home care is often supplemented with nursery school attendance or other group activities so the child can be with peers.

Family day care—that is, care in the home of another family with other children—is often cheaper and more flexible than center care and provides the same activities of home care with a stable care provider, but may not be as stimulating. Family day care homes can be, but are not always, licensed. Caregivers who are part of a larger umbrella network can give higher-quality care than can untrained caregivers.

Day care centers provide care and stimulating activities. The parent whose child goes to a day care center is sure of having child care available every day—at some centers from 7:00 A.M. until 7:00 P.M. Many centers have credentialed personnel who have been trained to work with children, and many centers have play equipment and supplies not found in most home-care situations. All centers provide opportunities for contact with same-age children.

Older, better-educated mothers are more likely to have children in self-care, perhaps because they are more available by phone, live in safe neighborhoods, and children have activities and sports that are supervised.[56] Working-class parents and parents of different ethnic groups prefer to have children supervised.

Availability, Affordability, and Quality of Day Care

We have described the kinds of care possible, but how affordable and available are they?

In 2010 in all regions of the country, the average cost of full-time center-based care for an infant and a four-year-old exceeded the annual median rent payment in every state.[57] In dollar amounts, depending on the state, for full-time, center-based care, parents can pay as much as $18,000 for infants; $14,000, for four-year-olds; and $10,400 for school-age children; in family day care, $12,000 for infants, $11,000 for four-year-olds, and $9,000 for school-age children. As noted, families receive little governmental support in arranging child care.[58]

Quality of Care during Infancy and Early Childhood

Quality of care is the major determiner of the effects of nonparental child care on children, and is measured in two ways.[59] *Structural measures* look at the amount of teacher or caregiver training/experience, staff turnover, salaries, and recommended staff ratios. Currently the recommended ratios of adults to children are 1:3 for infants, 1:4 for toddlers, and 1:7 for preschoolers. The number of children recommended for groups is six in infancy, eight in toddlerhood, and fourteen in the preschool years.

Process *measures* examine two aspects of caregiving for children—that is, sensitive, responsive interactions and appropriate activities in a safe, stimulating setting. Observations can focus on the caregiver's sensitive and stimulating behavior in response to all children or on the individual child's experiences of positive care. Since structural and process measures all reflect aspects of good care, they generally are related to each other.

In both center care and family day care, the quality of the interactions with the caregiver—the positive, sensitive responsiveness of the caregiver—is the best measure of the quality of the care.[60] Caregivers' salaries are good measures of caregiver stability; when salaries are high, caregivers stay.

In high-quality day care settings, children build secure attachments to teachers and develop the many positive social qualities associated with early secure attachment to parents.[61] The child uses this figure as a safe base for exploring the world, just as he or she uses the secure attachment with the mother or father. In the child's first thirty months, it is important for the teacher to remain the same; but after thirty months, the teacher can change and the child-teacher relationship will still remain stable.

There are, of course, confounding factors. Highly motivated, educated, stable parents seek out high-quality care for children.[62] Those infants who go into low-quality care often have parents who are less organized and use less appropriate socialization practices. A vicious cycle may develop for the infant in low-quality care. Highly stressed families give less attention to the child, and the child goes into a day care setting with few adults to interact with and little to do. Thus, they have cumulative risks for problems in development.

Federal law requires that states have standards to ensure the health and safety of children in child care, but states vary widely in specific laws and the degree to which they monitor and inspect family day care and child-care centers.[63] Some, but not all, states have set up requirements for staff training and ratios of adults to children. Those states that have stricter standards have fewer centers offering poor-quality care. Insisting on stricter standards for teacher training and adult–child ratios was related to more sensitive caregiving for children.

Availability of Good Quality Care

Most experts agree that shortages exist in services for infants and school-age children. Recent studies have found that, even when available, day care is most often of mediocre quality.[64] Observations of care in centers and family day care found that in centers, 14 percent were of sufficiently high quality to promote development, 74 percent were of mediocre quality, and 12 percent were of such low quality as to be unstimulating and unable to fully meet children's health and safety needs. Forty percent of care for infants and toddlers was described as low quality.

In family day care homes, 9 percent were found to be of good quality, 56 percent of adequate or custodial quality, and 35 percent of inadequate quality. The average family day care provider was described as "nonresponsive or inappropriate in interactions with children close to half the time."[65]

In a national study of the early caregiving experiences of toddlers and preschoolers, positive caregiving was very or somewhat characteristic for 39 percent of children, and somewhat or very uncharacteristic for 61 percent.

While good-quality care is expensive to provide because it requires recommended staffing ratios, as well as educated and trained staff members who stay, the fees charged to parents for good-quality care are not that different from those for mediocre care. Parents need training and awareness to identify quality care. When they compared parents' ratings of quality to their own, researchers found that parents identified as good quality what researchers described as mediocre.[66] Parents of all education and income levels tend to overestimate the quality of the caregiving their children get.

Parents also tend to overestimate their level of communication with caregivers who see themselves as professionals and want parents to consult them for information and skill-building.[67] Caregivers also want family information to understand children, and they want to give information to help parents understand what has happened in the day. But there is little time for conversation. Caregivers often want to talk in the mornings when parents are in a hurry, but they are rushed when parents pick up children and have time to talk.

Adaptation to Nonmaternal Care

In evaluating research, we must keep in mind first that a selection process related to mothers' education, personality, and interests determines who, in fact, chooses to return to work once children are born. Second, the meaning of maternal employment in a child's life depends on (1) the child's characteristics (age, sex, temperament), (2) family characteristics (education and socioeconomic level, fathers' involvement in the home, mother's satisfaction with working), (3) work characteristics (the number of hours the mother works, the level of her stress at work), and, perhaps most important, (4) the nature of the child's substitute care. Because so many factors influence the effects of day care, our understanding of its effects is more limited than we would like.[68]

Children enter care early in infancy and the stability and quality of that care can promote positive development. Parents who decided early on the type of care they preferred were more likely to have that type of care and to obtain higher quality care when infants were six months old.[69] Most parents preferred some form of relative care in their own or the relative's home, but family day care and center care were the most stable forms of care.[70]

Studying the stability of child care of infants from six to fifteen months, researchers found that 61 percent of infants had stable care over that period of time, although many infants had more than one kind of care.[71] Two aspects of care predicted the development of positive qualities—quality of day care (at fifteen months and the average quality of care from six to fifteen months) and multiple care arrangements with relatives predicted language comprehension. Poor quality of care negatively predicted language and cognitive performance. Multiple care arrangements with family and nonfamily caregivers predicted poorer language comprehension and more behavior problems.[72]

Parents worry that nonmaternal care may interfere with children's secure attachments to mothers. While research in the 1980s suggested this possibility, the findings from the National Institute of Child Health and Human Development Study of Child Care and Youth Development indicated it is mothers' warmth and sensitivity that determined children's attachment security: "Child care by itself constitutes neither a risk nor benefit for the development of the infant–mother attachment."[73]

Currently, there are concerns that day care represents a challenging situation for young children. Large numbers of infants, toddlers, and preschoolers show increases in cortisol, a stress-sensitive hormone, over the course of the day in day care centers and family day care homes in contrast to decreasing levels of cortisol during the day when children are at home.[74]

Increases in daytime cortisol are most often seen in family day care homes when caregivers are intrusive and overcontrolling. Boys with rising cortisol levels are described as angry and aggressive, and girls with rising cortisol levels are described as anxious, vigilant, and cautious in their behavior.

Following preschool children in family day care for six months and tracking cortisol levels revealed that rising daytime cortisol levels at first assessment predicted anxious, worried moods and anxious, inhibited, and vigilant behavior six months later.[75] Increases in anxious moods were especially likely in poor quality day care. Those children with more inhibited temperament showed decreases in anxiety and inhibited behavior when in supportive, warm care, but inhibited anxious children in day care centers arousing stressful reactions developed more anxious, inhibited behavior. Thus, the biological quality of the child's temperament and the quality of the day care interacted to predict the effects of day care.

The cortisol increases in day care settings and the emotional outbursts and demands for attention toddlers show at home suggest that in these early years of day care, parents must help children learn to manage their emotional reactions. Parents must be especially sensitive and responsive to help young children establish emotional balance. "Parents need to be especially attentive to children and their needs, responding sensitively to fusses and cries when they are together, thereby providing the emotion-regulating support that children typically do not obtain from care providers in a group setting."[76]

Cognitive and Social Stimulation

We know that early and continuing intervention programs that stimulate cognitive development promote intellectual growth during the school years and reduce grade retention and the need for special programs in the elementary school years.[77] These programs stimulate intellectual growth in children from economically disadvantaged families. The most successful programs also stimulate social and emotional competence seen in adulthood, as we described in Chapter 2. Children in "double jeopardy" experiencing risk factors for development at home and at day care had high levels of behavior problems and lower levels of prosocial behaviors as reported by mothers and caregivers.[78] When, however, children at risk from the home environment went into high-quality day care, their behavior problems and prosocial behaviors resembled those of children from average risk backgrounds. High-quality day care enabled children from high-risk families to learn more controlled and more prosocial behaviors.

National Study on the Effects of Day Care

To respond to concerns about the effects of day care, the National Institute of Child Health and Human Development recruited a network of researchers and, in 1991, a sample of 1,364 newborns and their families to participate in extensive assessments and observations of children at home and at day care and later in school from the age of one month through childhood.

The babies were first seen at one month, then at six, fifteen, twenty-four, thirty-six, and fifty-four months, with phone calls at scheduled intervals as well. The research has focused on the family and day care qualities that predict children's intellectual and social-emotional functioning, and their relationships with peers. Children were tested, then observed at home, at day care, and in the laboratory setting. Ratings were obtained from and about parents and day care workers. The group of researchers presented data about the children's functioning up to the age of fifty-four months. These were the basic findings at that point in the data analysis:[79]

1. Sensitive, responsive parenting consistently and strongly predicted children's competence in all areas at all ages.

2. High-quality day care was defined as day care that provided sensitive, responsive caregiving as well as language and intellectual stimulation. High-quality care predicted intellectual skills and most social-emotional behaviors, as well as some peer ratings to a modest degree.

3. Quantity of child care, or the number of hours children spent in child care, related to children's behavior in different ways. At twenty-four and thirty-six months, a greater number of hours in day care was related to verbal and cognitive skills but to more problem behaviors at thirty-six and fifty-four months and more conflict with the caregiver at fifty-four months. Children were also observed to show more negative behavior with a peer at fifty-four months as well.

4. The only form of day care related to child outcomes was center care. In early childhood, more time in center care predicted greater language and cognitive skills, but it also predicted more behavior problems. At fifty-four months, more time in center care predicted positive peer relationships.

The researchers discussed the usefulness of these findings for parents of young children. "The primary conclusion is that parenting matters much more than does child care, so parents might make decisions that allow them to have quality time with their children."[80] Some mothers may decide to cut back the number of hours they work so they can spend more quality time with their children, and others may decide that cutting back hours would create such financial stress for the family that parenting would be negatively affected.

The researchers highlighted that "exclusive maternal care was not related to better or worse outcomes for children. There is, thus, no reason for mothers to feel as though they are harming their children if they decide to work."[81] High-quality day care clearly contributes to all children's competence.

When the sample was seen after entrance into elementary school, in the third grade and again at the end of sixth grade, conclusions were similar:[82]

1. Parenting was a stronger and more consistent predictor of development than early child-care experiences.

2. Higher quality of care of any kind predicted higher vocabulary scores.

3. More exposure to center-based care predicted teachers' reports of problem behaviors such as noncompliance, aggressiveness, and blaming others for problems.

Nonparental Care during Later Childhood and Adolescence

As in the early years, quality after-school care is related to effective functioning.[83] Contemporaneous after-school day care that is not high quality is also related to children's being rated as noncompliant by teachers and less well liked by peers. Research found that low-income third-graders in formal after-school programs receive better grades in math, reading, and conduct than do children with other forms of care, including maternal care. From about the fifth grade on, children in self-care behave and perform similarly whether an adult is present or not.

Lack of supervision and monitoring in early adolescence, however, is related to increased use of alcohol, cigarettes, and marijuana. Eighth-graders in self-care for more than eleven hours a week—whether from dual- or single-earner families, from high- or low-income families, with good or poor grades, or active or nonactive in sports—were more likely than those not in self-care to use these substances.[84]

In adolescence, maternal employment is associated with self-confidence and independence.[85] The benefits are more pronounced for girls who obtain good grades and think of careers for themselves, most likely because their mothers serve as role models of competence.

Gender Differences

Boys and girls have more egalitarian views of gender roles when mothers are employed and fathers are more involved in child care.[86] Sons of employed mothers see women as more competent and men as more emotionally expressive and warm. Daughters of employed mothers have more egalitarian gender roles.

INTEGRATING FAMILY AND WORK TO GET AN ADAPTIVE FIT

As children grow, day care needs change, and sometimes work changes as well, so parents, whether married or single, look for that combination of work and time at home that enables them to meet children's needs most effectively. Dual earners have more income and flexibility in attaining a workable fit, but all parents have to find the best fit they can.

Dual-Earner Families

After interviewing 150 families, Francine Deutsch identified four patterns of working and parenting, which she termed *equal sharers, 60–40 couples, 75–25 couples,* and *alternating shifters*.[87] Families sometimes moved among these patterns. Families with infants were sometimes unequal sharers, becoming equal sharers over time. Even within the types of families, there were many variations. Equal sharers could be providing all the day care with flexible work hours, or they could have child care and work the same hours outside the home.

Alternating shifters tended to have working-class occupations, as it is these types of occupations that offer daytime and evening shifts. Women's income in alternating-shift families was often very important, and women felt they had power and received appreciation for their contributions.

Patterns of work influenced parents' ways of being with children but not the total amount of time they spent with children. Equal-sharing couples spent the same amount of time with children as did the other three groups of couples, but equal-sharing mothers were alone with children less frequently than were the other mothers. Equal-sharing fathers compensated for this, as they were alone with children more often than were fathers of the other groups. Furthermore, equal-sharing parents were more often together with children than were parents of the other groups.

Couples in the four groups did not differ markedly in politics, education, or class, but they did vary in how they negotiated the everyday issues of child-care and household tasks. Couples who wanted equal sharing of parenting and working made every effort to distribute both kinds of tasks equally and to find friends who supported their decisions. Deutsch recommends that parents be proactive in making daily choices that enable both parents to have careers and be parents. That means scaling back work—limiting work hours per day, workdays per week, travel, overtime—and letting family obligations shape work behavior. When both parents make adjustments, neither one has the traditional career.

An interview study of middle-class men and women in dual-earner families looked at families at different points in the life cycle—some before or after having children but most in the child-rearing stages of life.[88] This study focused on middle managers and professionals, as these people not only determine their own fates but also tend to shape the work lives of people they supervise. Sampling couples from upstate New York rather than those from an urban area may have resulted in an overrepresentation of families who have scaled back working demands, however.

In this sample, few participants had dual-career families in which both parents were highly involved in work and both were single-mindedly pursuing work goals. Dual-career couples usually had no children at home, or they hired help to meet many of the family demands. The vast majority of couples relied on one of three strategies for scaling back work demands to carve out time for the family. Although most couples had an egalitarian gender ideology, choices in day-to-day behaviors often resulted in traditionally gendered roles for men and women.

The three work–family strategies were termed *placing limits, job-versus-career,* and *trading-off.* Couples who placed limits (about 30 percent) turned down jobs or promotions that required relocation or traveling, refused overtime hours, and limited the number of hours worked. Women often did this when a child was born, and men sometimes did this when careers became established and parenting involvement grew. Job-versus-career strategies (relied on by about 40 percent) involved one parent's having an absorbing career and the other parent's having a job that produced income but was subordinated to the needs of the family and the parent with the career. In about two-thirds of these families, men had the career and women had the job, but in one-third, the wife had the career and the man the job. Often, chance or early advancement or opportunity determined which parent had the career. In the trading-off group, parents shifted back and forth between jobs and careers, depending on family needs and career opportunities.

When these strategies do not work, men and women may change jobs or retire from the workforce for a period before returning. While we think of this as a women's strategy, research finds that in a two-year period, about one-third of men do it and 42 percent of women do it.[89] Parents are most likely to make changes when work to family spillover is highly negative, work is seen as inflexible and not family friendly, or a life change such as birth of a child has occurred. Middle-class families with dual incomes have more choices and do seek for optimal opportunities to balance both work and family responsibilities.

Single Parents

As we noted earlier, single mothers' income is unstable and many changes in their work lives occur as a result of layoffs or work factors they cannot control. Many single mothers, however, make the same choices as dual-earner parents: to seek jobs that better fit families' needs, working evening or night shifts so relatives can care for children, staying with a poorer-paying job because employers permit them to take time off for family needs.[90] Their choices are more constrained than dual-earner couples, and regardless of what they choose, they experience many demands on their time and limited resources to meet their families' needs.

WAYS TO IMPROVE WORKING PARENTS' LIVES

A variety of programs, both public and private, can help working parents.

Parenting Programs

Mark Sanders and his colleagues at the University of Queensland have applied the principles of Positive Parenting to the special needs of working parents and designed and evaluated an eight-hour program, titled Workplace Triple P, to reduce parental stress at key times like leaving and returning home and to increase parents' skills in managing these transitions.[91] The program, carried out with volunteers in small groups, focused on two areas: coping skills, like deep breathing, muscle relaxation, challenging negative thoughts for managing parents' stress; and parent-skill training to promote children's development like engaging in activities, and skills to manage children's behavior problems.

At the end of the training, parents reported lower levels of personal stress, greater feelings of self-efficacy and greater satisfactions at work, and greater effectiveness with children. These gains were maintained over a twelve-month period so the training produced lasting benefits for parents at work and at home.

Parental Leave for Care of Family Members and Self

As we noted earlier, a combination of the FMLA and the California PFLI, financed by an employee-paid payroll tax, would enable all parents to take paid leave for six weeks at the birth or adoption of a child and to take time off to care for a sick family member. FMLA benefits could be extended to part-time employees and employees in small companies with under fifty employees.

An analysis of PFLI in California has found it did not eliminate jobs as predicted and did not affect overall employment in any discernible way.[92] Employers found the program had either no effect or a positive effect on productivity, and there was no cost increase to business. Eighty-three percent of low-wage job earners who used it returned to their work compared to 74 percent who were unaware of the benefit or did not use it because their job was not protected.

Care for Family Members When Working

Approximately 15.3 million children under the age of six require care while parents work and 9 million people over age sixty-five need long-term care.[93] Dependent care tax credits and spending accounts for dependent care help middle-income families, and subsidies for eligible low-income parents could help, as currently in one analysis of benefit payments, less than half who were eligible received child-care subsidies.

States have begun to experiment with providing pre-kindergarten classes as part of the educational system, paid for by public funding or public lottery. In Oklahoma, 99 percent of school districts offer pre-kindergarten programs, and research found that the programs benefitted all who attended. The National Institute for Early Education Research found that only sixteen of thirty-eight statewide universal pre-kindergarten programs receive enough funding to provide high-quality programs for children. So, though difficult to provide funding, it is possible for state programs to help families.

Flexible Working Hours and Places

As noted earlier, giving workers flexibility in times and places reduces working parents' stress and increases their satisfactions with life.[94] While most employees want such flexibility, it is generally available only to high-earning employees. Most employees do not abuse the privileges, and employers benefit because employees are more engaged in work and more likely to remain at that job, reducing the costs of hiring and training new workers.

Investments in Growth or Remediation of Problems?

Recall in Chapter 2 the discussion of the Canadian program Better Beginnings, Better Futures, funding an expansion of community programs for children from ages four to eight, devised by people in the community to meet their needs as they saw them.[95] The programs paid for themselves in seven years by reducing the needs for remedial education. The programs were so successful they are being extended to all Canadian families. Relying on community planning to determine selection of programs in addition to a core set of services is a model that the United States can follow even in recessionary times, but it does require investing money for children's growth in order to save money later by not having to remedy problems.

A PRACTICAL QUESTION: HOW DO WORKING PARENTS TAKE CARE OF THEMSELVES?

Studies we have reviewed suggest ways parents can increase their resources relative to their demands at work and in the family. Focusing on what is positive in life, using humor, using problem-solving strategies to deal with specific obstacles, reaching out for help from other people, and turning to work and community resources for help are all ways to increase resources to deal with work and family demands.

Nonprofit organizations help parents as well. For example, the National Association of Child Care Resource and Referral Agencies (www.naccrra.org)[96] provides parents with information (e.g., about child care, parenting, state licensing laws), connects parents with day care in their area, monitors states' activities in licensing and supervising child care, collects data and does research, and advocates policies to ensure quality care for children.

The Families and Work Institute (www.familiesandwork.org)[97] provides parents with information about work policies and laws, and parenting information about integrating work and family life.

Working parents who take care of themselves can take better care of their children. Exercising regularly, eating a balanced diet, making sure they have private time for thinking and pursuing interests, and finding time for pleasurable time with family and friends reduce fatigue and stress. Parents and families have to figure out what works for them.

The life of the working parent is challenging, but increasing resources can reduce demands and make life more enjoyable for all family members.

MAIN POINTS

Work
- has a strong effect on family life and is influenced by what parents experience at home
- develops adults' skills and provides many benefits and emotional resources
- can create stress that disrupts parenting skills

Among the many strategies parents use to navigate the flow of work and family, parents

- place primary importance on spending time with children to meet their needs and reduce couple time
- create time for children and family by sharing the workload at home
- maintain control of work demands through problem-solving methods
- build support systems at work and use high-quality child care

Children's nonparental care

- is not as predictive of children's development as are parental qualities
- in early childhood promotes competence when children have warm, supportive caregivers
- promotes development of all children when it is of high quality

Effectively combining working and parenting

- requires that parents make daily decisions to share the workload at home
- involves parents' devoting time to sustaining relationships

EXERCISES

1. Write a diary entry of a workday for an employed father who has an infant child whose mother is also employed full-time. How does he coordinate his work life and his home life on that day, and how does he coordinate his activities with his wife's in the care of their child? Do they spend time with each other? Does he get any time to himself? Or write a diary entry of a weekend day of an employed mother with a teenage son and an early adolescent daughter. How does she spend her time with her children and husband? What does she do in the home and outside the home, with family and friends? Does she get any time alone?

2. Imagine you had a child under age five—infant, toddler, or preschooler. Investigate day care options in the community for a child of that age. Investigate family day care in the area and compare the quality and the cost of care with that available in a center (www.nccrra.org is a good resource for doing this).

3. Design an ideal day care program for infants or toddlers, specifying the number of caregivers, their qualities, the physical facilities, and the daily routine.

4. Imagine what your family and work life would be like if you were a single parent with a toddler and a school-age child. Write diary entries for a day during the week describing work, day care, and transportation.

5. Write a short paper containing advice you could give to a parent of the same sex as you who feels frustrated and pressured trying to care for two teenagers and an aging parent while trying to work full-time.

ADDITIONAL READINGS

Christensen, Kathleen and Schneider, Barbara. *Workplace Flexibility: Reconfiguring 20th-century Jobs for a 21st-century Workforce.* Ithaca: Cornell University Press, 2010.

Drago, Robert W. *Striking a Balance: Work, Family, Life.* Boston: Dollars & Sense, 2007.

Galinsky, Ellen. *Ask the Children: What America's Children Really Think about Working Parents.* New York: Morrow, 1999.

Steiner, Leslie Morgan, ed. *Mommy Wars.* New York: Random House, 2006.

Zigler, Edward, Marsland, Katherine, and Lord, Heather. *The Tragedy of Child Care in America.* New Haven, CT: Yale University Press, 2009.

13

Parents by Adoption and Parents by Reproductive Technology

CHAPTER TOPICS

In this chapter, you will learn about:

- The many forms of adoption
- Ways society can provide supports for adoptees, birth parents, and adoptive parents
- Ways adoption and ART affect parenting and children
- Current issues that affect both adoption and ART

Test Your Knowledge: Fact or Fiction (True/False)

1. All adopted children at one point or another want to search for their biological parents.
2. After all the stress of finding children to adopt, it takes adoptive parents time to become sensitive caregivers for children.
3. Parents talk to children many times about adoption as children's understanding of adoption changes over time.
4. ART parents have planned and worked together to conceive children, and they become responsive caregivers who work together well as parents.
5. Currently parents who have used ART are advised not to tell children about the donations of eggs and sperms and surrogacy because the public reaction would be negative.

About 10 to 15 percent of couples have trouble conceiving their children,[1] and when they do, they turn to assisted reproductive technology (ART) and adoption to create their families. This chapter discusses the feelings couples have when they cannot conceive, and the paths to adoption and to assisted reproductive technology. We look at how relying on assisted reproductive technology and adoption affects parenting and children, and resources that help families function well.

People seek adoption and assisted reproductive technology (ART) help with a variety of feelings. Couples and individuals who have been unable to conceive children turn to ART with hope and optimism. The third who conceive and deliver babies happily rear their children.[2] Those who are not able to deliver babies often turn to adoption with feelings of disappointment, sadness, and frustration that they cannot carry out the basic biological imperative of reproducing their young. Adam Pertman, adoptive parent and executive director of the Evan B. Donaldson Adoption Institute, an education, research, and policy institute, wrote that he will someday have to explain to his children that adoption was his "second choice" but, he wrote, "The mistake many people make with that knowledge is concluding that second choice means second best. We adoptive parents know better. To love my son and daughter any more than I do, I would have to grow a second heart."[3]

And some individuals come straight to adoption enthusiastically as David Marin described in his book, *This Is US: The New All-American Family*. He had divorced and did not want to wait to find a wife and have a stable marriage before he became a father. When he told coworkers that he was adopting three children, he was amazed as people privately told him they were adopted or had adopted children. "Instead of adoption being grand, it was a source of shame, a scar covered by long sleeves. I didn't get it!"[4] He was thrilled with his adopted children, and they, with him.

In this chapter, we look at how adopting and relying on ART influence parenting, parents, and children.

WHEN PARENTS ADOPT

Between 2 and 4 percent of children in the United States are thought to be adopted; about half are adopted by biological relatives and other kin such as stepparents, and about half by adults not biologically related to them.[5] But there is no systematic counting of adoptions so we do not know for sure how many there are. The Census Bureau reported that in 2008, 55,000 children were adopted from foster care, and in 2006, the most recent year of statistics, 12,782 immigrant orphans were adopted in this country.[6] In this country we have agency-arranged and now privately arranged adoptions as well, but we do not know how many more adoptions there are beyond about 68,000. This chapter focuses on those children adopted by people not related to them.

Changes in the Nature of Adoption

Historically, adopted children were the offspring of single women, but in the last four decades, fewer babies were available for adoption because abortions decreased births to single women, and increases in social acceptability enabled more single women to keep their babies.[7] Parents wanting to adopt a child looked to other sources for children such as orphanages in Europe, Latin America, and Asia. China is the country from which children are most frequently adopted now.

Currently, as noted, a large number of children are adopted from foster care placements after being removed from their homes because of abuse or neglect. These children are likely to be older because opportunities must be given to parents to improve their parenting, and children are more likely to be of African American and Latino backgrounds.[8] In addition, there are increases in privately arranged

Box 13-1
EXTENDED FAMILIES

Because families are created in many ways, we now have new family members. Open adoption is one in which birth parent or parents have shared knowledge and some form of continuing contact with their child and the adoptive parents. It creates ties that can meet everyone's needs and removes many of the mysteries of adoption to the benefit of all. Birth parents know what is happening in the child's life, the child knows who the biological parent is, how he or she resembles that parent, and why the parent chose adoption for the child. The adoptive parents can answer children's questions about their family history. They also gain a clearer understanding of their own role in their child's life and fear less that the biological parent will come and take the child away. In many ways adoptive parents gain confidence in their own importance to their child.

A major advantage is that birth parents emerge from the shadows and become real individuals who had difficulties and made the best choice they could to give their child a happy, healthy life. Adam Pertman, who adopted two children and wrote the book *Adoption Nation,* described his family's experiences with two open adoptions:

> The kids are delighted and so are Judy and I. We now have a way of getting answers to medical and genealogical questions (among others), and most wonderfully, we all care about one another and feel we're members of an extended family. Counterintuitive as it may seem—and true to the research into open adoption—there's no role confusion, no divided loyalty, or any of those sorts of concerns. Some parents may have different experiences, but I'm deeply grateful for this transformation in our lives.*

Even if birth parents remain unknown, adoptive parents may include them in their mental pictures of family. Christina Frank describes her many thoughts about the birth mother of her Vietnamese daughter, Lucy. When Lucy's birth mother left the child at a clinic, she left only a short note giving her birth date, and the brief explanation, "A family situation."**

As Mrs. Frank walked the streets of Hanoi, she looked at every woman, wondering if she were the one. When she returned to the United States with the baby, and people commented, "How could a mother give up her child?" Mrs. Frank felt fiercely protective of the mother, thinking Americans could not understand the poverty and desperate circumstances in some countries that would lead a mother to give up her child. While she said nothing the first time anyone made that remark, she later would reply that only a "fool would question the reasons behind *my* daughter's birth mother's decision." She wrote, "By then, Lucy was not the only new member of my family. I had come to think of her birth mother and all her biological relatives as family too."***

*Adam Pertman, "And Then Everything Changed," in *Like No Other Love,* eds. Pamela Kruger and Jill Smolowe (New York: Riverhead, 2005), 213–214.
**Christina Frank, "She Is among Us," in *Like No Other Love,* eds. Kruger and Smolowe, p. 15. (New York: Riverhead, 2005)
***Ibid., p.19.

adoptions of infants in this country. Privately arranged adoptions are organized by professionals like doctors, lawyers, and adoption facilitators, who find babies, often of European American background, for European American couples. Such adoptions are not screened by agencies and can be very expensive.

Adults previously excluded from adoption—older, single, gay or lesbian, disabled, or poor people—are now approved for adoption.[9] Preliminary research indicates that these adoptive parents experience great satisfaction in their roles as parents and have good placement outcomes. Children adopted by single parents do as well as those adopted by young couples, even though single people tend to adopt more difficult children. In addition, legislation has enabled foster parents to adopt children in their care. Greater openness about adoption, along with greater awareness of the adoption process because of adoptions by celebrities and the adoptions of children from other countries, has improved people's perceptions of adoption and adoptive parents.[10] Some companies now offer parental leave for adoption. Celebrities talk about their own experiences as adopting parents or adopted children, and children from other countries talk about their two cultures of origin. Children are now less likely to be teased and made to feel different because they are adopted.

Open Adoption

In the past, adopting parents had limited or no information or contact with biological or birth parents. Currently, adoptive and birth parents are given greater access to information about and more contact with each other. In some instances, the birth mother selects the adopting parents and maintains ongoing contact with the child and the family; this is referred to as open adoption. The adopted child is sometimes included in the birth mother's family and activities as well. More open adoption has helped remove the element of secrecy from the adoption process. *All* the child's parents can know what is happening to the child, and the child can know them all as well. Children learn that birth parents have love for them though they cannot provide for them.

Research on open adoptions suggests that the birth mothers show better adjustment after placement than birth mothers who do not maintain contact.[11] Adoptive parents also seem to feel better because they are less fearful of losing children and they have a better understanding of birth parents so they can answer children's questions more completely. As rated by adoptive parents, children in open adoptions appear to have fewer problems than do other adopted children though this is not always a consistent finding. Sometimes there are no differences. Teens who experienced contact with birth mothers and other birth family members like grandparents and birth fathers reported fewer problems with angry feelings and noncompliant behaviors.[12]

Transracial Adoptions within the United States

When the number of children available for adoption decreased in the 1970s, adoptive parents looked outside their own ethnic groups for children to rear. Criticism followed with complaints that these children would lose their cultural heritage, but legislation in the 1990s made it illegal to use race as an obstacle to

African American adoptees reared by parents of another ethnic group often wished for more opportunities to be with other African American and biracial children.

adoption.[13] As adoptions of foster care children increase, adoptions of children of ethnic groups differing from adoptive parents increase.

Studies of children adopted in the United States and growing up with parents of different ethnic/racial backgrounds from themselves find that these children are psychologically well adjusted without behavioral or emotional problems.[14] While some studies have reported these children have positive racial identities, other studies find a higher percentage of ambivalent or confused racial identities in adoptees placed across racial/ethnic lines. These difficulties are greatly reduced when parents provide experiences that enable children to develop a positive racial identity, as parents adopting children from other countries are required to do.

Detailed interviews with a sample of adopted biracial African American/European American adults raised by European American parents revealed that some realized their adoption was necessary because their European American, birth mothers' families would not rear a biracial child.[15] All the adoptees between the ages of nineteen and thirty-two expressed gratitude for their adoptive families and for the opportunities they had as a result of adoption: good education, becoming racially open with others, and increased abilities to relate to many different kinds of people.

Yet many faced challenges as they were frequently the only person of their ethnic group, and they felt alone and distant from others because they did not look like them. One man described himself as constantly feeling on the outside like the movie character ET, watching human children play from the closet, curious and fascinated by them. Another said she wondered what her parents could possibly teach her because their life experiences were so different from hers.

As we saw in Chapter 8, European American parents often raise their children without ethnic socialization, and these parents raised their adopted children in a colorblind way, but most adopted children feel as much attention should be given to their racial socialization as to their academic education. Adoptees wish for more opportunities to be with African American and biracial people, opportunities "to blend in" and feel like everyone else.

Parents often failed to prepare them for racial discrimination, and when it happened, failed to realize the depth of the pain. As a result, children had to navigate their racialized world without the benefit of parental guidance and wisdom. The small number who felt their parents were supportive described their parents' attitude as one of "joining (children) on a journey, challenging themselves to see the world through their child's multiracial eyes."[16]

One woman said she did not need her parents to know what it felt like to be called "n----r." "All I needed to know is that they were there for me. That when I hurt, it did hurt them. They may not understand, but it did hurt them."[17] That was the caring support she needed. One suspects that in today's world with greater awareness of diversity, parents would be sensitive and connect children to their cultural heritage and help them cope with discrimination.

In addition to living in an ethnically different world and dealing with discrimination on their own, adoptees felt a third challenge was explaining their transracial upbringing to African American peers who sometimes saw it as a liability and viewed them negatively because they did not have the usual cultural references or spoke in what seemed like a "stuck-up" manner.

As adults most adoptees live in diverse cities and areas of the country where they may have more opportunities to connect with other biracial young adults who meet to discuss issues. They are grateful for their advantages but want more ways to share their unique experiences with others who understand.

International Adoptions

When parents adopt children from other countries, they must meet all the criteria for adoption in that country as well as those of the state in which they live. The United States has signed the resolution of the Hague Convention on International Adoption, an internationally agreed-on set of criteria to safeguard children's rights.[18]

Parents' Concerns about Effects of Early Institutionalization   Because babies were not readily available in the United States, many adoptive parents turned to other countries for infant adoption. A major concern of adopting parents centers on the trauma children may have experienced in orphanages or other settings prior to adoption and the effects of such trauma on attachment and later psychological development.[19] The identified effects of early institutionalization depend on:

- the quality of the early physical and medical care, nutritional level, and the consistency and responsiveness of the caregiver
- the length of the time spent in such care
- the age at which the child is assessed following adoption

In South Korea, infants were placed in foster care homes with excellent medical care and nutrition, with consistent, trained caregivers.[20] These children had few delays at the time of adoption. In Eastern Europe, infants were placed in orphanages where they experienced little medical care, poor nutrition, little cognitive stimulation, and little personal attention; there were delays at the time of adoption. The less time spent in the institution, the fewer the problems at the time of adoption. Infants spending less than six months had negligible effects but children spending longer times, in some studies over six months,[21] in other studies over twelve or eighteen months, can show more difficulties.[22]

A fifteen-year follow-up study with assessments when adoptees were four, six, eleven, and fifteen years of age found that children who lived in profoundly deficient Romanian orphanages more than six months were more likely to develop a core, deprivation-specific syndrome of four difficulties that led to increases in peer problems, emotional problems, and rule-breaking behaviors at ages eleven and fifteen.[23] The core syndrome consisted of difficulties in social understanding and appropriate social behaviors, inattention, and cognitive difficulties. Children seemed to have a hard time understanding others, but at the same time, an enormous desire to relate to them. They also had difficulties focusing their attention and sustaining cognitive skills. Although the core syndrome of difficulties was present earlier, the emotional problems and rule-breaking behaviors were not seen until ages eleven and fifteen.

Parents of children with the core syndrome were as sensitive and responsive caretakers as parents of children without the indications of the core syndrome, so the difficulties appeared not to result from parents' interactions with children, but possibly from the early deprivation that may change neural development in ways that do not manifest themselves until later ages when more complex behaviors are required.

Although parents appear sufficiently sensitive and responsive to their children, there are suggestions from research that children may require especially high levels of certain kinds of stimulation. For example, they may require extended time in joint attention and turn-taking activities with parents so that they develop the ability to wait and take turns, anticipate reactions, and better understand how people respond in interactions. They may also require more stimulation to develop verbal and executive function skills as described in Chapter 3.

It is possible that as children move through adolescence and into young adulthood, there will be improvement in their skills with peers and emotional and behavioral control because the brain will have achieved greater maturity, and they will have had more practice in these skills.

Providing Appropriate Cultural Socialization for Children   As occurs with domestic transracial adoptions, children's adjustment is eased when parents form a new family ethnic identity.[24] Parents provide experiences that connect not just the child, but the whole family, to the child's ethnic group of origin. This may mean learning a new language or new customs, celebrating new holidays, or living in new areas where there are more families of the child's origins. Such a child needs models of the culture and opportunities to have friends of his or her group of origin.

Currently, organizations form tours to countries where children were adopted, in order to acquaint children with the geographical regions and, in some instances, with birth families, though this is rare because usually records do not exist.

Since many of the adoptive American parents tend to be European American, middle- and upper-middle-class people, it is not easy for parents to prepare children for experiences of bias they themselves have never had. Parents who are aware of the differential treatment of racial and ethnic groups in this country are more likely to give their children cultural information about their country of origin, to involve them in cultural activities related to their countries, and to participate themselves in postadoption groups. They also think it important to prepare children for bias.[25]

Mothers of adopted Asian children were more likely to provide cultural socialization for children when they themselves felt connected to Asian culture.[26] They got their children involved in activities and taught them about Asian culture. They started cultural socialization early in the preschool years and continued consistently through adolescence. They also prepared children for experiencing bias, helping children counteract difficult experiences. Mothers did not start this until children were around eight and reached a peak in the years from twelve to fourteen, dropping off in later adolescence.

While cultural socialization was related to mothers' reports of lower levels of aggressive, noncompliant problem behaviors, preparation for bias was related to older children's higher levels of aggressive, oppositional behaviors.

Talking about Adoption and Children's Understanding of It

When parents feel secure, they neither overemphasize the fact of adoption nor do they deny that adoptive families have certain differences.[27] They are open to talk to children about their reactions and their views. They can explain the different ways to form a family, and they accept that their child has links to two families—to them and to biological parents. Much of the information in this section pertains to children whose adoptions are not open either because parents chose not to or because it was impossible, as in many international adoptions, to know who the biological parents were.

The general advice is to tell children they are adopted sometime in the toddler and preschool years.[28] Adoption, however, is not something you explain once or twice when the child is young and then forget about. Recent research evidence suggests that most preschoolers may not understand what adoption is even when parents have explained it to them and they refer to themselves as adopted. While many preschoolers confuse adoption and birth, making no distinction between the two ways of having children, still others grasp the basic facts. By the age of six, most children can understand that there are two paths to parenthood—birth and adoption—and they understand that adoption makes the child a permanent member of the family.

In the toddler and preschool years, children focus on the happy experiences of adoption—parents having children they want and children coming to live with people who love them. Between ages seven to eleven, children begin to think about adoption in new ways. They understand that adoption is not the usual way families grow.

Box 13-2
FIRST PERSON NARRATIVE*

Adam Pertman, adoptive father and, as noted, current executive director of the Evan B. Donaldson Adoption Institute, describes not only his own experiences with adoption but those of birth parents, adoptive parents, adults who learned of their adoption as adults, and other adoptees. Their stories often extend over many years so one has a sense of how people and their extended families change over time. Information about the history and current legal status of adoption in different states is woven through the narratives, increasing our understanding of the complexities of the adoption process and the vulnerabilities of the participants.

Pertman believes that as society adapts to the needs of adopted children, the needs of other children are better met as well. For example, as teachers substitute drawing a family "orchard" with all current family members instead of the traditional family "tree" with genetic roots that adopted children have difficulties completing, then children of gay/lesbian parents with parents of the same gender, and children of divorced and remarried parents who have a large array of family feel more comfortable as well.

Distilling his experience of what works in adoption and is beneficial for all parties, Pertman strongly advocates for counseling of all parties around adoption, for open adoptions, and for better control of the influence of money in driving the adoption system.

*Adam Pertman, *Adoption Nation: How the Adoption Revolution Is Transforming Our Families—and America* (Boston: Harvard Common Press, 2011).

They understand families are usually made up of blood or biological relations and they are not biologically related to their adoptive family. They learn that out in the world somewhere, they have biological parents, grandparents, and perhaps brothers and sisters. And they begin to wonder about them, and why the birth parents gave the child up for adoption.

Children become more preoccupied with questions about whether they were given up for adoption because parents felt there was something wrong with them.[29] Children have a variety of feelings, some anger and fears and some vague, lingering doubts about themselves. They may feel intensely angry at their biological parents for abandoning them or angry at their adoptive parents for taking them away. They may have vague feelings of being different, not like other children; they may feel sad not knowing who or where their biological parents are. Children may worry that adoptive parents will give them up, and there will be no one to care for them. Some may develop feelings that are too much to handle. All these intense feelings may account for the fact that adopted children on average begin to show psychological and mood problems in the elementary school years. In the case of open adoptions, children may know much more about their biological parents but still have some questions about the need for adoption and still retain feelings of being different from other children.

When children become teenagers, their questions about adoption may focus on identity issues. "What are my roots in this world?" "How am I like my biological parents?"

As sexual interest increases in adolescence, children's interest in their own conception and birth may also increase. They fantasize about their biological parents. Though the fantasies start in early childhood, teens may think about searching.

Searching for Birth Parents

A careful longitudinal study of internationally adopted young adults in The Netherlands found four different patterns regarding searching:[30]

- about one-third were uninterested and not searching for parents
- another third were interested in finding their biological parents but were not searching for them
- about one-third were searching—almost half of the searching group (14 percent of the sample) had reunited with their birth parents and the remainder of the group (18 percent of the sample) was still searching

Personal and social data on the adopted sample were available at three time periods—early adolescence, late adolescence, and young adulthood, ages twenty-four to thirty. In adulthood, the members of the groups resembled each other in their school success, levels of education and professional status, and their rates of marriage and having children. So in the major markers of adulthood, the groups were alike. However, the adults differed in their experience of adoption with the greatest contrasts occurring between those still searching for their biological parents and those who were not interested and were not searching.

The searchers:

- were preoccupied with adoption
- felt less positive about their adoption experience, feeling they were intellectually and psychologically different from their adoptive parents
- were older at the time of placement; boys had not experienced more abuse, but more early abuse than boys in other groups and girls less than girls in other groups
- even as teens, were interested in searching for biological parents and wanted to have close relationships with them
- had more worries and problem behaviors in adolescence
- continued to describe themselves as nervous and depressed in young adulthood.

Those who were not interested in finding their biological parents:

- felt positive about their adoptive experiences
- even in adolescence, had been uninterested in finding their biological parents
- as adults, felt they were similar to their adoptive parents both psychologically and intellectually,
- had more contact with adoptive parents
- as teens and adults, reported the fewest worries and problems of the groups.

Searchers who had reunited with their biological parents reported that as teens they had a great interest in searching, but now in adulthood, they were no longer preoccupied with adoption issues. Reunited searchers reported fewer worries and problems in adolescence and young adulthood than continuing searchers but more than uninterested nonsearchers. Reuniting with biological parents brought them satisfaction, but their worries remained at the same childhood level. Worries and preoccupations did not appear to spur the search, and worries did not decrease after reuniting with biological parents.

Gender differences were found as girls were more interested and preoccupied with searching, as was also found in other studies, but they did not necessarily do more searching.

In other studies most searchers were pleased to have reunited with their parents and maintained the contact over a period of years.[31] Many who established contact reported decreases in feelings of loss and rejection. A small number, about one in three, thought of the biological parent as a parent, but half thought of the parent as a friend or relative, and about 18 percent continued to feel distant from the parent. The reunion brought some adopted children closer to their adoptive parents, but about one in six felt it had led to a decline in their relationships with adoptive parents.

A recent study following adopted teens through adolescence and into young adulthood found that contact with biological family members increases teens' conversations with adoptive parents about adoption, how it occurred, and what it means in teens' lives.[32] One of the reasons that contact with biological family members may be positive is that conversations about adoption stimulate teens' thinking about what adoption means to them, and they construct a more integrated sense of identity.

Parenting Behaviors of Adopting Parents

Many adopting parents come to parenthood with feelings of sadness at not having a biological child and anxiety from the intense scrutiny they have undergone to determine their suitability as parents. One can imagine their feeling self-conscious and uncertain in their parenting behaviors.[33]

However, a study comparing the parenting strategies of parents who adopted a child at birth, parents who relied on donor insemination and ART, and parents who conceived a child naturally found few differences among the parenting behaviors of the three groups.[34] When children were between four and eight, adopting mothers did not differ from mothers of naturally conceived children in warmth, sensitivity, or attachment to their children. Mothers using donor insemination and ART were warmer and more involved than were the other two groups. Teachers and psychiatric evaluation judged children in the three groups as functioning equally well, with no problems.

When these children were twelve, the adopting parents continued to have warmth and control similar to that of parents of naturally conceived children. Again, psychiatric evaluation and teachers' assessments indicated that children, too, continued to function well in all three groups, with no significant differences among them.

Mothers of adopted children, however, described their children as having problems of rule-breaking and aggressiveness, but a more objective assessment did not present such a picture. Thus, the parenting behaviors of parents who adopted a child at birth seem quite similar to those of parents who have naturally conceived a child.

And the behavioral effects of their parental actions with children are the same as they are in biologically related families. For example, even though mothers do not share any genetic relationship with children, their sensitive responses with babies and secure attachments they form with babies uniquely predicted children's social and intellectual competence at age seven.[35] Similarly, when parents have problems, adopted children are affected as biological children would be. For example, parents' marital conflicts when infants are nine months old predict toddlers' sleep difficulties nine months later.[36] Mothers' depressive symptoms predict toddlers' acting out and aggressive behavior eighteen months later.[37]

Family communication patterns can create a shared reality and sense of solidarity that is important in adoptive families. Greater communication might well, for example, have helped the searching teens and young adults in the Dutch study to feel similar to their adoptive parents from whom they felt so different. Observing the communication patterns of teens and their family members in adoptive and biologically related two-parent families, researchers identified four patterns with similar proportions of adoptive and nonadoptive families in each.[38]

These types of communication intensified or reduced problem behaviors:

- Consensual pattern—parents and children were warm and open, expressing their views and listening to others, and each family member tried to influence others' attitudes and behavior to support family rules and structure (7 percent of adoptive and 4 percent of nonadoptive families fell in this pattern).

- Pluralistic pattern—parents and children were cool and distant and spoke about their thoughts and feelings, but did little to persuade others to adopt their standards of behavior (30 percent of adoptive and 30 percent of nonadoptive families fell into this pattern).

- Protective pattern—parents did not encourage open expression of views but insisted that children meet their standards and do what parents considered appropriate (20 percent of adoptive and 26 percent of nonadoptive families fell here).

- Laissez faire—nobody in the family spoke or listened or tried to influence each other so there was neither conversation nor pressure to agree to family standards (41 percent of adoptive and 40 percent of nonadoptive families fell here).

Researchers then looked at the rates of angry, externalizing behavior problems (as measured by self and others' reports) for adoptive and nonadoptive teens in the four communication groups. In general, adoptive teens were more sensitive to difficulties in family communication patterns as seen in their having more problems than nonadoptive teens did. For example, adoptive children had the most problems in families using laissez faire patterns (27 percent of adoptive teens had problems compared to 8 percent of nonadoptive) and protective patterns (18 percent of adoptive teens had problems compared to 4 percent of nonadoptive). Adoptive children appear more sensitive to the neglect of laissez faire parents and to the overcontrol of protective parents. These two groups incorporate between 60 and 66 percent of the families in the two samples.

In families using consensual forms of communication both adoptive and non-adoptive teens had low rates of problems (3 percent for adoptive teens and 0 percent for nonadoptive teens). Combining an emphasis on individual expression with conformance to parents' standards, this style of communication incorporates the basic principles of authoritative parenting. About the same percentages of teens developed problems in families using pluralistic forms of communication—17 percent for adoptive and 12 percent for nonadoptive. Communication without parental control and standards appeared to produce the most problems for nonadoptive teens.

Overall, the study indicates that just as in biological families, the same principles of respect for individuality, open communication, and structured standards for children are related to competent functioning and the reduction of problems. Still, even when parents are sensitive, warm and supportive, and open in communication, adopted adolescents appear to observers, to be less warm with parents than nonadopted teens, and there is more conflict between adopted teens and their parents than between nonadopted children and their parents.[39] There may be stressors specific to adoption that make teens more angry and willing to engage in conflict than nonadopted teens or there may be temperamental differences between parents and children that intensify conflict on teens' part.

A major parenting task with adopted children, then, is to keep channels of communication open, help children feel comfortable in the family so they can express their vague and their intense feelings to their parents without worrying about hurting or upsetting parents. Parents can help children by accepting and acknowledging all feelings and using problem-solving strategies to raise potential solutions. If parents feel they are not helpful, they can obtain counseling for children. Talking over the typical problems adoptive children experience with a neutral third party can be very useful for them.

A major set of feelings that require resolution, according to those who counsel adopted children, are the numerous feelings of loss—loss of their biological family and extended relatives, of their ethnic background, of their medical history, of the feelings of a secure place in the world with people who will not abandon you.[40]

As infants, they may feel a sense of loss when they are separated from their biological family, their culture, and language that has surrounded them. Those feelings may be reflected in passivity and mild withdrawal for a period of time. But it is often not until the school years and adolescence that such feelings are strong. They may continue to exist in adulthood as well, and are often intensified by the birth of their own children. Parents' sensitive and responsive interactions with children can help them accept and acknowledge these feelings of loss.

Children's Behaviors

There are suggestions that adopted children may have more problems in the school years with teachers seeing them as less socially and emotionally mature and their being seen in mental health clinics for psychological problems like aggressiveness and academic problems.[41] They represent 5 percent of clinic populations when they are 2 percent of the general population. Several possible factors may account for these statistics. Children may be more vulnerable because of genetic predispositions of biological parents and prenatal and immediate postnatal environments, and adoptive parents may be more alert to difficulties and want to see them addressed.

Studies of adult functioning of adopted children reveal that by early and middle adulthood, they resemble adults reared in biological families.[42] In a study comparing adopted adults with friends, the two groups were similar with respect to life satisfaction, purpose in life, intimacy, and substance use.[43] The adopted adults, however, reported lower self-esteem than did friends, though the difference of 1.5 points was small, and greater depression. More of the adopted sample (30 percent) fell in the clinical range of depression than did the sample of friends (19 percent), but 70 percent of the adopted adults fell within the normal range when the figure for the average sample was 80–85 percent. Adopted adults seeking their biological families reported lower self-esteem and greater depression than did other adopted adults. Still, all adopted adults expressed insecurity about adult attachments. They formed relationships with peers but expressed greater discomfort in the relationships than did their friends.

A meta-analysis of 101 studies on behavior problems and mental health referrals for internationally adopted children and teens included a total of 25,000 adopted children and 80,000 controls.[44] The conclusion was that most adopted children were doing well despite the medical and psychological adversities many experienced prior to their adoption. While they received more mental health services, the difference in adjustment with controls was modest.

David Brodzinsky and Ellen Pinderhughes caution that focusing on the problems of adopted children in comparison to the problems of children in the general population obscures the real benefits of adoption for children.[45] Controlled international studies comparing the adjustment of adopted children in comparison to the adjustment of children living in conditions from which adopted children come consistently finds adoptive children are functioning more effectively. Other studies comparing adopted children with children who were reared by parents who had considered giving them up for adoption or were ambivalent about keeping them found that adopted children functioned better. Adopted children also functioned more effectively than children in institutions, or long-term foster care, or poverty.

Adoption clearly provides benefits to children even though children will have to manage feelings of loss, deal with whatever mysteries exist about biological parents, and have a more complex path to identity formation.

A PRACTICAL QUESTION: CAN A THREE-SESSION INTERVENTION ENHANCE ADOPTIVE PARENTS' SENSITIVITY TO PROMOTE SECURE ATTACHMENT?

In The Netherlands, babies are adopted primarily from foreign countries and many of them come to adoptive homes after stressful experiences of separation from the biological mother or deficient care in institutional or foster placements. Their neuroendocrine systems may respond to the stress by shutting down so babies are initially less responsive, and their signals more difficult to interpret, making it harder for parents to respond in sensitive ways.[46] Many of these babies had been noted to develop disorganized attachments to mothers at twelve months.[47]

In Chapter 3 we described the use of video-feedback interventions to increase parents' positive, sensitive caregiving with their children. This method was used with adoptive parents in The Netherlands to increase their responsive interactions with their babies and promote secure attachments with infants. Babies were adopted from Sri Lanka, South Korea, and Colombia. The intervention with mothers consisted of four home visits with video-feedback and a book on sensitive caregiving when babies were five, six, nine, and twelve months. Mother-child interactions were observed in the laboratory in the Strange Situation Procedure at twelve and eighteen months.[48]

On the home visits, mothers were shown excerpts from the videotape, illustrating mothers' positive, sensitive interactions, and home visitors talked about babies' needs for warm, close relationships with mothers and their needs for opportunities to explore, also describing babies' signals of gestures and vocalizations that tell mothers what they need. In reviewing the video tapes excerpts, home visitors "spoke" for the babies and interpreted their signals.

At twelve months, mothers who received video-feedback were significantly more sensitive than mothers in two control groups and had significantly higher rates of secure attachments—at—twelve months, 90 percent in the intervention group and 70 percent in the control group, and at eighteen months, 90 percent with secure attachments in the intervention group and 73 percent in the control group. In a second subsample of adoptive parents with birth children, the intervention was not so successful initially, but by eighteen months, 79 percent of the video-feedback group had secure attachments compared to 75 percent in the control group. The intervention also reduced disorganized attachments to 6 percent in the intervention group as compared to 22 percent in the control group.

The three-session intervention also had long-term effects for children in adoptive families with birth children. Those girls whose mothers received the feedback intervention in infancy had greater ego resiliency and ego control at age seven, and both boys and girls whose mothers received the intervention had fewer internalizing problems than children in the control group. The video-feedback system may have taught parents to respond empathically and sensitively to children's sad and anxious feelings, thus reducing children's worries. The fact that the intervention did not predict long-term functioning for children in families without birth children may be that those families without birth children had more stressful events in their lives like illnesses, and one would expect greater discontinuity in children's behavior. Further, the ratings in that group had less variation, and so statistical properties may have made a difference in predictive power.

Based on the positive results of the study, all new adoptive families in The Netherlands are permitted to apply for four video-feedback sessions at a low fee in the first two and a half years after the adoption.

PARENTS WHO USE ASSISTED REPRODUCTIVE TECHNOLOGY

In Chapter 4, we described the different forms of reproductive technology and identified legal and ethical issues. Here we describe parenting and discuss strategies for dealing with ethical issues.

Box 13-3
EXTENDED FAMILIES

Because families are created in many ways, we now have new family members. Assisted reproductive technologies also create new families. Men can donate sperm to a bank many times. Many different women can use batches of the sperm, and sometimes buy and freeze several batches to create full siblings later. While the banks generally keep no records of whether or how many children are born of the sperm, families have organized Internet registries so that siblings and donors can sign up to locate each other by the donor's number. While only a few hundred donors have signed up, seven thousand siblings have signed up. Over a thousand children have connected with their half siblings and a much smaller number of donors and their offspring.*

In one instance, a donor was found to have fathered twenty-one children under the age of three living in very diverse families—four in lesbian couple families, three in heterosexual couple families, and six in single-parent families. These families post pictures of all the children on a website they created and describe children's ongoing development and their response to such demands as toilet training. The families hope to take a vacation together in the future.

The Donor Siblings Registry enables both older children and mothers to connect and share experiences via e-mail. One sixteen-year-old who had learned only three years before that her parents used donor sperm to conceive her felt angry at her parents' lying to her for so many years. She shared this with her half-sister, fifteen, who had known for years. Both girls confided that in crowds, they always looked to see if there was a six-foot tall, blond-haired man with blue eyes present.

When siblings get together, many feel a great sense of familiarity. They introduce them to others as half-brothers or half-sisters whereas they use the word "donor" to refer to the biological father.

One mother who corresponds with eight other women who used the same man's sperm feels that knowing other children has helped her son feel more connected to a man who has been a very shadowy figure. Knowing the other children has helped him to see his father as a person. "It's not a phantom person out there anymore."**

One mother whose daughter is one of the twenty-one siblings feels thrilled as she wants her daughter to have "family," which she cannot provide. She plans to go on the vacation with the other families and hopes to become close to one or two other families so that in the event she dies of high blood pressure, which she developed during the pregnancy, perhaps one of the other mothers or couples would be guardians for her daughter.

As more and more matches are made between siblings and between donors and offspring, we may have the kind of extended family situations created with open adoptions. Desire for a connection to our biological roots is a powerful force drawing people together.

*Jennifer Egan, "Wanted A Few Good Sperm," *New York Times Magazine,* 19 March 2006, p. 44.
**Amy Harmon, "Hello, I'm Your Sister: Our Father Is Donor 150," *New York Times,* 20 November, 2005, p. A20.

Parenting of Parents Relying on ART

Major studies find that the parenting of ART users resembles that of parents who naturally conceived their children.[49] Even though parents have experienced numerous anxieties about having children and numerous medical procedures, these difficulties do not detract from their parenting. In the transition to parenting, both ART parents and those parents conceiving naturally experienced less stress when prebirth expectations for parent-child relationships in the first year were positive.[50] Because ART partners work closely in the process of conception, they appear to adapt to their parenting partnership and share caregiving more quickly so they experience less negative stress in the first year.

When compared with parents who naturally conceived children, mothers in donor insemination families were described as warmer, more sensitive, and more responsive when children were in early elementary school and again at age twelve.[51] Children in these families thought their mothers were as warm as other mothers. Interviewers described fathers in donor insemination families as more detached in matters of discipline when children were twelve, but mothers and children did not perceive any differences in these fathers' behaviors. Teachers' ratings and psychiatric assessment of the records revealed that the children in all these groups were equally competent and as socially skilled as children reared by parents who had had no difficulties in conceiving.

In studies comparing the parents using sperm and egg donors with parents who naturally conceived their children, the differences between parents, when children were one, favored the parents using egg and sperm donations.[52] These parents had more positive parent-child relationships and were more emotionally involved with the child than parents who conceived their children without ART. Similar findings occurred when parents using surrogate mothers and egg donations were compared

Both ART parents and parents conceiving naturally experienced less stress in the transition to parenthood when prebirth experiences were positive.

with parents who naturally conceived their children; parents using surrogacy and donors were found to have higher psychological well-being and more positive parent-child relationships when children were age one than parents who naturally conceived their children.[53]

When children were ages two and three, families using surrogacy and egg and sperm donors were seen again with parents and children naturally conceived.[54] At these ages, parents using ART continued to be warmer and more interactive with their children than parents normally conceiving children. Children in all groups were functioning well, indicating that the use of ART appeared to have no negative effects on parents or children. A major hypothesis accounting for the positive differences in families using donor and surrogate arrangements is that those seeking parenthood through those means are highly motivated parents who truly enjoy their children and parent them in a sensitive and effective way.

When families relying on surrogacy and egg donors or conceiving naturally were seen again when children were seven, children's functioning, as measured by parents' and teachers' questionnaires, observation, and psychological evaluation of behavior was similar in all groups.[55] Parents were alike in their level of positive warmth and sensitivity with children, and alike in their level of negative behavior expressed in anger and criticism. However, mothers and children in families using surrogacy and egg donations were rated as less mutually responsive and cooperative in their interactions than mothers and children in families not using ART. Since genetic connection between mothers and children was missing in egg donor families and in two-thirds of families using surrogacy, it was speculated that it was the lack of genetic connection that may have reduced mother-child reciprocity rather than the lack of giving birth to the child as all egg donor mothers not using surrogacy gave birth to their children, and they were seen as less responsive in interactions.

However, comparing families relying on egg and sperm donors who had or had not disclosed information to children with naturally conceiving families when children were seven revealed that the differences in the mothers' ratings were coming primarily from mothers' responsiveness in families that had not disclosed information to children.[56] Mothers in donor families disclosing information to children were very similar to naturally conceiving mothers in levels of warmth and sensitivity and only marginally lower in mutual reciprocity. It was speculated that keeping secrets in families may create tension that reduces mutually responsive interactions between mothers and children.

Telling Children

The Ethics Committee of the American Society for Reproductive Medicine strongly recommends that prior to donations, donors and receiving parents get counseling and agree on the release of donor information to the child.[57] The committee urges reproductive clinics and sperm banks to have policies about how and when to release information to donor offspring.

When ART was initiated, parents were encouraged not to tell children because of possible negative social reactions, but over time, professional opinion has changed, and now the Ethics Committee of the American Society for Reproductive Medicine encourages parents to tell children. In interviews, parents who tell children say they do so because they don't want to lie and have family secrets; they want children to be able to trust them, and they believe their children have a right to the knowledge. One parent said, "Everyone has a right to know about their origin. . . . I don't understand what you are afraid of if you haven't told them! It's not shameful or strange."[58]

Yet parents who do not tell and do not plan to tell give three general reasons: fears that the knowledge will stigmatize children, fear that the knowledge will weaken the relationship between the child and the parent not biologically related to the child, and fear that disclosure will add stress for the child or family at a time when the family is already coping with illness or unemployment.[59]

Studies show that parents who are most likely to disclose early are parents who know children are likely to learn later: parents using surrogacy where many people know there was no pregnancy; single mothers, lesbian singles, or couples where child may later learn there was no father involved. Heterosexual couples where no one knows about sperm or egg donations are those most likely to want to keep secrets.[60] While many may plan not to tell the child, more than half have told another adult so disclosure from someone outside the family is a real possibility.

The guidelines for telling children are similar to those for telling children about adoption. Parents themselves must first feel comfortable with the facts before talking to children. They then explain them in simplest terms early in children's lives if possible so they grow up hearing about it. Reading books to young children about the many ways families are formed gives children some understanding of the basic concepts. Donors and surrogate parents can be described as helpers who make it possible for parents to have children. Conversations will occur many times and on many levels as children grow, and parents must be alert to feelings or questions children may have difficulty expressing.

When children learn early, by five or six, they are curious and accept the information; as adolescents, they may want to meet the donor, know other family members.[61] When children learn at older ages, for example adolescence or adulthood, some are angry and confused, wondering about the half of their biological identity they do not know, but many appreciate the honesty of their parents. In many cases, they are sympathetic to the fathers using sperm donors, and knowledge does not weaken the parent-child bond as was feared.

Sometimes, it explains parents' behavior to the child. One twenty-one-year-old responded sympathetically to his father's not being his and his twin brother's biological father, "I guess one of the good parts of all this is that now Pop isn't lugging that awful secret around anymore. Maybe the drinking and misery won't be as bad now that he knows we love him, fertile or not."[62]

So openness about surrogacy and donor eggs and sperm has positive benefits for children as knowing about adoptions has for adoptees. Currently in many countries, donor offspring are guaranteed the right to meet donors, and it will be interesting to observe how many do meet them. While many ART parents feel there is no need to know, advances in medicine may make it very important for children to have knowledge of biological parents' and extended families' medical history throughout adulthood.

Contemporary Issues in Adoption and ART Parenting

Adam Pertman, writing about adoption,[63] and Debora Spar, writing about ART,[64] both express similar concerns for parents and families. Both recognize that parents want very much to create families, and public sector adoptions are open to all, but both regret that the costs involved in conceiving one's own child through ART or seeking an infant through private adoptions or international adoptions are so high that prospective parents must be people of financial means or have excellent medical insurance to pay for ART. Countries like Israel make ART available to all women through health coverage, and it would be possible to do that in this country so there could be equal access for all women.

Both authors urge greater transparency in fees for services that vary widely, and in credentialing people involved in the work. With the exception of the medical personnel involved in ART, there is little credentialing or regulation of private adoption lawyers, facilitators, private agencies, sperm banks, or the procedures many of these places follow so medical information on birth parents or donors is stored and available for offspring when they seek it.

Pertman believes strongly that openness in adoption has benefitted birth parents, adoptive parents, and their children, and guidelines used in adoption can be used in ART families as well. He believes all parties should have access to counseling services before and after the formation of the family, much as the Ethics Committee of the American Society for Reproductive Medicine recommends. He insists that all children have a right to know their genetic history and to meet biological relatives if they wish to do so because the information can be important for medical treatments and for psychological well-being and a sense of rootedness in the world. When one adoptee or ART offspring is denied information, that person's children and descendants lack access as well, so many are affected.

As adoption and ART are more widely discussed and better understood, public pressure may insist on needed changes. Both adoption and ART are important means of forming families and require attention to be as effective and fair as possible to all involved.

MAIN POINTS

Changes in adoption and ARTs
- enable people who would have been childless in the past to have children now
- mean that parents have to find ways to be open with adopted children and ART offspring

Adoptive parents
- are a diverse group of adults who adopt an increasingly diverse group of children
- increasingly involve contact with birth parents and their relatives in open adoptions
- are as effective caregivers as biological parents

Adopted children

- confront additional issues in development
- deal with issues of having two families
- are by and large well-adjusted adults with few differences from age-mates
- function well when parents encourage open communication and give behavioral guidelines
- often overcome deficits of early institutional care if they spend only short times in institutions and are adopted at young ages

Parents using ART

- are warmer and more sensitive with infants, toddlers, and preschool children than parents naturally conceiving their children
- may be less mutually responsive with seven-year-old children than normatively conceiving parents, especially if they have not disclosed ART to children
- tell children about donor assistance because they do not like secrets in the family and believe children have a right to know and decide not to tell because they believe telling might damage parent-child relationship and burden children with unnecessary information

Children of ART parents

- in careful assessments function as well as children naturally conceived by parents at all ages thus far assessed
- show no negative psychological effects of ART use

EXERCISES

1. Imagine that you and your partner want to adopt a baby. What adoption agencies are available in your area to help you? Are there lawyers and doctors who specialize in arranging such an adoption? What would be the cost of adoption through a community agency? Can you adopt a baby through the foster care system?

2. Imagine you and your partner require donor sperm or eggs. Investigate the resources in your area, the costs, and the requirements for people using them.

3. If you were the adoptive parent of a child from China, how would you provide cultural socialization for the child; what resources are available in your area?

4. Imagine that you have adopted a nine-year-old foster care child of an ethnic background different from yours. Select an ethnic group different from your own and describe how you would socialize your child.

5. Imagine that you have a child from donor sperm or donor egg. Research the books available to read to young children. What would you tell your child and when would you start?

ADDITIONAL READINGS

Ehrensaft, Diane. *Mommies, Daddies, Donors, Surrogates: Answering Tough Questions and Building Strong Families.* New York: Guilford, 2005.

Finn, Holly. *The Baby Chase: An Adventure in Fertility.* Bylne.com, 2011, available as an American Kindle Single.

Kruger, Pamela and Smolowe, Jill, eds. *A Love Like No Other: Stories from Adoptive Parents.* New York: Riverhead, 2005.

Pertman, Adam. *Adoption Nation: How the Adoption Revolution Is Transforming Our Families—and America.* Boston: Harvard Common Press, 2011.

Spur, Debora. *The Baby Business: How Money, Science, and Politics Drive the Commerce of Conception.* Boston: Harvard Business School Press, 2006.

14

Parenting When Unmarried

CHAPTER TOPICS

In this chapter, you will learn about:

- Teen parents and their children
- Experiences of unmarried mothers and their children
- Fathers' roles in children's lives
- Programs that help unmarried parents and their children

Test Your Knowledge: Fact or Fiction (True/False)

1. When teen mothers have stable living arrangements and use positive parenting principles, their children function competently.
2. Babies born to unmarried parents are most often conceived in the context of romantic relationships.
3. When families are matched for education and income, children in low-stress single-mother families are indistinguishable from children in two-parent families.
4. As family structures have changed and young couples are more likely to live together, marriage is less valued.
5. Unmarried fathers usually have little role in their children's lives once they are born.

Economic and social changes in the last fifty years have led to an increasing number of children living with unmarried parents. How is life different for children and their parents in these households? How can society support families and decrease the stress many experience? This chapter focuses on the unmarried parents who give birth to 40 percent of the babies born in this country. It describes the stresses they face and the strengths many bring or develop in the course of rearing children.

CHANGING FAMILY STRUCTURES

As noted in Chapter 1, the twentieth century brought many changes in family life. At midcentury, the traditional nuclear family provided the center of people's emotional lives and feelings of closeness for their entire lives. By the 1960s, economic and social changes led to changes in family life. Women sought careers, and as fewer jobs were available to support families, both parents were expected to work outside the home.[1] In the 1980s an increasing number of women who had postponed marriage and children to meet work demands, considered having babies on their own before their biological clock made it hard to conceive.

The secularization of social values led to a focus on self-interest and self-growth. Marriage and children were postponed, divorces and remarriages increased, and there was a growing acceptance of premarital sex. As couples lived together in growing numbers, the number of children born to unmarried parents grew to its present number of 40 percent of all births, and 52 percent of births to women under thirty.[2] Of interest and importance is the fact that most of these babies were born to parents in a romantic relationship, whether they lived together or not.[3] Most unmarried parents care about each other; as we noted in Chapter 4, they value marriage as a future goal but they view children as possible in their present circumstances.

Depictions of single-parent families, whether resulting from divorce or births to unmarried parents, have been negative in popular magazine and scientific journals since 1900.[4] In about 1970, negative depictions of divorced families declined, but depictions of families headed by unmarried parents remain negative. Recall Table 1.2 (page 18) showing the American public's continuing concerns regarding single-parent families.

Table 1.1 (page 17) describes the living arrangements of American children, revealing that 60 percent live with their married biological or adoptive parents, and 40 percent, in other family structures. In the next four chapters, we look at how living in different family structures influences parents' behavior and children's growth. This chapter focuses on parenting in homes with unmarried parents: teen mothers and fathers, parents who were not married at the time of the child's birth, or single mothers by choice. In Chapter 15, we look at parents who were married and then divorce, and the stepfamilies the majority of divorced parents form. In Chapter 16, we look at parents and children in gay/lesbian/transgendered families relying on adoption and ART. In Chapter 17, we look at foster families.

Some parents and children move back and forth between these groups, living in all these kinds of families, e.g., starting with teen parents who later marry, divorce, and then cohabit, so information in all four chapters may be useful to some families. President Obama, for example, was born to a married couple who later divorced. He lived with his single mother, and then in a stepfamily when she remarried. He later lived with his two grandparents, and as an adolescent spent time with his mother who was again a single parent.

Births to unmarried mothers are twice as likely for African American women and Latina women as for European American women.[5] Cohabiting with the child's father increases intended and unintended pregnancies for all three groups, but Latinas are more likely to plan births with cohabiting fathers than the other two groups, and European American women are more likely to marry the fathers than African American or Latina mothers. African American women are more likely than the other two groups to have births when not cohabiting with fathers.

TEEN PARENTS

Teen parents are those who have children under the age of twenty, and most are single parents (about 80 percent).[6] Although the teen birth rate has generally declined in the last two decades,[7] the United States has the highest rate of babies born to teen mothers of any of the industrialized countries in the world. Although teens engage in similar levels of sexual activity as teens in Western Europe, they do not use contraceptives as effectively.[8] African American teens tend to be sexually active early and to have more teen births, followed by Latina adolescents, and then European American teens.

It is not necessarily parents' young age that accounts for the stresses they and their children experience.[9] When the young children of teen parents are compared to the children of mothers' sisters who had their children at older ages, the cousins perform at similar levels on cognitive tests, suggesting it is not young age but parents' family experiences that are important. When similar comparisons are made when children are adolescents, the adolescents of teen mothers are more likely to have been retained in school than their cousins, suggesting mothers' young age may influence that school outcome.

The Stressful Road to Teen Parenthood

The difficulties many teen parents have experienced and bring to parenting start early and fall into five main categories: (1) the teens' social backgrounds, (2) early family relationships with their own parents, (3) their own personality characteristics, (4) their relationships with peers,[10] and (5) their experience of sexual abuse.[11] The social backgrounds of adolescents who become teen parents contain such risk factors as being the child of an adolescent mother, living in a single-parent home with a parent who has limited education, living in poverty, and living in a community with a high level of poverty and welfare assistance.

The family relationships of adolescent parents often embody change and conflict. Their parents are less involved and less affectionate than parents of teens who do not have teen pregnancies, and they provide less monitoring as well. With parental supervision, teens headed in the direction of deviant behavior tend to stay involved in school and avoid pregnancy.[12]

Teen parents' own personality characteristics in childhood predict later teen pregnancy as early as eight years of age. In longitudinal studies, researchers found that eight-year-old girls who were described by peers as aggressive or aggressive and withdrawn were more likely to be teen mothers than were those girls who were low or average on aggression and withdrawal.[13] In addition, the prospective mothers were more likely to have school and conduct problems in elementary and high school and were more likely to drop out. In grade school, they were more likely to be rejected by peers, and in high school more likely to have deviant friends who broke rules and engaged in high-risk behaviors.

Early maturation and high rates of sexual activity increase girls' chances of becoming pregnant as teens.[14] Studies comparing adolescent mothers with teens who did not have babies have found that adolescent mothers are less independent, less certain of themselves, and less trusting of others. They have a diffuse sense of identity and greater susceptibility to depression. Teen mothers also have experienced more sexual abuse in childhood or early adolescence; in one study, 65 percent had been sexually abused—61 percent by several perpetrators.[15]

Most studies of adolescent parents have focused on mothers.[16] Research has followed samples of boys to determine the characteristics of those who become adolescent fathers. In many instances, they share the qualities of the mothers.[17] They are from low-income families in which parents often have problems with antisocial behavior. Their parents use ineffective disciplinary techniques and do not monitor the boys well. By early adolescence, these boys begin to engage in deviant, rule-breaking activities. They also have little academic success. Another study identified similar risk factors but concluded that the accumulation of risks, not any one of them, was most predictive of adolescent fatherhood.[18]

Teen Parents' Transitions to Parenthood

Interviews with pregnant African American teen mothers' reveal stages they go through as they develop identities as mothers.[19] Their own initial reactions to learning they were pregnant were often negative, as were the reactions of their mothers and friends. Teen mothers felt others looked down on them and felt they were shameful; their mothers were disappointed, sometimes angry and rejecting, and sometimes overwhelmed with the prospect of another child to care for. About half of the fathers were positive, about one quarter ambivalent, and about one quarter negative, with 14 percent denying paternity.

Teen mothers felt the pregnancy brought many negative changes. Teens were no longer attractive, no longer able to be involved in their usual activities. They were no longer teens with freedom and a bright future, but old ladies looking forward to more responsibilities in the future.

Although they lost their old identities, many teens were able to gain a new view of themselves as mothers, good mothers able to care for a new life. To become good mothers, many realized they had to give up negative behaviors, control their anger. "I changed a lot . . . I was more nicer, calmer, things like that . . . I stopped fighting, arguing a lot. I was trying to do better."[20]

What enabled teens to change was the care and support they received from their mothers, extended family members like aunts and grandmothers, their own fathers, and the fathers of their babies. The concern, advice, affection, and help they received gave teen mothers a sense of being connected to others who supported their new identities as mothers. From the support teens gained confidence that they could cope and become the mothers they wanted to be. Recall in Chapter 4, group support was seen as so important for stressed mothers that obstetrical care was provided in a group format that enabled pregnant mothers to talk over their worries with other mothers; the program resulted in a 33 percent decrease in premature births.[21]

The warmth and support that the extended family gave to teen mothers not only increased mothers' capacities for growth but also served as a model for the positive emotional atmosphere the teen mothers would be called upon to provide for their infants.

Teen Mothers' Relationships with Their Own Mothers

After the births of their babies, most teen mothers live with their own mothers as 1996 legislation mandated that to receive government assistance minor teens had to live with a parent or parental guardian and remain in school until graduating from high school.[22] Three kinds of relationships have been observed in teen mothers' relationships with their mothers, the grandmothers:

- replace teen mothers as mothers of the child,
- assist teen mothers and supplement their care as needed,
- assist and teach teens how to be good mothers so teen mothers serve as apprentices and learn from their mothers. The apprentice model has succeeded in helping mothers become effective mothers.

A two-year study following African American teen mothers and their babies found that when grandmothers in three-generation households were direct and demanding in a family atmosphere of low conflict with teens, then teen mothers were not harsh or controlling with their infants.[23] When there was low conflict between grandmothers and mothers, and grandmothers respected teens' autonomy and supported their growing independence, then teen mothers were positive and nurturing with their babies. Grandmothers had the usual task of encouraging teens' growing initiative and autonomy, while at the same time teaching and modeling the complex role of caregiver. Grandmothers and daughters did best when conflict remained low and teens served as apprentices to grandmothers who took pleasure in their daughters' growing competence as a parent.

Grandmothers in the study reported feeling left out of interventions and programs for teen mothers and their children. Yet many grandmothers play a pivotal role in the success of their daughters, and they want information on child development and want groups to talk with other grandmothers and get support for maintaining positive relationships with their daughters and grandchildren and the babies' fathers.

In families of Latina pregnant teens followed from the last trimester of pregnancy through the babies' first year, prenatal stresses such as the unplanned nature of the pregnancy, the financial stresses a new baby creates, and the anticipation of problems all predicted conflict and problematic relationships when babies were one-year-old.[24] Contrary to predictions for African American teens and midwestern pregnant teens to be discussed in a later section, teen mothers' preparation for parenthood predicted greater family conflict and decreases in family cohesion rather than positive outcomes.

Conflict was lower and cohesion increased when Latino families held strong values regarding the importance of family values and obligations, and held traditional beliefs about gender roles and teen mothers' gaining status in the family through having children.

Relationships with Babies' Fathers

Although teen mothers and fathers are usually not married, they are most often romantically involved and teen fathers are generally positive about the pregnancies, and want to be involved in the births and participate in babies' care.[25] About 25 percent of adolescent fathers live with their infants, and a national survey suggests that about 57 percent visit weekly in the first two years of life. The percentage of those visiting drops as the children grow older—from 40 percent when the child is between two and four and a half to 27 percent when the child is four and a half to seven.[26] African American fathers continue to be involved with children. Only 12 percent of African American fathers have no contact with their children, whereas 30 percent of European American fathers and 37 percent of Latino fathers have no contact. Adolescent fathers are more likely to be involved when other people in the environment support their involvement. (See the interview in Chapter 4 with James Levine.)

Like many fathers, teen fathers see their main role as that of being a good provider, and mothers agree.[27] But fathers' circumstances may limit their ability to provide financial resources to mothers. Fathers may still be in school or have low-wage jobs or be unemployed so like teen mothers, they have to adjust their ideals with their current realities. They may be able to give only limited amounts of money as their families of origin may depend on their income. Teen mothers and fathers have to work together to balance the needs of the new family and the needs of both families of origin. The abilities of teen parents to resolve their differences and meet each others' needs helps them to build a coparenting relationship so they can care for their child even if they do not remain a couple.

Fathers also see their role as being there for their child, supporting the child, doing whatever is possible to help him or her.[28] The roles of providers and supporters are related as fathers are more likely to remain involved with their children if they are working and providing for children. As we shall see, fathers' ongoing support of mothers and their children promotes children's competence even if fathers are not living with mothers or romantically involved with them. Fathers' support also increases mothers' effectiveness as a parent; mothers are more positive and less controlling with their infants when they have a good relationship with fathers. These are the same qualities we saw were important in relationships of married couples: positive emotions and support promote maternal competence.

Dads need all the parent training mothers do because they are especially uneasy around crying, fussy babies when they do not understand crying and fussiness and lack strategies for dealing with the distress.[29] Couples' groups of the kinds organized by the Cowans described in Chapter 6 can prevent relationship problems in the transition to parenting and help parents find ways to talk to each other.

Like mothers, fathers benefit from the positive feelings of extended family members. They gain confidence also from special groups for young fathers focused on pursuing job training or further schooling to increase occupational success and from being able to talk to other young fathers.[30]

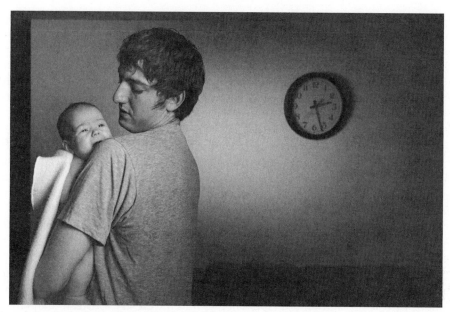

Teen dads need all the parent training that mothers do because they are especially uneasy around crying babies.

Resilient Teens' Parenting

Many teen parents and their children experience problems just described, but many do not. In a longitudinal study in Baltimore, about 75 percent of teen mothers were working in adulthood and not in need of any social services. Delaying a second pregnancy and getting more education predicted greater stability.[31]

A detailed study of Midwestern teen mothers of diverse backgrounds identified characteristics of mothers and children related to children's cognitive, academic, and socioemotional competence as children moved through elementary school. Prior to children's birth, mothers' cognitive readiness to have children, a measure based on mother's knowledge of children and developmental milestones, her expectations of children, her parenting style in response to children's behavior, and attitudes about being mothers predicted children's academic performance on reading achievement and math tests and their ability to cooperate and follow rules in school at age ten.[32] Adding several other measures of mothers' prebirth qualities like IQ, emotional stability, and social status did not improve prediction of children's behavior based on mothers' cognitive readiness to parent.

A three-item measure of postnatal instability—number of residential moves, school changes, and mothers' romantic partners—also predicted reading scores and children's behavioral problems at age ten with instability related to less effective functioning.[33] So two important factors in predicting outcomes for children of teen mothers are mother's readiness to care for children and her postnatal ability to provide stable living arrangements for them.

Resilient children attained developmental milestones in academic work, emotional stability, and social competence. At age five, 31 percent of children were described as resilient, and at age fourteen, 29 percent. Resilient children came primarily from homes described as "low adversity." Mothers had self-esteem, confidence, gained education, and had job stability. Those resilient children living in adverse environments experienced support from adults outside the immediate family such as fathers or grandparents.

A model describing a process of risk or resilience for children included mothers' prebirth qualities reflecting psychological adjustment, ability to learn, absence of a history of abuse or substance abuse, and the presence of support from fathers, friends, and parents.[34] These qualities helped mothers develop a cognitive readiness for caring for children. Cognitive readiness and infants' characteristics predicted mothers' effective parenting techniques that, in turn, predicted children's competence.

The child's relationship with their mothers was the most important source of support in coping with negative life events, but three other factors combined to yield an overall measure of social support.[35] (1) positive relationships with fathers, (2) family's religious involvement, and (3) children's participation in sports and community activities. Fathers' involvement included financial support, emotional support, caregiving, and other help. When children were age fourteen, 69 percent had some contact with fathers. Although only 8 percent lived with their fathers, fathers were important figures, as 37 percent described fathers as their most important male role model.

Fathers' positive support was related to lower levels of aggressiveness and noncompliance at school and, for sons, to higher levels of reading achievement. Fathers' support was especially important when mothers were considered to have many difficulties functioning. Contact with fathers prevented the increase in children's emotional problems.

The family's involvement in religious activities helped both mothers and children. Compared to mothers low on religious involvement, those mothers involved in church communities had higher self-esteem, more positive and less harsh parenting behaviors, greater educational and occupational success, and their children had fewer behavior problems. Churches may have provided social supports such as job opportunities and child care that enabled mothers to work. A third protective factor was the child's participation in community activities and sports.

Other studies have found that teen mothers of resilient children were more child-centered and more authoritative in their parenting, praising children and communicating rules in a positive way.[36]

In brief, the qualities most likely to stimulate children's development and adaptability are parenting qualities of mothers and fathers—sensitive, responsive, authoritative maternal caregiving, fathers' support and positive relationships with children—children's participation in active community pursuits, having supports from grandparents, a stable lifestyle and involvement in church activities that give a sense of a larger order and meaning to life as well as practical help with the everyday demands of life. These are the same qualities that predict competence in two-parent families. They are just harder to achieve when you are trying to find your own identity and at the same time cope with more than the usual number of stressors.

Risks in Teen Parenting

If stress is high and teen parents do not get education and support, their expectations of children are often unrealistic, and as a result their parenting is often insensitive and unresponsive to children's needs.[37] They are also less likely to provide verbal and cognitive stimulation for their children than older parents. This is true of both mothers and fathers in their interactions with children.[38]

Their children are at risk for problems as shown in a very detailed study of teen mothers and their children. Although most infants were healthy and cognitive measures indicated they were developing well in the first year, social-emotional measures indicated some difficulties at six months, and at one year of age, 63 percent of babies were described as having insecure attachments to mothers.[39] This was a higher rate of insecure attachments than has been found in low-income families.

In the toddler years, language delays were seen, and cognitive delays were noted at age three. In one study, 72 percent of children had at least one area of delay at age three, and 44 percent had two or more areas of delay.[40] Mothers noted anxious, worried moods and aggressive behaviors by age three. In the school years, children continued to have delays in language, cognitive, and social-emotional skills.

By adolescence, problems with impulse control and emotional regulation were marked, just as had occurred with their parents. Teens of adolescent mothers are more likely than others to become teen parents (in one study, 40 percent of girls and 21 percent of boys);[41] still, the majority of children of teenage mothers do not themselves become teen parents. Even when they delay childbearing, however, children of teen mothers are not as competent and well adjusted in early adulthood as are the children of those mothers who delayed pregnancy until their twenties.

Programs for Adolescent Parents

Because of risk factors for children and their parents, much attention has been given to programs for teen parents, and these programs can be divided into those aimed at (1) preventing the first teen pregnancy, (2) those aimed at helping teen parents cope with pregnancy, birth, and caregiving of children, and (3) those helping teens successfully negotiate the transition to adulthood so they can complete their educations, get stable jobs, form satisfying relationships with partners, and raise their children.[42]

Pregnancy prevention programs often start in adolescence and focus on sex education, successful use of contraceptives, and social skills to assert opinions with partners. Some successful educational programs reduce sexual activity and increase contraceptive use, but even greater use of contraceptives occurs when teens have ready access to low-cost contraceptives.[43]

Programs also seek to decrease sexual activity by promoting other activities and developing other skills so teens have alternative pursuits.[44] Programs to increase educational opportunities have had success in decreasing sexual activity and pregnancies, and programs encouraging participation in community service work have also been effective. Reviewing all the difficulties teen parents experienced early in grade school highlights the need for these programs to begin early to help children develop competence in early elementary school. If schools stimulate academic and social competence and children have fun with peers, children will be less likely to disengage from school in frustration and engage in impulsive, deviant behaviors like substance use and high-risk sexual activity.

Once teens are pregnant, programs are useful to provide information on children's needs and developmental patterns, effective ways to form secure attachments, engaging with infants and providing stimulating activities, and positive parenting strategies for dealing with problem behaviors typical of the age.[45] Many parenting programs also include home visits in the first three years. The most lasting effects are achieved when visits start prenatally and when they help young teens prevent a second pregnancy.

A large national parenting program has as its goal the prevention of child abuse and neglect, which is more frequent among teen parents than older parents.[46] The program provides teens a new mental model of what it means to be a parent. In addition, it teaches parenting skills in a one-on-one relationship, emphasizing positive caregiving and stimulating children's behavior. It teaches parents how to play and attend to children. Parents then teach these skills to one other family member.

A third kind of program helps teen parents make the transition to adulthood, connecting them with educational and community resources so they can complete their education and compete in the job market.[47] Such programs also help teen parents form positive relationships with the other parent so that parents can work together to rear their children.

UNMARRIED COHABITING AND SINGLE PARENTS

Concerned about the increasing number of babies born to unmarried parents and uncertain about how parents and children fared in these families, social scientists at Princeton and Columbia Universities initiated a study of 5,000 babies born in cities of over 200,000 in the years of 1998–2000, oversampling the babies of unmarried mothers.[48] The study, titled Fragile Families and Child Well-being Study (FFCWS), included interviews with mothers and fathers in the hospital, and then again when children were one, three, and five years of age with observations of children recorded at those times. Three-quarters of the sample were unmarried parents, 50 percent cohabiting and 30 percent romantically involved with each other.

Table 14.1 reveals the many vulnerabilities of unmarried parents, both cohabiting and single, who resemble each other on many characteristics. Although 80 percent of all three samples of mothers were employed in the previous year, the economic resources were very different for married parents compared to both groups of unmarried parents. This is because unmarried parents had much lower educational levels due, in part, to the large number of teen mothers in the single group who had not completed their education (34 percent compared to 4 and 18 percent in the married and cohabiting groups of mothers); poverty was also more widespread in the unmarried samples.

Although all three groups of mothers were similar in levels of depression with about 13 to 16 percent being depressed, unmarried mothers were more likely to have additional stresses from excessive drinking and illegal drug use and from

■ **TABLE 14-1**
CHARACTERISTICS OF MOTHERS IN FRAGILE FAMILIES AND
CHILD WELL-BEING STUDY*

	Age of Mothers	Education: % Less Than High School	% College Graduate
Married	29	18	36
Cohabiting	25	41	2
Single	22	49	2

	Mothers' Mean Earnings	Household Income	% in Poverty
Married	$25,618	$55,057	14
Cohabiting	$11,433	$26,548	32
Single	$10,764	$18,662	53

	% Heavy Drinking	% Illegal Drug Use	% Fathers in Jail
Married	2	0.3	8
Cohabiting	8	8	32
Single	8	8	45

*Adapted from: Ariel Kalil and Rebecca M. Ryan, "Mothers' Economic Conditions and Sources of Support," *Future of Children 20* (2010): 39–61.

fathers' incarceration. Unmarried parents were also three times more likely than married parents to have ties with previous partners with whom they had children to care for (35 and 38 percent of single and cohabiting parents compared to 12 percent of married parents).

When low-income, unmarried mothers experience the many stresses detailed in Table 14.1, having access to support from friends, relatives, and the child's father provide a sense of security that reduces mothers' stress levels and enables them to parent more effectively.[49] When mothers in the FFCWS sample reported they had individuals who could lend them money, give them a place to live, provide emergency child care, then mothers' reported lower levels of anxiety and depression, and their children had fewer worries.

In a study of African American single mothers, support came from others who served as a coparent to the single mothers: maternal grandmothers (31 percent of families), biological fathers (26 percent), maternal aunts (11 percent), older sisters (11 percent), and others (21 percent).[50] When the coparent relationship was a positive one, mothers were warmer in their interactions with their children and more consistent in monitoring them, and mothers reported children performed better in school and had fewer social problems than when the coparent relationship had conflict.

Mothers who reported positive coparenting support from fathers over time after dissolution of the relationship were mothers who had more committed relationships with fathers prior to the dissolution. If mothers became involved in a new romantic relationship, then they reported a decline in coparenting support.[51]

A major factor interfering with mothers' abilities to form supportive relationships with biological fathers or new partners is mothers' distrust of men.[52] In one study, 96 percent of low-income unmarried mothers reported they distrusted men, but did have relationships with them. About 22 percent were able to work through issues of trust and have satisfying relationships but three-quarters of the women leaped into relationships or had compartmentalized relationships that ended in disappointment, confirming their beliefs about men's reliability. Age, ethnicity, and education did not distinguish the groups that could and could not establish trustworthy relationships, but the childhood experience of physical and/or sexual abuse did. Seventy-five percent of women who did not form trusting relationships with men experienced childhood abuse compared to 31 percent of women who formed trusting bonds.

Even when single mothers have known childhood adversity and struggle with economic worries, mothers who have optimistic temperaments and focus on the positive in life are able to maintain warm relationships with their children and manage their behavior effectively so children achieve academically and enjoy school.[53]

Children of Unmarried Parents

Children born to unmarried mothers take many paths to adulthood; no one outcome characterizes them all.[54] Many family changes and limited resources create the parental strain and parenting difficulties that are associated with children's behavior problems in the first three years of life.[55] Across all ethnic groups, partner changes that occur significantly more often in single-parent households predict parents' reports of children's anxious and depressed moods and their aggressive behaviors at age three. The greater the number of changes, the greater is the increase in children's problem behaviors. Parents' stress and declining parenting skills independently account for the relationship between partner changes and problem behaviors. The reverse relationships are not statistically significant, indicating that children's problem behaviors and parents' stress do not predict partner changes.

FFCWS data for the first five years indicate that family instability (number of moves and family changes) predicts lower scores on measures of verbal skills and cognitive development.[56] However, with respect to aggressive behavior problems, living with an unmarried parent, regardless of the level of stability in the family, predicted the development of such behaviors. When children lived in cohabiting families, stability of the family minimized the risk of such problems.

Parents living in single-mother and in cohabiting families report that their children aged six to seventeen have a greater number of school difficulties, peer problems, more worries and anxieties, and, in high school, mood and school problems and noncompliant and less trustworthy behavior than are reported for children living with their married biological parents.[57] When economic and parental resources are controlled, differences between children six to eleven disappear with the exception of school difficulties, but in the adolescent years, differences between children in single- and two-parent homes are found at every economic and social level.

Protective factors in the child, the mother, the parent-child relationship, and the larger social context buttress children from stress and predict positive outcomes for them. Eight protective factors were divided into four categories:

- the child's characteristics (positive sociability and attentiveness),
- maternal qualities (efficacy and low risk of depression),
- parenting qualities (positive parent-child relationship and fathers' involvement),
- qualities of the larger social context (social support and few difficult life experiences).

In a sample of disadvantaged, never-married mothers, families averaged three out of the eight protective factors, and 20 percent of families had five or more protective factors.

Protective factors assessed when children were eighteen and twenty-one months of age predicted measures of cognitive and social functioning at preschool age.[58] All protective factors except the father's involvement predicted competent psychological functioning, as measured by low aggressive, anxious, depressed, hyperactive, dependent, and withdrawn behaviors.

Only the child's characteristics and positive parent-child relationship predicted cognitive competence, as measured by higher scores on a school-readiness test. The most important aspect of the parent-child relationship for later well-being was the absence of harsh discipline. Economic disadvantage may have its greatest impact on families by intensifying maternal distress that leads to harsh discipline. The more protective factors in the child's family, the better the child functioned. Nevertheless, even the children with the greatest number of protective factors scored below average, at the 32nd percentile, on the measure of school readiness.

In predicting adult outcomes, research indicates children in stable living situations generally got more education and were economically self-sufficient and independent in adulthood.[59] Stability could come through adoption to two parents, through living in a stable single-parent family, or living in a three-generational family with single mother and grandparents. Living with grandparents without the mother was related to lower educational attainment and to a higher probability of leaving home by age eighteen.

The evidence from many studies, then, suggests that there is no single outcome for children of never-married and single mothers. When children (1) have stable living arrangements, and (2) experience positive parenting, they have greater social and cognitive competence.

Programs to Promote Parents' and Children's Effectiveness

The first programs directed at unmarried fathers sought to collect child support payments from them as a way of increasing mothers' economic resources.[60] The program had limited results because many unmarried fathers lacked jobs, but when fathers did make support payments, then they were more likely to stay connected to children. A second form of intervention sought to encourage marriage between unmarried parents, but in the absence of skills for solving conflicts and working together, marriages resulted in parents and children living in angry conflict. As a result, the focus has shifted to improving couples' relationships by developing emotional coping skills and problem-solving strategies so whether they live together, marry or not, they can coparent. The couples groups devised by Carolyn and Philip Cowan and described in Chapter 6 have proven a successful intervention to improve low income and unmarried parents' skills in getting along and working together to rear children and increase stability in their children's lives.[61]

A second category of interventions focuses on increasing economic resources for fragile families through food programs, health care, and general assistance.[62] Families' economic resources are increased through work programs that advance occupational skills of both mothers and fathers or through proposed monetary funds available to families at times of emergencies.

A third kind of intervention focuses on providing services directly to promote children's development and well-being through home visiting programs and high-quality preschool education programs.[63]

At times of family disruptions, programs for divorced parents and children should include unmarried parents and their children as well because family separations are as painful and difficult even if parents are not married.

SINGLE MOTHERS BY CHOICE

A small number of women make a conscious choice to have a child alone through adoption, assisted reproductive technology, or very occasionally through an unplanned pregnancy as a relationship or marriage ended. Strong desires for a child along with the feeling that they have lost the opportunity to do this under the ideal circumstances of marriage to a loved partner spur women to consider this option. These mothers are in some way the mirror image of the mothers we have just been discussing. This is a relatively homogeneous subgroup of unmarried mothers.[64] They are well educated, European American women who are in their mid- to late-thirties. They have good incomes and satisfying jobs, and many have changed lifestyles in advance of having children (e.g., buying a home, moving closer to relatives who can be a support group. See first person narrative. They are, however, only a small proportion of unmarried parents, in the FFCWS, only about 2 percent of unmarried mothers).[65]

Children of Advantaged Single Mothers

A careful study of single-parent and married-couple families matched for parents' education, income, area of residence, and age and gender of the child observed maternal and child interactions when the child was in the preschool years and a second time when children were ages eight to thirteen.[66]

In the preschool years, single mothers reported more stress than did mothers in two-parent families. Single mothers had to work longer hours and were more worried about finances than were their married counterparts. The greatest difference between these two groups of mothers, however, was that single mothers had fewer social and emotional supports when their children were young. It was precisely this

Living near extended family members provides support for single mothers and their children.

kind of support that predicted optimal parent-child interactions in both single- and two-parent families. When single mothers had socioemotional support, their children's behavior was similar to that of children in two-parent families.

In the preschool years, observations of mothers' and children's behaviors during a mother-directed teaching task revealed few differences between single and married parents, with the exception that single mothers had difficulty managing the behaviors of sons, who were often noncompliant and resistant to mothers' requests. In the years eight to thirteen, however, teachers described children of single mothers as less socially competent, less successful academically, and more problematic in behavior than children of married parents.

Stressful life events in single-mother families had a more direct impact on mothers' parenting and on children's behavior than it did in two-parent families. Single mothers with high stress were less nurturing and less effective in parenting, and children living in high-stress single-parent homes, independent of parenting, showed more problems. Stressful life events affected children directly and indirectly through mothers' parenting. Teachers and mothers described school-age children living in homes where mothers had high stress levels as having the most problems.

The behavior of children living in single-parent homes with low stress was similar to that of children in two-parent homes. It is the stress level that is critical, perhaps because there are not two parents to manage the stress and care for children. It points to the importance of a strong support system for single mothers even when they have the same educational and income level as two-parent families.

Jane Mattes founded Single Mothers by Choice (SMC), a national organization, to provide information and resources for mothers on the many options for handling the common challenges mothers face as they conceive and rear children.[67]

Box 14-1
FIRST PERSON NARRATIVE*

Wanting to become a mother but divorced, thirty-six years old, and fearful she would not be able to conceive if she waited to find the right husband, journalist Mikki Morrissette decided to become a single mother by choice (SMC) using donor sperm from a friend to conceive her daughter. Almost six years later she had a son using sperm from the same donor, and while pregnant met and later married her husband, a widower who was raising two teenage children, one, a special-needs daughter with aggressive behavior problems.

Her book, *Choosing Single Parenthood*, describes her thoughts and experiences as a Choice Mother, as she refers to herself, and also pulls together information from psychologists, psychotherapists, and other social scientists, as well as from other mothers and their children to give a very full picture of the rewards and difficulties of rearing children alone. She provides guidelines for answering the questions single mothers typically ask themselves before becoming Choice Moms: Will they have the psychological and economic resources to raise a child alone? Do they have a network of friends and relatives who will support them as mothers? Are they making a selfish choice? Will their children have difficulties because of growing up in a single-parent household? Will their children blame them for becoming single mothers by choice and not giving them fathers?

She raises and provides women's answers to the charge that it is selfish for a single mother to give birth to a child to satisfy her personal desire to be a parent when the child will lack a father and miss important experiences growing up. She says mothers must feel comfortable with their own answers to that charge because at some point they will have to explain their decision to their children, and that can be done most effectively when mothers feel comfortable with their choice. She states Choice Mothers have to accept that others may feel they are selfish even if they themselves feel they are not because they have sacrificed to have a child and have preferred having a child alone to trapping a husband in a loveless marriage in order to satisfy their needs for a child. If mothers believe they are being selfish to give birth to a child alone, they can wait until they do have a husband or adopt a child who has no parent.

Her conversations with teen and adult children of Choice Mothers provide children's points of view. Although the children were all volunteers and do not make up a representative sample so we cannot draw firm conclusions, their statements are still valuable. Almost all indicated they were not angry at mothers or sad at not having a father in their life. They would like to have had a father, and many were curious as to what it would have been like, but mothers had arranged relationships with men for both sons and daughters so children had men in their lives to model. Several said they missed having a sibling, someone to interact with and someone to provide more family life and activity.

All children, whether adopted or conceived by donor sperm, felt they had a right to know their biological father and his family. They did not want a strong relationship so much as they wanted to learn about the missing pieces of their biological inheritance just as children adopted into two-parent families did. Those who did meet fathers wanted to see the resemblance between them: Did they have funny ears or big feet? Did they like science or music? Were they active? And they wanted to know about fathers' extended families as well.

> **Box 14-1**
> **CONTINUED**
>
> Choice mothers expressed no regrets at rearing a child on their own. Like all parents, they felt the laughter, love, and connections to others that children brought into their lives far outweighed any difficulty involved.
>
> Written with her son, Sam Lamott, Anne Lamott's memoir, *Some Assembly Required: A Journal of My Son's First Son,*** chronicles the first year in the life of her grandson, Jax, born to young, unmarried parents whose romantic relationship had come apart from tensions and disagreements when they learned Amy, Jax's mother, was expecting a child she was determined to raise.
>
> Sam's determination to be a father was fueled by the absence of his father in the early years of his life. Even though Sam had wonderful male mentors like his uncles and his grandfather and he and his father forged closer bonds as Sam grew older and approached adulthood, still the early loss of his father's love strengthened Sam's resolve to be part of his son's life, "Even though I was too young, and too terrified and confused, to be a dad, I promised God and Jax that I would show up and be the best father I could be."***
>
> Amy and Sam moved in together and cared for Jax while at the same time forging a mutual bond that could support their caregiving. The book illustrates the powerful role that supportive grandparents and extended family members play in supplementing income, giving emotional support, and providing a stable structure that nourishes both parents and their baby. With this strong insulating layer of love and caring, parents can rear a happy, thriving baby who draws all family and friends together even when parents are sometimes at odds with each other.
>
> *Mikki Morrissette, *Choosing Single Motherhood: The Thinking Woman's Guide* (Boston: Houghton Mifflin, 2008).
> **Anne Lamott with Sam Lamott, *Some Assembly Required: A Journal of My Son's First Son* (New York: Riverhead Books, 2012).
> ***Ibid., pp. 252–253.

FATHERS' ROLE IN CHILDREN'S LIVES

We saw in Chapter 12 that fathers' increased role in dual-earner families benefits children as well as mothers who are both working and rearing children. How does diminished contact with fathers affect children?

Fathers' Presence or Absence

Using data from several longitudinal samples, Sara McLanahan and Julien Teitler report the consequences of father presence and absence for children's development, along with the factors underlying those consequences.[68] They report that, compared to children growing up in two-parent families with fathers present, children growing up apart from fathers have lower grades, achieve less education, are more likely to drop out of school, and are less likely to get and keep a job.

Adolescent girls in father-absent homes were more likely to initiate sexual activity at an early age and to have a teen birth or a birth outside of marriage. In one study, 11 percent of adolescent girls in two-parent families had a teen birth, compared with 27 percent of girls in father-absent families. Father absence had a greater effect on the risk for teen births for European American and Latina teens than for African American teens.

The effects of father presence on educational attainment did not vary as a result of gender or racial or ethnic status of the family. Boys and girls of all ethnic groups had increased educational attainment when fathers were present. It did not seem to matter when fathers' absence occurred or how long it lasted. Nor did it matter what family structure the child lived in, with one exception: children in homes with widowed mothers did nearly as well as children in two-parent families. In general, father absence matters more than the circumstances causing it, except in the case of widowhood.

Fathers' Contributions to Children's Lives

McLanahan and Teitler identified three aspects of fathers' contributions: financial, social, and community. Fathers' financial contribution improves the resources available for child rearing. Without the additional resources, families may not have services such as health care and may live in poorer neighborhoods with poorer schools and fewer community services. They estimate that reduced income accounts for approximately 50 percent of the effects of father absence.

These researchers estimate that about half the disadvantage of father-absent homes results from poorer parent-child relationships, poorer relationships with adults, and a loss of resources in the community. As noted, it is extremely difficult for one parent to provide as much time, attention, and balance in parenting as two parents; nevertheless, some single-parent mothers do establish low-conflict homes in which children's functioning improves.

Paul Amato conducted new analyses of data to determine fathers' contributions to children's lives.[69] He looked at both mothers' and fathers' contributions in terms of human, financial, and social capital. *Human capital* refers to parents' skills, abilities, and knowledge that contribute to achievement in our culture. A useful measure of human capital is parents' education. *Financial capital* refers to the economic resources available to the family to purchase needed goods and services. *Social capital* refers to family and social relationships available to promote children's development.

Amato distinguished between the benefits of the coparental relationship and those of the parent-child relationship. In a positive coparental relationship, the child views a model of how two people relate, cooperate, negotiate, and compromise. Children who learn these skills tend to get along better with peers and later partners. In providing a unified authority structure to children, two parents teach that authority is consistent and rational. Amato writes, "Social closure between parents helps children to learn and internalize social norms and moral values. Also, a respect for hierarchical authority, first learned in the family, makes it easier for young people to adjust to social institutions that are hierarchically organized, such as schools and the workplace."[70]

Looking at many studies, Amato demonstrates that children's well-being is positively associated with (1) the father's education, (2) the father's income, (3) the quality of the coparental relationship, and (4) the quality of the parent-child relationship. These relationships hold in two- and one-parent families as well, even in studies with controls for mothers' contributions.

In his own longitudinal study, Amato interviewed individuals originally studied as children and followed up to early adulthood. He has found that fathers' education and income are related to children's education and that children's education has positive implications for such areas as friendships, self-esteem, and life satisfaction. Fathers' characteristics appear to account for more variance in children's education, self-esteem, and lack of psychological distress than do mothers' characteristics. Mothers' characteristics account for more variance in children's developing kin ties and close friends than do fathers' characteristics. Fathers' and mothers' characteristics account for equal amounts of variance in life satisfaction. Amato summarizes,

> Current research suggests that fathers continue to be important for their contributions of human and financial capital. Current research also suggests, however, that children benefit when fathers are involved in socioemotional aspects of family life . . . the current trend for fathers to be less involved in their children's lives (due to shifts in family structure) represents a net decline in the level of resources available for children.[71]

Studies show that nonresidential fathers who confine their activities with children to fun outings play a minimal role in children's development. Amato concludes that fathers matter "to the extent that they are able to provide appropriate support, guidance, and monitoring—especially if this occurs in the context of cooperation between the parents."[72]

Unmarried Fathers

In the future, we may have more unmarried fathers like David Marin, men who are similar to Choice Mothers, with good incomes and education, no romantic partner but a strong desire to parent, but at present there is no research on such a sample.[73]

Currently most research is on unmarried fathers who cohabit or reside separately from their children. Men need not be married and living with children to have a positive impact. As we saw, the children of teen mothers benefited from their relationships with their fathers in the same ways as children living with biological fathers—namely in the areas of school performance and reduced aggressiveness. Boys especially got better grades when fathers were involved.[74]

Fathers also need not be biological fathers to have an impact. Social fathers, defined as men who live with a young child's mother, had a positive impact on children's lives when they were highly engaged with the child.[75] High levels of engagement with children predicted lower levels of aggressive behaviors and better health in children regardless of whether the father was a biological or social father. Social fathers did not diminish the positive relationships children had with their biological nonresident fathers. They seemed to compliment them.

Nonresident unmarried fathers were most likely to stay highly involved over a two-year period when they had positive relationships with mothers, and each parent had positive relationships with the other's parents.[76] The extended family, positively supporting both parents, helped fathers to stay involved. The major variable, however, was the parents' romantic involvement. When parents were romantically involved, fathers were engaged. When the romantic relationship ended, fathers decreased their contact. If the romance resumed, fathers became more engaged. One of the policy implications is that if parents get training in relationship and communication skills, they may be better able to continue the romantic relationship that holds the family together.

Children certainly want their fathers involved in their lives. Survey responses of college students whose parents divorced during childhood revealed that 70 percent of men and women believe that equal time with both parents is the best living arrangement after divorce; less than 10 percent of students wanted less time with fathers.[77]

Benefits to Fathers of Engagement with Their Children

We have seen that it is good for children when fathers are active participants in their lives. It is also good for fathers. Unmarried fathers who cohabit or contribute financially to their children earn higher wages and work more hours over a five-year period than unwed fathers who do not cohabit or contribute to children's care.[78] Using data from the FFCWS, researchers found that men who stayed involved with their children over time became more stable and more mature individuals as a result. Data suggested that engaged fathers make constructive life changes for their children that they will not make for themselves or for the mothers of their children.[79] Recall in Chapter 1, the positive changes many parents felt in their own lives as a result of becoming parents.

Encouraging Fathers' Participation

James Levine has written extensively on the advantages for children of fathers' increased involvement regardless of whether fathers are married to mothers.[80] He identifies three lessons he has learned over the years.

The first important ingredient in successfully involving fathers is the recognition that fathers want to be involved and can be effective parents with preparation and help. Second, single fathers need a support network that guides their behavior. Third, women play a key role in supporting men as fathers.

Fathers who confine their activities with children to fun outings play a minimal role in children's lives. Fathers matter when they provide appropriate support, guidance, and monitoring with children.

In this chapter we have seen there are many vulnerabilities and many forms of intervention that can help families of unmarried parents. Yet we are living in a recessionary economy in which all levels of government help are reduced. This requires that we look to individual and voluntary community efforts to provide the parenting classes and relationship and communication skills classes that are so helpful to these parents. All of us in our individual and community activities can look for opportunities to extend positive support to these families particularly as they are often grappling with many stresses. Increasing community park and recreational activities, calling in people from the Search Institute as described in Chapter 1 to benefit the whole community, are initiatives we can all take.

MAIN POINTS

Family structures have changed over the last forty years with

- parents marrying later
- an increase in unmarried couples living together and marrying later
- increasing number of babies born to unmarried parents who have a child by a previous partner
- increase in single women having children alone by choice

Teen parents

- come to parenting having experienced many difficulties and less parental support
- are more effective parents when they understand children's development and their needs and are able to respond sensitively to children
- are helped by programs that support parents' caregiving and their transition to adulthood

Children of teen parents are more likely to develop effective behaviors when

- mothers are stable, sensitive caregivers
- fathers are positive and involved with children
- family receives support from communities like religious groups
- children themselves are involved in athletic and community activities

Unmarried parents

- are a heterogeneous group that includes many parents with less education and fewer economic resources and a small group of parents with education, good jobs and resources
- regardless of resources need to build a support group that will support their efforts as unmarried parents
- need to make provisions as best they can for child to have contact with nonresident biological parent

When compared to children in two-parent families, children in unmarried parent families are at greater risk for

- resistant, noncompliant behaviors at age three
- school problems, peer problems, and anxiety and worry when in elementary school years
- school and mood problems as well as concompliant behaviors in high school

- problems when mothers are under high levels of stress but not at risk when single mothers had the same levels of stress as parents in married families

Men make positive contributions to children's development when

- they provide their human, financial, and social capital to the family
- the social context encourages their involvement

EXERCISES

1. Explore what programs are available in your community for teen mothers and teen fathers. How do teen parents meet requirements for high school graduation in the local high schools? Are there programs that care for infants at school while mothers attend classes?

2. Explore what programs are available in the community for the mothers of teen parents so they can get information and support to teach and support their daughters in becoming effective parents.

3. Look in the community to determine what training is available for unmarried parents in relationship and communication skills so they can improve and maintain their relationships.

4. Explore the programs available in the community to teach parenting skills to unmarried fathers who are not teens. Are there support groups for unmarried fathers? occupational training groups for unmarried men and women who are not teens?

5. Look at the activities in your community and see how some can be adapted to meet the needs of unmarried parents who live there.

ADDITIONAL READINGS

Connor, Michael E. and White, Joseph L., eds. *Black Fathers: An Invisible Presence in America.* Mahwah, NJ: Erlbaum, 2006.

Lamott, Anne with Sam Lamott. *Some Assembly Required: A Journal of My Son's First Son* (New York: Riverhead Books, 2012).

Mattes, Jane. *Single Mothers by Choice: A Guidebook for Single Women Who Are Considering or Have Chosen Motherhood.*, 2nd ed. New York: Times Books, 1997.

Marin, David. *This Is US: The New All-American Family.* United States: Exterminating Angel Press, 2011.

Morrissette, Mikki. *Choosing Motherhood: The Thnking Woman's Guide.* Boston: Houghton Mifflin, 2008.

15

Parenting in Divorced Families and Remarried Families

CHAPTER TOPICS

In this chapter, you will learn about:

- Process of divorce and the intense feelings and changes parents and children experience

- Actions parents can take to help children function well during the divorce and afterward

- Experiences of parents and children in stepfamilies

- The actions parents can take to help children function well in stepfamilies

Test Your Knowledge: Fact or Fiction (True/False)

1. Most adults are so traumatized and financially burdened by divorce that only a minority remarry and form new families.
2. A collaborative divorce process offers parents opportunities for arriving at divorce agreements without going through adversarial legal court proceedings.
3. As long as parents in conflict stay married, their children experience fewer problems than those children whose parents divorce.
4. Feelings of anger and loss naturally disappear over time in divorced families.
5. With all the stresses of divorce and remarriage, the same principles of authoritative parenting that have positive effects in intact families do not provide benefits in stepfamilies.

In this chapter we focus on parenting when parents decide to dissolve the legal ties that bind them together. We look at how parents and children fare in this process and at actions that can decrease difficulties for all involved. We then look at how families repartner and form new families and actions that can ease that transition.

The parenting issues discussed in Chapters 14, 15, and 16 overlap as single unmarried parents, regardless of gender orientation, may marry or cohabit and have the experience of forming a stepfamily, and divorced parents may have similar experiences to those of single unmarried parents once the divorce is complete. The particular experiences of gay/lesbian/transgendered families are discussed in Chapter 16. In Chapter 15, we focus first on divorcing parents who dissolve a legal partnership, though the pain and necessity for negotiations apply to all who have lived together and decide to separate, and then on remarried or repartnered parents.

The majority of American women are estimated to marry by the age of thirty: 81 percent of European American women, 77 percent of Latina women, and 52 percent of African American women marry with those having the highest levels of education marrying most frequently.[1] While the divorce rate of American families increased in the 1950s, 1960s, and 1970s, it has leveled off and even decreased a bit. It is estimated that between 40 to 50 percent of marriages will end in divorce.[2] Asian Americans and Latina families have the lowest rates of divorce, and African American families, the highest. Of those who divorce, the large majority will marry again—about two-thirds of women and three-quarters of men; 60 percent of these marriages end in divorce.[3] So, in this chapter we discuss experiences that affect large numbers of men, women, and children.

DIVORCED PARENTS

Both men and women seeking divorce say communication problems, incompatibility, and marital unhappiness led to the divorce. Wives, who initiate divorces in about 66 percent of cases, are also likely to cite serious emotional and behavioral problems like extramarital affairs, physical spousal abuse, problematic levels of drinking, and neglect of children, whereas husbands are more likely to cite daily interpersonal stresses like wives' whining, nagging, and faultfinding.[4] Several demographic factors make it more likely parents will divorce: young age, low levels of education, being from a divorced family, cohabiting premaritally, and having a child premaritally.[5]

When adults marry, they make formal, legal, and sometimes religious commitments to stay together for life, so when couples find it necessary to divorce, feelings of deep disappointment and grief accompany the process.[6] These feelings are especially painful for the large majority of men and women who did not initiate the divorce; in one study, only 20 percent of divorces were sought by both spouses.[7] Couples who have cohabited may also experience similar difficulties in separating and finding mutually agreed upon solutions for their children.

The Grief Process

On the basis of clinical work and research, Robert Emery describes the grief cycle that the process of divorce triggers.[8] We discuss this first because if parents do not cope effectively with their grief, their feelings can interfere with successful solutions in the process of divorce.

Grief is a complicated combination of feelings of anger, sadness, love, and longing for the marriage that was. When individuals lose a loved one or a valued job, they go through the cycle of feelings at varying rates but they have to accept the loss. In the divorce process, the loss is not a complete loss of the relationship but a changed nature of the relationship. Once couples have children, they will always be involved with each other even when children are grown and independent because there are weddings and holidays and special occasions to be arranged, so the grief process is more complicated.

Emery says in the beginning of the divorce process, adults swing through cycles of love, anger, and sadness with each feeling experienced separately and intensely, and parents are often at different stages of feelings from their spouses. Over time, feelings decrease in intensity and begin to blend together with love mixed with anger, or sadness tinged with love and longing for the marriage, and eventually the emotions all blend together, resulting in a realistic, integrated set of feelings about the marriage.

Emery says parents sometimes get stuck in one of these feelings, often anger, that dominates parents' feelings and their decisions about children. Anger may be justified; hanging on to it may protect the parent from other feelings like sadness or fear, and may make them feel powerful rather than helpless. However, decisions made in anger often do not help children or parents themselves. To manage their own anger and cope with the anger of the other parent, Emery suggests that parents harness their angry feelings by:

- accepting all their feelings about the divorce, writing about them or talking to friends or a therapist about them
- not responding to partners' provocations
- maintaining a neutral, business-like approach to solving problems, speaking only briefly
- deciding to focus on the most important issues and letting unimportant issues go
- being pleasant and emotionally neutral with spouse or partner when in the presence of the children
- examining one's own role in the marital problems
- remembering the good times and the fun even though there is sadness at the loss

Emery believes parents never completely get over the grief because that would mean giving up memories of all the love and hope they had when they entered the marriage that created their children, but they cope with grief and move beyond it to establish appropriate boundaries and new relationships with their spouses.

Children too experience grief though they may not go through the cycle of emotions as their parents do. They have lost their family as they have known it, and parents' task, according to Emery, is to help the child through the grief process, encouraging children to express their emotions to parents even though parents' actions are the cause of pain. Parents can take other actions as well: permitting children to have their own emotional reactions; helping children gain insight into feelings and find words to express them; talking about one's own feelings as is appropriate; and finally reducing losses from the divorce as much as possible so that although parents are not together, children still have their friends, their activities, and typical childhood experiences.

The Process of Divorce

Mavis Hetherington, who has carried out careful longitudinal studies of intact, divorced, and remarried families for four decades, describes four basic facts about divorce: (1) divorce is not a single event but an event that triggers many changes for children and parents over time; (2) changes associated with marital transitions have to be viewed as changes in the entire family system—parents, children, and extended family members; (3) the entire social milieu—peer group, neighborhood, school, friendship network—influences an individual's response to the transition; and (4) there is great diversity in the ways children and parents respond to marital transitions.[9] Most studies of families in transition focus on European American middle-class families, and we do not know how widely we can generalize these findings.

The changes of divorce—new households, changes in finances, changes in parents' and children's moods and behaviors, increased responsibilities in caring for children alone—all create stress for parents. Religious beliefs can increase or decrease the stress of divorce.[10] When people believe divorce is breaking sacred vows, they are more likely to report depression at the time of divorce. If divorcing adults focus on feelings of guilt, and loss of trust in God to prevent bad outcomes, they are more likely to be depressed a year later. When, however, religious people feel their beliefs give them strength in coping with stress and motivate them to avoid anger and find effective solutions, these people feel greater optimism about the future and have more positive relationships with others a year later.

Observing parents and children reveals that it takes around two years to adapt to all the changes and establish new patterns of life. Two major factors influence how children and their parents fare: parents' abilities' to (1) maintain positive authoritative parenting behaviors, and (2) put aside the anger that many parents feel toward the other parent and the divorce so they can work together cooperatively.

We have seen that at all ages and in all ethnic groups, parents' ability to be warm and supportive, respectful of children's individually yet consistent in enforcing appropriate limits, promotes children's competence and well-being. In all the changes and emotional upheaval of divorce, parents' continuing reliance on authoritative techniques helps children to feel secure and cared for.

The anger seen in many divorces is a major predictor of children's mood problems and later behavior problems.[11] Just as in two-parent families, parents' skill in supporting each others' parenting when living separately helps parents and children do well. Hetherington estimates that only about 25 percent of parents in her studies were able to put aside their own issues and focus on children's needs, coordinating their efforts to solve problems and, to coordinate rules and regulations in the two homes. Sometimes a crisis like a child's illness or accident sparked the cooperation.

About 50 percent of parents in Hetherington's samples practiced what she termed "parallel" parenting, in which each parent went his or her own way, ignoring the other parent as much as possible. Each parent had his or her rules; children were expected to adapt to them, and often children did.

About 25 percent of parents engaged in ongoing conflict, sometimes for years. Parents took every opportunity to criticize the other parent's actions. Children have a variety of feelings—anger, sadness, hopelessness—and these feelings are the most frequent predictors of ongoing problems for children.

Like Hetherington, Emery describes three kinds of divorces that he terms the cooperative divorce, the distant divorce, and the angry divorce, and describes visitation schedules and actions designed to address the particular needs in each situation.[12] Even in the event of an angry divorce, he encourages parents to sit down and talk to each other with a neutral mediator and come up with schedules that meet their needs. He did a controlled study and found that when parents met together with a mediator and negotiated their own settlement, twelve years later, their children were more likely to have weekly contact with nonresidential parents than when parents went immediately to the legal system for solutions (28 percent as compared to 9 percent) and were more likely to talk weekly or more often on the telephone with parents (59 percent compared to 14 percent).

Very little time was required to resolve issues, an average of five hours, about half the time in the legal system, and the benefits were great. He advises, "In approaching legal issues, you should try to work things out fairly and try again. And again. And again—even if things do not work out now, or tomorrow, or the next day. That way . . . you at least will have the solace of knowing you tried."[13]

Telling Children

When a couple decides to divorce, it is best if both parents together tell the children about the divorce before one parent leaves. Parents explain the reasons appropriate to the child's age and express their regret and sadness that divorce was the only alternative. Judith Wallerstein, who has followed divorced families, advises parents to indicate to the child that parents had problems in the marriage that could not be fixed, and the remedy is to separate, but both parents are committed to the care of the children. She states parents should indicate they know the pain their decision causes and are truly sorry for causing it.[14]

Parents can help children most by providing emotional support.[15] Parents are urged to (1) communicate with the child about the new changes, explaining in simple language the reasons for each change that occurs, and (2) reduce the child's suffering, where possible, by giving reassurance that the child's needs will be met. Many children get little information and support as they go through the initial turmoil of divorce. Often no one talks to them, no one listens to them talk about their feelings or answers their questions, and few relatives give added help and support.

Parents need to say clearly and often, when opportunities arise, that the divorce was *not* caused by the children but was caused by difficulties between the parents. In addition, parents need to remember that children worry about them and how they are doing. Parents cannot always confine their own intense reactions to times when the children are not present, but parents can try to do so.

There are many things divorcing parents should not say. First, they should not burden their children with their own negative views of each other. Second, they should not blame the other parent for all the problems. Third, they should not ask children to take sides—children usually need and want to be loyal to both parents.

Children's Immediate Reactions to Divorce

Emotional reactions to divorce, common to children of all ages, include sadness, fear, depression, anger, confusion, and sometimes relief; the predominant emotions vary with the child's age and family circumstances.[16] Even young children verbalize very intense feelings. A three-year-old described divorce, "When Mom and Dad hate each other and your family is dead."[17] And a five-year-old said, "It's when someone signs a paper, someone leaves home, and then kids cry."[18]

In the preschool years, children are sometimes protected because they do not understand the ramifications of a divorce.[19] When they do, they may feel abandoned and overwhelmed; they may worry that some rule breaking they did caused the divorce. They may regress and start wetting their pants or having temper tantrums. Five- to seven-year-old children understand better but they do not have the coping mechanisms of older children, and they are likely to express sadness and grief.

Children experience fear as they may believe only a father can keep the family safe, or only a mother can care for them if sick, and they worry that if one parent can leave, maybe a second parent can leave. As children get older, they may worry more about being responsible for parents' difficulties.

Thus far, we have seen the reactions of children who regret their parents' divorce, but about 10 percent of children feel relieved when their parents divorce.[20] Often, these are older children who have witnessed violence or severe psychological suffering on the part of a parent or other family member. These children feel that dissolution of the marriage is the best solution, and progressing from a conflict-ridden home to a more stable environment with one parent helps these children's overall level of adjustment and functioning.

Children's behavioral reactions to the divorce vary, depending on the personal and family characteristics—the level of conflict, the child's age, gender, and temperament, parents' emotional reactions, the amount of time with each parent.[21] Children often feel sad at not living with both parents and become anxious they will lose the parent they live with as well. Young boys frequently express their anger and fearfulness in aggressive, noncompliant behavior that creates even further distance with mothers who feel overwhelmed. Sensitive boys with irritable, reactive temperaments often feel both anxiety and anger, and their behavior drives others away so they do not get the support they need. Young girls get along better with mothers because girls more often are understanding of mothers and compliant, so mothers and daughters grow closer.

Children in divorced families resist mothers' authority. Mothers are more successful and the children have fewer problems when another adult like a grandparent reinforces the mother's authority. Adolescents may feel caught between divorced parents whose conflicts intensify adolescents' anxiety, depression, and poor adjustment.

Even when parents have high conflict with each other, adolescents can do well, provided parents do not put them in the middle. The feeling of being caught between parents contributes to these children's problems.

Although many children of divorce show aggressive and insecure behaviors in adolescence, others are caring, competent teenagers who cooperate with divorced parents and make significant contributions to family functioning. Still others are caring, responsible teenagers who worry that they will be unable to meet the demands placed on them. The aggressive, insecure children who have many difficulties do not have a single caring adult in their lives. Their parents are neglectful, disengaged, and authoritarian, and the children cannot find support outside the family.

When children have ongoing relationships with both parents, they are more likely to adjust well following the divorce process. Fathers are more likely to maintain relationships with their sons than with their daughters. In fact, many mothers relinquish custody of older sons to fathers because they feel sons need a male role model.

Parents' Reactions to Divorce

About thirty-five years ago when much divorce research began, mothers usually had primary legal custody (responsibility for children) and physical custody (place the child lived), and fathers saw children every other weekend. This arrangement paralleled family life in two-parent homes where mothers had primary responsibility for caregiving. As fathers in two-parent families took a more active role in family life and child care, they wanted more time with children when the marriages dissolved. In addition, research was demonstrating that increased contact with fathers was beneficial for boys and girls. Shared physical and legal custody became more accepted in many states unless some particular problem prevented a parent from being responsible for children. Still, mothers often get the larger share of physical custody. In 1998, only 12 percent of fathers received it though more wanted it.[22]

Mothers   In families mothers have had the role of nurturing parent, understanding feelings and communicating feelings with children. In the first one to two years after the divorce, custodial mothers are preoccupied, sometimes anxious and depressed. These mood changes are difficult for children because just at the time children are most in need of nurturance, mothers often have less to give.

Mothers are trying to establish independent households with less money and often with the stress of ongoing legal proceedings. Financial pressures increase, and mothers often seek more work and have to get more day care. When mothers are financially comfortable, their children show fewer problems than children living with a mother with financial pressures. In response to all the stress, mothers' parenting strategies often change, and mothers become more permissive or harsh or neglectful, and children resist their requests. Mothers often give preadolescents freedom and choices, but are restrictive and limiting with their adolescents. Parenting difficulties are most marked in the first two years following the divorce, but imbalances between freedom and limits may continue.

Fathers are more comfortable and practical with setting limits with children.

Over time, mothers' reactions to divorce are diverse. Seventy-five percent of divorced custodial mothers report that at the end of two years, they feel happier than they did in the last year of the marriage. Many of these women go on to develop independent lives and careers that increase their self-esteem. Some divorced women, however, report depression, loneliness, and health problems six to eleven years after the divorce. Still, they do not have as many problems as do nondivorced women in high-conflict marriages, who are more depressed and anxious and have more physical problems.

Fathers   When fathers are custodial parents, they face many of the problems of custodial mothers, feeling overwhelmed as they take full responsibility for children. However, they usually have established work schedules, and, on average, they have greater income than divorced mothers, so the sources of stress fall mainly in the area of being fully responsible parents.

Fathers differ from mothers in being more comfortable and practiced in setting limits with children and enforcing them in a matter-of-fact way with younger children. Fathers are not so used to understanding children's feelings and emotional needs, especially when children are young and not as logical as fathers might expect. Their parenting experiences with children greatly expand their understanding of others' feelings and their patience, and many fathers report this a major gain of caring for children, a gain that helps them in all their relationships. With adolescent children fathers may have the same trouble as mothers, giving too much freedom and not enforcing the limits.

Noncustodial fathers have the challenge of maintaining close relationships with children when they see them for briefer periods of time. As a reaction, and especially right after the divorce, noncustodial fathers tend to become either permissive/indulgent or disengaged parents. They are less likely to be disciplinarians and more likely to play the role of recreational companion than are custodial mothers because they do not want the little time they have with children, taken up with limit setting.

And many times noncustodial fathers do not stay involved. Noncustodial fathers are most likely to stay involved when they feel they play an important role in their children's lives and their long-term development.

Hetherington advises parents going through a divorce to take an active role in shaping their lives—get support from others, use resources at work or in the community, plan for long-term goals (e.g., getting more education, different jobs), avoid impulsive decisions, and be aware that cohabiting relationships involve higher rates of relationship break-ups before and after marriages. She observes, however, that, "The effects of a new intimate relationship are so profound it is worth repeating my findings: after a divorce, nothing heals as completely as a new love. True for women, this finding is even more true for men, who, being less socially adept and more emotionally isolated, often feel unsupported in the early years without a new partner."[23]

Protective Factors for Children

Protective factors for children as they adjust to divorce include qualities of the child, supportive aspects of the family system, and external social supports.[24] The child's age, sex, and intelligence serve as protection. Younger children appear less affected than elementary school children or early adolescents at the time of the divorce or remarriage. Because they are becoming increasingly independent of the family, late adolescents seem less affected than younger children. Boys appear to suffer more difficulties at the time of the divorce, and girls appear to have more problems at the time of the mother's remarriage. Intelligence can help children cope with the stress.

The child's temperament also influences the process of divorce. An easy, adaptable temperament is a protective factor. In contrast, children with a difficult temperament are more sensitive and less adaptable to change; they can become a focal point for parental anger. In part, they elicit the anger with their reactive behavior; in part, they provide a convenient target for parental anger that may belong elsewhere.

We have already touched on some forms of family interaction that are protective—reduced conflict between the parents, authoritative parenting, structure and organization in daily life. Mothers must be especially firm and fair in establishing limits with boys, as their tendency is to develop a vicious repetitive cycle of complaining and fighting.

Siblings and grandparents are potential supports. When family life is harmonious after divorce, then sibling relationships resemble those in intact families. When conflict between parents arises, siblings fight, with the greatest difficulty occurring between older brothers and younger sisters.

Grandparents can support grandchildren directly with time, attention, and special outings and privileges that help ease the pain of the divorce. Many grandchildren credit their grandparents with their own stability and happiness following the divorce. Grandparents provide support indirectly by helping one of the parents. In fact, returning to live in the home of one's parents is a solution many young parents choose when they do not have the resources to live on their own. Grandparents can be loving, stable baby-sitters who enrich children's lives in ways that no one else can. The mother can work and carry on a social life, knowing that her child is well cared for in her absence. This arrangement also usually reduces living expenses. When the mother and grandparents agree on child-rearing techniques and the mother is respected in the household as a mature adult, this solution may be attractive.

School is another major source of support for children. Authoritative, kind teachers and peer friendships give pleasure and a sense of esteem to children. Educational and athletic accomplishments contribute to feelings of competence that stimulate resilience, and many children find mentors in these activities.

Some protective factors lie beyond a parent's control, including the age, sex, and temperament of the child, but many lie within it, such as setting aside anger, establishing structure, monitoring behavior, and seeking out external supports for children.

Long-Term Consequences for Children of Divorce

A longitudinal study following families with four- to seven-year-old children and observing qualities of divorced families before and after the divorce finds that children of divorce have problems years before the divorce.[25] When compared with children whose parents remain together, those children living in families in which parents will later divorce have significantly greater problems with aggressive, noncompliant behaviors and anxious/depressed moods before the divorce. After the divorce, their aggressive, rule-breaking behaviors decrease, but anxious/depressed moods increase further. These are the same emotions and behaviors Hetherington noted in her samples of children studied twenty years earlier. Despite greater understanding of divorce, and attempts to make things easier for families, children still suffer ongoing anger, depression, and sadness at the dissolution of their families.

Six years following the divorce, three-quarters of children were doing well in Hetherington's groups, but 25 percent showed difficulties in aggressive/impulsive behaviors and depressed moods (compared to 10 percent in nondivorced families).[26] Other studies, too, have found that in comparison to children in nondivorced families, children of divorce have an increased risk for problems in cognitive and social competence. The differences are small, and there is much overlap in the functioning of the two groups.

When assessed in young adulthood at age twenty-four, 20 percent of Hetherington's sample reported continued problems in the area of impulsive, rule-breaking behavior and in the area of depression. Nevertheless, 80 percent scored within the average range on measures of psychological functioning, and many were doing very well.[27] In comparison, 10 percent of children in two-parent married families showed clinical levels of problems.

Judith Wallerstein, reporting on an adult follow-up of her intensively studied group of divorced children begun in 1971, described the consequences of divorce as serious and pervasive for her adult study members, especially in the area of establishing intimate ties with others.[28] Her statements about serious long-term consequences for children of divorce provoked discussions regarding the exact nature of these consequences.

Paul Amato, analyzing data from adult children of divorce collected in 2000, found that these adults reported high levels of well-being, relatively little discord in their own marriages, and close relationships with fathers in many families.[29] Conversely, some children from nondivorced families reported low levels of well-being, discord in marriages, and distant relationships with fathers. So, like Hetherington, he found diversity of outcomes with most adults of divorced parents doing well, and some children of intact parents having problems. Amato concluded that although divorce negatively affects some children and is a risk factor for later social and emotional functioning, the majority of children do well.

He believes is important to identify the conditions of divorce that lead to negative outcomes and those leading to positive outcomes. He found that children who experienced only one divorce and no other marital transitions reported a sense of well-being similar to that of children who grew up in nondivorced families. Further, when the divorce ended a marriage with intense marital discord, children reported feeling better in adulthood than those adults who continued to live in high-conflict marriages. So, stability and limiting conflict are two factors identified as protective factors in other research as well. Having ongoing contact with fathers is also important. Surveys of college students whose parents divorced when they were children revealed that 70 percent of men and women believed equal time with both parents was the best living arrangement after divorce even though less than 10 percent had experienced it.

Given the negative effects of divorce, many wonder whether it is better for parents to stay together than to divorce. The answer depends on the nature of the conflict in the marriage, the various changes that follow the divorce, the quality of the postdivorce family relationships, and the degree to which the custodial parent relies on authoritative parenting.[30]

When married parents have intense conflicts, children have emotional and behavior problems. Following a divorce, many children have behavior problems for the first two years. If parents of high-conflict marriages divorce and the conflict ends, then children's well-being improves over time, and the turmoil of the divorce is worth it because stability follows and children do well. If parents continue to fight after the divorce, then children suffer and parents might as well stay in high-conflict marriages and spare children the problems of the divorce process. It is hard to tell in advance, though, whether parents can end the conflicts after they end the marriage.

Some suggest that the mood and behavioral problems of children of divorced parents are due not to economic and psychological stressors but to genetic factors.[31] Parents with irritable temperaments and angry personality traits may find it difficult to get along with other adults so they remain single or get divorced. They pass on these personality traits to their children who then have problems.

Reviewing both twin and adoptive studies, Amato found little evidence of simple genetic inheritance, but there was some suggestion that there may be a gene x environment interaction. One study found that adolescents with a certain genetic polymorphism were more likely to develop delinquent behaviors when living with a single parent than when living with two parents.

Whatever genetic influences affect children of single parents in terms of temperamental dispositions, the behavior of children is improved and problems decreased when their single mothers learn more effective ways of relating to them.[32] For example, single mothers of young boys aged six to ten received fourteen weeks of training in positive parenting, using consistent rewards for positive behaviors and consistent negative consequences like time-outs for aggressive behaviors. Families were followed for thirty months. Teachers' ratings and test scores revealed children of trained mothers declined in aggressive behaviors and increased in adaptability at school. Children themselves reported they got along better with peers and felt less depressed. Mothers, too, felt less depressed and they advanced at work and socially. Follow-up data nine years later revealed that mothers who received the fourteen weeks of training had improved educational and occupational levels and increased incomes.[33]

Community Resources

The legal system has changed, making it easier for both parents to continue to be involved in the care of children. When parents have difficulty coming to agreement about custody issues, many states now provide court mediation services. Counselors help parents explore children's and parents' needs and reach agreement on reasonable living arrangements.

Further, laws have been passed to make it easier for single mothers to obtain child support payments decreed by the court. This is imperative because, as noted, mothers who are single heads of household have incomes far below those of other family units.

Court services in many states have organized psychoedueational programs for divorcing families. Children attend a group with same-age peers while each parent attends a different parent group. The groups last for six to ten weeks and cover experiences many parents and children have in the process of divorce. In addition to providing information on the psychological experiences common to the divorce process, the groups give a family member opportunities to talk without other family members present. These groups also provide coping strategies that children and parents can use and ways for children to raise sensitive topics with parents. Parents and children report they like the program and benefit from it even though as yet there are no random controlled studies of its effects.

A Collaborative Divorce Process

Lawyers and counselors separately recognized the damage and difficulties that an adversarial legal system creates for families, and some joined together to form the International Academy of Collaborative Professionals to offer a different way for parents to bring their marriages to an end. The process helps parents put their anger and intense feelings aside, put children's needs first, and focus on the family's future.[34]

The process includes several professionals working as a team to help the couple work out agreements that reflect their short- and long-term goals. Couples who wish a collaborative divorce agree to keep all the discussions and information gathered confidential; if either parent seeks litigation in the courts, the team does not participate, and all the information gathered remains confidential.

Each parent has both a collaborative lawyer and a divorce coach, and the couple also has a child mental health specialist who advises on the needs of the children, and a financial specialist to give advice on finances. Working with his or her divorce coach, each parent discusses feelings about the marriage, the divorce, and the hoped-for future. Coaches help parents recognize unacknowledged feelings and help them communicate feelings calmly in discussions with the other parent. The child specialist meets with each parent and with the child or children alone and helps parents understand and focus on children's needs in custody arrangements. The financial consultant gives information and options on ways to handle parents' needs for money.

Discussing serious differences in a calm atmosphere helps parents make good decisions at an emotional and challenging time in life. The team meets many times until the divorce agreement is concluded. The team of experts remains available to be reconvened in the future if circumstances change or difficulties arise. Proponents of the process say it is cheaper than the cost of lengthy, expensive litigation that creates bitterness but does not provide consensual solutions.

REMARRIAGE

About 65 percent of divorced women and 75 percent of divorced men marry again, and half of the adults have children. Many repartner without marriage, but we know less about these relationships, so we focus on remarriage.[35] Remarriage provides many benefits to parents. First, it provides emotional closeness, intimacy, and sexual satisfaction. In caring relationships, parents feel greater self-esteem, contentment, and happiness.[36] Second, parents have someone with whom they can share both the financial and caregiving responsibilities. We know most about remarried families that consist of the custodial mother, her children, and the stepfather, who may or may not have children, but there are an increasing number of studies of families with resident fathers and stepmothers. Few studies focus on marriages of single mothers who have children, even though these may have many characteristics of stepfamilies.

Challenges of Stepfamilies

Stepparenting is more demanding than parenting in intact families for several reasons. First, a stepparent does not have long-standing emotional bonds with the children to help all of them overcome the feelings of frustration and stress that occur as a result of remarriage.[37]

Box 15-1
FIRST PERSON NARRATIVE

Psychologist Robert Emery's book *The Truth about Children and Divorce** describes his own divorce experiences, the experiences of divorcing couples he has worked with for twenty-five years, and his research on the positive effects of couples' finding their own solutions for their children rather than seeking solutions from the legal system. The first-person experiences of numerous couples followed over time give readers a keen sense of the intense feelings and conflicts aroused in divorce and how they interfere with parents' caring for their children. The case examples translate research concepts like authoritative parenting and handling anger into real life events and show the many different ways divorcing parents can solve problems and meet their children's needs. Seeing how couples change over time enables readers to understand that adamant opinions and habits do shift in response to events and nonjudgmental responses so the book provides a hopeful and optimistic view that people can change and make positive decisions for their children.

While Emery's book focuses primarily on parents' experiences and choices in divorce, Joanne Pedro-Carroll** focuses in greater detail on children's experiences in divorce and remarriage. From her work as a school psychologist, she became convinced that programs could be established in schools that could prevent children's emotional problems at stressful times, and that divorce was a main source of children's stress. Obtaining her doctorate in clinical psychology, she has had a primary role in establishing programs in schools and in carrying out research to show their effectiveness.

Like Emery, she translates research concepts like divided loyalties into children's experiences in everyday life. From listening to children and from her research, she guides parents to decisions that put children's needs first. She has different suggestions for families with differing levels of cooperation.

She follows children over time so one can see how their reactions change in response to parents' behaviors. She sums up children's most frequent pieces of advice for parents as follows: Let children know the good things they do, be truthful about the divorce but do not go into great detail, avoid fighting in front of children, tell children it is okay to love both parents, don't try to buy loyalty or affection with gifts and trips, see the divorce as children see it, tell children you love them even if you think they already know.

Second, a stepfamily includes more people than does a nuclear family, so it has different needs and interests to consider. There are husbands and wives, their biological children, ex-spouses, stepbrothers and stepsisters, half-brothers and half-sisters, and stepgrandparents. Parents have the multiple tasks of solidifying and maintaining marital ties while sustaining relationships with their biological children and promoting positive sibling relationships.

Third, members of stepfamilies have memories of the earlier marriage and may feel sadness at its loss and ambivalence about the present family, where there is less time for each member. Children may feel that the new marriage is depriving them of their parent. Parents must accept those feelings as realistic—there is less time

Divorced with one son when she married her husband who had three children, Susan Philips became curious about the experiences of children in stepfamilies. Finding little available from stepchildren themselves, she interviewed dozens of young adults who had grown up in stepfamilies. She presented ten narratives in her book, *Stepchildren Speak*.*** This group represents a broader range of social and ethnic backgrounds than is usually found in divorced and remarried studies, and we can see vividly how the stress of limited resources complicates the processes of divorce and remarriage and makes growing up so much harder.

These ten narratives illustrate the many ways children's childhoods changed following divorce and remarriage, how understanding children could be of parents' problems, how eager children are to have good relationships with everyone, and how little it took to win a child's affection and loyalty. Each person sums up their experiences with advice to parents, stepparents, children, and stepchildren. While much of the advice is similar to research guidelines like avoid criticizing the other parent, go slow in establishing new partnerships, some suggestions were new. Children were advised to have their own interests and activities at school because they could serve as a great source of satisfaction and comfort; parents were advised to let children get to know stepparents as individuals—their pasts, their interests—and let stepparents get to know children as people with special strengths and interests because stepparents and stepchildren might have ways to connect besides their role in the family. Finally, most advised stepparents to be parent-like but not take on the role of parent. One young man said it very poetically, "You have to offer the child the opportunity to see that strength can be garnered, help can be won, and security had, they need only gravitate toward you. . . . You can provide that godfatherly sense of 'I am a new sanctuary for you.'"****

*Robert E. Emery, *The Truth about Children and Divorce: Dealing with the Emotions So You and Your Children Can Thrive* (New York: Penguin, 2006).
**JoAnne Pedro-Carroll, *Putting Children First: Proven Parenting Strategies for Helping Children Thrive through Divorce* (New York: Penguin, 2010).
***Susan Philips, *Stepchildren Speak: 10 Grown-Up Stepchildren Teach Us How to Build Healthy Stepfamilies* (Vancouver, WA: AWYN, 2005).
****Ibid., p. 46.

for each child. Conversely, the parents may feel that the children are intruding on the marriage.

Fourth, anger and frustration with former spouses and relatives may present the stepfamily with ongoing irritations and problems that dampen the mood in the stepfamily. Fifth, there are no clear guidelines for being a stepparent. There are few enough for biological parents, but the role of stepparent remains even vaguer. The stepparent must create his or her role according to his or her individual personality, the ages and sexes of the children, and the family's living arrangements. Stepparents who are forewarned about the problems of stepparenting and who think and talk in advance about how to cope with these problems can find their new roles rewarding and exciting.

Mavis Hetherington identifies four myths that create unrealistic expectations for parents as they enter stepfamilies:[38]

The nuclear family myth—that family members will love and be close to each other, and children will respect both parents in the home

The compensatory myth—the new spouse and family will be everything that the first family and marriage were not

Instant love expectations—the stepparent and children will form instant, close, loving bonds

Rescue fantasy—the new parent will solve all the child-rearing and financial problems in the family and everything will be fine.

If parents can be realistic about their own contributions to difficulties and family problems, and work through problems as they arise in the stepfamily, then remarried couples are as happy as nondivorced couples after five or six years. Not everyone works through problems, and about 60 percent of remarriages end in divorce, often in the first few years.

Types of Mother and Stepfather Families

From his ten-year study of one hundred stepfamilies made up of custodial mothers, stepfathers, and young children and a controlled sample of one hundred non-divorced families, James Bray has provided a basic understanding of developmental issues facing stepfamilies.[39] His major findings include the following:

1. A stepfamily has a natural cycle of changes and transition points.
2. A stepfamily takes many years to form a basic family unit.
3. The greatest risk to the stepfamily occurs in the first two years, when about 25 percent of remarriages fail.
4. In a stepfamily, there is no honeymoon period of high satisfaction followed by a gradual decrease, as there is in a first marriage; in a stepfamily, marital satisfaction starts at a moderate level and builds up from there or decreases to the point of divorce.
5. A stepfamily has four basic tasks to achieve cohesion:
   a. Integrating the stepfather into the family
   b. Creating a satisfying second marriage
   c. Separating from the ghosts of the past
   d. Managing all the changes
6. A stepfamily eventually takes one of three forms: *neotraditional, matriarchal,* or *romantic*. Neotraditionals almost always succeed, matriarchals succeed much of the time, and romantics face great risk of divorce.

The neotraditional family is described as a "contemporary version of the 1950s, 'white-picket fence family'; it is close-knit, loving, and works very well for a couple with compatible values."[40] The matriarchal family is one in which the wife-mother is a highly competent woman who directs and manages all the family activities. The romantic family seeks everything the neotraditional family does but wants it all immediately, as soon as the marriage occurs. The romantic family is at great risk for not surviving the conflicts and changes of the first two years. The three types of families do not differ in the crises and turning points they face, but they do differ in their expectations and their willingness to change their expectations and their behaviors to solve the problems they confront.

The first cycle of change that stepfamilies experience in the process of their formation occurs in the first two years of the remarriage. In this stressful period, all members of the family try to find ways to live together, deal with ex-spouses and noncustodial parents, and form a stable unit that brings *everyone* happiness. By the end of two years, the second cycle begins; family members find mutually satisfying ways of getting along, and a family unit is established. Tensions are reduced, and happy stepfamilies resemble nondivorced families. A third cycle of change occurs when children move into adolescence and become more insistent on independence and individuality.

Neotraditional families successfully navigate the changes because they give up unrealistic expectations and because they communicate feelings and solve problems.

Bray describes the neotraditional family as having the ability to (1) identify and express feelings clearly; (2) identify and understand other family members' thoughts, feelings, and values so differences are bridged; (3) resolve conflicts; (4) state a complaint so the other person feels empathy; (5) establish new rituals that help define the family as a unit; and (6) accept other family members. Romantic families seek the same cohesiveness and close ties that neotraditional families do, but they find it very difficult to give up unrealistic expectations and solve the problems at hand.

Bray reports that despite the crises and difficulties of remarriage, many stepfamilies succeed and form stable, cohesive family units that give all members a sense of warmth and accomplishment. A significant number of stepfamilies do not succeed, however, and dissolve the marriages because the parents do not have the commitment to work through the problems to reach a joint resolution. A third group of families stay together and seem happy enough, but they lack a sense of vitality and seem to "just get by." These families do not want open communication or to really understand each other and instead choose habitual ways of relating to each other. Bray asked successful families what got them through all the stressful periods. "The consistent answer was commitment. Commitment to a life together, not just getting by but living and loving fully, communicating about issues, building a stable family, and enjoying a good life together."[41]

Types of Father and Stepmother Families

In a study of fathers rearing children with stepmothers, stepmothers had many of the same difficulties as stepfathers—uncertainty about their role in the family, uncertainty about how to establish relationships with stepchildren and whether to discipline.[42] The majority of stepmothers relied on one of three role models: the nuclear, the extended, or the couple. In the nuclear model, stepmothers expected

INTERVIEW
with the late Emily Visher and the late John Visher

Emily Visher, a clinical psychologist, and John Visher, a psychiatrist, were founders of the Stepfamily Association and authors of such books as Stepfamilies: Myths and Realities *and* Old Loyalties, New Ties: Therapeutic Strategies with Stepfamilies.

You have worked with stepparents and stepfamilies for many years, so I want to talk to you about what you feel are the important things for parents to do in order to ease the difficulties that can arise in stepfamilies.

E. Visher: We talk about a parenting coalition that is the joining of all the adults in the child's life. For example, you see, there could be three or four parenting adults—if both parents have remarried, there will be four. If those adults can somehow develop a working relationship around raising the children, the loyalty conflicts of the children will be much less. The adults will get a lot out of it, too, because there is less tension, and better relationships develop between stepparent and stepchild.

We chose the word *coalition* because it means a temporary alliance of separate entities for accomplishing a task. The households and couples are separate, and it is a temporary alliance among all the adults. The task they are working on together is raising the children. Families can flounder on the basis of the stepparent's trying to be a parent and the children saying basically, "I've got a mother or a father." We have moderated panels of teenagers in stepfamilies, and we always ask them, "What do you want your stepparents to be? What is their role?" I don't think we have ever heard anyone say anything other than "a friend." The difficulty is that by "friend," they mean something very different. They don't mean a pal; it's closer than that.

They are able to talk to the stepparent in a meaningful way that is different from the way they would talk to a parent. They are freer to talk to a stepparent because they are not so involved. One teenager on a panel said she wanted her stepfather to be her friend, and then later she said, "I love my stepfather, and I've never told him." She's saying she wants a friend, but she has very deep feelings for him. He was in the back of the room and heard her.

J. Visher: Another major tip is to develop realistic expectations about what it is going to take to make everything work. So many people feel that they have failed after a few weeks or months, that the remarriage has faltered because things are chaotic. It takes four or five years for things to settle down and for people really to get satisfaction out of the whole family relationship.

Working out the parenting coalition so that it is at least civil makes an enormous difference to everybody. The children can go through the remarriage smoothly if there is no constant warfare. Sometimes parents who divorce or separate are tied together in bonds of anger. The anger can reflect an inadequate separation between the biological parents. They keep together by fighting.

E. Visher: Truman Capote said, "It's easy to lose a good friend, but it's hard to lose a good enemy." The anger ties you together. Hostility eats you up, and you are not free to go on.

J. Visher: Most people don't understand how much damage they are doing to themselves and to the children. Sometimes people say, "How can I work with that S.O.B. when I couldn't even stay married to him?" We say maybe you can split off the part that does not want to be married to him and share the parenting experience.

E. Visher: What the children need from that parent is different from what the spouse needed.

What can you do to decrease the hostility?

J. Visher: One thing is to trade assurances between the households that you are not trying to take the child away from them or trying to get the child to like you better. Often, in a single-parent household, the parent is afraid of further loss, afraid that the ex-spouse and his or her new spouse will encourage the child to stay there and the child will want to because it is a more attractive place or there is more money. This fear fuels the anger and makes the parent cling to the child more and try to influence the child to turn against the other parent.

E. Visher: So we think that sometimes the anger is not left over from the former marriage but has to do with the fear that builds up between the two households, the fear of more loss. The other household becomes a threat, and the ex-spouses become like enemies rather than like people trying to raise a child. The parents are afraid of each other, and they are not aware that the anger substitutes for fear. If they are more aware of it, they can deal with it.

Also important is the guilt the remarried parent feels. He or she feels guilty that the children have been unhappy through the death or divorce and then the remarriage. That parent has a real investment in its being a big, happy family right away. Yet they have difficulty setting limits for the children who live there or visit. The stepparent goes up the wall.

Sometimes they feel that to form a good couple relationship and make that primary is a betrayal of their relationship with their child. The parent-child relationship is different from the relationship with the spouse.

J. Visher: There may be an unusually strong bond between parent and child; perhaps it has lasted for many years, and the new spouse is a rival. It becomes a power struggle between spouse and child for the loyalty of the biological parent. The child is sometimes suddenly out of a job as confidant.

E. Visher: I don't think people realize the change for the children, that now they have to share. One mother described that she and her daughter had lived together for five years. When she came home from work, she talked to her daughter. Now that she is remarried, she talks to her husband. That one little thing is not so little, as the daughter has to share her mother.

If people are aware of the losses for the children in the new structure, they can acknowledge those changes with the children and do things differently—sit down with the children alone and talk. When children sense their feelings are accepted, they will talk about them. One stepmother commented to her stepson that when the father talked to the son, she felt left out, and she wondered if he felt left out when the father talked to her. He agreed he did, and they talked about it. There was not a lot they could change, but after they had the talk, they got along better.

J. Visher: We hope that as people are more informed, they will be able to deal more effectively with the situation.

to take the same role as the biological mother and to focus energy on the family unit, disciplining children and expecting children would distance themselves from the other parent and family, and look to her as the primary caregiving person. These mothers were disappointed and frustrated when children rejected them as the primary parent.

In the extended model, stepmothers were similar to nuclear mothers in wanting to be important figures in their stepchildren's lives but mainly as coparent with the biological parent. They also saw the family as an extended unit and wanted their own family to be very involved with stepchildren and the whole family unit.

About a third of stepmothers used a couple model and focused on forming a strong marital relationship with the biological father, believing that a strong marriage would benefit everyone. They believe that the biological parents should have primary responsibility for raising the children. While these stepmothers are warm and friendly with stepchildren, they leave discipline to the biological parent. Research suggests that the couple model may be most effective as stepmothers are less stressed and stepchildren have fewer pressures on them.

Parents' Behaviors over Time

There are no differences in how biological parents parent their own children in nondivorced and remarried families. Regardless of family status, mothers and fathers are warmer, more supportive, and closer to their biological children than to their stepchildren, and their children are more often closer to them.[43]

No matter what the age of a child at a parent's remarriage, stepfathers initially feel less close to their stepchildren than to their biological children, and they do not monitor behavior as well as fathers do in intact families. When children are

Girls often feel angry at the loss of the close relationship with their mothers.

relatively young at the time of the remarriage, stepfathers may be able to build relationships with stepchildren by taking on the role of a warm and supportive figure and forgoing the role of disciplinarian until a relationship is established. Young boys have an easier time building relationships, while young girls often feel angry at the loss of the close relationship with mothers. Girls resist stepfathers and direct angry, negative behavior to the custodial mother.[44]

When children are early adolescents at the time of the remarriage, there appears to be little adaptation to the new family over a two-year period.[45] Children are negative and resistant and, as a result, stepfathers remain disengaged, critical, and distanced from the day-to-day monitoring of children. When, however, stepparents can be authoritative parenting figures—warm, positive, appropriate in monitoring—then children's adjustment improves. With adolescents, stepparents fare better when they are authoritative from the start.

Adolescents at the time of the remarriage are often unwilling to become involved with stepparents, and they frequently retreat from the families and establish strong relationships with families of friends. At the same time, they become more argumentative with the biological parents, both custodial and noncustodial. Adolescents feel closer to noncustodial mothers than to noncustodial fathers.[46]

In stepfamilies, marital happiness has a different relation to children's behavior than it has in intact families.[47] In nondivorced families, marital happiness is related to children's competent functioning and positive relationships with parents. In stepfamilies, marital happiness is related to children's negative and resistant behavior with parents. Girls may especially resent the loss of the close relationship with their custodial mother.

Relationships with siblings are less positive and more negative in remarried families than in nondivorced families.[48] Although girls tend to be warmer and more empathetic than boys, they are almost equally aggressive. As siblings become adolescents, they become more separated from each other. Interestingly, relationships with their stepsiblings appear less negative than relationships with their own siblings.

Children's Behavior over Time

Children's adjustment in stepfamilies varies. Often, initial declines in cognitive and social competence follow the remarriage, but when boys are young and stepparents are warm and authoritative, problem behaviors improve, and boys in these stepfamilies show levels of adjustment similar to those of boys in nondivorced families. Young girls continue to have more acting-out and defiant behavior problems than do girls in intact or divorced families.[49] Most gender differences in adjustment disappear at early adolescence, when both boys and girls have more problems.

Still, large-scale surveys of teens living with biological parents and stepparents find that many adolescents feel close to stepparents when relationships were formed early. In a study of 1,100 teens living with mothers and stepfathers, but still seeing nonresidential fathers, 91 percent of teens felt close to mothers, 61 percent felt close to stepfathers, and 41 percent felt close to nonresidential fathers.[50] About 25 percent of teens reported feeling close to both fathers and 24 percent felt close to neither.

When marriage or repartnering occurred in adolescence, mother-teen close-ness decreased if the stepfather was cohabiting but not if the stepfather married the mother. Mother-teen closeness prior to the stepfather's entry predicted teen-stepfather closeness after marriage.[51] Stepfamily formation had little effect on teens' relationship to nonresidential fathers.

When teens reported close relationships to stepfathers and fathers, or even to stepfathers alone, teens had better grades, more positive moods, and less aggressive, noncompliant behaviors.[52] Close relations with the two fathers were part of a generally close family in which parents got along with each other, and the teen felt close to both. Those adolescents who felt close to neither parent tended to be girls, were older, and were more likely to have been born outside of marriage. Parents in the home did not get along well, and these teens reported the more anxious or depressed moods, more aggressive behaviors, and poor grades.

Close relationships between teens and both fathers may occur, in part, because stepfathers go out of their way to include fathers in the child's life.[53] One study found that about 40 percent of stepfathers went out of their way to encourage non-residential fathers' phone calls, visiting, and participation in children's lives because they saw children were happier and because stepfathers too had children in other households that they wanted more time with.

When teens live with biological fathers and stepmothers and still see non-residential mothers, 92 percent reported having close relationships with fathers, 67 percent had close relationships with stepmothers, and 60 percent had close relationships with biological mothers.[54] In these families, it was teens who had close relationships with biological fathers and mothers who had the more positive moods, less aggressive behaviors, and less substance use. Closeness with step-mothers did not predict teens' well-being.

At all ages, a small subsample of children in remarried families, like children in divorced families, have poorer school performance, more problems in social respon-sibility, and more rule-breaking behaviors than do children in intact families. Still, the majority do well. Between two-thirds and three-quarters of children in remar-ried families score within the average range on assessment instruments. Although this falls below the comparable figure of 90 percent for children of nondivorced parents, it indicates that most children in remarried families are doing well.[55]

As with children of divorced families, children of remarried families are at a dis-advantage in early adulthood.[56] Compared with children of nondivorced parents, they are more likely to leave home at an early age, less likely to continue in school, and more likely to leave home as a result of conflict. As adults, they feel they can rely less on their families. Still, responses vary and many of these children feel close to and supported in stepfamilies.

Many of the difficulties stepfamilies encounter can be avoided or lessened if they are anticipated and prepared for. Stepfamilies can strengthen their ties in many ways, such as nurturing relationships, finding personal space and time, and build-ing trust. Although divorce and repartnering involve many changes and stresses, families do well when they rely on the same strategies that have beneficial effects in two-parent families, namely open communication of feelings, respect for others' points of views, and authoritative parenting.

MAIN POINTS

The process of divorce

- involves a grief cycle both parents and children experience
- is a major disruption for all family members
- involves many changes for children that can include fewer economic resources as well as a new neighborhood, a new school, and new friends
- places stress on children and parents, which can be reversed if parents establish low-conflict divorced homes and use authoritative parenting

Protective factors for children at the time of divorce include

- a child's age, sex, intelligence, and temperament
- manageable amounts of stress and appropriate support from grandparents and other relatives
- educational and athletic accomplishments that contribute to children's feelings of competence and stimulate resilience

Children's behavior

- becomes more problematic at the time of divorce but improves as time passes
- is less carefully monitored in single-parent than in dual-parent homes in early adolescence
- improves when parents resolve their anger and use authoritative parenting

Stepfamilies

- often have unrealistic expectations about how quickly closeness and cohesiveness of family members will develop
- need empathy and communication skills to work through the crises and conflicts that occur in the first two years
- parenting tasks at times of partner and marital transition include
- maintaining positive emotional relationships with children and including nonresidential parents
- learning effective conflict-resolution skills
- relying on authoritative parenting strategies
- modeling positive relationships with the extended family
- encouraging children to have positive experiences in their own social world

EXERCISES

1. Imagine that your married brother, sister, or friend came to you and said he or she was getting a divorce and wanted advice on how to minimize the pain of the divorce for the children, ages five and ten. What would you say?

2. If possible, attend divorce court for a morning and summarize the cases presented there. What issues do parents seem to disagree about? What issues about children arise? Do you agree with the judge's ruling and why?

3. Explore the workshops for divorcing parents and children in your area. How expensive are they? How readily available?

4. Suppose your brother, who has one child from a previous marriage, told you he was going to marry a woman who has two children from a previous marriage. What advice could you offer your brother to ease adjustments for all in the new marriage? In a class discussion, share your ideas on how to advise your brother.

5. Imagine that your remarried brother, sister, or friend is experiencing increased conflict with his or her stepson who is now a teenager. What questions would you ask about conflicts and what advice might you give in helping them to decrease conflicts? What guidelines would you give your relative or friend?

ADDITIONAL READINGS

Bray, James H., and Kelly, John. *Stepfamilies: Love, Marriage, and Parenting in the First, Decade.* New York: Broadway Books, 1998.

Emery, Robert E. *The Truth about Children and Divorce: Dealing with the Emotions so You and Your Children Can Thrive.* New York: Penguin, 2006.

Hetherington, E. Mavis, and Kelly, John. *For Better or Worse: Divorce Reconsidered.* New York: Norton, 2002.

Pedro-Carroll, JoAnne. *Putting Children First: Proven Parenting Strategies for Helping Children Thrive through Divorce.* New York: Penguin, 2010.

Philips, Susan. *Stepchildren Speak: 10 Grown-up Stepchildren Teach Us How to Build Healthy Stepfamilies.* Vancouver, WA: AWYN Publications, 2005.

16

Parenting in Lesbian and Gay Families

CHAPTER TOPICS

In this chapter, you will learn about:

- Lesbian and gay parents' decision to parent

- Parenting experiences in rearing children

- Children's experiences growing up in lesbian and gay families

- The challenges of family life

Test Your Knowledge: Fact or Fiction (True/False)

1. Young adults who grew up in lesbian and gay families were not aware as children of the pressures parents felt to demonstrate effective parenting.
2. Lesbian and gay parents often choose open adoption as a way to have children because then there is complete honesty about parents' family life.
3. Most lesbian partners who are awaiting the adoption of a child believe it is important to make a deliberate plan for including male relatives and friends in their children's lives.
4. One-third of prospective gay fathers say they want to provide children with the happy childhoods they never had.
5. Lesbian mothers who have a biological connection with children often have more power in the couple relationship and make more decisions than the nonbiological parent.

In this chapter we focus on the experiences of lesbian and gay parents as they make the decision to become parents and as they rear their children. We look at the experiences of their children, and their recollections as young adults of what their experiences were in childhood. We detail the special stresses and strengths of these families.

Lesbian and gay parents share many of the experiences of parents described in the last three chapters. Many decided to use assisted reproductive technology (ART) to conceive a child and turned to adoption when ART was not successful. They may be single parents, but they are more likely living with partners to whom they are not married. Their partnerships may end, and they know all the pain of divorce and difficulties of sharing custody or perhaps having no contact with a child they have raised as their own.

So, they have all the special stresses of parents in the last three chapters as well as the stress of being stigmatized for their sexual preferences and denied the legal and social benefits married couples enjoy.[1] We devote this chapter to describing their experiences in the parenting process because their experiences are more complex than those of other parents, and because we seek to understand the strategies they use so that they and their children function effectively and competently despite the added layers of stress. Their strategies may be helpful to other families dealing with difficult circumstances as well.

Lesbian and gay parents are a heterogeneous group.[2] In early studies, most lesbian and gay parents had children in the context of heterosexual marriages and then divorced and adopted a lesbian or gay identity, rearing their children alone or with partners of the same sex. These families faced not only all the stresses of remarried families but also the pressure of prejudice against lesbian and gay parents. Much of the initial research done on lesbian and gay parents and their children was conducted in order to prevent parents' being denied custody of and visitation with their children.

More recently, research has focused more on lesbian and gay parents who choose parenthood after proclaiming a lesbian or gay identity. Parents are usually living with partners and choose to have a child through ART, surrogate parenthood, or adoption. The child may have a biological relationship with one parent, with the other parent becoming a coparent through legal adoption of the child, or the child may have no biological relationship with either parent. A single lesbian or gay person may have a child in the same way.

More research has been carried out primarily with lesbian mothers and their children because they are more numerous.[3] Research has relied on European American, middle-class families, and there are fewer studies of working class and ethnic lesbian and gay families. Further, the focus has often remained on the characteristics of parents and children, and only recently has research begun to focus on the family processes within these families followed over time.

STRESS IN THE ABSENCE OF LEGAL PROTECTIONS

Since 2000, many countries, among them Canada, Norway, South Africa, Spain, and The Netherlands, have passed legislation enabling same-sex couples to marry and enjoy all the benefits and supports of married couples.[4] Within the United States six states and Washington, D.C., have passed similar legislation, and the state of California is engaged in court battles to permit same-sex marriage. Such laws give symbolic recognition to the status of same-sex partnerships and psychological benefits for same-sex parents and their children.

Many young adult children of lesbian and gay parents report same-sex marriage would have given them and their families both psychological and material benefits. One woman commenting on the symbolic significance of same-sex marriage said,

"Marriage would make those relationships real to other people. It would make them understand that it's such a real thing. These are real people, they want real families, they want real relationships. Because it's a nationally recognized process to get married. . . . That's what you do when you're in love with someone and you want to have a family."[5]

Young adults feel they and their families were denied material benefits freely given to heterosexual parents and their families, and their denial impacted families in many ways. For example, one teen could not drive her nonbiological mother's car because she was not legally her daughter. Sometimes, family members were denied the medical benefits of the nonlegal parent. And sometimes, families had to pay thousands of dollars to sign papers so a child could visit a nonlegal parent in the hospital. This lack of benefits was dispiriting to families.

Married Canadian lesbian and gay adults report that the greater closeness in financial and other affairs has added a greater depth of feeling in their relationship.[6] In giving legal status to the couple's partnership, same-sex marriage gives both parents a legal tie to each other, and each of them, a legal tie to their children, giving children access to both parents' insurance and other resources, and giving the family access to public services such as court proceedings like custody determinations in the event of parental separation.

When both parents do not automatically have equal legal ties to children, parents and children feel stress. When only one parent has a legal tie as occurs when states do not permit adoptions by same-sex parents and do not approve petitions to have a parent added as a coparent, then one parent has all of the responsibility and legal control of children. If families dissolve their partnership, courts may take no role in custody determinations, and the parent with the legal tie can eliminate the other parent from the child's life even if there is a strong attachment between the child and that parent.

The lack of equal protection for both parents results in greater stress for parents.[7] For example, lesbian mothers in the United States report significantly more worries about discrimination and legal difficulties such as partner's rights to their children or worries about losing their rights to their children than lesbian mothers in Canada where same-sex marriage equalizes the rights of lesbian, gay, and heterosexual families. Similarly, American children of lesbian mothers report more teasing and exclusion from social groups than children of lesbian mothers in The Netherlands where same-sex marriage became law in 2000, creating a more approving social climate for lesbian mothers and their children.[8] Understanding the greater vulnerability of these parents and their children, let us look at how they decide to parent and carry out their roles.

DECISION TO PARENT AND PATHWAYS TO PARENTHOOD

Advances in ART have enabled both women and men in same-sex relationships to consider having a child biologically related to at least one of the parents, and changes in the social climate have enabled women and men to consider adopting a child, so many more lesbian and gay couples and individuals are having children.

Figures from the 2000 Census suggest that one in five gay couples is raising a child and one in three lesbian couples has a child. Since 2000 those numbers have likely increased.[9]

Reasons for Having Children

Gay men who decided to become parents gave three broad reasons for wanting children:[10] finding psychological and personal fulfillment in being a parent, satisfying partner's desire to have a child and form a family, and seeking to enhance one's future personal security. Gay men gave various ways in which parenthood was fulfilling: it enabled them to re-create the happy family times they had enjoyed with their parents growing up; they enjoyed being with children and wanted to make children's lives better, often through adoption; they also thought that rearing children was a basic part of life. These are the same kinds of reasons that heterosexual parents give.

The men gave five general reasons for seeking parenthood at that time: their age, relationship-related reasons (stability of the relationship, partner's mutual desire for a child), work stability, life change and special events (getting to know other gay parents, moving to a home where they could have children), and considering it the next stage of life.

Lesbians often cite their desire to experience conceiving and bearing a child biologically related to them as a major reason.[11] Like gay men, some lesbian mothers come to parenting because their partners want to have a family. In eight of twenty-five lesbian couples using alternative insemination to have a child, the nonbiological mothers did not want a child, but were willing to become parents to support their partners' desire and found they enjoyed parenthood.

Pathways to Parenthood

Having decided to become parents, lesbians and gays have to select the routes to parenthood that meet their needs. Lesbians may rely on heterosexual sex with a friend, alternative insemination with donor sperm from a friend or clinic, more advanced ART methods, surrogacy, and public or private adoption. Gay men may rely on surrogacy and adoption, public or private.[12]

The methods vary in cost with alternative insemination being the cheapest with costs of $500 to $1,000, more involved ART interventions using medications and in vitro fertilization, ranging from $8,000 to $10,000 per cycle; surrogacy costing between $115,000 and $150,000. Although public adoptions cost little, ranging from $0 to $2,500, in contrast to private adoptions costing between $8,000 and $40,000, public adoptions require that biological parents relinquish or lose parental rights, and that can take years to process as David Marin found when he adopted his children. In addition, there are few infants available in public adoptions.

At the same time parents consider cost, they also have to consider the options available to them in their area. Some states do not permit adoptions to lesbian and gay parents. Parents often apply to adopt as single parents and later petition to have the second parent identified as a coparent, but states need not approve the petition.

While some parents apply as single parents for international adoptions, countries like China and Guatemala now require single parents to supply affidavits of heterosexuality. If states do not permit coadoption, parents have to consider other legal means like a private contract or power of attorney, to give the second parent the ability to have an active role in children's lives, and children's ability to see the parent if he or she is hospitalized.

Donor selection is also an issue when lesbian women choose alternative insemination. Between 30 and 45 percent of lesbian women, depending on the study, choose a known donor because they want to have personal knowledge and history of the donor, and their children to know the donor and have contact with him while they are growing up, but they do not want the donor to be involved as an equal parent.[13] Other women select an unknown donor with the possibility of children's contacting the donor when they are eighteen as they do not want an intrusive figure who will want to parent or, perhaps, want shared custody.

Many prospective lesbian and gay parents seek open adoptions through private agencies. They think openness is best so children will have connections with birth parents and can have information about their birth families and circumstances of their adoptions and continuing relationships with birth parents.[14] Lesbian and gay parents also appreciate having their same-sex partnerships known to birth parents and not having to pretend they are single parents.

Another issue is the child's last name, including the possibility of a hyphenated name or only the name of the legal parent. And there is also the question of what the child will call each parent to distinguish between them yet give both parents the title of mother or father. Some choose "Mommy" and "Mama" or "Daddy" and "Papa."

Parents research clinics and medical personnel as well as persons in adoption agencies to locate those who understand their special needs and treat them with respect and sensitivity.

TRANSITION TO PARENTING

Although there are some similarities in the experiences of lesbian, gay, and heterosexual parents, lesbian and gay couples have somewhat different transitions to parenthood from those of heterosexual parents because being a parent has not always been taken for granted as a possibility and because there is not a simple route to having a child. For example, until recently, gay men believed they had renounced the possibility of being fathers when they identified themselves as gay so when they first chose to become fathers, they were older and more likely to be European American men with good incomes and higher social status than men who had not chosen fatherhood.[15]

When parenthood became possible, they found themselves thinking about becoming fathers. Interacting with children and caring for them, e.g., nieces and nephews or friends' children, awakened desires to rear their own children, and they decided to pursue the option. They recognized they might face barriers. With determination, they found adoption agencies or identified egg donors and surrogate mothers to participate in the process of having a biological child. For some gay men, the biological connection was an important one, but for others, it was not. With time, the men achieved their goals. Studies on their children have not yet been reported.

In the transition to parenthood, lesbian partners' experiences are similar to those of heterosexual couples when both groups are adopting.[16] Both groups of parents reported similar levels of psychological well-being. All prospective parents experienced some anxiety and tension about the adoption process. A subsample of both lesbian and heterosexual parents reported feelings of depression related to their unsuccessful efforts to conceive a child. Both groups of parents sought support from their families and friends for their decision to adopt. Women, both lesbian and heterosexual, were more likely to receive family and friend support than were men. Lesbian women, however, received less family support than heterosexual women did, particularly if they had been with their partner a short time. Partners who had been together a longer time received more family support. Friend support was sufficiently strong so lesbian partners did not suffer any loss of overall well-being.

Interviews in the last trimester with lesbian partners about to have their first child by means of donor insemination found that all women, both the biological mothers and their co-mother partners, considered that men would play a role in their child's life.[17] They were not looking for a traditional father figure, but they were thinking about men who would interact with their children and would be a good model of what it means to be a man. All the women knew men—fathers, brothers, gay and straight friends—who could take this role.

The women could be grouped into three categories. The largest group, forty of the sixty lesbian women, termed "deliberate," made very definite plans about how to include men. A group of fifteen, termed "flexible," thought they would let circumstances dictate how men were included. A final group of five, termed "ambivalent," were uncertain how important it was to include men.

These women's views were subject to change once the baby arrived. At the interview when babies were three months old, three flexible mothers had become very deliberate about including men because they saw that their babies responded differently to men. Mothers' thinking about including men in their children's lives appeared part of being a sensitive parent who wanted to provide their child with the best possible experiences.

Lesbian women's transition to parenthood appeared much like that reported for heterosexual couples.[18] Like heterosexual couples, lesbian parents reported a decline in feelings of love in the partnership and an increase in conflict from the last trimester of the pregnancy to three months after the birth. New demands on time and less time available for the partner relationship seemed to account for some of the changes, but personality characteristics, relationship qualities as well as family support, played a role in minimizing or increasing the changes.

In lesbian partnerships, the biological mother takes primary care of the child in the earliest months, but nonbiological co-mothers often report an immediate attachment to the child and take a larger role when the child is twelve months or older.[19] There was more equal sharing of child care and household work in lesbian partnerships than in heterosexual marriages. Lesbian partners also report a high level of relationship satisfaction and greater satisfaction with the division of labor. Co-mothers were seen as more knowledgeable about child care and more willing to assume equal care of the child than were heterosexual fathers.

A study comparing single and coupled lesbian mothers with single and coupled heterosexual mothers found that (1) single heterosexual and lesbian mothers were warmer and more positive with their children than were coupled heterosexual mothers, and all lesbian mothers were more interactive with their children than were single heterosexual mothers, and (2) single heterosexual and lesbian mothers reported more serious, though not more frequent, disputes with children than did coupled heterosexual mothers.[20]

Gay fathers also experience a decline in relationship quality across the transition to parenting due to the same kind of factors that impact heterosexual and lesbian parents:[21] sleep deprivation, less couple time to check in and talk to each other, having difficulties balancing work and family responsibilities. Some gay fathers also included differences in parenting behaviors and beliefs as a source of conflict. Gay fathers relied on the same strategies detailed for couples in Chapter 4: being proactive in bringing up differences and talking about them before they fester and become conflicts, finding collaborative solutions to the problems that satisfy both parents.

If one parent has a biological connection to the child, or if the biological mother is nursing and has more physical contact with the child, inequities may build in the couple relationship and have to be collaboratively worked out just as they build in heterosexual parent relationships. For example, the non-nursing mother can always use expressed milk and bottle-feed the child. If such issues are not resolved, they can provide a major source of dissatisfaction in the partnership.

While lesbian and gay parents have greater stress in the process of becoming parents, they still share many experiences common to all couples.

PARENTING OF LESBIAN AND GAY PARENTS

The largest group studied has been lesbian mothers. Concerns first focused on divorced lesbian mothers' mental health and on their sex-role behavior and its effects on children.[22] Most early studies compared lesbian and heterosexual mothers and found no differences between them on self-concept, overall psychological adjustment, psychiatric status, sex-role behavior, or interest in children and child rearing. Divorced lesbian mothers were more likely to be living with partners and more worried about custody issues than were divorced heterosexual mothers.

Later studies on lesbian mothers who became mothers when living with lesbian partners were summarized as follows:

> Research has repeatedly shown that lesbian parent couples have high levels of shared employment, decision-making, parenting, and family work, in part in the service of an egalitarian ideology. . . . Lesbian couples also averaged higher satisfaction with their relationships with each other and with each other's parenting. . . . Lesbian DI (donor insemination) mothers had a strong desire for children and devoted a great deal of time and thought to choosing parenthood, and they tended to equal or surpass heterosexual married couples in time spent with children, parenting skills, and warmth and affection.[23]

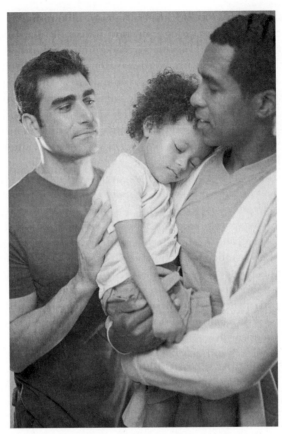

Gay couples coparent more equally than heterosexual couples.

Much less is known about divorced gay fathers and gay fathers in partner rela-tionships.[24] There is no research comparing the psychological stability of gay and heterosexual divorced fathers, perhaps because men did not often seek physical custody after divorce. Research comparing their parenting behaviors suggests that gay fathers are more responsive, more careful about monitoring, and more likely to rely on authoritative parenting strategies than are heterosexual divorced fathers. Studies of the family lives of gay fathers, teen sons, and fathers' partners indicate greater family happiness when the partner has a good relationship with the adoles-cent boy.

Gay couples, like lesbian couples, coparent more equally than their hetero-sexual counterparts.[25] Coparenting equally does not mean sharing every task equally as gay parents tend to specialize in certain tasks depending on their inter-ests and aptitudes with one parent perhaps doing more child care and one doing more housework or cooking.

Gay fathers were more likely than other groups of parents to use positive par-enting strategies and to avoid spanking their children. They were open about their same-sex relationships at children's schools and with children's friends.

Box 16-1
FIRST PERSON NARRATIVE

*How It Feels to Have a Gay or Lesbian Parent: A Book by Kids for Kids of All Ages** is a compilation of the stories of twenty-eight children ranging in age from seven to twenty-eight years, collected by a counselor who wanted a book to give children of gay and lesbian parents who were in the divorce process with heterosexual parents, and nothing was available.

The book lacks stories from children who were born into lesbian and gay families, but many of these children lived with their lesbian and gay parents and their partners. They all dealt with discrimination against their parents as well as disapproval from some friends and sometimes their other parent. They talk about how they coped and dealt with the confusion and pain they experienced. The stories are also full of love for their parents and partners.

Their stories illustrate the strengths that children in research reported they gained in their families. They were caring, understanding, and accepting of all the adults in their lives even when they were sometimes irrational. They are honest and direct and tell their stories with clarity.

This is a moving book that draws readers into the stories and translates the dry facts and statistics of research into the vivid events of everyday life.

*Judith E. Snow, *How It Feels to Have a Gay or Lesbian Parent: A Book by Kids for Kids of All Ages* (New York: Routledge, 2009).

Most of the studies just detailed are of European American, middle-class, educated parents. Information from national data sets provides samples of lesbian mothers raising a significant number of children in areas where they represent a very small concentration of lesbian/gay parents, i.e., South Carolina and Alaska. These working-class lesbian mothers of different ethnic backgrounds appear to have more traditional ways of sharing parenting duties with one parent being a more maternal figure, and the other, a more paternal figure.

Special Challenges

When both parents are mothers and the child prefers one mother, the other may feel hurt and jealous, feeling she is rejected as a nurturer.[26] Mothers may attribute the preference to temperamental similarities or to a genetic connection if there is one, but both parents have to find ways to feel comfortable with the situation or make changes that resolve the hurt feelings. One mother, for example, feeling inadequate and left out because she did not want the role of a typical mother and felt her child gravitated to the other mother, realized she preferred a more paternal role. She constructed her role as that of "lesbian dad" and felt much more comfortable. Gay fathers may have the same problem and have to resolve it as well.

Parents worry that their children will be stigmatized because of parents' partnerships and be teased and bullied at schools. Parents try to live in areas where their families will be accepted and enroll their children in schools that appreciate diversity and accept many kinds of families.

There is not only discrimination against children, but sometimes parents are restricted from participating in all school activities, not going on school trips or helping in classrooms, or being told only one parent can participate in school. Parents model positive behavior when they respond in an assertive, confident way, directly addressing school authorities about their exclusion. In approaching schools and other public arenas, parents can keep in mind the survey results reported in Chapter 1 that most people in the country accept lesbian and gay parents as either being good for society or not making any difference one way or the other (53 percent), and only 43 percent believing gay/lesbians' having children is bad for society.[27]

When they deal with schools about teasing and bullying of their children, parents can point out that a safe school environment is important for all children, and parents will be happy to participate in forming parents' groups and helping schools provide such environments.

Benefits of Growing Up in Lesbian and Gay Families

Interviews with four hundred lesbian and gay parents revealed that despite the stigmatization they and their children may experience, parents identified certain benefits of growing up in families with lesbian and gay parents.[28] Children were:

- understanding and accepting of different points of view
- open in talking about their feelings and problems
- free of the restrictions of traditional role models

Talking about their childhood experiences growing up with lesbian and gay parents, adolescents and young adults identify similar benefits:

- being accepting and nonjudgmental of a broad range of beliefs, cultures, and political views
- having broad definitions of "family" and valuing communities of chosen friends
- valuing honesty and truthfulness in relationships after having sometimes hidden secrets as children
- being more comfortable with gender nonconformity

Parents believe their support system of extended family members became more involved and supportive as children developed, and they were able to develop a friendship network oriented around family activities. Their children describe the family and extended family friendships as important supports for them as well.

Growing up, many children felt discriminated against at school because of parents' sexual orientation.

CHILDREN OF LESBIAN AND GAY PARENTS

In this section we review how children and adolescents learned of and responded to parents' sexual orientations, how they managed their reactions, their overall psychological adjustment, and the supports they relied on.

Responding to Parents' Sexual Orientations

Abbie Goldberg reviewed many studies, including her own work, to describe how children learned of and responded to parents' sexual orientations.[29] Information came from parents' reports and from adolescents' and young adults' descriptions. When children were born into families headed by lesbian and gay parents, they became aware of parents' sexual orientation gradually. Parents may have casually talked about their different form of family life; children may have noticed differences with other families; and there may have been a particular event that made them aware of the difference. Just as children in heterosexual families have a time when they see their parents as sexual beings, so children of lesbian and gay parents may have a moment when they realize what their parents' sexual orientation means and that some people do not approve.

When children have lived with parents as heterosexuals and parents then identify themselves as lesbian or gay, children may learn in two basic ways: parents may tell them directly, explaining the reasons for a divorce or the beginning of a same-sex partnership or in response to a child's questions; or parents may indicate their orientation indirectly, taking children to a same-sex social event like a gay/lesbian parade or socializing with other lesbian or gay families, or by leaving reading material around.

Children's reactions vary. When children learn gradually and live in a supportive social climate, they may feel it is "no big deal" to have same-sex parents. In one study, the majority of children appear to have a mild or neutral reaction with only a small percentage feeling angry or ashamed. Over time children's reactions were largely indifferent or positive, with again, a small number being angry or ashamed.

When children were told, two big worries were common: that other children would reject them or others would think they were gay or lesbian. All children in these families had to decide how and how much to disclose to friends about their family relationships. One study found that they used three main strategies to handle their worries:

- boundary control in which children sought (a) to control parents' behavior by asking parents to act in a certain way like coming separately to school events or sleeping in separate bedrooms when friends slept over; (b) to control their own behavior, e.g., by not going certain places with parents; and (c) to control peers' behavior, for example, not inviting friends to their home
- nondisclosure in which children told no one
- selective disclosure in which children told only certain people

While one sample of ten-year-olds were very open with 57 percent completely open with friends, 39 percent open with selective friends, and only 4 percent hiding the information, selective disclosure appeared the common strategy, telling some friends and telling others only as circumstances required. When children lived with openly lesbian or gay parents, they had less choice, and some parents reported they knew children did not invite friends to the home to avoid telling them. Keeping parents hidden can create family tensions. Parents may understand why children do not want them to come to school together, and they do not put pressure on children, but they may be hurt and at the same time want to encourage more positive ways of handling problems. Parents can talk to children to discuss children's feelings and to assert that the problem is not parents' same-sex orientation but society's stigmatizing disapproval of it. Young adults reported later that it was very helpful to them when parents understood and did not put pressure on them to disclose.

In lesbian families using donor sperm, there is no simple trend regarding the effects on children of knowing or not knowing the donor. Children with known and unknown donors did not appear to differ in psychological adjustment in two studies, and while some children wanted contact and to know donors, a large number did not care. The results may change as children get older. In two studies, knowing made a difference with boys who knew the donor showing more problems, and in another, not knowing the donor was related to more problems.

Young Adults' Reports of Growing Up in Lesbian and Gay Families

Growing up, many young adults reported feeling discriminated against at school not just by peers but by school personnel who allowed disparaging comments to be made by other students and who made no attempt to present a positive picture of lesbian and gay people or of their history.[30]

Some young adults also reported feeling under a microscope as people were judging them, and indirectly their parents. They felt they had had to be seen as "successful" or "well-adjusted," especially if there was a news item that drew attention to gay and lesbian people. Some also knew their parents experienced pressure to be seen as good parents, and so children wanted to be "psychologically healthy" in order to demonstrate parents' competence and reduce parents' worries.

As adults, many reported they realized that hiding their parents' sexual orientation was stressful for them. Even though they thought secrecy was sometimes necessary, they realized later it was a heavy burden.

As adults, only half of the sample were completely open about their parents' sexual orientation, and some said they were open as a way of educating people about lesbian and gay parents. A second group was selective and sometimes disclosed information as a way of testing the value of a possible friendship. A third group did not routinely disclose information as they thought it was irrelevant and did not matter, and because it was not part of their identity.

In talking about supports in their childhoods, young adults referred to three: their parents, their extended family members, and their friends. Parents who were positive, confident role models, who were open about their own sexual orientations and able to create a supportive climate for communication, were helpful. When family members could talk about the disapproval some people felt for their way of life, and parents and children could talk about how to respond to questions or teasing and how to handle exclusions, children felt better able to deal with problems. Extended family members created a supportive network and also served as role models for how to handle difficulties. Good friends created fun times and also gave children feelings of being included and connected.

Psychological Adjustment of Children

Research has focused on three questions—the nature of children's gender identity, their psychological stability, and their social relationships with other children. With respect to gender identity, there is no evidence that children of lesbian and gay parents have an increased likelihood of having a lesbian/gay gender identity or same-sex sexual orientation. However, many do have less sex-stereotyped interests and activities.[31]

Children living with lesbian and gay parents are as well adjusted and socially competent as children living with heterosexual parents. Children of lesbian parents show no special problems with self-concept or with depression or self-esteem. The results of research indicate that family process variables operate in much the same way in lesbian and gay families as in heterosexual families—that is, when parents are warm and involved, as many lesbian and gay parents are, their children do well.

The most detailed research has been carried out with data from the National Longitudinal Study of Adolescent Health, a national sample of children from grades 7 to 12 in eighty different schools around the country.[32] Adolescents filled out questionnaires at school, and a subsample of 12,105 were interviewed at home. One parent, preferably the resident mother, was interviewed and filled out questionnaires regarding characteristics of the home, the parents, and the parent-teen relationship. In addition, peers also rated the teens on social relationships, and schools provided grades. This study is especially important because people outside the family (peers) are describing children as well as parents and teens themselves, and schools provided grades.

Children whose parent reported being in a same-sex marriage or marriage-like relationship with a same-sex partner were identified and matched with teens from families headed by a heterosexual couple. Forty-four children of lesbian partners were found. Because only six teens lived in homes with gay men parents the study was restricted to forty-four living with lesbian parents.

Reports from adolescents, their parents, peers, and school provided a picture of adolescents' functioning in a variety of areas—psychological stability, relationships with parents, academic success, dating and romantic relationships,[33] social friendships and peer acceptance,[34] substance use and delinquent activities, and experiences of victimization.[35] In all these areas of behavior, adolescents of lesbian couples were functioning as well as teens from families headed by heterosexual couples. Their dating and romantic attachments were similar, and both teens and peers reported the children of lesbian parents as well accepted as those in the control group.

Although gender type of family did not predict differences in teens' behavior, the quality of parent-teen relationships did predict teens' behavior. Regardless of sexual orientation of parents, parents' reports of close relationships with their teens predicted adolescents' psychological stability, their competence in school and social relations, and their lower rates of substance use and delinquent activity. So, it is the quality of parent-teen relationships that predict positive qualities, not the gender orientation.

This study with carefully collected data on a national sample that included 38 percent of teens of non-white background provides strong evidence that children living in lesbian couple families are doing as well as children in traditional families. Unlike children of divorce, remarriage, or adoption, there does not appear to be a small core who have problems with worried, depressed moods or angry, oppositional behaviors.

DISSOLUTIONS OF PARENTS' RELATIONSHIPS

Like heterosexual families, lesbian and gay parents sometimes decide to separate. The estimates are that between 40 and 50 percent of families will experience this process in the course of children's growing up.[36] The reasons given are those often given in heterosexual relationships: increasing incompatibility, differing views on parenting and rearing children, difficulties in sharing family responsibilities, and financial disagreements.

In Chapter 15 we saw the pain divorce recreates for all involved. In lesbian and gay families there may be no mechanisms or agencies to help parents find the best solutions for children, and no agencies specifically charged with looking after the welfare of children. Parents can seek a collaborative divorce process, but as noted, if one parent has sole custody, that may not be possible. Still, for the sake of children, parents should try to follow the guidelines of Chapter 15.

MANAGING STRESSES IN LESBIAN AND GAY FAMILIES

We have seen the many stresses that lesbian and gay parents and their children experience. Yet all the studies of both parents and their children attest to their strengths and resilience that result in effective functioning even though families experience more than the average amount of stress. Several factors may be responsible:

- parents planned carefully for having children and how they would meet children's needs
- parents had middle-class resources to meet stresses that came primarily from outside the home
- parents emphasized equality in adult relationships and sharing household tasks
- parents established a climate of open and honest communication and willingness to talk about problems
- parents encouraged children's individuality and a broad range of independent interests
- parents' understanding of children's behavior with respect to hiding parents' orientation and willingness to put children's needs first

Planning for family needs, creating a family atmosphere of equality between parents and open communication and warmth with children, as well as encouraging individuality—all these behaviors appear to compensate for the added stresses parents and children experience and enable them to function effectively. Furthermore, disapproval and hostility came from people outside the home and not inside, and families often had resources to find schools and neighborhoods where they would be more likely to be accepted. The quality of lesbian/gay parenting has gained support from many including President Obama, who in May 2012, endorsed same-sex marriage saying, in part, he recognized that same-sex parents are as loving, caring and committed as heterosexual parents.[37]

MAIN POINTS

Lesbian and gay parents and their children feel added stress from
- society's failure to give symbolic recognition to parents' union and their family relationships
- social disapproval and exclusion
- denial of material benefits freely accorded to heterosexual parents and their families

Lesbian and gay parents

- share child care and household tasks more equally than heterosexual parents
- make the transition to parenthood much as heterosexual partnered parents do
- are open and honest in communication with children

Children of lesbian and gay parents

- function as well psychologically and socially as children from two-parent heterosexual families
- believe they are less judgmental and more accepting of diverse points of view
- are less stereotyped in interests and activities

EXERCISES

1. Investigate the laws of your state regarding lesbian and gay parent adoption and coparent adoption of children in lesbian and gay partnerships.

2. Research the availability of public and private adoption services for lesbian and gay parents as well as policies of any fertility clinics.

3. Research the availability of parenting classes for lesbian and gay parents in your area. Are there special groups where they can get information and support? Are they included in the regular prebirth classes at the local hospital?

4. Have small groups consider the possible reasons that the children of lesbian partners function so well. While children of divorced, remarried, and single-parent families all have a subgroup of children who have significantly more problems than children living in biological two-parent families, from the research at hand this does not seem to be true with the children of lesbian partners.

5. In groups, have students discuss how they, if they were the children of lesbian and gay parents, would want friends to react when they told them about their parents' relationships.

ADDITIONAL READINGS

Clunis, D. Merilee and Green, G. Dorsey. *The Lesbian Parenting Book: A Guide to Creating Families and Rearing Children.* 2nd ed. New York: Seal Press, 2003.

Garner, Abigail. *Families Like Mine: Children of Gay Parents Tell It Like It Is.* New York: Harper, 2004.

Goldberg, Abbie E. *Lesbian and Gay Parents and Their Children: Research on the Family Life Cycle.* Washington, DC: American Psychological Association, 2010.

Mallon, G. *Gay Men Choosing Parenthood.* New York: Columbia University Press, 2004.

Snow, Judith E. *How It Feels to Have a Gay or Lesbian Parent: A Book by Kids for Kids of All Ages.* New York: Routledge, 2009.

17

Parenting in Challenging Times

CHAPTER TOPICS

In this chapter, you will learn about:

- Systems Perspective
- Illness
- Death in the Family
- Maltreatment
    - Forms
    - Family Risk Factors
    - Children's Reactions

- Interventions and Prevention
- Foster Families
- National Disaster and War
    - Natural Disaster
    - Terrorism
    - Military Families
- Challenge model of intervention

Test Your Knowledge: Fact or Fiction (True/False)

1. Childhood is a time of health and energy, and physical problems in the family concern parents' and grandparents' health.
2. Children who experience one form of maltreatment often experience several others.
3. In foster homes, children are able to deal with the problems that brought them there, and so they have fewer problems when they leave.
4. Disasters and national violence are so overwhelming that families can do little to minimize their effects.
5. Most families of deployed service members cope with the numerous stresses involved in having a parent in harm's way.

When traumatic events occur, parents face difficult challenges. What reactions can parents expect from children? What can parents do to manage their own reactions and help children cope? What can parents do to protect children from violence and enable them to feel secure in a world that is sometimes unsafe? How can they help children develop resilience in challenging times?

In previous chapters, we have talked about the moderately stressful events of life like school and peer problems. In Chapters 14 and 15 we talked about the losses and sadness of divorce, and separations from biological parents. Here, in this chapter, we talk about many other major traumatic events: illness and death, abuse, neglect, and violence in the home, the community, and the nation. We also look at foster parenting and parenting when one or both parents are in the military. Sadly, some people experience several major losses and traumas, and ironically and unfairly, experience all the moderately stressful life events as well. (See Box 17-1.)

This chapter focuses on how parents help themselves and their children cope with the challenges of illness, death in the family, neglect, abuse, community and national disaster, and violence and the parenting that takes place around these events.

SYSTEMS PERSPECTIVE

In Chapter 3, we described the ABC-X family stress theory developed by Reuben Hill[1] (pages 97–98), and Table 17-1 provides this broad conceptual framework for understanding how trauma impacts families and how each member copes with severe stress depending on the resources of the family and the community, and we use the framework to understand how children and parents cope with extraordinary stresses.

While treatment programs provide significant help in the process of coping, parents must remember that children who experience many adversities in the course of life often get help from their own daily activities.[2] Data from two longitudinal studies indicate that adverse experiences like a parent's psychological problems increase children's problem behavior but when children are able to engage positively in school activities, that activity serves to buffer the child from the increase in problem behaviors that would ordinarily occur. Engaging in valued activity appears to give the child a sense of self-worth, control, and social connection.

ILLNESS AND DEATH

We think of childhood as a time of health and energy. Yet, over 10 percent of children have serious or chronic illnesses.[3] The most common chronic illnesses are asthma, which affects from 4 to 9 percent of children, diabetes, cerebral palsy, human immunodeficiency virus (HIV), cystic fibrosis (a genetic disorder involving many symptoms and daily treatments), cancer, sickle cell disorder, juvenile rheumatoid arthritis, and hemophilia. In addition, up to 20 percent of children between the ages of five and seventeen suffer from chronic headaches, and many others from bowel and stomach pains.[4]

Illnesses differ in their symptoms, treatments, pain involved, and life-threatening potential, but all create stress and worry and require interventions. They interrupt family's daily schedules and activities. We discuss special sources of stress for children and parents and special strategies for maintaining family closeness and effectiveness.

> ### Box 17-1
> ## THE MANY STRESSES THAT CAN COME YOUR WAY*
>
> In the book *Conquering Your Child's Chronic Pain*, Dr. Lonnie Zeltzer describes the case of Damien, whom she treated for pain related to his sickle cell disease. Up to the age of eleven or twelve, he rarely came to the hospital with complaints of pain. He was a happy boy, doing well at school, and having fun with his brothers.
>
> When he entered middle school, however, he began to have school difficulties and his grades started to drop; in retrospect he seemed to have a learning disability with math. At thirteen, he experienced a traumatic event, but said nothing to the doctors who were overseeing his medical care.
>
> When Dr. Zeltzer met him, he was a quiet thirteen-year-old boy who said little about himself or his life when he came for medical visits to control the pain that was causing him increasing difficulties. Gradually, over a two-year period he told Dr. Zeltzer details of the trauma. His older brother had joined a gang and was killed in a gang-related shooting. Damien had worshipped him and blamed himself for his brother's death. Damien had telephoned his brother and asked him to come home and help him repair his bicycle. They were walking to the store to get parts for the bike when a car came by and someone shot his brother.
>
> Damien blamed himself because if he had not called, his brother would not have been on the street that day. Following the death, Damien began to have symptoms of anxiety and flashbacks of the shooting. He felt on alert, startled easily, and he could not sleep at night. Tired during the day, he had even greater difficulty with school-work, and his grades dropped further. Furthermore, the adrenaline that was racing through his system was making the pain of the sickle cell disease worse.
>
> He was also having problems with peers. Sickle cell disease stunted his growth, and bullies at school began to tease him for his shortness. To escape the teasing, he began to cut school with his friends. His parents, caught up in their own grief, tried to handle Damien's problems by yelling and predicting that Damien would meet the same fate as his brother.
>
> At this time, Damien's pain became unmanageable because he stopped taking his medications regularly, refused help from his parents, skipped his regular doctors' appointments, and began to show up in the Emergency Room at irregular intervals for pain-killing medications. Medical staff became concerned he was using street drugs and gave him only minimal pain medications in the Emergency Room. As a result, Damien ended up screaming for pain medications.
>
> One can see how a combination of physical illness, his particular age, and most of all the trauma of his brother's death put Damien on a downhill course. Had he and his parents been able to talk about his brother's death and Damien received psychological help for his symptoms of posttraumatic stress disorder at the time they began, he and his parents might have been spared much psychological pain.
>
> *From: Lonnie K. Zeltzer and Christina Blackett Schlank, *Conquering Your Child's Chronic Pain* (New York: HarperCollins, 2005).

■ **T A B L E 17-1**
FRAMEWORK FOR UNDERSTANDING IMPACT OF TRAUMA AND DISASTERS
ON FAMILIES*

Pre-event Adjustment of Family:

    Health, psychological adjustment, skills of each family member

    Family resources (financial, psychological support)

    Previous stresses, traumas, disasters in last two-three years

    Community resources

Characteristics of Trauma, Disaster:

    Severity of harm/damage/losses

    Duration

    Degree to which it triggers cascade of other stresses

Family Members' Experiences in Trauma, Disaster:

    Direct or indirect involvement

    Extent of damages, losses of family

Family's Resources for Dealing with Trauma, Disaster:

    Emotional coping skills of all family members

    Problem-solving skills of all family members

    Support system

    Financial resources

Community Resources for Helping Families

Outcomes for Children and Families over Time

*Adapted from: Sharon J. Price and Christine A. Price (With Patrick C. McKenry, posthumously) "Families Coping with Change: A Conceptual Overview," in *Families and Change: Coping with Stressful Events and Transitions*, 4th ed., eds. Sharon J. Price, Christine A. Price, and Patrick C. McKenry (Thousand Oaks, CA: Sage, 2010), 1–23.

Children's Understanding of Their Bodies and Illness

Part of children's stress in illness comes from lack of information. Children do not have clear conceptions of their bodies and illness, and so they may not understand what is happening or they may have upsetting misconceptions of what is or has happened and their role in causing the illness.

Young children get their ideas about their bodies from colloquial expressions, their own bodily sensations, and from time devoted to that part of the body.[5] For example, they think "nerves" give you courage. One little girl thought hair was the most important part of the body because her mother spent so much time brushing it. It is wise to remember that children may hear parts of conversations about their illness and misinterpret what they hear. With increasing age, children's concepts of the body become more accurate, but their notions of how the body works remain rudimentary even in early adolescence. For example, one thirteen-year-old girl thought lungs were in the throat and one was for breathing and one was for eating.

Their thoughts about illness also expand and become more detailed with age.[6] In the preschool years, children think of illness as a single symptom caused by a rays from. In these years, children sometimes think illness is caused by an immoral act—you are bad and you get punished. As children move into elementary school years, they see illness as several symptoms that are caused by germs, dirt, and—still—bad behavior. Direct contact with germs or dirt causes illness and it can be avoided if you stay away from direct contact with the cause.

Parents and health professionals must explore with children all their ideas about their physical functioning and what they think is the cause of their illness. When given accurate information in words they can understand, children, even in preschool years, can develop scripts about what they must do and why in order to get over the illness or to control symptoms.

Anxiety and Fear of the Unknown

Children get anxious about shots and blood tests with which they have had experience, and procedures they do not understand. Parents give accurate information about whether a shot will be given and reassure the child that the pain will be brief and helps keep the child well. When a child starts to cry, the parent can sympathetically comment that when things hurt, people cry, and it is okay to cry.

A parent can reduce a child's anxiety by encouraging the child to talk about feelings, clarifying any misconceptions, and giving the child strategies to reduce the nervousness by slowing down breathing or focusing on other thoughts. If the child is very young, it is helpful for the child to have a favorite toy or object to bring along. If a parent cannot reduce the child's anxiety, then consultation with a pediatric or clinical psychologist can be useful because elevated anxiety can increase symptoms and obstruct healing.

Guilt

As noted, children often think that illness is a punishment for something they have done or have not done, and so they feel guilty, making the illness experience even worse because they believe they caused it themselves. Parents can be alert for any indication of such feelings and even raise the topic in a casual way, saying, "Sometimes children believe they caused their illnesses. Do you ever feel this way?" Even if the child's behavior played a part in an accident or an injury, parents can reassure the child that everyone makes a mistake from time to time, and, most often there is not such a heavy penalty. Or the parent can say he or she knows the child did not intend to get injured. Sometimes parents are at a loss for words, as they never would have imagined the way in which their child felt responsible for the illness.

Box 17-2
FIRST PERSON NARRATIVE*

Journalist Melinda Blau collaborated with psychologist Karen Fingerman to write *Consequential Strangers*, integrating Fingerman's research on the importance of people on the peripheries of our social circles with Blau's interviews with additional researchers and individuals who talked about the roles "consequential strangers" play in their daily lives.

The term "stranger" is misleading because these people are not strangers; they are all known to us. Although they are not family members or close friends, we see them regularly and the first-person accounts of the authors and others illustrates their significant contributions to the quality of our lives. They are the parents we see when picking children up at day care or the parents who sit with us in the stands watching children's swim teams or soccer matches. They are people at work who, though not in our department, have a friendly word or share a great recipe, or are classmates in our exercise class. They are happy to see us, listen to our worries, give us advice and support. In everyday life they help us feel connected and important to others, and they help us function more effectively.

At times of trouble, these consequential supporters may provide things no loving family or friend can. They are coparents in the support groups for parents whose children have a rare illness or a special disability or they are other patients with amputations or debilitating diseases. They know what we are going through, and they can often connect us to crucial resources or provide tips based on their own experience. And they are sources of inspiration and encouragement.

The first-hand accounts provide a valuable look into community life in twenty-first-century America and suggest that if we all increase our consequential encounters just a little, we may be able to increase the social atmosphere of trust and support described in Chapter 1 as an antidote to the stress from living in challenging times.

*Melinda Blau and Karen L. Fingerman, *Consequential Strangers: Turning Everyday Encounters into Life-Changing Moments* (New York: W. W. Norton, 2009).

Pain

Pain is a common element of many illnesses, and is stressful for children and parents. In the past, medical personnel minimized the pain that children felt, believing that it was different from that of adults, and so they often failed to treat it effectively with medication. Since pain is a subjective experience it is difficult to determine how much pain a child has.

Dr. Lonnie Zeltzer, Director of the University of California at Los Angeles Pediatric Pain Program, writes in her book for parents, "I believe that if a child complains of pain, the pain is real and the child is suffering. The job of parents and physicians is to figure out what might have started the pain and, more importantly, what is keeping the pain going. Typically the pain is continuing not because of one single thing such as torn cartilage but more commonly from an array of factors."[7] Parents work with medical personnel to plan a comprehensive pain relief program that includes medication, relaxation exercises, physical exercises, and a generally healthy lifestyle.

Anger and Irritability over Restrictions and Demands

Many illnesses restrict fun activities and at same time, often impose frustrating demands of daily treatments or regimes. Asthmatic children must measure oxygen flow each day and do breathing treatments. Diabetic children must test their blood sugar and adjust insulin accordingly. Sometimes the procedures are painful and all cut into time that children would rather spend elsewhere.

Parents must cope with children's resistance and also insist calmly that treatments be completed. It requires parents' organization to allow enough time for children to carry out the tasks and for monitoring to ensure completion. Parents must also keep their own emotions under control when children complain and direct their anger at the illness to parents who are there and can respond. Listening to children's feelings and accepting them while staying problem-focused is difficult, but when parents do that, children usually comply after their feelings have been heard. Adolescents may have the most difficulties even after years of compliance because they want very much to do what their peers are doing and because they want their independence, and illness limits it.

Engaging the child in problem solving to eliminate the most irritating aspects of the treatments helps, but parents must convey that although they understand the child's reasons for anger, the restrictions must be followed and treatments must still be completed. When everyone in the family follows the restrictions of the ill child—if that is feasible and healthy—then the child feels less alone and less limited. For example, it is possible for everyone in the family to follow a diet very similar to that of the child with diabetes with no refined sugars, limited carbohydrates like bread, many vegetables, and several smaller meals during the day at home. No candy is eaten at home. Brothers and sisters can have some sugary treats at school or with friends, but at home, everyone eats a diet very similar to that of the person who is restricted. Furthermore, healthy lifestyles advised for all children with illnesses are followed by all family members. Everyone in the family joins with the ill child to the degree that is possible.

Sources of Stress for Parents and Strategies for Successful Coping

Parents' distress comes from many sources:[8]

1. Worries and uncertainties about what the illness and treatments involve and the possible lasting effects of the illness
2. Feelings of guilt that they did not prevent and cannot cure the illness, and such guilt may be intensified if the illness is a genetic one
3. Feelings of helplessness at not having control over what is happening to their child and not being able to fix it
4. Financial burdens from the cost of the illness and treatment
5. Feelings of inadequacy at meeting everyone's needs—the child's, their other children's, their spouse's, their own, their extended family members', the needs of the workplace

6. Disruption of work life, needing time off, diminished work performance

7. Disruption of social ties to extended family and friends

Parents cope with all these stresses by clear and effective communication with everyone involved, expressing feelings and concerns and listening to others. They help sick children ask their questions and express their worries, and they find time to talk with other children in the family and their partner and relatives. They try to keep pace with work demands if they can. Research indicates that it is the mother who is often the linchpin in this situation.[9] If she gets information and accepts the diagnosis, family stress is reduced. Fathers feel greater marital satisfaction, and are more helpful and supportive. Children also feel more secure attachments to mothers when mothers accept the diagnosis.

Effective problem solving and organization also help parents with the many extra activities involved with illness. Scheduling relatives and friends to help out with chores and provide support reduces stress. Parents must also take some time to unwind even if it is only a few minutes at the end of the day.

Other strategies to reduce the stress of illness include:[10]

1. Forming a collaborative partnership with health-care providers, working as a team, sharing information and concerns, presenting the child's point of view

2. Balancing the needs of all family members, especially siblings, so that their needs are not ignored

3. Focusing on the positive aspects of the situation—help and support given, seeing the cooperation and caring of brothers and sisters, working together as a family

4. Emphasizing the commitment all family members feel toward the family and helping everyone in it do well

5. Maintain ties to friends and extended family members

6. Be flexible with family roles and let others take on new roles to get things done

7. Separating the illness from the child; and treating the sick child as nearly as possible like a healthy child, even if the child is dying; they have chores within their capacities, go to school, and receive discipline like other children

Death in the Family

We look at this problem from the point of view of the child because more children are losing a parent in war. When a parent dies, nothing is the same. Earl Grollman writes, "Never again will the world be as secure a place as it was before. The familiar design of family life is completely disrupted."[11] While there are differences in the ways that children and parents grieve, there are also many similarities, and we touch on them first and then move to what is unique for children and parents.

For the child the death of a parent is "the worst loss."[12] The child has lost the figure he or she depended upon for security in life, and the parent has lost his or her life companion. John Bowlby described four phases of the grief process: (1) a period of numbing lasting for hours or weeks in which the person has taken in the fact of the death but has not registered it emotionally because the pain is so great; (2) a period of protest and yearning in which the person refuses to accept the fact of the death and searches for the parent; (3) a period of sadness and despair in which the reality of the death has sunk in emotionally and life without that person seems unbearable; and (4) a period of reorganization of life to go on without that person.[13]

Bowlby did not think of these as clear-cut stages but rather as a "succession of phases." It is possible to move back and forth between two phases while moving in the direction of adapting to and accepting the fact of the person's death.[14] Thus, a person can move from feeling sad to being engaged in reorganization and then back to feeling sad again. Bowlby also believed it is not necessary to detach completely from the memory of the person; it is possible to reorganize your life in a meaningful way and still have a continuing sense of the dead person's presence in your life.

There is no specific length of time for grieving. Children may proceed through the phases of grief more rapidly than adults. It used to be thought that about a year was the usual length of mourning, and to be sad and grieving after a year indicated problems. Now, we realize it may take two or more years before people have reorganized their lives and are on a steady emotional keel most of the time. Still, there will always be reminders and sudden experiences of intense grief. Psychological consultation is often recommended when the usual reactions to grief persist in intense ways that disrupt daily functioning. However, sometimes getting immediate professional advice eases the process of mourning and prevents the development of problems.

Children's Special Needs   A child's developmental level and temperament will guide what is said to the child about the death. At the Dougy Center for Grieving Children, counselors have four guiding principles:

- "Grief is a natural and expectable response to loss.
- Each individual carries within him an innate capacity to heal.
- The duration and intensity of grief is unique for each individual.
- Caring and acceptance are helpful to a person in resolving grief."[15]

Talking to Children   One has to give as much accurate information as possible to children in words that they can understand.[16] Very young children think of death as a reversible condition, and it is not until they are five to seven that they understand it is irreversible. So little children may ask when the parent is returning. Regardless of their initial understanding, as they get older and their thinking becomes more mature, they may have new questions and new reactions they want to discuss. So, the initial explanation of the death is the beginning of conversations that will extend over the years.

Parents are sometimes told to wait for children to ask questions, but children may not know enough to ask questions at the time, and only later may have the words or thoughts they need answers to.[17] For example, a preschooler refused to go to bed after her infant sister died of SIDS because she thought she too would die in her sleep. She did not volunteer this information until her mother asked her what was upsetting her at bedtime.

Parents have to be aware that children are prone to feel guilt and to blame themselves for the death of a loved one. One family was surprised to learn that their daughter blamed herself for a family death. She was not present, but blamed herself because she thought the death was God's punishment for not saying her prayers at night.

Ways Children's Reactions Differ from Adults   The Dougy Center lists several ways in which children's grief differs from adults.[18] First, children are more physical in their expressions of grief. They may want to ride a bike, shoot baskets, or run as a way of dealing with grief. They also may have more physical complaints of stomachaches or headaches. Second, children are less verbal, and sometimes parents think they are not grieving because they are not talking about it. They may use imaginative play or actions rather than words to express grief. Third, children express their anger about the death more directly and may do more quarreling or arguing or simply express anger at everyone and life in general.

Fourth, children may be more attuned to parents' needs and feelings than parents realize. As a result, they may behave in ways that they think will please or help their parents. For example, if they see that their questions upset a parent, they may stop asking them even though they are still confused about the death. Fifth, children need breaks from grieving; parents may find it hard to understand that they can become immersed in an activity and not grieve. Parents misinterpret that as not caring for the dead person, but children do have the ability to live in the moment. They can grieve intensely and then happily be with friends.

Helping Children Grieve   Joan Huff, program director at the Dougy Center, believes that parents create a supportive emotional climate in which children feel safe to go through the process of grieving.[19] To create such a climate she advises:

- In age-appropriate terms, give accurate, detailed information about the death and answer all questions; be prepared to continue discussions in the future.

- Reassure children that the remaining parent will continue to nurture and care for them, and though the grief process may last an extended period of time, they will always be taken care of.

- "Keep your children with you, and include them in family and religious observances: viewings, funerals, burials, wakes, and the like. The question of at what age children should attend funerals comes up frequently. Talking with children, I hardly ever heard a child complain he was forced to attend a funeral against his will. Much more often, children complained that they had been sent away, excluded from this profoundly important event in their family's life."[20] If children are babies or toddlers, other relatives can hold them or supervise them. In the future, it is valuable for them to know that they were there with the rest of the family even though they do not remember it.

- Talk to children about what they want to do with their parent's possessions; parents make the final decision but get input from children.

- Express your grief in front of your children so they receive permission to grieve as well; parents may worry that their grief may overwhelm children; certainly in extreme form, wailing or sobbing can overwhelm them, so it is wise to try to strike a balance between expressing your feelings so children feel free to grieve also and expressing them so intensely that children are overwhelmed and afraid.

- Structure observances of the death so that all close family members are included and have a role—lighting a candle on anniversaries, making a donation in the name of the person.

Parents' Special Needs   We all live with the assumption that we will grow up, marry, raise children, live for many years after children are grown, and then die when we are old and infirm. The untimely death of a young parent violates our sense of the order of life events and arouses fear that other frightening events or another untimely death can occur as well. Parents' expectations about life are dashed and they have many of the emotional reactions children have—anger, guilt, fear, insecurity. One father said, "When you lose a child, you lose a piece of yourself. You lose your illusions. You lose reason and predictability; all the order falls out of the universe. And you lose your future."[21] The same feelings exist when you lose your husband or wife.

Parents need as much support and nurturance as their young children at this devastating time, and yet they also have the responsibility for providing and looking after other family members. So what helps them cope? Living in an emotionally safe environment with people who respect that they will grieve in their own individual way and who give them support as they find their way enables adults to get through the process of grieving.

Helpful strategies include:[22]

- Talking to other people, sometimes in a group of people who have suffered a similar loss like Compassionate Friends; talking to other family members and staying connected; expect to have to educate them about the grief process as you experience it.

- Knowing that life will not always be this painful; you will get through this experience; however painful it is, however many ups and downs you experience, you will survive.

- Striving for balance in your life with physical exercise, healthy eating, and little pleasures to offset the pain that you are experiencing.

- Seeking a spiritual or broader connection to provide meaning in life; many people find help in a religious or spiritual understanding of the event; others seek meaning by becoming involved in groups to prevent the kind of tragedy that happened to them; still others find meaning and vitality to their lives by providing services to others, e.g., bringing pets or plants or services to people in nursing homes.
- Valuing what they do have rather than focusing on what they have lost.

VICTIMIZATION AND ADVERSITY

David Finkelhor and his coworkers have focused on a broad range of stresses in childhood including:[23]

Disasters: increased risk of death, bereavement, physical harm, loss of basic human necessities like food and water caused by human or natural means (fires, hurricanes, tornados)

Victimization: physical/psychological harm to individuals caused by other individuals who are violating society's norms (assaults, physical/sexual abuses, neglect, bullying, robberies)

Adversity: other daily events that are associated with psychological suffering but are not caused by individuals but rather by life circumstances (ill parent, parent incarcerated)

A telephone survey regarding stressful experiences of 2,030 children from ages two to seventeen was carried out in 2001–2002. A representative national sample of parents was interviewed about the experiences of their children ages two to nine, and children ten to seventeen were interviewed regarding how many experiences of the above kind occurred in the course of a lifetime and how many in the past year. Finkelhor and his colleagues believe that experiences of victimization prior to or at the time of disasters can intensify the emotional reactions to disaster.

The survey, believed to be the first of its kind, revealed that 14 percent of children ages two to seventeen had been exposed to one disaster in their lifetime, and 4 percent had experienced a disaster in the past year. The most common disasters were tornados (27 percent), hurricanes (24 percent), earthquakes (18 percent), and fires (14 percent). Finkelhor and his colleagues were surprised that of the seventy children who had experienced a disaster in the previous year, only two had been referred for counseling.

Table 17-2 presents percentages of other forms of victimization.

One can see that victimizations are the more common forms of trauma in children's lives with one in three children experiencing some form of victimization, and one in seven children experiencing some form of disaster. Victimization was related to depression among two- to nine-year-old disaster survivors and to depression and anger among ten- to seventeen-year-old disaster survivors. Children exposed to victimization only or victimization and disaster had more difficulties in psychological adjustment than those children who experienced neither.

■ **T A B L E 17-2**
RESULTS OF SURVEY ON DISASTER, VICTIMIZATION, AND ADVERSITY
IN CHILDREN AGES 2 TO 17*

Experienced disaster during lifetime	14
Experienced disaster in last year	4
Of those who experienced any disaster, percent experienced more than one	25
Victimization in lifetime	
Sexual victimization	14
Child maltreatment	20
Witnessing family violence	11
Witnessing other form of violence	17
Experienced at least one form of victimization	36
Among children 10–17, correlation between lifetime experience of disaster and:	
Lifetime experience of sexual victimization	.86
Lifetime experience of maltreatment	.29
Adversity	.13
Major violence	−.15

*From: Katherine A. Becker-Blease, Heather A. Turner, and David Finkelhor, "Disasters, Victimization, and Children's Mental Health," *Child Development 81* (2010): 1040–1052.

CHILD MALTREATMENT

Family violence and child maltreatment are traumatic to children, more traumatic than community and national disaster and violence because it is personal and most often occurs at the hands of the very individuals who were expected to protect the child. In addition to the pain or damage of the abuse itself, the child experiences a great loss of trust in parents and authority in general that cannot be easily restored.

We look at a bioecological view of abuse, then at the definitions, incidence, and prevalence of maltreatment, factors that place families at high risk for maltreatment, the problems children experience as a result of such experiences, and finally forms of intervention and prevention.

Bioecological View of Maltreatment

Using Urie Bronfenbrenner's ecological model presented in Chapter 3, researchers describe risk and protective factors for maltreatment at the cultural, community, family, and individual levels of experience.[24] Cultural beliefs that physical force is an acceptable way to settle differences, that children are property and one can spank them if one wishes, and that sexual prowess is a sign of masculinity are macrosystemic cultural beliefs that contribute to abuse.

At the *exosystemic level*, community factors, such as the absence of supervised play areas and recreational activities for children and the social isolation of poor neighborhoods, contribute to increased risk for abuse. Factors at the community level can interact with factors at the family level. For example, a neighborhood with high unemployment and drug addiction may in turn add to the distress of an unemployed father, who then becomes more physically punishing with his son.

Children experience violence at the *microsystemic level* in daily interactions with siblings, parents, peers, and teachers. Both parents and children bring their individual characteristics to these interactions. Parents who mistreat children have their own difficult pasts, as we will see. They interact with children in many negative ways besides the actual abuse. Children's individual characteristics such as health also can influence the likelihood of abuse, as we shall see.

Finally, children experience violence at the *ontogenic level*—that is, in how they develop as individuals—in their attachment relationship with the parent, their regulation of emotion, self-concept, peer relationships, and adaptation to school and learning.

The model also has implications for interventions that can help families and provide protective factors for them. First, there are interventions at the microsystemic level, with the individual and the family—helping them deal with the situation, the feelings that arise from it, and the problems that ensue.

Then there are interventions at the exosystemic level—helping parents and children reach out to social agencies and social structures such as schools and community organizations to get support to enable the family to cope. Community agencies also identify high-risk parents and provide, often in the home, training and modeling in appropriate caregiving and help parents adopt effective problem-solving skills.

Finally, there are interventions at the *macrosystemic level*—changing the societal views of violence and sexuality that permit victimization of children. Although this is a complicated process, giving all parents training in effective caregiving and child-rearing strategies also makes abuse less likely.[25]

Incidence and Definitions of Maltreatment

Table 17-3 presents the number of maltreatment reports made to government agencies and the number of substantiated victims of abuse in 2008, along with the forms of maltreatment and the ages and sexes of children who were maltreated. In 2007, 1,500 children died as a result of maltreatment.[26] It is estimated 90 percent of abusers are parents.[27] This is not surprising since 80 percent of the cases involve physical abuse and neglect, and parents are the primary providers of daily care.

From 1990 to 2004, social scientists have documented significant decreases in physical and sexual abuse cases.[28] However, the overall number of cases increased 26 percent during that time, and neglect became the most frequent form of maltreatment, increasing from 49 to 62 percent of cases.[29] It is not clear what has caused the declines in physical and sexual abuse and what has led to the increase

■ **TABLE 17-3**
VICTIMS OF CHILD MALTREATMENT IN 2008*

Total Number of Reports: Investigated	2,024,094
Victims of Substantiated Abuse:	773,792
Neglect	71%
Physical abuse	16%
Sexual abuse	9%
Emotional abuse	7%
Medical neglect	2%
Sex of Victims:	
Boys	48%
Girls	52%
Age of Victims:	
1 and Under	19%
2 to 5	25%
6 to 9	22%
10 to 13	18%
14 to 18	16%

*U.S. Census Bureau *Statistical Abstract of the United States: 2011,* 130th ed. (Washington, DC: U.S. Government Printing Office, 2010).

in neglect and overall number of cases. Perhaps there have been cultural changes in beliefs that led to decreases in these two areas.

Definitions of maltreatment are difficult because we do not have an agreed-upon code of what is acceptable parental care and discipline, so it is hard to define when a parent's behavior is unacceptable. In addition, we have cultural and ethnic differences within our country as to what is acceptable discipline. Immigrants from other countries have cultural traditions that include more severe hitting and hitting with objects, and parents who cannot give up these traditions are more likely to be reported as abusive.

There are ethnic differences in the number of maltreatment reports made to Child Welfare Services.[30] Since maltreatment is more likely to occur in poor families of low socioeconomic status, and more Native American, African American, and Latinos/as are living below the poverty level, these groups may well have higher reports of child maltreatment because of poverty. There are suggestions that when European Americans and African Americans are carefully matched for poverty and neighborhood social organization, European American families have more child maltreatment.[31] Racial bias may play a role, however, as one study found that substance-abusing, pregnant African American women were ten times more likely to be reported to authorities than European American women despite the fact that the rates of pregnancy drug tests were the same for the two groups.[32] Once infants were in foster care, agency caseworkers had less contact and made fewer case plans for African American families.

Dante Cicchetti and Sheree Toth define four major areas of abuse as follows:[33]

Physical abuse: the infliction of bodily injury on a child by other than accidental means.

Sexual abuse: sexual contact or attempted sexual contact between a caregiver or other responsible adult and a child for purposes of the caregiver's gratification.

Neglect: The failure to provide minimum care and the lack of appropriate supervision.

Emotional maltreatment: Persistent and extreme thwarting of a child's basic emotional needs.

Other forms of abuse to the child are *moral–legal–educational* maltreatment that involves failure to help the child develop appropriate moral and social values (e.g., involving the child in selling drugs)[34] and exposure to domestic or family violence. Exposure to family violence is included as a form of abuse because, although the violence is directed to another person, it traumatizes children and negatively affects their behavior.[35]

Some consider *community violence* a form of maltreatment because children are threatened, robbed, assaulted, stabbed, or shot, or witness these acts directed against others, and they suffer from it in the same ways that they do when they experience neglect or physical abuse.[36]

Prevalence

Incidence figures reported in Table 17-3 are reports of the new cases investigated in a year. Prevalence figures report the total number of people who have had such experiences. There are no statistics on the prevalence of family violence, but it is estimated that between three and ten million children are exposed to it, beginning *in utero*.[37] Sixteen percent of women questioned in prenatal clinics reported spousal abuse, and half of them reported several incidents.

Determining the incidence and prevalence of sexual abuse in childhood is extremely difficult, as the acts are taboo, secret, and most are not reported. Estimates are that one in four girls and one in six boys has experienced some form of sexual abuse by age eighteen.[38]

When David Finkelhor and his colleagues carried out a survey of victimizations that occurred over a year's time, 70 percent of the 1,400 children had experienced one or more victimizations with the mean number of different kinds being 2.8 victimizations in the course of a year. Eighteen percent of the children had four or more victimizations and were termed polyvictims.[39] Polyvictims did not differ in gender, ethnicity, place of residence, or socioeconomic status. They did tend to be older and to live in single-parent families or in stepfamilies. Polyvictimized children had more serious forms of victimization like sexual abuse or physical abuse, were most likely to have psychological symptoms of trauma like anxiety and depression, and had more general adversities like illnesses, accidents, and family stresses.

This research also points to the importance of inquiring about a whole range of victimizations that may have occurred for individuals when a report of abuse is made rather than focus just on the one area of initial complaint. Clinicians make the same suggestion. They believe understanding the broad range of victimizations many children experience will permit a better matching of treatment program to the child's needs.

Factors That Place Families at High Risk for Maltreatment

In looking at family risks for maltreatment, it is important to recall that some abuse is experienced outside the home with strangers, and the child's family may have taken all possible protective actions to prevent maltreatment, yet it occurred—perhaps at a reliable babysitter's or on the school grounds.

When research was first carried out on families and children who were abused, the search was for single factors that led to each kind of abuse, and the specific problem that resulted from the abuse. While we distinguish the major forms of abuse listed above, they are not so much separate problems as several different ways children experience violence and trauma in a family setting.[40] Some of the many predisposing characteristics are listed in Table 17-4.

The predisposing factors also indicate forms of intervention and prevention with home visiting programs to help parents with babies, parenting programs to help parents develop greater parenting skills, programs that help parents relieve the emotional distress they are under, and intervention programs that seek to improve the social context that parents and children inhabit.

Children's Neurobiological Responses to Maltreatment

Parents can understand children's reactions better when they are aware of the many neurobiological changes associated with abuse in childhood.[41] Maltreatment creates fear that activates the brain to produce hormones that, in turn, trigger the adrenal glands to produce cortisol as well as other hormones. High levels of cortisol help the body respond to stress. Cortisol triggers the brain to shut down the stress response system and return to normal levels of arousal when stress has passed.

Cortisol not only helps the body respond to stress, it also regulates the daily pattern of arousal, alertness, and attention.[42] In human beings, cortisol is elevated in the morning and gradually declines during the day and early evening as individuals get ready to sleep. Ongoing stress disrupts the usual patterns of cortisol release and children show atypical patterns, with some children showing low levels in the morning and throughout the day, and some high. When continuously low, children may be less responsive and alert and attentive.

When fear is ongoing as it sometimes is in maltreatment, and the body maintains high levels of cortisol, there can be changes in the immune system and changes in the memory area of the brain.[43] Some children who have symptoms of ongoing

■ **T A B L E 17-4**
FACTORS THAT PUT FAMILIES AT RISK FOR MALTREATMENT

Child Characteristics*

Age, youngest and teens are at greatest risk

Low birth weight, prematurity

Medical problems

Difficult temperament, overactive

Parent Characteristics*

Parental history of childhood abuse, Substance abuser

Increase daily stress, job loss, illness and limited coping skills

Unrealistic expectations of child

Harsh discipline

Social Context**

Living in poverty

Social isolation of families, little support network

Greater number of marital problems

*Sandra T. Azar, "Parenting and Maaltreatment," in *Handbook of Parenting*, 2nd ed., ed. Marc
H. Bornstein, vol. 4: *Social Conditions and Applied Parenting* (Mahwah, NJ: Erlbaum, 2002), 361–388.
**Fred Wulczyn, "Epidemiological Perspectives on Maltreatment Prevention," *Future of Children* 19
(2009): 39–66.

hyperarousal show declines in intellectual functioning, attention, and memory. Not all children show these changes, and they are often reversible when stress subsides. Still, they are of concern, and a major reason for prompt attention to these symptoms. As we will see, infants experience symptoms of hyperarousal, and interventions can calm their stress response systems.

Children's Psychological Responses to Maltreatment

Children often respond to maltreatment with symptoms of posttraumatic stress disorder (PTSD).[44] The symptoms have been described in terms of adults' reactions to stress and adults' ability to verbalize their reactions, and have to be translated to fit children's level of development and their reactions. PTSD refers to a cluster of reactions that follow exposure to an unusual, threatening stress that arouses fear, helplessness, and horror in the person. The person suffers from:

- repetitive recollections of the event or dreams about it or relives it—in children, the repetitive themes can occur in play.

- symptoms of feeling numb, uninterested in usual activities, avoiding activities or thoughts that serve as reminders of the stress, feeling dissociated and detached from the events yet at the same time, feeling a sense of a shortened future.

- heightened emotional arousal, with difficulties sleeping, concentrating, being startled easily, and feeling irritable and on alert for another disaster.

A diagnosis is not made until the person has had such symptoms for more than a month.

Traumatic events often trigger children's self-blame, and it may play a role in the continuing existence of difficulties.[45] The more adolescents blame themselves, the more serious the behavior changes. Even though adolescents, and probably children as well, give the perpetrator primary responsibility for the abuse, the majority of victims of all kinds of abuse consider that they too deserve blame because they did not prevent or avoid the abuse. Blaming oneself and feeling ashamed intensify feelings of depression and withdrawal that can continue on into adulthood.

Changes in behavior are associated with the severity of the abuse and the age at which it occurred as well as the identity of the perpetrator. Some research suggests that the earlier the abuse occurred and the longer it lasted, the more behavioral effects are seen.[46] Those who experienced abuse in infancy and the toddler years still showed differences in behavior from nonmaltreated children in the school years, and those abused in preschool were especially prone to developing aggressive and bullying behavior in the school years. The speculation is that ongoing stress is more disorganizing to the individual in periods in which the person is developing an understanding of the world and refining basic ways of relating to people.

Parental maltreatment very often results in a disorganized/disoriented form of attachment in which the child happily approaches the parent on some occasions, and then at other times avoids the parent. Such attachments occur in as many as 80 percent of maltreated children and do not provide a secure base for exploration or a positive inner working model of relationships.[47]

When maltreatment occurs early in life and continues, children have great difficulty in understanding others' reactions and ways of thinking, and they find it hard to understand others' points of view.[48] As preschoolers, they have a more negative view of themselves and their relationships with their mothers, and they begin to become aggressive.[49]

Physical abuse has been associated with peer problems regardless of the sex, socio-economic status, or stress level of the abused person.[50] The abusive experience in the family appears to lead to distortions in how people relate to each other and what is required to get along. As noted earlier, this is especially sad because children then lose a major source of support in coping with their problems. Abuse and violence damage children's trust in their parents and their peers and decrease their capacity for positive relationships, thus removing an important resource for such children.

Maltreated children also may have difficulties with emotional control, in part because their feelings are intense and in part because they do not have appropriate ways of expressing them verbally.[51] They may express their feelings in aggressive, demanding behaviors or in silent retreats from others. In either way, they are more likely to have peer problems because they do not have good control of their feelings. Because of their intense feelings, it will also be harder for them to focus and concentrate on schoolwork so they may develop academic problems.

The impact of sexual abuse depends very much on the child and the specific circumstances of the abuse. Even in a fairly narrowly defined form of abuse, children's responses can differ widely depending on the frequency of the event and the perpetrator and the actions that followed disclosure.[52] For example, girls aged six to sixteen who experienced sexual abuse of genital contact or penetration within the family responded differently depending on the frequency of the abuse and whether the family member was the biological father or a nonbiological father-figure such as a stepfather or mother's boyfriend. Parents have to always pay attention to how their child experienced and reacted to the event. Not only does maltreatment have adverse effects on children's development in childhood, but it also predicts later depression, substance abuse, conduct problems, and poor health.[53]

Intervention and Prevention

The first step in intervention is to ensure the safety of the mistreated child. This can take several forms. In violent families at risk for imminent harm, it may mean getting the safe parent and children to a shelter. In physically and sexually abusive families, it may mean removing the abusive family member from the home, or it may mean out-of-home placement for the child in the event there is no other parent or relative to care for the child.

While studies reveal that foster care has potential benefit for the children it serves[54] (a more detailed discussion follows), a small, but carefully controlled study suggests that out-of-home placement with strangers may place an extra layer of stress for children already under emotional siege.[55]

Interventions with Young Children   A recently developed intervention for infants and toddlers and their foster care parents has helped to reduce the hyperarousal and behavioral difficulties that often follow when children are removed from their parents and placed with strangers.[56] A ten-hour manualized program carried out in the foster home with an experienced professional teaches foster care parents of infants and toddlers to (1) follow the child's lead, (2) touch and cuddle infants to soothe them, and (3) allow the child to express emotions so he or she can learn to regulate them. Hyperarousal, as measured by atypical patterns of cortisol production, decreased following this program and resembled those of children not in foster care. The cortisol pattern of a control group receiving a psychoeducational program remained significantly different from the group not in foster care.

Home visitation programs, parenting programs, and psychotherapy can be instituted to prevent abuse or help children and families cope with the many effects of maltreatment.[57] Home visitation programs can help young mothers with few resources to provide adequate care for children. One program following families at high risk from pregnancy to the child's fifteenth birthday found that regular nurse visits during pregnancy and the first two years of life resulted in less maltreatment in these homes, and when maltreatment occurred, fewer problem behaviors in children. The nurse was able to form a relationship with the mother, give information on early child development and care, and connect the mother to other resources.

Recall the intervention with mothers in Chapter 7 (see page 236) that empowered mothers to examine their own beliefs about children's behaviors and take action to solve problems. That intervention, added to a home visiting program, dramatically reduced the incidence of physical maltreatment in the group.[58]

The relationship the home visitor formed with the mothers seems critical. In two studies of treatment for abusing mothers—mothers of infants and mothers of preschool children—mothers received home visits and counseling that focused on either (1) the transmission of parenting information and skill-building or (2) helping mothers build positive mother-child attachments by means of infant- or preschool-mother psychotherapy. In the latter form of visit, the focus was on helping mothers see connections between their past and present relationships with others and their way of relating to their children in the present.

Both kinds of visits, lasting about an hour and a half and occurring each week for a year, had significant impacts. In the study of infants, infants in the infant-mother psychotherapy group went from 3.6 percent with secure attachments at twelve months to 61 percent secure attachments at the end of the year; in the psycho-educational group, there was a similar increase, from 0 percent secure attachments to 54 percent secure attachments.[59] The control maltreated group who received community services went from 0 percent secure attachments to 1.9 percent. The study indicated that attachment did not need to be the focus of the home visits in order for attachment classification to change. Further, the study showed interventions could reverse the effects of maltreatment and perhaps interrupt the persistent course of problems that could be expected without intervention.

When mothers of preschoolers received the intensive parent psychotherapy sessions for a year, their preschoolers decreased their negative views of themselves and their parents, and increased their positive views of themselves.[60]

Interventions with Older Children   Improving mothers' parenting skills decreased aggressive, noncompliant behaviors of children living with domestic violence. Children who made the transition from shelters to new living situations benefited when mothers participated in a supportive program that not only helped mothers develop problem-solving skills, but also taught them new strategies for rearing children—focusing on nurturing skills and positive parenting strategies, giving attention to approved behaviors, increasing communication skills, giving negative nonphysical consequences for disapproved behaviors, and problem solving at times of conflict.[61]

Therapists came to the home and worked with mothers during an eight-month period, after they left the shelters, for an average number of twenty-three one-and-a-half-hour visits. Students offered support and served as models for children during the visits. Mothers were not the source of the aggressive problems, but different child management styles, particularly the avoidance of physical punishment, significantly helped children.

Two years after the intervention, children's behaviors were compared to those children in a control group whose mothers received community services and one contact a month with the researchers. Children whose mothers had received training had far fewer problems with aggressive, noncompliant behavior (15 percent of children compared to the control's 53 percent). Mothers reported their children were happier and had better social relationships with others. Furthermore, mothers were less likely to have used physical discipline than mothers in the control group and less likely to have returned to the abusive partner.

Applying these same forms of intervention with parents who had physically abused their young children resulted in only 8 percent of repeated abuse in the intervention group in the eight months following the intervention whereas the repeat rate was 28 percent of the group receiving the usual Children's Protective Services interventions.[62]

An effective program for physically abused children and their parents, Multisystemic Therapy for Child Abuse and Neglect (MST-CAN), was provided in the home with more intensive services for families.[63] A treatment team consisted of a trained therapist, a psychiatrist, and twenty-four-hour-a-day, seven days a week emergency consultations to deal with family crises. The program was individualized to the needs of the particular family and with attention to reducing everyone's emotional distress. Families were helped to build a support network. The program was more effective than an enhanced outpatient clinic treatment program in reducing children's psychological problems, parents' psychological distress, parenting behaviors associated with maltreatment, and youths' out-of-home placement. Although MST-CAN families had lower rates of repeated abuse in an eight-month follow-up after the end of treatment, the rates in both groups were low, and the differences not significant though the other differences between the groups were.

A form of cognitive-behavioral therapy first used to help traumatized sexually abused children, Trauma-Focused Cognitive-Behavioral Therapy (TF-CBT), has been adapted and proved successful with many other forms of maltreatment—physical abuse, school violence, and community violence.[64] The program includes both children and parents and draws on strategies from many sources: (1) psychoeducation gives children and parents knowledge about trauma or abuse, common reactions to it, and effective ways of coping and preventing it in the future: (2) cognitive-behavioral therapy strategies to manage intrusive thoughts and feelngs and to desensitize the child and family to upsetting thoughts and places: (3) family therapy to help children and parents deal with the maltreatment: (4) relaxation and stress management training to deal with symptoms of hyperarousal: (5) problem-solving skills to achieve future goals. The program has been used with individual children and their families and with groups and varies from twelve to twenty sessions. Many well-controlled studies have documented its effectiveness in reducing symptoms of trauma and abuse and increasing children's and parents' well-being.

So all forms of intervention involve increasing parents' skills with children. If parents have been the source of abuse, then they learn new patterns of relationships. Even when parents are not the source of the maltreatment, increasing their skills in helping children regulate feelings, cope with stresses, and develop problem-solving strategies helps children overcome problems. Supporting activities that give children feelings of self-worth and control also reduce problems.

Interrupting the Cycle of Abuse

Positive relationships appear to be critical to breaking the cycle of maltreatment and ongoing socioemotional problems. In a longitudinal study in Minnesota, children were followed into adulthood, and it was possible to compare adults abused as children who did not continue this pattern to determine what helped them avoid it.[65] Researchers looked at the 30 percent of the sample who provided good care to their infants and compared them with the 40 percent who abused their children (30 percent of abused children provided borderline care). Three kinds of positive relationships helped young adults escape the cycle of abuse. Mothers who in childhood had emotionally supportive relationships with an adult outside the family or received emotional support in psychotherapy did not abuse their infants. The third form of positive relationship was with a partner in adulthood. None of these factors were found in the lives of mothers who continued the abuse. Nonabusing mothers also tended to have come to terms with their childhood experiences of abuse and been able to form an integrated sense of self.

Community Intervention

Because home visiting and parenting programs have been less effective in decreasing abuse than anticipated, programs are now being offered at the community-wide level as a way to have greater impact.[66]

Recall in Chapter 6 (pages 201–202) the use of the Triple P-Positive Program to reduce abuse in Ransom County, South Carolina. The program presents a community-wide educational program that includes media messages about positive parenting principles, ways to handle everyday problems, access to parenting information at community agencies like day care, and access to parenting programs in groups, at home, or online.

As noted, the program has been effective in slowing the rate of growth in child abuse reports and reducing the number of children removed from the home and the number of hospital admissions for abuse.

Strengths of Effective Programs

The strengths of those programs that have been most effective in helping children and families dealing with abuse: (1) have provided services in the home at times convenient to families so completion rates are high; (2) are tailored to the needs of the individual children and families though they are evidence-based and rely on sound theories; (3) not only provide parenting skills but ways to reduce parents' emotional distress; (4) provide ready access to service with consultants available when crisis comes; and (5) help parents and children build strong bridges to other people and community agencies.

FOSTER FAMILIES

Foster parents care for children whose parents cannot care for them, for a variety of reasons. Parents may have died and left no relatives or friends to care for the child. Parents may have been incarcerated or hospitalized for psychiatric or medical reasons, and no relatives or friends could step in to provide care. But most often, children live in foster families because parents' care has been found to be neglectful or abusive.

Approximately 300,000[67] children are taken into foster care each year, and approximately 500,000[68] children live in foster care, some with biological relatives but a half or more with nonrelatives. At present, the average length of stay in foster care is twenty-two months. About 20–25 percent of children will not return to their biological parents to live. Children of ethnic groups with high rates of poverty such as Native American, African American, and Latina/o families are overrepresented among children going into foster care.

The major law governing foster care is the Adoption and Safe Family Act (ASFA), passed by Congress in 1997.[69] Its main thrust is to provide services for families at high risk of abuse so children can remain with biological parents. These services include, for example, parenting programs, anger management programs, and therapy. If, however, children are removed from the home, the second main thrust of the program is to motivate parents to make changes in their behavior within about eighteen months. Agencies and parents set up plans for change, with periodic checks to note progress. If changes are not made, and if the child cannot be returned to the biological parents within about eighteen months, then parental rights are terminated. This is to maximize the possibility that the child can be adopted and have a permanent home. Before the time frame was established, some children were in foster care for years, waiting for parents to change, and by the time parents' rights were terminated, children were considered hard to adopt because they were older.

Foster parents need special training to understand what children have been through.

Foster Parents

There is no national registry of foster parents, and our knowledge about them is based on small surveys. They are generally married (60 percent), with an average education of high school level; about half are of middle-class background, 15 percent are of upper-middle-class background, and 35 percent are of working-class background. Still, 40 percent are single parents, and many have limited financial resources.[70]

Adults who become foster parents give several reasons: (1) to have children, (2) to be altruistic, and (3) to help deprived children. People who foster for these reasons receive higher ratings as parents than adults who become parents to nurture children. The latter group of parents may feel disappointed when children do not respond to their nurturance.[71]

Foster parents undertake a daunting challenge.[72] They have all the stresses and strains that any parent experiences, plus several others. The children who come into their homes arrive with a history of difficult life experiences—the death of a parent, physical or sexual abuse, neglect—and they are often dealing with strong emotional reactions to those experiences. In addition, they have the stress of being separated from their parents, brothers and sisters, and often friends as well. Finally, there is the stress of living with a new family, adjusting to new rules and expectations. Children may express their anger, disappointment, or sadness in their interactions with their foster parents, and resist efforts to follow the family routines. Foster parents, like stepparents, have had no previous attachment relationship with children, and it is such ties that often motivate children to cooperate. Building such relationships at times of crisis is difficult. A further difficulty for foster parents is that they have to relinquish the ties when children leave their care.

Because of the numerous sources of difficulties, foster parents need to be trained to understand what children have been through, to be patient, sensitive, and warm yet firm and supportive in helping children meet age-appropriate demands at home and at school. One study found that, when foster parents learned ways to stimulate verbal and cognitive development of preschoolers, the children had fewer emotional and behavioral problems, perhaps because they felt more competent.

The Web of Foster Care Relationships

In carrying out their caregiving responsibilities, foster parents are enmeshed in a web of what can be competing responsibilities.[73] First, they are to provide good care to the children, and they often feel strongly protective of them. Second, they are to work with the agency workers, helping to implement reunification programs with biological parents. Third, they work with biological parents, helping them and their children to establish effective patterns of interaction, sometimes arranging or supervising visits, sometimes helping parents' understand children's feelings. Looming over the system are the judge and court, who make final decisions about what will happen with children.

When there is clear communication and everyone is working together for the child's best interests, such a system can work well. But competing interests can easily surface. Foster parents may feel critical of parents and the protective agencies if they feel not enough is being done to safeguard the child. Birth parents may feel angry that children were taken, because parents had little help and support to do well, and frustrated that they are competing for their children with foster parents who have more resources. Agency workers may feel frustrated with many cases and many demands on them.

Foster Children

There is less research than we would like on contemporary foster children. In the earlier days of foster care, older children typically came to these homes from stable families because of the death or absence of a parent. As child maltreatment cases have increased, children come to foster care with many emotional and behavioral problems. As drug abuse has increased among young women, infants have been sent to foster care from the hospital, and they make up a growing percentage of children in foster care.[74] Little is known about their attachment experiences and how foster care will affect their development over time, because there can be many moves within the foster-care system.

A small, well-controlled study provides information on children's experiences in foster care.[75] Following a sample of high-risk families (at risk because of the young age of mothers, parents' low levels of education, poverty income, unstable environments) as children progressed through childhood to adulthood, University of Minnesota researchers were able to select three groups of children: (1) children who were maltreated and remained with the maltreating parent, (2) children who were removed from the home but lived with relatives or family friends, and (3) children who went into foster care with strangers. In 70 percent of the cases, removal from the home was for parental maltreatment or neglect, and in 30 percent, it was because of the death of a parent, homelessness, or a parent's being incarcerated. The remainder of the high-risk sample served as a control group of children who were not maltreated or placed in foster care.

There was detailed information on these children prior to the abuse and the removal from the family as well as after they left foster care. Prior to placement, maltreated children at home and those going into out-of-home placement showed more behavior problems than the control group, and those who stayed at home and those who were in out-of-home care did not differ from each other. Age at entry and length of time out of the home did not predict later functioning.

As soon as placement occurred, behavior problems of foster children sharply increased. Those who remained at home had no such spike. At the time of release from foster care, those leaving foster care had slightly higher levels of emotional and behavioral problems than those who had remained at home. Both groups of maltreated children continued to have more problems than those in the control group who did not experience maltreatment. Assessments of all groups of children in adolescence up to age seventeen and a half revealed that those who stayed at home with the maltreating parent had slightly fewer problems than those who went into foster care. Going into foster care may well place an extra layer of stress on children and increase the behavior problems children have even after they leave foster care. Those who went into homes with familiar adults were less anxious, depressed, and withdrawn than those who went into foster care with strangers. Although this study is small, there were many controls for the social status of the groups and for the children's behavior ratings, as they were done by teachers, not by social workers or parents, who might have been less objective.

Support for the stressfulness of foster care with strangers comes from the fact that those children who go into foster homes of working-class and lower socioeconomic-status families, which are more like the families children lived in before foster care, have greater success, perhaps because the child feels more familiar with the routines and values expressed there.[76]

Sadly, children in foster care are at increased risk for abuse.[77] More reports of abuse are made about children in foster families than those in families in the general community, but the rate of substantiation is much lower for children in foster families. Existing studies indicate that, although the abuse rate may be higher in foster families than in community families, the rate is lower in foster families than is the rate of repeated abuse when children remain with biological parents. Furthermore, foster parents may not always be the abusers; it may be the biological parent on a visit or someone else living in the foster home. Abuse is more likely to be reported in foster families with a younger mother, lower income, poorer health of the foster parents, and a crowded situation where foster children slept together.

The largest study of children leaving foster care provided some good news and some bad news about their experiences.[78] The good news is that, at age seventeen, 90 percent of the group of 732 young people leaving foster care in Illinois, Wisconsin, and Iowa, felt optimistic about the future. More than half felt "lucky" to have been placed in foster care, and an even larger percentage felt "mostly satisfied" with their foster-care experience.

The bad news is that this sample of youth experienced more difficulties in their growing-up years than a national sample of young people their age, and they faced the future with fewer skills. In comparison to the national group, the foster-care group was more likely to have been held back a year in school, twice as likely to have been suspended, and four times as likely to have been expelled. Though most at age seventeen were in the last grades of high school, they were reading, on average, at the seventh-grade level.

The foster-care sample was much more likely to have received counseling and medication for psychological problems, and a large number had had conflict with the law—one-fifth reported conviction for a crime, and more than half had been arrested.

When followed up at age nineteen, the group still "wrestled" with worse problems than the national sample of nineteen-year-olds.[79] More than a third had no high school diploma—the comparable figure for the national sample was 10 percent—and they were more likely to be unemployed, pregnant, unable to pay rent, and sometimes hungry and homeless. Those who remained in foster care beyond their eighteenth birthdays were more likely to be in school or a training program to prepare for the future.

It is important to point out that the appropriate comparison group may not be a broad national sample of same-aged youths but a sample of poorer youths who have known many difficulties as well, or a group of children who were maltreated and did not go to foster care, as in the Minnesota study. The children exiting foster care have suffered many negative experiences, including poverty and traumatic events of abuse. Studies of mistreated children suggest that they had many emotional problems when they entered foster care, and even with counseling, it has not remedied them.

Richard Wexler, executive director of the National Coalition for Child Protection Reform, says, "What these results should tell us is that we've got to stop throwing so many children into foster care in the first place. What you can see is, regardless of what the problems were going in, foster care surely didn't fix them."[80] Despite all the problems, it is important to recall that half the children felt that they were lucky to have been in foster care. Box 17-3 describes innovations in foster care that may make it more effective.

Kinship Foster Care and Nonrelative Foster Care

As suggested in the Minnesota study, kinship foster care has some advantages. It appears to provide more stability.[81] Children are less likely to be moved from it, and biological parents appear to keep in closer contact with children, with 56 percent visiting at least once a month and 19 percent visiting four or more times a month; the comparable figures in nonrelative foster care are 32 percent once a month and 3 percent four or more times a month. In addition, abuse is less likely to be reported in kinship foster families than in nonrelative foster families. Some foster-care professionals have expressed concern that, in kinship foster homes, children may receive fewer services and may be exposed to the influences that created difficulties for the parent, but kinship foster homes do appear to provide greater stability, and children seem to have fewer problems there.

Termination of Parental Rights

In our country, the tie between biological parent and child is considered so important that it is severed only because the parent cannot meet his or her responsibilities to provide adequate care for the child for an extended period of time. Even if a child has been placed for adoption and has lived happily for two or three years with adoptive parents as the only parents he or she has known, the courts will return the child to a competent biological father who did not know of the child's existence before adoption and who seeks the child out as soon as he learns he has one.[82] Parents' rights can be relinquished voluntarily, as when young parents give up a baby for adoption. Parents' rights are terminated when they have demonstrated to a court that they are unable to care for the child or children for an extended period of time. These decisions are not easy, for there can be mitigating circumstances that make it hard to meet the time limit—loss of a job or place to live, time in jail. Still, the court is concerned about the child's right to permanent placement with parents who can care for him or her. The child's interest will be considered only if the parent has proved unable or unwilling to make changes to become a competent parent.

Box 17-3
INNOVATIVE FOSTER CARE PROGRAMS

Two innovative programs seek to build a more effective, supportive foster-care system for everyone involved.

In 1998, New York City established the family-to-family program* to create an open family system in which biological and foster parents meet with each other, plan the care of the children, and have ongoing contact as parents work toward having children live at home again. Meetings are initially held in agency offices where biological parents can meet the foster parents, give information about their child's routines and habits, and can express their preferences for things like church attendance, dress rules, and hairstyles.

When visiting starts, parents sometimes come to the foster homes a number of times before they start unsupervised visits. Parents frequently maintain relationships with each other and children go back to visit after they return to their biological parents. Foster parents become part of the extended family system. In many ways, foster parents and biological parents form the kind of relationship we referred to in Chapter 4 as coparenting, even though foster parents are more like mentors to parents in the beginning.

The program in New York is a voluntary one unless court prohibition forbids it, and about 60 percent of parents have had some contact with foster parents. The program requires special training for agency workers and for foster parents who frequently feel critical of parents because of their child maltreatment. The program has resulted in children's returning to their biological families about three months sooner than under the older system. The rate at which parental rights are terminated remains the same, but the parent has better understanding that he or she cannot provide an effective level of care.

In the midwest, Brenda Eheart, an Illinois sociologist concerned that many foster children were not able to return to their biological parents, started a program she called "Generations of Hope," to re-create for foster children the kind of close and caring social ties she had had growing up in a small town.** She was able to negotiate the purchase of part of a decommissioned Air Force Base and organized a community to live there. She advertised for adults who would become foster parents with the goal of adopting the children. She also advertised for older adults who would live there, volunteer services to care for children, tutoring them and teaching them skills in exchange for reduced rent of comfortable homes. And she contacted the Illinois Department of Children and Family Services for hard-to-place children.

Her program provides therapy, tutoring, and respite services for children and families. Eheart compares her program with state programs of residential centers. In those programs, which are expensive, children have to leave at age eighteen. She summarizes her program, "We give children a childhood, a sense of permanence." Older adults as well as children have gained from the program because they have important, useful jobs, and they too have community connections.

*Leslie Kaufman, "Birth Parents Retaining a Voice in New York Foster Care Model," *New York Times,* June 3, 2004, A1.
**Lou Ann Walker, "A Place Called Hope," *Parade Magazine,* July 7, 2002, 10–12.

DISASTERS

In this section, we discuss local and national disasters and children's and parents' responses to them.

Natural Disasters

In our country we have seen the devastating effects of powerful hurricanes on the southern coast of the United States, and there is reason to think that we are in a phase of weather cycles or changes that will produce a continuation of such disasters.[83] Hurricane Katrina damaged large sections of several southern states, killed thousands of people, and upended the lives of hundreds of thousands of individuals and their families. Survivors are scattered around the country, and while many will get their lives back together, it will take individuals, communities, and state agencies years to rebuild the structure of life as residents there once knew it.

Natural disasters vary in their predictability, and unpredictability increases stress. Hurricanes can be anticipated and sometimes escaped, but earthquakes and tornados are sudden and unpredictable. Even when predicted, the unprecedented damage of Hurricane Katrina was not planned for, and the country saw the anguished faces of families seeking safety or seeking loved ones whose whereabouts were unknown.

The effects of a natural disaster depend on its duration, which is usually short-lived in comparison to abuse or community violence that may be ongoing, and on the amount of damage it wreaks. In general, in the first year after the disaster,

Natural disaster like Hurricane Katrina have upended the lives of thousands of victims.

moderate to severe symptoms of PTSD are found in 30–50 percent of children who experience the effects of the disaster. Children who had problems prior to the disaster are more likely to have more serious problems after the disaster or to have their own difficulties intensified by the disaster.

When compared to teens not affected by Hurricane Katrina, teens living in relocation camps two months after the hurricane showed depressed levels of salivary cortisol and increased salivary alpha amylase that is often associated with chronic stress.[84] Girls reported significantly more depression than boys in the camp and higher levels than either control boys or girls. Boys in relocation camps showed significantly less aggressiveness than the other three groups, perhaps reflecting their feelings of loss of status and control as a result of damage experienced in the hurricane.

These boys may be similar to a sample of teens living in relocation camps after Hurricane Katrina who reported lower levels of self-esteem and higher levels of depression and distress when their families relied on community agencies for help.[85] Teens may be especially sensitive to feelings of social stigmatization and vulnerable to feelings of helplessness when family members do not have resources for managing independently.

While many children show a decrease in negative feelings with the passage of time, 28 percent of children were still experiencing enough symptoms of distress to qualify for psychological treatment three years after Hurricane Katrina.[86] Those children who had the most difficult time recovering were those who had experienced a major loss before or after the hurricane, had limited family connections, and reported ongoing financial, family, and school difficulties.

A study of Sri Lankan youth exposed to civil war, the tsunami, and daily personal stresses such as poverty, marital conflict, and abuse found that while disasters like war and the tsunami had a direct effect on feelings of depression, it was primarily the daily hassles that were the major sources of stress.[87] The researchers pointed to the importance of community-wide, psychosocial approaches strengthening the systems that support children's daily routines and activities as they contribute more significantly to children's recovery than trauma-focused services that do not necessarily strengthen the major sources of children's strength.

Massage therapy was found to be helpful in reducing elementary school children's feelings of anxiety and depression following Hurricane Andrew in Florida.[88] Children who reported many symptoms of PTSD were assigned to receive back massages twice weekly for thirty minutes or to a control group who watched a video while sitting on the lap of a research assistant for the same amount of time. Children who received massages had lower levels of anxiety and depression, and reduced levels of cortisol, indicating less stress after the massages. Parents were taught to give their children back massages.

TF-CBT therapy, as noted, has proven useful with traumatized children. Other useful interventions for reactions following disasters include school programs that help children process events, normalize their reactions of immediate distress, and give creative outlets for expression of feelings are useful. If schools are not in session, then such programs can be carried out at community centers.

Managing Fears of National Violence

On September 11, 2001, Americans across the country and people around the world witnessed via television the tragic and violent deaths of three thousand people killed in the terrorist attacks in New York, Washington, D.C., and Pennsylvania. All joined with their families and communities in mourning their deaths. Americans have since lived with the fears of possible terrorist killings through bombs, bio-chemical agents released in the air or in the mail, and shootings. These fears have been heightened as the nation has engaged in war overseas. At the national level, we are now experiencing the ongoing fears people in inner cities have experienced for years, and the research on handling fear and stress in that situation can be applied to our present national tragedy.

Research after the Oklahoma City bombing revealed that symptoms following a terrorist attack can be long-lived. School-age children who lived a hundred miles away from Oklahoma City and suffered no physical or direct contact with the bombing were studied two years after the bombing. Almost a third of the children indicated knowing a friend who knew someone who had been injured or killed. Twenty percent of the children described bomb-related symptoms that decreased their level of functioning at home or in school.[89]

In studies of children's worries following the September 11 bombings, research-ers found that children had fewer worries after the September bombings than they had in June 2000.[90] Parents made a great effort to talk to children about their fears and concerns, and children felt reassured. Children who were chosen as panel mem-bers to discuss these studies stated they wanted parents to talk to them about their everyday concerns such as bullying and television violence like they talked to them after September 11. They recommend that parents push at times to get information even if children say they are not worried because children will not talk spontane-ously about their worries for fear of burdening their parents. One researcher com-mented, "When things are 'normal,' children seem to feel most alone and helpless in their fear, and unlike Code Orange times, parents can be clueless about kids' anxiety, and kids know that."

Like studies of children's reactions following natural disasters, studies of chil-dren's responses to the 9/11 attacks over time reveal that it is the ongoing stresses in people's lives that intensify problems after attacks. Preschool children whose mothers suffered from depression and PTSD three years after the attacks were more likely to have problems controlling their emotional reactions and their aggressive feelings than children whose mothers suffered from depression only or had no symptoms.[91] Both mothers and teachers agreed in identifying children's problems.

When New York City (NYC) teens and their mothers were assessed fifteen months after the 9/11 bombings, both teens and their mothers had elevated rates of PTSD (4 percent in teens and 20 percent in mothers) and depression (12 percent in teens and 20 percent in mothers), but it was exposure to community violence as a victim or witness that predicted teens' distressed feelings, not exposure to the bombings.[92] There was no information on other stressors in mothers' lives to carry out a comparable analysis.

Parents want to know what to do to help their children in these scary times. Parents, as we have learned, are the most important figures in helping children cope with trauma and stress of all kinds, and their most important role is to talk to children. Here, as well as at the chapter's end, are suggestions parents can use.[93]

1. Examine and manage their own fears, because children model their responses on their parents' behavior.

2. Turn off the television and radio when their children are awake to reduce the stress of repeated exposure to visual images and discussion of the tragedies.

3. Listen and observe children to determine their level of stress, as reflected in eating, sleeping, and level of energy. Parents should respond to children's questions and concerns in a supportive way.

4. Give honest statements of reassurance—saying they and the government are working to keep children safe, not promising that nothing bad will happen.

5. Respond in age-appropriate ways when talking to children. Preschoolers do not need the level of information and discussion useful for older children.

6. Maintain daily activities and routines, as familiar patterns of behavior provide reassurance and feelings of security.

7. Have a friend's phone number outside the community whom all family members can call to report safety and whereabouts in the event of a community disaster.

8. Appreciate and comment on the good things in life today—for example, the family's being together, the closeness with friends. Feelings of enjoyment provide a reserve of strength to deal with stress when it comes.

9. Read stories about the country's history that inspire and give confidence that we can survive and flourish in times of struggle and adversity (e.g., getting to the Pacific Coast from St. Louis, getting to the moon, surviving the battles of the Revolution and of the War of 1812, when the White House burned).

10. Volunteer with children in some activity to make a part of the world a better place. We cannot directly influence those who might wish to hurt us now, but we can increase the pleasure and joy some people get out of life.

In all these difficult situations, the family remains the main source of support for children. Agencies and therapies can help, but it is individuals who are close and have a sense of the child's individuality who are truly helpful. If parents cannot do this, other relatives or family friends, teachers, or day care workers can step in.

HOMELESS FAMILIES

Homelessness increased in the 1980s and 1990s when the number of low-cost housing decreased and poverty remained high. While homelessness occurs in rural areas, we know primarily about it from studies of urban homelessness. It is difficult to have an accurate estimate of how many people are homeless but in 2006–2007, it is estimated that about 500,000 people in families were served in shelters and transitional housing.[94] Over 80 percent of families are headed by single mothers with two or three children. The median stay in a homeless facility is thirty days.

Social scientists divide the causes of homelessness into three categories: structural, individual, and social. Structural causes (reduced number of low-rent housing and high levels of poverty) are the most important predictors with poverty being the major factor. Individual factors include domestic violence, unemployment, mothers' psychological problems, and lower educational levels. Social factors are having a reduced social support network.

In 2007, the United States Conference of Mayor's Survey listed the major causes of homelessness as poverty (57 percent), domestic violence (39 percent), unemployment (26 percent), and family disputes (17 percent). In many ways homeless families and low-income housed families have similar problems.

Homeless Mothers

It is important to emphasize the diversity of homeless mothers and their children.[95] While one can draw a portrait of the average homeless mother as unmarried, with less than high school education, with a limited social network, and an increased number of psychological problems and traumatic childhood abuse, 15 percent of homeless mothers are married and 27 percent have post–high-school education. While homeless mothers have higher rates of psychological problems such as depression, their rates of depression are similar to those of low-income housed mothers, and are thought to be the result of long-standing poverty. Their rates of alcohol and drug abuse are also higher than those in the general population

Parenting is difficult in shelters because families have limited spaces, structured rules limit what parents can do and when, and children may have more stress in shelters.

Though it is difficult, mothers seek to restabilize their families and report using such coping techniques as:

- taking action to identify and solve problems
- getting social support and accepting help
- enduring the hard times patiently
- thinking positively and relying on religious beliefs
- helping others

Homeless Children

Like their mothers, homeless children are a diverse group who have all the usual stresses of childhood, the added stresses of being poor, and the additional stress of being homeless.[96] Children feel distress at uncertain living conditions, and many have had the added trauma of living in homes with domestic violence.

Studies suggest that their level of psychological stability is closely related to their mothers' stability rather than to being homeless. While they have more problems than the average child in the population and they sometimes are found to have more difficulties than low-income housed children, the pattern of difficulties is similar to that of low-income housed children.

When homeless children's school performance, behavior problems, and psychological adaptability are assessed, samples are diverse with some children doing well and some very poorly in the three areas. The main differences between the two groups were that those children doing poorly were more likely to have been physically or sexually abused and their mothers were having greater emotional problems. In one study, eighteen percent of homeless children were likely to have contact with Children's Protective Services in the five years after leaving a shelter.

Services

While emergency and transitional housing services are an essential safety net, the most important goal is to help families move toward restabilization and independent living through job and housing assistance. Researchers have concluded that primary emphasis should be placed on getting permanent housing as quickly as possible and reintegrating the family into the community. When permanent housing is obtained and vulnerable families receive added services to meet their needs, they are able to maintain their independence.

Interventions

In addition to general mental health and community services, three innovative forms of intervention have been identified.[97] First, there is provision of mental health services for families in primary health-care facilities rather than mental health clinics. Health-care workers appear easier to relate to, and families do not feel the stigmatization of having psychological problems.

Second, a seven-week summer program aimed at helping children by empowering them and building self-esteem and positive work habits through behavioral strategies to enable them to perform better at school. Weekly discussions touched on such topics as anger management, problem solving and social skills, positive classroom behavior, and relaxation techniques. Parents also had opportunities for parenting classes. Mothers and teachers reported children's behavior and emotional regulation were now typical for their age.

A third innovative program was a Multi-Family Group in which parents and children from several families met with a facilitator for a "retreat" that occurred on a Friday night and all day on Saturday to focus on strengthening families, giving them opportunities to have fun together, but also to improve skills in communication, problem solving, and managing stress. Families got ideas from each other and felt support from others in a similar situation.

These innovative programs seek to give parents skills in an atmosphere of fun and respect.

Box 17-4
FIRST PERSON NARRATIVE

Lauralee Summer moved twenty times before she was twelve years old, staying no more than six months in any one place. She lived in shelters, spent part of eighth grade in foster care, and in high school lived with her mother in an apartment they shared with another mother and her daughter. In high school, she joined the wrestling team and won a wrestling scholarship to Harvard. National stories with such titles as, "Homeless to Harvard" led to her being interviewed on television where she was asked, "What was it like to be homeless?" At the time, she had no immediate answer, and this memoir is her thoughtful response.

Growing up, she thought her life was "nothing extraordinary." She knew her family lacked money and all the restrictions that brought, but it was not until she was in college that she felt the pain and degradation of being homeless. In looking back at her life, she identifies the many "buffers and boosters" who helped her achieve her goals: her mother and her emphasis on reading and independent thinking, her teachers and high school that emphasized individuality, her wrestling coaches who taught her persistence, discipline, and team effort, wrestling itself that connected her with her body and gave her sense of self, connecting with her biological father, and her college experiences.

It is a well-told memoir of an extraordinary childhood and adolescence. Ms. Summer attended graduate school after Harvard.

*Lauralee Summer, *Learning Joy from Dogs without Collars* (New York: Simon & Schuster, 2003).

MILITARY FAMILIES

Of all the families discussed in this book, these families face the greatest challenges because family members are participating in military conflicts abroad where one or both parents face injury or death on a regular basis. That most families cope with the numerous stresses involved is a testament to their strength, especially when other families around them are living lives without these stresses.

In the United States at the present time, there are 1.4 million active duty service members and their families include 1.2 million children.[98] The National Guard and Reserves include another 900,000 service members with 700,000 children, so almost 2 million children live in military families, with 25 percent under the age of five.[99] At any one time, about 700,000 children experience the deployment of a parent to a war zone.

In the best of times, children in these families experience added stresses of multiple moves, separations from loved ones on duty, and the influence of strict military culture.[100] But living on military bases with other families who share similar challenges provides support. In times of war, there are longer separations and the risk of injury and death for loved ones. Injuries, when they occur, may influence family life and all family members for decades.

Military families are very diverse and include single-parent families, dual-parent families in which both parents are in service, regular military service members, and

National Guard and Reservists who live in communities with less support and less understanding and quick orders for deployment with marked drops in income during deployment.

Families cope best when they value the military lifestyle and see meaning in the sacrifices they make. When spouses are self-reliant and active in coping with problems, have a strong support system, and have an optimistic view of the future, families do well. When families have additional stresses to those of military life—young children, low pay, no support system, added psychological problems—they do less well.

Deployment Cycle

Deployment is the most stressful experience for military families because the service member is at risk of death. It consists of four stages: pre-deployment (notification to actual departure), deployment (time away from family in war zone), reunion (return to family), and post-deployment (period of adjustment in the family, with many facing future deployments). Children's responses depend on the child's age, the specific family context, the child's temperament, and personal qualities.[101]

Pre-Deployment   About 15 percent of families rate this period as the most stressful time in the cycle. Service members are doing their regular jobs and are also preparing to leave. Their family members have many emotional reactions. Even young infants can sense changes in the family and become more irritable, not eating or not sleeping well. Preschoolers may be confused, unhappy, or crying at the impending departure. Older children may have a clearer understanding of the dangers involved, and many feel sad and angry at the impending separation. Teens may retreat from their feelings and deny they are concerned.

Deployment   Families have to reorganize to take on the tasks that the service member did. The remaining spouse has all the burdens of a single parent in addition to the worry about the safety and welfare of the absent parent. The caregiving parent's stable mood and ability to maintain the usual family routines help children cope. However, their eating and sleeping can be disrupted, especially at times of anxiety. Older schoolchildren may be more aware of the dangers for the absent parent and have physical complaints, moodiness, and trouble completing schoolwork. They may resist the usual rules. Teens may try to take the place of the absent parent and help with chores and enjoy their greater role in the family. Some feel worried and depressed and have school problems. Twenty-nine percent of families find the midpoint of deployment the most stressful time.

A primary task in this period is maintaining contact with the absent parent. This can be done in many ways—phone, cell phone, e-mail, video calls, and letters. Families can stay close, and the absent parent can be involved in daily events when contact is frequent, but there may have to be ground rules about what is shared. If all the details of everyday life are shared, an absent parent may worry about what is happening at home and feel helpless to solve problems. Distracting worries may interfere with work and cause mistakes or injuries. Knowing certain details of a parent's surroundings can also increase the family's worries.

Reunion   Everyone is happy, and expectations are high for the reunion. However, everyone in the family has changed. Everyone is older, and their experiences have led to new skills and abilities and new feelings. It is easiest to see with babies who are toddlers and talkers when their parent returns. Caregiving parents have taken on many new jobs and feel independent and pleased at their skills. The returning service member has perhaps experienced the biggest changes in war. Everyone has to get reacquainted and get back in the family routines. If contact has been close, this is much easier.

Post-Deployment   This is a period of readjustment for the family. The absent parent is incorporated back in the family, and roles change. Spouses may find it hard to give up making all the decisions. Service members may find it hard to forget their wartime experiences, or they may miss the friends and close relationships of their military unit. Many live with the certainty that they will have to redeploy and go through the same cycle again in six to twelve months, so happiness is short-lived.

There is limited help given to families in this readjustment period, as little is known about the processes involved, especially about the process for single parents and for dual-parent military families. Some service members settle back into routine family life with minimal difficulties. Others find it hard to be around young children and feel irritable at the noise and chaos. Some may suffer from depression or PTSD that was not diagnosed at the time of return. When families are close to a base, there are more services available to help with the readjustment process. Those in the Guard or Reserves have to seek help in the private community where professionals are less likely to have experience in military problems.

A major problem is also the military's past history of minimizing psychological difficulties and encouraging a "tough it out" attitude that delays getting needed help. Because of the traumatic nature of their experiences, returning service members are more emotionally vulnerable, and, as has been found, at greater risk for domestic violence and child abuse. So, if problems do not subside, help must be sought quickly. Outside agencies such as Head Start have partnered with military bases and installations to give training to their staffs to help them be sensitive to children's reactions in the deployment cycle.[102] Teachers have been able to refer families for needed services, and have been active in helping community agencies understand the needs of military families. Schools for older children have also provided group programs when there are a sizeable number of children to participate.

Family Challenges

While many military families function well despite all the stresses involved in military service, war and killing present traumas that make it hard for many veterans to settle back into routine life. It is estimated that one-third of returning soldiers suffer significant distress with PTSD depression and substance abuse being common problems in the group.[103] Depending on the sample, between 20 to 40 percent of wives of men with psychological problems also report problems of depression but more in relation to their own lives and past experiences than in response to their husbands' problems.[104] When husbands are depressed, marital dissatisfaction often follows.[105]

Young children three to eight have increased health-care visits for health and emotional problems while parents are in deployment. Children five to twelve show an increase in feelings of anxiety and depression as well as aggressive behaviors and school problems. Teens show similar emotional reactions of sadness and anger, and their school performance and peer relationships suffer during deployment.[106]

Services

The military seeks to prevent problems with educational information on deployment stresses for families. General services provided for all can focus on building general stress management coping skills to prevent psychological problems in the deployment cycle.[107]

When problems arise, services should be organized and offered by providers who are knowledgeable about and respectful of the military culture. Cognitive behavioral programs have many advantages for dealing with psychological problems as they are evidence-based, structured, and can address the variety of problems that children and parents experience.

Services must be sustained and available for long periods of time as families may have increases in problems with subsequent deployments. These families have given much to their country and deserve the highest levels of services on an ongoing basis.

THE CHALLENGE MODEL

Therapy can help children deal with the effects of certain traumatic events and troubled family situations. Some therapists have become concerned, however, that certain forms of intervention so emphasize the pain and damaging effects of these difficulties that children and adults believe they are doomed to emotionally impoverished lives as a result of the trauma.

Steven Wolin and Sybil Wolin have developed a *challenge model* of development.[108] Although adversity brings stress, harm, and vulnerability to the individual, Wolin and Wolin believe it also stimulates the person to branch out, to take measures to protect him- or herself, and find other sources of strength that promote development. Although the individual experienced pain, the focusing is on developing resiliencies that can limit the pain and promote accomplishment and satisfaction.

In their book *The Resilient Self*, Wolin and Wolin identify seven resiliencies that help individuals rebound in the face of difficult circumstances:

1. *Insight*—[developing] the habit of asking tough questions and giving honest answers

2. *Independence*—drawing boundaries between yourself and the troubled people around you; keeping emotional and physical distance while satisfying the demands of your conscience

3. *Relationships*—[building] intimate and fulfilling ties to other people that balance a mature regard for your own needs with empathy and the capacity to give to someone else

4. *Initiative*—taking charge of problems; exerting control; [acquiring] a taste for stretching and testing yourself in demanding tasks

5. *Creativity*—imposing order, beauty, and purpose on the chaos of your troubling experiences and painful feelings

6. *Humor*—finding the comic in the tragic

7. *Morality*—[developing] an informed conscience that extends your wish for a good personal life to all of humankind.[109]

Their book describes the many ways resiliencies grow in childhood, adolescence, and adulthood and offers an optimistic approach that encourages survivors of traumas and difficult childhood experiences to review their lives in terms of the strengths they have developed. As a result, people experience pride in their ability to overcome hardships—whether as a result of violence or abuse or natural disasters such as floods and earthquakes—and confidence in their capacity to make further changes as needed. In focusing on pain and the sources of pain in the past, the damage model tends to discourage individuals, because the past cannot be changed and the pain undone. In contrast, the challenge model asserts that life can be satisfying, joyful, and productive even with the pain and scars of the past.

MAIN POINTS

Chronic illness
- affects 4–9 percent of children
- changes child's and family's routines
- brings feelings of worry, helplessness
- makes great demands on child and family
- requires parents build an alliance with health-care providers
- build and maintain a positive support system

When a parent dies
- children feel many emotions which they are more likely to express in physical, motoric activity when they are young
- children need parents' help and encouragement in talking about feelings
- children worry about remaining parent
- remaining parent needs to get support and people with whom to talk
- takes individual amounts of time before people are able to reorganize their lives

An ecological/transactional model of community violence and child maltreatment

- describes characteristics of the child, parent, and environment that increase the risk of violence
- describes violence at several ecological levels: the macrosystem, the exosystem, the microsystem, and the ontogenic, or personal, level
- has implications for types of intervention at the various ecological levels

Child maltreatment

- includes many forms—individual (physical/emotional abuse, neglect), family (domestic violence), and school/community (assaults, shootings)
- includes a broader array of victimizations that increase the level of symptoms children have
- includes 18 percent of children who have had four or more victimizations in a year
- requires organized community interventions to prevent family violence

Risks for maltreatment include

- social characteristics of family (e.g., poverty status, neighborhood violence)
- parents' personal characteristics (history of abuse, substance use, psychological stability)
- child's characteristics (medical problems, overreactive temperament)

Children's response to maltreatment include

- neurobiological hyperarousal
- PTSD
- disorganized/disoriented attachment to parent
- poor peer relations
- poor emotional regulation and feelings of self-blame
- depression

Interventions to help

- separating child from abuser
- parenting interventions so parents learn parenting skills as well as ways to help children cope
- home visiting programs to promote parents' skills and positive relationships with children
- activities that promote feelings of self-worth, control, and social connections
- community programs that provide information and help in many forms readily available to family
- multisystemic family therapy that offers a wide variety of services in homes
- interrupt cycle of abuse by providing a supportive adult outside the family, therapist, or supportive partner in adulthood

Foster parenting

- involves the satisfactions and challenges of providing care for children who are dealing with difficult life experiences
- involves many other people and agencies and the ongoing supervision of parents
- has difficulty helping children overcome problems they enter with, but innovative programs provide useful interventions

Homeless mothers and their children

- have all the problems of low-income housed people and added stress of being homeless
- are a diverse group with some children doing well and some poorly with two basic factors related to doing poorly—child's experience of abuse and mother's emotional stability
- are in shelters primarily because of poverty and domestic violence
- are able to maintain independence when they have stable housing and added services to meet their needs

Military families

- include 1.2 million children
- have more stresses than most families because of separations from loved ones and increased risk of harm
- experience stages in deployment process
- by and large cope well with the many difficulties involved

The challenge model

- focuses on strengths people develop to cope with negative family experiences or other traumas
- identifies seven resiliencies: insight, independence, relationships, initiative, creativity, humor, and morality
- presents an optimistic view of people's capacity to create satisfying lives despite the scars of painful experiences

EXERCISES

1. Imagine that a close friend told you that her four-year-old twin boys fought so hard each day that they often inflicted injuries so she had to take them to the Emergency Room for treatment. What would you say to her about sibling victimization and what would you advise her to do?

2. Divide into groups of four and describe the general information you would choose to include in an eight-session parenting course for men and women who have physically abused their children. Share your group's results with the entire class. What elements were chosen by only one or two groups? Combine

the best information from all groups and come up with one eight-session program. If possible, compare it with a program offered in your area, such as parental stress.

3. Divide into groups of four and describe a parenting program for adolescent mothers and fathers to prevent physical child abuse. Is it identical to the program designed for those who have already committed abuse? In what ways does it differ?

4. Imagine that you had unlimited money to go into a low-income housing project in a high-crime area. What kinds of programs would you devise to help children cope with the violence they witness around them?

5. Think about what you most feared as a young child. What would you tell a nine-year-old brother or sister who is afraid of being kidnapped on the street? Of experiencing an earthquake or hurricane or flood?

ADDITIONAL READINGS

Cohen, Judith A., Mannarino, Anthony P., and Deblinger, Esther. *Treating Trauma and Traumatic Grief in Children and Adolescents*. New York: Guilford, 2006.

Dodge, Kenneth A. and Coleman, Doriane Lambelet. *Preventing Maltreatment: Community Approaches*. New York: Guilford, 2009.

Finkelhor, David. *Childhood Victimization: Violence, Crime and Abuse in the Lives of Young People*. New York: Oxford University Press, 2008.

Summer, Lauralee. *Learning Joy from Dogs without Collars*. New York: Simon & Schuster, 2003.

Zelter, Lonnie K. and Schlank, Christinne Blackett. *Conquering Your Child's Chronic Pain*. New York: HarperCollins, 2005.

E P I L O G U E

We have looked at parenting behaviors in many different circumstances. We have discussed parenting children of all ages living in families of diverse values and goals and in diverse family structures with one or two parents, who are sometimes of the same sex. We have looked at parenting in ordinary times and in times of special stress such as divorce or trauma. No matter what the age of the child; no matter whether the child is a biological or an adopted child, a child with special gifts or special needs, or a child with the usual gifts and needs; no matter whether parents are married, single, or remarried—four basic principles stand out.

The four basic principles are straightforward. First, parents give children positive attention. Positive attention does not mean accepting and approving all behaviors. It does mean that parents view children in terms of their special qualities and strengths, and that parents maintain their positive view of children while helping them make needed changes in behavior.

Second, parents provide support for the growth of children's competence by modeling positive behavior, guiding children's behavior, and teaching them problem-solving skills to deal with challenges. Third, parents talk about what is happening, listen to children's feelings, and answer children's questions so children have a clear understanding of situations and a chance to express their concerns. Fourth, parents deal with unresolved anger and hostility directed at the child or expressed to or about others in the child's presence. The persistence of such feelings destroys children's good feelings and their effectiveness in the world.

Relying on these four principles, parents can help children grow and realize their potential. No matter how strong the desire, parents cannot guarantee children a problem-free life, especially in these historical times, but they can guarantee children a lifetime attachment that provides the support and help necessary to grow and to meet life's challenges.

Throughout the book, we have seen that parents benefit from support as they go about rearing the next generation. In our individualistic society, this support usually comes from individuals and voluntary organizations. Government programs do not give much help to the vast array of parents, though such programs are effective in providing services—for example, home visiting programs for parents of infants or early childhood stimulation programs for children with special needs.

In most parents' lives, support comes primarily from marital partners, extended family members such as grandparents, friends, coworkers, and organizations like CHADD (Children and Adults with Attention Deficit Disorder) designed to help special groups of parents and children. More recently, organizations like the National Parenting Association have addressed the broader needs of all parents.

Further, parents themselves have followed the Youth Charter plan of William Damon to organize the entire community to address the needs of all youth. This is vitally important for all of us, because children are the future of our society.

If you are not a parent or grandparent, you may wonder what you can do to help parents. First, every one of us can give parents the respect and acknowledgment for their hard work and sacrifice that our society generally withholds from parents.

Second, with whatever your special skills, you may be able to take actions in your everyday life to support parents and parenting. A single individual has tremendous power, as the actions of Barbara Barlow illustrate.[1] A pediatric surgeon at Harlem Hospital in New York, she became concerned at the growing number of preventable injuries she was treating. Children fell from open windows, were hit by automobiles while playing in the street, and were victims of violence.

In 1988, Barlow started Harlem Hospital's Injury Prevention Project (IPP) with a grant from the Robert Wood Johnson Foundation. With a staff of three, she worked to rebuild playgrounds and parks in the community, making them safe places to play. She photographed all the parks and playgrounds and took the information to the Parks Department and the Board of Education. The Parks Department has since made nearly all the parks in the area safe. Private funding was obtained, and with the suggestions of teachers and students, eight new parks were built.

The IPP has expanded to include activities that foster children's competence. For example, an in-hospital art program allows patients to express their feelings about illness and hospitalization. Children have exhibited and sold their work, with half of the profits going to the children and half to the art program. The IPP also sponsors baseball teams, a soccer team, a dance program serving two hundred children, and a greening program in which children can grow vegetables and flowers.

Since the implementation of this program, major injuries to children in Harlem have decreased by 37 percent. Motor vehicle accidents have decreased by 50 percent, and fewer children fall from windows. In addition, dancers, athletes, artists, and gardeners have developed skills they would not have been able to develop without the programs.

An increase in violent injuries led Barlow to start the Anti-Violence Project, which contains several specific programs for (1) teaching children how to stay safe, (2) helping children deal with violence after they experience it, and (3) teaching the children, their parents, and educators conflict resolution techniques and other ways to avoid violence.

Funding for all these programs comes from individuals, corporations, foundations, and fees from Barlow's speaking engagements. Barlow concludes,

> You have to give to get in this world, and we give a lot. We put in lots of hard work, but it's immensely satisfying. There is no such thing as not being able to make things better. In any community, every individual can make a tremendous difference if they truly care, if they look around to see what needs to be done.[2]

NOTES

CHAPTER ONE

1. U.S. Census Bureau, *Statistical Abstract of the United States: 2009,* 128th ed. (Washington, DC: U.S. Government Printing Office, 2008).

2. Amy Chua, "Why Chinese Mothers Are Superior," *Wall Street Journal,* January 8–9, 2011, C1.

3. "Our Readers Roar: What Makes a Good Parent," *Wall Street Journal,* January 15–16, 2011, C2.

4. Amy Chua, "The Tiger Mother Talks Back," *Wall Street Journal,* January 15–16, 2011, C2.

5. Ayelet Waldman, "In Defense of the Guilty, Ambivalent, Preoccupied Western Mom," *Wall Street Journal,* January 15–16, 2011, C1.

6. Gerard Baker, "Larry Summers vs. Tiger Mom," *Wall Street Journal,* January 29–30, 2011, C3.

7. *Time,* May 2, 2011.

8. Marc H. Bornstein, "Parenting Science and Practice," in *Handbook of Child Psychology,* 6th ed., eds. William Damon and Richard M. Lerner, vol. 4: *Child Psychology in Practice,* eds. K. Ann Renninger and Irving E. Sigel (Hoboken, NJ: Wiley, 2006), 893–949.

9. Lois Wladis Hoffman and Jean Denby Manis, "The Value of Children in the United States: A New Approach to the Study of Fertility," *Journal of Marriage and the Family 41* (1979): 583–596.

10. Donald G. McNeil, Jr., "Demographic 'Bomb' May Only Go Pop!," *New York Times,* August 29, 2004, Section 4, 1.

11. Personal Communication.

12. Hoffman and Manis, "The Value of Children."

13. Gerald Y. Michaels, "Motivational Factors in the Decision and Timing of Pregnancy," in *The Transition to Parenthood,* eds. Gerald Y. Michaels and Wendy Goldberg (New York: Cambridge University Press, 1988), 23–61.

14. Arthur T. Jersild et al., *The Joys and Problems of Child Rearing* (New York: Bureau of Publications, Teachers College, Columbia University, 1949).

15. William Morris, ed., *The American Heritage Dictionary of the English Language* (Boston: American Heritage Publishing and Houghton Mifflin, 1969).

16. Diana Baumrind and Ross A. Thompson, "The Ethics of Parenting," in *Handbook of Parenting,* 2nd ed., ed. Marc H. Bornstein, vol. 5: *Practice Issues in Parenting* (Mahwah, NJ: Erlbaum, 2002), 3.

17. Bornstein, "Parenting Science and Practice."

18. Jay Belsky, "The Determinants of Parenting: A Process Model," *Child Development 55* (1984): 83–96.

19. Urie Bronfenbrenner and Pamela A. Morris, "The Bioecological Model of Human Development," in *Handbook of Child Psychology,* 6th ed., eds. William Damon and Richard M. Lerner, vol. 1: *Theoretical Models of Human Development,* ed. Richard Lerner (Hoboken, NJ: Wiley, 2006), 793–828.

20. Belsky, "Determinants of Parenting."

21. Richard M. Lerner, Elizabeth E. Sparks, and Laurie D. McCubbin, "Family Diversity and Family Policy," in *Handbook of Family Diversity,* eds. David H. Demo, Katherine R. Allen, and Mark A. Fine (New York: Oxford University Press, 2000), 391.

22. Baumrind and Thompson, "The Ethics of Parenting."

23. Belsky, "Determinants of Parenting."

24. Ibid.

25. Pauline M. Pagliocca et al., "Parenting and the Law," in *Handbook of Parenting,* 2nd ed., ed. Bornstein, vol. 5, 463–485.

26. Baumrind and Thompson, "The Ethics of Parenting."

27. Laura Landro, "Parents Barred from Teen Health Files," *Wall Street Journal,* August 8, 2005, Dl.

28. Pagliocca et al., "Parenting and the Law."

29. Baumrind and Thompson, "The Ethics of Parenting."

30. Margaret B. Neal and Leslie B. Hammer, *Working Couples Caring for Children and Aging Parents: Effects on Work and Well-Being* (Mahwah, NJ: Erlbaum, 2007).

31. Christopher J. Ruhm, "Policies to Assist Parents with Young Children," *Future of Children* 21 (2011): 37–65, Footnote 4.

32. Mark K. Rank, "As American as Apple Pie: Poverty and Welfare," in *Shifting the Center: Understanding Contemporary Families,* 3rd ed., ed. Susan J. Ferguson (New York: McGraw-Hill, 2007), 739–745.

33. U.S. Census Bureau, *Statistical Abstract of the United States: 2009.*

34. Sylvia Hewlett and Cornel West, *War against Parents* (Boston: Houghton Mifflin, 1998).

35. Steve Farkas et al., *A Lot Easier Said Than Done: Parents Talk about Raising Children in Today's America* (New York: Public Agenda, 2002).

36. Ibid.

37. Marian J. Bakermans-Kranenburg et al., "Experiential Evidence for Differential Susceptibility: Dopamine D4 Receptor Polymorphism (DRD4 VNTR) Moderates Intervention Effects on Toddlers' Externalizing Behavior in a Randomized Controlled Trial," *Developmental Psychology* 44 (2008): 293–300.

38. Ibid.

39. Adele Diamond et al., "Preschool Program Improves Cognitive Control," *Science* 318 (2007): 1387–1388.

40. Michael I. Posner and Mary K. Rothbart, *Educating the Human Brain* (Washington, DC: American Psychological Association, 2007).

41. Susan Saulny, "They Stand When Called Upon and When Not," *New York Times,* February 25, 2009, A1.

42. Ibid., A15.

43. Farkas et al., *A Lot Easier Said Than Done.*

44. Steve Farkas et al., *Kids These Days: What Americans Really Think about the Next Generation* (New York: Public Agenda, 1997).

45. Ibid.

46. Ellen Galinsky, *Ask the Children: What American Children Really Think about Working Parents* (New York: Morrow, 1999).

47. Jay Belsky and John Kelly, *The Transition to Parenthood* (New York: Delacorte, 1994), 23.

48. Vern Bengtson, "Beyond the Nuclear Family: The Increasing Importance of Multigenerational Bonds," *Journal of Marriage and Family* 63 (2001): 1–16.

49. Ibid., p. 5.

50. Steven H. Zarit and David J. Eggebeen, "Parent-Child Relationships in Adulthood and Later Years," in *Handbook of Parenting,* 2nd ed., ed. Marc H. Bornstein, vol. 1: *Children and Parenting* (Mahwah, NJ: Erlbaum, 2002), 135–161.

51. U.S. Census Bureau, *Statistical Abstract of the United States: 2011.*

52. Bengtson, "Beyond the Nuclear Family," 7.

53. Claude S. Fischer, *Still Connected: Family and Friends in America Since 1970* (New York: Russell Sage Foundation, 2011).

54. www.childstats.gov/americaschildren/famsoc1.asp. Table Family 1.B. Percentage of Children Ages 0–17 Living in Various Family Arrangements, 2008.

55. Pew Social & Demographic Trends, "The Public Renders a Split Verdict on Changes in Family Structure," downloaded from www.pewsocialtrends.org/2011/02/16.

56. Joseph E. Illick, *American Childhoods* (Philadelphia: University of Pennsylvania, 2009).

57. U.S. Census Bureau, *Statistical Abstract of the United States: 2011.*

58. Ibid.

59. Hirokazu Yoshikawa, *Immigrants Raising Citizens: Undocumented Parents and Their Young Children* (New York: Russell Sage Foundation, 2011).

60. "Public Favors Tougher Border Controls and Path to Citizenship," www.pewresearchcenter.org, downloaded 2011, February 27.

61. U.S. Census Bureau, *Statistical Abstract of the United States: 2011.*

62. Sabrina Tavernise, "In Census, Minorities Show Gains in Youth," *New York Times,* February 5, 2011, A10.

63. U.S. Census Bureau, *Statistical Abstract of the United States: 2011.*

64. "Reading between the Poverty Lines," *New York Times,* November 20, 2011, Sunday Review, 10.

65. Daniel T. Lichter and Elaine Wethington, "Chaos and Fortunes of American Children: A Historical Perspective," in *Chaos and Its Influence on Children's Development: An Ecological Perspective,* eds. Gary W. Evans and Theodore D. Wachter (Washington, DC: American Psychological Association, 2010), 15–32.

66. Richard Wilkinson and Kate Pickett, *The Spirit Level: Why Equality Is Better for Everyone* (London: Penguin, 2010).

67. Don Peck, "How a New Jobless Era Will Transform America," *Atlantic*, March, 2010, 42–56.

68. Tamar Lewin, "Once in First Place, Americans Now Lag in Attaining College Degrees," *New York Times*, July 23, 2010, A10.

69. Sam Dillon, "Many Nations Passing U.S. in Education, Expert Says," *New York Times*, March 10, 2010, A21.

70. Donna Gordon Blankinship, "Most in Poll Blame Parents for School Ills," *San Francisco Chronicle*, December 12, 2010, A16.

71. Victoria J. Rideout, Ulla G. Foehr, and Donald F. Roberts, "Generation M2: Media in the Lives of 8- to 18-Year-Olds," Kaiser Family Foundation Report No. 8010, January, 2010, www.kff.org.

72. U.S. Census Bureau, *Statistical Abstract of the United States: 2011*.

73. Hilary Stout, "Play's the Thing," *New York Times*, January 5, 2011, D11.

74. Matthew J. Bundick et al., "Thriving across the Lifespan," in *The Handbook of Life-Span Development*, ed. Richard M. Lerner, vol. 1: *Cognition, Biology, and Methods*, ed. Willis F. Overton (Hoboken, NJ: Wiley, 2010), 882–923.

75. Anne C. Petersen, "Inconvenient Truths: Behavioral Research and Social Policy," in *Development and Prevention of Problems: From Genes to Social Policy*, eds. Richard E. Tremblay, Marcel A. G. van Aken, and William Koops (New York: Psychology Press, 2009), 229–245.

76. Peter L. Benson, *All Kids Are Our Kids: What Communities Must Do to Raise Caring and Responsible Children and Adolescents*, 2nd ed. (San Francisco: Jossey-Bass, 2006).

77. Judith Rich Harris, *The Nature Assumption: Why Children Turn Out the Way They Do* (New York: Free Press, 1998).

78. Martha J. Cox et al., "Systems Theory and Cascades in Developmental Psychopathology," *Development and Psychopathology* 22 (2010): 497–506.

79. NICHD Early Child Care Research Network, Trajectories of Physical Aggression from Toddlerhood to Middle Childhood, *Monographs of the Society for Research in Child Development*, 69, serial no. 278 (2004).

80. Darya Bonds McClain et al., "Developmental Cascade Effects of the New Beginnings Program on Adolescent Adaptation Outcomes," *Development and Psychopathology* 22 (2010): 771–784.

81. Gerald R. Patterson, Marion S. Forgatch, and David S. DeGarmo, "Cascading Effects Following Intervention," *Development and Psychopathology* 22 (2010): 949–970.

82. Tricia K. Neppl et al., "Intergenerational Continuity in Parenting Behavior: Mediating Pathways and Child Effects," *Developmental Psychology* 45 (2009): 1241–1256.

83. Anne Shaffer et al., "Intergenerational Continuity in Parenting Quality: The Mediating Role of Social Competence," *Developmental Psychology* 45 (2009): 1227–1240.

84. June Lichtenstein Phelps, Jay Belsky, and Keith Crnic, "Earned Security, Daily Stress, and Parenting: A Comparison of Five Alternative Models," *Development and Psychopathology* 10 (1998): 21–38.

85. Sandra T. Azar, "Parenting and Child Maltreatment," in *Handbook of Parenting*, 2nd ed., ed. Marc H. Bornstein, vol. 4: *Social Conditions and Applied Parenting* (Mahwah, NJ: Erlbaum, 2002), 361–388.

86. Personal communication with Steven Wolan.

87. Ibid.

88. Jeffrey Marx, *Season of Life* (New York: Simon & Schuster, 2003), 141.

89. Daniel J. Siegel and Mary Hartzell, *Parenting from the Inside Out: How a Deeper Self-Understanding Can Help You Raise Children Who Thrive* (New York: Penguin, 2003), 4.

90. Ibid., p. 248.

91. Katherine Ellison, *The Mommy Brain: How Motherhood Makes Us Smarter* (New York: Basic Books, 2005).

92. James J. Dillon, "The Role of the Child in Adult Development" *Journal of Adult Development* 9 (2002): 267–275.

93. Ibid., p. 271.

94. Ibid., p. 272.

95. Jersild et al., *The Joys and Problems of Child Rearing*, 122.

CHAPTER TWO

1. William Morris, ed., *The American Heritage Dictionary of the English Language* (Boston: American Heritage Publishing Co., 1969).

2. Sara Harkness and Charles Super, "Culture and Parenting," in *Handbook of Parenting*, 2nd ed., ed. Marc H. Bornstein, vol. 2: *Biology and Ecology of Parenting* (Mahwah, NJ: Erlbaum, 2002), 253–280.

3. Shinobu Kitayama, Sean Duffy, and Yukiko Uchida, "Self as Cultural Mode of Being," in *Handbook of Cultural Psychology*, eds. Shinobu Kitayama and Dov Cohen (New York: Guilford, 2007), 136–174.

4. Melvin Konner, "Evolutionary Foundations of Cultural Psychology," in *Handbook of Cultural Psychology*, eds. Kitayama and Cohen, 77–105.

5. Kitayama, Duffy, and Uchida, "Self As Cultural Mode of Being."

6. Sara Harkness, Charles M. Super, and Caroline Johnston Mavridis, "Parental Ethnotheories about Children's Socioemotional Development," in *Socioemotional Development in Cultural Context*, eds. Xinyin Chen and Kenneth H. Rubin (New York: Guilford, 2011), 73–98.

7. Richard E. Nisbett, *The Geography of Thought: How Asians and Westerners Think Differently . . . and Why* (New York: Free Press, 2003).

8. Harkness, Super, and Mavridis, "Parental Ethnotheories about Children's Socioemotional Development."

9. Sara Harkness and Charles M. Super, "Themes and Variations: Parental Ethnotheories in Western Cultures," in *Parental Beliefs, Behaviors, and Parent-Child Relations*, eds. Kenneth H. Rubin and Ock Boon Chung (New York: Psychology Press, 2006), 61–79.

10. Kitayama, Duffy, and Uchida, "Self as Cultural Mode of Being."

11. Patricia M. Greenfield, "Linking Social Change and Developmental Change: Shifting Pathways of Human Development," *Developmental Psychology* 45 (2009): 401–418.

12. Nisbett, *The Geography of Thought*, 229.

13. Michael J. Chandler et al., "Personal Persistence, Identity Development, and Suicide," *Monographs of the Society for Research in Child Development 68*, serial no. 273 (2003).

14. Mary Gauvain and Ross D. Parke, "Socialization," in *Handbook of Cultural Developmental Science*, ed. Marc H. Bornstein (New York: Psychology Press, 2010), 239.

15. Konner, "Evolutionary Foundations of Cultural Psychology."

16. Barbara Fiese et al., "A Review of 50 Years of Research on Naturally Occurring Family Routines and Rituals: Cause for Celebration," *Journal of Family Psychology* 16 (2002): 381–390.

17. Daphne Blunt Bugental and Joan E. Grusec, "Socialization Processes," in *Handbook of Child Psychology*, 6th ed., eds. William Damon and Richard M. Lerner, vol. 3: *Social, Emotional, and Personality Development*, ed. Nancy Eisenberg (Hoboken, NJ: Wiley, 2006), 366–428.

18. Rogers Brubaker, *Ethnicity without Groups* (Cambridge, MA: Harvard University Press, 2004).

19. Jean L. Briggs, "Mazes of Meaning: How a Child and a Culture Create Each Other," in *Interpretive Approaches to Socialization*, eds. William A. Corsaro and Peggy J. Miller, *New Directions for Child Development*, no. 66 (San Francisco: Jossey Bass, 1992), 25.

20. Konner, "Evolutionary Foundations of Cultural Psychology."

21. Tara Callaghan et al., "Early Social Cognition in Three Cultural Contexts," *Monographs of the Society for Research in Child Development 76*, serial no. 299 (2011).

22. Jonathan Tudge, *The Everyday Lives of Young Children: Culture, Class, and Child Rearing in Diverse Societies* (New York: Cambridge University Press, 2008).

23. Harkness and Charles M. Super, "Themes and Variations."

24. Leslie A. Roberts et al., "International Comparisons of Behavioral and Emotional Problems in Preschool Children: Parents' Reports from 24 Societies," *Journal of Clinical Child and Adolescent Psychology 40* (2011): 456–467.

25. Reed W. Larson and Suman Verma, "How Children and Adolescents Spend Time across the World: Work, Play, and Developmental Activities," *Psychological Bulletin 125* (1999): 701–736.

26. Edoard Mackery and Luc Faucher, "Social Construction and the Concept of Race," *Philosophy and Science 72* (2005): 1208–1219.

27. Andrew M. Penner and Aliyah Saperstein, "How Social Status Shapes Race," *Proceedings of the National Academy of Sciences 105* (2008): 19628–19630.

28. U.S. Census Bureau, *Statistical Abstract of the United States: 2011*, 130th ed. (Washington, DC: United States Government Printing Office, 2010).

29. Ibid., p. 5.

30. John Branch, "The Journey toward Acceptance," *New York Times,* November 9, 2009, D1.
31. Ibid., D4.
32. Susan Saulny, "Black? White? Asian? More Young Americans Choose All of the Above," *New York Times,* January 30, 2011, A1.
33. Ross D. Parke and Raymond Buriel, "Socialization in the Family: Ethnic and Ecological Perspectives," in *Handbook of Child Psychology,* 6th ed., eds. Damon and Lerner, vol. 3, 465.
34. Robert H. Bradley et al., "The Home Environments of Children in the United States: Part II: Relations with Behavioral Development through Age Thirteen," *Child Development* 72 (2001): 1868–1886.
35. William E. Cross, Jr., "A Two-Factor Theory of Black Identity: Implications for the Study of Identity Development in Minority Children," in *Children's Ethnic Socialization: Pluralism and Development,* eds. Jean S. Phinney and Mary Jane Rotheram (Beverly Hills, CA: Sage, 1987), 117–133.
36. Catherine S. Tamis-Le Monda and Karen E. McFadden, "The United States of America," in *Handbook of Cultural Developmental Science,* ed. Bornstein, 299–322.
37. Ibid.
38. Sabrina Tavernise, "Poverty Reaches a 52-Year Peak Government Says," *New York Times,* September 14, 2011, A1.
39. Daniel J. Hernandez, Nancy A. Denton, and Suzanne E. Macartney, "Children in Immigrant Families: Looking to America's Future," *Social Policy Report* 22 (3) (2008): 1–22.
40. Cynthia Garcia Coll and Lee M. Pachter, "Ethnic and Minority Parenting," in *Handbook of Parenting,* 2nd ed., ed. Marc H. Bornstein, vol. 4: *Social Conditions and Applied Parenting* (Mahwah, NJ: Erlbaum, 2002), 7.
41. Marc H. Bornstein and Linda R. Cote, "Immigration and Acculturation," in *Handbook of Cultural Developmental Science,* ed. Bornstein, 531– 552.
42. Julia Preston, "Illegal Immigrant Parents Pass a Burden, Study Says," *New York Times,* September 21, 2011, A21.
43. Cynthia Garcia Coll and Laura A. Szalacha, "The Multiple Contexts of Middle Childhood," *Future of Children* 14 (2) (2004): 81–97.
44. Margaret Burchinal et al., Examining the Black-White Achievement Gap among Low-Income Children Using the NICHD Study of Early Childhood and Youth Development," *Child Development* 82 (2011): 1404–1420.
45. Garcia Coll and Szalacha, "The Multiple Contexts of Middle Childhood," 89.
46. Geoffrey L. Cohen et al., "Recursive Processes in Self-Affirmation: Intervening to Close the Minority Achievement Gap," *Science* 324 (2009): 400–403.
47. Tina Hoff, Liberty Greene, and Julia Davis, *National Survey of Adolescents and Young Adults: Sexual Health and Knowledge, Attitudes and Experiences* (Menlo Park, CA: Kaiser Family Foundation, 2003).
48. John W. Berry, "Acculturation," in *Handbook of Socialization: Theory and Research,* eds. Joan E. Grusec and Paul D. Hastings (New York: Guilford, 2007), 543–558.
49. Gene H. Brody et al., "Perceived Discrimination and the Adjustment of African American Youths: A Five-Year Longitudinal Analysis with Contextual Moderation Effects," *Child Development* 77 (2006): 1170–1189.
50. Gene H. Brody et al., "Linking Perceived Discrimination to Longitudinal Changes in African American Mothers' Parenting Practices," *Journal of Marriage and Family* 70 (2008): 319–331.
51. Steven R. Beach et al., "Change in Caregiver Depression as a Function of the Strong African American Families Program," *Journal of Family Psychology* 22 (2008): 241–252.
52. Melanie Killen, Adam Rutland, and Martin D. Ruck, "Promoting Equity, Tolerance, and Justice," *Social Policy Report* 24 (2011): 1–26.
53. Frances E. Aboud, "The Formation of In-Group Favoritism and Out-Group Prejudice in Young Children: Are They Distinct Attitudes?" *Developmental Psychology* 39 (2003): 48–60.
54. Meagan M. Patterson and Rebecca S. Bigler, "Preschool Children's Attention to Environmental Messages about Groups," *Child Development* 77 (2006): 847–860.
55. Killen, Rutland, and Ruck, "Promoting Equity, Tolerance, and Justice."
56. Jennifer H. Pfeifer, Christia Spears Brown, and Jaana Juvonen, "Teaching Tolerance in Schools: Lessons Learned since *Brown v.*

Board of Education about the Development and Reduction of Children's Prejudice," *Social Policy Report 21* (2) (2007).

57. Killen, Rutland, and Ruck, "Promoting Equity, Tolerance, and Justice."

58. Jean M. Twenge and Jennifer Crocker, "Race and Self-Esteem: Meta-Analyses Comparing Whites, Blacks, Hispanics, Asians, and American Indians and Comment on Gray-Little and Haldahl (2000)," *Psychological Bulletin 64* (2002): 703–716.

59. Erika Hoff, Brett Laursen, and Twila Tardif, "Socioeconomic Status and Parenting," in *Handbook of Parenting,* 2nd ed., ed., Bornstein, vol. 2, 231–252.

60. Betty Hart and Todd R. Risley, *Meaningful Differences in the Everyday Experiences of Young American Children* (Baltimore: Brookes, 1995).

61. Annette Lareau, *Unequal Childhoods: Class, Race, and Family Life* (Berkeley: University of California Press, 2003).

62. Sandra L. Hofferth, "Linking Social Class to Concerted Cultivation, Natural Growth and School Readiness," in *Disparities in School Readiness: How Families Contribute to Transitions into School,* eds. Alan Booth and Ann C. Crouter (New York: Erlbaum, 2008), 199–205

63. Robert Serpell et al., "Intimate Culture of Families in the Early Socialization of Literacy," *Journal of Family Psychology 16* (2002): 391–405.

64. Joseph A. Buckhalt, Mona El-Sheikh, and Peggy Keller, "Children's Sleep and Cognitive Functioning: Race and Socioeconomic Status as Moderators of Effects," *Child Development 78* (2007): 213–231.

65. Allison J. Pugh, *Longing and Belonging: Parents, Children, and Consumer Culture* (Berkeley: University of California Press, 2009).

66. Vonnie C. McLoyd, Nikki L. Aikens, and Linda M. Burton, "Childhood Poverty, Policy, and Practice," in *Handbook of Child Psychology,* 6th ed., eds. William Damon and Richard M. Lerner, vol. 4: *Child Psychology in Practice,* eds. K Ann Renninger and Irving E. Seigel (Hoboken, NJ: Wiley, 2006), vol. 4, 700–775.

67. U.S. Census Bureau, *Statistical Abstract of the United States: 2011,* 130th ed.

68. Mary E. Corcoran and Ajay Chaudry, "The Dynamics of Childhood Poverty," *Future of Children 7* (2) (1997): 40–54.

69. McLoyd, Aikens, and Burton, "Childhood Poverty, Policy, and Practice."

70. Jeanne Brooks-Gunn and Greg J. Duncan, "The Effects of Poverty on Children," *Future of Children 7* (2) (1997): 55–71.

71. Gary W. Evans, "The Environment of Childhood Poverty," *American Psychologist 59* (2004): 77–92.

72. Ibid.

73. Romina M. Barros, Ellen Silver, and Ruth E. K. Stein, "School Recess and Group Classroom Behavior," *Pediatrics 123* (2009): 431–436.

74. Gary W. Evans, "A Multimethodological Analysis of Cumulative Risk and Allostatic Load among Rural Children," *Developmental Psychology 39* (2003): 924–933.

75. Eric Dearing, Kathleen McCartney, and Beck A. Taylor, "Within-Child Associations between Family Income and Externalizing and Internalizing Problems," *Developmental Psychology 42* (2006): 237–252.

76. National Institute of Child Health and Human Development Early Child Care Network, "Duration and Developmental Timing of Poverty and Children's Cognitive and Social Development from Birth through Third Grade," *Child Development 76* (2005): 795–810.

77. Dearing, McCartney, and Taylor, "Within-Child Associations between Family Income and Externalizing and Internalizing Problems."

78. Suniya S. Luthar and Shawn Latendresse, "Comparable 'Risks' at the Socioeconomic Status Extremes: Preadolescents Perceptions of Parenting," *Development and Psychopathology 14* (2005): 2–30.

79. John M. Love et al., "The Effectiveness of Early Head Start for Three-Year-Old Children and Their Parents: Lessons for Policy and Programs, "*Developmental Psychology 41* (2005): 885–901.

80. David L. Kirp, "Life Way after Head Start," *New York Times Magazine,* November 21, 2004, 32–38.

81. Jeffrey Mervis, "Past Successes Shape Effort to Expand Early Intervention," *Science 333* (2011): 952–956.

82. Ray DeV. Peters et al., "Better Beginnings, Better Futures Project: Findings from Grade 3 to Grade 9," *Monographs of the Society for Research in Child Development 75,* serial no. 297 (2009).

83. Tammy L. Mann, "Findings from the Parent-Child Project and the Impact

of Values on Parenting Reflections in a Scientific Age," *Zero to Three 20* (December 1999-January 2000): 3–8.

84. Ibid., p. 8.

85. Vivian J. Carlson and Robin L. Harwood, "Understanding and Negotiating Cultural Differences Concerning Early Developmental Competence: The Six Raisin Solution," *Zero to Three 20* (December 1999-January 2000): 19–24.

86. Ibid, p.24.

CHAPTER THREE

1. Marc H. Bornstein et al., "Parenting Knowledge: Experiential and Sociodemographic Factors in European American Mothers of Young Children," *Developmental Psychology 46* (2010): 1677–1693.

2. Zero to Three, *Parenting Infants and Toddlers Today: Research Findings* (Washington, DC: Hart Research, 2009).

3. Ross A. Thompson, "The Development of the Person: Social Understanding, Relationships, Conscience, Self," in *Handbook of Child Psychology*, 6th ed., eds. William Damon and Richard M. Lerner, vol. 3: *Social, Emotional, and Personality Development*, ed. Nancy Eisenberg (Hoboken, NJ: Wiley, 2006), 24–98.

4. Mario Mikulincer and Philip R. Shaver, *Attachment in Adulthood: Structure, Dynamics, and Change* (New York: Guilford, 2007).

5. Ibid.

6. Zero to Three, *Parenting Infants and Toddlers Today*.

7. Ibid.

8. Lenore Skenazy, *Free-Range Kids: How to Raise Safe, Self-Reliant Children (Without Going Nuts with Worry)*. (San Francisco: Jossey-Bass, 2009).

9. Amy Chua, *Battle Hymn of the Tiger Mother* (New York: Penguin, 2011).

10. "Our Readers Roar: What Makes A Good Parent," *Wall Street Journal*, January 15-16, 2011, C2.

11. Amy Chua, "The Tiger Mother Talks Back," *Wall Street Journal*, January 15–16, 2011, C2.

12. Judith Warner, "No More Mrs. Nice Mom," *New York Times Magazine*, January 16, 2011, 11–12.

13. Annie Murphy Paul, "The Roar of the Tiger Mom," *Time*, January 31, 2011, 34–41.

14. Trip Gabriel, "Children and Stress: A Movie Hits Home," *New York Times*, December 9, 2010, A20.

15. Valerie French, "History of Parenting: The Ancient Mediterranean World," in *Handbook of Parenting*, 2nd ed., ed. Marc H. Bornstein, vol. 2: *Biology and Ecology of Parenting* (Mahwah, NJ: Erlbaum, 2002), 345–376.

16. Ibid.

17. Ibid.

18. Linda A. Pollock, *Forgotten Childhood: Parent-Child Relations from 1500 to 1900* (New York: Cambridge University Press, 1983).

19. Ibid., p. 268.

20. Ibid., p. 270.

21. International Human Genome Sequencing Consortium, "Finishing the Euchromatic Sequence of the Genome," *Nature 431* (2004): 931–945.

22. Michael J. Meaney, "Epigenetic and the Biological Definition of Gene x Environment Interactions," *Child Development 81* (2010): 41–79.

23. Marian J. Bakermans-Kranenburg et al., "Effects of an Attachment-Based Intervention on Daily Cortisol Moderated by Dopamine Receptor D4: A Randomized Control Trial on 1- to 3-Year-Olds Screened for Externalizing Behavior," *Development and Psychopathology 20* (2008): 805–820; Marian J. Bakermans-Kranenburg et al., "Experiential Evidence for Differential Susceptibility: Dopamine D4 Receptor Polymorphism (DRD4 VNTR) Moderates Intervention Effects on Toddlers' Externalizing Behavior in a Randomized Controlled Trial," *Developmental Psychology 44* (2008): 293–300.

24. Patrick O. McGowan et al., "Epigenetic Regulation of the Glucocorticoid Receptor in Human Brain Associates with Childhood Abuse," *Nature Neuroscience 12* (2009): 342–348.

25. Peter Huttenlocher, *Neural Plasticity: The Effects of Environment on the Development of the Brain* (Cambridge, MA: Harvard University Press, 2002).

26. Ibid.

27. Ibid.

28. Louis Cozolino, *The Neuroscience of Human Relationships: Attachment and the Developing Social Brain*

(New York: Norton, 2006); Sandra Blakeslee, "Cells That Read Minds," *New York Times,* January 10, 2006, D1.

29. Bruce D. Perry, "Incubated in Terror: Neurodevelopmental Factors in the Cycle of Violence," in *Children in a Violent Society,* ed. Joy D. Osofsky (New York: Guilford, 1997), 124–149.

30. Blakeslee, "Cells That Read Minds."

31. Charles A. Nelson III, Kathleen M. Thomas, and Michelle DeHaan," Neural Bases of Cognitive Development," in *Handbook of Child Psychology,* 6th ed., eds. William Damon and Richard M. Lerner, vol. 2: *Cognition, Perception, and Language,* eds. Deanna Kuhn and Robert S. Siegler (Hoboken, NJ: Wiley, 2006), 3–57.

32. Huttenlocher, *Neural Plasticity.*

33. Jay N. Giedd et al., "Brain Development during Childhood and Adolescence: A Longitudinal MRI Study," *Nature Neuroscience 2* (1999): 861–863.

34. Huttenlocher, *Neural Plasticity.*

35. Ibid., p. 215.

36. Mary Dozier et al., "Foster Children's Diurnal Production of Cortisol: An Exploratory Study," *Child Maltreatment 11* (2006): 189–197.

37. Clancy Blair, Douglas Granger, and Rachel Peters Razza, "Cortisol Reactivity Is Positively Related to Executive Function in Preschool Children Attending Head Start," *Child Development 76* (2005): 554–567.

38. Gary W. Evans and Michelle A. Shamberg, "Childhood Poverty, Chronic Stress, and Adult Working Memory," *Proceedings of the National Academy of Sciences 106* (2009): 6545–6549.

39. Hermann Englert, "Sussing Out Stress," *Scientific American Mind 14* (2004): 56–57.

40. Stephen W. Porges and C. Sue Carter, "Neurobiological Bases of Social Behavior across the Life Span," in *Handbook of Lifespan Development,* vol. 2: *Social and Emotional Development,* eds. Michael E. Lamb and Alexandra M. Freund (Hoboken, NJ: Wiley, 2010), 9–50.

41. Mary K. Rothbart and John E. Bates, "Temperament," in *Handbook of Child Psychology,* 6th ed., eds. Damon and Lerner, vol. 3, 100.

42. Ibid.

43. Ibid.

44. Jerome Kagan et al., "The Preservation of Two Infant Temperaments into Adolescence," *Monographs of the Society for Research in Child Development 72,* serial no. 287 (2007).

45. Rothbart and Bates, "Temperament."

46. Denise L. Newman et al., "Antecedents of Adult Interpersonal Functioning: Effects of Individual Differences in Age 3 Temperament," *Developmental Psychology 33* (1997): 206–217.

47. Daniel Hart, Robert Atkins, and Suzanne Fegley, "Personality and Development in Childhood: A Person-Centered Approach," *Monographs of the Society for Research in Child Development 68,* serial no. 271 (2003).

48. Terrie E. Moffitt et al., "A Gradient of Childhood Self-Control Predicts Health, Wealth, and Public Safety," *Proceedings of the National Academy of Sciences 108* (2011): 2643–2650.

49. Kagan et al., "The Preservation of Two Infant Temperaments into Adolescence".

50. Rothbart and Bates, "Temperament."

51. Ibid.

52. Ibid.

53. Adele Diamond et al., "Preschool Program Improves Cognitive Control," *Science 318* (2007): 1387–1388.

54. Michael I. Posner and Mary K. Rothbart, *Educating the Human Brain* (Washington, DC: American Psychological Association, 2007).

55. Annie Bernier, Stephanie M. Carlson, and Natasha Whipple, "From External Regulation to Self-Regulation: Early Parenting Precursors of Young Children's Executive Functioning," *Child Development 81* (2010): 326–339.

56. Annie Bernier et al. "Relations between Physiological and Cognitive Regulatory Systems: Infant Sleep Regulation and Subsequent Executive Functioning," *Child Development 81* (2010): 1739–1752.

57. Diamond et al., "Preschool Program Improves Cognitive Control;" Elena Bodrova and Deborah J. Leong, *Tools of the Mind: The Vygotskian Approach to Early Childhood Education,* 2nd ed. (Upper Saddle River, NJ: Pearson Prentice-Hall, 2007).

58. Adele Diamond and Kathleen Lee, "Interventions Shown to Aid Executive Function Development in Children 4 to 12 Years Old," *Science 333* (2011): 959–964.

59. Thompson, "The Development of the Person," 43.

60. Michael Lewis, Candace Feiring, and Saul Rosenthal, "Attachment over Time," *Child Development* 71 (2000): 707–727; L. Alan Sroufe and Byron Egeland, "Attachment from Infancy to Early Adulthood in a High-Risk Sample: Continuity, Discontinuity, and Their Correlates," *Child Development* 71 (2000): 695–702.

61. L. Alan Sroufe et al., *The Development of the Person: The Minnesota Study of Risk and Adaptation from Birth to Adulthood* (New York: Guilford, 2005).

62. Thompson, *The Development of the Person.*

63. Melvin Konner, *The Evolution of Childhood: Relationships, Emotion, Mind* (Cambridge, MA: Belknap Press, 2010).

64. Albert Bandura, *Self-Efficacy: The Exercise of Control* (New York: Freeman, 1997).

65. Laura E. Berk, *Awakening Children's Minds: How Parents and Teachers Can Make a Difference* (New York: Oxford, 2001).

66. David F. Bjorklund and Anthony D. Pellegrini, "Child Development and Evolutionary Psychology," *Child Development* 71 (2000): 1687–1708; David F. Bjorklund, Jennifer L. Yunger, and Anthony D. Pellegrini, "The Evolution of Parenting and Evolutionary Approaches to Childrearing," in *Handbook of Parenting,* 2nd ed., ed. Bornstein, vol. 2, 3–30.

67. Bjorklund and Pellegrini, "Child Development and Evolutionary Psychology."

68. Herbert Ginsburg and Sylvia Opper, *Piaget's Theory of Intellectual Development* (Englewood Cliffs, NJ: Prentice-Hall, 1969); Jean Piaget and Barbel Inhelder, *The Psychology of the Child* (New York: Basic Books, 1969).

69. Jean Piaget, *The Child's Conception of the World* (Paterson, NJ: Littlefield, Adams & Co., 1963).

70. E. Mark Cummings and Jennifer S. Cummings, "Parenting and Attachment," in *Handbook of Parenting,* 2nd ed., ed. Marc H. Bornstein, vol. 5: *Practical Issues in Parenting* (Mahwah, NJ: Erlbaum, 2002), 35–58.

71. Erik H. Erikson, *Childhood and Society,* 2nd ed. (New York: Norton, 1963).

72. Erik H. Erickson, "Human Strength and the Cycle of Generations," in *Insight and Responsibility* (New York: Norton 1964), 109–157.

73. Urie Bronfenbrenner and Pamela A. Morris, "The Bioecological Model of Human Development," in *Handbook of Child Psychology,* 6th ed., eds. William Damon and Richard M. Lerner, vol. 1: *Theoretical Models of Human Development,* ed. Richard M. Lerner (Hoboken NJ: Wiley, 2006), 793–828.

74. Urie Bronfenbrenner, "Growing Chaos in the Lives of Children: How Can We Turn It Around?" in *Parenthood in America,* ed. Jack C. Westman (Madison: University of Wisconsin Press, 2001), 197–210.

75. Philip A. Cowan, Douglas Powell, and Carolyn Pape Cowan, "Parenting Interventions: A Family Systems Perspective," in *Handbook of Child Psychology* , 5th ed., ed. William Damon, vol. 4: *Child Psychology in Practice,* eds. Irving Sigel and K. Ann Renninger (New York: Wiley, 1998), 3–72.

76. Sharon J. Price and Christine A. Price (with Patrick McKenry posthumously), "Families Coping with Change: A Conceptual Overview," in *Families & Change: Coping with Stressful Events and Transitions,* 4th ed., eds. Sharon J. Price, Christine A. Price, and Patrick C. McKenry (Thousand Oaks, CA: Sage, 2010), 1–23.

77. Gary W. Peterson, Charles B. Hennon, and Terence Knox, "Conceptualizing Parental Stress with Family Stress," in *Families & Change,* eds. Price, Price, and McKenry, 25–49.

78. Kenneth H. Rubin et al., "Parenting Beliefs and Behaviors: Initial Findings from the International Consortium for the Study of Emotional Development (ICSSED)," in *Parenting Beliefs, Behaviors, and Parent-Child Relations: A Cross-Cultural Perspective,* eds. Kenneth H. Rubin and Ock Boon Chung (New York: Psychology Press, 2006), 81–103.

79. Haim G. Ginott, *Between Parent and Child* (New York: Avon, 1969).

80. Thomas Gordon, *P.E.T.: Parent Effectiveness Training* (New York: New American Library, 1975).

81. Rudolf Dreikurs with Vicki Soltz, *Children: The Challenge* (New York: Hawthorn, 1964).

82. Anne Hulbert, *Raising America* (New York: Alfred A. Knopf, 2003).

83. T. Berry Brazelton and Stanley I. Greenspan, *The Irreducible Needs of Children* (Cambridge, MA: Perseus, 2000).

84. Dr. Phil McGraw, *Family First: Your Step by Step Plan for Creating a Phenomenal Family* (New York: Free Press, 2004).

85. Deborah Carroll and Stella Reid with Karen Moline, *Nanny 911: Expert Advice for All Your Emergencies* (New York: HarperCollins, 2005).

86. Ibid., p. xvii.

87. Ibid., p. xviii.

88. Diana Baumrind, "The Development of Instrumental Competence through Socialization," in *Minnesota Symposium on Child Psychology*, ed. Ann D. Pick, vol. 7 (Minneapolis: University of Minnesota Press 1973), 3–46.

89. Ibid., pp. 42–43.

90. Gerald R. Patterson et al., *A Social Learning Approach to Family Intervention,* vol. 1: *Families with Aggressive Children* (Eugene, OR: Castalia, 1975).

91. Gerald R. Patterson and Philip A. Fisher, "Recent Developments in Our Understanding of Parenting: Bidirectional Effects, Causal Models, and the Search for Parsimony," in *Handbook of Parenting,* 2nd ed., ed. Bornstein, vol. 5, 59–88.

92. Gerald R. Patterson, "The Early Development of the Coercive Family Process," in *Antisocial Behavior in Children and Adolescents,* eds. John B. Reid, Gerald R. Patterson, and James Snyder (Washington, DC: American Psychological Association, 2002), 25–44.

93. Femmie Juffer, Marian J. Bakermans-Kranenburg, and Marinus van IJzendoorn, "Methods of Video-Feedback Programs to Promote Positive Parenting Alone with Sensitive Discipline and with Representational Attachment Discussion," in *Positive Parenting: An Attachment-Based Intervention,* eds. Femmie Juffer, Marian J. Bakermans-Kranenburg, and Marinus van IJzendoorn (New York: Erlbaum, 2008), 11–23.

94. Marinus van IJzendoorn., Marian J. Bakermans-Kranenburg, and Femmie Juffer," Video-Feedback Intervention to Promote Positive Parenting: Evidence-Based Intervention for Enhancing Sensitivity and Security," in *Positive Parenting,* eds. Juffer, Bakermans-Kranenburg, and van IJzendoorn, 193–202.

CHAPTER FOUR

1. Pamela J. Smock and Fiona Rose Greenland, "Diversity in Pathways to Parenthood: Patterns, Implications, and Emerging Research Directions," *Journal of Marriage and Family* 72 (2010): 576–593.

2. Ibid.

3. U.S. Census Bureau, *Statistical Abstract of the United States: 2011,* 130th ed. (Washington, DC: U.S. Government Printing Office, 2010).

4. David Lykken, "Parental Licensure," *American Psychologist* 56 (2001): 885–894.

5. Christoph Heinicke, "The Transition to Parenting," in *Handbook of Parenting,* 2nd ed., ed. Marc H. Bornstein, vol. 3: *Being and Becoming a Parent* (Mahwah, NJ: Erlbaum, 2002), 363–388.

6. John G. Borkowski, Thomas I. Whitman, and Jaelyn R. Farris, "Adolescent Mothers and Their Children: Risks, Resilience, and Development," in *Risk and Resilience: Adolescent Mothers and Their Children Grow Up,* eds. John G. Borkowski et al. (Mahwah, NJ: Erlbaum, 2007), 1–34.

7. Jennifer Corbett Dooren, "Healthy Diet May Cut Risk of Birth Defects," *Wall Street Journal,* October 4, 2011, D2.

8. Michael C. Lu, *Get Ready to Get Pregnant* (New York: Harper, 2009).

9. Paul R. Amato et al., "Precursors of Young Women's Family Formation Pathways," *Journal of Marriage and Family* 70 (2008): 1271–1286.

10. Ibid.

11. D. Wayne Osgood et al., "Six Paths to Adulthood: Fast Starters, Parents without Careers, Educated Partners, Educated Singles, Working Singles, and Slow Starters," in *On the Frontier of Adulthood: Theory, Research, and Public Policy,* eds. Richard A. Settersten, Jr., Frank F. Furstenberg, Jr., and Ruben C. Rumbaut (Chicago: University of Chicago Press, 2005), 320–355.

12. Paul Amato et al., "Precursors of Young Women's Family Formation Pathways;" Robert Schoen and Paula Tufis, "Precursors of Nonmarital Fertility in the United States," *Journal of Marriage and Family* 65 (2003): 1030–1040.

13. Osgood et al., "Six Pathways to Adulthood."

14. Elizabeth Fussell and Frank F. Furstenberg, Jr., "The Transition to Adulthood during the Twentieth Century: Race, Nativity, and Gender," in *On the Frontier of Adulthood,* eds. Settersten Jr., Furstenberg, Jr., and Rumbaut, 29–75.

15. Katie Zezima, "More Women Than Ever Are Childless, Census Finds," *New York Times,* August 19, 2008, A12.

16. Tanya Koropeckorj-Cox and Gretchen Pendell, "The Gender Gap in Attitudes about Childlessness in the United States," *Journal of Marriage and Family 69* (2007): 899–915.

17. Joyce C. Abma and Gladys M. Martinez, "Childlessness among Older Women in the United States: Trends and Profiles," *Journal of Marriage and Family 68* (2006): 1045–1056.

18. Julia M. McQuillan et al., "Frustrated Fertility: Infertility and Psychological Distress among Women," *Journal of Marriage and Family 65* (2003): 1007–1018.

19. Melinda Beck, "The Birth-Control Riddle," *Wall Street Journal,* April 20, 2010, D1.

20. Pamela Daniels and Katy Weingarten, *Sooner or Later: The Timing of Parenthood in Adult Lives* (New York: W. W. Norton, 1983).

21. Jeanette M. Connor and James E. Dewey, "Reproductive Health," in *Well-Being: Positive Development across the Life Course,* eds. Marc H. Bornstein et al. (Mahwah, NJ: Erlbaum, 2003), 99–107.

22. Smock and Greenland, "Diversity in Pathways to Parenthood."

23. Kelly Musick, "Planned and Unplanned Childbearing among Unmarried Women," *Journal of Marriage and Family 64* (2002): 915–929.

24. Andrew J. Cherlin, "Demographic Trends in the United States: A Review of Research in the 2000s," *Journal of Marriage and Family 72* (2010): 403–419.

25. Mylene Lachance-Grzela and Genevieve Bouchard, "The Well-Being of Cohabiting and Married Couples during Pregnancy: Does Pregnancy Planning Matter?" *Journal of Social and Personal Relationships 26* (2009): 141–159.

26. Julia F. Klavsli and Margaret Tresch Owen, "Stable Maternal Cohabitation, Couple Relationship Quality, and Characteristics of the Home Environment in the Child's First Two Years," *Journal of Family Psychology 23* (2009): 103–106.

27. Lachance-Grzela and Bouchard, "The Well-Being of Cohabiting and Married Couples during Pregnancy."

28. Jacinta Bronte-Tinkew et al., "Resident Fathers' Pregnancy Intentions, Prenatal Behaviors, and Links to Involvement with Infants," *Journal of Marriage and Family 69* (2007): 977–990.

29. Cherlin, "Demographic Trends in the United States."

30. Musick, "Planned and Unplanned Childbearing."

31. Cherlin, "Demographic Trends in the United States."

32. Lachance-Grzela and Bourchard, "The Well-Being of Cohabiting and Married Couples during Pregnancy."

33. Klavsli and Owen, "Stable Maternal Cohabitation Couple Relationship Quality."

34. Musick, "Planned and Unplanned Childbearing."

35. Tamar Lewin, "Unwed Fathers Fight for Babies Placed for Adoption by Mothers," *New York Times,* March 19, 2006, A1.

36. Smock and Greenland, "Diversity in Pathways to Parenthood."

37. Cherlin, "Demographic Trends in the United States."

38. Jennifer S. Barber, William G. Axinn, and Arland Thornton, "Unwanted Childbearing, Health, and Mother-Child Relationships," *Journal of Health and Social Behavior 40* (1999): 231–257.

39. Henry P. David, Zdenek Dytrych, and Zdenek Matejcek, "Born Unwanted," *American Psychologist 58* (2003): 224–229.

40. Adam Pertman, *Adoption Nation* (New York: Perseus, 2000), 47–48.

41. Melinda Beck, "Surprising Causes of Male Infertility," *Wall Street Journal,* June 28, 2011, D3.

42. McQuillan et al., "Frustrated Fertility."

43. Smock and Greenland, "Diversity in Pathways to Parenthood."

44. U.S. Census Bureau, *Statistical Abstract of the United States: 2011.*

45. Carol Harkness, *The Infertility Book,* 2nd ed. (Berkeley, CA: Celestial Arts, 1992).

46. Jennifer Vanderbes, "What's That Ticking Sound? The Male Biological Clock," *Wall Street Journal,* June 25–26, 2011, C3.

47. Andrew Yarrow, *Latecomers: Children of Parents over 35* (New York: Free Press, 1991).

48. Xi-Kuan Chen et al., "Paternal Age and Adverse Birth Outcomes: Teenager or 40+, Who Is at Risk?" *Human Reproduction 23* (2008): 1290–1296.

49. Stephanie Belloc, "Father's Age a Factor in Infertility," Paper presented at the European Society of Human Reproduction and Embryology, Barcelona, Spain, July 6, 2008.

50. Emma M. Frans et al., "Advancing Paternal Age and Bipolar Disorder," *Archives of General Psychiatry 65* (2008): 1034–1040.

51. Susan Golombok, "Parenting and Contemporary Reproductive Technologies," in *Handbook of Parenting,* 2nd ed., ed. Bornstein, vol. 3, 339–360.

52. J. Reefhuis et al., "Assisted Reproductive Technology and Major Structural Birth Defects in the United States," *Human Reproduction 24* (2008): 360–366.

53. Debora Spar, *The Baby Business: How Money, Science, and Politics Drive the Commerce of Conception* (Cambridge, MA: Harvard University Press, 2006).

54. U.S. Census Bureau, *Statistical Abstract of the United States: 2011.*

55. National Center on Birth Defects and Developmental Delays, "Assisted Reproductive Technology and Major Structural Birth Defects United States."

56. Golombok, "Parenting and Contemporary Reproductive Technologies."

57. Pam Belluck, "From Stem Cell Opponents, an Embryo Crusade, *New York Times,* June 2, 2005, A1.

58. Pam Belluck, "It's Not So Easy to Adopt an Embryo," *New York Times,* June 12, 2005, section 4, 5.

59. Belluck, "From Stem Cell Opponents."

60. Spar, *The Baby Business.*

61. Lori B. Andrews, "Designer Babies," *Reader's Digest,* July 2001, 72.

62. Spar, *The Baby Business.*

63. Jacqueline Mroz, "From One Sperm Donor, 150 Children," *New York Times,* September 6, 2011, D1.

64. Spar, *The Baby Business.*

65. Cynthia Lightfoot, Michael Cole, and Sheila R. Cole, *The Development of Children,* 6th ed. (New York: Worth, 2009).

66. Ibid.

67. Edward Zigler et al., *The First Three Years and Beyond* (New Haven, CT: Yale University Press, 2002).

68. Ibid.

69. Annie Murphy Paul, *Origins: How the Nine Months before Birth Shape the Rest of Our Lives* (New York: Free Press, 2010).

70. Shirley S. Wang, "Programming a Fetus for a Healthier Life," *Wall Street Journal,* July 5, 2011, D3.

71. Paul, *Origins.*

72. Ibid.

73. Elysia P. Davis, and Curt A. Sandman, "The Timing of Prenatal Exposure to Maternal Cortisol and Psychosocial Stress Is Associated with Human Infant Cognitive Development," *Child Development 81* (2010): 131–145.

74. Ibid.; Janet A. Di Pietro et al., "Prenatal Antecedents of Newborn Neurological Maturation," *Child Development 81* (2010): 115–130.

75. Jeanette R. Ickovics et al., "Group Prenatal Care and Perinatal Outcomes," *Obstetrics and Gynecology 110* (2007): 330–339.

76. Claire Westdahl et al., "Social Support and Social Conflict as Predictors of Prenatal Depression," *Obstetrics and Gynecology 110* (2007): 134–140.

77. Sue Shellenbarger, "Why Worries About Baby Are Bad for Baby," The *Wall Street Journal,* March 31, 2010, D1.

78. Ellen Galinsky, *Between Generations: The Six Stages of Parenthood* (New York: Times Books, 1981).

79. Paul, *Origins.*

80. Melissa Curran et al., "Representations of Early Family Relationships Predict Marital Maintenance during Transition to Parenthood," *Journal of Family Psychology 19* (2005): 189–197.

81. Ross D. Parke and Barbara J. Tinsley, "Family Interaction in Infancy," in *Handbook of Infant Development,* 2nd ed., ed. Joy Doniger Osofsky (New York: Wiley, 1987), 579–641.

82. Jay Belsky and John Kelly, *The Transition to Parenthood* (New York: Delacorte Press, 1994).

83. Galinsky, *Between Generations.*

84. Myra Leifer, "Psychological Changes Accompanying Pregnancy and Motherhood," *Genetic Psychology Monographs 95* (1977): 55–96.

85. James McHale. *Charting the Bumpy Road of Coparenthood: Understanding the Challenges of Family Life,* (Washington, DC: Zero to Three, 2007).

86. Susan Goldberg and Barbara DiVitto, "Parenting Children Born Preterm," in *Handbook of Parenting,* 2nd ed., ed. Marc H. Bornstein, vol. 1: *Children and Parenting* (Mawa, NJ: Erlbaum, 2002), 329–354.

87. Heideliese Als et al.,"Early Exposure Alters Brain Function and Structure," *Pediatrics 113* (2004): 846–857.

88. Martina Jotzo and Christian F. Poets, "Helping Parents Cope with the Trauma of Premature Birth: An Evaluation of a Trauma-Preventive Psychological Intervention," *Pediatrics* 115 (2005): 915–919.

89. Ruth Feldman et al., "Testing a Family Intervention Hypothesis: The Contribution of Mother-Infant Skin-to-Skin Contact (Kangaroo Care) to Family Interaction, Proximity, and Touch," *Journal of Family Psychology* 17 (2003): 94–107.

90. Sari Goldstein Ferber and Imad R. Makhoul, "The Effect of Skin-to-Skin Contact (Kangaroo Care) Shortly after Birth on the Neurobehavioral Responses of the Term Newborn: A Randomized, Controlled Trial," *Pediatrics* 113 (2004): 858–865.

91. Carolyn Pape Cowan and Philip A. Cowan, *When Partners Become Parents* (New York: Basic Books, 1992).

92. Philip A. Cowan, Carolyn Pape Cowan, and Virginia Knox, "Marriage and Fatherhood Programs," *Future of Children* 20 (2010): 205–230.

93. Philip A. Cowan and Carolyn Pape Cowan, "After the Baby: Keeping the Couple Relationship Alive," *NCFR (National Council on Family Relations) Report,* Summer, 2011, F1–F2, F5.

94. Aly Frei and Pamela Jordan, "A New 'Vaccine' for Expectant Parents?" *NCFR (National Council on Family Relations) Report,* Summer, 2011, F12–F13.

95. Galinsky, *Between Generations.*

96. Kathryn E. Barnard, Colleen E. Moriset, and Susan Spieker, "Preventive Interventions: Enhancing Parent-Infant Relationships," in *Handbook of Infant Mental Health,* ed. Charles H. Zeanah, Jr. (New York: Guilford, 1993), 386–401.

97. Amy Wolfson, Patricia Lacks, and Andrew Futterman, "Effects of Parent Training on Infant Sleeping Patterns, Parents' Stress, and Perceived Parental Competence," *Journal of Consulting and Clinical Psychology* 60 (1992): 41–48.

CHAPTER FIVE

1. David G. Myers. "Close Relationships and Quality of Life," in *Well-Being: The Foundations of Hedonic Psychology,* eds. Daniel Kahneman, Ed Diener, and Norbert Schwartz (New York: Russell Sage Foundation, 1999), 374–391.

2. Linda C. Mayes et al., "Social Relationships as Primary Rewards: The Neurobiology of Attachment," in *Handbook of Developmental Social Neuroscience,* eds. Michelle De Haan and Megan R. Gunnar (New York: Guilford, 2009), 342–377.

3. Ashley Montague, *Touching,* 2nd ed. (New York: Harper & Row, 1978).

4. Tiffany Field, "Infant Massage Therapy," in *Handbook of Infant Mental Health,* 2nd ed., ed. Charles H. Zeanah, Jr. (New York: Guilford, 2000), 494–500.

5. Urs A. Hunziker and Ronald G. Barr, "Increased Carrying Reduces Crying: A Randomized Controlled Trial," *Pediatrics* 77 (1986): 641–647.

6. Field, "Infant Massage Therapy."

7. Tiffany Field, "The Effects of Mother's Physical and Emotional Availability on Emotion Regulation," in *Development of Emotion Regulation: Biological and Behavioral Considerations,* ed. Nathan A. Fox, *Monographs of the Society for Research in Child Development 59,* serial no. 240 (1994): 208–227.

8. James A. Coan, Hillary S. Schaefer, and Richard J. Davidson, "Lending a Hand: Social Regulation of the Neural Response to Threat," *Psychological Science* 17 (2006): 1032–1039.

9. Barbara L. Frederickson, "The Role of Positive Emotions in Positive Psychology: The Broaden-and-Build Theory of Positive Emotions," *American Psychologist* 56 (2001): 218–226.

10. Ann S. Masten, "Ordinary Magic: Resilience Processes in Development," *American Psychologist* 56 (2001): 227–238.

11. Charles C. Carlson and John C. Masters, "Inoculation by Emotion: Effects of Positive Emotional States on Children's Reactions to Social Comparison," *Developmental Psychology* 22 (1986): 760–765.

12. Dorothy C. Briggs, *Your Child's Self-Esteem* (Garden City, NY: Doubleday, 1970), 61–62.

13. Haim G. Ginott, *Between Parent and Child* (New York: Avon, 1969).

14. John M. Gottman, Lynn Fainsilber Katz, and Carole Hooven, "Parental Meta-Emotion Philosophy and the Emotional Life of Families: Theoretical Models and Preliminary Data," *Journal of Family Psychology* 10 (1996): 243–268.

15. John Gottman with Joan DeClaire, *The Heart of Parenting: Raising an Emotionally Intelligent Child* (New York: Simon & Schuster, 1997).

16. Ibid.

17. Beverly J. Wilson and John M. Gottman, "Marital Conflict, Repair, and Parenting," in *Handbook of Parenting*, 2nd ed., ed. Marc H. Bornstein, vol. 4: *Social Conditions and Applied Parenting* (Mawa NJ: Erlbaum, 2002) 227–258.

18. Thomas Gordon, *P.E.T. in Action* (New York: Bantam Books, 1978); Thomas Gordon, *Teaching Children Self-Discipline* (New York: Random House, 1989).

19. Gordon with Sands, *P.E.T. in Action*, 47.

20. Judy Dunn, Jane Brown, and Lynn Beardsall, "Family Talk about Feeling States and Children's Later Understanding of Others' Emotions," *Developmental Psychology* 27 (1991): 448–455.

21. Adele Faber and Elaine Mazlish, *Liberated Parents/Liberated Children* (New York: Avon Books, 1975).

22. John A. Clausen, Paul H. Mussen, and Joseph Kuypers, "Involvement, Warmth, and Parent-Child Resemblance in Three Generations," in *Present and Past in Middle Life*, ed. Dorothy H. Eichorn et al. (New York: Academic Press, 1981), 299–319.

23. Reed W. Larson and David M. Almeida, "Emotional Transmission in the Daily Lives of Families: A New Paradigm for Studying Family Process," *Journal of Marriage and the Family* 61 (1999): 5–20.

24. Denise E. Kennedy and Laurie Kramer, "Improving Emotion Regulation and Sibling Relationship Quality: The More Fun with Sisters and Brothers Program," *Family Relations* 57 (2008): 567–578.

25. Engel, *The Stories Children Tell* (New York: Freeman, 1999), 189.

26. Ibid.

27. Barbara H. Fiese and Kathleen A. T. Marjinsky, "Dinnertime Stories: Connecting Family Practices with Relationship Beliefs and Child Adjustment," in *The Stories That Families Tell: Narrative Coherence, Narrative Interaction and Relationship Beliefs*, eds. Barbara H. Fiese et al. *Monographs of the Society for Research in Child Development* 64 (2) serial no. 257 (1999): 52–68.

28. Arnold J. Sameroff and Barbara H. Fiese, "Narrative Connections in the Family Context: Summary and Conclusions," in *The Stories That Families Tell*," eds. Fiese et al., 122.

29. Robert H. Bradley and Robert F. Corwyn, "Productive Activity and the Prevention of Behavior Problems," *Developmental Psychology* 41 (2005): 89–98.

30. Richard Louv, *The Last Child in the Woods: Saving Our Children from Nature-Deficit Disorder*, rev. ed. (Chapel Hill, NC: Algonquin Books of Chapel Hill, 2008).

31. Benedict Carey, "Families? Every Hug and Fuss, Taped, Analyzed, and Archived," *New York Times*, May 23, 2010, A1.

32. Louv, *The Last Child in the Woods*.

33. Thomas E. Gordon, *PET: Parent Effectiveness Training* (New York: New American Library, 1975).

34. John H. Grych, "Marital Relationships and Parenting," in *Handbook of Parenting*, 2nd ed., ed. Bornstein, vol. 4 203–225.

35. Marcie C. Goeke-Morey, E. Mark Cummings, and Lauren M. Papp, "Children and Marital Conflict Resolution: Implications for Emotional Security and Adjustment," *Journal of Family Psychology* 21 (2007): 744–753.

36. E. Mark Cummings et al., "Interparental Discord and Child Adjustment: Prospective Investigations of Emotional Security as an Explanatory Mechanism," *Child Development* 77 (2006): 132–152.

37. Patrick T. Davies et al., "Children's Insecure Representations of the Interpersonal Relationship and Their School Adjustment: The Mediating Role of Attention Difficulties," *Child Development* 79 (2008): 1570–1582.

38. Tina D. Du Rocher Schudlich et al., "Observed Infant Reactions during Live Interparental Conflict," *Journal of Marriage and Family* 73 (2011): 221–235.

39. Sarah J. Schoppe-Sullivan, Alice C. Schermerhorn, and E. Mark Cummings, "Marital Conflict and Children's Adjustment: Evaluation of the Parenting Process Model," *Journal of Marriage and Family* 69 (2007): 1118–1134.

40. Thao Ha et al., "Marital Quality, Parenting, and Adolescent Internalizing Problems: A Three-Wave Longitudinal Study," *Journal of Family Psychology* 23 (2009): 263–267.

41. E. Mark Cummings et al., "Evaluating a Brief Prevention Program for Improving Marital Conflict in Community Families," *Journal of Family Psychology* 22 (2008): 193–202.

42. Rand D. Conger and Katherine J. Conger, "Resilience in Midwestern Families: Selected Findings from the First Decade of a Prospective Longitudinal Study," *Journal of Marriage and Family 64* (2002): 361–373.

43. Ibid.

44. Suzanne Bartholomae and Jonathan Fox, "Economic Stress and Families," in *Families & Change: Coping with Stressful Events and Transitions*, 4th ed., eds. Sharon J. Price, Christine A. Price, and Patrick C. McKenry (Los Angeles: Sage, 2010), 185–209.

45. Tytti Solantaus, Jenni Leinonen, and Raija-Leena Punamaki, "Children's Mental Health in Times of Economic Recession: Replication and Extension of the Family Economic Stress Model in Finland," *Developmental Psychology 40* (2004): 412–429.

46. Hee-Kyung Kwon et al., "Marital Relationships Following the Korean Economic Crisis: Applying the Family Stress Model," *Journal of Marriage and Family 65* (2003): 316–325.

47. Isik A. Aytac and Bruce H. Rankin, "Economic Crisis and Marital Problems in Turkey: Testing the Family Stress Model," *Journal of Marriage and Family 71* (2009): 756–767.

48. SabrinaTavernise, "Recession Study Finds Hispanics Hit the Hardest," *New York Times,* July 26, 2011, A1.

49. Michael Luo and Megan Thee-Brennan, "Emotional Havoc Wreaked on Workers and Family," *New York Times,* December 15, 2009, A1.

50. APA Stress Survey: Children Are More Stressed than Parents Realize," www.apapracticecentral.org/update/2009/11-23/stress-survey.aspx. Downloaded July 19, 2011.

51. Christopher Munsey, "The Kids Aren't All Right," *Monitor on Psychology,* January 2010, 23–25.

52. Michael Winerip, "Teacher, My Dad Lost His Job. Do we Have to Move?" *New York Times,* January 31, 2011, A1.

53. Suzanne M. Bianchi, John P. Robinson, and Melissa A. Milkie, "*Changing Rhythms of American Family Life* (New York: Russell Sage, 2006).

54. Carey, "Families?"

55. Lynn Craig and Killian Mullan, "Parenthood, Gender, and Work-Family Time in the United States, Australia, Italy, France, and Denmark," *Journal of Marriage and Family 72* (2010): 1344–1361.

56. John P. Robinson and Geoffrey Godbey, *Time for Life* (University Park: Pennsylvania State University Press, 1997).

57. Keith Crnic and Christine Low, "Everyday Stresses and Parenting," in *Handbook of Parenting,* 2nd ed., ed. Marc H. Bornstein, vol. 5: *Practical Issues in Parenting* (Mahwah, NJ: Erlbaum, 2002), 243–267; Theodore Dix, "The Affective Organization of Parenting: Adaptive and Maladaptive Processes," *Psychological Bulletin 110* (1991): 3–25.

58. Ernest N. Jouriles, Christopher M. Murphy, and K. Daniel O'Leary, "Effects of Maternal Mood on Mother-Son Interaction Patterns," *Journal of Abnormal Child Psychology 17* (1989): 513–525.

59. John U. Zussman, "Situational Determinants of Parenting Behavior: Effects of Competing Cognitive Activity," *Child Development 51* (1980): 772–780.

60. Crnic and Low, "Everyday Stresses and Parenting."

61. Crnic and Low, "Everyday Stresses and Parenting"; Jay Belsky, Keith Crnic, and Sharon Woodworth, "Personality and Parenting: Exploring the Mediating Role of Transient Mood and Daily Hassles," *Journal of Personality 63* (1995): 905–929.

62. W. Edward Craigshead et al., "Psychosocial Treatments for Major Depressive Disorder," in *A Guide to Treatments That Work,* 3rd ed., eds. Peter E. Nathan and Jack M. Gorman (New York: Oxford University Press, 2007), 289–307.

63. Sheryl H. Goodman and Sarah G. Brand, "Infants of Depressed Mothers: Vulnerabilities, Risk Factors, and Protective Factors for the Later Development of Psychopathology," in *Handbook of Infant Mental Health),* 3rd ed., ed. Charles H. Zeanah, Jr. (New York: Guilford, 2009), 153–170.

64. Paul Ramchandani et al., "Paternal Depression in the Postnatal Period and Child Development: A Prospective Population Study," *Lancet 365* (2005): 2201–2205.

65. R. Neal Davis et al., "Fathers' Depression Related to Positive and Negative Parenting Behaviors with 1-Year-Old Children," *Pediatrics 127* (2011): 612–618.

66. Craigshead et al., "Psychosocial Treatments for Major Depressive Disorder."

67. Goodman and Brand, "Infants of Depressed Mothers."

68. Ibid.

69. Misaka N. Natsuaki et al., "Genetic Liability, Environment, and the Development of Fussiness in Toddlers: The Roles of Maternal Depression and Parental Responsiveness," *Developmental Psychology* 46 (2010): 1147–1158.

70. Sharon E. Ashman, Geraldine Dawson, and Heracles Panagiotides, "Trajectories of Maternal Depression over 7 Years: Relations with Child Psychophysiology and Behavior and Role of Contextual Risks," *Development and Psychopathology* 20 (2008): 55–77.

71. Katherine H. Shelton and Gordon T. Harold, "Interpersonal Conflict, Negative Parenting, and Children's Adjustment: Bridging Links Between Parents' Depression and Children's Psychological Distress," *Journal of Family Psychology* 22 (2008): 712–724.

72. Irene J. Kim Park et al., "Convergence among Multiple Methods of Measuring Positivity and Negativity in the Family Environment: Relation to Depression in Mothers and Their Children," *Journal of Family Psychology* 22 (2008): 123–134.

73. Myrna M. Weissman et al., "Remissions in Maternal Depression and Child Psychopathology: A Star*D-Child Report," *Journal of American Medical Association 295* (2006): 1389–1398.

74. Ashman, Dawson, and Panagiotides, "Trajectories of Maternal Depression over 7 Years."

75. Ibid.

76. William R. Beardslee et al., "A Family-Based Approach to the Prevention of Depressive Symptoms in Children at Risk: Evidence of Parental and Child Change," *Pediatrics 112* (2003): 119–131.

77. Christine Timko, Ruth C. Cronkite, and Rudolf H. Moos, "Do Parental Stressors and Avoidance Coping Mediate between Parental Depression and Offspring Depression? A 23-Year Follow-up," *Family Relations 59* (2010): 121–135.

78. Jessica M. Fear et al., "Parental Depression and Interparental Conflict: Children

and Adolescent Self-Blame and Coping Responses," *Journal of Family Psychology* 23 (2009): 762–766.

79. Karin T. M. van Doesum et al., "A Randomized Controlled Trial of a Home-Visiting Intervention Aimed at Preventing Relationship Problems in Depressed Mothers and Their Infants," *Child Development 79* (2008): 547–561.

80. Beardslee et al., "A Family-Based Approach to the Prevention of Depressive Symptoms in Children."

81 William R. Beardslee et al., "Long-term Effects from a Randomized Trial of Two Public Health Interventions for Parental Depression," *Journal of Family Psychology 21* (2007): 703-713.

82. Timko, Cronkite, and Moos, "Do Parental Stressors and Avoidance Coping Mediate between Parental Depression and Offspring Depression?"

83. Charles P. O'Brien and James McKay, "Psychopharmacological Treatments for Substance Use Disorder," in *A Guide to Treatments That Work,* 3rd ed., eds. Nathan and Gorman, 145–177.

84. Neil W. Boris, "Parental Substance Abuse," in *Handbook of Infant Mental Health,* ed. Zeanah, 171–196.

85. John W. Finney, Paula L. Wilbourne, and Rudolf H. Moos, "Psychosocial Treatments for Substance Uses Disorders," in *A Guide to Treatments That Work,* 3rd ed., eds. Nathan and Gorman, 179–202.

86. Boris, "Parental Substance Abuse."

87. Rina Das Eiden, Felipa Chavez, and Kenneth E, Leonard, "Parent-Infant Interactions among Families with Alcoholic Fathers," *Development and Psychopathology 11* (1999): 745–762.

88. Boris, "Parental Substance Abuse."

89. Linda C. Mayes and Sean D. Truman, "Substance Abuse and Parenting," in *Handbook of Parenting,* 2nd ed., ed. Bornstein, vol. 4, 329–359.

90. Andrea M. Hussong et al., "Characterizing The Life Stressors of Children of Alcoholic Parents," *Journal of Family Psychology 22* (2008): 819–832.

91. Carol Pape Cowan and Philip A. Cowan, *When Partners Become Parents* (New York: Basic Books, 1992), 142.

92. Ellen P. Edwards, Rina Das Eiden, and Kenneth E. Leonard, "Behavior Problems in

18- to 36-Month-Old Children of Alcoholic Fathers: Secure Mother Infant Attachment as a Protective Factor," *Development and Psychopathology* 18 (2006): 395–407

93. Mona El-Sheikh and Joseph A. Buckhalt, "Parental Problem Drinking and Children's Adjustment: Attachment and Family Functioning as Moderators of Risk," *Journal of Family Psychology* 17 (2003): 510–520.

94. Boris, "Parental Substance Abuse."

95. Nancy Suchman et al., "Parenting Interventions for Drug-Dependent Mothers and Their Young Children: The Case for an Attachment-Based Approach," *Family Relations* 55 (2006): 211–226.

96. Nancy Suchman, Cindy DeCoste, and Linda Mayes, "The Mothers and Toddlers Program: An Attachment-Based Intervention for Mothers in Substance Abuse Treatment," in *Handbook of Infant Mental Health,* 3rd ed., ed. Zeanah, 485–499.

97. Melissa A. Barnett et al., "Grandmother Involvement as a Protective Factor for Early Childhood Social Adjustment," *Journal of Family Psychology* 24 (2010): 635–645.

98. Jane L. Pearson et al., "Black Grandmothers in Multigenerational Households: Diversity in Family Structures on Parenting in the Woodlawn Community," *Child Development 61* (1990): 434–442.

99. Peter K. Smith and Linda M. Drew, "Grandparenthood," in *Handbook of Parenting,* 2nd ed., ed. Marc H. Bornstein, vol. 3: *Being and Becoming a Parent* (Mahwah, NJ: Erlbaum, 2002), 141–172.

100. Ibid., p. 147.

101. Ibid.

102. Ibid.

103. Natalie Angier, "Weighing the Grandma Factor," *New York Times,* November 5 2002, D1.

104. Smith and Drew, "Grandparenthood."

105. Peter C. Scales, Peter L. Benson, and Eugene C. Roehlkepartain, *Grading Grownups: American Adults Report on Their Real Relationships with Kids* (Minneapolis: Lutheran Brotherhood and Search Institute, 2001).

106. Jay D. Schvaneveldt, Marguerite Fryer, and Renee Ostler, "Concepts of 'Badness' and 'Goodness' of Parents as Perceived by Nursery School Children," *Family Coordinator 19* (1970): 98–103.

107. John R. Weisz, "Autonomy, Control, and Other Reasons, Why 'Mom Is the Greatest': A Content Analysis of Children's Mother's Day Letters," *Child Development 51* (1980): 801–807.

CHAPTER SIX

1. Steve Farkas et al., *A Lot Easier Said Than Done: Parents Talk about Raising Children in Today's America* (New York: Public Agenda, 2002).

2. Kees Keizer, Siegwart Lindenberg, and Linda Steg, "The Spreading of Disorder," *Science 322* (2008): 1681–1685.

3. Joan E. Grusec and Maayan Davidov, "Integrating Different Perspectives on Socialization Theory and Research," *Child Development 81* (2010): 687–709.

4. George W. Holden, "Child Rearing and Developmental Trajectories; Positive Pathways, Off-Ramps, and Dynamic Processes," *Child Development Perspectives 4* (2010): 197–204.

5. Lynn Okagaki and Gary E. Bingham, "Parents' Social Cognitions and Their Parenting Behaviors," in *Parenting: An Ecological Perspective,* 2nd ed., eds. Tom Luster and Lynn Okagaki (Mahwah, NJ: Erlbaum, 2005), 3–33.

6. Melissa A. Barnett et al., "Independent and Interactive Contributions of Parenting Behaviors and Beliefs in the Prediction of Early Childhood Behavior Problems," *Parenting: Science and Practice 10* (2010): 43–59.

7. Okagaki and Bingham, "Parents' Social Cognitions."

8. Barnett et al., "Independent and Interactive Contributions of Parenting Behaviors."

9. Bruce J. Ellis and W. Thomas Boyce, "Differential Susceptibility to the Environment: Toward an Understanding of Sensitivity to Developmental Experiences and Context," *Development and Psychopathology 23* (2011): 1–5.

10. Ross A. Thompson, Sara Meyer, Meredith McGinley, "Understanding Values in Relationships: The Development of Conscience," in *Handbook of Moral Development,* eds. Melanie Killen and Judith Smetana (Mahwah, NJ: Erlbaum, 2006), 267–297.

11. Gerald R. Patterson and Philip A. Fisher, "Recent Developments in Our Understanding of Parenting: Bidirectional Effects, Causal Models, and the Search for Parsimony," in *Handbook of Parenting,* 2nd ed., ed. Marc H. Bornstein, vol. 5: *Practical Issues in Parenting* (Mahwah, NJ: Erlbaum, 2002), 59–88.

12. Thomas S. Weisner, "Well-Being, Chaos, and Culture: Sustaining a Meaningful Daily Routine," in *Chaos and Its Influence on Children's Development: An Ecological Perspectives,* eds. Gary W. Evans and Theodore D. Wachs (Washington, DC: American Psychological Association, 2010), 211–224.

13. Barbara Fiese et al., "A Review of Fifty Years of Research on Naturally Occurring Family Routines and Rituals: Cause for Celebration," *Journal of Family Psychology 16* (2002): 381–390.

14. Barbara Rogoff, "Cognition as Collaborative Process," in *Handbook of Child Psychology,* 5th ed., ed. William Damon, vol. 2: *Cognition, Perception, and Language,* eds. Deanna Kuhn and Robert S. Siegler (New York: Wiley, 1998), 679–744.

15. Ibid.

16. Fiese et al., "A Review of Fifty Years of Research."

17. Robert Serpell et al., "Intimate Culture of Families in the Early Socialization of Literacy," *Journal of Family Psychology 16* (2002): 391–405.

18. Rudolf Dreikurs with Vicki Soltz, *Children: The Challenge* (New York: Hawthorn, 1964).

19. Ibid., p. 39.

20. Ibid.

21. Femmie Juffer, Marian J. Bakermans-Kranenburg, and Marinus van IJzendoorn, "Methods of Video-Feedback Programs to Promote Positive Parenting Alone with Sensitive Discipline and with Representational Attachment Discussion," in *Positive Parenting: An Attachment-Based Intervention,* ed. Femmie Juffer, Marian J. Bakermans-Kranenburg, and Marinus van IJzendoorn (New York: Erlbaum, 2008), 11–23.

22. U.S. Census Bureau, *Statistical Abstract of the United States: 2011,* 130th ed. (Washington, DC: U.S. Government Printing Office, 2010).

23. Elizabeth L. Pollard and Mark L. Rosenberg, "The Strengths-Based Approach to Child Well-Being: Let's Begin with the End in Mind," in *Well-Being: Positive Development across the Life Course,* eds. Marc H. Bornstein et al. (Mahwah, NJ: Erlbaum, 2003), 13–21.

24. Farkas et al., "A Lot Easier Said Than Done."

25. Jerica M. Berge et al., "Are Parents of Young Children Practicing Healthy Nutrition and Physical Activity Behaviors? *Pediatrics 127* (2011): 881–887.

26. Hillary L. Burdette and Robert C. Whitaker, "Resurrecting Free Play in Young Children: Looking Beyond Fitness and Fatness to Attention, Affiliation, and Affect," *Archives of Pediatric and Adolescent Medicine 159* (2005): 46–50.

27. David A. Sleet and James A. Mercy, "Promotion of Safety, Security, and Well-Being," in *Well-Being,* ed. Bornstein, 81–97.

28. Wanda M. Hunter et al., "Injury Prevention Advice in Top-Selling Parenting Books," *Pediatrics 116* (2005): 1080–1088.

29. Linda C. Mayes and Sean D. Truman, "Substance Abuse and Parenting," in *Handbook of Parenting,* 2nd ed. ed. Marc H. Bornstein, vol. 4: *Special Conditions and Applied Parenting* (Mahwah, NJ: Erlbaum, 2002), 329–359.

30. Caroline H. Leavitt, Thomas F. Tonniges, and Martha F. Rogers, "Good Nutrition: The Imperative for Positive Development," in *Well-Being,* ed. Bornstein, 35–49.

31. Anthea M. Magarey et al., "A Parent-Led Family-Focused Treatment Program for Overweight Children Aged 5 to 9 Years: The PEACH RCT," *Pediatrics 127* (2011): 214–222.

32. Kristine A. Madsen, Ashley E. Weedn, and Patricia B. Crawford, "Disparities in Peaks, Plateaus, and Declines in Prevalence of High BMI among Adolescents," *Pediatrics 126* (2010): 434–442.

33. Julie C. Lumeng, Valerie P. Castle, and Carey N. Lumeng, "The Role of Pediatricians in the Coordinated National Effort to Address Childhood Obesity," *Pediatrics 126* (2010): 574–575.

34. Magarey et al., "A Parent-Led Family-Focused Treatment Program for Overweight Children."

35. Jeanette M. Connor, "Physical Activity and Well-Being," in *Well-Being,* ed. Bornstein, 65–79.

36. Charles H. Hillman et al., "The Effect of Acute Treadmill Walking on Cognitive Control and Academic Achievement in Preadolescent Children," *Neuroscience 159* (2009): 1044–1054.

37. Public Broadcasting Station Program, "Need to Know," February 11, 2011.

38. Connor, "Physical Activity and Well-Being,"

39. Angie L. Cradock et al., "Neighborhood Social Cohesion and Youth Participation in Physical Activity in Chicago," *Social Science & Medicine 68* (2009): 427–435.

40. Rachel Ruiz et al., "The Relationship between Hispanic Parents and Their Preschool-Aged Children's Physical Activity," *Pediatrics 127* (2011): 888–895.

41. Beth Azar, "Wild Findings in Animal Sleep," *Monitor on Psychology,* January 2006, 54–55.

42. James C. Spilsbury et al., "Sleep Behavior in an Urban U.S. Sample of School-age Children," *Archives of Pediatric and Adolescent Medicine 158* (2004): 988–994.

43. Ronald E. Dahl and Mona El-Sheikh, "Considering Sleep in a Family Context: Introduction to the Special Issue," *Journal of Family Psychology 21* (2007): 1–3.

44. Annie Bernier et al., "Relations between Physiological and Cognitive Regulatory Systems: Infant Sleep Regulation and Subsequent Executive Functioning," *Child Development 81* (2010): 1739–1752.

45. Avi Sadeh, Reut Gruber, and Amiram Raviv, "The Effects of Sleep Restriction and Extension On School-Age Children: What a Difference an Hour Makes," *Child Development 74* (2003): 444–455.

46. Joseph A. Buckhalt, Mona El-Sheikh, and Peggy Keller, "Children's Sleep and Cognitive Functioning: Race and Socioeconomic Status as Moderators of Effects," *Child Development 78* (2007): 213–231.

47. Marc Weissbluth, *Healthy Sleep Habits, Happy Child* (New York: Fawcett, 1999).

48. Alice M. Gregory and Thomas G. O'Connor, "Sleep Problems in Childhood: A Longitudinal Study of Developmental Change and Association with Behavioral Problems," *Journal of the American Academy of Child and Adolescent Psychiatry 41* (2000): 964–971.

49. Emma K. Adam, Emily K. Snell, and Patricia Pendry, "Sleep Timing and Quantity in Ecological and Family Context: A Nationally Representative Time-Diary Study," *Journal of Family Psychology 21* (2007): 4–19.

50. Mona El-Sheikh et al., "Child Emotional Insecurity and Academic Achievement: The Role of Sleep Disruptions," *Journal of Family Psychology 21* (2007): 2.

51. Jeanne Brooks-Gunn and Elizabeth Hirschhorn Donahue, "Introducing the Issue," *Future of Children 18* (2008): 3–10.

52. Victoria J. Rideout, Ulla G. Foehr, and Donald F. Roberts, "Generation M2: Media in the Lives of 8- to 18-Year-Olds," Kaiser Family Foundation Report Number 8010, January 2010, www.kff.org.

53. Victoria Rideout and Elizabeth Hamel, "The Media Family: Electronic Media in the Lives of Infants, Toddlers, Preschoolers, and Their Parents," Kaiser Family Foundation, Report No. 7500, May, 2006, www.kff.org

54. Rideout, Foehr, and Roberts, "Generation M2."

55. Ibid.

56. Rideout and Hamel, "The Media Family."

57. Ibid.

58. American Academy of Pediatrics, "Children, Adolescents, and Television," *Pediatrics 107* (2001): 423–426

59. Rideout, Foehr, and Roberts, "Generation M2."

60. Ibid.

61. Ibid.

62. Ibid.

63. Patricia M. Greenfield, "Technology and Informal Education: What Is Taught, What Is Learned," *Science 323* (2009): 69–71.

64. Matt Richtel, "Hooked on Gadgets and Paying a Mental Price," *New York Times,* June 7, 2010, A1.

65. Gwenn Schurgin O'Keefe and Kathleen Clark-Pearson, "Clinical Report—The Impact of Social Media on Children, Adolescents, and Families," *Pediatrics 127* (2011): 800–804.

66. Ibid.

67. Jill Tucker, "Teens Show, Tell Too Much Online," *San Francisco Chronicle,* August 10, 2009, A1.

68. Jan Hoffman, "A Girl's Nude Photo and Altered Lives," *New York Times,* March 27, 2011, A1.

69. Ibid., p. A19.

70. Tucker, "Teens Show, Tell Too Much Online."

71. Rideout and Hamel, "The Media Family."

72. U.S. Census Bureau, "Statistical Abstract of the United States: 2011."

73. Richtel, "Hooked on Gadgets and Paying a Mental Price."

74. Elizabeth Bernstein, "Your BlackBerry or Your Wife," *Wall Street Journal,* January 11, 2011, D1.

75. Brooks-Gunn and Hirschhorn Donahue, "Introducing the Issue."

76. Ibid.

77. Thomas N. Robinson, "Reducing Children's Television Viewing to Prevent Obesity: A Randomized Controlled Trial," *Journal of the American Medical Association 282* (1999): 1561–1567; Thomas N. Robinson et al., "Effects of Reducing Children's Television and Video Game Use on Aggressive Behavior: A Randomized Controlled Trial," *Archives of Pediatric and Adolescent Medicine 155* (2001): 17–23.

78. Rideout, Foehr, and Roberts, "Generation M2."

79. American Academy of Pediatrics, "Children, Adolescents, and Television."

80. Rideout, Foehr, and Roberts, "Generation M2."

81. Rideout and Hamel, "The Media Family."

82. Rideout, Foehr, and Roberts, "Generation M2."

83. Tara Parker-Pope and Fidelity Barringer, "Panel Adds to Debate over Cancer Risk of Cell Phone Radiation," *New York Times,* June 1, 2011, A12.

84. Henry K. Lee, "Girl's Death Points Out Tragic Cost of Texting and Driving," *San Francisco Chronicle,* May 20, 2011, A1.

85. Victoria Rideout, Donald F. Roberts, and Ulla G. Foehr, "Generation M: Media in the Lives of 8- to 18-Year-Olds," Kaiser Family Foundation Report No. 7251, March 2005, www.kff.org.

86. Molly Baker, "My Grandparents R My BFF," *Wall Street Journal,* May 9, 2011, R4.

87. Robin Dunbar, "You've Got to Have (150) Friends," *New York Times,* December 26, 2010, Week in Review, 15.

88. Ibid.

89. Bernstein, "Your BlackBerry or Your Wife."

90. Elizabeth Bernstein, "Making 2011 the Year of Great Relationships," *Wall Street Journal,* December 28, 2010, D1.

91. Bob Egelko, "Violent Video Games Ban Doomed by Free Expression Concerns," *San Francisco Chronicle,* June 28, 2011, A1.

92. W. Douglas Evans, "Social Marketing Campaigns and Children's Media Use," *Future of Children 18* (2010): 181–203.

93. Greenfield, "Technology and Informal Education," 71.

94. Dreikurs with Soltz, *Children: The Challenge.*

95. Patricia Chamberlain and Gerald R. Patterson, "Discipline and Child Compliance in Parenting," in *Handbook of Parenting,* ed. Marc H. Bornstein, vol. 4: *Applied and Practical Parenting* (Mahwah, NJ: Erlbaum, 1995) 205–225.

96. Brigitte Vittrup, George W. Holden, and Jeanell Buck, "Attitudes Predict the Use of Physical Punishment: A Prospective Study of the Emergence of Disciplinary Practices," *Pediatrics 117* (2006): 2055–2064.

97. Elizabeth T. Gershoff et al., "Parent Discipline Practices in an International Sample: Associations with Child Behaviors and Moderation by Perceived Normativeness," *Child Development 81* (2010): 487–502.

98. Vittrup, Holden, and Buck, "Attitudes Predict the Use of Physical Punishment"; Michael Regalado et al., "Parents' Discipline of Young Children: Results from the National Survey of Early Childhood Health," *Pediatrics 113* (2004): 1952–1958.

99. Vonnie C. McLoyd and Julia Smith, "Physical Discipline and Behavior Problems in African American, European American, and Hispanic Children: Emotional Support as a Moderator," *Journal of Marriage and Family 64* (2002): 40–53.

100. Vittrup, Holden, and Buck, "Attitudes Predict the Use of Physical Punishment."

101. Zero to Three, *Parenting Infants and Toddlers Today: Research Findings* (Washington, DC: Hart Research Associates, 2009). Download at www.zerotothree.org/parentsurvey.

102. Vittrup, Holden, and Buck, "Attitudes Predict the Use of Physical Punishment."

103. Regalado et al., "Parents' Discipline of Young Children"; Matthew R. Sanders et al., "What Are the Parenting Experiences of Fathers? The Use of Household Survey Data to Inform Decisions about the Delivery of Evidence-Based Parenting Interventions," *Child Psychiatry and Human Development 41* (2011): 562–581; Catherine A. Taylor et al., "Use of Spanking for 3-Year-Old Children and Associated Intimate Partner Aggression or Violence," *Pediatrics 126* (2010): 415–424.

104. Regalado et al., "Parents' Discipline of Young Children"; Sanders et al., "What Are the Parenting Experiences of Fathers?"

105. McLoyd and Smith, "Physical Discipline and Behavior Problems"; Taylor et al., "Use of Spanking"; Lisa J. Berlin et al., "Correlates and Consequences of Spanking and Verbal Punishment for Low-Income White, African American, and Mexican American Toddlers," *Child Development 80* (2009): 1403–1420.

106. Berlin et al., "Correlates and Consequences of Spanking."

107. Gershoff et al., "Parent Discipline Practices."

108. Murray A. Straus and Michael Donnelly, "Theoretical Approaches to Corporal Punishment," in *Corporal Punishment of Children in Theoretical Perspective,* eds. Michael Donnelly and Murray A. Straus (New Haven, CT Yale University Press, 2005), 3.

109. Vittrup, Holden, and Buck, "Attitudes Predict the Use of Physical Punishment."

110. Berlin et al., "Correlates and Consequences of Spanking."

111. Eric P. Slade and Lawrence S. Wissow, "Spanking in Early Childhood and Later Behavior Problems: A Prospective Study of Infants and Young Toddlers," *Pediatrics 113* (2004): 1321–1330.

112. Diana Baumrind, Robert E. Larzelere, and Philip A Cowan, "Ordinary Physical Punishment: Is It Harmful? Comment on Gershoff (2002)," *Psychological Bulletin 128* (2002): 580–589; Jennifer E. Lansford et al., "Trajectories of Physical Discipline: Early Childhood Antecedents and Developmental Outcomes," *Child Development 80* (2009): 1385–1402.

113. George W. Holden, "Pespectives on the Effects of Corporal Punishment."

114. Jennifer E. Lansford et al., "Physical Discipline and Children's Adjustment: Culture Normativeness as a Moderator," *Child Development 76* (2005): 1234–1246.

115. Elizabeth Thompson Gershoff, "Corporal Punishment by Parents and Child Behaviors and Experiences: A Meta-Analysis and Theoretical Review," *Psychological Bulletin 128* (2002): 539–579; Lansford et al., "Trajectories of Physical Discipline;" Berlin et al., "Correlates and Consequences of Spanking."

116. Baumrind, Larzelare, and Cowan, "Ordinary Physical Punishment."

117. Gershoff, "Corporal Punishment."

118. Ibid.

119. McLoyd and Smith, "Physical Discipline and Behavior Problems;" Berlin et al., "Correlates and Consequences of Spanking."

120. Lansford et al., "Trajectories of Physical Discipline"; Taylor et al., "Use of Spanking."

121. Lansford et al., "Trajectories of Physical Discipline"; Berlin et al., "Correlates and Consequences of Spanking."

122. Sanders et al., "What Are the Parenting Experiences of Fathers?"; Taylor et al., "Use of Spanking."

123. Gershoff, "Corporal Punishment."

124. Ibid.

125. Berlin et al., "Correlates and Consequences of Spanking."

126. Slade and Wissow, "Spanking in Early Childhood."

127. Baumrind, Larzelare, and Cowan, "Ordinary Physical Punishment."

128. Gershoff et al., "Parent Discipline Practices."

129. McLoyd and Smith, "Physical Discipline and Behavior Problems."

130. Taylor et al., "Use of Spanking."

131. Lawrence S. Wissow, "What Clinicians Want to Know about Teaching Families New Disciplinary Tools," *Pediatrics 98* (1996): 1815–1828.

132. Matthew R. Sanders, "Triple P-Positive Parenting Program as a Public Health Approach to Strengthening Parenting," *Journal of Family Psychology 22* (2008): 506–517; Ireen deGraaf et al., "Effectiveness of the Triple P-Positive Parenting Program on Parenting: A Meta-Analysis," *Family Relations 57* (2008): 553–566.

133. Sanders, "Triple P-Positive Parenting Program," 507.

134. deGraaf et al., "Effectiveness of the Triple P-Positive Program."

135. Ronald J. Prinz, "Toward a Population-Based Paradigm for Parenting Intervention for Child Maltreatment and Promotion of Child Well-Being," in *Preventing Child Maltreatments: Community Approaches,* eds. Kenneth A. Dodge and Doriane Lambelet Coleman (New York: Guilford, 2009), 55–67.

136. Carolyn Pape Cowan and Phillip A. Cowan, *When Partners become Parents* (New York: Basic Books, 1992).

137. Carolyn Pape Cowan, Philip A. Cowan, and Gertrude Heming, "Two Variations of a Preventive Intervention for Couples: Effects on Parents and Children during the Transition to School," in *Family Context of Parenting in Children's Adaptation to Elementary School,* eds. Philip A. Cowan et al. (Mahwah, NJ: Erlbaum, 2005), 277–312.

138. Carolyn Pape Cowan, Philip A. Cowan and Jason Barry, "Couples' Groups for Parents of Preschoolers: Ten-Year Outcomes of a Randomized Trial," *Journal of Family Psychology* 25 (2011): 240–250.

139. Gene H. Brody et al., "The Strong African-American Families Program: Translating Research into Prevention Programming," *Child Development* 75 (2004): 900–917.

140. Camille Smith, Ruth Perou, and Catherine Lesesne, "Parent Education," *Handbook of Parenting,* 2nd ed., ed. Marc H. Bornstein, vol. 4: *Social Conditions and Applied Parenting,* 405.

141. Arnold Gesell and Frances L. Ilg, *The Child from Five to Ten* (New York: Harper & Row, 1946), 308.

142. Grace Hechinger, *How to Raise a Street-Smart Child* (New York: Ballantine, 1984).

143. Lenore Skenazy, *Free-Range Kids: How to Raise Safe, Self-Reliant Children (Without Going Nuts with Worry)* (San Francisco: Jossey-Bass, 2009).

CHAPTER SEVEN

1. Thomas Anders, Beth Goodlin-Jones, and Avi Sadeh, "Sleep Disorders," in *Handbook of Infant Mental Health,* 2nd ed., ed. Charles H. Zeanah, Jr. (New York: Guilford, 2000), 326–338.

2. Marc Weissbluth, *Crybabies* (New York: Arbor House, 1984).

3. Ibid.

4. Ross Thompson, "The Development of the Person: Social Understanding, Relationships, Conscience, Self," in *Handbook of Child Psychology,* 6th ed., eds. William Damon and Richard M. Lerner, vol. 3: *Social, Emotional and Personality Development,* ed. Nancy Eisenberg (Hoboken, NJ: Wiley, 2006), 24–98.

5. Ibid.

6. Tiffany Field, "The Effects of Mother's Physical and Emotional Availability on Emotion Regulation," in *Development of Emotion Regulation: Biological and Behavioral Considerations,* ed. Nathan A. Fox, *Monographs of the Society for Research in Child Development* 59, serial no. 240 (1994): 208–227.

7. Jayne Standley, "Music Therapy in the NICU: Promoting Growth and Development of Premature Infants," *Zero to Three* 23, no. 1 (2002): 23–30.

8. Thompson, "The Development of the Person."

9. Ruth Feldman, Charles W. Greenbaum, and Nurit Yirmiya, "Mother-Infant Affect as an Antecedent of the Emergence of Self-Control," *Developmental Psychology* 35 (1999): 223–231.

10. Thompson, "The Development of the Person."

11. Gabriela Markova and Maria Legerstee, "Contingency, Imitation, and Affect Sharing: Foundations of Infants' Social Awareness," *Developmental Psychology* 42 (2006): 132–141.

12. Robin Hornick, Nancy Eisenhoover, and Megan Gunnar, "The Effects of Maternal Positive, Neutral, and Negative Affect Communication on Infant Responses to New Toys," *Child Development* 58 (1987): 936–944.

13. James P. McHale, *Charting the Bumpy Road of Coparenthood: Understanding the Challenges of Family Life* (Washington, DC: Zero to Three, 2007).

14. Martina Jotzo and Christian F. Poets, "Helping Parents Cope with the Trauma of Premature Birth: An Evaluation of a Trauma-Preventive Psychological Intervention," *Pediatrics* 115 (2005): 915–919.

15. Susan Goldberg and Barbara DiVitto, "Parenting Children Born Preterm," in *Handbook of Parenting,* 2nd ed., ed. Marc H. Bornstein, vol. 1: *Children and Parenting* (Mahwah, NJ: Erlbaum, 2002), 329–354.

16. Carole Muller Nix and Francois Ansermet, "Prematurity Risk Factors and Protective Factors," in *Handbook of Infant Mental Health*, 3rd ed., ed. Charles H. Zeanah, Jr. (New York: Guilford, 2009), 180–196.

17. Karli Treyvaud et al., "Parenting Behavior Associated with the Early Neurobehavioral Development of Very Preterm Children," *Pediatrics 123* (2009): 555–561.

18. Mark T. Greenberg and Kenneth Crnic, "Longitudinal Predictors of Developmental Status and Social Interaction in Premature and Full-Term Infants at Age Two," *Child Development 59* (1988): 544–553.

19. Goldberg and DiVitto, "Parenting Children Born Preterm."

20. Marilyn Stern and Katherine A. Hildebrandt, "Prematurity and Stereotyping: Effects on Mother-Infant Interaction," *Child Development 57* (1986): 308–315.

21. Cynthia I. Zarling, Barton J. Hirsch, and Susan Landry, "Maternal Social Networks and Mother-Infant Interactions in Full-Term and Very Low Birthweight, Preterm Infants, *Child Development 59* (1988): 178–185.

22. Glenn Affleck et al., "Effects of Formal Support on Mothers' Adaptation to the Hospital-to-Home Transition of High-Risk Infants," *Child Development 60* (1989): 488–501.

23. Thompson, "The Development of the Person."

24. Susan Crockenberg and Esther Leerkes, "Infant Social and Emotional Development in Family Context," in *Handbook of Infant Mental Health,* 2nd ed., ed. Charles H. Zeanah, Jr., 60–90.

25. Herbert Ginsburg and Sylvia Opper, *Piaget's Theory of Intellectual Development* (Englewood Cliffs, NJ: Prentice-Hall, 1969; Jean Piaget and Barbel Inhelder, *The Psychology of the Child* (New York: Basic Books, 1969).

26. Ellen Galinsky, *Mind in the Making: The Seven Essential Life Skills Every Child Needs* (New York: HarperCollins, 2010).

27. Rachel Wu et al., "Infants Learn About Objects from Statistics and People," *Developmental Psychology 49* (2011): 1220–1229.

28. Paul L. Harris, "Social Cognition," in *Handbook of Child Psychology,* 6th ed., eds. William Damon and Richard M. Lerner,

vol. 2: *Cognition, Perception, and Language,* eds. Deanna Kuhn and Robert S. Siegler (Hoboken, NJ: Wiley, 2006), 811–858.

29. Alison Gopnik, *The Philosophical Baby: What Children's Minds Tell Us about Truth, Love, and the Meaning of Life* (New York: Farrar, Straus, and Giroux, 2009).

30. James V. Wertsch and Peeter Tulviste, "L. S. Vygotsky and Contemporary Developmental Psychology," *Developmental Psychology 28* (1992): 548–557.

31. Lois Bloom, "Language Acquisition in Its Developmental Context," in *Handbook of Child Psychology,* 5th ed., ed. William Damon, vol. 2: *Cognition, Perception, and Language,* eds. Deanna Kuhn and Robert S. Siegler (New York: Wiley, 1998), 309–370.

32. Michael H. Goldstein, Jennifer A. Schwade, and Marc H. Bornstein, "The Value of Vocalizing: Five-Month-Old Infants Associate Their Own Vocalizations with Responses from Caregivers," *Child Development 80* (2009): 636–644.

33. Bruna Pelucchi, Jessica F. Hay, and Jenny R. Saffran, "Statistical Learning in a Natural Language by 8-Month-Old Infants," *Child Development 80* (2009): 674–685.

34. Shannon M. Pruden et al., "The Birth of Words: Ten-Month-Olds Learn Words through Perceptual Salience," *Child Development 77* (2006): 266–280.

35. Betty Hart and Todd R. Risley, *Meaningful Differences in the Everyday Experiences of Young American Children* (Baltimore: Brookes, 1995).

36. Elaine Reese and Rhiannon Newcombe, "Training Mothers in Elaborative Reminiscing Enhances Children's Autobiographical Memory and Narrative," *Child Development 78* (2007): 1153–1170.

37. Hart and Risley, *Meaningful Differences.*

38. Michael Cole, Sheila R. Cole, and Cynthia Lightfoot, *The Development of Children,* 5th ed. (New York: Worth, 2005).

39. Michael Lewis, "The Emergence of Human Emotions," in *Handbook of Emotions,* 2nd ed., eds. Michael Lewis and Jeannette M. Haviland-Jones (New York: Guilford, 2000), 265–280.

40. Theodore Dix et al., "Autonomy and Children's Reactions to Being Controlled: Evidence that Both Compliance and Defiance May Be Positive Markers in Early Development," *Child Development 78* (2007): 1204–1221.

41. Lenneke R. A. Alink et al., "The Early Childhood Aggression Curve: Development of Physical Aggression in 10- to 50-Month-Old-Children," *Child Development* 77 (2006): 954–966.

42. Florence L. Goodenough, *Anger in Young Children* (Minneapolis: University of Minnesota Press, 1931).

43. Claire B. Kopp, "Regulation of Distress and Negative Emotions: A Developmental View," *Developmental Psychology* 25 (1989): 343–354.

44. Galinsky, *Mind in the Making.*

45. Marion Radke-Yarrow et al., "Learning Concern for Others," *Developmental Psychology* 8 (1973): 240–260; Herbert Wray, *Emotions in the Lives of Young Children,* Department of Health, Education, and Welfare Publication no. 78–644 (Rockville, MD: National Institute of Mental Health, 1978); Carolyn Zahn-Waxler et al., "Development of Concern for Others," *Developmental Psychology* 28 (1992): 126–136.

46. Thompson, "The Development of the Person."

47. Deborah Stipek, Susan Recchia, and Susan McClintic, "Self-Evaluation in Young Children," *Monographs of the Society for Research in Child Development* 57, serial no. 226 (1992).

48. Harriet L. Rheingold, Kay V. Cook, and Vicki Kolowitz, "Commands Cultivate the Behavioral Pleasure of Two-Year-Old-Children," *Developmental Psychology* 23 (1987): 146–151.

49. Susan Harter, "The Self," in *Handbook of Child Psychology,* 6th ed., eds. William Damon and Richard M. Lerner, vol. 3: *Social, Emotional, and Personality Development,* ed. Nancy Eisenberg (Hoboken, NJ: Wiley, 2006), 505–571.

50. Claire B. Kopp, "Antecedents of Self-Regulation: A Developmental Perspective," *Developmental Psychology* 18 (1982): 199–214; Susan D. Calkins, "Early Attachment Processes and the Development of Emotional Self-Regulation," in *Handbook of Self-Regulation,* eds. Roy F. Baumeister and Kathleen D. Vohs (New York: Guilford, 2004), 324–339.

51. Donelda J. Stayton, Robert Hogan, and Mary D. Salter Ainsworth, "Infant Obedience and Maternal Behavior: The Origins of Socialization Reconsidered," *Child Development* 42 (1971): 1057–1069.

52. Kopp, "Antecedents of Self-Regulation."

53. Brian E. Vaughn et al., "Process Analysis of the Behavior of Very Young Children in Daily Tasks," *Developmental Psychology* 22 (1986): 752–759.

54. Kenneth H. Rubin, William M. Bukowski, and Jeffrey G. Parker, "Peer Interactions, Relationships, and Groups," in *Handbook of Child Psychology,* 6th ed., eds. Damon and Lerner, vol. 3, 571–645.

55. Marianne S. De Wolff and Marinus van IJzendoorn, "Sensitivity and Attachment: A Meta-Analysis on Parental Antecedents of Infant Attachment," *Child Development* 68 (1997): 571–591.

56. Clancy Blair et al., "Salivary Cortisol Mediates Effects of Poverty and Parenting on Executive Functions in Early Childhood," *Child Development* 82 (2011): 1970–1984.

57. W. Roger Mills-Koonce et al., "Father Contributions to Cortisol Responses in Infancy and Toddlerhood," *Developmental Psychology* 47 (2011): 388–395.

58. Michael F. Lorber and Byron Egeland, "Infancy Parenting and Externalizing Problems from Childhood through Adulthood: Developmental Trends," *Developmental Psychology* 45 (2009): 909–912.

59. Michael F. Lorber and Byron Egeland, "Parenting and Infant Difficulty: Testing a Mutual Exacerbation Hypothesis to Predict Early Onset Conduct Problems," *Child Development* 82 (2011): 2006–2020.

60. Jutta Heckhausen, "Balancing for Weaknesses and Challenging Developmental Potential: A Longitudinal Study of Mother-Infant Dyads in Apprenticeship Interactions," *Developmental Pychology* 23 (1987): 762–770.

61. Ross D. Parke, "Fathers and Families," in *Handbook of Parenting,* 2nd ed., ed. Marc H. Bornstein, vol. 3: *Being and Becoming a Parent* (Mahwah, NJ: Erlbaum, 2002), 27–73.

62. W. Jean Yeung et al., "Children's Time with Fathers in Intact Families," *Journal of Marriage and Family* 63 (2001): 136–154.

63. Ibid.

64. Parke, "Fathers and Families."

65. Kathryn E. Barnard and JoAnne E. Solchany, "Mothering," in *Handbook of Parenting,* 2nd ed., ed. Bornstein, vol. 3, 3–25.

66. Parke, "Fathers and Families."

67. Jay Belsky, Bonnie Gilstrap, and Michael Rovine, "The Pennsylvania Infant and Family Development Project I: Stability

and Change in Mother-Infant and Father-Infant Interaction in a Family Setting at One, Three, and Nine Months," *Child Development 55* (1984): 692–705.

68. Marc H. Bornstein, "Parenting Infants," in *Handbook of Parenting,* 2nd ed, ed. Bornstein, vol. 1, 3–43.

69. T. Berry Brazelton and Stanley I. Greenspan, *The Irreducible Needs of Children* (Cambridge, MA: Perseus, 2000).

70. Patricia M. Greenfield, Lalita K. Suzuki, and Carrie Rothstein-Fisch, "Cultural Pathways through Human Development," in *Handbook of Child Psychology,* 6th ed., eds. William Damon and Richard M. Lerner, vol. 4: *Child Psychology in Practice,* ed. K. Ann Renninger and Irving E. Sigel (Hoboken, NJ: Wiley, 2006), 665–775.

71. Sylvia M. Bell and Mary D. Salter Ainsworth, "Infant Crying and Maternal Responsiveness," *Child Development 43* (1972): 1171–1190.

72. Esther M. Leerkes, A. Nyena Blankson, and Marion O'Brien, "Differential Effects of Maternal Sensitivity to Infant Distress and Nondistress on Social-Emotional Functioning," *Child Development 80* (2009): 762–775.

73. Judy Dunn, *Distress and Comfort* (Cambridge, MA: Harvard University Press, 1977), 23.

74. Ian St. James-Roberts et al., "Infant Crying and Sleeping in London, Copenhagen, and When Parents Adopt 'Proximal' Form of Care," *Pediatrics 117* (2006): e1146–e1155.

75. Elizabeth Anisfeld et al., "Does Infant Carrying Promote Attachment? An Experimental Study of the Effects of Increased Physical Contact on the Development of Attachment," *Child Development 61* (1990): 1617–1627.

76. Suzi Tortora, "Studying the Infant's Multisensory Environment: A Bridge Between Biology and Psychology," *Zero to Three 24* (May, 2004), 13–24.

77. Jodi A. Mindell, *Sleeping through the Night,* rev. ed. (New York: HarperCollins, 2005).

78. William A. H. Sammons, *The Self-Calmed Baby* (Boston: Little, Brown, 1989).

79. Gilda Morelli et al., "Cultural Variations in Infants' Sleeping Arrangements: Questions of Independence," *Developmental Psychology 28* (1992): 604–613.

80. Peter S. Blair, Jon Heron, and Peter J. Fleming," Relationship between Bed

Sharing and Breastfeeding: Longitudinal, Population-Based Analysis," *Pediatrics 126* (2010): e1119–e1126.

81. Jacqueline M. T. Henderson et al., "Sleeping through the Night: The Consolidation of Self-regulated Sleep across the First Year of Life," *Pediatrics 126* (2010): e1081–e1087.

82. Richard Ferber, *Solve Your Child's Sleep Problems,* rev. ed. (New York: Simon & Schuster, 2006).

83. Mindell, *Sleeping through the Night.*

84. Ibid.

85. Task Force on Sudden Infant Death Syndrome, "The Changing Concept of Sudden Infant Death Syndrome: Diagnostic Coding Shifts, Controversies Regarding the Sleeping Environment, and New Variables to Consider in Reducing Risk," *Pediatrics 116* (2005): 1245–1255.

86. Ibid.; Ferber, *Solve Your Child's Sleep Problems;* Mindell, *Sleeping through the Night.*

87. William Sears, Introduction to *Attachment Parenting* by Katie Allison Granju with Betsy Kennedy (New York: Pocket Books, 1999).

88. Katie Allison Granju with Betsy Kennedy, *Attachment Parenting* (New York: Pocket Books, 1999), 9.

89. Ibid., p. 10.

90. St. James-Roberts et al., "Infant Crying and Sleeping."

91. Deborah Laible and Ross A. Thompson, "Early Socialization: A Relationship Perspective," in *Handbook of Socialization: Theory and Research,* eds. Joan E. Grusec and Paul D. Hastings (New York: Guilford, 2007), 181–207.

92. Ibid.

93. J. Heidi Gralinski and Claire B. Kopp, "Everyday Rules for Behavior: Mothers' Requests to Young Children," *Developmental Psychology 29* (1993): 573–584.

94. Cheryl Minton, Jerome Kagan, and Janet A. Levine, "Maternal Control and Obedience in the Two-Year-Old," *Child Development 42* (1971): 1873–1894.

95. Marja C. Paulussen-Hoogeboom et al., "Child Negative Emotionality and Parenting from Infancy to Preschool: A Meta-Analytic Review," *Developmental Psychology 43* (2007): 438–453.

96. Thompson, "The Development of the Person."

97. Grazyna Kochanska, Nazam Aksan, and Mary E. Joy, "Children's Fearfulness as a Moderator of Parenting in Early Socialization: Two Longitudinal Studies," *Developmental Psychology 43* (2007): 222–237.

98. Ibid.

99. Marc H. Bornstein, "On the Significance of Social Relationships in the Development of Children's Earliest Symbolic Play: An Ecological Perspective," in *Play and Development: Evolutionary, Sociocultural, and Functional Perspectives,* eds. Artin Goncu and Suzanne Gaskins (Mahwah, NJ: Erlbaum, 2007), 101–129.

100. Linda R. Cote and Marc H. Bornstein, "Child and Mother Play in Three U.S. Cultural Groups: Comparisons and Association," *Journal of Family Psychology 23* (2009): 355–363.

101. Robert H. Bradley and Robert F. Corwyn, "Productive Activity and the Prevention of Behavior Problems," *Developmental Psychology 41* (2005): 89–98.

102. Robert H. Bradley and Robert F. Corwyn, "Externalizing Problems in Fifth Grade: Relations with Productive Activity, Maternal Sensitivity, and Harsh Parenting from Infancy through Middle Childhood," *Developmental Psychology 43* (2007): 1390–1401.

103. Helen Raikes et al., "Mother-Child Bookreading in Low-Income Families; Correlates and Outcomes during the First Three Years of Life," *Child Development 77* (2006): 924–953.

104. Ellen Galinsky, *Between Generations: The Six Stages of Parenthood* (New York: Basic Books, 1981).

105. McHale, *The Bumpy Road of Coparenthood.*

106. Martin Pinquart and Daniela Teubert, "Effects of Parenting Education with Expectant and New Parents: A Meta-Analysis," *Journal of Family Psychology 24* (2010): 323.

107. Marc S. Schulz, Carolyn Pape Cowan, and Philip A. Cowan, "Promoting Healthy Beginnings: A Randomized Control Trial of a Preventive Intervention to Preserve Marital Quality during the Transition to Parenthood," *Journal of Consulting and Clinical Psychology 74* (2006): 20–31.

108. Kate Harwood, Neil McLean, and Kevin Durkin, "First-Time Mothers' Expectations of Parenthood: What Happens When Optimistic Expectations Are Not Matched by Later Experiences?" *Developmental Psychology 43* (2007): 1–12.

109. Linda Gilkerson, Larry Gray, and Nancy Mark, "Fussy Babies, Worried Families, and a New Service Network," *Zero to Three 25* (January 2005), 34–41.

110. Ibid.

111. Daphne Blunt Bugental et al., "A Cognitive Approach to Child Abuse Prevention," *Journal of Family Psychology 16* (2002): 243–258.

112. *Zero to Three 28* (November 2007), 48.

113. Claire Lerner and Amy Laura Dombro, *What's Best for My Baby and Me?"* (Washington, DC: Zero to Three Press, 2006).

114. Patricia K. Coleman and Katherine H. Karraker, "Self-Efficacy and Parenting Quality: Findings and Future Applications," *Developmental Review 18* (1997): 47–85.

CHAPTER EIGHT

1. Allison Gopnik, Andrew N. Meltzer, and Patricia K. Kuhl, *The Scientist in the Crib* (New York: Morrow, 1999).

2. Jean Piaget and Barbel Inhelder, *The Psychology of the Child* (New York: Basic Books, 1969).

3. Michelle M. Chouinard, "Children's Questions: A Mechanism for Cognitive Development," *Monographs of the Society for Research in Child Development 72,* serial no. 286 (2007).

4. Brandy N. Frazier, Susan A. Gelman, and Henry M. Wellman, "Preschoolers Search for Explanatory Information within Adult-Child Conversations," *Child Development 80* (2009): 1592–1611.

5. Melissa A. Koenig and Paul L. Harris, "Preschoolers Mistrust Ignorant and Inaccurate Speakers," *Child Development 76* (2005): 1261–1277.

6. Rebecca A. Williamson, Andrew N. Meltzoff, and Ellen Markman,"Prior Experiences and Perceived Efficacy Influence 3-Year-Olds' Imitation," *Developmental Psychology 44* (2008): 275–285.

7. Ross A. Thompson, "The Development of the Person: Social Understanding, Relationships, Conscience, Self," in *Handbook of Child Psychology,* 6th ed., eds. William Damon and Richard M.

Lerner, vol. 3: *Social, Emotional, and Personality Development,* ed. Nancy Eisenberg (Hoboken, NJ: Wiley, 2006), 24–98.

8. Clancy Blair, Douglas Granger, and Rachel Peters Razza, "Cortisol Reactivity Is Positively Related to Executive Function in Preschool Children Attending Head Start," *Child Development* 76 (2005): 554–567.

9. Lisa A. Turner and Burke Johnson, "A Model of Mastery Motivation for At-Risk Preschoolers," *Journal of Educational Psychology* 95 (2003): 495–505.

10. Lois Bloom, "Language Acquisition in Its Developmental Context," in *Handbook of Child Psychology,* 5th ed., ed. William Damon, vol. 2: *Cognition, Perception, and Language,* eds. Deanna Kuhn and Robert S. Siegler (New York: Wiley, 1998), 309–370.

11. Betty Hart and Todd R. Risley, *Meaningful Differences in the Everyday Experiences of American Children* (Baltimore: Brookes, 1995).

12. Ibid.

13. NICHD Early Child Care Research Network, "Pathways to Reading: The Role of Oral Language in the Transition to Reading," *Developmental Psychology* 41 (2005): 428–442.

14. Thompson, "The Development of the Person."

15. Inge Bretherton et al., "Learning to Talk about Emotions: A Functionalist Perspective," *Child Development* 57 (1986): 529–548.

16. Thompson, "The Development of the Person."

17. Michael Lewis and Margaret Wolan Sullivan, "The Development of Self-Conscious Emotions," in *Handbook of Competence and Motivation,* eds. Andrew J. Elliott and Carol S. Dweck (New York: Guilford, 2005), 185–201.

18. Daniel B. M. Haun and Michael Tomasello, "Conformity to Peer Pressure in Preschool," *Child Development* 82 (2011): 1759–1767

19. Lewis and Sullivan, "The Development of Self-Conscious Emotions."

20. NICHD Early Child Care Research Network, "Trajectories of Physical Aggression from Toddlerhood to Middle Childhood," *Monographs of the Society for Research in Child Development* 69 serial no. 278 (2004).

21. Kristin A. Buss, "Which Fearful Toddlers Should We Worry about? Context, Fear, Regulation, and Anxiety Risk," *Developmental Psychology* 47 (2011): 804–819.

22. Liat Sayfan and Kristin Hansen Lagattuta, "Grown-Ups Are Not Afraid of Scary Stuff but Kids Are: Young Children's and Adults' Reasoning about Children's, Infants,' and Adults' Fears," *Child Development* 79 (2008): 821–835.

23. Jerome Kagan and Nancy Snidman, "Temperamental Factors in Human Development," *American Psychologist* 46 (1991): 856–862; Paul D. Hastings et al., "Parental Socialization, Vagal Regulation, and Preschoolers' Anxious Difficulties: Direct Mothers and Moderated Fathers," *Child Development* 79 (2008): 45–64.

24. Kenneth H. Rubin et al., "Parenting Beliefs and Behaviors: Initial Findings from the International Consortium for the Study of Emotional Development (ICSSED)," in *Parenting Beliefs, Behaviors, and Parent-Child Relations: A Cross-Cultural Perspective,* eds. Kenneth H. Rubin and Ock Boon Chung (New York: Psychology Press, 2006), 81–103.

25. Hastings et al., "Parental Socialization, Vagal Regulation, and Preschools' Anxious Difficulties."

26. Rubin et al., "Parenting Beliefs and Behaviors."

27. Xinyin Chen et al., "Early Childhood Behavioral Inhibition and Social and School Adjustment in Chinese Children: A 5-Year Longitudinal Study," *Child Development* 80 (2009): 1692–1704.

28. Liat Sayfan and Kristin Hansen Lagattuta, "Scaring the Monsters Away: What Children Know about Managing Fears of Real and Imaginary Creatures," *Child Development* 80 (2009): 1756–1774.

29. Kristin Hansen Lagattuta, "Thinking About the Future Because of the Past: Young Children's Knowledge about the Causes of Worry and Preventative Decisions," *Child Development* 78 (2007): 1492–1509.

30. Jack P. Shonkoff, "Protecting Brains, Not Simply Stimulating Minds," *Science* 333 (2011): 982–983.

31. Arthur J. Reynolds et al., "Age 26 Cost-Benefit Analysis of the Child-Parent Center Early Education Program," *Child Development* 82 (2011): 379–404.

32. William Roberts and Janet Strayer, "Parents' Responses to the Emotional Distress of Their Children: Relations with Children's Competence," *Developmental Psychology* 23 (1987): 415–422.

33. Amanda Sheffield Morris et al., "The Influence of Mother-Child Emotion Regulation Strategies on Children's Expression of Anger and Sadness," *Developmental Psychology* 47 (2011): 213–225.

34. Ross Thompson, "How Emotional Development Unfolds Starting at Birth," *Zero to Three* 32 (January 2012): 6–11.

35. Richard A. Fabes et al., "Preschoolers Attributions of the Situational Determinants of Others' Naturally Occurring Emotions," *Developmental Psychology* 24 (1988): 376–385.

36. Nancy Eisenberg, Richard A. Fabes, and Tracy L. Spinrad, "Prosocial Development," in *Handbook of Child Psychology*, 6th ed, eds. Damon and Lerner, vol. 3: 646–718.

37. Susan Harter, "The Self," in *Handbook of Child Psychology*, 6th ed., eds. Damon and Lerner, vol. 3: 505–570.

38. Jeffrey R. Measelle, "Children's Self-Perceptions as a Link between Family Relationship Quality and Social Adaptation to School," in *The Family Context of Parenting in Children's Adaptation to Elementary School*, eds. Philip A. Cowan et al. (Mahwah, NJ: Erlbaum, 2005), 163–187.

39. Harter, "The Self."

40. Diane N. Ruble, Carol Lynn Martin, and Sheri A. Berenbaum, "Gender Development," in *Handbook of Child Psychology*, 6th ed., eds. Damon and Lerner, vol. 3: 858–932.

41. Susan Golombok and Robyn Fivush, *Gender Development* (New York: Cambridge University Press, 1994), 111.

42. Diane N. Ruble et al., "The Role of Gender Constancy in Early Gender Development," *Child Development* 78 (2007): 1121–1136.

43. Susan A. Gelman, Marianne G. Taylor, and Simone P. Nguyen, "Mother-Child Conversations about Gender," *Monographs of the Society for Research in Child Development* 69, serial no. 275 (2004).

44. Ruble, Martin and Berenbaum, "Gender Development."

45. Carolyn Zahn-Waxler, "Warriors and Worriers: Gender and Psychopathology,"

Development and Psychopathology 5 (1993): 79–89.

46. Ross D. Parke and Raymond Buriel, "Socialization in the Family: Ethnic and Ecological Perspectives," in *Handbook of Child Psychology*, 6th ed., eds. Damon and Lerner, vol. 3, 465.

47. Brett Laursen and Vickie Williams, "The Role of Ethnic Identity in Personality Development," in *Pathways to Successful Development: Personality in the Life Course*, eds. Lea Pulkkinen and Avshalom Caspi (New York: Cambridge University Press, 2002), 203–226.

48. Margaret O'Brien Caughey et al., "The Influence of Racial Socialization Practices on the Cognitive and Behavioral Competence of African American Preschoolers," *Child Development* 73 (2002): 1611–1625.

49. Judith G. Smetana, "Social-Cognitive Domain Theory: Consistencies and Variations in Children's Moral and Social Judgments," in *Handbook of Moral Development*, eds. Melanie Killen and Judith G. Smetana (Mahwah, NJ: Erlbaum, 2006): 119–153.

50. Kristin Hansen Lagattuta, Larry Nucci, and Sandra Leanne Bosacki, "Bridging Theory of Mind and the Personal Domain: Children's Reasoning about Resistance to Parental Control," *Child Development* 81 (2010): 616–635.

51. Smetana, "Social-Cognitive Domain Theory."

52. Victoria Talwar and Kang Lee, "Social and Cognitive Correlates of Children's Lying Behavior," *Child Development* 79 (2008): 866–881.

53. Angela D. Evans, Fen Xu, and Kang Lee, "When All Signs Point to You: Lies Told in the Face of Evidence," *Developmental Psychology* 47 (2011): 39–49.

54. Victoria Talwar and Kang Lee, "A Punitive Environment Fosters Children's Dishsonesty: A Natural Experiment," *Child Development* 82 (2011): 1751–1758.

55. Daniel Hart, Robert Atkins, and Suzanne Fegley, "Personality Development in Childhood: A Person-Centered Approach," *Monographs of the Society for Research in Child Development* 68, serial no. 272 (2003).

56. Parke and Buriel, "Socialization in the Family."

57. Thompson, "The Development of the Person."

58. Femmie Juffer, Marian J. Bakermans-Kranenburg, and Marinus H. van IJzendoorn, eds., *Promoting Positive Parenting: An Attachment-Based Intervention* (New York: Erlbaum, 2007); Judi Mesman et al., "Extending the Video-Feedback Intervention to Sensitive Discipline: The Early Intervention of Antisocial Behavior," in *Promoting Positive Parenting,* eds. Juffer, Bakermans-Kranenburg, and van IJzendoorn, 171–191.

59. James P. McHale, *Charting the Bumpy Road of Coparenthood* (Washington, DC: Zero to Three, 2007).

60. Laura E. Berk, *Awakening Children's Minds* (New York: Oxford, 2001).

61. Susan H. Landry et al., "A Responsive Parenting Intervention: The Optimal Timing across Early Childhood for Impacting Maternal Behaviors and Child Outcomes," *Developmental Psychology 44* (2008): 1335–1353.

62. Stuart I. Hammond et al., "The Effects of Parental Scaffolding on Preschoolers' Executive Functioning," *Developmental Psychology 48* (2012): 271–281.

63. Parke and Buriel, "Socialization in the Family."

64. Philip A. Cowan, Isabel Bradburn, and Carolyn Pape Cowan, "Parents' Working Models of Attachment: The Intergenerational Context of Parenting and Children's Adaptation to School," in *The Family Context of Parenting in Children's Adaptation to Elementary School,* eds. Cowan et al., 209–235.

65. Campbell Leaper, "Parenting Boys and Girls," in *Handbook of Parenting,* 2nd ed., ed. Marc H. Bornstein, vol. 1: *Children and Parenting* (Mahwah, NJ: Erlbaum, 2002), 189–225; Ruble, Martin, and Berenbaum, "Gender Development."

66. Campbell Leaper, "Gender Affiliation, Assertion, and the Interactive Context of Parent-Child Play," *Developmental Psychology 36* (2000): 381–393.

67. Beverly I. Fagot, "Parenting Boys and Girls," in *Handbook of Parenting,* ed. Marc H. Bornstein, vol. 1: *Children and Parenting* (Mahwah, NJ: Erlbaum, 1995), 163–183.

68. Leaper, "Parenting Boys and Girls."

69. Gelman, Taylor, and Nguyen, "Mother-Child Conversations."

70. Lacy J. Hilliard and Lynn S. Liben, "Differing Levels of Gender Salience in Preschool Classrooms: Effects on Children's Attitudes and Intergroup Bias," *Child Development 81* (2010): 1787–1798.

71. Gelman, Taylor, and Nguyen, "Mother-Child Conversations."

72. Peggy Orenstein, *Cinderella Ate My Daughter* (New York: HarperCollins, 2011).

73. Ruble, Martin, and Berenbaum, "Gender Development."

74. Jeanette Hsu, "Marital, Quality, Sex-Typed Parenting, and Girls' and Boys' Expression of Problems Behaviors," in *The Family Context of Parenting in Children's Adaptation to Elementary School,* eds. Cowan et al., 139–162.

75. Caughey et al., "The Influence of Racial Socialization Practices."

76. Melanie Killen, Adam Rutland, and Martin D. Ruck, "Promoting Equity, Tolerance, and Justice on Childhood," *Social Policy Report 25* (2011): 1–26.

77. Cecilia Wainryb, Beverly A. Brehl, and Sonia Matwin, "Being Hurt, and Hurting Others: Children's Narrative Accounts and Moral Judgments of Their Own Interpersonal Conflicts," *Monographs of the Society for Research in Child Development 70,* serial no. 281 (2005).

78. Peggy J. Miller, "Personal Storytelling as a Medium of Socialization in Chinese and American Families," Child Development 68 (1997): 557–568.

79. Robert Serpell et al., "Intimate Culture of Families in the Early Socialization of Literacy," *Journal of Family Psychology 16* (2002): 391–405.

80. Geetha B. Ramani and Robert S. Siegler, "Promoting Broad and Stable Improvements in Low-Income Children's Numerical Knowledge through Playing Number Board Games," *Child Development 79* (2008): 375–394.

81. Catherine S. Tamis-LeMonda, Ina C. Uzgiris, and Marc H. Bornstein, "Play in Parent-Child Interaction," in *Handbook of Parenting,* 2nd ed., ed. Marc H. Bornstein, vol. 5: *Practical Issues in Parenting* (Mahwah, NJ: Erlbaum, 2002), 221–241.

82. McHale, *Charting the Bumpy Road of Coparenthood.*

83. Nazli Baydar, April Geek, and Jeanne Brooks-Gunn, "A Longitudinal Study of

the Effects of the Birth of a Sibling during the First 6 Years of Life," *Journal of Marriage and the Family 59* (1997): 939–956; Nazli Baydar, Patricia Hyle, and Jeanne Brooks-Gunn, "A Longitudinal Study of the Effects of the Birth of Sibling during Preschool and Early Grade School Years," *Journal of Marriage and the Family 59* (1997): 957–965.

84. Robert B. Stewart et al., "The Firstborn's Adjustment to the Birth of a Sibling: A Longitudinal Assessment," *Child Development 58* (1987): 341–355.

85. Judy Dunn, "Siblings and Socialization," in *Handbook of Socialization: Theory and Research,* eds. Joan E. Grusec and Paul D. Hastings (New York: Guilford, 2007), 309–327.

86. Judith F. Dunn, Robert Plomin, and Denise Daniels, "Consistency and Change in Mothers' Behavior toward Young Siblings," *Child Development 57* (1986): 348–356; Judith F. Dunn, Robert Plomin, and Margaret Nettles, "Consistency of Mothers' Behavior Toward Infant Siblings," *Developmental Psychology 21* (1985): 1188–1195.

87. Dunn, "Siblings and Socialization."

88. Carollee Howes, "Peer Interaction of Young Children," *Monographs of the Society for Research in Child Development 53,* serial no. 217 (1987).

89. Kenneth H. Rubin, William M. Bukowski, and Jeffrey G. Parker, "Peer Interactions, Relationships, and Groups," in *Handbook of Child Psychology,* 6th ed., eds. Damon and Lerner, vol. 3, 571–645.

90. Ibid.

91. Ibid.

92. Ibid.

93. Richard Ferber, *Solve Your Child's Sleep Problems,* rev. ed. (New York: Simon & Schuster, 2006).

94. Patty Khule, "Sleep Trouble in School-Aged Kids," *USA Weekend,* November 15–17, 2002, 16.

95. Ferber, *Solve Your Child's Sleep Problems.*

96. Ibid., p. 163.

97. Ibid.

98. Jodi Mindell, *Sleeping through the Night,* rev. ed. (New York: HarperCollins, 2005).

99. Ross A. Thompson and Sara Meyer, "Socialization of Emotion Regulation in the Family," in *Handbook of Emotion Regulation,* ed. James J. Gross (New York: Guilford, 2007), 249–268.

100. Thomas Gordon with Judith Gordon Sands, *P.E.T. in Action* (New York: Bantum Books, 1978).

101. John D. Krumboltz and Helen B. Krumboltz, *Changing Children's Behavior* (Englewood Cliffs, NJ: Prentice-Hall, 1972).

102. Stanley Turecki and Leslie Tonner, *The Difficult Child* (New York: Bantum Books, 1972).

103. Dunn, "Siblings and Socialization."

104. Gordon with Sands, *P.E.T. in Action.*

105. Rudolf Dreikurs with Vicki Soltz, *Children: The Challenge* (New York: Hawthorn, 1964).

106. Kenneth H. Rubin and Kim B. Burgess, "Parents of Aggressive and Withdrawn Children," in *Handbook of Parenting,* 2nd ed., ed. Bornstein, vol.1, 383–418.

107. Carolyn Webster-Stratton, M. Jamila Reid, and Mary Hammond, "Preventing Conduct Problems, Promoting Social Competence: A Parent and Teacher Training Partnership in Head Start," *Journal of Child Clinical Psychology 30* (2001): 283–302.

108. Paul D. Hastings et al., "The Development of Concerns for Others in Children with Behavior Problems," *Developmental Psychology 36* (2000): 531–546.

109. Rubin and Burgess, "Parents of Aggressive and Withdrawn Children."

110. National Center for Birth Defects and Developmental Disabilities, "Autistic Spectrum Disorders Overview," www.cdc.gov/ncbddd/autism/overview.htm, 4/7/2008.

111. Linda Gilkerson and Frances Stott, "Parent-Child Relationships in Early Intervention with Infants and Toddlers with Disabilities and Their Families," in *Handbook of Infant Mental Health,* 2nd ed., ed. Charles H. Zeanah, Jr. (New York: Guilford, 2000), 460.

112. Penny Hauser-Cram et al. "Children with Disabilities," *Monographs of the Society for Research in Child Development 66,* serial no. 266 (2001).

113. Berk, *Awakening Children's Minds,* 180.

114. Ellen Galinsky, *Between Generations: The Six Stages of Parenthood* (New York: Times Books, 1981).

115. McHale, *Charting the Bumpy Road of Coparenthood,* 252.

116. Measelle, "Children's Self-Perceptions."

117. Carolyn Pape Cowan, Philip A. Cowan, and Gertrude Heming, "Two Variations of a Preventive Intervention for Couples: Effects on Parents and Children during

the Transition to School," in *The Family Context of Parenting in Children's Adaptation to Elementary School*, eds. Cowan et al., 163–187.

CHAPTER NINE

1. Clancy Blair, "School Readiness: Integrating Cognition and Emotion in a Neurobiological Conceptualization of Children's Functioning at School Entry," *American Psychologist* 57 (2002): 111–127.
2. W. Andrew Collins, Stephanie D. Madsen, and Amy Susman-Stillman, "Parenting during Middle Childhood," in *Handbook of Parenting,* 2nd ed., ed. Marc H. Bornstein, vol. 1: *Children and Parenting* (Mahwah, NJ: Erlbaum, 2002), 73–101.
3. Robert S. Siegler, "Microgenetic Analyses of Learning," in *Handbook of Child Psychology*, 6th ed., eds. William Damon and Richard M. Lerner, vol. 2: *Cognition, Perception, and Language,* eds. Deanna Kuhn and Robert S. Siegler (Hoboken, NJ: Wiley, 2006), 464–510.
4. Emilie Phillips Smith et al., "Opportunities for Schools to Promote Resilience in Children and Youth," in *Investing in Children, Youth, Families, and Communities: Strength-Based Research and Policy, eds.* Kenneth I. Maton et al. (Washington, DC: American Psychological Association, 2004), 213–231.
5. Allan Wigfield et al., "Development of Achievement Motivation," in *Handbook of Child Psychology*, 6th ed., eds. William Damon and Richard M. Lerner, vol. 3: *Social, Emotional and Personality Development,* ed. Nancy Eisenberg (Hoboken, NJ: Wiley, 2006), 933–1002.
6. Ibid.
7. Ibid.
8. Jennifer A. Fredricks and Jacquelynne S. Eccles, "Children's Competence and Value Beliefs from Childhood through Adolescence: Growth Trajectories in Two Male-Typed Domains," *Developmental Psychology 38* (2002): 519–533.
9. Jennifer A. Fredricks, Sandra Simpkins, and Jacquelynne S. Eccles, "Family Socialization, Gender, and Participation in Sports and Instrumental Music," in *Developmental Pathways through Middle Childhood: Rethinking Contexts and Diversity as Resources,* eds. Catherine R. Cooper et al. (Mahwah, NJ: Erlbaum, 2005), 41–62.
10. Eva M. Pomerantz, Wendy S. Grolnick, and Carrie E. Price, "The Role of Parents in How Children Approach Achievement: A Dynamic Process Perspective," in *Handbook of Competence and Motivation,* eds. Andrew J. Elliot and Carol S. Dweck (New York: Guilford, 2005), 259–278.
11. Ibid.
12. Eva M. Pomerantz, Qian Wang, and Florrie Fei-Yin Ng, "Mothers' Affect in the Homework Context: The Importance of Staying Positive," *Developmental Psychology 41* (2005): 414–427.
13. Smith et al., "Opportunities for Schools to Promote Resilience in Children and Youth."
14. Margaret Burchinal et al., "Examining the Black-White Achievement Gap among Low-Income Children Using the NICHD Study of Early Child Care and Youth Development," *Child Development 82* (2011): 1404–1420.
15. Duane E. Thomas et al., "The Influence of Classroom Aggression and Classroom Climate on Aggressive-Disruptive Behavior," *Child Development 82* (2011): 751–757; Joseph A. Durlak et al., "The Impact of Enhancing Students' Social and Emotional Learning: A Meta-Analysis of School-Based Universal Interventions," *Child Development 82* (2011): 405–432.
16. Nancy G. Guerra, Kirk R. Williams, and Shelby Sadek, "Understanding Bullying and Victimization during Childhood and Adolescence: A Mixed Methods Study," *Child Development 82* (2011): 295–310; Drew Nesdale and Michael J. Lawson, "Social Groups and Children's Intergroup Attitudes: Can School Norms Moderate the Effects of Social Group Norms?" *Child Development 82* (2011): 1594–1606.
17. Bridget K. Hamre and Robert C. Pianta, "Can Instructional and Emotional Support in the First-Grade Classroom Make a Difference for Children at Risk of School Failure?" *Child Development 76* (2005): 949–967.
18. Heidi Gazelle, "Class Climate Moderates Peer Relations and Emotional Adjustment in Children with an Early History of Anxious Solitude: A Child X Environment Model," *Developmental Psychology 42* (2006): 1179–1192.
19. Annie Lowrey, "A Study Links Good Teachers to Lasting Gain," *New York Times,* January 6, 2012, A1.

20. Karin S. Frey and Diane Ruble, "What Children Say about Classroom Performance: Sex and Grade Differences in Perceived Competence," *Child Development* 58 (1987): 1066–1078.

21. Wigfield et al., "Development of Achievement Motivation."

22. Deborah Stipek, "Children as Unwitting Agents in Their Developmental Pathways," in *Developmental Pathways through Middle Childhood*, eds. Cooper et al. 99–120.

23. NICHD Early Child Care Research Network, "Trajectories of Physical Aggression from Toddlerhood to Childhood," *Monographs of the Society for Research in Child Development* 69, serial no. 278 (2004).

24. Mona El Sheikh et al., "Child Emotional Insecurity and Academic Achievement: The Role of Sleep Disruptions," *Journal of Family Psychology* 21 (2007): 29–38.

25. Bonnie J. Leadbeater and Wendy L. G. Hoglund, "The Effects of Peer Victimization and Physical Aggression on Changes in Internalizing from First to Third Grade," *Child Development* 80 (2009): 843–869.

26. Wigfield et al., "Development of Academic Motivation."

27. Patricia M. Greenfield, Lalita K. Sazuki, and Carrie Rothstein-Fisch, "Cultural Pathways through Human Development," in *Handbook of Child Psychology*, 6th ed., eds. William Damon and Richard M. Lerner, vol. 4: *Child Psychology in Practice*, eds. K. Ann Renninger and Irving E. Sigel (Hoboken, NJ: Wiley, 2006), 655–699.

28. Laura T. Zionts, "Examining Relationships between Students and Teachers: A Potential Extension of Attachment Theory," in *Attachment in Middle Childhood*, eds. Kathryn A. Kerns and Rhonda A. Richardson (New York: Guilford, 2005), 231–254.

29. Cynthia T. Garcia Coll, Laura A. Szalacha, and Natalia Palacios, "Children of Dominican, Portuguese, and Cambodian Immigrant Families: Academic Attitudes and Pathways during Middle Childhood," in *Developmental Pathways through Middle Childhood*, eds. Cooper et al., 207–233.

30. Andrew J. Fuligni et al., "Family Obligation and the Academic Motivation of Young Children from Immigrant Families," in *Developmental Pathways through Middle Childhood*, eds. Cooper et al., 261–282.

31. Greenfield, Suzuki, and Rothstein-Fisch, "Cultural Pathways through Human Development."

32. Carolyn Saarni et al., "Emotional Development: Action, Communication, and Understanding," in *Handbook of Child Psychology*, 6th ed., eds. Damon and Lerner, vol. 3, 226–299.

33. Dayna Fuchs and Mark H. Thelen, "Children's Expected Interpersonal Consequences of Communicating Their Affective State and Reported Likelihood of Expression," *Child Development* 59 (1988): 1314–1322.

34. Saarni et al., "Emotional Development."

35. Kaoru Yamamoto et al., "Voices in Unison: Stressful Events in the Lives of Children in Six Countries," *Journal of Child Psychology and Psychiatry* 28 (1987): 855–864.

36. Elaine Shaw Sorensen, *Children's Stress and Coping* (New York: Guildford, 1993).

37. Steven R. Asher et al., "Peer Rejection and Loneliness in Childhood," in *Peer Rejection in Childhood*, eds. Steven R. Asher and John D. Coie (Cambridge, UK: Cambridge University Press, 1990), 253–273.

38. Susan L. Isley et al., "Parent and Child Expressed Affect and Children's Social Competence: Modeling Direct and Indirect Pathways," *Developmental Psychology* 35 (1999): 547–560.

39. Gary W. Ladd, "Peer Rejection, Aggressive or Withdrawn Behavior, and Psychological Maladjustment from Ages 5 to 12: An Examination of Four Predictive Models," *Child Development* 77 (2006): 822–846.

40. Ann S. Masten et al., "Developmental Cascades: Linking Academic Achievement and Externalizing and Internalizing Symptoms over 20 Years," *Developmental Psychology* 41 (2005): 733–746.

41. Jennifer L. Altshuler and Diane N. Ruble, "Developmental Changes in Children's Awareness of Strategies for Coping with Uncontrollable Stress," *Child Development* 60 (1989): 1337–1349.

42. Sorensen, *Children's Stress and Coping.*

43. Molly Reid et al., "My Family and Friends: Six to Twelve-Year-Old Children's Perceptions of Social Support," *Child Development* 60 (1989): 907.

44. Mary J. Levitt, Nathalie Guacci-Franco, and Jerome L. Levitt, "Convoys of Social Support in Childhood and Early Adolescence," *Developmental Psychology 29* (1993): 811–818.

45. Susan Harter, "The Self," in *Handbook of Child Psychology,* 6th ed., eds. Damon and Lerner, vol. 3, 505–570.

46. Janet J. Boseovski, "Evidence for 'Rose-Colored Glasses': An Examination of the Positivity Bias in Young Children's Personality Judgments," *Child Development Perspectives 4* (2010): 212–218.

47. Diane N. Ruble, Carol Lynn Martin, and Sheri A. Berenbaum, "Gender Development," in *Handbook of Child Psychology,* 6th ed., eds. Damon and Lerner, vol. 3, 858–932.

48. Joel Szkrybalo and Diane N. Ruble, "God Made Me a Girl: Sex-Category Constancy Judgments and Explanations Revisited," *Developmental Psychology 35* (1999): 392–402.

49. Susan Golombok et al., "Developmental Trajectories of Sex-Typed Behavior in Boys and Girls: A Longitudinal General Population Study of Children Aged 2.5–8 Years," *Child Development 79* (2008): 1583–1593.

50. Lynn S. Liben and Rebecca S. Bigler, "The Developmental Course of Gender Differentiation," *Monographs of the Society for Research in Child Development 67,* serial no. 269 (2002); Diane N. Ruble and Carol Lynn Martin, "Commentary: The Developmental Course of Gender Differentiation," *Monographs of the Society for Research in Child Development 67,* serial no. 269 (2002).

51. Frances E. Aboud, "The Development of Ethnic Self-Identification and Attitudes," in *Children's Ethnic Socialization,* eds. Jean S. Phinney and Mary Jane Rotheram (Beverly Hills, CA: Sage, 1987), 32–55.

52. Sandra L. Hofferth and John F. Sandberg, "How American Children Spend Their Time," *Journal of Marriage and Family 63* (2001): 295–308.

53. Margaret O'Brien Caughey et al., "Neighborhood Matters: Racial Socialization of African American Children," *Child Development 77* (2006): 1220–1236.

54. Melissa Faye Jackson et al., "Classroom Contextual Effects of Race on Children's Peer Nominations," *Child Development 77* (2006): 1325–1337.

55. Travis Wilson and Philip C. Rodkin, "African American and European American Children in Diverse Elementary Classrooms: Social Integration, Social Status, and Social Behavior," *Child Development 82* (2011): 1454–1469.

56. Rebecca S. Bigler, Cara J. Averhart, and Lynn S. Liben, "Race and the Workforce: Occupational Status, Aspirations, and Stereotyping Among African American Children," *Developmental Psychology 39* (2003): 572–580.

57. Frances E. Aboud, "The Formation of In-Group Favoritism and Out-Group Prejudice in Young Children: Are They Distinct Attitudes?" *Developmental Psychology 39* (2003): 48–60.

58. Christia Spears Brown et al., "Ethnicity and Gender in Late Childhood and Early Adolescence: Group Identity and Awareness of Bias," *Developmental Psychology 47* (2011): 463–471.

59. Cari Gillen-O'Neel, Diane N. Ruble, and Andrew J. Fuligni, "Ethnic Stigma, Academic Anxiety, and Intrinsic Motivation in Middle Childhood," *Child Development 82* (2011): 1470–1485.

60. Susan Harter, "Causes, Correlates, and the Functional Role of Global Self-Worth: A Life-Span Perspective," in *Competence Considered,* eds. J. Kolligian and Robert Sternberg (New Haven, CT: Yale University Press, 1990), 67–97.

61. Jean M. Twenge and Jennifer Crocker, "Race and Self-Esteem: Meta-Analysis Comparing Whites, Blacks, Hispanics, Asians, and American Indians and Comment on Gray-Little and Hofdahl (2000)," *Psychological Bulletin 128* (2002): 371–408.

62. Tamara J. Ferguson, Hedy Stegge, and Ilse Damhuis, "Children's Understanding of Guilt and Shame," *Child Development 62* (1992): 827–839.

63. Hazel J. Marcus and Paula S. Nurius, "Self-Understanding and Self-Regulation in Middle Childhood," in *Development during Middle Childhood,* ed. W. Andrew Collins (Washington, DC: National Academy Press, 1984), 147–183.

64. Nancy Eisenberg et al., "Relations among Positive Parenting, Children's Effortful Control, and Externalizing Problems: A

Three-Wave Longitudinal Study," *Child Development 76* (2005): 1055–1071.

65. Melanie Killen et al., "How Children and Adolescents Evaluate Gender and Racial Exclusions," *Monographs of the Society for Research in Child Development 67*, serial no. 271 (2002).

66. Eliot Turiel, "The Development of Morality," in *Handbook of Child Psychology,* 6th ed., eds. Damon and Lerner, vol. 3, 789–857.

67. Collins, Madsen, and Susman-Stillman, "Parenting during Middle Childhood."

68. Cathryn Booth-LaForce et al., "Attachment and Friendship Predictors of Psychosocial Functioning in Middle Childhood and the Mediating Roles of Social Support and Self-Worth," in *Attachment in Middle Childhood,* eds. Kerns and Richardson, 161–188.

69. Ellen Moss et al., "Stability of Attachment During the Preschool Period," *Developmental Psychology 41* (2005): 773–783.

70. Ellen Moss et al., "Quality of Attachment at School Age: Relations between Child Attachment Behavior, Psychosocial Functioning and School Performance," in *Attachment in Middle Childhood,* eds. Kerns and Richardson, 189–211.

71. Jonathan F. Mattanah, "Authoritative Parenting and the Encouragement of Children's Autonomy," in *The Family Context of Parenting in Children's Adaptation to Elementary School,* eds. Philip A. Cowan et al. (Mahwah, NJ: Erlbaum, 2005), 119–138.

72. Collins, Madsen, and Susman-Stillman, "Parenting during Middle Childhood."

73. Laura Wray-Lake, Ann C. Crouter, and Susan M. McHale, "Developmental Patterns in Decision-Making across Middle Childhood and Adolescence: European American Parents' Perspectives," *Child Development 81* (2010): 636–651.

74. Graeme Russell and Alan Russell, "Mother-Child and Father-Child in Middle Childhood," *Child Development 58* (1987): 1753–1585.

75. Frances K. Grossman, William S. Pollack, and Ellen Golding, "Fathers and Children: Predicting the Quality and Quantity of Fathering," *Developmental Psychology 24* (1988): 822–891.

76. Molly Reid, Sharon Landesman Ramey, and Margaret Burchinal, "Dialogues with Children about Their Families," in *Children's Perspectives on the Family,* eds. Inge Bretherton and Malcolm W. Watson, *New Directions for Child Development 48* (San Francisco: Jossey-Bass, 1990), 5–28.

77. Eleanor E. Maccoby, "Middle Childhood in the Context of the Family," in *Development during Middle Childhood,* 184–239.

78. Carolyn Pape Cowan, Philip A. Cowan, and Gertrude Heming, "Two Variations of a Preventive Intervention for Couples: Effects on Parents and Children during the Transition to School," in *The Family Context of Parenting in Children's Adaptation to Elementary School,* eds. Philip A. Cowan et al., 277–312.

79. Caughey et al., "Neighborhood Matters: Racial Socialization of African American Children."

80. Ibid.

81. Susan M. McHale et al., "Mothers' and Fathers' Racial Socialization in African American Families: Implications for Youth," *Child Development 77* (2006): 1387–1402.

82. Caughey et al., "Neighborhood Matters: Racial Socialization of African American Children."

83. Carolyn Bennett Murray and Jelani Mandara, "Racial Identity Development in African American Children: Cognitive and Experiential Antecedents," in *Black Children,* 2nd ed., ed. Harriette Pipes McAdoo (Thousand Oaks, CA: Sage, (2002), 73–96.

84. Po Bronson and Ashley Merryman, *Nurture Shock: New Thinking about Children* (New York: Twelve Books, 2009).

85. Collins, Madsen, and Susman-Stillman, "Parenting during Middle Childhood;" Wyndol Furman and Richard Lanthier, "Parenting Siblings," in *Handbook of Parenting,* 2nd ed., ed. Bornstein, vol. 1, 165–188.

86. Ibid.

87. Clare M. Stocker and Lise Youngblade, "Marital Conflict and Hostility Links with Children's Siblings and Peer Relationships," *Journal of Family Psychology 13* (1999): 598–609.

88. Clare M. Stocker, Rebecca A. Burwell, and Megan L. Briggs, "Sibling Conflict in Middle Childhood Predicts Children's Adjustment in Early Adolescence," *Journal of Family Psychology 16* (2002): 50–57.

89. Gene H. Brody et al., "Sibling Relationships in Rural African American Families," *Journal of Marriage and the Family 61* (1999): 1046–1057.

90. Kenneth H. Rubin, William M. Bukowski, and Jeffrey G. Parker, "Peer Interactions, Relationships, and Groups," in *Handbook of Child Psychology,* 6th ed., eds. Damon and Lerner, vol. 3, 571–645.

91. Ibid.

92. Nicki R. Crick and Jennifer Grotpeter, "Relational Aggression, Gender, and Social-Psychological Adjustment," *Child Development 66* (1995): 710–722.

93. Ibid.

94. Dan Olweus, "Annotation: Bullying at School: Basic Facts and Effects of a School-Based Intervention Program," *Journal of Child Psychology and Psychiatry 35* (1994): 1171–1190.

95. Nicki R. Crick and Jennifer K. Grotpeter, "Children's Treatment of Peers: Victims of Relational and Overt Aggression," *Development and Psychopathology 8* (1996): 367–380.

96. David Schwartz et al., "Peer Group Victimization as a Predictor of Children's Behavior Problems at Home and in School," *Development and Psychopathology 10* (1998): 87–99.

97. Guerra, Williams, and Sadek, "Understanding Bullying and Victimization during Childhood and Adolescence."

98. Karen D. Rudolph, "Developing Relationships, Being Cool, and Not Looking Like a Loser: Social Goal Orientation Predicts Children's Responses to Peer Aggression," *Child Development 82* (2011): 1518–1530.

99. Avi Sadeh, Reut Gruber, and Amiram Raviv, "The Effects of Sleep Restriction and Extension in School-Age Children: What a Difference an Hour Makes," *Child Development 74* (2003): 444–455.

100. Kristen L. Bub, Joseph A. Buckhalt, and Mona El-Sheikh, "Children's Sleep and Cognitive Performance: A Cross-Domain Analysis of Change over Time," *Developmental Psychology 47* (2011): 1504–1514.

101. Alice M. Gregory and Thomas G. O'Connor, "Sleep Problems in Childhood: A Longitudinal Study of Developmental Change and Association with Behavioral Problems," *Journal of Academy of Child and Adolescent Psychiatry 41* (2002): 964–971.

102. Emma K. Adam, Emily K. Snell, and Patricia Pendry, "Sleep Timing and Quantity in Ecological and Family Context: A Nationally Representative Time-Diary Study," *Journal of Family Psychology 21* (2007): 4–19.

103. El-Sheikh et al., "Child Emotional Insecurity and Academic Achievement."

104. Ross W. Greene, *The Explosive Child: A New Approach for Understanding and Parenting Easily Frustrated, Chronically Inflexible Children* (New York: HarperCollins, 2010).

105. Conduct Problems Prevention Research Group, "The Effects of the Fast Track Preventive Intervention on the Development of Conduct Disorder across Childhood," *Child Development 82* (2011): 331–345.

106. Martin E. P. Seligman, *The Optimistic Child* (Boston: Houghton Mifflin, 1995).

107. Marlene Jacobs Sandstrom and John D. Coie, "A Developmental Perspective on Peer Rejection: Mechanisms of Stability and Change," *Child Development 70* (1999): 955–966.

108. Sherri Oden and Steven R. Asher, "Coaching Children in Social Skills for Friendship Making," *Child Development 48* (1977): 495–506.

109. Alan E. Kazdin and Moira K. Whitley, "Treatment of Parental Stress to Enhance Therapeutic Change among Children Referred for Aggressive and Antisocial Behavior," *Journal of Consulting and Clinical Psychology 71* (2003): 504–515.

110. Durlak et al., "The Impact of Enhancing Students' Social and Emotional Learning."

111. Olweus, "Annotation: Bullying at School."

112. Antti Karna et al., "A Large-Scale Evaluation of the KiVa Antibullying Program, Grades 4–6," *Child Development 82* (2011): 311–330.

113. Karin S. Frey et al., "Reducing Playground Bullying and Supporting Beliefs: An Experimental Trial of the Steps to Respect Program," *Developmental Psychology 41* (2005): 479–491.

114. Joyce L. Epstein and Mavis G. Sanders, "Family, School, and Community Partnerships," in *Handbook of Parenting,* 2nd ed., ed. Marc H. Bornstein, vol. 5, *Practical Issues in Parenting* (Mahwah, NJ: Erlbaum, 2002), 407–437.

115. Ellen Galinsky, *Between Generations: The Six Stages of Parenthood* (New York: Times Books, 1981).

116. Cowan, Cowan, and Heming, "Two Variations of a Prevention Program for Couples."

117. Jennifer C. Ablow, "When Parents Conflict or Disengage: Children's Perceptions of Parents' Marital Distress Predict School Adaptation," in *The Family Context of Parenting in Children's Adaptation to Elementary School,* eds. Philip A. Cowan et al., 189–208.

118. Kazdin and Whitley, "Treatment of Parental Stress to Enhance Therapeutic Change."

119. Cowan, Cowan, and Heming, "Two Variations of a Prevention Program for Couples."

120. John B. Reid, Gerald R. Patterson, and James Snyder, eds., *Antisocial Behavior in Children and Adolescents* (Washington, DC: American Psychological Association, 2002).

121. Joan Beck, *Effective Parenting* (New York: Simon & Schuster, 1976).

122. Emmy E. Werner and Ruth S. Smith, *Overcoming the Odds* (Ithaca, NY: Cornell University Press, 1992), 177.

123. Robert Coles, *The Spiritual Life of Children* (Boston: Houghton Mifflin, 1990), 127.

CHAPTER TEN

1. Elizabeth J. Susman and Alan Rogol, "Puberty and Psychological Development," in *Handbook of Adolescent Psychology,* 2nd ed., eds. Richard M. Lerner and Laurence Steinberg (New York: Wiley, 2004), 15–44.

2. Bruce J. Ellis and Marilyn J. Essex, "Family Environments, Adrenarche, and Sexual Maturation: A Longitudinal Test of a Life History Model," *Child Development 78* (2007): 1799–1817.

3. Jay Belsky et al., "Family Rearing Antecedents of Pubertal Timing," *Child Development 78* (2007): 1302–1321.

4. Ellis and Essex, "Family Environments, Adrenarche, and Sexual Maturation."

5. Belsky et al., "Family Rearing Antecedents of Pubertal Timing."

6. Ibid.

7. Susman and Rogol, "Puberty and Psychological Development."

8. Ibid.

9. Heidemarie Blumenthal et al., "Elevated Social Anxiety among Early Maturing Girls," *Developmental Psychology 47* (2011): 1133–1140.

10. L. LaBerge et al., "Development of Sleep Patterns in Early Adolescence," *Journal of Sleep Research 10* (2001): 59–67.

11. W. Andrew Collins and Laurence Steinberg, "Adolescent Development in Interpersonal Context," in *Handbook of Child Psychology,* 6th ed., eds. William Damon and Richard M. Lerner, vol. 3: *Social, Emotional, and Personality Development,* ed. Nancy Eisenberg (Hoboken, NJ: Wiley, 2006), 1003–1067.

12. Ronald E. Dahl, "Adolescent Brain Development: Vulnerabilities and Opportunities," *Annals of the New York Academy of Sciences 1021* (2004): 1–22.

13. Laurence Steinberg et al., "Age Differences in Sensation Seeking and Impulsivity as Indexed by Behavior and Self-Report: Evidence for a Dual System Model," *Developmental Psychology 44* (2008): 1764–1778.

14. John Tierney, "What's New? A Penchant for Novelty Has Benefits," *New York Times,* February 14, 2012, D1.

15. Susman and Rogol, "Puberty and Psychological Development."

16. Jay N. Giedd et al., "Brain Development during Childhood and Adolescence: A Longitudinal MRI Study," *Nature Neuroscience 2* (1999): 861–863.

17. Ibid., 863.

18. Steinberg et al., "Age Differences in Sensation Seeking and Impulsivity as Indexed by Behavior and Self-Report."

19. K. Paige Harden and Elliot M. Tucker-Drob, "Individual Differences in the Development of Sensation Seeking and Impulsivity during Adolescence: Further Evidence for a Dual System Model," *Developmental Psychology 47* (2011): 739–746.

20. Collins and Steinberg, "Adolescent Development in Interpersonal Context."

21. Herbert Ginsburg and Sylvia Opper, *Piaget's Theory of Intellectual Development* (Englewood Cliffs, NJ: Prentice-Hall, 1969); Jean Piaget and Barbel Inhelder, *The Psychology of the Child* (New York: Basic Books, 1969).

22. Allan Wigfield et al., "Development of Achievement Motivation," in *Handbook of Child Psychology,* 6th ed., eds. Damon and Lerner, vol. 3, 933–1002.

23. Allan Wigfield and A. Laurel Wagner, "Competence, Motivation, and Identity Development during Adolescence," in *Handbook of Competence and Motivation,* eds. Andrew J. Elliott and Carol S. Dweck (New York: Guilford, 2005), 222–239.

24. Lisa S. Blackwell, Kali Trzesniewski, and Carol S. Dweck, "Implicit Theories of Intelligence Predict Achievement across an Adolescent Transition: A Longitudinal Study and an Intervention," *Child Development* 78 (2007): 246–263.

25. Reed W. Larson et al., "Continuity, Stability, and Change in Daily Emotional Experiences across Adolescence," *Child Development* 73 (2002): 1151–1165.

26. Josien Schneiders et al., "Mood Reactivity to Daily Negative Events in Early Adolescence: Relationship to Risk for Psychopathology," *Developmental Psychology* 42 (2006): 543–554.

27. Lisa Flook and Andrew J. Fuligni, "Family and School Spillover in Adolescents' Daily Lives," *Child Development* 79 (2008): 776–787.

28. Ibid.

29. Lisa Kiang et al., "Ethnic Identity and the Daily Psychological Well-Being of Adolescents from Mexican and Chinese Backgrounds," *Child Development* 77 (2006): 1338–1350.

30. Mary J. Levitt, Nathalie Guacci-Franco, and Jerome L. Levitt, "Convoys of Social Support in Childhood and Early Adolescence: Structure and Function," *Developmental Psychology* 29 (1993): 811–818.

31. Reed W. Larson, "Toward a Psychology of Positive Youth Development," *American Psychologist* 55 (2000): 170–183.

32. Ibid., p. 170.

33. Susan Harter, "The Self," in *Handbook of Child Psychology,* 6th ed., eds. Damon and Lerner, vol. 3, 505–570.

34. Erik H. Erikson, *Childhood and Society,* 2nd ed. (New York: Norton, 1963).

35. James F. Marcia, "Identity in Adolescence," in *Handbook of Adolescent Psychology,* ed. Joseph Adelson (New York: Wiley, 1980), 159–187.

36. Harold D. Grotevant, "Adolescent Development in Family Contexts," in *Handbook of Child Psychology,* 5th ed., ed. William Damon, vol. 3: *Social, Emotional, and Personality Development,* ed. Nancy Eisenberg (New York: Wiley, 1998), 1097–1149.

37. Harter, "The Self."

38. Kali H. Trzesniewski et al., "Low Self-Esteem during Adolescence Predicts Poor Health, Criminal Behavior, and Limited Economic Prospects during Adulthood," *Developmental Psychology* 42 (2006): 381–390.

39. Jennifer L. Yunger, Priscilla R. Carver, and David G. Perry, "Does Gender Identity Influence Children's Psychological Well-Being?" *Developmental Psychology* 40 (2004): 572–582.

40. Brooke C. Corby, Ernest V. E. Hodges, and David G. Perry, "Gender Identity and Adjustment in Black, Hispanic, and White Preadolescents," *Developmental Psychology* 43 (2007): 261–266.

41. Ann C. Crouter et al., "Development of Gender Attitude Traditionality across Middle Childhood and Adolescence," *Child Development* 78 (2007): 911–926.

42. Susan McHale et al., "Links Between Sex-Typed Time Use in Middle Childhood and Gender Development in Early Adolescence," *Developmental Psychology* 40 (2004): 868–881.

43. Crouter et al., "Development of Gender Attitude Traditionality."

44. Jean S. Phinney, "Stages of Ethnic Identity Development in Minority Group Adolescents," *Journal of Early Adolescence* 9 (1989): 34–49.

45. Kiang et al., "Ethnic Identity and the Daily Psychological Well-Being of Adolescents from Mexican and Chinese Backgrounds."

46. Eleanor K. Seaton, Krista Maywalt Scottham, and Robert M. Sellers, "The Status Model of Racial Identity Development in African American Adolescents: Evidence of Structure, Trajectories, and Well-Being," *Child Development* 77 (2006): 1416–1426.

47. Gene H. Brody et al., "Perceived Discrimination and the Adjustment of African American Youths: A Five-Year-Longitudinal Analysis with Contextual Moderation Effects," *Child Development* 77 (2006): 1170–1189.

48. Aprile D. Benner and Su Yeong Kim, "Experiences of Discrimination among Chinese American Adolescents and the Consequences for Socioemotional and Academic Development," *Developmental Psychology* 45 (2009): 1682–1694.

49. Wim Meeus et al., "Personality Types in Adolescence: Change and Stability and Links with Adjustment and Relationships: A Five-Wave Longitudinal Study," *Developmental Psychology* 47 (2011): 1181–1195.

50. Nancy Eisenberg and Amanda Sheffield Morris, "Moral Cognitions and Prosocial Responding in Adolescence," in *Handbook of Adolescent Psychology,* 2nd ed., eds. Lerner and Steinberg, 155–188.

51. Reed Larson and Maryse H. Richards, "Daily Companionship in Late Childhood and Early Adolescence: Changing Developmental Contexts," *Child Development* 62 (1991): 284–300.

52. Brian K. Barber, Heidi E. Stolz, and Joseph A. Olsen, "Parental Support, Psychological Control, and Behavioral Control: Assessing Relevance across Time, Culture, and Method," *Monographs of the Society for Research in Child Development 70,* serial no. 282 (2005).

53. Christina Hardway and Andrew J. Fuligni, "Dimensions of Family Connectedness among Adolescents with Mexican, Chinese, and European Backgrounds," *Developmental Psychology* 42 (2006): 1246–1258.

54. Barber, Stolz, and Olsen, "Parental Support, Psychological Control, and Behavioral Control."

55. Judith G. Smetana, "Adolescent-Parent Conflict: Resistance and Subversion as Developmental Process," in *Conflict, Contradiction, and Contrarian Elements in Moral Development and Education,* ed. Larry Nucci (Mahwah, NJ: Erlbaum, 2005), 69–91.

56. Andrew J. Fuligni, "Authority, Autonomy, and Parent-Adolescent Conflict and Cohesion: A Study of Adolescents from Mexican, Chinese, Filipino, and European Backgrounds," *Developmental Psychology* 34 (1998): 782–792.

57. Judith G. Smetana, "Concepts of Self and Social Convention: Adolescents' and Parents' Reasoning about Hypothetical and Actual Family Conflicts," in *Development during the Transition to Adolescence: Minnesota Symposium on Child Psychology,* vol. 21, eds. Megan R. Gunnar and W. Andrew Collins (Hillsdale, NJ: Erlbaum, 1988), 79–122.

58. Smetana, "Adolescent-Parent Conflict."

59. Eisenberg and Morris, "Moral Cognition and Prosocial Responding in Adolescence."

60. Judith G. Smetana, "It's 10 O'Clock: Do You Know Where Your Children Are? Recent Advances in Understanding Parental Monitoring and Adolescents' Information Management," *Child Development Perspectives* 2 (2008): 19–25.

61. Judith G. Smetana et al., "Disclosure and Secrecy in Adolescent-Parent Relationships," *Child Development* 77 (2006): 201–217.

62. Barber, Stolz, and Olsen, "Parental Support, Psychological Control, and Behavioral Control."

63. Eva S. Lefkowitz, Marian Sigman, and Terry Kit-fong Au, "Helping Mothers Discuss Sexuality and AIDS with Adolescents," *Child Development* 71 (2000): 1383–1394.

64. Nancy Eisenberg et al. "Understanding Mother-Adolescent Conflict Discussions: Concurrent and Across-Time Prediction from Youths' Dispositions and Parenting," *Monographs of the Society for Research in Child Development 73,* serial no. 290 (2008).

65. Martha A. Rueter and Rand D. Conger, "Reciprocal Influences between Parenting and Adolescent Problem-Solving Behavior," *Developmental Psychology* 34 (1998): 1470–1482.

66. Mary Pipher, *Reviving Ophelia* (New York: Ballantine Books, 1994), 283.

67. William Pollock, *Real Boys* (New York: Henry Holt, 1998), xxiv.

68. Susan M. McHale et al., "Mothers' and Fathers' Racial Socialization in African American Families: Implications for Youth," *Child Development* 77 (2006): 1387–1402.

69. Velma McBride Murry et al., "Parental Involvement Promotes Rural African American Youths' Self-Pride and Sexual Self-Concepts," *Journal of Marriage and Family* 67 (2005): 627–642.

70. Gene H. Brody et al., "The Strong African American Families Program: Prevention of Youths' High-Risk Behavior and a Test of a Model of Change," *Journal of Family Psychology* 20 (2006): 1–11.

71. Andrew J. Supple et al., "Contextual Influences on Latino Adolescent Ethnic Identity and Academic Outcomes," *Child Developmental* 77 (2006): 1427–1433.

72. Ronald L. Simons et al., "Discrimination, Crime, Ethnic Identity, and Parenting as Correlates of Depressive Symptoms among African American Children: A Multilevel Analysis," *Development and Psychopathology* 14 (2002): 371–393.

73. Supple et al., "Contextual Influences on Latino Adolescent Ethnic Identity and Academic Outcomes."

74. Patrick T. Davies et al., "Child Emotional Security and Interparental Conflict," *Monographs of the Society for Research in Child Development 67,* serial no. 270 (2002).

75. Gene H. Brody et al., "Linking Perceived Discrimination to Longitudinal Changes in African American Mothers' Parenting Practices," *Journal of Marriage and Family 70* (2008): 319–331.

76. Judy Dunn, "Siblings and Socialization," in *Handbook of Socialization: Theory and Research,* eds. Joan E. Grusec and Paul D. Hastings (New York: Guilford, 2007), 309–327.

77. Cheryl Slomkowski et al., "Sisters, Brothers, and Delinquency: Evaluating Social Influence during Early and Middle Adolescence," *Child Development 72* (2001): 271–283.

78. Kenneth H. Rubin, William M. Bukowski, and Jeffrey G. Parker, "Peer Interactions, Relationships, and Groups," in *Handbook of Child Psychology,* 6th ed., eds. Damon and Lerner, vol. 3, 571–645.

79. Kathleen Mullan Harris and Shannon E. Cavanagh, "Indicators of the Peer Environment in Adolescence," in *Key Indicators of Child and Youth Well-Being,* ed. Brett V. Brown (Mahwah, NJ: Erlbaum 2008), 259–278.

80. Kathleen B. McElhaney, Jill Antonishak, and Joseph P. Allen, "'They Like Me, They Like Me Not': Popularity and Adolescents' Perceptions of Acceptance Predicting Social Functioning over Time," *Child Development 79* (2008): 720–731.

81. Laurence Steinberg, *You and Your Adolescent: The Essential Guide for Ages 10–25* (New York: Simon & Schuster, 2011).

82. Patti M. Valkenburg and Jochen Peter, "Preadolescents' and Adolescents' Online Communication and Their Closeness to Friends," *Developmental Psychology 43* (2007): 267–277.

83. Rubin, Bukowski, and Parker, "Peer Interactions, Relationships, and Groups."

84. Amanda J. Rose, Wendy Carlson, and Erika M. Waller, "Prospective Associations of Co-Rumination with Friendship and Emotional Adjustment: Considering the Socioemotional Trade-Offs of Co-Rumination," *Developmental Psychology 43* (2007): 1019–1031.

85. Rubin, Bukowski, and Parker, "Peer Interactions, Relationships, and Groups."

86. Karen Nylund et al., "Subtypes, Severity, and Structural Stability of Peer Victimization: What Does Latent Class Analysis Say?" *Child Development 78* (2007): 1706–1722.

87. Adrienne Nishina and Jaana Juvonen, "Daily Reports of Witnessing and Experiencing Peer Harassment in Middle School," *Child Development 76* (2005): 435–450.

88. Victoria Kim, "Free Speech, Schools, and Cyber-bullying," *Los Angeles Times,* August 3, 2008, A1.

89. Don Dinkmeyer and Gary D. McKay, *STEP/TEEN Systematic Training for Effective Parenting of Teens* (Circle Pines, MN: American Guidance Service, 1983).

90. Adele Faber and Elaine Mazlish, *How to Talk So Kids Will Listen and Listen So Kids Will Talk* (New York: Rawson Wade, 1980).

91. Tori DeAngelis, "Web Pornography's Effects on Children," *Monitor on Psychology,* November 2007, 50–52.

92. Myrna B. Shure with Roberta Israeloff, *Raising a Thinking Preteen* (New York: Henry Holt, 2000).

93. Larson, "Toward a Psychology of Positive Youth Development," 170.

94. Dahl, "Adolescent Brain Development."

95. Larson, "Toward a Psychology of Positive Youth Development," 177.

96. Ibid., p. 179.

97. Ibid.

98. Rubin, Bukowski, and Parker, "Peer Interactions, Relationships, and Groups."

99. Ibid.

100. Ibid.

101. James Garbarino and Ellen deLara, *And Words Can Hurt Forever* (New York: Free Press, 2002).

102. Linda A. Jackson et al., "Does Home Internet Use Influence the Academic Performance of Low-Income Children?" *Developmental Psychology 42* (2006): 429–435.

103. Jan Hoffman, "I Know What You Did Last Math Class," *New York Times,* May 4, 2008, Sunday Styles, 1.

104. Ellen Galinsky, *Between Generations: The Six Stages of Parenthood* (New York: Times Books, 1981).

105. William Damon, *The Youth Charter: How Communities Can Work Together to Raise Standards for All Children* (New York: Free Press, 1997).

106. Ibid., p. ix.

CHAPTER ELEVEN

1. Ronald E. Dahl, "Adolescent Brain Development: A Period of Vulnerabilities and Opportunities," *Annals of the New York Academy of Science 1021* (2004): 1–22.

2. Centers for Disease Control and Prevention, "Youth Risk Behavior Surveillance—United States, 2009." Surveillance Summaries, June 4, 2010. MMWR Report 2010, 59 (No. SS–5).

3. Ibid.

4. Ritch C. Savin-Williams and Lisa M. Diamond, "Sex," in *Handbook of Adolescent Psychology,* 2nd ed., eds. Richard M. Lerner and Laurence Steinberg (Hoboken, NJ: Wiley, 2004), 189–231.

5. Ibid.

6. Centers for Disease Control and Prevention, "Youth Risk Behavior Surveillance."

7. Tina Hoff, Liberty Greene, and Julia Davis, *National Survey of Adolescents and Young Adults: Sexual Health Knowledge, Attitudes and Experiences* (Menlo Park, CA: Kaiser Family Foundation, 2003).

8. Ibid.

9. Centers for Disease Control and Prevention, "Youth Risk Behavior Surveillance."

10. Jerald G. Bachman et al., *The Education-Drug Use Connection: How Successes and Failures in School Relate to Adolescent Smoking, Drinking, Drug Use, and Delinquency* (New York: Erlbaum, 2008).

11. Laurie Chassin et al., "Adolescent Substance Use," in *Handbook of Adolescent Psychology,* 2nd ed., eds. Lerner and Steinberg, 665–696.

12. Hoff, Greene, and Davis, *National Survey of Adolescents and Young Adults.*

13. Susan T. Ennett et al., "The Social Ecology of Adolescent Alcohol Misuse," *Child Development 79* (2008): 1777–1791.

14. Bachman et al., *The Education-Drug Use Connection.*

15. Megan E. Patrick and John E. Schulenberg, "How Trajectories of Reasons for Alcohol Use Relate to Trajectories of Binge Drinking: National Panel Data Spanning Late Adolescence to Early Adulthood," *Developmental Psychology 47* (2011): 311–317.

16. Joyce A. Martin et al., "Annual Summary of Vital Statistics: 2006," *Pediatrics 121* (2008): 788–801.

17. Hoff, Greene, and Davis, *National Survey of Adolescents and Young Adults.*

18. Kerry M. Green and Margaret E. Ensminger, "Adult Social Behavioral Effects of Heavy Adolescent Marijuana Use among African Americans," *Developmental Psychology 42* (2006): 1168–1178.

19. Bachman et al., *The Education-Drug Use Connection.*

20. Ibid., p. 30.

21. Centers for Disease Control and Prevention, "Youth Risk Behavior Surveillance."

22. Judith Owens, Katherine Belon, and Patrick Moss, "Impact of Delaying School Start Time on Adolescent Sleep, Mood, and Behavior," *Archives of Pediatric and Adolescent Medicine 164* (2010): 608–614.

23. Karen Bartsch, "Adolescents' Theoretical Thinking," in *Early Adolescent Perspectives on Research, Policy, and Intervention,* ed. Richard M. Lerner (Hillsdale, NJ: Erlbaum, 1993), 143–157.

24. Laurence Steinberg et al., "Age Differences in Future Orientation and Delay Discounting," *Child Development 80* (2009): 28–44.

25. Dahl, "Adolescent Brain Development."

26. Ibid.

27. Margo Gardner and Laurence Steinberg, "Peer Influence on Risk Taking, Risk Preference, and Risky Decision Making in Adolescence and Adulthood: An Experimental Study," *Developmental Psychology 41* (2005): 625–635.

28. Jacquelynne S. Eccles, "Schools, Academic Motivation, and Stage-Environment Fit," in *Handbook of Adolescent Psychology,* 2nd ed., eds. Lerner and Steinberg, 125–153.

29. Ibid.

30. Ibid.

31. Ibid.

32. W. Andrew Collins and Laurence Steinberg, "Adolescent Development in Interpersonal Context," in *Handbook of Child Psychology,* 6th ed., eds. William Damon and Richard M. Lerner, vol. 3: *Social, Emotional, and Personality*

Development, ed. Nancy Eisenberg (Hoboken, NJ: Wiley, 2006), 1003–1067.

33. Jerald G. Bachman et al., "Twelfth-Grade Student Work Intensity Linked to Later Educational Attainment and Substance Use: New Longitudinal Evidence," *Developmental Psychology 47* (2011): 344–363; Kathryn C. Monahan, Joanna M. Lee, and Laurence Steinberg, "Revisiting the Impact of Part-Time Work on Adolescent Adjustment: Distinguishing between Selection and Socialization Using Propensity Score Matching," *Child Development 82* (2011): 96–112.

34. Dahl, "Adolescent Brain Development."

35. Michael A. Busseri et al., "A Longitudinal Examination of Breadth and Intensity of Youth Activity Involvement and Successful Development," *Developmental Psychology 42* (2006): 1313–1326.

36. Nikki Pearce Dawes and Reed Larson, "How Youth Get Engaged: Ground-Theory Research on Motivational Development in Organized Youth Programs," *Developmental Psychology 47* (2011): 259–269.

37. Dustin Wood, Reed W. Larson, and Jane R. Brown, "How Adolescents Come to See Themselves as More Responsible through Participation in Youth Programs," *Child Development 80* (2009): 295–309.

38. Joseph L. Mahoney, Angela L. Harris, and Jacquelynne S. Eccles, "Organized Activity Participation, Positive Youth Development, and the Overscheduling Hypothesis," *Social Policy Report 20* (4) (2006): 1–30.

39. Susan Harter, "The Self," in *Handbook of Child Psychology,* 6th ed., eds. Damon and Lerner, vol. 3, 505–570.

40. J. Scott Brown, Sarah O. Meadows, and Glen H. Elder, Jr., "Race-Ethnic Inequality and Psychological Distress: Depressive Symptoms from Adolescence to Young Adulthood," *Developmental Psychology 43* (2007): 1295–1311.

41. Inge Seiffge-Krenke, Kaisa Aunala, and Jari-Erik Nurmi, "Changes in Stress Perception and Coping During Adolescence: The Role of Situational and Personal Factors," *Child Development 80* (2009): 259–279.

42. Emily A. Impett et al., "Girls' Relationship Authenticity and Self-Esteem Across Adolescence," *Developmental Psychology 44* (2008): 722–733.

43. Harter, "The Self."

44. Monisha Pasupathi and Timothy Hoyt, "The Development of Narrative Identity in Late Adolescence and Emerging Adulthood: The Continued Importance of Listeners," *Developmental Psychology 45* (2009): 558–574.

45. Harter, "The Self."

46. Nancy L. Galambos, "Gender and Gender Role Development in Adolescence," in *Handbook of Adolescent Psychology,* 2nd ed., eds. Lerner and Steinberg, 233–262.

47. Erica S. Weisgram, Rebecca S. Bigler, and Lynn S. Liben, "Gender Values, and Occupational Interests among Children, Adolescents, and Adults," *Child Development 81* (2010): 778–796.

48. Galambos, "Gender and Gender Role Development in Adolescence."

49. Janet S. Hyde et al., "Gender Similarities Characterize Math Performers," *Science 321* (2008): 495.

50. Jack Block, "Some Relationships Regarding the Self from the Block and Block Longitudinal Study," paper presented at the Social Science Research Council conference on Selfhood, Stanford, CA, October 1985.

51. Campbell Leaper and Christia Spears Brown, "Perceived Experiences with Sexism among Adolescent Girls," *Child Development 79* (2008): 685–704.

52. Ibid.

53. Ritch C. Savin-Williams, *The New Gay Teenager* (Cambridge, MA: Harvard University Press, 2005).

54. Lisa M. Diamond, "Female Bisexuality From Adolescence to Adulthood: Results From a 10-Year Longitudinal Study," *Developmental Psychology 44* (2008): 5–14.

55. Savin-Williams and Diamond, "Sex."

56. V. Paul Poteat, "Peer Group Socialization of Homophobic Attitudes and Behavior during Adolescence, *Child Development 78* (2007): 1830–1842.

57. Anthony R. D'Augelli, Arnold H. Grossman, and Michael T. Starks, "Parents' Awareness of Lesbian, Gay, and Bisexual Youths' Sexual Orientations," *Journal of Marriage and Family 67* (2005): 474–482.

58. Laurie Hetherington and Justin A. Lavner, "Coming to Terms with Coming Out: Review and Recommendations for Family Systems-Focused Research," *Journal of Family Psychology 22* (2008): 329–343.

59. Michael A. Busseri et al., "On the Association between Sexual Attraction and Adolescent Risk Behavior Involvement: Examining Mediation and Moderation," *Developmental Psychology* 44 (2008): 69–80.

60. Savin-Williams, *The New Gay Teenager*.

61. Kenneth J. Zucker, "Gender Identity Development and Issues," *Child and Adolescent Psychiatric Clinics of North America 13* (2004): 551–568.

62. Kelly D. Drummond et al., "A Follow-Up Study of Girls with Gender Identity Disorder," *Developmental Psychology 44* (2008): 34–45.

63. Amy K. Marks, Flannery Patton, and Cynthia Garcia Coll, "Being Bicultural: A Mixed-Methods Study of Adolescents' Implicitly and Explicitly Measured Multiethnic Identities, *Developmental Psychology* 47 (2011): 270–288.

64. Andrew J. Fuligni et al., "Stability and Change in Ethnic Labeling among Adolescents from Asian and Latin American Immigrant Families," *Child Development 79* (2008): 944–956.

65. Tiffany Yip, Elinor K. Seaton, and Robert M. Sellers, "Interracial and Intraracial Contact, School-Level Diversity, and Change in Racial Identity Status among African American Adolescents," *Child Development 81* (2010): 1431–1444.

66. Kerstin Pahl and Niobe Way, "Longitudinal Trajectories of Ethnic Identity among Urban Black and Latino Adolescents," *Child Development 77* (2006): 1403–1415.

67. Melissa L. Greene, Niobe Way, and Kerstin Pahl, "Trajectories of Perceived Adult and Peer Discrimination among Black, Latino/a, and Asian American Adolescents: Patterns and Psychological Correlates," *Developmental Psychology 42* (2006): 218–236.

68. Pahl and Way, "Longitudinal Trajectories of Ethnic Identity among Urban Black and Latino Adolescents."

69. Renee V. Galliher, Matthew D. Jones, and Angie Dahl, "Concurrent and Longitudinal Effects of Ethnic Identity and Experiences of Discrimination on Psychosocial Adjustment of Navajo Adolescents," *Developmental Psychology 47* (2011): 509–526.

70. Nancy Rumbaugh Whitesell et al., "Developmental Trajectories of Personal and Collective Self-Concept among American Indian Adolescents," *Child Development 77* (2006): 1487–1503.

71. Jean S. Phinney and Mona Devich-Navarro, "Variations in Bicultural Identification among African-American and Mexican-American Adolescents," *Journal of Research on Adolescence 7* (1997): 3–32.

72. Maria Wong et al., "Behavioral Control and Resiliency in the Onset of Alcohol and Illicit Drug Use: A Prospective Study from Preschool to Adolescence," *Child Development 77* (2006): 1016–1033; Lisa J. Crockett et al., "Psychological Profiles and Adolescent Adjustment: A Person-Centered Approach," *Development and Psychopathology 18* (2006): 195–214.

73. Bachman et al., *The Education-Drug Use Connection*.

74. Wong et al. "Behavioral Control and Resiliency in the Onset of Alcohol and Illicit Drug Use"; Crockett et al., "Psychological Profiles and Adolescent Adjustment.

75. Crockett et al. "Psychological Profiles and Adolescent Adjustment.

76. Scott J. South, Dana L. Haynie, and Sunita Bose, "Residential Mobility and the Onset of Adolescent Sexual Activity," *Journal of Marriage and Family 67* (2005): 499–514.

77. David B. Henry et al., "Peer Selection and Socialization Effects on Adolescent Intercourse Without a Condom and Attitudes about the Costs of Sex," *Child Development 78* (2007): 825–838.

78. Bachman et al., *The Education-Drug Use Connection*.

79. Elizabeth A. Pomery et al., "Families and Risk: Prospective Analyses of Familial and Social Influences on Adolescent Substance Use," *Journal of Family Psychology 19* (2005): 560–570.

80. Ibid.

81. Steinunn Gestsdottir and Richard M. Lerner, "Intentional Self-Regulation and Positive Youth Development in Early Adolescence: Findings from the 4-H Study of Positive Youth Development," *Developmental Psychology 43* (2007): 508–521.

82. Bachman et al., *The Education-Drug Use Connection*.

83. Michael D. Resnick et al., "Protecting Adolescents from Harm," *Journal of the American Medical Association 278* (1997): 823–832.

84. Pamela Ebstyne King and James L. Furrow, "Religion as a Resource for Positive Youth Development: Religion, Social Capital, and Moral Outcomes," *Developmental Psychology 40* (2004): 703–713.

85. Fritz K. Oser, W. George Scarlett, and Anton Bucher, "Religious and Spiritual Development throughout the Life Span," in *Handbook of Child Psychology*, 6th ed., eds. William Damon and Richard M. Lerner, vol. 1: *Theoretical Models of Human Development*, ed. Richard M. Lerner (Hoboken, NJ: Wiley, 2006), 942–998.

86. Anna B. Lopez, Virginia W. Huynh, and Andrew J. Fuligni, "A Longitudinal Study of Religious Identity and Participation during Adolescence," *Child Development 82* (2011): 1297–1309.

87. Joseph P. Allen, "The Attachment System in Adolescence," in *Handbook of Attachment*, 2nd ed., eds. Jude Cassidy and Phillip R. Shaver (New York: Guilford, 2008), 424.

88. Kee Jeong Kim et al., "Parent-Adolescent Reciprocity in Negative Affect and Its Relation to Early Adult Social Development," *Developmental Psychology 37* (2001): 775–790.

89. Diana Baumrind, "The Influence of Parenting Style on Adolescent Competence, and Problem Behavior," paper presented at the American Psychological Association Meetings, New Orleans, LA, August 1989, 16.

90. Collins and Steinberg, "Adolescent Development in Interpersonal Context."

91. Mark E. Feinberg, Marni L. Kan, and E. Mavis Hetherington, "The Longitudinal Influence of Coparenting Conflict on Parental Negativity and Adolescent Maladjustment," *Journal of Marriage and Family 69* (2007): 687–702.

92. Feinberg, Kan, and Hetherington, "The Longitudinal Influence of Coparenting Conflict on Parental Negativity and Adolescent Maladjustment"; Megan E. Baril, Ann C. Crouter, and Susan M. McHale, "Processes Linking Adolescent Well-Being, Marital Love, and Coparenting," *Journal of Family Psychology 21* (2007): 645–654.

93. Collins and Steinberg, "Adolescent Development in Interpersonal Context."

94. Andrew J. Fuligni, Vivian Tseng, and May Lam, "Attitudes toward Family Obligations among American Adolescents with Asian, Latin American, and European Backgrounds," *Child Development 70* (1999): 1039.

95. Hoff, Greene, and Davis, *National Survey of Adolescents and Young Adults.*

96. Hetherington and Lavner, "Coming to Terms with 'Coming Out.'"

97. Velma McBride Murry et al., "Parental Involvement Promotes Rural African American Youths' Self-Pride and Sexual Self-Concepts," *Journal of Marriage and Family 67* (2005): 627–642.

98. Kimberly A. Updegraff et al., "Adolescent Sibling Relationships in Mexican American Families: Exploring the Role of Familism," *Journal of Family Psychology 19* (2005): 512–522.

99. Mark E. Feinberg et al., "Differential Association of Family Subsystem Negativity on Siblings' Maladjustment: Using Behavior Genetic Methods to Test Process Theory," *Journal of Family Psychology 19* (2005): 601–610.

100. Pomery et al., "Families and Risk."

101. Collins and Steinberg, "Adolescent Development in Interpersonal Context."

102. Wyndol Furman, "Friends and Lovers: The Role of Peer Relationships in Adolescent Romantic Relationships," in *Relationships as Developmental Contexts: The 30th Minnesota Symposium on Child Development,* eds. W. Andrew Collins and Brett Laursen (Hillsdale, NJ: Erlbaum, 1999), 133–154.

103. Duane Buhrmester, "Intimacy and Friendship, Interpersonal Competence, and Adjustment during Preadolescence and Adolescence," *Child Development 61* (1990): 1101–1111.

104. B. Bradford Brown, "Adolescents' Relationships with Peers," in *Handbook of Adolescent Psychology,* 2nd ed., eds. Lerner and Steinberg, 363–394.

105. Ibid.

106. Ibid.

107. Ibid.

108. Geoffrey L. Ream and Ritch C. Savin-Williams, "Reciprocal Associations between Adolescent Sexual Activity and Quality of Youth-Parent Interactions," *Journal of Family Psychology 19* (2005): 171–179.

109. Ann M. Meier, "Adolescent First Sex and Subsequent Mental Health," *American Journal of Sociology 112* (2007): 1811–1847.

110. Ream and Savin-Williams, "Reciprocal Associations between Adolescent Sexual Activity and Quality of Youth-Parent Interactions."

111. Frederick J. Zimmerman, "Children's Media Use and Sleep Problems: Issues and Unanswerable Questions," Kaiser Family Foundation Report No. 7674, June 2008, www.kff.org.

112. Emma K. Adam, Emily K. Snell, and Patricia Pendry, "Sleep Timing and Quantity in Ecological and Family Context: A Nationally Representative Time-Diary Study," *Journal of Family Psychology 21* (2007): 4–19.

113. Alice M. Gregory et al., "Family Conflict in Childhood: A Predictor of Later Insomnia," *Sleep 29* (2006): 1063–1067.

114. Adam, Snell, and Pendry, "Sleep Timing and Quantity in Ecological and Family Context."

115. David Ludwig with Suzanne Rostler, *Ending the Food Fight* (New York: Houghton Mifflin, 2007).

116. Ibid.

117. G. Terence Wilson, Carlos M. Grilo, and Kelly M. Vitousek, "Psychological Treatment of Eating Disorders," *American Psychologist 62* (2007): 199–216.

118. Mark Chavez and Thomas R. Insel, "Eating Disorders: National Institute of Mental Health's Perspective," *American Psychologist 62* (2007): 159–166.

119. Wilson, Grilo, and Vitousek, "Psychological Treatment of Eating Disorders."

120. Erin Calhoun Davis and Lisa V. Friel, "Adolescent Sexuality: Disentangling the Effects of Family Structure and Family Context," *Journal of Marriage and Family 63* (2001): 669–681.

121. Rebekah Levine Coley, Elizabeth Votruba-Drzal, and Holly S. Schindler, "Fathers' and Mothers' Parenting Predicting and Responding to Adolescent Sexual Risk Behavior," *Child Development 80* (2009): 808–827.

122. Jonathan D. Klein and the Committee on Adolescence, "Adolescent Pregnancy: Current Trends and Issues," *Pediatrics 116* (2005): 281–286.

123. Rinka M. P. Van Zundert et al., "Pathways to Alcohol Use among Dutch Students in Regular Education and Education for Adolescents with Behavioral Problems: The Role of Parental Alcohol Use, General Parenting Practices, and Alcohol-Specific Parenting Practices," *Journal of Family Psychology 20* (2006): 456–467.

124. Michael S. Robbins et al., "The Efficacy of Structural Ecosystems Therapy with Drug Abusing/Dependent African American and Hispanic American Adolescents," *Journal of Family Psychology 22* (2008): 51–61.

125. Deborah M. Capaldi and Mike Stoolmiller, "Co-occurrence of Conduct Problems and Depressive Symptoms in Early Adolescent Boys: III. Prediction to Young Adult Adjustment." *Development and Psychopathology 11* (1999): 59–84.

126. Ibid., p. 78.

127. Alice W. Pope and Karen L. Bierman, "Predicting Adolescent Peer Problems and Antisocial Activities: The Relative Roles of Aggression and Dysregulation," *Developmental Psychology 35* (1999): 335–346.

128. Capaldi and Stoolmiller, "Co-occurrence of Conduct Problems and Depressive Symptoms in Early Adolescent Boys."

129. Nicola M. Curtis et al., "Dissemination and Effectiveness of Multisystemics Treatment in New Zealand: A Benchmaking Study," *Journal of Family Psychology 23* (2009): 119–129.

130. Dante Cicchetti and Sheree L. Toth, "The Development of Depression in Children and Adolescents," *American Psychologist 53* (1998): 221–241.

131. Donald H. McKnew, Leon Cytryn, and Herbert Yahraes, *Why Isn't Johnny Crying?* (New York: Norton, 1983).

132. Cicchetti and Toth, "The Development of Depression in Children and Adolescents."

133. Harold S. Koplewicz, *More Than Moody: Recognizing and Treating Adolescent Depression* (New York: Putnam, 2002).

134. Jennifer J. Connor and Martha A Rueter, "Parent-Child Relationships as Systems of Support or Risk for Adolescent Suicidality," *Journal of Family Psychology 20* (2006): 143–155.

135. Julia A. Graber, "Internalizing Problems during Adolescence," in *Handbook of Adolescent Psychology*, 2nd ed., eds. Lerner and Steinberg, 587–626.

136. Anne C. Petersen et al., "Depression in Adolescence," *American Psychologist 48* (1993): 135–168.

137. Brown, Meadows, and Elder, Jr., "Race-Ethnic Inequality and Psychological Distress."

138. Ibid., p. 308.

139. Arin M. Connell and Thomas J. Dishion, "Reducing Depression among At-Risk Early Adolescents: Three-Year Effects of a Family-Centered Intervention Embedded within Schools," *Journal of Family Psychology 22* (2008): 574–585.

140. Collins and Steinberg, "Adolescent Development in Interpersonal Context."

141. W. Andrew Collins et al., "Conflict Processes and Transitions in Parent and Peer Relationships," *Journal of Adolescent Research 12* (1997): 179–198.

142. Robert B. McCall, Cynthia Evahn, and Lynn Kratzer, *High School Underachievers.* (Newbury Park, CA: Sage, 1992).

143. Anthony L. Burrow and Patrick L. Hill, "Purpose as a Form of Identity Capital for Positive Youth Adjustment," *Developmental Psychology 47* (2011): 1196–1206.

144. William Damon, *The Path to Purpose: Helping Our Children Find Their Calling in Life* (New York: Free Press, 2008), 131.

145. Marcia Herrin and Nancy Matsumoto, *The Parent's Guide to Childhood Eating Disorders* (New York: Holt, 2002).

146. Koplewicz, "*More Than Moody.*

147. Harold J. Koplewicz, "More then Moody: Recognizing and Treating Adolescent Depression," *Brown University Child and Adolescent Newsletter 18,* December 24, 2002, 7.

148. Jane E. Brody, "Adolescent Angst or a Deeper Disorder? Tips for Spotting Serious Symptoms," *New York Times*, December 24, 2002, D5.

149. Nikki Babbit, *Adolescent Drug and Alcohol Abuse: How to Stop It and Get Help for Your Family* (Sebastopol, CA: O'Reilly, 2000).

150. Laurence Steinberg and Wendy Steinberg, *Crossing Paths: How Your Children's Adolescence Triggers Your Own Crisis* (New York: Simon & Schuster, 1994).

151. Gail S. Goodman, Robert E. Emery, and Jeffrey J. Haugaard, "Developmental Psychology and the Law: Divorce, Child Maltreatment, Foster Care, and Adoption," in *Handbook of Child Psychology,* 5th ed., ed. William Damon, vol. 4: *Child Psychology in Practice,* eds. Irving E. Sigel and K. Ann Renninger (New York: Wiley, 1998), 775–784.

152. Jeffrey Jensen Arnett, "Conceptions of the Transition to Adulthood: Perspectives from Adolescence through Midlife," *Journal of Adult Development 8* (2001): 133–143.

153. D. Wayne Osgood et al., "Six Paths to Adulthood: Fast Starters, Parents without Careers, Educated Partners, Educated Singles, Working Singles, and Slow Starters," in *On the Frontier of Adulthood: Theory, Research, and Public Policy.* eds. Richard A. Settersten, Jr., Frank F. Furstenberg, Jr., and Ruben C. Rumbaut (Chicago: University of Chicago Press, 2005), 320–355.

154. John Schulenberg et al., "Early Adult Transitions and Their Relation to Well-Being and Substance Use," in *On the Frontier of Adulthood,* eds. Settersten, Furstenberg, and Rumbaut, 417–453.

155. Nancy L. Galambos, Erin T. Barker, and Harvey J. Krahn, "Depression, Self-Esteem, and Anger in Emerging Adulthood: Seven-Year Trajectories," *Developmental Psychology 42* (2006): 350–365.

156. Ibid.

157. Schulenberg et al., "Early Adult Transitions and Their Relation to Well- Being and Substance Use."

158. John E. Schulenberg and Nicole R. Zarrett, "Mental Health during Emerging Adulthood: Continuity and Discontinuity in Courses, Causes, and Functions," in *Emerging Adults in America: Coming of Age in the 21st century,* eds. Jeffrey Jensen Arnett and Jennifer Lynn Tanner (Washington, DC: American Psychological Association, 2006), 135–172.

159. Carol L. Gohm et al., "Culture, Parental Conflict, Parental Marital Status, and the Subjective Well-Being of Young Adults," *Journal of Marriage and the Family 60* (1998): 319–344.

160. Moncrieff Cochran, "Parenting and Personal Social Networks," in *Parenting: An Ecological Perspective,* eds. Tom Luster and Lynn Okagaki (Hillsdale, NJ: Erlbaum, 1993), 149–178.

161. Robert F. Shoeni and Karen E. Ross, "Material Assistance from Families

during the Transition to Adulthood," in *On the Frontier of Adulthood,* eds. Settersten, Furstenberg, and Rumbaut, 396–416.

162. Cochran, "Parenting and Personal Social Networks."

163. Shoeni and Ross, "Material Assistance from Families during the Transition to Adulthood."

164. Osgood et al., "Six Paths to Adulthood."

165. E. Michael Foster and Elizabeth J. Gifford, "The Transition to Adulthood for Youth Leaving Public Systems: Challenges to Policies and Research," in *On the Frontier of Adulthood,* eds. Settersten, Furstenberg, and Rumbaut, 501–533.

166. Steven L. Gortmaker et al., "An Unexpected Success Story: Transition to Adulthood in Youth with Chronic Physical Health Conditions," *Journal of Research on Adolescence 3* (1993): 333.

167. John Mollenkopf et al., "The Ever Winding Path: Ethnic and Racial Diversity in the Transition to Adulthood," in *On the Frontier of Adulthood,* eds. Settersten, Furstenberg, and Rumbaut, 454–500.

168. Jean S. Phinney, "Ethnic Identity Exploration in Emerging Adulthood," in *Emerging Adults in America,* eds. Arnett and Tanner, 117–134.

169. William S. Aquilino, "Family Relationships and Support Systems in Emerging Adulthood," in *Emerging Adults in America,* eds. Arnett and Tanner, 193–217.

170. Ibid.

171. Erica Goode, "Students' Emotional Health Worsens," *San Francisco Chronicle,* 3 February 2003, A9.

172. Ray Delgado, "Report on College Drinking's Toll Shows Health Crisis, Experts Say," *San Francisco Chronicle,* April 10, 2002, A7.

173. Katherine S. Newman, *The Accordion Family: Boomerang Kids, Anxious Parents, and the Private Toll of Global Competition* (Boston: Beacon Press, 2012.)

CHAPTER TWELVE

1. U.S. Census Bureau, *Statistical Abstract of the United States: 2011,* 130th ed., (Washington, DC: U.S. Government Printing Office, 2010).

2. Suzanne M. Bianchi, "Changing Families, Changing Workplaces," *Future of Children 21* (2011): 15–36.

3. Ibid.

4. Lynn Craig and Killian Mullan, "Parenthood, Gender, and Work-Family Time in the United States, Australia, Italy, France, and Denmark," *Journal of Marriage and Family 72* (2010): 1344–1361.

5. Christopher J. Ruhm, "Policies to Assist Parents with Young Children," *Future of Children 21* (2011): 37–65.

6. Ibid.

7. Mark A. Schuster, Paul J. Chung, and Katherine D. Vestal, "Children with Health Issues," *Future of Children 21* (2011): 91–116.

8. Ruhm, "Policies to Assist Parents with Young Children."

9. Ibid.

10. Alison Earle, Zitha Mokomane, and Jody Heymann, "International Perspectives on Work-Family Policies: Lessons from the World's Most Competitive Economies," *Future of Children 21* (2011): 191–210.

11. Ibid.

12. Suzanne M. Bianchi and Melissa A. Milkie, "Work and Family Research in the First Decade of the 21st Century," *Journal of Marriage and Family 72* (2010): 705–725.

13. Bianchi, "Changing Families, Changing Workplaces."

14. Patricia Voydanoff, *Work, Family, and Community: Exploring Interconnections* (New York: Psychology Press, 2007).

15. Bianchi, "Changing Families, Changing Workplaces."

16. Ibid.

17. Maureen Perry-Jenkins et al., "Working-Class Jobs and New Parents' Mental Health," *Journal of Marriage and Family 73* (2011): 1117–1132.

18. Julie E. Press, Jay Fagan, and Lynda Laughlin, "Taking Pressure Off Families: Child Care Subsidies Lessen Mothers' Work-Hour Problems," *Journal of Marriage and Family 68* (2006): 155–171.

19. E. Jeffrey Hill et al., "Workplace Flexibility: Work Hours and Work-Life Conflicts," *Journal of Family Psychology 24* (2010): 349–355.

20. Ellen Galinsky, *Ask the Children: What America's Children Really Think about Working Parents* (New York: Morrow, 1999).

21. Marc S. Schulz, "Parents' Work Experiences and Children's Adaptation to School," in *The Family Context of Parenting in Children's Adaptation to Elementary School,* eds. Philip A. Cowan et al. (Mahwah, NJ: Erlbaum, 2005), 237–253.

22. Ariel Kalil and Kathleen M. Ziol-Guest, "Single Mothers' Employment Dynamics and Adolescent Well-Being," *Child Development 76* (2005): 196–211.

23. Galinsky, *Ask the Children.*
24. Ibid.
25. Ibid.
26. Ibid.
27. Rena L. Repetti and Jennifer Wood, "Effects of Daily Stress at Work on Mothers' Interactions with Preschoolers," *Journal of Family Psychology 11* (1997): 90–108.
28. Lisa B. Story and Rena Repetti, "Daily Occupational Stressors and Marital Behavior," *Journal of Family Psychology 20* (2006): 690–700.
29. Lyndall Strazdins et al., "Unsociable Work? Nonstandard Work Schedules, Family Relationships, and Children's Well-Being," *Journal of Marriage and Family 68* (2006): 394–410.
30. Wen-Jui Han and Liana E. Fox, "Parental Work Schedules and Children's Cognitive Trajectories," *Journal of Marriage and Family 73* (2011): 962–980.
31. JoAnn Hsueh and Hirokazu Yoshikawa, "Working Nonstandard Schedules and Variable Shifts in Low-Income Families: Associations with Parental Psychological Well-Being, Family Functioning, and Child Well-Being," *Developmental Psychology 43* (2007): 620–632.
32. Rachel Dunifon, Ariel Kalil, and Ashish Bajracharya, "Maternal Working Conditions and Child Well-Being in Welfare Leaving Families," *Developmental Psychology 41* (2005): 851–859.
33. Galinsky, *Ask the Children.*
34. Rosalind Chait Barnett and Karen C. Gareis, "Parental After-School Stress and Psychological Well–Being," *Journal of Marriage and Family 68* (2006): 101–108.
35. Joseph G. Grzywacz, David M. Almeida, and Daniel A. McDonald, "Work-Family Spillover and Daily Reports of Work and Family Stress in the Adult Labor Force," *Family Relations 51* (2002): 28–36.
36. Margaret B. Neal and Leslie B. Hammer, *Working Couples Caring for Children and Aging Parents: Effects on Work and Well-Being* (New York: Erlbaum, 2007).
37. David J. Maume, "Gender Differences in Restricting Work Efforts Because of Family Responsibilities," *Journal of Marriage and Family 68* (2006): 859–869.
38. Neal and Hammer, *Working Couples Caring for Children and Aging Parents.*
39. Galinsky, *Ask the Children.*
40. Suzanne M. Bianchi, John P. Robinson, & Melissa A. Milkie, *Changing Rhythms of American Family Life* (New York: Russell Sage, 2006).
41. Michael E. Lamb and Lieselotte Ahnert, "Nonparental Child Care: Context, Concepts, Correlates, and Consequences," in *Handbook of Child Psychology,* 6th ed., eds. William Damon and Richard M. Lerner, vol. 4: *Child Psychology in Practice,* eds. K. Ann Renninger and Irving E. Sigel (Hoboken, NJ: Wiley, 2006), 950–1016; Shira Offer and Barbara Schneider, "Multitasking among Working Families: A Strategy for Dealing with the Time Squeeze," in *Workplace Flexibility: Realigning 20th-Century Jobs for a 21st Century Workforce,* eds. Kathleen Christensen and Barbara Schneider (Ithaca: Cornell University Press, 2010), 43–56.
42. Belinda Campos et al., "Opportunity for Interaction? A Naturalistic Observation Study of Dual-Earner Families after Work and School," *Journal of Family Psychology 23* (2009): 798–807.
43. Bianchi, Robinson, and Milkie, *Changing Rhythms of American Family Life.*
44. Kevin M. Roy, Carolyn Y. Tubbs, and Linda M. Burton, "Don't Have No Time: Daily Rhythms and the Organization of Time for Low-Income Families," *Family Relations 53* (2004): 168–173.
45. Ibid.
46. Galinsky, *Ask the Children.*
47. Ann C. Crouter and Susan M. McHale, "The Long Arm of the Job Revisited: Parenting in Dual-Earner Families," in *Parenting: An Ecological Perspective,* 2nd ed., eds. Tom Luster and Lynn Okagaki (Mahwah, NJ: Erlbaum, 2005), 275–296.
48. Gregory Petit, "After-School Experience and Social Adjustment in Early Adolescence: Individual, Family, and Neighborhood Risk Factors," paper presented at the Meetings of the Society for Research in Child Development in Washington, DC, April 11, 1997.
49. Jean L. Richardson et al., "Substance Use among Eighth-Grade Students Who Take Care of Themselves after School," *Pediatrics 84* (1989): 556–566.
50. Galinsky, *Ask the Children.*
51. Ibid., p. 232.
52. Lamb and Ahnert, "Nonparental Care," 951.
53. Ibid.
54. Ibid.

55. Edward F. Zigler, Matia Finn-Stevenson, and Nancy W. Hall, *The First Three Years of Life and Beyond* (New Haven, CT: Yale University Press, 2002).

56. Lamb and Ahnert, "Nonparental Care."

57. National Association of Child Care Resource and Referral Agencies, *Parents and the High Cost of Child Care: 2011 Update,* Arlington, VA, 2011.

58. Zigler, Finn-Stevenson, and Hall, *The First Three Years of Life and Beyond.*

59. Lamb and Ahnert, "Nonparental Care."

60. Carollee Howes, Deborah A. Phillips, and Marcy Whitebook, "Thresholds of Quality Implications for the Social Development of Children in Center-Based Child Care," *Child Development 63* (1992): 449–460.

61. Cheryl D. Hayes, John L. Palmer, and Martha Zaslow, eds., *Who Cares for America's Children* (Washington, DC: National Academy Press, 1990).

62. Carollee Howes, Catherine C. Matheson, and Claire B. Hamilton, "Maternal, Teacher, and Child Care History Correlates of Children's Relationships with Peers," *Child Development 65* (1994): 264–273.

63. National Association of Child Care Resource and Referral Agencies, *We Can Do Better: NACCRRA Rankings of State Child Care Center Standards and Oversight* (Arlington, VA: 2007).

64. Suzanne W. Helburn and Carollee Howes, "Child Care Cost and Quality," *Future of Children 6* (2) (1996): 62–82.

65. Ibid., p. 69.

66. Ibid.

67. Lamb and Ahnert, "Nonparental Care."

68. Ibid.

69. Rachel A. Gordon and Robin S. Hognas, "The Best Laid Plans: Expectations, Preferences, and Stability of Child Care Arrangements," *Journal of Marriage and Family 68* (2006): 373–393.

70. Henry Tran and Marsha Weinraub, "Child Care Effects in Context: Quality, Stability, and Multiplicity in Nonmaternal Child Care Arrangements during the First 15 Months of Life," *Developmental Psychology 42* (2006): 566–582.

71. Ibid.

72. Taryn W. Morrissey, "Multiple Child-Care Arrangements and Young Children's Behavioral Outcomes," *Child Development 80* (2009): 59–76.

73. NICHD Early Child Care Research Network, "The Effects of Infant Child Care on Infant-Mother Attachment Security: Results of the NICHD Study of Early Child Care," *Child Development 68* (1997): 876.

74. Sarah E. Watamura et al., "Morning to Afternoon Increases in Cortisol Concentrations for Infants and Toddlers at Child Care: Age Differences and Behavioral Correlates," *Child Development 74* (2003): 1006–1020; Megan R. Gunnar et al., "The Rise in Cortisol in Family Day Care: Associations with Aspects of Care Quality, Child Behavior, and Child Sex," *Child Development 81* (2010): 851–869.

75. Megan R. Gunnar et al., "The Import of the Cortisol Rise in Child Care Differs as a Function of Behavioral Inhibition," *Developmental Psychology 47* (2011): 792–803.

76. Lamb and Ahnert, "Nonparental Care," 975.

77. Ibid.

78. Sara Enos Watamura et al., "Double Jeopardy: Poorer Social-Emotional Outcomes for Children in the NICHD SECCYD Experiencing Home and Child Care Environments That Confer Risk," *Child Development 82* (2011): 48–65.

79. NICHD Early Child Care Research Network, "Child Care Effect Sizes for the NICHD Study of Early Child Care and Youth Development," *American Psychologist 61* (2006): 99–116.

80. Ibid., p. 111.

81. Ibid.

82. Jay Belsky et al., "Are There Long-Term Effects of Early Child Care?" *Child Development 78* (2007): 681–701.

83. Lamb and Ahnert, "Nonparental Care."

84. Richardson et al., "Substance Use among Eighth Grade Students."

85. Lois Wladis Hoffman, "Effects of Maternal Employment in the Two-Parent Family," *American Psychologist 44* (1989): 283–292.

86. Ross D. Parke and Raymond Buriel, "Socialization in the Family: Ethnic and Ecological Perspectives," in *Handbook of Child Psychology,* 6th ed., eds. William Damon and Richard M. Lerner, vol. 3: *Social, Emotional, and Personality Development,* ed. Nancy Eisenberg (Hoboken, NJ: Wiley, 2006), 429–504.

87. Francine M. Deutsch, *Having It All: How Equally Shared Parenting Works* (Cambridge, MA: Harvard University Press, 1999).

88. Penny Edgell Becker and Phyllis Moen, "Scaling Back: Dual-Earner Couples' Working Family Strategies," *Journal of Marriage and the Family* 61 (1999): 995–1007.

89. Phyllis Moen and Qinlei Huang, "Customizing Careers by Opting Out or Shifting Jobs: Dual Earners Seeking 'Fit,'" in *Workplace Flexibility,* eds. Christensen and Schneider, 73–94.

90. Roy, Tubbs, and Burton, "Don't Have No Time."

91. Matthew R. Sanders, Helen M. Stallman, and Mala McHale, "Workplace Triple P: A Controlled Evaluation of a Parenting Intervention for Working Parents," *Journal of Family Psychology* 25 (2011): 581–590.

92. Heather Boushey, "The Role of the Government in Work-Family Conflict," *Future of Children* 21 (2011): 163–190.

93. Ibid.

94. Galinsky, *Ask the Children.*

95. Ray DeV. Peters et al., "Better Beginnings, Better Futures Project: Findings from Grade 3 to Grade 9," *Monographs of the Society for Research in Child Development,* 75, serial no. 297 (2009).

96. The National Association of Child Care Resource and Referral Agencies (www.naccrra.org).

97. Families and Work Institute (www.familiesandwork.org).

CHAPTER THIRTEEN

1. Holly Finn, *The Baby Chase: An Adventure in Fertility* (published by Byline.com in 2011, available as an Amazon Kindle Single).

2. Ibid.

3. Adam Pertman, *Adoption Nation: How the Adoption Revolution Is Transforming Our Families and America,* 2nd ed. (Boston: Harvard Common Press, 2011), 45.

4. David Marin, *This Is US: The All-American Family* (United States: Exterminating Angel Press, 2011).

5. David M. Brodzinsky and Ellen Pinderhughes, "Parenting and Child Development in Adoptive Families," in *Handbook of Parenting,* 2nd ed., ed. Marc H. Bornstein, vol. 1: *Children and Parenting* (Mahwah, NJ: Erlbaum, 2002), 279–311.

6. U.S. Census Bureau, *Statistical Abstract of the United States: 2011,* 130th ed. (Washington, DC: U.S. Government Printing Office, 2010).

7. Pertman, *Adoption Nation.*

8. Ibid.

9. Brodzinsky and Pinderhughes, "Parenting and Child Development in Adoptive Families."

10. Pertman, *Adoption Nation.*

11. Brodzinsky and Pinderhughes, "Parenting and Child Development in Adoptive Families."

12. Lynn Von Korff, Harold D. Grotevant, and Ruth G. McRoy, "Openness Arrangements and Psychological Adjustment in Adolescent Adoptees," *Journal of Family Psychology* 20 (2006): 531–534.

13. Pertman, *Adoption Nation.*

14. Brodzinsky and Pinderhughes, "Parenting and Child Development in Adoptive Families."

15. Gina Miranda Samuels, "'Being Raised by White People': Navigating Racial Difference among Adopted Multiracial Adults," *Journal of Marriage and Family* 71 (2009): 80–94.

16. Ibid., p. 91.

17. Ibid.

18. Pertman, *Adoption Nation.*

19. Brodzinsky and Pinderhughes, "Parenting and Child Development in Adoptive Families."

20. Jacqueline Bruce, Amanda R. Tarullo, and Megan P. Gunnar, "Disinhibited Social Behavior among Internationally Adopted Children," *Development and Psychopathology* 21 (2009): 157–171.

21. Michael Rutter et al., "Deprivation-Specific Psychological Patterns: Effects of Institutional Deprivation," *Monographs of the Society for Research in Child Development 75,* serial no. 295 (2011).

22. Amanda R. Tarullo, Melissa C. Garvin, and Megan R. Gunnar, "Atypical EEG Power Correlates with Indiscriminately Friendly Behavior in Internationally Adopted Children," *Developmental Psychology* 47 (2011): 417–431.

23. Megan R. Gunnar, "Commentary on SRCD Monograph: Deprivation-Specific Psychological Patterns: Effects of Institutional Deprivation," *Monographs of*

the *Society for Research in Child Development 75,* serial no. 295 (2011): 232–247.

24. Brodzinsky and Pinderhughes, "Parenting and Child Development in Adoptive Families."

25. Richard M. Lee et al., "Cultural Socialization in Families with Internationally Adopted Children," *Journal of Family Psychology 20* (2006): 571–580.

26. Kristen E. Johnston et al., "Mothers' Racial, Ethnic, and Cultural Socialization of Transracially Adopted Asian Children," *Family Relations 56* (2007): 390–402.

27. Brodzinsky and Pinderhughes, "Parenting and Child Development in Adoptive Families."

28. Ibid.

29. David M. Brodzinsky, Marshall D. Schechter, and Robin Marantz Henig, *Being Adopted: The Lifelong Search for Self* (New York: Anchor Books, 1992).

30. Wendy Tieman, Jan van der Ende, and Frank C. Verhulst, "Young Adult International Adoptees' Search for Birth Parents," *Journal of Family Psychology 22* (2008): 678–687.

31. Mary Dozier and Michael Rutter, "Challenges to the Development of Attachment Relationships Faced by Young Children in Foster and Adoptive Care," in *Handbook of Attachment: Theory, Research, and Clinical Applications,* 2nd ed., eds. Jude Cassidy and Philip R. Shaver (New York: Guilford, 2008), 698–717.

32. LynnVon Korff and Harold D. Grotevant, "Contact in Adoption and Adoptive Identity Formation: The Mediating Role of Family Conversation," *Journal of Family Psychology 25* (2011): 393–401.

33. Brodzinsky and Pinderhughes, "Parenting and Child Development in Adoptive Families."

34. Susan Golombok, "Parenting and Contemporary Reproductive Technologies," in *Handbook of Parenting,* 2nd ed., ed. Marc H. Boorstein, vol. 3: *Being and Becoming a Parent* (Mawah, NJ Erlbaum, 2002), 339–360.

35. Geert-Jan J. M. Stams et al., "Maternal Sensitivity, Infant Attachment, and Temperament in Early Childhood Predict Adjustment in Middle Childhood: The Case of Adopted Children and Their Biologically Unrelated Parents," *Developmental Psychology 38* (2002): 806–821.

36. Anna M. Mannering et al., "Longitudinal Associations between Marital Instability and Child Sleep Problems across Infancy and Toddlerhood in Adopted Families," *Child Development 82* (2011): 1252–1256.

37. Caroline K. Pemberton et al., "Influence of Parental Depressive Symptoms on Adopted Toddler Behaviors: An Emerging Developmental Cascade of Genetic and Environmental Effects," *Development and Psychopathology 22* (2010): 803–818.

38. Martha A. Rueter and Ascan F. Koerner, "The Effect of Family Communication Pattern on Adopted Adolescent Adjustment," *Journal of Marriage and Family 70* (2008): 715–727.

39. Martha A. Reuter et al., "Family Interactions in Adoptive Compared to Nonadoptive Families," *Journal of Family Psychology 23* (2009): 58–66.

40. Brodzinsky, Schecter, and Henig, *Being Adopted.*

41. Brodzinsky and Pinderhughes, "Parenting and Child Development in Adoptive Families."

42. Gail S. Goodman, Robert E. Emery, and Jeffrey J. Haugaard, "Developmental Psychology and Law: Divorce, Child Maltreatment, Foster Care, and Adoption," in *Handbook of Child Psychology,* 5th ed., ed. William Damon, vol. 4: *Child Psychology in Practice,* eds. Irving E. Sigel and K. Ann Renninger (New York: Wiley, 1998), 775–874.

43. Diane Borders, Judith M. Penny, and Francine Portnoy, "Adult Adoptees and Their Friends: Current Functioning and Psychosocial Well-Being," *Family Relations 49* (2000): 407–418.

44. Femmie Juffer and Marinus H. van IJzendoorn, "Behavior Problems and Mental Health Referrals of International Adoptees," *Journal of the American Medical Association 293* (2005): 2501–2515.

45. Brodzinsky and Pinderhughes, "Parenting and Child Development in Adoptive Families."

46. Dozier and Rutter, "Challenges to the Development of Attachment Relationships."

47. Femmie Juffer, Marinus H. van IJzendoorn, and Marian J. Bakermans-Kranenburg, "Supporting Adoptive Families with Video-Feedback Intervention," in *Promoting Positive Parenting: An Attachment-Based*

Intervention, ed. Femmie Juffer, Marian J. Bakermans-Kranenburg, and Marinus H. van IJzendoorn (New York: Erlbaum, 2008), 139–153.

48. Ibid.

49. Susan Golombok, "Parenting and Contemporary Reproductive Technologies," in *Handbook of Parenting,* 2nd ed., ed. Bornstein, vol. 3, 339–360.

50. Marjo Flyks et al., "Prenatal Expectations in Transition to Parenthood: Former Infertility and Family Dynamic Considerations," *Journal of Family Psychology* 23 (2009): 779–790.

51. Golombok, "Parenting and Contemporary Reproductive Technologies."

52. Susan Golombok et al., "Parenting Infants Conceived by Gamete Donations," *Journal of Family Psychology* 18 (2004): 443–452.

53. Susan Golombok et al., "Families Created Through Surrogacy Arrangements: Parent-Child Relationships in the 1st Year of Life," *Developmental Psychology* 40 (2004): 400–411.

54. Susan Golombok et al., "Non-genetic and Non-gestational Parenthood: Consequences for Parent-Child Relationships and the Psychological Well-Being of Mothers, Fathers, and Children at Age 3," *Human Reproduction* 21 (2006): 1918–1924.

55. Susan Golombok et al., "Families Created through Surrogacy: Mother-Child Relationships and Children's Psychological Adjustment at Age 7," *Developmental Psychology* 47 (2011): 1579–1588.

56. Susan Golombok et al., "Children Conceived by Gamete Donation: Psychological Adjustment and Mother-Child Relationships at Age 7," *Journal of Family Psychology* 25 (2011): 230–239.

57. Ethics Committee of the American Society for Reproductive Medicine, "Informing Offspring of Their Conception by Gamete Donation," *Fertility and Sterility* 81 (2004): 527–531.

58. A. P. Lalos, C. Gottleib, and D. Lalos, "Legislated Right for Donor-Insemination Children to Know Their Genetic Origin: A Study of Parental Thinking," *Human Reproduction* 22 (2007), 1762.

59. Diane Ehrensaft, *Mommies, Daddies, Donors, Surrogates: Answering Tough Questions and Building Strong Families* (New York: Guilford, 2005).

60. E. Lycett et al., "School-aged Children of Donor Insemination: A Study of Parents' Disclosure Patterns," *Human Reproduction* 20 (2005): 810–819.

61. Vasanti Jadva et al., "The Experiences of Adolescents and Adults Conceived by Sperm Donation: Comparisons by Age of Disclosure and Family Type," *Human Reproduction* 24 (2009): 1909–1919.

62. Ehrensaft, *Mommies, Daddies, Donors, Surrogates,* 169.

63. Pertman, *Adoption Nation.*

64. Debora L. Spar, *The Baby Business: How Money, Science, and Politics Drive the Commerce of Conception* (Boston: Harvard Business School Press, 2006).

CHAPTER FOURTEEN

1. Andrew J. Cherlin, "The Deinstitutionalization of American Marriage," *Journal of Marriage and Family* 66 (2004): 848–861.

2. Isabel Sawhill, Adam Thomas, and Emily Monea, "An Ounce of Prevention: Policy Prescriptions to Reduce the Prevalence of Fragile Families," *Future of Children* 20 (2010): 133–155.

3. Andrew J. Cherlin, "Demographic Trends in the United States: A Review of Research in the 2000s," *Journal of Marriage and Family* 72 (2010): 403–419.

4. Margaret L. Usdansky, "A Weak Embrace: Popular and Scholarly Depictions of Single-Parent Families," *Journal of Marriage and Family* 71 (2009): 209–225.

5. Judith Musick, "The Special Role of Parenting in the Context of Poverty: The Case of Adolescent Motherhood," in *Threats to Optimal Developmental: Integrating Biological Psychological and Social Risk Factors,* ed. Charles A. Nelson (Hillsdale, NJ: Erlbaum, 1994), 179–216.

6. Mignon R. Moore and Jeanne Brooks-Gunn, "Adolescent Parenthood," in *Handbook of Parenting,* 2nd ed., ed. Marc H. Bornstein, vol. 3: *Being and Becoming a Parent* (Mawah, NJ Erlbaum, 2002), 173–214.

7. Rob Stein, "Teenage Birthrate Has Plummeted to Record Low," *San Francisco Chronicle,* December 22, 2010, A9.

8. Charles M. Blow, "Let's Talk about Sex," *New York Times,* September 6, 2008, A23.

9. Judith A. Levine, Clifton R. Emery, and Harold Pollack, "The Well-Being of

Children Born to Teen Mothers," *Journal of Marriage and Family* 69 (2007): 105–122.

10. Lianne Woodward, David M. Fergusson, and L. John Horwood, "Risk Factors and Life Processes Associated with Teenage Pregnancy: Results of a Prospective Study from Birth to Twenty Years," *Journal of Marriage and Family* 63 (2001).

11. Musick, "The Special Role of Parenting in the Context of Poverty."

12. Laura V. Scaramella et al., "Predicting Risk for Pregnancy by Late Adolescence: A Social Contextual Perspective, *Developmental Psychology* 34 (1998): 1233–1245.

13. Lisa A. Serbin et al., "Intergenerational Transfer of Psychosocial Risk in Women with Childhood Histories of Aggression, Withdrawal, or Aggression and Withdrawal," *Developmental Psychology* 34 (1998): 1242–1262.

14. Woodward, Fergusson, and Horwood, "Risk Factors and Life Processes."

15. Musick, "The Special Role of Parenting in the Context of Poverty."

16. Joy D. Osofsky, Della M. Hann, and Claire Peebles, "Adolescent Parenthood: Risks and Opportunities for Mothers and Infants," in *Handbook of Infant Mental Health,* ed. Charles H. Zeanah, Jr. (New York: Guilford, 1993), 106–119.

17. Ibid.

18. Terrence P. Thornberry, Carolyn A. Smith, and Gregory J. Howard, "Risk Factors for Teenage Fatherhood," *Journal of Marriage and the Family* 59 (1997): 505–522.

19. Sarah Jane Brubaker and Christine Wright, "Identity Transformation and Family Caregiving: Narratives of African American Teen Mothers," *Journal of Marrriage and Family* 68 (2006): 1214–1228.

20. Ibid., p. 1225.

21. Jeanette R. Ickovics et al., "Group Prenatal Care and Perinatal Outcomes," *Obstetrics and Gynecology* 110 (2007): 330–339.

22. Sydney L. Hans and Matthew J. Thullen, "The Relational Context of Adolescent Motherhood," in *Handbook of Infant Mental Health,* 3rd ed., ed. Charles H. Zeanah, Jr. (New York: Guilford, 2009), 214–229.

23. Katie Sellers et al., "Adolescent Mothers' Relationships with Their Own Mothers: Impact on Parenting Outcomes," *Journal of Family Psychology* 25 (2011): 117–126.

24. Patricia L. East and Nina C. Chien, "Family Dynamics across Pregnant Latina Adolescents' Transition to Parenthood," *Journal of Family Psychology* 24 (2010): 709–720.

25. Brubaker and Wright, "Identity Formation and Family Caregiving."

26. Ross D. Parke and Raymond Buriel, "Socialization in the Family: Ethnic and Ecological Perspectives, in *Handbook of Child Psychology,* 5th ed., ed. William Damon, vol. 3: *Social, Emotional, and Personality Development,* ed. Nancy Eisenberg (New York: Wiley, 1998), 463–552.

27. Hans and Thullen, "The Relational Context of Adolescent Motherhood."

28. Ibid.

29. Ibid.

30. Ibid.

31. Frank F. Furstenberg, Jr., J. Brooks-Gunn, and S. Philip Morgan, *Adolescent Mothers in Later Life* (Cambridge, England: Cambridge University Press, 1990).

32. John G. Borkowski, Thomas I. Whitman, and Jaelyn R. Farris, "Adolescent Mothers and Their Children: Risks, Resilience, and Development," in *Risk and Resilience: Adolescent Mothers and Their Children Grow Up,* eds. John G. Borkowski et al. (Mahwah, NJ: Erlbaum, 2007), 1–34; Jaelyn R. Farris, Leann E. Smith, and Keri Weed, "Resilience and Vulnerability in the Context of Multiple Risks," in *Risks and Resilience,* eds. Borkowski et al., 179–204.

33. Farris, Smith, and Weed, "Resilience and Vulnerability in the Context of Multiple Risks."

34. Borkowski, Whitman, and Farris, "Adolescent Mothers and Their Children."

35. Kimberly S. Howard et al., "Overcoming the Odds: Protective Factors in the Lives of Children," in *Risk and Resilience,* eds. Borkowski et al., 205–232.

36. Tom Luster and Julie Laser Haddow, "Adolescent Mothers and Their Children," in *Parenting: An Ecological Perspective,* 2nd ed. eds. Tom Luster and Lynn Okagaki (Mahwah, NJ: Erlbaum 2005), 73–101.

37. Ibid.

38. Moore and Brooks-Gunn, "Adolescent Parenthood"; Beverly I. Fagot et al., "Becoming an Adolescent Father: Precursors and Parenting," *Developmental Psychology* 34 (1998): 1217.

39. Borkowski, Whitman, and Farris, "Adolescent Mothers and Their Children,"

40. Ibid.

41. Moore and Brooks-Gunn, "Adolescent Parenthood."

42. Cynthia J. Schellenbach, Bonnie J. Leadbeater, and Kristen Anderson Moore, "Enhancing the Developmental Outcomes of Adolescent Parents and Their Children," in *Investing in Children, Youth, Families, and Communities: Strengths-Based Research and Policy*, eds. Kenneth I. Maton et al. (Washington, DC: American Psychological Association, 2004), 117–136.

43. Sawhill, Thomas, and Monea, "An Ounce of Prevention."

44. Ibid.

45. Ibid.

46. John G. Borkowski, Jaelyn R. Farris, and Keri Weed, "Toward Resilience: Designing Effective Prevention Programs," in *Risk and Resilience*, eds. Borkowski et al., 259–278.

47. Schellenbach, Leadbeater, and Moore, "Enhancing the Developmental Outcomes of Adolescent Parents and Their Children."

48. Sara McLanahan et al., "Introducing the Issue," *Future of Children 20* (2010): 3–16.

49. Rebecca M. Ryan, Ariel Kalil, and Lindsay Leininger, "Low-Income Mothers' Private Safety Nets and Children's Socioemotional Well-Being," *Journal of Marriage and Family 71* (2009): 278–297.

50. Sarah E. Shook et al., "The Mother-Coparent Relationship and Youth Adjustment: A Study of African American Single-Mother Families," *Journal of Family Psychology 24* (2010): 243–252

51. Claire M. Kamp Dush, Letitia E. Kotila, and Sarah J. Schoppe-Sullivan, "Predictors of Supportive Coparenting after Relationship Dissolution Among At-Risk Parents," *Journal of Family Psychology 25* (2011): 356–365.

52. Linda M. Burton et al., "The Role of Trust in Low-Income Mothers' Intimate Unions," *Journal of Marriage and Family 71* (2009): 1107–1124.

53. Zoe E. Taylor et al., "Life Stress, Maternal Optimism, and Adolescent Competence in Single Mother, African American Families," *Journal of Family Psychology 24* (2010): 468–477.

54. William S. Aquilino, "The Life Course of Children Born to Unmarried Mothers: Child Living Arrangements and Young Adult Outcomes," *Journal of Marriage and Family 58* (1996): 293–310.

55. Cynthia Osborne and Sara McLanahan, "Partnership Instability and Child Well-Being," *Journal of Marriage and Family 69* (2007): 1065–1083.

56. Jane Waldfogel, Terry-Ann Craigie, and Jeanne Brooks-Gunn, "Fragile Families and Child Well-Being," *Future of Children 20* (2010): 87–112.

57. Susan L. Brown, "Child Well-Being in Cohabiting Families," in *Just Living Together*: Implications of Cohabitation on Families, Children, and Social Policy, eds. Alan Booth and Ann C. Crowter (Mahwah, NJ, Erlbaum, 2002) 173–187; Susan L. Brown, "Family Structure and Child Well-Being: The Significance of Parental Cohabitation," *Journal of Marriage and Family 66* (2004): 351–367.

58. Martha J. Zaslow et al., "Protective Factors in the Development of Preschool-Age Children of Young Mothers Receiving Welfare," in *Coping with Divorce, Single Parenting, and Remarriage*, ed. E. Mavis Hetherington (Mahwah, NJ: Erlbaum, 1999), 193–223.

59. Aquilino, "The Life Course of Children Born to Unmarried Mothers."

60. Robert I. Lerman, "Capabilities and Contributions of Unwed Fathers, *Future of Children 20* (2010): 63–85.

61. Philip A. Cowan, Carolyn Pape Cowan, and Virginia Knox, "Marriage and Fatherhood," *Future of Children 20* (2010): 205–230.

62. Ariel Kalil and Rebecca M. Ryan, "Mothers' Economic Conditions and Sources of Support in Fragile Families," *Future of Children 20* (2010): 39–67.

63. Waldfogel, Craigie, and Brooks-Gunn, "Fragile Families and Child Well-Being."

64. Marsha Weinraub, Danielle L. Horvath, and Mary B. Gringlas, "Single Parenthood," in *Handbook of Parenting*, 2nd ed., ed. Bornstein, vol. 3, 109–140.

65. Kalil and Ryan, "Mothers' Economic Conditions and Sources of Support in Fragile Families."

66. Weinrab, Horvath, and Gringlas, "Single Parenthood."

67. Jane Mattes, *Single Mothers by Choice*, 2nd ed. (New York: Times Books, 1997).

68. Sara McLanahan and Julien Teitler, "The Consequence of Father Absence," in *Parenting and Child Development in Nontraditional Families*, ed. Michael E. Lamb (Mahwah, NJ: Erlbaum, 1999), 83–102.

69. Paul R. Amato, "More Than Money: Men's Contributions to Their Children's Lives," in *Men in Families: When Do They Get Involved? What Difference Does It Make?* eds. Alan Booth and Ann C. Crouter (Mahwah, NJ: Erlbaum, 1998), 241–278.
70. Ibid., p. 244.
71. Ibid., pp. 271–272.
72. Ibid., p. 257.
73. David Marin, *This Is US: The New All-American Family* (United States: Exterminating Angel Press, 2011).
74. Howard et al., "Overcoming the Odds."
75. Sharon H. Bzostek, "Social Fathers and Child Well-Being," *Journal of Marriage and Family 70* (2008): 950–961.
76. Rebecca M. Ryan, Ariel Kalil, and Kathleen M. Ziol-Guest, "Longitudinal Patterns of Nonresident Fathers' Involvement: The Role of Resources and Relations," *Journal of Marriage and Family 70* (2008): 962–977.
77. William V. Fabricius, "Listening to Children of Divorce: New Findings that Diverge from Wallerstein, Lewis, and Blakeslee," *Family Relations 52* (2003): 385–396.
78. Lerman, "Capabilities and Contributions of Unwed Fathers."
79. Jay Fagan et al., "Pathways to Paternal Engagement: Longitudinal Effects of Risk and Resilience on Nonresident Fathers," *Developmental Psychology 45* (2009): 1389–1405.
80. James A. Levine with Edward W. Pitt, *New Expectations: Community Strategies for Responsible Fatherhood* (New York: Families and Work Institute, 1995).

CHAPTER FIFTEEN
1. Andrew J. Cherlin, "Demographic Trends in the United States: A Review of Research in the 2000s," *Journal of Marriage and Family 72* (2010): 403–419.
2. Mark A. Fine, Lawrence H. Ganong, and David H. Demo, "Divorce: A Risk and Resilient Perspective," in *Families and Change: Coping with Stressful Events and Transitions,* 4th ed., eds. Sharon J. Price, Christine A. Price, and Patrick C. McKenry (Los Angeles: Sage, 2010), 211–233.
3. Megan M. Sweeney, "Remarriage and Stepfamilies: Strategic Sites for Family Scholarship in the 21st Century," *Journal of Marriage and Family 72* (2010): 667–684.
4. Fine, Ganong, and Demo, "Divorce."
5. Ibid.
6. Ibid.
7. Elizabeth J. Krumrei, Annette Mahoney, and Kenneth I. Pargament, "Divorce and the Divine: The Role of Spirituality in Adjustment to Divorce," *Journal of Marriage and Family 71* (2009): 373–383.
8. Robert E. Emery, *The Truth about Children and Divorce: Dealing with the Emotions So You and Your Children Can Thrive* (New York: Penguin, 2006).
9. E. Mavis Hetherington, "An Overview of the Virginia Longitudinal Study of Divorce and Remarriage with a Focus on Early Adolescence," *Journal of Family Psychology 1* (1993): 39–56.
10. Krumrei, Mahoney, and Pargament, "Divorce and the Divine."
11. E. Mavis Hetherington and John Kelly, *For Better or For Worse: Divorce Reconsidered* (New York: Norton, 2002).
12. Emery, *The Truth about Children and Divorce.*
13. Ibid., p. 139.
14. Judtith S. Wallerstein and Sandra Blakeslee, *Second Chances* (New York: Ticknor & Fields, 1989).
15. Judith S. Wallerstein and Joan B. Kelly, *Surviving the Breakup* (New York: Basic Books, 1980).
16. Ibid.
17. Pauline H. Tessler and Peggy Thompson, *Collaborative Divorce* (New York: HarperColllins, 2006), 130.
18. Ibid.
19. Hetherington and Kelly, *For Better or For Worse.*
20. Wallerstein and Kelly, *Surviving the Breakup.*
21. E. Mavis Hetherington and Margaret Stanley-Hagan, "Parenting in Divorced and Remarried Families," in *Handbook of Parenting,* 2nd ed., ed. Marc H. Bornstein, vol. 3: *Being and Becoming a Parent* (Mahwah, NJ: Erlbaum, 2002) 287–315.
22. Ibid.
23. Hetherington and Kelly, *For Better or For Worse,* 80.
24. Ibid.
25. Lisa Strohschein, "Parental Divorce and Child Mental Health Trajectories," *Journal of Marriage and Family 67* (2005): 1286–1300.

26. Hetherington and Kelly, *For Better or For Worse.*
27. Ibid.
28. Judith S. Wallerstein, Julia M. Lewis, and Sandra Blakeslee, *The Unexpected Legacy of Divorce* (New York: Hyperion, 2000).
29. Paul R. Amato, "Reconciling Divergent Perspectives: Judith Wallerstein, Quantitative Family Research, and Children of Divorce," *Family Relations* 52 (2003): 332–339.
30. Hetherington and Kelly, *For Better or For Worse.*
31. Paul R. Amato, "Research on Divorce: Continuing Trends and New Developments," *Journal of Marriage and Family* 72 (2010): 650–666.
32. Charles R. Martinez, Jr. and Marion Forgatch, "Preventing Problems with Boys' Noncompliance: Effects of a Parent Training Intervention for Divorcing Mothers," *Journal of Consulting and Clinical Psychology* 69 (2001): 416–428.
33. Gerald R. Patterson, Marion S. Forgatch, and David DeGarmo, "Cascading Effects Following Intervention," *Development and Psychopathpology* 22 (2010): 949–970.
34. Tessler and Thompson, *Collaborative Divorce.*
35. Sweeney, "Remarriage and Stepfamilies."
36. Wallerstein and Blakeslee, *Second Chances.*
37. Fitzhugh Dodson, *How to Discipline with Love* (New York: Rawson Associates, 1977).
38. Hetherington and Kelly, *For Better or For Worse.*
39. James H. Bray and John Kelly, *Stepfamilies: Love, Marriage, and Parenting in the First Decade* (New York: Broadway Books, 1998).
40. Ibid., p. 16.
41. Ibid., p. 265.
42. Hetherington and Kelly, *For Better or For Worse.*
43. E. Mavis Hetherington and Kathleen M. Jodl, "Stepfamilies as Settings for Child Development," in *Stepfamilies: Who Benefits? Who Does Not?* eds. Alan Booth and Judy Dunn (Hillsdale, NJ: Erlbaum, 1994), 55–79.
44. Ibid.
45. Hetherington, "An Overview of the Virginia Longitudinal Study of Divorce and Remarriage with a Focus on Early Adolescence."
46. Hetherington and Stanley-Hagan, "Parenting Divorced and Remarried Families."
47. Ibid.
48. Ibid.
49. Ibid.
50. Valarie King, "The Antecedents and Consequences of Adolescents' Relationships with Stepfathers and Nonresident Fathers," *Journal of Marriage and Family* 68 (2006): 910–928.
51. Valarie King, "Stepfamily Formation: Implications for Adolescent Ties to Mothers, Nonresident Fathers, and Stepfathers," *Journal of Marriage and Family* 71 (2009): 954–968.
52. King, "The Antecedents and Consequences of Adolescents' Relationships with Stepfathers and Nonresident Fathers."
53. William Marsiglio and Ramon Hinojosa, "Managing the Multifather Family: Stepfathers as Father Allies," *Journal of Marriage and Family* 69 (2007): 845–862.
54. Valarie King, "When Children Have Two Mothers: Relationships with Nonresident Mothers, Stepmothers, and Fathers," *Journal of Marriage and Family* 69 (2007): 1178–1193.
55. Hetherington and Kelly, *For Better or For Worse.*
56. Lynn White, "Stepfamilies over the Life Course: Social Support," in *Stepfamilies,* eds. Booth and Dunn, 109–137.

CHAPTER SIXTEEN

1. Abbie E. Goldberg and Katherine A. Kuvalanka, "Marriage (In)equality: The Perspectives of Adolescent and Emerging Adults With Lesbian, Gay, and Bisexual Parents," *Journal of Marriage and Family* 74 (2012): 45.
2. Charlotte J. Patterson, "Lesbian and Gay Parenthood," in *Handbook of Parenting,* 2nd ed., ed. Marc H. Bornstein, vol. 3: *Being and Becoming a Parent* (Mahwah, NJ: Erlbaum, 2002), 317–338.
3. Timothy J. Biblarz and Evren Savci, "Lesbian, Gay, Bisexual, and Transgender Families," *Journal of Marriage and Family* 72 (2010): 480–497.

4. Abbie E. Goldberg, *Lesbian and Gay Parents and Their Children: Research on the Life Cycle* (Washington, DC: American Psychological Association, 2010).

5. Goldberg and Kuvalanka, "Marriage (In)equality," 45.

6. Goldberg, *Lesbian and Gay Parents and Their Children*.

7. Danielle N. Shapiro, Christopher Peterson, and Abigail J. Stewart, "Legal and Social Contexts and Mental Health among Lesbian and Heterosexual Mothers," *Journal of Family Psychology* 23 (2009), 255–262.

8. Biblarz and Savci, "Lesbian, Gay, Bisexual, and Transgender Families."

9. Goldberg, *Lesbian and Gay Parents and Their Children*.

10. Abbie E. Goldberg, Jordan B. Downing, and April M. Moyer, "Why Parenthood and Why Now? Gay Men's Motivation for Pursuing Parenthood," *Family Relations 61* (2012): 157–174.

11. Goldberg, *Lesbian and Gay Parents and Their Children*.

12. Ibid.

13. Ibid.

14. Abbie E. Goldberg et al., "Lesbian, Gay, and Heterosexual Couples in Open Adoption Arrangements: A Qualitative Study," *Journal of Marriage and Family 73* (2011): 502–518.

15. Dana Berkowitz and William Marsiglio, "Gay Men: Negotiating Procreative, Father, and Family Identities," *Journal of Marriage and Family 69* (2007): 366–381.

16. Abbie E. Goldberg and JuliAnna Z. Smith, "Social Support and Psychological Well-Being in Lesbian and Heterosexual Preadoptive Couples," *Family Relations 57* (2008): 281–294.

17. Abbie E. Goldberg and Katherine R. Allen, "Imagining Men: Lesbian Mothers' Perceptions of Male Involvement during the Transition to Parenthood," *Journal of Marriage and Family 69* (2007): 352–365.

18. Abbie E. Goldberg and Aline Sayer, "Lesbian Couples' Relationship Quality across the Transition to Parenthood," *Journal of Marriage and Family 68* (2006): 87–100.

19. Patterson, "Lesbian and Gay Parenthood."

20. Charlotte J. Patterson and Raymond W. Chan, "Families Headed by Lesbian and Gay Parents," in *Parenting and Child Development in Nontraditional Families*, ed. Michael E. Lamb (Mahwah, NJ: Erlbaum, 1999), 191–219.

21. Goldberg, *Lesbian and Gay Parents and Their Children*.

22. Patterson, "Lesbian and Gay Parenthood."

23. Biblarz and Savci, "Lesbian, Gay, Bisexual, and Transgender Families."

24. Patterson, "Lesbian and Gay Parenthood."

25. Biblarz and Savci, "Lesbian, Gay, Bisexual, and Transgender Families."

26. Goldberg, *Lesbian and Gay Parents and Their Children*.

27. Pew Social & Demographic Trends, "The Public Renders a Split Verdict on Changes in Family Structure," downloaded from www.Pewsocialtrends,org./2011/02/16.

28. Goldberg, *Lesbian and Gay Parents and Their Children*.

29. Ibid.

30. Ibid.

31. Patterson, "Lesbian and Gay Parenthood."

32. Jennifer L. Wainwright, Stephen T. Russell, and Charlotte J. Patterson, "Psychosocial Adjustment, School Outcomes, and Romantic Relationships of Adolescents with Same-Sex Parents," *Child Development* 75 (2004): 1886–1898.

33. Ibid.

34. Jennifer L. Wainwright and Charlotte J. Patterson, "Peer Relations among Adolescents with Female Same-Sex Parents," *Developmental Psychology 44* (2008): 117–126.

35. Jennifer L. Wainwright and Charlotte J. Patterson, "Delinquency, Victimization, and Substance Use among Adolescents with Female Same-Sex Parents," *Journal of Family Psychology 20* (2006): 526–250.

36. Goldberg, *Lesbian and Gay Parents and Their Children*.

37. Kenji Yoshino, "For Obama, It's about the Children," *New York Times* Sunday Review, May 13, 2012, 11.

CHAPTER SEVENTEEN

1. Sharon J. Price and Christine A. Price (with Patrick C. McKenry, posthumously), "Families Coping with Change: A Conceptual Overview," in *Families and Change: Coping with Stressful Events and Transitions*, 4th ed., eds. Sharon J. Price, Christine A. Price, and Patrick C. McKenry (Thousand Oaks, CA: Sage, 2010), 1–23.

2. Irwin N. Sandler et al., "Adversities and Public Policy," in *Investing in Children, Youth, Families, and Communities,* eds. Kenneth I. Maton et al. (Washington, DC: American Psychological Association, 2004), 31–49.

3. Barbara G. Melamed, "Parenting the Ill Child," in *Handbook of Parenting,* 2nd ed., ed. Marc H. Bornstein, vol. 5: *Practical Issues of Parenting* (Mahwah, NJ: Erlbaum, 2002), 329–348.

4. Lonnie K. Zeltzer and Christine Blackett Schlank, *Conquering Your Child's Chronic Pain* (New York: HarperCollins, 2005).

5. Elizabeth Gellert, "Children's Conceptions of the Content and Functions of the Human Body," *Genetic Psychology Monographs* 65 (1962): 293–405.

6. Roger Bibace and Mary E. Walsh, "Developmental States of Children's Conceptions of Illness," in *Health Psychology,* eds. George C. Stone, Frances Cohen, and Nancy E. Adler (San Francisco: Jossey-Bass, 1979), 285–301.

7. Zeltzer and Schlank, *Conquering Your Child's Chronic Pain,* 32.

8. Melamed, "Parenting the Ill Child."

9. Ibid.

10. Ibid.

11. Earl Grollman, "Prologue," in *Explaining Death to Children,* ed. Earl Grollman (Boston: Beacon, 1967), 15

12. Barbara D. Rosoff, *The Worst Loss* (New York: Henry Holt, 1994).

13. John Bowlby, *Attachment and Loss,* vol. 3, *Loss, Sadness, and Depression* (New York: Basic Books, 1980).

14. Ibid.

15. Rosoff, *The Worst Loss,* 108.

16. Ibid.

17. Ibid.

18. Ibid.

19. Ibid.

20. Ibid., p. 128.

21. Ibid., p. 14.

22. Ibid.

23. Katherine A. Becker-Blease, Heather A. Turner, and David Finkelhor, Disasters, Victimization, and Children's Mental Health," *Child Development* 81 (2010): 1040–1052.

24. Dante Cicchetti and Michael Lynch, "Toward an Ecological/Transactional Model of Community Violence and Child Maltreatment: Consequences for Child Development," *Psychiatry* 56 (1993): 96–118.

25. Sandra T. Azar, "Parenting and Maltreatment," in *Handbook of Parenting,* 2nd ed., ed. Marc H. Bornstein, vol. 4: *Social Conditions and Applied Parenting* (Mahwah, NJ: Erlbaum, 2002), 361–388.

26. Christina Paxson and Ron Haskins, "Introducing the Issue," *Future of Children* 19 (2009): 3–27.

27. Edward F. Zigler, Matia Finn-Stevenson, and Nancy W. Hall, *The First Three Years and Beyond* (New Haven, CT: Yale University Press, 2002.)

28. David Finkelhor and Lisa Jones, "Why Have Child Maltreatment and Child Victimization Declined?" *Journal of Social Issues* 62 (2006): 685–716.

29. U.S. Census Bureau, *Statistical Abstract of the United States:* 2007, 126th ed. (Washington, DC: Government Printing Office, 2006).

30. Katherine Elliott and Anthony Urquiza, "Ethnicity, Culture, and Child Maltreatment," *Journal of Social Issues* 62 (2006): 787–809.

31. Fred Wulczyn, "Epidemiological Perspective on Maltreatment Prevention," *Future of Children* 19 (2009): 39–66.

32. Gregory K. Fritz, "The Foster Care System: Can't Live with It and Can't Live without It," *Brown University Child and Adolescent Behavior Newsletter,* March 2004, 7.

33. Dante Cicchetti and Sheree L. Toth, "Developmental Psychopathology and Preventive Intervention," in *Handbook of Child Psychology,* 6th ed., eds. William Damon and Richard M. Lerner, vol. 4: *Child Psychology in Practice,* eds. K. Ann Renninger and Irving E. Sigel (Hoboken, NJ: Wiley, 2006), 497–547.

34. Gail S. Goodman, Robert E. Emery, and Jeffrey J. Haugaard, "Developmental Psychology and Law: Divorce, Child Maltreatment, Foster Care, and Adoption," in *Handbook of Child Psychology,* 5th ed., ed. William Damon, vol. 4: *Child Psychology in Practice,* eds. Irving E. Sigel and K. Ann Renninger (New York: Wiley, 1998), 775–874.

35. John W. Fantuzzo and Wanda K. Mohr, "Prevalence and Effects of Child Exposure to Domestic Violence," *Future of Children* 9, (3) (1999): 21–32.

36. Judith A. Cohen et al., "Psychosocial Interventions for Maltreated and Violence-Exposed Children," *Journal of Social Issues* 62 (2006): 737–766.

37. Lucy Salcido Custer, Lois A. Weithorn, and Richard E. Berman, "Domestic Violence and Children: Analysis and Recommendations," *Future of Children 9* (3) (1999): 4–20.

38. Sally Zierler, "Studies Confirm Long-Term Consequences of Childhood Sexual Abuse," *Brown University Child and Adolescent Newsletter 8* (1992): 3.

39. David Finkelhor, Richard K. Ormrod, and Heather A. Turner, "Polyvictimization and Trauma in a National Longitudinal Cohort," *Development and Psychopathology 19* (2007): 149–166.

40. Wulczyn, "Epidemiological Perspective on Maltreatment Prevention."

41. Tiffany Watts-English et al., "The Psychobiology of Maltreatment in Childhood," *Journal of Social Issues 62* (2006): 717–736.

42. Mary Dozier et al., "Developing Evidence-Based Interventions for Foster Children: An Example of a Randomized Clinical Trial with Infants and Toddlers," *Journal of Social Issues 62* (2006): 767–785.

43. Watts-English et al., "The Psychobiology of Maltreatment in Childhood."

44. American Psychiatric Association, *Diagnostic and Statistical Manual of Mental Disorders,* 4th ed. (Washington, DC: American Psychiatric Association, 1994).

45. Robin McGee, David Wolfe, and James Olson, "Multiple Maltreatment, Attribution of Blame, and Adjustment among Adolescents," *Development and Psychopathology 13* (2001): 827–846.

46. Jody Todd Manly et al., "Dimensions of Child Maltreatment and Children's Adjustment: Contributions of Developmental Timing and Subtype," *Development and Psychopathology 13* (2001): 759–782.

47. Robert E. Emery and Lisa Laumann-Billings, "An Overview of the Nature, Causes, and Consequences of Abusive Family Relationships: Toward Differentiating Maltreatment and Violence," *American Psychologist 53* (1998): 121–135.

48. Dante Cicchetti et al., "False Belief Understanding in Maltreated Children," *Development and Psychopathology 15* (2003): 1067–1091.

49. Sheree L. Toth et al., "The Relative Efficacy of Two Interventions in Altering Maltreated Preschool Children's Representational Models: Implications for Attachment Theory," *Development and Psychopathology 14* (2002): 877–908.

50. Dante Cicchetti, "An Odyssey of Discovery: Lessons Learned through Three Decades of Research on Child Maltreatment," *American Psychologist 59* (2004): 731–741.

51. Manley et al., "Dimensions of Child Maltreatment."

52. Penelope K. Trickett et al., "Variants of Intrafamilial Sexual Abuse Experience: Implications for Short- and Long-Term Development," *Development and Psychopathology 13* (2001): 1001–1019.

53. Paxson and Haskins, "Introducing the Issue."

54. Goodman, Emery, and Haugaard, "Developmental, Psychology, and Law."

55. Catherine R. Lawrence, Elizabeth A. Carlson, and Byron Egeland, "The Impact of Foster Care on Development," *Development and Psychopathology 18* (2006): 57–76.

56. Dozier et al., "Developing Evidence-Based Interventions for Foster Children."

57. John Eckenrode et al., "Child Maltreatment and the Early Onset of Problem Behaviors: Can a Program of Nurse Home Visitation Break the Link?" *Development and Psychopathology 13* (2001): 873–890.

58. Daphne Blunt Bugental et al., "A Cognitive Approach to Child Abuse Prevention," *Journal of Family Psychology 16* (2002): 243–258.

59. Cicchetti and Toth, "Developmental Psychopathology and Preventive Intervention."

60. Toth et al., "The Relative Efficacy of Two Interventions in Altering Maltreated Preschool Children's Representational Models."

61. Renee McDonald, Ernest N. Jouriles, and Nancy A. Skopp, "Reducing Conduct Problems Among Children Brought to Women's Shelters: Intervention Effects 24 Months Following Termination of Services," *Journal of Family Psychology 20* (2006): 127–136.

62. Ernest N. Jouriles et al., "Improving Parenting in Families Referred for Child Maltreatment: A Randomized Controlled Trial Examining Effects of Project Support," *Journal of Family Psychology 24* (2010): 328–338.

63. Cynthia Cupit Swenson et al., "Multisystemic Therapy for Child Abuse and Neglect: A Randomized Effectiveness Trial," *Journal of Family Psychology 24* (2010): 497–507.

64. Cohen, "Psychosocial Interventions for Maltreated and Violence-Exposed Children."

65. Sroufe et al., *The Development of the Person.*

66. Deborah Daro and Kenneth A. Dodge, "Creating Community Responsibility for Child Protection Possibilities and Challenges," *Future of Children 19* (2009): 67–93.

67. George K. Fritz, "The Foster Care System: Can't Live with It and Can't Live without It," *Brown University Child and Adolescent Behavior Newsletter,* March 2004) 7.

68. Jeffrey Haugaard and Cindy Hazan, "Foster Parenting," in *Handbook of Parenting,* 2nd ed., ed. Marc H. Bornstein, vol. 1: *Children and Parenting* (Mahwah, NJ: Erlbaum, 2002), 313–327.

69. Ibid.

70. Ibid.

71. Ibid.

72. Ibid.

73. Ibid.

74. Ibid.

75. Lawrence, Carlson, and Egeland, "The Impact of Foster Care on Development."

76. Haugaard and Hazan, "Foster Parenting."

77. Goodman, Emery, and Haugaard, "Developmental, Psychology, and Law."

78. Monica Davey, "Youths Leaving Foster Care Are Found Facing Obstacles," *New York Times,* February 24, 2004, A10.

79. Monica Davey, "Those Who Outgrow Foster Care Struggle, Study Finds," *New York Times,* May 19, 2005, A14.

80. Ibid.

81. Goodman, Emery, and Haugaard, "Developmental, Psychology, and Law."

82. Ibid.

83. Annette M. LaGreca and Mitchell J. Prinstein, "Hurricanes and Earthquakes," in *Helping Children Cope with Disasters and Terrorism,* eds., Annette LaGreca et al. (Washington DC: American Psychological Association, 2002), 107–138.

84. Jacob M. Vigil et al., "Sex Differences in Salivary Cortisol, Alpha-Amylase, and Psychological Functioning," *Child Development 81* (2010): 1228–1240.

85. Jacob M. Vigil and David C. Geary, "A Preliminary Investigation of Family Coping Styles and Well-Being among Adolescent Survivors of Hurricane Katrina," *Journal of Family Psychology 22* (2008): 176–180.

86. Mindy E. Kronenberg et al., "Children of Katrina: Lessons Learned about Postdisaster Symptoms and Recovery," *Child Development 81* (2010): 1244–1259.

87. Gaithri A Fernando, Kenneth E. Miller, and Dale E. Berger, "Growing Pains: The Impact of Disaster-Related and Daily Stressors on the Psychological and Psychosocial Functioning of Youth in Sri Lanka," *Child Development 81* (2010): 1192–1210.

88. LaGreca and Prinstein, "Hurricanes and Earthquakes."

89. Robin H. Gurwitch et al., "The Aftermath of Terrorism," in *Helping Children Cope with Disasters and Terrorism,* eds. LaGreca et al., 327–357.

90. Deborah Smith, "Everyday Fears Trump Worries about Terrorism," *Monitor on Psychology,* May 2003, 22–23.

91. Claude M. Clemtob et al., "Impact of Maternal Posttraumatic Stress Disorder and Depression Following Exposure to the September 11 Attacks on Preschool Children's Behavior," *Child Development 81* (2010): 1129–1141.

92. Elizabeth T. Gershoff et al., "Exposure to 9/11 among Youth and Their Mothers in New York City: Enduring Associations with Mental Health and Sociopolitical Attitudes," *Child Development 81* (2010): 1142–1160.

93. Joshunda Sanders, "What to Tell Kids about War," *San Francisco Chronicle,* March 19, 2003, A21.

94. Elizabeth W. Lindsey and Christina A. Sanchez, "Homeless Families: An Extreme Stressor," in *Families & Change,* eds. Price, Price, and McHenry, 357–379.

95. Ibid.

96. Ibid.

97. Ibid.

98. American Psychological Association, "The Psychological Needs of U.S. Military Service Members and Their Families: A Preliminary Report," 2007, Retrieved January, 2009 from www.apa.org/releases/MilitaryDeploymentTaskForceReport.pdf.

99. Julia Yeary, "Operation Parenting Edge: Promoting Resiliency through Prevention," *Zero to Three 27* (July 2007), 7–12.

100. American Psychological Association, "The Psychological Needs of U.S. Military Service Members and Their Families."

101. Ibid.

102. Yeary, "Operation Parenting Edge."

103. Helen Verdeli et al., "The Case for Treating Depression in Military Spouses," *Journal of Family Psychology* 25 (2011): 488–496.

104. Keith D. Renshaw et al., "Distress in Spouses of Service Members with Symptoms of Combat-Related PTSD: Secondary Traumatic Stress or General Psychological Distress?" *Journal of Family Psychology* 25 (2011): 461–469.

105. Leanne K. Knoblock and Jennifer A. Theiss, "Depressive Symptoms and Mechanisms of Relational Turbulence as Predictors of Relationship Satisfaction among Returning Service Members," *Journal of Family Psychology* 25 (2011): 470–475.

106. Christianne Esposito-Smythers et al., "Military Youth and the Deployment Cycle: Emotional Health Consequences and Recommendations for Intervention," *Journal of Family Psychology* 25 (2011): 497–507.

107. Ibid.

108. Steven J. Wolin and Sybil Wolin, *The Resilient Self* (New York: Villard Books, 1993).

109. Ibid., p. 5–6.

EPILOGUE

1. Amy Arner Sgarro, "A Surgeon and Her Community," *Vassar Quarterly,* Spring, 1993, 10–13.

2. Ibid., p. 13

C R E D I T S

Photo Credits

Page 4: Dex Image/Punchstock; 15: Big Cheese Photo/Punchstock; 39: Rolf Bruderer/ Blend Images LLC; 56: Don Bayley/Getty Images; 86: JGI/Jamie Grill/Blend Images LLC; 101: Design Pics/Ron Nickel; 125: Science Photo Library/Photolibrary; 130: Ingram Publishing/Superstock; 139: Brand X Pictures/Jupiterimages; 163: Jose Luis Palaez Inc./Blend Images LLC; 181: Jose Luis Palaez Inc./Blend Images LLC; 185: Onoky/Superstock; 213: Bananastock/PictureQuest; 234: Design Pics/Kristy-Anne Glubish; 253: Dex Image/Punchstock; 257: David De Lossy/Getty Images; 277: Pixtal/AGE Fotostock; 298: Drew Myers/Corbis; 322: Royalty-Free/Corbis; 325: Robert Daly/Getty Images; 356: L. Mouton/PhotoAlto; 358: Stockbyte/Punchstock; 388: Jose Luis Palaez Inc./Blend Images LLC; 393: Anderson Ross/Blend Images LLC; 411: Image Source/Veer; 423: Tetra Images/Getty Images; 435: Brand X Pictures/ Jupiterimages; 443: E. Audras/PhotoAlto; 458: Buccina Studios/Getty Images; 470: Design Pics/Kristy-Anne Glubish; 482: Image Source/Veer; 485: Stockbyte/ Punchstock; 514: Ale Ventura/AGE Fotostock; 520: Michael Rieger/FEMA.